RESEARCH IN
THE SOCIOLOGY
OF WORK

Volume 1 • 1981

RESEARCH IN THE SOCIOLOGY OF WORK

A Research Annual

Editors: RICHARD L. SIMPSON
Department of Sociology
University of North Carolina at Chapel Hill

IDA HARPER SIMPSON
Department of Sociology
Duke University

VOLUME 1 • 1981

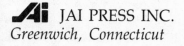 JAI PRESS INC.
Greenwich, Connecticut

CONTENTS

LIST OF CONTRIBUTORS

William H. Friedland	Project on Social Impact Assessment and Values, University of California, Santa Cruz
James A. Geschwender	Department of Sociology, State University of New York at Binghamton
Richard Hamilton	Department of Sociology, McGill University,
T. Anthony Jones	Department of Sociology, University of North Carolina at Chapel Hill
Morton Klass	Department of Anthropology, Barnard College, Columbia University
Henry A. Landsberger	Department of Sociology, University of North Carolina at Chapel Hill
David Lockwood	Department of Sociology, University of Essex, Colchester, England
John R. Logan	Department of Sociology, State University of New York at Stony Brook
John Low-Beer	Department of Social Sciences, York College, City University of New York
Paul M. Lubeck	College 8, University of California, Santa Cruz
Elizabeth Mutran	Department of Sociology University of Akron

Margaret Peil

Centre of West African Studies
The University of Birmingham, England

Richard Sandbrook

Department of Political Economy, University
of Toronto

Lawrence Schofer

419 West Mt. Pleasant Avenue, Philadelphia,
Pennsylvania

Ida Harper Simpson

Department of Sociology, Duke University

Richard L. Simpson

Department of Sociology, University of North
Carolina at Chapel Hill

James Wright

Department of Sociology
University of Massachusetts–Amherst

INTRODUCTION

When we invited the authors to contribute to this volume, we described its topic as follows:

> The theme will be variations in the nature and degree of "worker consciousness," conditions favoring or impeding its development, and its consequences when it arises in countries and historical periods representing different stages or patterns of industrialization. By worker consciousness we mean workers' identities and societal imagery based on their places in systems of work relations which override the identities of kinship, ethnicity, or other nonwork roles and affiliations. Worker consciousness as we are using the term may or may not imply class consciousness in a Marxian sense. . . . Workers may express it by acting collectively or as individuals. . . . We leave it to chapter authors to decide what aspects of worker consciousness (or lack of it) they wish to examine, and whether to use the term.

The response was gratifying. All authors addressed aspects of the theme. Chapters concern a variety of times and places.

Several authors treat ways in which nonwork statuses can impair worker consciousness or working-class solidarity and action. Sandbrook analyzes how continued attachments to rural and kin networks retard proletarianization of the emergent tropical African working class. Peil shows that social networks away from work in three African countries were not built around work associates but around kinship and neighborhood. Klass discusses a factory in India where caste distinctions impaired the institutionalization of a rational bureaucratic system of recruiting and organizing work groups. Geschwender examines how Hawaiian capitalists manipulated national (racial) consciousness to divide workers. Schofer looks at national and religious cleavages that splintered the working class of Upper Silesia.

Two chapters suggest that sex differentiation may be the most deeply rooted obstacle to unified worker consciousness. Logan finds that Spanish urbanization and industrialization have done little to alter the traditional sexual division of labor and that women are still contained in the domestic sphere. I. Simpson and Mutran find that work status separates American working women's consciousness from that of housewives but does not overcome sex differences to build common interests on the part of working women and men.

Worker consciousness sometimes predominates over nonwork status consciousness. Hamilton and Wright's study finds few work-related attitudinal differences between college-educated and other U.S. blue-collar workers.

Nonwork and work affiliations may reinforce each other and enhance worker consciousness. Lubeck analyzes the role of Islamic nationalism in developing Nigerian working-class consciousness. Friedland shows how ethnic homogenization of California farm workers helped their unionization.

Several authors discuss other influences on worker consciousness and action. Landsberger reports that even under conditions very favorable to revolutionary class consciousness, Chilean and German workers oriented to short-run economistic interests more than to long-run revolutionary goals. Logan shows that rural-urban migration and affluence increased class consciousness among Barcelona textile workers. Jones argues that Soviet workers' class consciousness and militancy have been affected more by off-the-job concerns such as housing and consumer services than by job-related ones. Friedland shows how the growth of agribusiness with its need for a stable and skill-specialized labor force has helped the farm laborers' union movement. R. Simpson maintains that differing forms of community and workplace social structures, and the relations between these two structures, account for successes and failures of Southern U. S. textile unionism. Low-Beer argues that social backgrounds and socialization condition the effects of technological influences on class consciousness; he supports his contention with data from an Italian survey. Lockwood criticizes Marxist theories of proletarian class action. He argues that theorists must attend carefully to the complexities of the cultural and status orders as they relate to structural sources of consciousness and action.

We believe that this collection of papers achieves the aims we set out for the first volume in our series on sociology of work. Succeeding volumes will focus on different themes.

Richard L. Simpson
Ida Harper Simpson
Series Editors

RESEARCH IN
THE SOCIOLOGY
OF WORK

Volume 1 • 1981

WORKER CONSCIOUSNESS AND POPULIST PROTEST IN TROPICAL AFRICA

Richard Sandbrook

The organized working class in most advanced capitalist countries historically played a prominent role in the political struggles leading to the extension of democratic rights and the "welfare state." Elsewhere, the industrial proletariat was a participant, though never the central actor, in revolutionary upheavals. Is an analogous social-democratic or revolutionary role for workers likely in the peculiar circumstances of peripheral capitalism in Tropical Africa?

I. THE LIMITS OF PROLETARIANIZATION

The nature of these peculiar circumstances as they affect labor require adumbration. Not only is the urban wage-earning force in Middle Africa

Research in the Sociology of Work, Volume 1, pages 1–36
Copyright © 1981 by JAI Press Inc.
All rights of reproduction in any form reserved.
ISBN: 0-89232-124-5

1

relatively small, but it has also only recently achieved stability and remains only partially proletarianized. Roughly 40% of the population in these countries is typically economically active; the proportion of this in salaried, or wage, employment varies considerably—from between a quarter and a third in Zambia to under 5% in Mali and Niger (Doctor and Gallis, 1966: 150–173). Between a third and half of the *urban* labor forces are wage earners in the capitalist or modern sector. It is unusual for more than half of these to belong to trade unions.

Though small, the urban wage-earning force has become remarkably stable since the 1950s. Circular migration between town and country was the characteristic pattern for the bulk of African workers throughout most of the colonial period; indeed, the colonial authorities resorted to directly or indirectly coercive measures to generate an adequate labor supply until the Second World War. Even in the 1950s, an acute observer could comment that the distinction between "peasant" and "worker" was artificial in Africa in that most men were both at different times or simultaneously. In Walter Elkan's words (1960), "by and large it is wrong to equate the growth of towns . . . with the growth of an urban proletariat." However, a variety of factors since the 1950s have encouraged those with jobs to make a career of them—including a long-term need for cash in an increasingly monetarized economy, more attractive wage rates (in particular, scales rewarding long service), burgeoning unemployment, and increasing land shortages. The trend, even in the least-developed countries, has been towards labor turnover rates in the modern sector comparable to those in advanced capitalist countries. For example, a vast urban survey in Tanzania led to the conclusion that:

> . . . towns are no longer merely employment centres where a peasant goes for short periods to supplement his income. The urban labour force is now a modern labour force in the sense that its commitment to wage employment is not shared with a commitment to agricultural self-employment. Increasing stability has gone hand in hand with the increasing acquisition of skills, the acceptance of industrial discipline, and specialization, resulting in large part from the accumulation of experience and on the job training. . . . And the towns are no longer mere dormitories for transient workers, but now function as the locus of activity of a growing urban community (Richard Sabot, 1972: 191–192).

The same observation would apply throughout Africa. Survey upon survey reports that annual turnover rates are now much lower than before 1960 or 1950 (in the order of 5–15%) in the large firms and government, and that the proportion of urban workers resident in town for ten or twenty years is on the increase (see ILO, 1972: 92n; Bissman, 1969: 27; Grillo, 1973: 38; Berger, 1974: 207–210; Peil, 1968b: 11–13; Hinchliffe, 1973: 30).

Yet this stable work force remains only partially proletarianized. Proletarianization is the process of creating a "free" labor market by the separation of individuals from their means of production. But though most urban workers now apparently intend to remain in town for a considerable time, often until retirement, a majority of them still possess rights to land. In East Africa, for instance, roughly three-quarters of samples of industrial workers in the late 1960s and early 1970s acknowledged rights to land. Most workers are therefore not wholly dependent upon selling their labor power to survive (though the land to which many have access is too meagre to support a large family) (see Bissman, 1969: 28; Sabot, 1972: 215).

This retention of land rights would normally conduce to the maintenance of a rural orientation. There is in fact substantial evidence regarding the extensive rural links of many urban inhabitants. "Throughout Subsaharan Africa urban dwellers regularly visit their rural homes where they bring gifts, find wives, maintain land rights, build houses, intend to retire eventually, want to be buried; they receive gifts, offer hospitality to visitors from home, and help new arrivals in town" (J. Gugler, 1969: 146–147). Another practice reported in numerous surveys is that of making regular or irregular remittances to rural kin, the sum remitted constituting as much as 10–20% of a worker's take-home pay. In addition, it is not unusual for workers, along with their better-off urban townsmen, to support financially a village improvement society and/or ethnic union located in the city.[1]

Semiproletarianization, in sum, is evident structurally in the retention by most workers of land rights and culturally in their maintenance of ·extensive links to their rural homes. These two aspects are closely related. Workers (and urban dwellers in general) continue to fulfill their traditional obligations partly to ensure their economic security in an uncertain future. City people who intend to retire to their home villages feel constrained to ensure the good will and cooperation of their kin, both to safeguard their rights to land and to establish an honored place for themselves within local society. Furthermore, in the absence of a social welfare system, workers must perforce rely upon the generosity of kin and villagers should they fall upon hard times (occasioned perhaps by unemployment). However, they cannot expect generosity unless they themselves have been generous in the past. A rural orientation may thus connote not the tenacious hold of peasant conservatism upon workers, but a rational response to the exigencies of an insecure existence. Such an orientation is only likely to disappear, as suggested by Gibbal (1974) in his fascinating study of Abidjan, among the second-generation townsmen bereft of rural assets (see La Fontaine, 1970: 106–107; Ejiogu, 1968: 321; Waweru, 1976: 49–50). Needless to add, this component of the urban population, though now a minority in all cities, is rapidly growing.

If full proletarianization has generally not accompanied labor stabilization, what implications does this have for workers' consciousness? This is a difficult question to answer. On the one hand, to the extent that a worker possesses a continuing interest in the land, he cannot afford to ignore village politics and traditional ties. On the other hand, to the extent that he has made a career in town, he also cannot afford to ignore such urban problems as unemployment, wages, and the cost of living. These are the issues that normally engage the attention of trade unions. Semi-proletarianization should therefore not preclude the workers' attachment to collective organization and class solidarity.

But can this solidarity ever take a radical form, or do the circumstances of urban employment encourage militancy but not radicalism? There is little doubt that the preponderant (though not sole) tendency of trade unions in most African countries is to forego any overt political role, besides pressure-group tactics, in favor of concentration upon the defense of narrow economic interests. This "trade-union consciousness" makes no connections between sociopolitical grievances and the workers' specific industrial grievances and protests. Obviously, the political effect of such an orientation on the part of powerful sectors of the working class is to stabilize the development of peripheral capitalism. The explanation of this politically quiescent and even conservative behavior is often phrased in terms of the "labor aristocracy" thesis. If this thesis is generally sound, then the radical potential of the leading working-class sectors can be discounted. But is it sound?

II. A "LABOR ARISTOCRACY"?

Labor aristocracy, used descriptively, has long possessed considerable polemical appeal.[2] Considered as a theory of political behavior, however, it lacks both conceptual clarity and explanatory power. In the first place, ambiguity surrounds the stratum to which the theory refers. Various authors have typified any one of three strata of organized workers as labor aristocrats, while one (Lenin) used the term at various times to apply to all three: the trade union leadership, the skilled upper stratum, and the whole of the organized (especially urban) working class. In the case of African labor, Frantz Fanon (1965: 98) is, of course, the best known exponent of the view that the unionized urban workers as a whole are a relatively pampered and thus conservative force.[3] Giovanni Arrighi and John Saul (1973), on the other hand, initially identified the skilled and semiskilled workers in international corporations, along with the salariat ("elite" and "subelite"), as the labor aristocracy.[4] The empirical validity of each characterization will receive consideration below.

In the second place, the theory is deficient in explanatory power even when its referent is clear. The original Leninist formulation, at its most elegant, explained the alleged conservatism and Philistinism of certain leading segments of European working classes by reference to both their relatively privileged income position and the security of their employment. Both of these benefits were facilitated by the super-profits derived from the exploitation of non-Western areas by the monopolistic firms who employed the putative labor aristocrats. Translated into the African context, this theory, in its most complex form, can be summarized in three interrelated propositions:

1. The leading segment of the urban working class, employed either by state agencies, state corporations, or international corporations, has a privileged income position relative to the semiproletarianized peasants in town and the rural masses.
2. This privileged employment is secure owing to the monopolistic or oligopolistic power of their employers (especially because increased labor costs can typically be passed on to consumers or the public).
3. In these circumstances, the labor aristocrats can see their interests as linked to the persistence of peripheral capitalism and its attendant dominant classes, and as separate from those of the peasants and urban poor. Hence, the leading segment of the working class is both politically quiescent and conservative, and able to impose these orientations upon the labor movement as a whole.

Consider first a methodological problem with this formulation. While working classes at all times and in all places have been internally differentiated and privileged in comparison with other social forces, some of these working classes have assumed a radical orientation and others a conservative one. The fact of income differentials per se explains little. For the theory to possess any explanatory power, it must estimate the income differential that allegedly generates, in conjunction with secure employment, complacency and conservatism on the part of workers. Without some rough measure, the thesis easily collapses into a tautology: the labor aristocrats are conservative because they are relatively privileged and secure, and one knows that they are sufficiently privileged and secure because they are conservative. Only Arrighi and Saul, to their credit, offer a way to avoid tautology, by suggesting that the semi-skilled workers and others of the labor aristocracy earn three to five times the income of the unskilled workers.

But even if one could demonstrate the general applicability of such an income gap (which, I suggest below, is doubtful), the thesis would still be unconvincing. It is simply too crudely materialist in drawing an unmediated link between objective conditions and political behavior.[5] What counts in understanding the workers' political behavior is their perception of their place in society and of the desirability and possibility of structural change; it is doubtful that this is a function solely of differentials between a supposed labor aristocracy and those strata and classes below. The consciousness of workers is subject to many other influences—including, e.g., the workers' well-being relative to the bourgeoisie and salariat,[6] traditions of struggle or accommodation with the dominant classes, and the existence of a radical movement agitating for change.

If the logic of the theory is dubious, its empirical basis with respect to Tropical Africa is also generally unconvincing. That is to say, the gaps in living standards and lifestyles between a putative labor aristocracy and more deprived classes and strata are, with certain exceptions, too modest to generate in themselves conservatism on the part of the workers. Along with the emergence of permanent wage-labor forces in the 1950s and 1960s came the view, with supporters on both the Right and the Left, that the organized urban workers as a whole were extracting an unduly large share of the potential economic surplus—at the expense of peasants and/or employment generation (see Turner, 1966: 13). But the evidence now available, sparse as it is, suggests that this conception of African urban workers is largely unwarranted. Arthur Hazlewood's trenchant comment (1978: 90) with respect to the Kenyan proletariat can be more widely applied: the view that workers, even skilled ones, are relatively well-off could be "believed only by someone without experience of the way they live or with his nose firmly buried in the figures."

There is, obviously, not space in this paper to discuss all the studies bearing upon the contention of relative privilege. Luckily, some fairly exhaustive literature surveys are available which relate to the existence and extent of the urban-rural income differential. One of these (Allen, 1972: 61–92), covering the relevant literature to 1971, seeks as far as possible to control cost-of-living differences and size of household in comparing income levels. It concludes, on the basis of evidence about countries as diverse as Senegal, Zaire, Ghana, Zambia, Kenya, Tanzania, and Botswana, that the differentials between urban workers and peasants are (with the exception in particular of Zambia) modest or negligible (see also Hinchliffe, 1974; Knight, 1972; Greenhalgh, 1972; Hazlewood, 1978: 90–92). Another survey of wage rates in Francophone and Anglophone West Africa supports the notion that urban workers have not prospered. In general, "the pattern in West Africa since independence has been one of governments restraining changes in money wages, and allowing real wages to fall, sometimes steeply and usually for long periods of time, in face of rising prices. Only in Nigeria in 1964 was this pattern seriously disturbed and the policy behind it seriously breached" (Rimmer, 1970: 50). In considering relative well-being, one must recognize, in the first place, that urban workers bear a disproportionate part of the burden of rural poverty. Study after study has reported that these workers remit 20% or more of their income to relatives in the rural areas, and support large households in the towns. In the second place, statistics comparing the real incomes of peasants and urban workers are misleading in that these tend to underestimate the value of rural subsistence production (especially housing, food, and fuel) and ignore the added expenses of city living—such as transport to work and higher quality clothing. The net result of these factors is to diminish, or even in some cases eliminate, the per capita household income differential between peasants and workers.[7]

It is in the light of these considerations that the plight of urban workers in various countries is to be understood. In Ghana, for instance, a statistical study (Ewusi, 1971: 50, 52) found that the real minimum wage fell by 45% throughout the 1960s; by 1970, Accra's laborers were considerably worse off than they had been in 1939. Price inflation has also worked to the detriment of Ghana's skilled workers (Lisk, 1976: 368–370). Their real earnings in 1967 were only 70% of the 1963 level, and by 1972 these still stood at only 76.7% of the 1963 standard (which was itself below the 1959 real earnings). [Disposable incomes had fallen even more than these statistics would suggest, in that the rise in workers' *money* incomes meant that these became subject to income tax.] This was the context in which Ghana's Ministry of Health made a rather startling discovery in a 1971 survey (de Heer, 1972: 79–85). Although an average 69% of workers' take-home pay was spent on food purchases, "many" workers in Accra complained that they often had to rely upon kola nuts to dull their hunger pains after the middle of the month.

In the Ivory Coast, a sample survey of 1,000 manual workers in urban food-processing plants arrived at equally distressing conclusions. This survey sought to expose the roots of the low productivity and high rate of absenteeism of the largely immigrant workers from surrounding countries. The most important factor was found to be the workers' general physical debilitation; this was a consequence of nutritional deficiencies, of the prevalence of parasitical and endemic diseases, of alcoholism, and of a widespread psychological malaise associated with a sense of hopelessness and alienation from work (Esparre, 1967: 181–192).

But the situation of the skilled and unskilled workers in Kinshasa has probably been the worst. Here, the real minimum wage diminished by more than 50% in the first eight years of independence—and the economy has continued on its downward path since. An intensive, month-long household survey of the income and expenditure of a small sample concluded that workers' households could not survive on the diminishing real wages (Houyoux, 1970: 99–108). Consequently, all of the employed men engaged in spare-time employment or self-employment, all but one of their wives undertook petty trading, and only about half of the schoolage children actually attended school. Even so, the workers (skilled and unskilled) and their families could not afford to buy sufficient food (though 62% of total household expenditures went on this item). These families went hungry as often as those in the sample of unemployed.[8]

Of course, not all groups of urban workers are as wretched as these. The Zambian copper miners are perhaps the most clearly privileged workers' group in comparison to peasants. Indeed, one influential study of the comparative returns to agricultural cash production and urban labor in Zambia contended that it did not pay to engage in peasant commercial agriculture (Young, 1971: 91–94). A hard-working peasant who had in 1964 succeeded in attaining an income level equal to that of an urban worker was, by 1968, 30% poorer in absolute terms and more than twice as poorly off as the nonagricultural wage earner. While other writers have dismissed this contention as exaggerated on the basis of a new rural cost-of-living index, they still found the rural-urban differential to be substantial (see Fry, 1975: 730–738). The average real earnings of cash-cropping peasants rose by just over 32% between 1964 and 1971, whereas those for African wage earners increased by over 74%. Furthermore, peasants had probably fallen even farther behind in 1973–1974 owing to poor harvests. Among Zambian wage earners, it was the miners of the Copperbelt towns—whose average income throughout the 1960s was about twice the average for all other industrial sectors—who contributed disproportionately to this rural-urban income differential (see also Maimbo and Fry, 1971: 95–110; ILO, 1969: 9).

Has the relative privilege of these copper miners induced a conservative and politically quiescent orientation on their part? Yes and no—the evidence is ambiguous. It is the case that the Mineworkers Union qua union played no part in the nationalist struggle. While labor leaders in the 1950s and early 1960s championed nationalist causes in public and the rank and file joined nationalist parties in droves, the miners' union refused to stage politically motivated strikes and resisted efforts by the dominant United National Independence Party to control it. The politicization of the African miners was thus limited (though not absent) during the colonial period. Indeed, the miners have remained a steadfastly economistic lot to the present day, resisting attempts at governmental control of their union at the branch level and undertaking unofficial strikes in defiance of a ban on work stoppages (see Bates, 1971; chap. 7, 8; Henderson, 1973: 288–299).

Yet the case is not clear cut. In the first place, African trade unions catering for workers much less relatively privileged than these miners were also politically inactive during the colonial era; in fact, political quiescence on the part of unions was more the norm than the exception (see Berg and Butler, 1964: 340–381). This had much to do with the repressive power of the colonial state—in particular, the reasonable fear on the part of union leaders and members that political action by their unions would prompt curtailment of labor's collective bargaining and legal rights (see Sandbrook, 1975). In the second place, recent intensive interviews with a substantial sample of Zambian copper miners have revealed a political orientation that is far from conservative (Burawoy, 1972b). These workers clearly do not regard themselves as a beneficiary of a neo-colonial order. Instead, the African miners tend to conceive of

> . . . the union leadership, white management and black Government as three pillars of a corporate "power elite" determined to exploit and sap the workers of energy in the pursuit of increased profits to be used as much for their own private benefit as for the development of the country. It is not just that the miner feels "poverty-stricken" in comparison with the expatriate . . . but also that he feels inadequately treated by his own Government. . . . Their perspectives are coloured by a small black elite competing for higher standards of living in an attempt to emulate the whites (Burawoy, 1972a: 263).

These attitudes have prompted considerable industrial unrest in the mines, unrest that has increasingly been met by state coercion against the miners' informal leaders. In these circumstances, it is doubtful whether the miners can be regarded as a stabilizing influence within the Zambian political economy. Their political potential remains ambiguous.

If the urban unionized workers as a whole cannot generally by typified as a labor aristocracy, is it more valid to apply this thesis to the skilled workers alone? The existence of a skilled-unskilled wage differential is not at issue; the problem is to determine how wide this income gap must be in order to generate conservatism among skilled workers. Unfortunately, the studies in industrial sociology that would permit one to relate workers' political behavior to varying skill differentials do not exist. Arrighi and Saul (1973) suggest that the complacent labor aristocrats earn three to five times as much as the unskilled migrants. But as Table 1 shows, the interskill wage differential in Africa has not recently been that wide within any sector of economic activity surveyed. Although this differential varies both by activity and time, it is rare for a skilled worker to earn even twice as much as an unskilled laborer. In a substantial number of cases, the unskilled earn a wage as much as 70 or 80% of that of the skilled worker. This is particularly likely in Greater Accra, Metropolitan Lagos, and Dar-es-Salaam.

If the secular trend in the interskill wage differential favored the skilled workers in particular economic activities, then this could also provide some grounds for considering the latter labor aristocrats. Such data do not seem to exist on a comparative basis.[9] One can only tentatively argue that the pressure within most African countries has been towards the

Table 1.   Interskill Wage Differentials, Most Recent Year(s)

Economic Activity	Textile Manufacturing	Printing-Publishing	Machine Manufacturing	Construction
	unskilled wage × 100	unskilled wage × 100	unskilled wage × 100	laborer's wage × 100
	loom fixer's wage	machine compositor's wage	machine fitter's wage	plumber's wage
Dakar, Senegal (1969, 1970)	82 (1970)	49 (1969)	59 (1969)	62 (1969)
Ivory Coast, urban average (1975, 1976)	73 (1975)	42 (1976)	69 (1976)	72 (1976)
Douala, Cameroun (1976)	53	44	36	53
Greater Accra, Ghana (1974)	82	74	88	81
Greater Lagos, Nigeria (1970, 1973, 1974)	83 (1973)	70 (1970)	76 (1970)	76 (1974)
Lusaka, Zambia (1975, 1976)	89 (1976)	15* (1975)	44 (1976)	63 (1976)
Dar-es- Salaam, Tanzania (1972)	88	73	—	62

Source: Calculated from the International Labour Office's, *Bulletin of Labour Statistics,* 1969–1977, 2nd quarter, Appendix A.

*This figure is highly suspect; only two years earlier the Government had reported that the unskilled workers made the same wage as the machine compositor!

compression of interskill wage differentials. Insofar as most of these countries have suffered from a dearth of skilled manpower and an abundance of unskilled labor, this assertion may sound preposterous. Yet, in this area, as elsewhere in state-capitalist economies, institutional forces offset market ones. One such force is represented by trade unions. Where unions organize along industrial lines (as is the norm in Tropical Africa), union leaders will tend to favor the demands of the less-skilled workers who constitute the bulk of their members. Collective bargaining can thus lead to the compression of interskill differentials. Governments have represented another important influence on wage rates through minimum wage legislation, government wage rates, and income policy. Claiming to be guided by a "fair wages policy," official wage-determination agencies have often granted wage rates to unskilled labor higher than those warranted by the market. In the Nigerian Federal Civil Service, for instance, a laborer's minimum wage in 1953 amounted to just 57% of that of the skilled worker; by 1970, this had risen to 77%. In Kenya, the wage guidelines applied by the Industrial Court since August 1973 require higher proportionate increases for the lowest paid employees. Since then, the real wages of skilled workers have apparently declined, whereas those of the less skilled have, at worst, remained stationary (see Fajana, 1975: 164–165; 151–152; Cowan and Kinyanjui, 1977: 12, 13). Efforts by governments to maintain the pretense of their commitment to egalitarian policies have thus tended to favor the unskilled over the skilled wage earners.

I cannot pretend to have conclusively refuted in these few paragraphs the notion of skilled workers acting as a labor aristocracy. Indeed, it would be ridiculous even to attempt this. In general terms, one can only observe that skilled workers appear to be neither enjoying undue privilege nor enhancing their relative position. There are, of course, exceptions to this general rule. But one must also point out that those studies of African workers' political action that distinguish among skill levels *have not portrayed the skilled workers as politically quiescent and conservative.* The skilled have, indeed, often served either as the informal leaders of radical political action or at least as participants (see Stichter, 1975; Jeffries; Peace; see also Zeitlin, 1970).

There is one further aspect of the labor aristocracy thesis that requires a brief comment. To constitute a labor aristocracy, a group of organized workers must not only be relatively privileged, but also perceive itself as having interests separate from, and indeed opposed to, those of the lower strata or classes. One cannot infer that such a perception exists merely on the grounds of an income differential and the presence of a large industrial reserve army in the towns. Although the situation will vary from place to place, there are certain widely operating social and economic factors tending to associate urban workers with popular interests and grievances, to make them men of the people. These factors are only now receiving the consideration they deserve.

A. Common Residence, Lifestyles, and Aspirations

It must be remembered that those employed in the modern sector in African cities constitute only a half or less of the urban labor force. With the partial exception of miners and railwaymen, urban workers tend to live in the congested and usually unsanitary low-income residential areas side by side with those engaged in the petty capitalist and noncapitalist forms of production, in petty commerce, or unemployed. A consistent finding of anthropological studies of these neighborhoods in West, Central, and East African cities is the similarity of lifestyle among households of wage earners and non-wage earners. Workers are generally not an easily distinguishable or exclusive group within the common people. As well, urban workers, as much as their self-employed or unemployed neighbors, maintain diffuse links with their rural homes; the effect of this is presumably to promote a perception of the complementarity of workers' and peasants' interests and grievances.

Furthermore, if there is an aristocracy among the common people, this is not usually composed of workers. It was once thought that all self-employed individuals in urban small-scale activities were poor, eking out a living until they could obtain a secure job in the modern capitalist sector. This, we now know, is a myth. Although there is considerable variance even within a single informal occupation, many of the self-employed earn incomes higher than those employed in the modern sector. The best-off are generally the petite bourgeoisie of landlords, traders, transporters, small-scale manufacturers, and hotel or bar keepers. It is little wonder, then, that the successful petite bourgeoisie often constitute a reference group for their proletarian, subproletarian, and unemployed neighbors. Numerous studies, especially in West and Central Africa, report the prevalence of petite bourgeois aspirations among both skilled and unskilled workers, who aim to accumulate the initial capital to enter self-employment (see Peace, 1976: 288–289; Peil, 1972: 20; Lloyd, 1976: 111–113; Lubeck, 1975: 258–259; Le Brun and Gerry, 1976: 23–24; Jeffries, 1976: 276; Sandbrook and Arn, 1977: 37). This may well be an increasingly unrealizable dream. Nonetheless, the prevalence of popular petite bourgeois aspirations among even secure workers, combined with their often indistinguishable lifestyle and inclusive social ties, do not represent the sort of conditions conducive to the formation of a labor aristocracy (or a radical proletariat).

B. Multiple Job-holding and Alternation between Wage and Self-employment

The common practices among urban workers of multiple job-holding and alternation in employment may also dispose them to see their interests as generally congruent with those of the common people. In the first place, many of the urban self-employed are people who had initially been in wage-employment. For instance, 34% of a large sample of self-employed in the eight largest Tanzanian urban areas had a proletarian background. Even if this proportion is lower in other cities, there is doubtless considerable interchange and alternation, especially in those occupations (e.g., construction and crafts) closely tied to wage-employment opportunities. While some skilled workers become petty producers out of necessity, having been laid off by a large firm, others voluntarily leave wage employment to set up their own self-financed establishments. Conversely, petty producers who have fallen upon hard times will naturally seek skilled wage employment, though not necessarily as more than a temporary expedient (see Bienefeld, 1974: 34–36; King, 1977: 114–118; Mukenge, 1973: 472–475; Lloyd, 1976: 111–113; Koll, 1969: 21; Le Brun and Gerry, 1976: 23–24).

In the second place, it is common in African cities for a worker's household to contain at least one secondary earner in informal economic activities. This secondary earner may be the worker himself, who devotes part of his spare time to self-employment, or a wife and/or child may contribute a supplementary income by means of petty commerce, manufacturing, or services. One anthropologist studying a neighborhood in Accra (Hart, 1973: 66) has asserted that "multiple informal employment—both with and without simultaneous wage employment—is almost universal in the economic behaviour of Accra's subproletariat." This perhaps is an exaggeration; nonetheless, this practice of multiple job holding is common enough to receive mention in many detailed studies of African workers' domestic lives (see Joshi, et al., 1976: 58–59; Barnes, 1974: 55; Date-Bah, 1974: 169; Sandbrook and Arn, 1977: 36–37; Houyoux and Houyoux, 1970: 107; Mukenge, 1973: 466–468; Bienefeld, 1974: 34–36; Halpenny, 1972: 43–44; Boswell, 1975: 3). The effect of both multiple job holding and alternation between wage and self-employment is to blur the distinction between workers' and nonworkers' households. In this way, these practices tend to prevent the separation of a self-conscious labor aristocracy from the urban masses.

This section has sought to suggest that, if economism is a common tendency among organized labor in Africa, the labor aristocracy thesis provides no general explanation for this. This theory is, first, generally (though not invariably) empirically unsound in its application to either urban organized workers as a whole or skilled workers as a putative labor aristocracy. Secondly, it is vague conceptually and simplistic in its crude materialism. Political consciousness has more complex roots than the theory allows.

III. WORKERS AND URBAN POPULISM

An interim conclusion is that one should not construe economism as implying active support for the peripheral capitalist order. Acquiescence on the part of workers (to the extent that this obtains) is not tantamount to complicity in a class alliance underpinning a neo-colonial state. This is not to say that Africa's urban workers are destined to become a radical force at some point. It is rather to assert that one cannot preclude this possibility on the basis of the labor aristocracy thesis.

Is then a political role for African workers precluded by the absence of a vanguard group to politicize and mobilize them? Should one simply agree with Lenin that workers, left to themselves, are capable of only a "trade-union consciousness"? Indeed, workers in Africa have commonly had to rely inordinately upon their own resources, with precious little institutional support in their confrontations with employers and the state. There is not space here to expatiate upon the sad history of African trade unions; but the typical story, in country after country, of their rise and atrophy is apropos. Trade unions anywhere tend to have contradictory consequences for worker consciousness. On the one hand, they serve to integrate emergent proletariats into capitalist political economies by working within the rules established for industrial relations and political change. On the other hand, unions broaden and intensify working-class identities in the process of articulating and representing common interests and coordinating industrial action on a nationwide or inter-industry basis. But, in contemporary Africa, national union officials can more often be found stifling rank-and-file initiatives than articulating common grievances or coordinating industrial action. Of course, the state's efforts to emasculate organized labor go back to the latter's origins just before the Second World War; post-colonial regimes, regardless of professed political complexion, almost invariably extended and refined the existing panoply of labor controls and sanctions within a few years of independence (see Sandbrook and Cohen, 1976: 195–204). Where the state has essentially incorporated trade unions (above the grass-roots level) into its structure, workers must perforce find noninstitutional forms of protest—and these will inevitably be localized and sporadic.

In addition to the usual atrophy of union movements, working classes have been exposed to radical movements in few African countries. In those few cases where a radical party either assumed power or was permitted an oppositional role, the radical intellectuals have had a profound influence upon working-class action. In the Sudan, for instance, where a Communist Party operated openly for a considerable time, its leadership has been regarded as a major determinant of that labor movement's penchant for direct political action (see Taha, 1970: 242) (discussed further below). In Tanzania, since the move to the left in 1967, and especially since the Mwongozo Declaration of 1971, commentators have linked much of Dar-es-Salaam's industrial protest to TANU's propagation of such radical notions as the right of workers to participate in management and political decision making, and to be supervised by individuals who are neither "arrogant, extravagant, contemptuous, nor oppressive (Mwongozo Declaration, Clause 15)."[10]

It is the case, then, that along with the absence of a revolutionary vanguard went the absence or weakness of radical consciousness among the urban workers. In view of the limited proletarianization of the African labor forces and the weakness of emergent union movements, it is hardly surprising that, during the colonial period:

> . . . the political history of the African worker . . . indicates a locally based reactive political consciousness and activism rather than a broadly-based class consciousness. At no period during colonialism have African workers revealed such a high degree of political will and organization skill as to have proposed a major threat to colonial rule (Gutkind, 1974: 57).

Much the same could be said in general about the post-colonial period. While occasionally general strikes have contributed to the fall of regimes, the working class, possessing neither the requisite cohesion, organization, nor consciousness, saw power pass to the army instead of itself.

Yet it is incorrect to conclude from this that African workers, on their own, are capable only of trade-union consciousness. Applied to Africa, Lenin's formulation surely slights the workers' autonomous political role, thus distorting the historical record. The latter, by casting the discussion of workers' consciousness in terms of either "trade-union" or "social-democratic" (i.e., revolutionary) types, has obfuscated the range of possibilities. It is more fruitful to adhere to Lenin's more cryptic observation that "there is consciousness and consciousness." In some parts of Africa, segments of workers have evolved at least a "populist," if nonrevolutionary, political consciousness that transcends economism. Populism, of course, is not a specifically working-*class* consciousness. It is instead a mentality of the underprivileged as a whole who no longer accept the legitimacy of the existing distribution of power and wealth. Its prime feature is a tendency to hold an allegedly corrupt and supercilious elite personally responsible for an inegalitarian and oppressive social order and to invest all virtue and legitimacy in the common people. While such a perspective provides only a limited guideline for effective political action, it is nonetheless a form of consciousness that deserves serious consideration. That this mentality should have been achieved at all is no minor feat, inasmuch as educational and value systems tend to legitimate the *status quo*. That workers apparently manifest a special propensity for populist notions, and indeed for spearheading urban populist protest, requires some explanation.

On what basis can one talk with confidence about the existence of a populist political consciousness in Africa? There are two main methods of gauging the consciousness of particular groups of workers, and each has inherent shortcomings. In the historical approach, the researcher infers consciousness from the actual collective action of workers; but action is often ambiguous. The alternative, more common in Latin American than African labor studies, is the attribution of political orientations on the basis of a sample survey. The shortcomings in this methodology are too well known to require elaboration. Nonetheless, several recent West African studies that have sought to combine interview research with observation have suggested the saliency of populist orientations among the workers they studied (see Jeffries, 1976: 261–280; Sandbrook and Arn, 1977: Chap. 6; Peace 1976: 281–302; Gutkind, 1975: 11, 19, 20).

The historical approach cannot be dealt with so summarily. One must first decide what action will count as evidence of a populist mentality. In more politically developed countries, an oppositional consciousness would be manifested mainly in the workers' support for certain political parties or their participation in mass demonstrations, rallies, or riots. But in the circumstances of Tropical Africa, radical movements are not tolerated outside of Tanzania and the former Portuguese colonies, while mass demonstrations are suppressed and thus infrequent. Hence, the quintessence of workers' populist protest is the general or wildcat strike which supplements its economic demands with a political critique. Although African labor history is still relatively unexplored, it records many instances in which striking workers crystallized the inchoate sociopolitical grievances of the common people. In these cases, strikes with wide popular support represented essentially ephemeral protest movements.

A study of the strike literature permits the formulation of several generalizations respecting the consciousness and political potential of urban workers. In the first place, solidarity in strike action among workers from different sectors (as in general strikes), or between a particular group of workers and the subproletariat, depends upon the combination of a potent workers' economic grievance with popular political dissatisfaction. Inasmuch as the highly inegalitarian social structures of peripheral capitalist societies and the insensitivity of governments provide fertile ground for political disaffection, such a combination of grievances and interests is not unusual. In the second place, urban-based strikes in Africa can attain an immediate political impact disproportionate to the relatively small number of workers involved. This is due not only to the fragility of regimes and the paucity of strong institutions (excepting the army in some cases), but also to the concentration of workers within the urban seats of power, and the propensity of disaffected elements of the subproletariat and petite bourgeoisie to join the protest. Such labor protests, however, have only rarely led to any long-term sociopolitical change.

In the third place, the workers who have manifested the most solidarity and militancy, as measured by their propensity to strike, have been the dockers, railwaymen, and miners. In southern Nigeria, for instance, railway employees participated in a third of twenty strikes occurring between 1897 and 1939, dockers and marine workers in a fifth, and coal miners in a fifth. Of the remainder, all but two involved state employees. In Ghana in the 1970s, factory workers have evinced a growing militancy —accounting for almost half the strikes in 1972–1976—but earlier mining and "transport and communications" employees had the highest strike records (Hughes and Cohen, 1978: 39–40; Kraus, forthcoming: Table 3).

Dockers, railwaymen, and miners have also evidenced the highest propensity to act as the leading edge of popular urban protest. This is not surprising. Marx, Engels, and many others have observed that the political potential of workers—indeed their emergence as a distinct class— required the growth of large-scale enterprises. In the case of the early industrializers, these enterprises were typically factories. But in the peculiar circumstances of peripheral capitalism, the conglomeration of permanent workers initially occurs in mineral extraction, plantations, and the public services. The combination of limited industrialization—mostly undertaken in the post-war period and oriented to import substitution and raw-material processing—and the common reliance upon capital-intensive technologies, have restricted the size, and hence the power, of industrial labor. However, industrialization is proceeding apace in a few primate cities; in the future industrial workers may play a more central role within labor movements.

Consider briefly the major patterns revealed in the strike literature. General strikes with evident political implications have rarely occurred in Middle Africa, in part because national union federations have rarely preserved sufficient autonomy from the government to promote these. Nonetheless, such strikes have threatened or toppled governments in Senegal in May–June 1968, Ghana in 1950, 1961, and 1971, Nigeria in 1945 and 1964, the Congo-Brazzaville in 1963 and 1968, the Sudan in 1958 and 1964, and Madagascar in 1972.[11] In all these strikes, the workers' solidarity depended upon the fusing of a basic economic grievance to a widespread political disaffection. Support for most of these general strikes extended beyond the workers directly concerned to the urban masses. In three of the countries—Congo-Brazzaville, the Sudan, and Madagascar— general strikes formed part of the background to an overthrow of government; but power eventually passed to the military.

The most recent case, that of Madagascar, illustrates why this is the usual outcome. In the Tananarive demonstrations and riots of May 1972, which undercut the authority of President Tsiranana, widely regarded as a tool of French neo-colonialism, students and workers played a central role. A general strike declared on May 15 paralyzed the country's economy. But it is one thing to weaken and topple a regime, and quite another to install another in its place. The movement to oust Tsiranana was unorganized and poorly coordinated. The dominant goals, as expressed by the most militant and articulate elements involved in the revolt, were utopian and populist:

> They called for the destruction of hierarchies and for the establishment of equality for everyone. They designated as their objective the setting up of 'the state of little people' . . . in the form of a National Popular Congress which would realize their dream of direct democracy. This utopian construction was to be produced by the simple inversion of the hierarchical society and despotic power they were attacking (Althabe; 1978).

What inevitably happened, however, was that the chiefs of the armed forces picked up the power lying in the street. Appointed Prime Minister by Tsiranana in the midst of the crisis, the head of the General Staff proceeded to smash the power not only of the old regime, but also of the rebels seeking to realize popular power (Althabe, 1972: 205–243).

Dockworkers throughout the world evince a relatively high level of group solidarity and militancy. In Africa this segment of emergent working classes has instigated and animated many popular urban protests. The Lagos dockworkers had spearheaded a general strike as early as 1897; this, though lasting only three days and concerning only economic grievances, seriously embarrassed the colonial government. Later labor protests in Nigeria as well found the dockworkers at the forefront of the confrontation (Hopkins, 1966: 133–135; see also Melson, 1970: 784). The workers in ports along the Indian Ocean have also manifested a propensity for developing a group consciousness and leading ephemeral protest movements. Studies reveal this to have been the case in Mombasa, Dar-es-Salaam, and Zanzibar City. For instance, the 1948 Zanzibar General Strike has been characterized as "Zanzibar's 1905, the first mass demonstration of the Protectorate's urban work force . . . protesting against aspects of the existing social and economic order.[12]

The railways and railwaymen have played an important part in the development of African working classes. In the words of Michael Mason:

> Of all the undertakings of the colonial state, it was the railway which demanded the greatest supply of labor. For this reason, in much of Africa we can see the railway as the nursery of the working class. It is true that the earliest forms of labor organization and even some elements of labor consciousness emerged in connection with the African ports which often became capitals. But the growth of a working class in these waterfront towns was severely limited without a complementary growth of modern communication with the hinterland (Mason, 1978).

Strikes by railwaymen have a long history in most African countries; in Freetown, Sierra Leone, for instance, the first work stoppage occurred in 1919, with a second instance in 1926 (Conway, 1968: 49–59). In the immediate post-World War II period, there were a spate of railway strikes, some of which assumed the form of popular movements against colonial rule. This happened in Douala in 1945, and on the four railway networks in French West Africa in 1947.[13] Indeed, the latter strike was probably the longest in African union history, with most of the workers staying out for five months. Needless to say, these strikers could not have maintained their strike without the unstinting material assistance provided by kin and neighbors. In the Rhodesias during this period, the African railwaymen were also developing solidarity and eventually union organization through strike action and organizational work by labor leaders (Turner, 1976: 73–98). But in this case, the colonial government's prohibition of political action, backed by the evident will to employ coercion, prevented the combination of workers' grievances and popular urban demands. In the post-colonial period, the railway workers in both Ghana (in 1961 and 1971) and Nigeria (in 1964) have led or unreservedly backed general strikes that involved a political critique of the existing regime (see Jeffries, 1975: 784).

Miners are another group noted for their solidarity. As historical studies of strikes by the iron and diamond miners in Sierra Leone, gold miners in the Gold Coast, and copper miners in Northern Rhodesia (Zambia) have shown, some groups of African miners had achieved a remarkable collective consciousness well before the Second World War (Conway, 1968: 59–63; Greenstreet, 1972: 30–40; Perrings, 1977: 33–51). It was not unusual even at this early time for economic grievances to be mixed with political ones. In Nigeria, the famous Enugu colliery strike of 1949, though prompted by strictly economic demands, nevertheless attained a symbolic anticolonial significance with the death by shooting of twenty-one strikers (Akpala, 1965: 335–363; see also Smock, 1969). In southern Rhodesia, the African miners apparently developed a group consciousness in the earliest days of the mining industry. However, this could not be manifested through the creation of workers' organizations or political action owing to the oppressive milieu of the mining compound. Instead, worker consciousness was evident in two brief strikes before World War I, and in such covert forms of labor protest as desertion and resistance in day-to-day situations (Van Onselen, 1976).

Miners have continued to be an obstreperous group in post-colonial societies where authoritarian and hierarchical production relations continue unchanged, though usually with African managers and supervisors gradually replacing expatriates. While the distance of mines from major urban centers typically limits the capacity of miners to spark urban protests, their industrial actions are not infrequently tumultuous (since they are commonly unofficial and "illegal") and fraught with political implications.

Consider the hardy "economism" of the Ghanaian gold miners and its links with Ghana's evolving political economy. These workers engaged in a series of wildcat strikes, riots, and demonstrations in 1968–1970. In this period, the police fought with and shot miners on several occasions; striking workers threatened and beat mine managers and supervisors and (significantly) union officials; and the management of Ghana's richest mine requested the army to intervene to restore order and prevent the closure of its mine. Although various specific industrial grievances precipitated the unofficial strikes and demonstrations, an underlying cause was the miners' hostility toward the Africanized mine management who were supercilious and conspicuous in their consumption while the real incomes of the workers were declining. Yet the mines constituted only one specific instance of the elitism and widening income gaps among classes in post-colonial Ghana. Since the state owned most of the gold mines and was demonstrably unsympathetic to workers' grievances—having used its coercive apparatus to emasculate the Mineworkers' Union and crush the miners' protests—the strikes took on a political (though not a revolutionary) connotation. Some of the flavor of this is apparent in the following description of one wildcat strike at Tarkwa mine in June 1969:

> Before noon workers gathered at the shaft top and smashed doors and windows in the mine offices and chased clerical workers from the building. They started to march into Tarkwa. The Medical Officer, Mine Secretary, and Labor Controller were seized and severely beaten. The Managing Director was taken from his office, stripped and dressed in a miner's overalls and boots and made to carry mining tools at the head of the workers' procession. The miners marched into town, according to one witness "like an invading army." A platoon of police rushed to the mine to subdue what they described as an "insurrection." Miners clashed with police and after warning shots failed to disperse the workers, police opened fire and wounded four workers in the legs. . . .
>
>   The following day the strike continued. One thousand workers with bows, arrows, and other weapons gathered at the shaft top. Again police rushed to the mine and clashed with the workers. Tear gas failed to disperse them and again police fired on the workers, wounding three. Workers armed with sticks, stones, and iron rods fought with police at Akoon Gate and eleven more workers were arrested (Crisp, 1978: 4).

Factory workers, as I have mentioned, are generally a recent and relatively small addition to African labor forces. Yet there are indications that in future they may play an important political role. In Africa, as elsewhere, factory workers have quickly shown themselves capable of creating considerable solidarity and initiating concerted action in defense of their interests. Consider the case of Nigeria, a country with a high industrial potential owing to the size of its market and its resource endowment. Although industrial workers are by no means the largest sector of Nigeria's working class, manufacturing and repairs accounted for about one-third of all the workers involved in strikes between 1966 and 1971 inclusive. (Transport and communications supplied the second largest number of strikers.) In terms of the number of trade disputes and number of strikes, the relative militancy of the various sectors remained about the same, with manufacturing and repairs at the top of the list (see Sonubi, 1973: 228–233). This militancy is all the more remarkable when one considers that the number of strikes did not diminish among factory workers even after strikes were essentially banned in 1969.

In some instances, it is clear that striking Nigerian factory workers were animated by more than solely economic grievances. This was evident in early 1971, after private firms had refused to grant a cost of living award that a Wages and Salaries Review Commission had awarded to workers in public employment. The initial refusal of expatriate concerns to follow suit prompted the mobilization of industrial workers. For example, in Ikeja, an industrial estate in Metropolitan Lagos, the animus underlying the wildcat strikes and occasional violence of 1971 can be traced to the workers' antipathy to a grossly inegalitarian social order, in addition to the specific economic grievance. Moreover, this industrial action won support among Ikeja's self-employed, who obviously shared this same hostility (see Peace, 1974; Peace, 1976). In Kano, the third largest industrial center in Nigeria, the initial intransigence of factory employers in 1971 also sparked a solidary reaction on the part of the workers in some cases. This reaction, it should be noted, apparently took place in the *absence* of conditions that favored class action among Lagosian factory workers; these adverse conditions in Kano included the relatively small size of factories, the paternalistic or even blatantly oppressive labor-management practices of indigenous or Levantine owners, the relatively low educational level of workers, and the absence of trade unions. Yet, even under these circumstances, the Kano factory workers manifested an "early class consciousness" during the crisis, successfully defending their interests through the development of informal strike committees and the initiation of wildcat strikes (Lubeck, 1975: 123; see also Lubeck, 1976).

It is worth emphasizing, in the light of the militancy and occasional populist protest of the first-generation factory proletariat, that their numbers are rapidly expanding in some African primate cities. Consider again the striking case of Lagos. Black Africa's largest city (with 3.5 million inhabitants in 1976), metropolitan Lagos exemplifies the national trend of industrial concentration in one or two cities. By 1965 about one-third of Nigeria's total manufacturing plants in the modern sector was concentrated in metropolitan Lagos; in the following five years about half of all new manufacturing investment went to this area. Over half of this city's labor force (about 1.4 million people) was occupied in 1976 in informal economic activities, i.e., self-employment or employment in enterprises with fewer than ten employees. In the modern sector, the public service was the largest employer. While manufacturing and repair firms engaged only about half as many employees, this number was still considerably larger than those employed in the formal commercial sector. An estimated 112,000 employees worked in 1976 within 332 industrial establishments employing ten or more workers. Between 1965 and 1974 Lagos' formal industrial employment quadrupled; the growth in industrial employment in the 1970s has been at least 8% per annum. If these trends continue, there will, by 1980, be 138,000 employees within 439 industrial establishments, with an average number of employees each increasing from 266 in 1974 to 314. And there are grounds for believing that such trends will persist. Metropolitan Lagos' share of Nigeria's net investment has increased in the 1970s—to 73% in 1973. Moreover, the Port is to be expanded from twenty-three to fifty-nine berths between 1975 and 1980, while the Third National Development Plan states that seven further industrial estates are to be developed by the Lagos State Government by 1980. Finally, it is noteworthy that most heavy industry locates in Lagos. It accounts for about three-quarters of the value added on such commodities as chemicals, metals and machinery, and paper and printing (Lagos Master Plan Project Unit, 1976).

If it is likely that factory workers will assume a more important role in African labor movements and urban protests, what form will this role take? One probable pattern emerges from a study of collective industrial and political action in Cordoba, an industrial city in Argentina. When foreign capital established large automobile factories there in the 1950s to serve the local market, a modern and relatively well-educated proletariat was thereby grafted onto the existing "traditional" working class employed in indigenously owned small establishments. Subsequently, large-scale rural-urban migration prompted by the lure of comparatively lucrative factory employment created a burgeoning and involutionary tertiary sector. In these circumstances, radicalized students and the modern proletariat led a rebellion in May 1969 that received mass support. However, the absence of any clear ideological direction, owing to the predominance of Peronist ideology, weakened the alliance and lessened its political impact (Massari, 1975: 403–419). This pattern of urban protest with widespread popular support, linked to a populist ideology and led in part by a modern proletariat, may well become more common in Africa's expanding cities.

IV. FROM POPULIST TO WORKER POLITICAL CONSCIOUSNESS?

Populism, I have asserted, is a consciousness that workers, the petite bourgeoisie and the subproletariat can evince, but it is not a working-*class* consciousness. It is an oppositional mentality in which popular resentment is limited to a vague notion of a rich, powerful, and corrupt "they" who advance themselves by cheating "we," the people. It connotes rebelliousness, but not revolution. Indeed, populists are often those whose fondest desire is to get a piece of the action. Populist orientations tend to flourish in the flux of early capitalist development. Such orientations may be absorbed in a radical direction with the growth of class consciousness, though this is by no means inevitable. By the development of a working-class political consciousness I mean the emergence of a notion of a common, economically dominant class enemy, and a recognition that only the control or transformation of certain economic and political institutions through collective action would bring beneficial change.

A radical proletariat has, of course, only emerged anywhere under quite special conditions. True, the necessary condition for working-class formation—the concentration of permanent workers in large-scale workplaces—increasingly obtains in Tropical Africa. But the limited proletarianization of a largely first-generation urban wage-earning force doubtless impedes the deepening of worker consciousness. As well, the typical pattern of political suppression of radical movements or ideas nullifies a potential radicalizing influence upon workers in most countries. Is populism then to represent the acme of workers' political dissent?

Some would argue that one should never broach this sort of question in the abstract. They would say that worker consciousness can only be understood historically, within the concrete economic, political, social, and cultural configuration of a particular country. Guiding this historical analysis would be the proposition that consciousness emerges from, and in turn affects, the workers' experience of class subordination and conflict. This is in general true: indeed, it is a truism. But in any specific case study, one needs to explain why, if workers' experiences on the job are similar, they develop a differential consciousness. Generic politicizing and depoliticizing influences operate upon workers to which social scientists or historians must be sensitive in designing their studies.

A. Does "Tribalism" Impede Working-Class Formation?

This is an important and complex question, but one that I can only touch on here. There are two extreme positions that ought to be avoided: that ethnicity is simply derivative of class concepts, or alternatively that ethnic identities pre-empt consciousness, thereby preventing class formation. The former view derives from an overly enthusiastic adherence to a simplistic Marxism; the latter from the erroneous assumption that tribalism is the primordial and natural attachment of Africans.

My own position is that there is no conflict between class and ethnic (and religious) identities—up to a point. It is common for people to compartmentalize their identities, in the sense that they perceive that different identities are relevant in different social situations. "Thus, it is possible for the same person to join a trade union to advance his occupational interests, a communal association to promote his social or electoral objectives, and a religious interest group to lobby for educational reforms. In short, it is possible for an individual to be both a communal and a non-communal political actor" (Melson and Wolpe, 1970: 1127). In some areas of social life the appropriate identity is unambiguous. For instance, a class identity is obviously salient where employees confront a recalcitrant or oppressive employer as workers. In this case the trade union is the natural organizational focus of activities (provided it possesses some autonomy), not an ethnic association or religious group. It is therefore quite understandable why workers drawn from different (sometimes antagonistic) tribes generally evince a high degree of solidarity in industrial disputes. A trade-union consciousness is not incompatible with strongly held ethnic loyalties.[14]

But the relevancy of a particular identity is not so clear cut in all social situations. There are some ambiguous situations that need to be defined; it is here that leadership plays a role in shaping societal conflicts. For instance, it is not inevitable that people in Africa will perceive party politics or *coups d'état* in ethnic terms. Yet this is in fact often the popular perception of political events. Why is it that, in countries such as Nigeria, Kenya, or Zaire, ethnic identities are usually at the center of the political process?

Much research has gone into the investigation of the conditions under which ethnicity is politicized. It is widely accepted now that ethnic cleavages are the result of much more than merely cultural differences and traditional hostilities. Rather, solidarity along cultural-linguistic lines requires at least the following: a culturally plural society; a common arena or arenas of competition for the distribution of scarce resources and power; and a differential impact of modernization along cultural-regional lines. Even then, ethnic conflict is not inevitable. Leaders help to politicize ethnicity in the process of mobilizing a popular base. A symbiotic relationship emerges between politicians, who wish to advance their own positions, and their "people," who come to fear political domination and economic exploitation by a culturally distinct group allegedly organized for these ends. A politician thus gains a tribal power base by successfully manipulating the appropriate cultural symbols and by articulating and advancing his people's collective aspirations (which he himself probably helped define). Needless to add, national political figures will not be tempted to exploit ethnic loyalties where there exists, as in Tanzania, a large number of equally small ethnic groups (see Gulliver, 1969).

I have stated that ethnic and class identities are compatible only up to a point. It is now time to clarify this. Although a politicized ethnicity can coexist with a hardy trade-union consciousness and even an amorphous populism, it does obstruct the development of a worker consciousness encompassing solidarity in the *political* as well as the economic sphere. Where ethnic definitions of political life are entrenched, it is a difficult task to redefine political conflict in class terms. Such redefinition is not impossible. But, it is made even more unlikely where the state suppresses radical movements and ideas. In short, a politicized ethnicity is incompatible with a working-class political consciousness.

B. Occupational Communities and Class Formation

Politicization and class formation are functions of what happens off the job, as well as on. The concept of an "occupational community," found useful elsewhere in the explanation of working-class consciousness, deserves application in studies of African workers. It is not coincidental that two of the most politically assertive groups of workers—railwaymen and miners—normally constitute such communities, while two other assertive groups—dockworkers and factory workers—sometimes do. Occupational communities are characterized, first, by the tendency for people who work together, or who at least share a common occupation and economic activity, to spend their leisure time together. Secondly, these communities tend to be self-enclosed, that is, to act as reference groups for those who belong in matters of behavior and opinion. The structural bases for their formation include: shift-work, and the consequent throwing together of workers who jointly work awkward hours; physical isolation, as in some mining operations and railway estates; or simply the concentration of workmates within a common residential area (see Kerr and Siegel, 1954: 191–194; Bulmer, 1975: 61–92). The point is that interaction and communication both on and off the job can reinforce common views of the world and the legitimacy of shared grievances. They can, moreover, facilitate the socialization of new generations of workers in traditions of industrial and labor protest. Indeed, nonworkers living in the midst of a residentially based occupational community may also come to share the dominant political orientations of the working-class subculture. The little survey research on African workers relating to this topic confirms that the existence of such communities does influence the nature of working-class consciousness (see Lubeck, 1975: 151; Sandbrook and Arn, 1977: Chap. 6).

Not surprisingly, if an occupational community is culturally or ethnically homogeneous, this can reinforce the solidifying effect. This is well illustrated in the case of the militant gold miners in Ghana, who have a long history of labor protest. The dirty and hard underground work has, from the beginning, been left to the migrant workers from Northern Ghana and Francophone West Africa. These miners tend to live in communities around the mine with a high degree of regional-cultural homogeneity. Hence, these workers "live together, drink *pito* together, intermarry, and generally maintain their 'ethnic' lifestyle. Such cultural elements naturally find their way into political culture. This was quite evident when the workers of Tarkwa Goldfields marched into town singing Dagarti war songs, wielding their hunting weapons and simultaneously wearing their mining hats and boots" (Crisp, 1978: 21).

C. Education and Class Formation

Another politicizing factor that is largely unexplored is education in conjunction with other potentially frustrating influences. There has been a significant shift upwards in the educational achievement of urban manual, especially skilled, workers over the past fifteen years. This is one consequence of the successive devaluation of higher levels of formal qualifications. Owing to the disjunction between the expanding output from the schools and the slow growth of job opportunities, many job seekers wishing to remain in town have had to revise downwards their occupational expectations. Employers, at the same time, have sought to limit the pressure from job seekers by requiring a minimum educational qualification even for unskilled manual work. While the minimum for this required by relatively good employers is now completion of primary school (six to seven years of schooling), the average educational achievement of recent recruits may in fact be higher. This trend is illustrated by a large sample survey of manual and nonmanual labor markets in both rural and urban areas of the Cameroons in 1964–1965. Whereas 69% of the younger individuals with a post-primary education were currently engaged in manual work, only 15% of their older counterparts were so employed. In Kaduna, located in educationally underdeveloped northern Nigeria, a survey of textile workers in 1972 arrived at equally striking findings. Fully 72.5% of all the workers, *including daily paid operatives,* had at least completed primary school. Among Tema's factory workers, a survey in 1975 discovered that the bulk of the skilled (86%) and a majority of the unskilled had at least some middle-school education (Clignet, 1977: 67; Hinchliffe, 1973: 33–34; Sandbrook and Arn, 1977: Table 7; see also Peil, 1968a: 71–78).

The relationship between workers' educational achievement and politicization is clear in principle. One would expect that the better-educated workers who considered themselves deprived or oppressed would not only feel more frustrated by their situation, but would also be more capable of developing a theory of exploitation, than their less-educated colleagues. Whether this proposition is valid remains to be seen. The two surveys of workers bearing upon it—one conducted among Kano factory workers, the other among workers in Greater Accra—tend to confirm the link between education and working-class formation (see Lubeck, 1975: 250–251; Sandbrook and Arn, 1977: 54–57).

V. SUMMARY AND CONCLUSIONS

1. A stabilized labor force is a recent phenomenon in African countries. Even among those committed to long-term wage employment, semiproletarianization is the rule rather than the exception. This is manifest structurally in a worker's retention of rights to land and culturally in his cultivation of extensive linkages with his rural home.

2. "Economism," militant or otherwise, characterizes the activities of trade unions in most African countries. But this tendency cannot in general be explained by reference to the labor aristocracy thesis. This thesis is conceptually vague and empirically weak in relation to the bulk of workers' situations in Tropical Africa. It is also simplistic in its crude materialism: mediating between material conditions and the observable behavior of workers are perceptions. These are subject to the influence of a variety of objective and subjective conditions.

3. It is not true to say that workers, left to themselves, are capable only of trade-union consciousness. The available historical and survey evidence suggests that they can also, under certain conditions, develop at least a populist consciousness, and indeed constitute the leading edge of popular urban protest. This is especially true of dockworkers, railwaymen, miners, and factory workers. But populism, a pre-class political consciousness, is limiting in that it only promotes protest and rebellion against corrupt individuals and groups, not collective political action to control or reshape institutions. Moreover, the characteristically sporadic and localized nature of this protest, a function largely of the ubiquitous suppression of autonomous trade unionism and oppositional movements, reduces the long-term political import of populism.

4. It is important to study the conditions that tend to politicize workers in the absence of a radical party. This is a complex task, as there are many historical, structural, and subjective factors bearing upon working-class formation. Ethnicity is one such historical factor. Although a politicized ethnic identity is compatible with a trade-union consciousness and populist rebellion, it would seem to obstruct the emergence of a radical working-class consciousness. Two other potentially important factors de-

serving more attention include the role of occupational communities in creating working-class traditions and socializing new workers, and of the rising educational level of manual workers.

5. Any study of the political potential of African workers should focus upon the links between these and elements of the petite bourgeoisie, subproletariat, and peasantry. Under current conditions, any popular movement limited to workers is unlikely to have much long-term impact.

NOTES

1. There is a wealth of anthropological and sociological literature pertaining to the urbanite's retention of rural links. See J. Aldous, 1965: 107–116. For studies of specific cases, see T. S. Weisner, 1976: 199–223; Marc H. Ross, 1975: 44–54; G. P. Ferraro, 1973: 214–231; Grillo, 1973: 44–61; Sabot, 1972: 221–224; Abdul-Rahman Taha, 1970: 31; J. Middleton, 1969: 42–51; John Caldwell, 1969: 152; John Nabilia, 1974: 265–299; A. Adepoju, 1974: 127–136; S. Goddard, 1965: 21–29; and A. B. Diop, 1968: 301–307.

2. This section and the following two draw heavily upon my article, Sandbrook, 1977: 413–432.

3. A view close to that of Fanon has been argued by R. Kaplinsky, 1971: 15–21.

4. Saul has recently had second thoughts about the utility of his thesis. See his " 'The labour aristocracy' thesis reconsidered," in Sandbrook and Cohen (eds.), *The Development of an African Working Class*. In addition, Sharon Stichter has recently used the Arrighi-Saul version of the theory in "Imperialism and the rise of the labor aristocracy in Kenya" (1976–77).

5. A recent, more subtle, reformulation of the thesis that nonetheless fails to escape this crude materialism is in P. Waterman, 1975: 64–70.

6. As Marx and Engels observed long ago, workers could achieve considerable material advances and yet become increasingly disaffected: "although the enjoyments of the workers have risen, the social satisfaction that they give has fallen in comparison with the increased enjoyments of the capitalist, which are inaccessible to the worker, in comparison with the state of development of society in general. Our desires and pleasures spring from society; we measure them, therefore, by society and not by the objects which serve for their satisfaction. Because they are of social nature, they are of a relative nature." "Wage Labour and Capital", *Selected Works*, Vol. I (Moscow: Foreign Languages Publishing House, 1955: 94).

7. On this, see Allen, 1972:61–92; Hinchliffe, 1974; Knight, 1972; Greenhalgh, 1972; Hazlewood, 1978: 90–92; Rimmer, 1970; Mersadier, 1968: 252–254; Elliott, 1975: 295 (data on Yaoundé and Abidjan); ILO, 1972: 348–350; Joshi, et al., 1976: 40–41.

8. Professor Crawford Young has informed me that his studies of Zaire support this view of the situation. Recent statistics apparently reveal that real urban wages in Kinshasa were about 25% of the 1960 level and about the same as those prevailing in 1910! On the other hand, rural people are more highly taxed than urban dwellers, being subjected to export duties, head taxes, and semi-legal or illegal extortion.

9. The ILO's *Bulletin of Labor Statistics* has provided tables on wage rates by occupational categories only since 1969, and the data available on any particular African country is either nonexistent or discontinuous and incomplete.

10. On the nature of and background to, industrial unrest in Tanzania in the 1970s, see J. V. Mwapachu, 1973: 383–401 and M. A. Bienefeld, 1976: 250–256.

11. On Senegal, see: Cottingham, 1972: 208–213; and Waterman, 1970: 10. On Ghana,

see: Jeffries, 1975: 59–70, and St. Clair Drake and L. A. Lacy, 1966. On Nigeria, see: R. Cohen, 1974: 157–168, R. Melson, 1970: 771–787, and Braundi and Lettieri, 1964. On Congo-Brazzaville, see Friedland, 1965: 6–13 and Waterman, 1970: 10–11. On the Sudan, see: Taha, 1970: 92–94. On Madagascar, see: Althabe, 1978: 205–243.

12. See, on Mombasa, two reports issued by Kenya's colonial government: *Report of the Commission of Inquiry Appointed to Examine the Labour Conditions in Mombasa* (Nairobi, Kenya: Government Printer, 1939), and *Report of the Committee of Inquiry into Labour Unrest in Mombasa* (Nairobi, Kenya: Government Printer, 1945). On Dar-es-Salaam, see Iliffe, 1976: 49–72. On Zanzibar, see: Clayton, 1976.

13. On Douala, see: Joseph, 1974: 669–687. On the A.O.F., see: Surèt-Canale, 1978: 129–154, Allen, 1976: 99–125, and Ousmane Sembene, 1970.

14. A. L. Epstein developed the notion of the "principle of situational selection" (1958: 232–240). A useful theoretical discussion based upon this principle is in Melson and Wolpe, 1970: 1112–1130.

REFERENCES

Adepoju, A.
1974 "Rural-urban socio-economic links: The example of migrants in South-west Nigeria." Pp. 127–136 in Sami Amin (ed.), Modern Migrations in Western Africa. London: OUP.

Akpala, A.
1965 "The background to the Enugu colliery shooting incident in 1949." Journal of the Historical Society of Nigeria III, 2.

Aldous, J.
1965 "Urbanization, the extended family and kinship ties in West Africa." Pp. 107–116 in Pierre van den Berghe (ed.), Africa: Social Problems of Change and Conflict. San Francisco: Chandler.

Allen, C.
1972 "Unions, incomes and development." In Developmental Trends in Kenya, Proceedings of a seminar held at the Centre of African Studies, April 28–29, University of Edinburgh.
1976 "Union-party relationships in Francophone West Africa." Pp. 99–125 in Sandbrook and Cohen (eds.), The Development of an African Working Class. Toronto: University of Toronto Press.

Althabe, G.
1978 "Strikes, urban mass action and political change, Tananarive, 1972." Pp. 205–243 in Gutkind, Cohen, and Copans (eds.), African Labor History. Beverly Hills, Calif.: Sage.

Arrighi and Saul
1973 Essays on the Political Economy of Africa. New York: M. R. Press.

Barnes, Sandra
1974 Becoming a Lagosian. Ph.D. Dissertation, University of Wisconsin.

Bates, R.
1971 Unions, Parties, and Political Development: A Study of Mineworkers in Zambia. New Haven, Conn.: Yale University Press.

Berg, E. J., and J. Butler
1964 "Trade unions." Pp. 340–381 in James S. Coleman and Carl G. Rosberg (eds.), Political Parties and National Integration in Tropical Africa. Berkeley, Calif.: University of California Press.

Berger, Elena
  1974   Labour, Race, and Colonial Rule (in Northern Rhodesia). Oxford, U.K.:
         Clarendon Press.
Bienefeld, M. A.
  1974   The Self-Employed of Urban Tanzania. Discussion paper no. 54. University of
         Sussex, Institute of Development Studies.
  1976   "Socialist development and the workers in Tanzania." Pp. 250–256 in Sandbrook
         and Cohen (eds.), The Development of an African Working Class. Toronto: Uni-
         versity of Toronto Press.
Bissman, K.
  1969   "Industrial worker in East Africa." International Journal of Comparative Sociol-
         ogy X.
Boswell, David
  1975   "Business and petty trading in Robert's Compound (Lusaka) in 1964–65 and
         reflections on the situation in 1974." Report prepared for the Development Plan-
         ning Unit London: University College (March).
Braundi, E. R., and A. Lettieri
  1964   "The general strike in Nigeria." International Socialist Journal I (5–6).
Bulmer, M. I. A.
  1975   "Sociological models of the mining community." Sociological Review XXIII, 1.
Burawoy, M.
  1972a "Another look at the mineworker." African Social Research 14.
  1972b The colour of Class in the Copper Belt. Manchester, U.K.: University of Manches-
         ter Press.
Caldwell, John
  1969   African Rural-Urban Migration: The Movement to Ghana's Towns. New York:
         Columbia University Press.
Clayton, A.
  1976   The 1948 Zanzibar General Strike. Research Report 32. Uppsala, Sweden: Scan-
         dinavian Institute of African Studies.
Clignet, R.
  1977   The Africanization of the Labor Market: Educational and Occupational Segmenta-
         tions in the Camerouns. Berkeley, Calif.: University of California Press.
Cohen, R.
  1974   Labour and Politics in Nigeria, 1945–71. London: Heinemann.
Conway, H. E.
  1968   "Labour protest activity in Sierra Leone during the early part of the 20th century."
         Labour History, 15.
Cottingham, C.
  1972   Class, Politics and Rural Modernization: A Study of Local Political Change in
         Senegal. Ph.D. dissertation, University of California, Berkeley.
Cowan, M., and Kinyanjui, K.
  1977   Some Problems of Income Distribution in Kenya. Nairobi, Kenya; University of
         Nairobi, Institute of Development Studies.
Crisp, J.
  1978   "Union atrophy and worker revolt: Labour protest at Tarkwa goldfields, Ghana,
         1968–69." Unpublished paper. Birmingham, U.K.: University of Birmingham.
Date-Bah, E.
  1974   Societal Influences on Work Behaviour and Interaction of Ghanian Workers: A
         Case Study. Ph.D. dissertation. Birmingham, U.K.: University of Birmingham.

de Heer, N. A.
1972 "The food and nutrition of the adult worker." Ghana Academy of Arts and Sciences. Proceedings, X.

Diop, A. B.
1968 "L'Organisation de la famille africaine." En Groupes d'études dakaroises, Dakar en devenir. Paris: Présence Africaine.

Doctor, K. C., and H. Gallis
1966 "Size and characteristics of wage employment in Africa." International Labor Review 2: 150–173.

Drake, St. Clair, and L. A. Lacy
1966 "Government vs. the unions: The Sekondi-Takoradi strike, 1961." In G. Carter (ed.), Politics in Africa. New York: Harcourt Brace and World.

Ejiogu, C. N.
1968 "African rural-urban migrants in the main migrant areas of the Lagos Federal Territory." In J. C. Caldwell and C. Okonjo (eds.), The Population of Tropical Africa. London: Longman.

Elkan, W.
1960 Migrants and Proletarians: Urban Labour in the Economic Development of Uganda. London: OUP.

Elliott, Charles
1975 Patterns of Poverty in the Third World. New York: Praeger.

Epstein, A. L.
1958 Politics in an Urban African Community. Manchester, U.K.: Manchester University Press.

Esparre, P. L.
1967 "Le travailleur de Côte d'Ivoire: une intégration difficile à la société industrielle." Genève-Afrique VI, 2.

Ewusi, K.
1971 The Distribution of Monetary Incomes in Ghana. Technical Publication Series Number 14. ISSER. University of Ghana.

Fajana, F. O.
1975 "The evolution of skill wage differentials in a developing economy: The Nigerian experience." Developing Economies XVIII, 2.

Fanon, F.
1965 Wretched of the Earth. London: MacGibbon and Kee.

Ferraro, G. P.
1973 "Tradition or transition: Rural and urban kinsmen in East Africa." Urban Anthropology 2.

Friedland, W. H.
1965 "Paradoxes of African trade unionism: Organizational chaos and political potential." Africa Report X.

Fry, J.
1975 "Rural-urban terms of trade, 1960–73." African Social Research 19.

Gibbal, Jean-Marie
1974 Citadins et villageois dans la ville africaine: l'exemple d'Abidjan. Grenoble: Maspero.

Goddard, S.
1965 "Town-farm relationships in Yorubaland: A case study from Oyo." Africa 1: 21–29.

Greenhalgh, C.
  1972   "Income differentials in the eastern region of Ghana." Economic Bulletin of Ghana
         (2nd series) II, 3.
Greenstreet, M.
  1972   "Labour relations in the Gold Coast with special reference to the Ariston strike."
         Economic Bulletin of Ghana II, 3.
Grillo, R. D.
  1973   African Railwaymen: Solidarity and Opposition in an East African Labour Force.
         Cambridge, U.K.: Cambridge University Press.
Gugler, J.
  1969   "On the theory of rural-urban migration in Africa." In J. A. Jackson (ed.),
         Migration. Cambridge, U.K.: Cambridge University Press.
Gulliver, P. H.
  1969   "Introduction." In Gulliver (ed.), Tradition and Transition in East Africa: Studies
         of the Tribal Factor in the Modern Era. Los Angeles: University of California
         Press.
Gutkind, P. C. W.
  1974   The Emergent African Urban Proletariat. Occasional paper no. 8., McGill Uni-
         versity, Centre for Developing Area Studies.
  1975   "The view from below: Political consciousness of the urban poor in Ibadan."
         Cahiers d'études africaines XV, 1.
Gutkind, P. C. W., R. Cohen, and J. Copans (eds.)
  1978   African Labor History. Beverly Hills, Calif.: Sage.
Halpenny, P.
  1972   "Getting rich by being 'unemployed': Some political implications of 'informal'
         economic activities (in Kampala)." Paper delivered to Universities of East Africa
         Social Sciences Conference, Nairobi, Kenya.
Hart, K.
  1973   "Informal income opportunities and urban employment in Ghana." Journal of
         Modern African Studies XI, 1.
Hazlewood, A.
  1978   "Kenya: Income distribution and poverty." Journal of Modern African Studies 1:
         90.
Henderson, I.
  1973   "Wage-earners and political protest in colonial Africa: The case of Northern
         Rhodesia." African Affairs LXXII (July).
Hinchliffe, K.
  1973   "The Kaduna textile workers: Characteristics of an African industrial labour
         force." Savanna II (1).
  1974   "Labour aristocracy—A Northern Nigerian case study." Journal of Modern Africa
         Studies XII (1).
Hopkins, A. G.
  1966   "The Lagos general strike of 1897." Past and Present 35.
Houyoux, C., and J. Houyoux
  1970   "Les conditions de vie dans soixante familles à Kinshasa." Cahiers economiques
         et sociaux VII, 1.
Hughes, A., and Cohen, R.
  1978   "An emerging Nigerian working class: The Lagos experience." In Gutkind,
         Cohen, and Copans (eds.), African Labor History. Beverly Hills, Calif.: Sage.

Iliffe, J.
1976 "The creation of group consciousness: A history of the dockworkers of Dar-es-Salaam." Pp. 49–72 in Sandbrook and Cohen (eds.), The Development of an African Working Class. Toronto: University of Toronto Press.
ILO
1969 Report to the Government of Zambia on Income, Wages and Prices in Zambia. Lusaka, Zambia: Government Printer.
1972 Employment, Incomes, and Equality: A Strategy for Increasing Productive Employment in Kenya. Geneva: ILO.
Jeffries, R. D.
1975 "The labour aristocracy? A Ghana case study." RAPE 3.
1976 "Populist tendencies in the Ghanian trade union movement." In Sandbrook and Cohen (eds.), The Development of an African Working Class. Toronto: University of Toronto Press.
Joseph, R.
1974 "Settlers, strikers and sans travail: The Douala riots of 1945." Journal of African History XV, 4.
Joshi, Heather, et al.
1976 Abidjan: Urban Development and Employment in the Ivory Coast. Geneva: ILO.
Kaplinsky, R.
1971 "Myths about the 'revolutionary proletariat' in developing countries." Institute of Development Studies Bulletin 4: 15–21.
Kerr, C., and Siegel, A.
1954 "The interindustry propensity to strike." In A. Kornhauser, et al. (eds.), Industrial Conflict. New York: McGraw-Hill.
King, Kenneth J.
1977 The African Artisan: Education and the Informal Sector in Kenya. London: Heinemann.
Knight, J. B.
1972 "Rural-urban income comparison and migration in Ghana." Bulletin, Oxford University, Institute of Economics and Statistics XXIV, 2.
Koll, M.
1969 Crafts and Cooperation in Western Nigeria. Bertelsmann Universitatsverlag.
Kraus, J.
forth- "Strikes and labour power in a post-colonial African State: Ghana." In Peter
coming Waterman (ed.), Third-World Strikes.
LaFontaine, J. S.
1970 City Politics: A Study of Leopoldville. Cambridge, U.K.: Cambridge University Press.
Lagos Master Plan Project Unit
1976 "Master plan for metropolitan Lagos: Development of manufacturing industry in Lagos, 1976." Master Plan Bulletin No. 2 Mimeograph. Lagos, Nigeria: Ministry of Works and Planning (December).
LeBrun, O., and Gerry, C.
1976 "Petty producers and capitalism (in Dakar)." RAPE 3.
Lisk, F.
1976 "Inflation in Ghana, 1964–1975: Its effects on employment, income, and industrial relations." International Labour Review CXIII, 3.
Lloyd, P. C.
1976 Power and Independence: Urban Africans' Perception of Social Inequality. London: Routledge and Kegan Paul.

Lubeck, P.
1975 Early Industrialization and Social Class Formation Among Factory Workers in Kano, Nigeria. Ph.D. dissertation, Northwestern University.
1976 "Unions, workers and consciousness in Kano, Nigeria: A view from below." In Sandbrook and Cohen (eds.), The Development of an African Working Class. Toronto: University of Toronto Press.
Maimbo, F., and J. Fry
1971 "An investigation into the change in the terms of trade between the rural and urban sectors of Zambia." African Social Research 12.
Mason, M.
1978 "Working on the railway: Northern Nigeria, 1907–1912." In Gutkind, Cohen, and Copans (eds.), African Labor History. Beverly Hills, Calif.: Sage.
Massari, R.
1975 "Le 'Cordobazo'." Sociologie du travail XVII, 4.
Melson, R.
1970 "Nigerian politics and the general strike of 1964." In R. Rotberg and A. Mazrui (eds.), Protest and Power in Black Africa. New York: OUP.
Melson, R., and Wolpe, H.
1970 "Modernization and the politics of communalism." American Political Science Review LXIV, 4.
Mersadier, Y.
1968 "Les niveaux de vie." Groupes d'études dakaroises, Dakar en devenir. Paris: Présence Africaine.
Middleton, J.
1969 "Labour migration and associations in Africa: Two case studies." Civilisations 1: 42–51.
Mukenge, T.
1973 "Les hommes d'affaire zairois: du travail salarié a l'entreprise personnelle." Canadian Journal of African Studies VII, 3.
Mwapachu, J. V.
1973 "Industrial labour protest in Tanzania: An analysis of influential variables." The African Review III, 3.
Mwongozo Declaration, Clause 15, 28.
Nabilia, John
1974 The Migration of the Frafra of Northern Ghana. Ph.D. dissertation, Michigan State University.
Peace, A.
1974 "Industrial protest at Ikeja, Nigeria." In E. de Kadt and G. P. Williams (eds.), Sociology and Development. London: Tavistock.
1976 "The Lagos proletariat: Labour aristocrats or populist militants?" In Sandbrook and Cohen (eds.), The Development of an African Working Class. Toronto: University of Toronto Press.
Peil, M.
1968a "Aspirations and social structure: A West African example." Africa XXXVIII, 1.
1968b "The unemployment history of Ghanian factory workers." Manpower and Unemployment Research I, 2.
1972 "Male unemployment in Lagos." Manpower and Unemployment Research V, 2.
Perrings, C.
1977 "Consciousness, conflict and proletarianization: An assessment of the 1935 miners' strike on the Northern Rhodesian copperbelt." Journal of Southern African Studies IV, 1.

Rempel, H.
   1971   "The rural-to-urban migrant in Kenya." African Urban Notes 1.
Rimmer, D.
   1970   Wage Politics in West Africa. Birmingham, U.K.: University of Birmingham,
          Faculty of Commerce and Social Science, Occasional paper.
Ross, Marc H.
   1975   Grass Roots in an African City: Political Behavior in Nairobi. Cambridge, Mass.:
          MIT Press.
Rotberg, R., and A. Mazurui (eds.)
   1970   Protest and Power in Black Africa. New York: OUP.
Sabot, Richard
   1972   Urban Migration In Tanzania, Vol. II of the National Urban Mobility, Employment
          and Income Survey. Dar-es-Salaam: University of Dar-es-Salaam, Economic Re-
          search Bureau (September).
Sandbrook, Richard
   1975   Proletarians and African Capitalism: The Kenyan Case, 1960–72. Cambridge,
          U.K.: Cambridge University Press.
   1977   "The political potential of African workers." Canadian Journal of African Studies
          XI, 2.
Sandbrook, R. and J. Arn
   1977   The Labouring Poor and Urban Class Formation: The Case of Greater Accra.
          Monograph series no. 12 Centre for Developing-Area Studies, McGill University.
Sandbrook, R., and Cohen, R., eds.
   1976   The Development of an African Working Class. Toronto: University of Toronto
          Press.
Sembene, Ousmane
   1970   God's Bits of Wood. New York: Anchor Books.
Smock, D.
   1969   Conflict and Control in an African Trade Union: A Study of the Nigerian Coal
          Miners' Union. Stanford, Calif.: Hoover Institution Press.
Sonubi, O.
   1973   "Trade disputes in Nigeria, 1966–71." Nigerian Journal of Economic and Social
          Studies XV, 2.
Stichter, S.
   1975   "Workers, trade unions, and the Mau Mau rebellion." Canadian Journal of African
          Studies IX, 2.
   1976- "Imperialism and the rise of the labor aristocracy in Kenya." Berkeley Journal of
   1977   Sociology XXI.
Suret-Canale, J.
   1978   "The French West African railway workers strike, 1947–48." Pp. 129–154 in
          Gutkind, Cohen, and Copans (eds.), African Labor History. Beverly Hills, Calif.:
          Sage.
Taha, Abdul-Rahman
   1970   The Sudanese Labor Movement: A Study of Labor Unionism in a Developing
          Society. Ph.D. dissertation. University of California, Los Angeles.
Turner, A.
   1976   "The growth of railway unionism in the Rhodesias, 1944–1955." Pp. 73–98 in
          Sandbrook and Cohen (eds.), The Development of an African Working Class.
          Toronto: University of Toronto Press.
Turner, H. A.
   1966   Wage Trends, Wage Policies and Collective Bargaining: The Problems of Underde-
          veloped Countries. Cambridge, U.K.: Cambridge University Press.

Van Onselen, C.
   1976   Chibaro: African Mine Labour in Southern Rhodesia, 1900–1933. London: Pluto
           Press.
Waterman, P.
   1970   "Towards an understanding of African trade unionism." Presence Africaine 76.
   1975   "The 'labour aristocracy' in Africa: Introduction to a debate." Development and
           Change 3.
Waweru, James, and associates
   1976   Kenya, Progress Report No. 5: Results of the Socio-economic Survey, Report of
           the Low-Cost Housing and Squatter Upgrading Study to the World Bank. Nairobi,
           Kenya: August.
Weisner, T. S.
   1976   "The structure of sociability: Urban migration and rural-urban ties in Kenya."
           Urban Anthropology 2: 199–223.
Young, C. E.
   1971   "Rural-urban terms of trade." African Social Research 12.
Zeitlin, Maurice
   1970   Revolutionary Politics and the Cuban Working Class. New York: Doubleday-
           Anchor.

CLASS FORMATION AT THE PERIPHERY:

CLASS CONSCIOUSNESS AND ISLAMIC NATIONALISM AMONG NIGERIAN WORKERS

Paul M. Lubeck

Sociological studies of workers' consciousness during the early phases of capitalist industrialization often acknowledge two kinds of consciousness. One kind of consciousness emerges from and is directed by the concrete experience of wage labor in capitalist enterprises. It may vary by the labor process, the peculiarities of the labor market, or the historically developed inequality structure that precedes the introduction of industrial capitalism. This consciousness, however weakly or strongly held, refers to the bonds of solidarity among wage workers and some shared sentiment of domination by, or an antagonism toward, those who purchase and control their labor. When this sentiment of solidarity is widely held and workers

Research in the Sociology of Work, Volume 1, pages 37–70.

Copyright © 1981 by JAI Press Inc.

All rights of reproduction in any form reserved.

ISBN: 0-89232-124-5

take collective action against those who control and profit from their labor, this consciousness becomes class consciousness. To be sure, one may debate the revolutionary potential, the degree of class cohesion, or the permanence of this consciousness, but once class action is taken against management, those workers who support such action have achieved some minimal level of class consciousness.

Workers always enter into industrial wage labor for the first time with assumptions concerning the correct relationship between employee and employer, master and servant, or patron and client. Oftentimes, these norms are drawn from a precapitalist system or mode of production that, initially at least, exists side by side with industrial capitalism. Varying by social boundary and origin, the second kind of consciousness draws upon, and indeed is structured by, sentiments of community: the basis of this community may be defined in religious, ethnic, regional, racial, or linguistic terms. And the critical feature of membership in this community is acceptance of a common set of beliefs, ideologies, institutions, and organizations that orient and reproduce the community both materially and ideologically. When a community achieves significance in terms of size, or when membership is open rather than ascribed by birth alone, or when a distinct territory is claimed by that community, then such a group forms a *nation*. Hence, consciousness arising from and informed by the beliefs of such a community becomes *nationalist* consciousness.

The relationship between these two forms of consciousness is a tricky problem for social theory and social science. Both Marxian and orthodox sociology are replete with dichotomous labels describing the differences between them, e.g., revolutionary class consciousness versus cultural nationalism (see Lenin, 1968; Nairn, 1977), modern versus traditional (see Kahl, 1968; Inkeles and Smith, 1974), and committed versus uncommitted (see Feldman and Moore, 1960). Moreover, recent scholarship on the international division of labor and the effect of global inequality structures on workers' consciousness pose an additional complicating factor for any analysis of national and class consciousness (see Amin, 1976; Wallerstein, 1974, 1975).

If we assume, as I do, that the position of a state or region in the international division of labor and its particular experience of *incorporation* into the capitalist world economy has a determining effect upon the formation of nationalist consciousness, then effects of this structured inequality relationship operating at the global level must be integrated into our analysis. Implicit here is the rejection of explanations that rely on functionalist or cultural diffusionist explanations of ethnicity or ethnonationalism. At the same time, cultural values, or better, ideological assumptions and normative prescriptions are not irrelevant to our analysis. But these normative expressions are not suspended above history like Platonic essences. Rather the particular normative content of a nationalist ideology reacts to political and economic inequities, determined by that nation's position in the world economy, and in turn this *ethno-national reaction* determines the outlook and direction of the resulting nationalist perspective. To return to our problematic—the relationship of class and national consciousness in a peripheral proletariat—any explanation of class and nationalist consciousness must assess the continuing influence of reactive ethno-nationalism as an independent force arising from a region's structural position in the international division of labor over the long historical term.

The introduction of global or world systemic inequality structures to our discussion raises the question of how the latter form of inequality articulates with class and nationalist consciousness as expressed by a first generation industrial proletariat in the peripheral capitalist city of Kano, Nigeria. Like class consciousness, which emerges from a *division of labor* within an organization of production, popular reactions against imperialism, the international division of labor, or the inequities arising from surplus transfers from peripheral to core areas of the world economy correspond to a peripheral area's particular role in the global *division of labor*. Yet unlike class consciousness, workers' consciousness arising from global inequities is perceived in ethno-nationalist terms. That is to say, nationalist consciousness reflects a particular position in the world division of labor. Only then does this global inequity articulate with class consciousness at the level of social relations of production. To take the concrete example of Muslim northern Nigeria, we are confronted with a situation where capitalist social relations of production were introduced through violent conquest by Christians, who were perceived as the historical enemy of the Muslim community. Again, unlike Europe at a different moment in the historical evolution of capitalism as a global system, capitalist social relations did not develop from the internal logic of the historically prior precapitalist system. Muslim nationalism generated popular reactions in the form of milleniarian movements at the moment of incorporation and during the colonial era shaped the Muslim populations' perception of capitalist social relations, especially under industrialism, as both alien in the national sense and alienating in the interpersonal sense. For fundamentalist Muslim workers, therefore, inequalities arising from northern Nigeria's role in the international division of labor are not experienced directly but are mediated through Muslim nationalism at the regional level. At the micro-level involving the social relations of production, where the language, the technology, the raw material inputs, and the factory management are perceived as evidence of Christian capitalist domination, nationalist consciousness often converges with class consciousness in a complex articulation within a peripheral industrial proletariat (see Foster-Carter, 1978; Roxborough, 1976; Post, 1978).

In order to analyze our problematic and to provide the background for an historical understanding of the data to be presented, we must review the development of Islamic nationalism and peripheral capitalism in Nigeria so as to comprehend the structures and organizations that generate both *class* and *national* consciousness within a newly formed industrial proletariat.

Before moving to relations between Islamic nationalism and capitalism, contemporary Nigeria should be brought into perspective. As the most populous state in Africa (c. 80 million) and the second largest supplier of American petroleum imports, Nigeria has emerged as the regional power in black Africa. Oil revenue has funded an economic boom, state centralization at the federal level, and a spectacular disruption of the social order through increasing commercialization of land and housing, expansion of industrial production, and a high rate of inflation. In turn, these changes have undermined the peasantry and stimulated rural to urban migration. Even after a civil war waged by a centralized federal state, Nigeria possesses great regional disparities in educational attainment, industrialization and urbanization rates, and attachments to regional nationalisms. While most of the import substitution-type industries are located in the south, as will be the new petroleum-related industries, the northern urban centers of Kano and Kaduna have attracted foreign, multinational, and indigenous capital for light and medium forms of industrial production. Even with increased state centralization, however, the Muslim peoples of the north (i.e., Hausa, Fulani, Kanuri, and Nupe) have maintained a strong sense of Muslim nationalism. For example, during recent debates over the proposed constitution, Muslims demonstrated nationalist solidarity by unsuccessfully petitioning for a distinct court of appeals for Muslim law at the federal level. Let us examine the historical development of Muslim nationalism in the northern region where approximately half of Nigeria's population resides.

I. THE ORIGINS OF MUSLIM REGIONAL NATIONALISM: 1804–1904

While Islam was practiced among urban ruling strata at least since the year 1000, it was not until the holy war, or *jihad*, which founded the Sokoto Caliphate (1804), that Islamic law and an Islamic ruling class emerged to dominate the Hausa-speaking majority. Not only was the Caliphate the largest, most populous and most complexly organized state in precolonial West Africa, but the ideology of Islam allowed an inter-urban ruling class to emerge across separate emirates united under So-koto. Through conquest of non-Muslims and slave raiding, the emirates absorbed and resocialized populations into a more differentiated Muslim society. Though uneven in cultural and religious practice, the expanding Caliphate created a complex division of labor marked by long-distance trading, leather and textile handicrafts, a complex and hierarchical marketing system and, above all, a patrimonial Muslim state apparatus that extracted surplus from peasant and handicraft producers. With So-koto functioning as the political and religious center, Kano served as the economic center of this Muslim state system. Note that while the triumph of Muslims was occurring in northern Nigeria, the Muslim empires of North Africa declined and became subject to European imperialism. Thus, the emirates of the Sokoto Caliphate became a cultural periphery of that cultural area called Islamdom, all to its benefit; but because of the weakness of North African states and the ecological barrier posed by the Sahara, the Caliphate avoided becoming a political or economic vassal of the more technically advanced states of North Africa. Similarly, the distance from the Atlantic coast, where the slave and palm oil trade integrated southern Nigerian city states into the capitalist world econ-omy, also allowed the Muslim states of the north to develop distinctly Muslim institutions, cultural styles, and popular organizations until the first decade of the twentieth century (see Last, 1967; Smith, 1960; Adeleye, 1971).

After a century of autonomous Muslim rule dominated by a patrimonial state and by an urban resident, office-holding aristocracy, the *sarauta,* large numbers of Africans had become socialized either voluntarily or involuntarily into Muslim culture and social practice. Increasingly, Mus-lim scholars (*mallams*) intensified their influence through Koranic studies and by more advanced legal training for the performance of literate roles in the patrimonial bureaucracy or for participation in commercial ven-tures. Recent research shows the importance of literacy in Arabic script for tax records, long-distance trade, and the legal system. What is impor-tant for our understanding of national consciousness among industrial workers is that the origins of their Muslim national identity precede colonization and incorporation into the capitalist world economy. Fur-ther, as I shall develop below, rather than destroying the unity and intensity of Islamic nationalism, conquest and incorporation actually ex-panded the boundaries of Islamdom and intensified the commitment to Islamic cultural participation among the commoner stratum—the *tala-kawa.*

Viewed from above, the process of Islamization in the Sokoto

Caliphate depended upon a state apparatus that ruled through Muslim law, provided tax and commercial advantages to Muslims over non-Muslims, and enslaved nonbelievers who soon became Muslims. Yet among the commoners, the *talakawa*, Islamization occurred through informal schools, networks among the clerics or *mallams*, and dry-season migrations that combined commerce, handicraft production, and Koranic studies. In the city of Kano, the urban talakawa maintained a reputation for legal studies, in contrast to the scholars associated with the aristocracy who favored Arabic studies. Taken together the *mallams*, Koranic schools, and their multifunctional networks formed an organizational structure that created a multiethnic community of Muslims which increased in number at the expense of pre-Islamic community identities. Not only did religious and ethnic identities change but Islamic custom demanded changes in diet, dress, and health practices. Further, assimilation into the Islamic national identity altered social practices associated with daily time, seasonal festivals (e.g., *ramadan* fasting), and contact with the wider world through the obligation of the *Hajj* to Mecca. It is important to emphasize that the clerics, *mallams*, are informally and not hierarchally organized; they often hold many other occupations; and they perform rituals throughout an individual's life cycle, as well as acting as counselors to their communities. Finally, because Islam recognizes no division between the political and religious spheres, *mallams* interpret community sentiment toward legitimate authority. Accordingly, their approval is sought after by the ruling groups, and at the same time, oppressed groups look to them for leadership against tyranny.

Despite social divisions between rulers and ruled, and the uneven development of Islamic belief and practice within the Caliphate, a Muslim national identity had formed when Kano and the Caliphate were conquered. Rather than perceiving the British in racial or ethnic terms as Europeans, the invaders were perceived and responded to as Christians, the historical enemy of Muslim civilization. Because the Caliphate was conquered swiftly and the invaders met extensive resistance from both the aristocracy and the commoner strata, the very process of conquest by the historical enemy of Islam generated a nationalist reaction that intensified a colonized people's commitment to their Muslim national identity. From the perspective of global inequality and the world division of labor, this "reactive" Muslim national identity corresponded to the political and administrative boundaries of the Protectorate of Northern Nigeria, whose economic link to the world economy consisted of peasant-produced groundnut (peanut) exports. Thus, the political and economic structures imposed upon northern Nigeria corresponded to and reinforced Muslim nationalism during the colonial period (see Lubeck, 1979a).

II. ISLAMIC NATIONALISM, INCORPORATION, AND CAPITALIST DEVELOPMENT IN NORTHERN NIGERIA

Unlike southern Nigeria, where incorporation of the coastal areas occurred over several centuries and where missionaries and merchants had established linkages to European capitalist states, the incorporation of the Sokoto Caliphate was rapid and encountered widespread resistance from the rulers and the peasantry. Resistance to conquest took the form of *Mahdism*, a Muslim millenarian movement, which involved a withdrawal by rulers and their dependents to Muslim states to the east and a peasant revolt directed against British occupation. Note that in addition to revolts against exploitation by the urban resident aristocracy in Kano Emirate, villagers in Sokoto followed a local village head who declared himself *Mahdi* and demanded that the aristocracy expel the invaders. After successfully resisting a British force resulting in the death of British officers, a joint party of British occupation troops and those of the collaborating aristocracy put down the rebellion and destroyed the village of Satiru. Hence, by revolting against the domination of Christian conquerors and collaborating aristocrats, *talakawa* protest reflected the combined elements of class-based deprivation and Islamic nationalism.

Both Muslim resistance and declining support at home for imperialism encouraged the British to establish the indirect rule system, whereby the traditional prerogatives of the ruling class that did not offend European norms were buttressed by the technical superiority of the British. Emirs became salaried officials; Islamic institutions and practices were not to be disturbed by the British; and missionaries were forbidden from proselytizing in Muslim areas. Elsewhere Islam expanded under the *Pax Britannica:* colonial authorities posted Muslim district heads in non-Muslim areas; rail and motor road communications allowed formerly isolated Muslim communities in West Africa to communicate more freely; and Hausa became the favored language of colonial rule in the north. In general then, British policy encouraged Muslim nationalism by not undermining the traditional Muslim structures of domination. In fact, both the resistance to and the technical benefits of British colonialism appear to have increased the participation of urban dwellers and trading groups in Islamic brotherhoods (*tarika*), especially the Tijaniya and the already popular Qadiriya. Paden argues that increased participation in Islamic brotherhoods reduced ethnic differences among Muslims in urban centers such as Kano (see Paden, 1974).

That incorporation into the capitalist world economy actually intensified Islamic nationalism may be plausible, but a skeptic must ask whether integration into the capitalist world economy undermined the agrarian class structure of the emirate system. The answer is no. Unlike other areas of Africa where plantation, white-settler farms or mineral extraction required large-scale, semipermanent wage labor forces, peasant-produced groundnut (peanut) exports became the mainstay of the northern economy. Centered in Kano Emirate, with urban Kano serving as the railway center for the region, surplus continued to be extracted from peasants through taxation of producers and their export crops; all this required only slight modification of the traditional patrimonial bureaucracy. Further, by removing traditional checks on illegitimate power, incorporation intensified aristocratic exploitation of the peasantry. Until nationalist agitation during the postwar era, northern Nigeria remained a peasant-produced, groundnut-exporting area, dominated by a British-supported Muslim aristocracy and lacking a significant urban proletariat.

The postwar period brought some industrial production and a small urban wage-earning class. But more importantly, nationalist politics brought a *talakawa*-based opposition party—The Northern Elements Progressive Union (NEPU)—to champion the interests of the commoners against the legal and illegal exactions of the aristocracy. Illegal taxation, extortion, forced labor, bribe-taking, and a repressive system of police and courts were the issues that generated commoner support for NEPU in the urban centers and especially in Kano. As one might expect, *mallams,* Koranic students, and factions of Islamic brotherhoods became involved in supporting NEPU against the aristocracy's party, which possessed its own Muslim institutional following. What is important for our understanding of Muslim nationalism and class consciousness is that NEPU offered an anti-imperialist critique of the aristocracy's alliance with the British that was, at the same time, a class-based critique of aristocratic exploitation of the commoners. As articulated by NEPU, exploitation by an aristocracy supported by colonial authority violated Islamic principles of justice, representative government, and community consensus. For the tiny wage earning class, NEPU's contribution to working-class ideology was its linking of class-based protest to Muslim nationalism. NEPU had its greatest impact upon those trained in Islamic political theory or those not directly dominated by the aristocracy or its agencies, i.e., the urban population of traders, craftsmen, casual laborers, and Koranic students (see Sklar, 1963). The lasting historical impact of NEPU's program, however, derived not from its reform of the Native Authority system, which has been implemented by the military government, but in its legitimization of Islamic nationalist ideology to justify popular and class-based protest against recognized tyranny. Though the party of the traditional Muslim aristocracy controlled both the Northern Region and the Federation of Nigeria, tensions generated by regional nationalism soon destroyed the fragile federal state. Several military coups were followed by civil war. Ironically, the crisis of Nigerian unity contributed to the emergence of an urban proletariat.

Until the postwar colonial development schemes of the fifties, wage labor in Kano was limited to state employees and the foreign trading companies. Most of the latter were controlled by, and often clients of, the Muslim aristocracy who managed the Native Authority system created by indirect rule. Concerned largely with the export of groundnuts, the foreign trading firms employed labor in large numbers only during the harvest season. For most of the colonial period, therefore, the state sector was the largest employer of labor. Tax revenues from groundnut exports meant that the state employed labor in public works and infrastructural improvements as well as in governmental services such as sanitation, education, and courts. Just as no large wage labor class of northern Muslims emerged, colonial policy determined that land be controlled by the aristocracy and that a capitalist land market be thwarted.

As the merchant class grew in wealth and in influence by playing an intermediary role between foreign firms and northern peasants, British authorities encouraged an alliance between wealthy traders and Kano's aristocracy where the merchants were the subordinate partners. The general point here is that, with British support, no antagonist class emerged to challenge aristocratic domination of the society, nor did significant legal definitions of property or social relations of production change prior to the Nigerian Civil War. The civil war brought shortages of manufactured goods, and import substitution industries increased the existing industrial base of light, consumer-oriented and agro-processing industries. Together with a high rate of inflation, the war brought an increase in formal and informal sector wage workers. Further, both compulsory savings schemes and inflation brought working-class grievances, to which the military government promised redress at the conclusion of the war.

III. URBAN LABOR AND MUSLIM NETWORKS IN KANO

When the Nigerian political crisis had ended, Kano had become a separate state. Compared to others it possessed the most homogeneous Muslim population and, with the creation of additional states, Kano became the most populous state in the Federation of Nigeria. With an urban population of 750,000 to 1 million in the early seventies, Kano was the primate city of the region and the commercial, industrial, and communications center for all of northern Nigeria. Despite low levels of peasant income, the densely populated rural areas of Kano state provided a market for manufactured goods. Light industry located in Kano in order to produce commodities for this market. New industries brought new employment opportunities, such that the industrial labor force had reached 20,000 by 1972 and about 32,000 by 1978. Industrial and urban growth encouraged land speculation and cheap housing for recent migrants. The housing of migrants created many new migrant areas where the market rather than Muslim tradition determined social patterns and densities. After 1973, when the OPEC price increase initiated Nigeria's petroleum boom, capitalist forms of urban growth became more intense as state infrastructural projects stimulated further the emigration of rural workers to high wage urban centers.

Even before the petroleum boom stimulated industrial production, Kano's industrial labor force had expanded in number and in the proportion of Muslim and Hausa speakers. While an important minority of industrial workers were from Kano's established urban families, most workers were recent rural emigrants or peasants who commuted from the densely populated areas surrounding the urban perimeter of Kano. For the peasants, the transition marked a change from patrimonial political relations and peasant household production to an unevenly developed city that, despite all of its residual precapitalist institutions, was the most developed capitalist center in the region. Hence, relative to rural areas where capitalist social relations were absent or characterized by commercial and debtor forms of domination, urban Kano was a thriving capitalist center. Even though the proportion of wage earners was small, Kano's function as an export center of a wider capitalist world economy and as a center of state administration generated enormous income and residential inequities. Peasants who labored for a few shillings a day in a competitive urban labor market were exposed to styles of consumption practiced by the internationalized state and private sector bourgeoisie.

While exposure to the market and urban inequality were important socializing experiences for recent migrants, participation in Muslim institutional networks and the acquisition of Islamic learning also occurred at the same time. Many workers interviewed report that they migrated to Kano originally to study the Koran or to pursue other Islamic studies. Recording of career histories showed that a sizable minority of Hausa workers, who "wandered" with their *mallams,* entered urban Kano with the intention of passing on to a center of Islamic studies elsewhere, or to study with a well-known scholar who was in their network. Others report that upon coming to Kano in search of work they linked up with a resident whom they met in rural areas as Koranic students. One advantage of assuming the status of a Koranic student is that students are allowed by custom to beg for alms and to perform errands such as carrying packages at the market. Thus, to allow them to carry packages is a form of almsgiving. Still others continue to study Islamic texts in a community of scholars while working at a factory; some even report having pupils whom they teach daily. Rather than emigration representing a radical break between the traditional or precapitalist rural sector and the increasingly capitalistic urban sector, the Islamic networks illustrate how, despite radical differences between the two sectors, Islamic networks serve to connect the two sectors by integrating recent migrants into the urban labor market. Finally, several respondents report learning of the advantages of factory employment while Koranic students: here recruitment was directly from koranic school to factory.

It is important to emphasize that migrants from commoner origins perceive Islamic studies and institutions as hierarchically distributed. The most advanced legal studies, the most charismatic *mallams,* and the greatest rewards for their services are located in urban centers such as Kano. Urban-born workers also pursue Koranic studies with the traditional combination being one of trade and scholarship. Among the urban dwellers and a smaller minority of migrants, participation in Islamic brotherhoods also continues to be an important source of social integration.

Participation in Islamic brotherhoods requires members to undergo initiation rites, to follow prescribed rituals and prayers, and, most important, to meet collectively with brotherhood *mallams* for collective rituals. Brotherhood members are perceived by the Muslim community as stricter adherents of Islamic practices. Brotherhood affiliations and rituals have in the recent past been used to maintain or to shore up political alliances. For example, during the political party period, one faction of a brotherhood followed a distinct style of prayer in public which was perceived as an act of protest against the authorities. Normally brotherhood members continue to pursue Islamic studies and thus are among the most integrated into a Muslim national identity. What is important for our analysis of workers' consciousness is the fact that Islamic institutional participation and popular commitment to a distinct Muslim lifestyle and culture have not decreased with increases in urbanization and in industrial capitalism. Rather a popular urban culture exists—one that is maintained by simple Koranic schools and mosques at one level, and at a more affluent level, the elaborate social rituals associated with attending and returning from the *Hajj* to Mecca reinforce Muslim popular culture.

To summarize: a rapid rate of urbanization, an increase in the number and importance of wage laborers, and an intense regional Muslim nationalism are occurring at the same time in the lives and consciousness of first-generation factory workers. It is a situation of extreme uneven development where Islamic institutions provide security and an expression of community solidarity in a world that is rapidly undergoing the transition from patrimonial and household relations to capitalist social relations and dependence upon the market. While it is certain that Muslim factory workers experience the effects of these three social forces, the combined effects of these contradictory social forces upon workers' consciousness remains unknown. What effect does participation in Muslim organizations have upon urbanized and experienced factory workers? Does Islamic participation dilute commitment to class action or the development of class consciousness? Regarding literacy in Western script, rather than in Arabic script, are literates more committed to workers' struggles, class conflict, and class organizations than illiterate workers? These are some of the classical sociological questions that our survey data address. Before moving to an analysis of a survey of workers' consciousness, the events leading to class struggle and the design of the survey require mention.

IV. RESEARCHING WORKERS' CONSCIOUSNESS: THE ADEBO STRIKES

The events leading to a series of wildcat strikes in 1971 were precipitated by a report released by a federal government-appointed wage review commission, the Adebo Commission, which was empowered to review wages and salaries, losses due to inflation, and make recommendations to the federal government regarding an arrears payment. After pressure from both management and organized labor at the capital (Lagos), the Adebo Commission released an interim report acknowledging the loss of real income by urban wage earners and recommended a wage increase that was to be backdated to the nine previous months. This meant that an unskilled industrial worker was to receive up to eleven times his weekly income in one lump sum. Further, though the review commission possessed authority to recommend only for the public sector, private sector workers began industrial actions to require management to pay the Adebo rate and arrears. As an example of how the precapitalist sector may interact and combine with events in the modern or capitalist sector, one notes that the commission's announcement occurred just prior to a major Muslim festival when workers were pressed to purchase goods for their wives and dependents. Virtually all of the factories in Kano experienced some kind of industrial action. Because there were not any functioning trade unions in the factories, workers selected representatives to negotiate for their Adebo arrears award. Most of the large employers refused to pay immediately and protracted, often violent, strikes followed. Since most employers were Asian or Levantine, and not rationalized managerial capitalists, the owners and managers attempted to stall for time in order to lobby the government for an exemption for the private sector or even to lay off workers; thus reducing the cost of the arrears payments. Elsewhere I have analyzed the forms and tactics of class struggle that workers undertook to secure their arrears pay (see Lubeck, 1975). Let us move to the survey of workers' career histories and consciousness.

The research design called for a multimethod approach where qualitative data was collected by the researcher while resident in the oldest established workers' community in the city. Field ethnographic data were collected on: the urban labor market, workers' career and life histories, workers' organizations and trade unions, the Adebo and earlier strikes, and data on the laboring and popular classes. After eight months of field work, a demographic enumeration of the work force of the five largest employers of industrial labor was undertaken (N = 3,075). After a preliminary analysis of the workers' modal characteristics, a stratified random sample, based upon urban status, was drawn from workers who were: married, Hausa-Fulani, uneducated, between the ages of twenty and forty, and unskilled. Workers were separated into three urban status groups and approximately fifty were randomly selected from each urban status group: *Urbans,* i.e., lifetime residents of Kano; *Migrants,* i.e., rural-born migrants to Kano; and *Commuters,* i.e., workers who commuted from their villages in the densely populated periurban area surrounding urban Kano. After items for an interview schedule were pretested by formal and informal interviewing, 140 interviews were conducted in Hausa and completed by the researcher during the first five months of 1972. The interview schedule recorded data on: family and marriages, Islamic participation, work history, evaluation of industrial work, social ranking of occupations, ethnic tolerance, perceptions of social mobility, evaluation of western education, and a series of items measuring class consciousness (see Lubeck, 1979b).

V. WORKERS' CONSCIOUSNESS: TALAKAWA, LEBURORI, AND INDUSTRIAL WORKERS

Muslim workers conceive of themselves in several frames of reference. Virtually all perceive themselves as *talakawa;* that is, members of the commoner stratum who possess neither a highly skilled occupation, Western education, access to state patronage, or sufficient capital to be considered wealthy. Hence, the urban *talakawa* include small-scale traders, craftsmen, wage workers, and marginal service workers. *Talakawa* consciousness is rooted in the precolonial and precapitalist inequality system. It was reinforced by the political propaganda of NEPU, which attacked privilege and the alliance of wealth and power. The term *leburori* (singular: *lebura*) originates from the colonial occupational category of laborer. Muslim workers make a clear distinction between working as a day laborer in agriculture (kwadego) and working for a wage in the modern capitalist sector. During the colonial era, most *leburori* worked for the state, but now the term includes all modern-sector workers. Hausa-speaking workers refer to modern-sector employment as *"aikin bature,"* literally "the work of Europeans"; such a definition of modern wage labor reflects the Muslim nationalist perspective in which the origin of capitalist wage labor relations is associated with a foreign conquerer. The term *lebura* may also refer to the impoverished service workers who live in a working-class community such as barbers, washermen, butchers, or even petty traders. Of all the terms used to refer to wage workers, whether casually or formally employed, *lebura* is the most widely recognized and accepted by industrial workers.

Industrial workers perceive of themselves as both *talakawa* and *leburori* but often use the term *"akin comfani"* (company workers) to distinguish themselves from craft, informal sector, or state sector workers. Nevertheless, industrial workers do not form a distinct class but are integrated into the *leburori* as a whole; they do, however, experience special conditions of industrial work—rotating shifts, stricter discipline in their labor process, greater risk of disfiguring injuries, and an enormous concentration of labor at the work site. Rather than being perceived as privileged by the community or by themselves, industrial workers are regarded as possessing low status. For example, even though casual work such as cart pushing or porterage is uncertain relative to factory work, the researcher discovered several workers who preferred casual work because of the freedom of movement and the release from harsh supervision.

An important aspect of industrial workers' consciousness pertains to their career aspirations. Nearly 80% of workers interviewed aspired to enter small-scale trading in the bazaar economy of Kano: i.e., as peddlers, stall renters or shop owners. Factory work is seen as very insecure and as the "work of strength." Workers fear that once they are old or middle-aged, younger and cheaper workers will be recruited to replace them. This belief is encouraged by the supervisors' practice of selling jobs, and thus a rapid turnover of workers increases a supervisor's income. Further, because they have learned that in a factory all skilled jobs and most supervisory jobs are allocated to educated workers, they correctly perceive that the factory represents a closed mobility system. In contrast, the petty trading occupations are perceived as open, for despite the odds, traders may receive good fortune from Allah or from other mortals and eventually achieve a much higher social position than factory workers. One notes with irony that participants in the modernization process, in contrast to the assumptions of modernization theory, perceive upward social mobility through *achievement* to be much more likely in the traditional, informal sector than in the modern, industrial sector.

Critics of Marxist class analysis have questioned whether commonly held entrepreneurial aspirations contradict any attribution of class consciousness to West African factory workers (see, for example, Lloyd, 1975). Empirically, critics correctly point out that workers do aspire to enter the informal sector as independent traders. But their criticism overlooks the fact that the proletarianization of independent producers or traders has never been voluntarily accepted or evaluated positively by those who undergo proletarianization. Further, the question remains whether a response to a query concerning one's ideal occupation, a kind of dream question, is a reliable indicator of class formation, class consciousness, or a commitment to class action in a world that is not voluntary, but imposed upon the workers by forces beyond their individual control. It is critical to ask those who aspire to become petty traders if they expect to achieve this ideal occupational status. For example, in the Kano sample, 80% responded with "trader"; but when asked to evaluate their chances of achieving this occupational status, two-thirds responded that they had little or no chance of achieving their ideal. Among rural-origin migrants, the modal factory workers, those responding negatively reached 74%.

When two-thirds or three-quarters of workers interviewed are pessimistic about achieving their occupational ideal of commerce, then the aspiration of trading is unlikely to prevent class formation or prevent support for class actions or the formation of working-class organizations. Even if workers achieve their ideal of trading in a very competitive market, our analysis of cyclical career patterns suggest that they are more than likely to return to wage labor during a trade recession. Again, class formation and class struggle are not voluntary processes but arise from situations where workers are compelled to combine and act collectively in order to survive. In such a situation, therefore, it matters little what their ideal occupations may be.

VI. CLASS CONSCIOUSNESS: CONCEPT AND INDICATORS IN THE CONTEXT OF MUSLIM WORKERS

Several points should be made when "class consciousness" is applied to Muslim workers in a peripheral capitalist city such as Kano. The first concerns historical continuity and the continuing influence of precapitalist structures and ideologies such as Islamic nationalism. Moreover, while proletarianization forces workers to acccept human relations as commodity relations, just as in the case of western Europe, the fact that capitalist social relationships were forced upon the community by formal conquest rather than emerging from the internal development of precapitalist institutions adds an additional source of tension to class conflict. To be proletarianized in Kano, therefore, means that one is subjected to "*aikin bature*" without any of the traditional rights and duties associated with Muslim patrimonialism. This, we believe, adds the potential of Muslim national resistance to proletarianization that was absent in the case of Western Europe where, more often than not, religious authorities sanctioned the domination of capital over labor. A second point concerns the role of the peripheral capitalist state in defining class boundaries and the terms of class struggle. Not only is the role of the state different from Europe during an equivalent period, but workers who draw upon their experience with the colonial and national state naturally look to the state to define relations between capital and labor. Finally, there is an international dimension to the relationship between capital and labor and the regional relationship of northern Nigeria to the capitalist world system. Though indigenous capitalists are often the most exploitative, many workers perceive, perhaps in an unsystematic way, that the ideologies, machinery, and technical personnel of the system that is both exploiting them and transforming their society is alien and European in origin. This feature may add an additional tension to an emerging proletariat's feelings about class action and class organization.

Given these differences, how does the classical Marxist theory of class formation and class consciousness relate to the situation of recently proletarianized Muslim workers? To be sure, recently proletarianized workers may develop class awareness, take class action, and form workers' organizations, but it is unrealistic at this stage to expect them to develop an alternative societal vision, which the achievement of a revolutionary level of class consciousness necessarily entails. Hence, the level of class consciousness must correspond to the level of economic and social development of the city and the technical development of the social forces of production. Empirically this leads to inquiring about several dimensions of class consciousness that are appropriate to a peripheral urban center such as Kano. Scholars concerned with class consciousness as an historical and empirical problem generally agree that there are several dimensions of class consciousness appropriate here (see Meszaros, 1971; Hazelrigg, 1973; Mann, 1973; Foster, 1974). First, workers must be aware of their position in a class hierarchy and accept the relative permanence of this status. Second, at the level of consumption, workers must recognize that they are exploited by management through the wage relationship and are not receiving a fair share of the socially produced surplus in the form of wages. Third, workers must recognize that their collective class interest is antagonistic to that of management and must be willing to engage in class conflict, e.g., striking, in order to secure their class interest. Fourth, workers must be willing to form organizations to pursue class interests, regardless of prior status or social origin of fellow workers. Fifth, at a societal level workers must recognize the need to engage in political activity in order to create the conditions that will secure their class interests.

From these abstract concepts some empirical indicators were developed and administered to factory workers in the sample (N = 140). To repeat, workers enter into factory work with a clear understanding that they are *talakawa* and *leburori*. After ranking a number of occupations on a three-tier occupational status ladder, workers were asked to rank themselves according to their social rank. Over 80% ranked themselves on the bottom tier. Hence, as the data presented earlier on workers' expectations of achieving their ideal occupation indicate, factory workers not only recognize their class position, but the overwhelming majority do not expect to advance upwards from this class position. We take this evidence as affirming empirically that the first dimension of class consciousness is present throughout the sample.

Indicators for the remaining dimensions are based upon five items. The second indicator refers to class consciousness at the level of the wage relationship. Workers were asked to consider the value of their work and their wages and to discuss whether they believed their pay to be fair or unfair. Workers who considered their pay to be unfair were coded as satisfying the second dimension of class consciousness. The third attempts to discover those who are willing to engage in collective class conflict with management over the payment of the Adebo bonus. The Adebo payment in this instance serves to crystallize class struggle and class interest as the benefits to either party were known and visible to all. Workers who supported the Adebo strike have satisfied the third dimension of class consciousness. Because the researcher was interested in the process by which recently proletarianized workers legitimize class struggle according to their precapitalist ideological standards, which continue to articulate within emerging classes, a second item asked "if Islam agreed with striking for a fair reason." Besides indicating the process of proletarian legitimization, the second item offers a multiple indicator for the Adebo strike support item that is divorced from the specific event. Finally, it is also of interest to my theoretical argument to know how workers most integrated into Muslim institutions responded to this item.

For the fourth dimension of class consciousness, the willingness to organize at the factory level, workers were asked an open-ended item: what can workers do in this factory to help themselves? Respondents who favored collective organizations to negotiate with management or to strengthen workers' interests were considered to have satisfied the fourth dimension of class consciousness. Moving to politics at a societal level, workers were asked both positively and negatively phrased questions inquiring whether workers should engage in politics to satisfy workers' needs. Workers responding affirmatively were considered to have satisfied the fifth dimension.

With these indicators of class consciousness defined, let us move to some theoretically significant independent variables in order to verify the hypothesis that participation in capitalist social structures generates an increasing level of class consciousness among recently proletarianized workers.

VII. EXPLAINING CLASS CONSCIOUSNESS

According to the Marxian intellectual tradition, social activity and social relations of production, while mediated by many institutions, ideologies, and personal attributes, have a determining effect on individual and collective consciousness. In a situation such as Kano, the problem is to show that social participation in capitalist structures such as a peripheral capitalist city or modern wage-labor organizations or even the acquisition of modern education in the form of Western literacy explains levels of class consciousness among recently proletarianized workers.

Participation and residence in a peripheral capitalist city exposes wage workers to inequality on a world scale. Compared to rural areas or to the precapitalist period, capitalist social relations are highly developed in urban Kano. Great inequalities of wealth and consumption exist; the market rather than tradition is allocating housing and occupational opportunities for both urbans and migrants; for migrants and an increasing number of urbans, the housing market concentrates wage workers into densely inhabited residential areas where class and community reinforce each other; local and international capital are becoming increasingly powerful with a corresponding decline in the petty commodity sector which is composed of traders and craftsmen. The city then is more than a large, dense, and heterogeneous mass. Rather it is an outpost of an expanding capitalist world system, where the poor and the powerless become increasingly insecure as capitalist social relations and values overcome traditional Muslim structures. Further, the city is highly organized if compared to rural areas. To reside in Kano is to expose oneself to the competitive urban labor market as well as to the technical domination of industrial capitalism in work and in consumption. Finally, residence in a peripheral city such as Kano enables potential or actual proletarians to demystify the economic and political centers of power that surround

Table 1. Class Consciousness and Urban Residential Experience

Dimension of Consciousness	Variable: Years of Urban Experience	Positive or Agree: %	(N)	Statistics
Agrees That Pay is Unfair	High Urban* Experience	60.3	(78)	Gamma = .65 P < .00 Corrected χ^2 = 15.33
	Low Urban** Experience	24.6	(47)	
Adebo Strike Support	High Urban* Experience	64.2	(81)	Gamma = .50 P < .00 Corrected χ^2 = 8.87
	Low Urban** Experience	37.3	(59)	
Islamic Approval of Fair Strike	High Urban* Experience	65.0	(80)	Gamma = .59 P < .00 Corrected χ^2 = 13.33
	Low Urban** Experience	32.2	(59)	
Agreement with Organizing at the Factory Level	High Urban* Experience	58.2	(79)	Gamma = .53 P < .00 Corrected χ^2 = 8.69
	Low Urban** Experience	30.0	(50)	
Agreement with Workers Engaging in Politics	High Urban* Experience	43.6	(78)	Gamma = .48 P < .02 Corrected χ^2 = 5.65
	Low Urban** Experience	21.6	(51)	

*High = six years or more.
**Low = five years or less.

them. Urban life also allows urbans and migrants the freedom to discover the inequities that surround them through communication with others. Table 1 presents the relationship between years of urban residence and class consciousness.

As our theory predicts, workers who have resided and participated in peripheral capitalist urban social relations are much more likely to develop class consciousness than recent rural migrants and commuters.

If urban participation is important, then what effect does the experience of wage labor in large, complexly organized capitalist enterprises have upon the development of class consciousness? Here our theory of class formation argues that the experience of wage labor in large-scale enterprises socializes workers into a new identity, the urban proletariat, pre-

Table 2. Class Consciousness and Wage Labor Experience

Dimension of Consciousness	Variable: Number of Years in Modern Wage Labor	Positive or Agree: %	(N)	Statistics
Agrees that Pay is Unfair	High Number of Years*	51.4	(70)	Gamma = .26 P < .18 Corrected χ^2 = 1.79
	Low Number of Years**	38.5	(65)	
Adebo Strike Support	High Number of Years*	65.3	(72)	Gamma = .48 P < .00 Corrected χ^2 = 8.18
	Low Number of Years**	39.7	(68)	
Islamic Approval of Fair Strike	High Number of Years*	60.6	(71)	Gamma = .37 P < .03 Corrected χ^2 = 4.48
	Low Number of Years**	41.2	(68)	
Agreement with Organizing at the Factory Level	High Number of Years*	54.4	(68)	Gamma = .30 P < .12 Corrected χ^2 = 2.36
	Low Number of Years**	39.3	(61)	
Agreement with Workers Engaging in Politics	High Number of Years*	36.8	(68)	Gamma = .09 P < .77 Corrected χ^2 = .08
	Low Number of Years**	32.8	(61)	

*High = five years or more.
**Low = four years or less.

cisely because their labor is a commodity and thus prior skills and forms of social status are meaningless to the labor process and the needs of industrial capitalism. Table 2 presents the relationship between wage-labor experience and class consciousness.

The results are of theoretical interest. The strongest effect of wage labor is on support for the concrete event—the Adebo strike—where all respondents witnessed and benefited from the strike even if they did not participate in or support the strike. Hence, wage-labor experience appears to be important at the level of class conflict and to a lesser degree at the level of organizing at the factory level, where the relationship is modest as compared to support for the Adebo strike. But the data indicate that the political dimension of class consciousness does not emerge as strongly from the wage-labor experience as it does from urban residential experience. This difference confirms that in the absence of trade unions, wage-labor experience may move workers to organizing at the factory level but politically active class consciousness requires an organizational and ideological force that is external to the factory. Let us control for the effects of urban residential experience on the relationship between wage-labor experience and class consciousness. Table 3 presents this relationship for one dimension, support for the Adebo strike.

In order to simplify the data analysis, only the strongest dimension is included in Table 3. To summarize the others: when controlled by urban residential experience, "organizing at the factory level" remained in the same direction, but the degree of association declined to a lower level (Gamma = .20 and Gamma = .19 for high and low urban experience, respectively), and the level of statistical significance rose appreciably. Thus, when controlled by urban residential experience, our fourth dimension of class consciousness, organizing at the factory level, declined to a weak association. Regarding the second dimension, the fairness of pay, controlling for urban residential experience reduced the explanatory effects of wage labor to a negligible level. This finding and some other data not included here confirm that it is the experience of urban life and the exposure to great inequality of income that explain workers' evaluation of the fairness of their pay, not the degree of exposure to wage labor.

To return to Table 3, the data show that wage labor exerts a powerful effect upon workers' willingness to support class action. This effect is

Table 3. Strike Support by Wage Labor Experience Controlled by Urban Residential Experience

		Positive or Agree: %	(N)	Statistics
High Urban Residential Experience (6 years or more)	High Wage Labor Experience*	72.9	(48)	Gamma = .43 P < .08 Corrected χ^2 = 3.02
	Low Wage Labor Experience**	51.5	(33)	
Low Urban Residential Experience (5 years or less)	High Wage Labor Experience*	50.0	(24)	Gamma = .43 P < .16 Corrected χ^2 = 1.95
	Low Wage Labor Experience**	26.6	(35)	

*Five years or more.
**Four years or less.

independent of the degree of urban residence. In fact, the effect of urban residence and wage-labor experience is additive, for among recent migrants or commuters who lack wage-labor experience, slightly more than a quarter support the strike. But among those who are experienced in wage labor and who have lived in a city for some length of time, nearly three-quarters support the strike. While the data are cross-sectional and do not permit a linear or time series interpretation, they suggest that as the proletariat matures in an urban-industrial situation, class consciousness at the level of class action increases significantly.

One important attribute acquired by those workers integrated into capitalist social relations is literacy in Western script. Literacy enables workers to cope with the bureaucratic and economic structures that dominate them; it also allows them to communicate with other workers and to read newspaper accounts or literature concerning workers' struggles and trade union organizations in distant cities and regions. While education and literacy are often assumed to be correlated with middle-class norms, as embodied in the "modernity" literature, our theoretical assumption expects that literate workers will be leaders in working-class activities. Most important, literacy is expected to increase class awareness and thus literate workers should have a higher level of class consciousness, especially at the organizational and societal levels. Table 4 presents the relationship between literacy and class consciousness.

Table 4.   Class Consciousness and Literacy

Dimension of Consciousness	Variable: Literacy	Positive or Agree: %	(N)	Statistics
Agrees that Pay is Unfair	Literacy	66.7	(24)	Gamma = .50
	No Literacy	40.0	(110)	P < .03 Corrected χ^2 = 4.64
Adebo Strike Support	Literacy	75.0	(24)	Gamma = .53
	No Literacy	47.8	(115)	P < .03 Corrected χ^2 = 4.84
Islamic Approval of Fair Strike	Literacy	75.0	(24)	Gamma = .56
	No Literacy	45.6	(114)	P < .02 Corrected χ^2 = 5.72
Agreement with Organizing at the Factory Level	Literacy	75.0	(24)	Gamma = .63
	No Literacy	40.4	(104)	P < .00 Corrected χ^2 = 8.04
Agreement with Workers Engaging in Politics	Literacy	65.2	(23)	Gamma = .66
	No Literacy	27.6	(105)	P < .00 Corrected χ^2 = 10.22

The data confirm our expectations: literacy is correlated with class consciousness, not only at the level of commitment to class action but also at the factory organizational and political levels. Because most literate workers are long-time urban residents, we should examine the effects of literacy on class consciousness among workers with high urban residential experience. Table 5 presents this relationship. If compared with Table 4 the effect of literacy among workers with high urban residential experience varies only slightly: note that while the degree of association declines slightly for organizing at the factory dimension, the political engagement dimension maintains the same degree of association, even when controlling for the effect of urban residence.

To summarize: our analysis verifies the relationship between participation in capitalist social relations and the acquisition of class consciousness. Urban residential experience and literacy explain class consciousness at the levels of commitment to class action and at the factory organizational and political levels. Regarding workers' evaluations of the fairness of their share of the socially produced surplus, their pay, it is clear that the more workers are exposed to urban life, the more they believe their pay to be unfair irrespective of the amount received. The experience of wage labor in large enterprises explains class consciousness at the level of overt class conflict. Experienced workers, even without a

Table 5. Class Consciousness and Literacy Among High Urban Residents

Dimension of Consciousness	Variable: Literacy	Positive or Agree: %	(N)	Statistics
Agrees that Pay is Unfair	Literacy	71.4	(21)	Gamma = .34
	No Literacy	55.4	(56)	P < .31 Corrected χ^2 = 1.04
Adebo Strike Support	Literacy	81.0	(21)	Gamma = .52
	No Literacy	57.6	(59)	P < .10 Corrected χ^2 = 2.71
Islamic Approval of Fair Strike	Literacy	85.7	(21)	Gamma = .64
	No Literacy	56.9	(58)	P < .04 Corrected χ^2 = 4.41
Agreement with Organizing at the Factory Level	Literacy	76.2	(21)	Gamma = .51
	No Literacy	50.9	(57)	P < .08 Corrected χ^2 = 3.06
Agreement with Workers Engaging in Politics	Literacy	70.0	(20)	Gamma = .65
	No Literacy	33.3	57)	P < .01 Corrected χ^2 = 6.70

high degree of urban residential experience, are much more likely to engage in class struggle than their inexperienced counterparts. The relationship between wage-labor experience and willingness to organize at the factory is weaker when controlled by urban residential experience, but it does not disappear. Class consciousness at the level of political engagement does not emerge from wage-labor experience alone; rather, literacy and long urban residence appear to explain this dimension. The effect of literacy on political levels of class consciousness is straightforward and accounted for by our theoretical assumptions. However, the determining effects that urban residential experience has on the factory organizational and political engagement dimensions of class consciousness required that we search for more discrete institutional or organizational experiences present within urban life that may account for the effects of urban residence on these two dimensions.

VIII. CLASS CONSCIOUSNESS AND ISLAMIC NATIONALISM: THE EFFECT OF ISLAMIC INSTITUTIONAL PARTICIPATION

Until now our analysis verifies a classical materialist interpretation of class formation and class consciousness. But past political movements among the popular classes indicate that Islamic nationalist consciousness, as expressed through Islamic brotherhoods and the loosely organized networks of *mallams* and Koranic schools, is an important social force among Muslim workers. Furthermore, field data published elsewhere show how *mallams* who worked at factories organized strikes and trade unions, and even negotiated for Adebo settlements in some factories (see Lubeck, 1975). Workers critical of the discipline of the factory often cited the refusal of management to allow them to pray at the correct time as a grievance that had resulted in wildcat strikes in the past. These examples suggest that, while class consciousness is mediated by Muslim ideology, Islamic nationalism may play an *independent* role in the development of class consciousness within an unevenly developed and neophyte proletariat. The problem, then, is to understand the "articulation" or the relationship between the two social forces—urban-industrial capitalism and Islamic nationalism—within a single social category that is immersed in both. This raises the question: what is the combined effect of intense participation in Islamic institutions and proletarianization in a peripheral capitalist city? Again, to repeat an earlier comment, Islamic nationalism is not declining in the face of increased integration into capitalist social relations; rather, while economic and political institutions associated with the precapitalist system are being eroded by those of a capitalist state and economy, there is a popular nationalist reaction that affirms Islamic nationalism at the cultural and community levels. By assuming that the two social forces are in a *dialectical* relationship to each other, and not independent forces where the modern rises while the traditional declines, we are arguing implicitly that a possible outcome of the combined effect of Islamic nationalism and proletarianization is a higher or an additional level of class consciousness among those workers most integrated into Islamic organizations.

In order to empirically verify our argument for combined effects, two indicators of Islamic organizational participation were developed: participation in Islamic brotherhoods (i.e., *Tijaniya* and *Qadiriya*) and years of Koranic school participation. While the first indicator was easily defined by membership, years of Koranic school posed some difficulty because of our uncertainty over the content or meaning that a year of Koranic school attendance involves. Rather than dividing at the mid-point, as we have done with previous variables in order to create two categories, we decided to take the upper third of the distribution, that is, eight years and above as constituting high Koranic school participation. In considering this decision we noted that all workers who reported having a secondary occupation as a *mallam* were in the upper third. Let us examine the relationship of Islamic brotherhood participation and Koranic school participation to class consciousness in Tables 6 and 7 respectively.

Table 6. Class Consciousness and Islamic Brotherhood Participation

Dimension of Consciousness	Variable: Participation in Islamic Brotherhoods	Positive or Agree: %	(N)	Statistics
Agrees That Pay is Unfair	Participation	75.8	(33)	Gamma = .70
	No Participation	35.3	(102)	P < .00 Corrected χ^2 = 14.89
Adebo Strike Support	Participation	66.7	(33)	Gamma = .36
	No Participation	48.6	(107)	P < .11 Corrected χ^2 = 2.62
Islamic Approval of Fair Strike	Participation	75.8	(33)	Gamma = .61
	No Participation	43.4	(106)	P < .00 Corrected χ^2 = 9.29
Agreement with Organizing at the Factory Level	Participation	78.1	(32)	Gamma = .72
	No Participation	37.1	(97)	P < .00 Corrected χ^2 = 14.63
Agreement with Workers Engaging in Politics	Participation	57.6	(33)	Gamma = .57
	No Participation	27.1	(96)	P < .00 Corrected χ^2 = 8.75

Table 7.   Class Consciousness and Koranic School Participation

Dimension of Consciousness	Variable: Years of Koranic Schooling	Positive or Agree: %	(N)	Statistics
Agrees that Pay is Unfair	High Number of Years*	47.7	(44)	Gamma = .08 P < .82 Corrected χ^2 = .05
	Low Number of Years**	44.0	(91)	
Adebo Strike Support	High Number of Years*	66.7	(45)	Gamma = .40 P < .04 Corrected χ^2 = 4.29
	Low Number of Years**	46.3	(95)	
Islamic Approval of Fair Strike	High Number of Years*	66.7	(45)	Gamma = .44 P < .02 Corrected χ^2 = 5.58
	Low Number of Years**	43.6	(94)	
Agreement with Organizing at the Factory Level	High Number of Years*	67.5	(40)	Gamma = .54 P < .00 Corrected χ^2 = 8.36
	Low Number of Years**	38.2	(89)	
Agreement with Workers Engaging in Politics	High Number of Years*	51.2	(43)	Gamma = .48 P < .01 Corrected χ^2 = 6.49
	Low Number of Years**	26.7	(86)	

*Eight years or more (upper third).
**Seven years or less.

Without controlling for urban experience the results confirm our hypothesis. Not only is participation in Islamic brotherhoods correlated with strike support but brotherhood members who are more confident of and more integrated into Muslim national culture and institutions strongly agree that Islam agrees with striking for a fair reason. Thus the principle of class struggle for a just cause is more strongly held among brotherhood members than is their support for the strike itself. Koranic school participation is consistent with brotherhood participation in its effects but at a weaker level of association and a lower level of percent agreement. If one recalls that wage labor experience is only weakly correlated with workers' agreement with organizing at the factory, then one should note that the two Islamic participation variables show their highest correlation with the "organizing at the factory" dimension of class consciousness. Furthermore, class consciousness at the political level is also strongly correlated with the two Islamic participation variables. Before interpreting these correlations, let us control for the effect of urban residential experience, which we know to be correlated with both organizing at the factory level and political engagement. Tables 8 and 9 present the Islamic participation variables controlled by urban residential experience. Note that Islamic brotherhoods are virtually absent from the recent low urban residential group, so only high urban residential workers are included in Table 8.

To take Islamic brotherhood participation among workers with high urban residential experience first, we see that controlling for urban residence makes virtually no difference in terms of the strength of the Gamma correlations. Because brotherhoods have a political organizational background, it is plausible to argue that such organizational experiences in precapitalist organizations predispose those workers toward seeking organizational and political solutions to their problems. If one takes account of the ideological content of brotherhood beliefs and practices as well as the role brotherhoods played in resisting European imperialism, then one

Table 8. Class Consciousness and Islamic Brotherhood Participation Among High Urban Residents

Dimension of Consciousness	Variable: Participation in Islamic Brotherhoods	Positive or Agree: %	(N)	Statistics
Agrees That Pay is Unfair	Participation	80.8	(26)	Gamma = .62
	No Participation	50.0	(52)	P < .02 Corrected χ^2 = 5.63
Adebo Strike Support	Participation	76.9	(26)	Gamma = .41
	No Participation	58.2	(55)	P < .16 Corrected χ^2 = 1.94
Islamic Approval of Fair Strike	Participation	80.8	(26)	Gamma = .51
	No Participation	57.4	(54)	P < .07 Corrected χ^2 = 3.25
Agreement with Organizing at the Factory Level	Participation	84.6	(26)	Gamma = .74
	No Participation	45.3	(53)	P < .00 Corrected χ^2 = 9.54
Agreement with Workers Engaging in Politics	Participation	61.5	(26)	Gamma = .50
	No Participation	34.6	(52)	P < .04 Corrected χ^2 = 4.07

Table 9. Class Consciousness and Kornic School Participation with
High and Low Urban Residential Experience

| | High Urban Residential Experience | | | |
| | | | | |
Dimension of Consciousness	*Variable: Years of Koranic Schooling*	*Positive or Agree: %*	*(N)*	*Statistics*
Adebo Strike Support	High Number of Years*	68.8	(32)	Gamma = .16 P < .65 Corrected χ^2 = .21
	Low Number of Years**	61.2	(49)	
Islamic Approval of Fair Strike	High Number of Years*	75.0	(32)	Gamma = .36 P < .20 Corrected χ^2 = 1.67
	Low Number of Years**	58.3	(48)	
Agreement with Organizing at the Factory Level	High Number of Years*	74.2	(31)	Gamma = .52 P < .04 Corrected χ^2 = 4.32
	Low Number of Years**	47.9	(48)	
Agreement with Workers Engaging in Politics	High Number of Years*	61.3	(31)	Gamma = .54 P < .02 Corrected χ^2 = 5.42
	Low Number of Years**	31.9	(47)	

must conclude that there is an Islamic nationalist content to brotherhood
members' preference for organizational and political solutions.

If we examine Table 9, we see that for Koranic school participation the
same relationships hold, though with weaker degrees of correlation. Note
that among the low urban residential group, Koranic school participation
is strongly correlated with support for the strike and at a reasonable level
of statistical significance. This suggests that among recent rural emigrants, Koranic school participation predisposes them to supporting class
action. Turning to the relationship between Koranic school participation
and class consciousness among workers with high urban residential experience, Koranic school participation continues to be correlated with
organizing at the factory level and with political engagement, even when
the strong effect of high urban residential experience is controlled for. In
passing we should note that Koranic school participation in rural areas has
little effect on class consciousness, except for support for the Adebo

Table 9. (continued)

	Low Urban Residential Experience			
Dimension of Consciousness	Variable: Years of Koranic Schooling	Positive or Agree: %	(N)	Statistics
Adebo Strike Support	High Number of Years*	61.5	(13)	Gamma = .57 P < .08 Corrected χ² = 2.97
	Low Number of Years**	30.4	(46)	
Islamic Approval of Fair Strike	High Number of Years*	46.2	(13)	Gamma = .37 P < .38 Corrected χ² = .78
	Low Number of Years**	28.3	(46)	
Agreement with Organizing at the Factory Level	High Number of Years*	44.4	(9)	Gamma = .37 P < .52 Corrected χ² = .41
	Low Number of Years**	26.8	(41)	
Agreement with Workers Engaging in Politics	High Number of Years*	25.0	(12)	Gamma = .13 P < .94 Corrected χ² = .01
	Low Number of Years**	20.5	(39)	

*Eight years or more (upper third).
**Seven years or less.

strike. Thus, we conclude that it is the combination of Koranic schooling and residence in a peripheral capitalist city that generates support for the organizational and political dimensions of class consciousness.

To conclude, Islamic organizational participation has a clear and consistent relationship with class consciousness. Regarding the more advanced levels of class consciousness, that is, organizing at the factory and support for workers' political engagement as opposed to support for the strike event, it is noteworthy that the strength of the correlations between Islamic participation and dimensions of class consciousness increases among those dimensions that pertain to organizing at the factory and societal level. This suggests that workers who participate in urban Muslim organizations are more open to participating in urban working-class organizations. Again, this linkage between participation in urban religious organizations and a greater propensity to participate in working-class organizations is only suggested in the data. But it is plausible. For example, E. P. Thompson's (1963) interpretation of Methodism among recently proletarianized English workers also finds a linkage between the two forms of organizational participation: Methodist sects and trade union organizations. Despite the ideological differences between the two fundamentalist religions—Islam and Methodism—both relate positively to the social, emotional, and community needs of recently proletarianized workers. Because Muslim religious organizations are controlled by working-class or *talakawa* members and because for many, they offer the first form of urban social participation free of family and community-of-origin ties, it is plausible that Muslim organizational participation predisposes workers to participate in secular trade union organizations.

IX. THE CONVERGENCE OF CLASS AND NATIONAL CONSCIOUSNESS: A THEORETICAL ASSESSMENT

Thus far we have shown at the level of empirical generalization that class and nationalist consciousness do converge under specific conditions such that both participation in urban capitalist social relations and participation in urban Muslim organizations predict increasing levels of class consciousness. Yet our original question remains: how does the experience of global inequality deriving from northern Nigeria's mode of incorporation into and contemporary role in the international division of labor articulate with Islamic nationalist and class consciousness? Before returning to this question, let us first review the consequences of our empirical findings for the alternative explanations offered by modernization theory (see Inkeles and Smith, 1974).

For those readers familiar with structural-functionalist (see Smelser, 1959, 1963) or modernity approaches that purport to explain individual or collective change in "developing countries," it is obvious that our findings are incompatible with the expectations of modernization theory. Let us examine modernity theory as developed in the work of Inkeles. Modernity theory argues that the factory acts as a "school" for the resocialization of third-world factory workers into reflections of idealized middle-class managers. Accordingly, it is argued that as exposure to urban industrial organizations increases, factory workers are expected to avoid irrational conflict, to favor formally rational bureaucratic authority, and to reduce incrementally their belief in traditional religion. Such an ahistorical and reductionist approach, as we have seen, is incapable of explaining the data provided above, even though Nigeria was one of the six nations sampled in the Harvard project on modernity. Furthermore, if Inkeles' statement that the factory acts as a "school" for the acquisition of modernity is applied to these data, it is obvious that workers learn a great deal through factory experience; but "schooling" does not lead to harmonious emulation of management but instead predicts to commitment for class struggle at the factory.

Structural-functionalist predictions fare no better than modernity theory. Again the social disorganization explanation of industrial protest during early industrialization is not supported by the data. The opposite is true: the more integrated workers were into secondary groups, the more likely they were to support industrial protest. Hence, explanations of industrial protest that seek to explain changes in workers' consciousness cannot apply ahistorical idealizations of the western experience to the societies of the periphery any longer without acknowledging the historical relationship that exists between the core and the periphery. Rather, only an historical analysis of peripheral societies that acknowledges the creation of the periphery by the core can serve as a valid method of studying and generalizing about workers' consciousness in peripheral societies.

Throughout our analysis of workers' consciousness we have argued that Islamic nationalist consciousness need not be antagonistic to the emergence of class consciousness. While the relationship between participation in capitalist social relations and class consciousness among recently proletarianized workers needs little elaboration because it follows classical materialist and Marxian theoretical assumptions, the positive effect exerted by participation in Islamic organizations on class consciousness requires some discussion. Indeed there are many levels of explanation: *mallams* and those integrated into Muslim organizations are usually community leaders who have a "calling" in the Weberian sense to protest and lead the community against tyranny. And they carry such expectations and callings with them when they enter the factory labor force. In this Weberian sense the *mallams* are a status group within an emerging class. But this micro-level approach does not explain the vitality of Islamic nationalism in Kano, nor the world resurgence of Islamic nationalism and Islamic revitalization movements, nor the convergence of national and class consciousness among Kano's industrial workers.

In order to explain the convergence of national and class consciousness we must understand that Islamic nationalism is not merely the diffusion of an ancient religious culture, but is rather an active and dynamic worldwide movement that has resisted and reacted to the penetration of Western capitalism. Moreover, the ideological content of Islamic nationalism varies significantly as it reacts to and in turn is reinforced by both historical and contemporary confrontations with the expanding capitalist world economy. Under conditions that are conjunctural and contingent rather than absolute and immutable, reactive Islamic nationalism can bolster particular social classes and play a role in class struggle as in the case of Kano's industrial workers. Here it is important to remember that when workers are treated as a commodity or when the timing and discipline of factory production contradict established Muslim practice (e.g., a patron's obligation to his servants, the observance of prayer time), the response of workers to the erosion of their traditional rights takes the form of Islamic nationalism. Unlike the situation in Western Europe or Japan during an equivalent period of proletarianization, religious and nationalist affiliations overlap upon and reinforce class cleavages.

At the level of global inequality, class and national consciousness converge under specific conditions of industrial production where technology, factory organization, inputs, and managerial expertise are externally controlled and are perceived to be subordinated to the logic of a global economy. Hence it is the subordination of a Muslim region to the exigencies of a capitalist world economy that generates the tension necessary for the revitalization of Islamic nationalism in a city undergoing the transition to semi-industrial peripheral capitalism. Finally, just as capitalism as a system of social relations at the factory level generates class consciousness, Muslim northern Nigeria's historically evolved relationship to the capitalist world economy generates "reactive" Islamic nationalism, which combines with its own internal ideological logic to converge with class consciousness as expressed by a recently proletarianized working class.

What, then, explains the vitality and resurgence of Muslim nationalist consciousness in regions as different and as distant as Pakistan, Iran, Libya, and northern Nigeria? Clearly the particular ideological content of Muslim culture, which is imbedded in all sectors of society, and its preference for the unity of the religious and the political play an important role in Islamic revitalization movements. Equally important is the structural position held by Muslim states, especially OPEC members, in the international division of labor. All are technically dependent and thus subordinate to a world economy dominated by their historical ideological enemies: Christian Europe and America. Not only are these states dependent upon the core states' demand for their products, but the essential technical and managerial expertise is imported from the core states in such a way that the division of labor within peripheral Muslim states often reflects the division of labor between states in the world economy. Moreover, we should remember that only a tiny minority of the population blessed with connections to the state or to the world economy benefit from rapid petroleum-induced economic growth. Then one may comprehend why popular Muslim nationalist movements, whose members are drawn from the less dynamic sectors, are generated as a reaction to formal imperialism as in the case of Iran or to more subtle forms of subordination—to the exigencies of the capitalist world economy—as in the case of Kano, Nigeria.

REFERENCES

Amin, Samir
1976 Unequal Development. New York: Monthly Review.
Adeleye, Roland
1971 Power and Diplomacy in Northern Nigeria. London: Longman.
Feldman, Arnold, and Wilbert Moore
1960 Labor Commitment and Social Change in Developing Areas. New York: Social
Science Research Council.
Foster, John
1974 Class Struggle and the Industrial Revolution. New York: St. Martin's Press.
Foster-Carter, Adian
1978 "The Modes of Production Controversy." New Left Review 107.
Hazelrigg, Lawrence
1973 "Aspects of the Measurement of Class Consciousness." In M. Armer and A.
Grimshaw, Comparative Social Research. New York: Wiley.
Inkeles, Alex, and David Smith
1974 Becoming Modern. Cambridge, Mass.: Harvard University Press.
Kahl, Joseph
1968 The Measurement of Modernism. Austin: University of Texas Press.
Last, Murray
1967 The Sokoto Caliphate. London: Longman.
Lenin, V. I.
1968 National Liberation, Socialism and Imperialism. New York: International Publishers.
Lloyd, Peter
1975 "Perceptions of Class and Inequality Among the Yoruba of Western Nigeria." In
H. Safa and B. Du Toit, Migration and Development. The Hague: Mouton.
Lubeck, Paul
1975 "Unions, Workers and Consciousness in Kano, Nigeria." In R. Sandbrook and R.
Cohen, The Development of an African Working Class. London: Longman.
1979a "Islam and Resistance in Northern Nigeria." In W. Goldfrank, The World System
of Capitalism. Beverly Hills, Calif.: Sage.
1979b "The Value of Multiple Methods in Researching Third World Strikes." Development and Change 10, 2.
Mann, Michael
1973 Consciousness and Action Among the Western Working Class. London: Macmillan.
Meszaros, Istvan
1971 Aspects of History and Class Consciousness. London: Routledge and Kegan Paul.
Nairn, Tom
1977 The Break-up of Britain. London: New Left Books.
Paden, John
1974 Religion and Political Culture in Kano. Berkeley: University of California Press.
Post, Ken
1978 Arise Ye Starvelings. The Hague: Nijhoff.
Roxborough, Ian
1976 "Dependency Theory in the Sociology of Development: Some Theoretical Problems." West African Journal of Sociology and Political Science I, 1.
Sklar, Richard
1963 Nigerian Political Parties. Princeton: Princeton University Press.

Smelser, Neil
   1959   Social Change in the Industrial Revolution. Chicago: University of Chicago Press.
   1963   "Mechanisms of Change and Adjustment to Change." In W. Moore and B. Hose-
          litz (eds.), Industrialization and Society. The Hague: Mouton.
Smith, Michael G.
   1960   Government in Zauzau. London: Oxford University Press.
Wallerstein, Immanuel
   1974   The Modern World System. New York: Academic Press.
   1975   "Class-Formation in the Capitalist World Economy." Politics and Society 5:
          367–375.

WORKMATES, KIN AND FRIENDS:

THE SOCIAL CONTACTS OF WEST AFRICAN URBAN WORKERS

Margaret Peil

Most studies of African workers have concentrated on their relations in the workplace (van der Horst, 1964; Kapferer, 1972) or their trade union activities (Smock, 1969; Sandbrook and Cohen, 1975; Jeffries, 1978). Even when informal activities have been discussed (Grillo, 1973; Sandbrook and Arn, 1977), the emphasis has been on relations with workmates, minimizing the effects of socializing in the wider community and ignoring as irrelevant time spent with family and kin. Yet, as far back as 1956, Mitchell showed that social activities off the job often do not involve workmates. Amachree (1968), Pfeffermann (1968: 164–170), and King (1977) provide some evidence of the importance of kinship and

Research in the Sociology of Work, Volume 1, pages 71–104
Copyright © 1981 by JAI Press Inc.
All rights of reproduction in any form reserved.
ISBN: 0-89232-124-5

hometown ties for urban workers, but there is little evidence of the range of workers' contacts or how different types of workers spend their leisure time—factors that can have an important effect on their self-image and perception of their role and status in society. Studies of African towns often provide examples of the wide range of social contacts that urban residents develop (see Epstein, 1961, the classic description), but they seldom differentiate residents by the nature of their employment.

This paper aims to fill a gap by examining the relations of wage- and self-employed workers[1] at various occupational levels, with their work-mates, kin, and other friends. If consciousness of deprived or exploited position in the social order develops as a result of workplace relations, it should be fostered by frequent contacts with workmates off the job, where workers are free to express their ideas and influence each other. If, therefore, workers spend little of their spare time with people they work with but instead socialize mainly with family and friends who have different occupational experiences and aspirations, they are more likely to think in terms of communal than of workplace values. There is considerable evidence that this is the case.

On the other hand, Sandbrook and Arn (1977) argue that politically conscious workers in large-scale enterprises may be a potent force for changing values, especially in an isolated community, because they pass on ideas developed at work to friends in the informal sector of the economy. I will argue that urban isolation is difficult to maintain and rare in practice. Most factory operatives are surrounded by neighbors and friends who see success in terms of joining the capitalists rather than overthrowing them and who maintain strong links with home and kin because that is where their ultimate security lies. This severely limits the development of an organized working class and even widespread commitment to trade unionism on a continuing rather than a sporadic basis (see Cohen, 1972: 252).

The primary data come from a series of surveys in Ghana, Nigeria, and Gambia between 1966 and 1976. Interviews of 1432 workers in sixteen factories located in four towns and two villages in Ghana included some questions on their families and contacts outside the workplace. Later, interviews of about 200 people (drawn from sample censuses) in each of eight towns in the three countries focused on social relations with family, neighbors, and friends, some of whom were workmates. This makes it possible to examine comparatively the influence of urban social structure and the nature of the workplace as well as individual variables, such as occupation, education, age, etc., on social relations. Only men will be included in this discussion, because few women in the samples were in large-scale wage employment and the different pattern of female social relations would unduly complicate the discussion.

A mono-industrial town is more likely to have a self-conscious worker community than a metropolis, where people living in the same neighborhood and drinking at the same bars have widely differing occupations and orientations, or a provincial town where a small number of factory workers find their friends among a much larger number of men in self-employment in commerce or crafts or in the civil service. Thus, Jeffries (1977) demonstrates a continuity of ideology among railway workers in the "working class town" of Sekondi, and the common interest of market women and others in the progress of the town's major industry. The relative separation of Sekondi from the corridors of power is paralleled in towns centered on mining or wood processing. As in industrialized countries (Kerr and Siegel, 1954), relative isolation helps to develop an occupational community where integration or division have more to do with local than with national conditions and leadership, though conflicts may be phrased in universalistic terms.

Much of this discussion will focus on four towns with considerable factory employment, three of which also have or are near ports. Tema is a new industrial town and port about fifteen miles east of Accra, the capital of Ghana. Building started in the 1950s; almost all the housing is owned by the Tema Development Corporation (TDC). Many of Ghana's large factories are in its industrial estate. Ashaiman, about five miles inland, houses about a third of Tema's labor force in privately built houses on TDC land. Rents there have tended to be lower than in Tema, reflecting lower standards of accommodation and amenities. Tema residents often get their housing through their employer and tend to be older, better educated, and in more stable wage employment than people living in Ashaiman. More of the latter are long distance or recent migrants and working in the informal sector. Tema had about 83,000 people in 1970 and Ashaiman about 28,000.

The other two towns are in Nigeria. Kakuri was chosen because it is about the same size as Ashaiman, with living conditions at about the same level. It is about four miles south of Kaduna, the former capital of northern Nigeria, and houses mainly workers in an adjoining industrial estate. When built in the early 1960s, this was the largest industrial complex in northern Nigeria. Ajegunle is part of the Lagos metropolitan area, contiguous with but officially outside the boundary of Nigeria's capital city. It has few metropolitan services. Residents find employment in the nearby industrial estates of Apapa and Ijora, in the port, and in other jobs throughout the city; many spend considerable time each day getting to and from work. It has been growing rapidly for at least the last thirty years and had about 90,000 people when studied in 1972.

Sandbrook and Arn (1977) characterize Ashaiman as isolated in comparison to Nima, a low income area (with at least twice Ashaiman's population) within Accra. While the opportunities for employment are more limited in Ashaiman than for Nima residents, both can easily get to central Accra and participate, however vicariously, in national events to a greater extent than residents of most Ghanaian towns. Thus, the factors influencing worker consciousness in Ashaiman (as in Tema) seem likely to be their relatively advanced education (about two-fifths had completed ten years in school), recent arrival from the more developed southern part of Ghana, and commitment to urban, wage employment.

Ajegunle is even more central to the national political scene than Tema and Ashaiman, though its residents often feel isolated by the governmental neglect of their needs. This is a highly heterogeneous town, in no sense an occupational community. There were members of forty different ethnic groups in the Ajegunle sample, and more nonmanual workers and self-employed than in the other industrial towns (see Table 1). Kakuri is the most isolated, and the concentration of residents in wage employment makes this a more likely spot for an occupational community than the other three towns. However, many men living in Kaduna also work in these factories (Hinchliffe, 1973), and Kakuri residents often visit Kaduna, so they share in its provincial milieu rather than being an independent industrial town.

Table 1 shows that the four industrial towns have broadly similar male labor forces, but there are a few important differences. The preponderance of factory employment has given Kakuri the most selective labor force, whereas Ajegunle provides the most varied opportunities. The level of self-employment in commerce in Ajegunle shows the importance which the Yoruba of southwestern Nigeria give to independent entrepreneurship as well the shortage of wage employment. Tema houses many more clerks and administrators than Ashaiman—as is so often the case with government housing in developing countries. Ashaiman accommodates those who cannot find a room in Tema, so it has a much larger complement of unskilled workers and of craftsmen who are dependent on the construction industry. Unemployment was highest in Ghana, which was (and still is) facing severe economic problems. Many of the unemployed were recent arrivals looking for their first urban job; few were heads of households. As most people leave these towns when they retire, males over fifteen not in the labor force are usually completing their education.

The four service-center (administrative and commercial) towns are older and have more nonmigrant residents than the industrial towns. Aba and Abeokuta, with 300,000 and 200,000 population respectively when studied, are provincial towns in southern Nigeria. Aba grew rapidly because of the civil disturbances of the late 1960s; the other towns were growing rather slowly. Banjul and Serekunda are the only large towns in

Table 1. Occupation and Labor Force Participation, by Town, Males (Percentages)

| | Industrial Towns | | | | Service-Center Towns | | | |
| | Ghana | | Nigeria | | Nigeria | | Gambia | |
	Ashaiman	Tema	Ajegunle	Kakuri	Aba	Abeokuta	Banjul	Serkunda
Employment Sector								
Self-employed	14	13	24	10	42	36	17	28
Wage-employed	71	71	60	78	43	44	52	49
Unemployed	14	11	9	7	5	2	7	5
Not in labor force	1	5	7	5	10	18	24	18
Total	100	100	100	100	100	100	100	100
N	907	858	981	819	821	392	543	470
Occupation*								
Farmer, unskilled	30	13	15	5	10	8	12	16
Semiskilled manual	25	28	14	62	8	10	5	12
Skilled manual	32	18	20	13	19	15	18	27
Commerce	5	8	17	6	50	24	19	13
Clerical, uniformed	6	23	30	12	8	23	32	21
Professional, admin.	2	10	3	2	5	20	10	11
Total	100	100	100	100	100	100	100	100
N	846	770	843	733	709	326	406	371

Source: House censuses.
*Those with an occupation only.

75

Gambia and contain a high proportion of the country's wage employees; they had about 40,000 and 28,000 people respectively when studied. Banjul, the Gambian capital, is an island; Serekunda, about seven miles away, takes much of the overflow population. A high proportion of its residents work in Banjul.

Self-employment tends to be high in these towns, especially Aba, and about a fifth of the men were either retired or still in school. Manufacturing and semiskilled work are limited compared to industrial towns, and the government is the main employer. Several factories in Aba had not yet reopened and there was little alternative employment in 1972, so many new arrivals were involved in highly competitive trading or craft activities. In the other three towns, the proportion of professionals is relatively high, as their schools and hospitals serve a wide area.

I. INDUSTRIAL AND OCCUPATIONAL DIFFERENCES

The main independent variables to be examined are industrial sector and occupation. These are to a certain extent interrelated. Self-employed men (often referred to in the literature as the informal sector) will be compared to those working in large manufacturing plants (from 30 to 4500 workers), at the ports, for the government, or for other private employers (most in small-scale commerce, banking, construction, or services such as private schools and hospitals).

The self-employed are usually traders/businessmen or craftsmen, who may have one or more apprentices or employees but would seldom be considered capitalists in the Marxist sense. A few are professionals (mallams, prophets, and traditional healers, as well as lawyers); drivers and laborers may also be self-employed. The proportion of men in manufacturing in the industrial towns varies considerably, from three-fifths of those in wage employment in Kakuri and nearly half in Tema to only a fifth in Ajegunle. These tend to be classified as semiskilled (less than a year training), whereas the construction industry employs large numbers of skilled artisans. Government employees tend to be either unskilled laborers or white collar workers (clerks, administrators, and professionals), as are workers at ports. Skilled workers in government employment usually work for the Department of Public Works or the Electricity Corporation.

Because of recent growth and the nature of the jobs, workers in manufacturing are likely to be young, relatively well-educated men who are drawn to semiskilled work because it pays better than most alternatives open to them; quite a few have done routine clerical work or teaching but found these unrewarding and offering little opportunity for promotion. As these men's aspirations are frustrated, they become conscious of the large gap between their position and that of the government elite, who are seen as taking an increasing share of the "national cake"; the multinational corporation which employs them also seems to possess unlimited riches.

On the other hand, they may prefer (as British workers in similar circumstances do; see Goldthorpe, *et al.*, 1969: 65) to associate in their spare time with people who are not workmates and (in a more West African pattern) to think of their position in society as an individual rather than a group matter. Many see advancement in terms of starting a small business, though this is more true of Yoruba operatives than of Ghanaian ones (see Konings, 1978b: 41; Peace, 1979: chap. 3; Peil, 1972: 105; Waterman, 1976: 175).

Unlike the situation in developed countries, skilled workers in West Africa tend to have less education, or at least no more, than semiskilled men. Until recently, masters did not expect their apprentices to be literate and many boys were put to an apprenticeship rather than being sent to school. Many skilled construction workers run businesses of their own on the side. For most, construction work is insecure, with layoff or the need to move as projects finish. Craft guilds are often more important than unions for skilled workers, except for permanent employees of the Department of Public Works or manufacturing firms. The majority see themselves as carpenters, masons, or painters rather than as workers; they have more affiliation to the trade than to any place of employment. Given their educational background and entrepreneurial links, construction workers can be expected to be generally more conservative in outlook than men in manufacturing.

Dock workers, seamen, and others associated with ports may see themselves as having more in common than factory operatives or construction workers. Large numbers of them are unskilled, illiterate, long-distance migrants with less commitment to the town and less interest in building a future there than the workers so far discussed, but they work in large numbers in a confined environment and often have waiting time which they can spend together. The first recorded strike in West Africa may have been that of Gold Coast port laborers (Priestley, 1965).

In recent years, they have been mobilized for strike action against oppressive management (as in the state-owned Cargo Handling Company strike in Tema in 1968), but on the whole they have tended to seek individual rewards through theft or smuggling rather than participating in group action, with the possible penalty of losing their job. Permanent employees are supplemented by casual workers, who support themselves through periods of unemployment by working occasionally on the docks.

The government is by far the largest single employer in most African countries. The Ministries of Education, Public Works, and Defense employ the most workers. Government employees have in common a large, impersonal bureaucracy, which is seen as rich, inefficient, and unresponsive but as providing the most secure employment available. The Nigerian teachers have historically been the most militant government workers, but other groups have struck in recent years. In the past, wage increases in the public sector led the way to rises in the private sector, but recently large-scale private employers have been under considerable pressure to surpass public wage rates. This and rising inflation have lowered the satisfaction of public employees and increased their militancy.

Although they are in a minority in some departments, the majority of white collar employees work for the government. White collar workers have often provided the literate leadership for unions and other voluntary associations. With the spread of education, this has become less necessary, and Kraus (1977: 33) reports "pronounced cleavages between white collar and manual workers" in Ghana.[2] Should this be true, a self-conscious middle class would appear to be well developed. However, the cleavage seems to be between ordinary manual and nonmanual workers and the small sector of white collar workers who are "senior staff"—the well-educated and well-paid administrators. In most towns, the average salary and standard of living of most white collar workers is similar to that of skilled and semiskilled manual workers and they tend to share the same houses. A disparity of interests across the white/blue collar line is more apparent in industries that have historically differentiated between a white collar salariat and a largely illiterate manual labor force hired on daily wage terms (i.e., mining) than for the majority of clerical workers.

Small private firms tend to be doing manufacturing or construction under local entrepreneurs. Relations of workers with their employers are likely to be personal and a we/they barrier may have little relevance. Late wages, poor working conditions, and other forms of exploitation are often present, but dissatisfaction results in turnover rather than militancy. Workers are often homogeneous in background, and many find the milieu suits them better than a large firm with manifestly better conditions. Others simply cannot find alternative employment.

The last group to be considered are employees of the Ministry of Defense, mainly soldiers and other uniformed workers such as policemen and prison warders. Soldiers are an occupational community to a greater extent than miners, as they place more emphasis on esprit de corps and have a lower turnover. Only those living outside barracks were included in these studies, but Nigeria's army had expanded well beyond its available housing and quite a few soldiers were living in both Kakuri and Ajegunle. Policemen tend to share houses with other policemen, and so are also a living and working community, though less isolated than soldiers.

While most of the soldiers interviewed had civilian as well as military friends, they were more likely to spend considerable time with workmates and to count some of them among their friends than any other category of workers. The close ties among soldiers were also represented by several men who belonged to ex-servicemen's associations. In a country run by the army (as was the case in both Ghana and Nigeria at the time these studies were made), even ordinary soldiers have a consciousness of their position in society which is considerably stronger than that of the average employee, and this tends to be reflected in their behavior.

II. WORKMATES

Contacts with workmates may be limited to the workplace or include trade union activities and/or informal interaction in neighborhoods or places of public recreation such as bars, cinemas or football matches. Membership of trade unions will be examined first, then the use made of opportunities to interact with workmates on and off the job.

A. Unions

The hopes for trade unionism in Africa have been expressed by Waterman (1978: 85–86): unions are "the only permanent mass organization of any section of the labouring poor"; they "will remain the key organization for translating mass consciousness into organization, policy and activity." While this may be true, it merely indicates what a long way there is to go. So far, trade unions are of negligible importance to a large majority of urban residents except during brief periods of negotiation and strike activity, and many strikes are independent of unions if not actually opposed by union leaders. Relatively well-off teachers and civil servants are more likely to belong to a union than laborers, the true poor.

This is not to say that union activity is not of consuming interest to some workers much of the time and to many workers occasionally, but the attitude of national governments toward unions, the size and employment opportunities of a particular town, the nature of an individual's employment (occupational level and type of employer) and of his experience (age, education, marital status, ethnicity, length of residence, and of employment in this firm) are likely to influence his interest in union affairs. Thus, an historical or statistical approach which concentrates exclusively on records or an informant approach which relies on union activists is likely to give a false impression.

A problem that has dogged much of this research is that most of those who have engaged in it have had no systematic training in survey methods. While a few have tried small surveys, they know little about the techniques of conducting or analyzing them and instinctively mistrust them. As a result, the marginals from less than 100 interviews, often with poorly framed questions, tell us little about how the majority of workers feel about trade unions. Surveys can tell only part of the story, but they would be an invaluable supplement to balance the data.

If unions are to be effective mass organizations, they must draw in the masses, at least occasionally. So far, unions in West Africa have been highly selective (attracting mainly the easily organizable groups such as miners, railway workers, and teachers) and have suffered from numerous disabilities that have discouraged their potential clientele (see Davies, 1966; Cohen, 1974; Crisp, 1978b). The situation in Ghana and Nigeria shows the difficulties of two quite different patterns.

Ghana has had mandatory union membership for wage employees since 1958, except for a short period when the Busia regime made it voluntary. This gave union leaders the security of an assured income, but has been allied to government control, which made most strikes illegal and promoted a productionist ideology that many workers found has little relevance to their needs. Thus, with a few notable exceptions such as the railway workers and gold miners, unions have not held much interest for Ghanaian workers. Even in these cases, the local union movement has often been at odds with national leadership, which is easier for the government to control.

Jeffries (1977) found increasing interest in unionism among railway workers after the overthrow of the Nkrumah government, when the TUC was revitalized under new leadership. However, this appears to have been a local response that drew on the strong historical base and abundance of local leadership in Sekondi. Of the firms I studied between 1966 and 1968, only one (a printing press) appeared to have a union that engaged the workers' interest. Crisp (1978b: 16–23) reports that the miners at Tarkwa found the post-Nkrumah period as frustrating as the previous era. The Mine Workers' Union president had sold out to the government, and Branch officers increasingly distanced themselves from workers and resisted all attempts to oust them.

Where union democracy remains (mainly at branch level), militant workers use it to put pressure on local branch leaders (Konings, 1978a: 12). In this way, certain groups of workers employed by profitable multi-national corporations have been able to gain higher wages and better conditions, but the majority of workers are much less fortunate and get little for their union dues. Civil servants and dock workers have faced dismissal for striking, and employees of small, locally owned companies can be sacked for showing an inclination to form a union or resist unpaid overtime or other exploitative conditions. Thus, workers who feel they have a cause to defend often do not see the union as the logical place for this defense.

Nigerian unionism has, on the whole, been more entrepreneurial and overtly political than Ghanaian unionism (see Cohen, 1974). Large numbers of small unions have been run by men who were as interested in the economic and political rewards of the job as in forwarding worker concerns. Whereas the Ghana TUC has had a continuing existence, Nigeria has had numerous unstable central bodies. Several attempts have been made by union leaders to establish a political party for workers, but these have attracted few votes. Wolpe (1974: chap. 8) shows how geoethnic interests have proved far stronger than economic identity at the ballot box (see also Melson, 1971: 164).

In both Ghana and Nigeria, there appears to be a large gap between the rank and file and union leaders and, as in most voluntary associations, only a small proportion of union members are active. Konings (1978a: 12) reports that only 2% of the relatively militant workers he interviewed at the Valco plant in Tema could name any national union leader and only 12% thought these leaders did a good job. The University of Ibadan unionists interviewed by Cohen (1974: 267–271) were selected from the 280 out of 1000 members on the union books who showed some interest. In this case, about three-quarters could name a national leader, but only 59% had voted at a union meeting and only 6% thought union leaders in Lagos could be trusted. Insofar as union leaders have been unwilling to allow internal democracy or resist domination by the government, workers must forward their cause by other means (Crisp, 1978a: 98–99).

The questions asked about trade union membership varied from one project to another, but the overall conclusion is that trade union membership is either absent or irrelevant for the majority of potential members in the towns I studied. The word *union* is more likely to mean a group based on common ethnicity or hometown than on employment, because the union of members is more evident in these smaller, ascriptive societies.

The main study of Tema and Ashaiman asked about membership in mutual aid associations and savings societies. Trade unions have seldom been able to give aid to their members or do much to encourage saving, which is one reason why few potential members see them as filling important felt needs. Thus, it is not too surprising that no one mentioned a trade union (including one man who was a trade union official), though two drivers did mention a Drivers' Association. The pretest, which asked for membership in any occupational association, did somewhat better. Of 408 male heads of households, nine mentioned such an association. Five said they belonged to the TUC and four to occupational associations. Of these, four were clerical workers, three skilled craftsmen, and the last a surveyor. Thus, none of the semiskilled factory operatives or unskilled workers thought his nominal membership in a union was worth mentioning.

The method improved in the Nigerian and Gambian interviews. To assess the whole range of occupational affiliation, respondents were asked specifically about membership in any work group: trade union, craft guild, traders' association, or cooperative. Table 2 shows the results for four Nigerian and two Gambian towns. Membership in any form of occupational association is somewhat higher in Gambia than in Ghana, but considerably higher than either in Nigeria, especially in the provincial towns.

Membership in craft guilds (usually by the self-employed), cooperative societies, small groups of coworkers (i.e., a soldier's dining hall group), and traders' or professional associations (including a Native Doctor's Union) were listed as well as trade union membership. On the whole, unskilled workers are least likely to have any work affiliation and administrative or professional people most likely, though they are only average in Ajegunle and are surpassed by semiskilled workers in Serekunda. Clerical workers are high participants only in Aba, where skilled workers are below average. The variety between towns demonstrates the danger of relying on data from a single site, where local conditions are likely to have unexpected effects on the results.

Work groups appear to be relatively unimportant in towns with a high proportion of the labor force in manufacturing and more salient in provincial towns where traditional values and particularistic relationships are strong. Since the "vanguard of revolution" argument relies on the discontent of large-scale industrial workers, changes in the modus vivendi of unionism or the social environment of industrial towns seems to be necessary before popular enthusiasm will be effectively promoted.

It was hypothesized that the self-employed would be less likely to belong to occupational associations than men in wage employment, because they are often in competition with each other and the natural leaders would have little to gain from such an association unless it acted in their own interests. The exceptions might be small towns where restraint of trade is both necessary and possible. Lewis (1976) reports that market women in Abidjan, Ivory Coast, have great difficulty forming viable associations because ethnic heterogeneity and economic and cultural values lead them to stress competition rather than cooperation. Oyeneye (1979) found much higher membership in craft guilds in two Yoruba provincial towns than appears to be the case in Accra, Ibadan, or Lagos; in these smaller towns, the pressure to cooperate is strong and sanctions against noncooperation can be enforced.

Table 2. Membership in Work Associations by Occupation and Town (Percentages)*

Town	Unskilled	Semiskilled	Skilled	Commerce	Clerical	Professional, Administrative	Total
Aba	$33_{(18)}$	$53_{(15)}$	$29_{(34)}$	$40_{(43)}$	$75_{(20)}$	$79_{(19)}$	$48_{(149)}$
Ajegunle	$50_{(14)}$	$54_{(11)}$	$60_{(30)}$	$58_{(26)}$	$45_{(31)}$	$68_{(25)}$	$57_{(137)}$
Kakuri	$19_{(21)}$	$40_{(30)}$	$44_{(36)}$	$37_{(19)}$	$31_{(45)}$	$33_{(12)}$	$34_{(163)}$
Banjul	$27_{(11)}$	$22_{(69)}$	$24_{(33)}$	$25_{(12)}$	$18_{(22)}$	$33_{(6)}$	$24_{(153)}$
Serekunda	$0_{(18)}$	$14_{(14)}$	$12_{(25)}$	$22_{(36)}$	$9_{(33)}$	$23_{(26)}$	$14_{(152)}$
	$9_{(22)}$	$56_{(16)}$	$14_{(36)}$	$16_{(19)}$	$10_{(30)}$	$21_{(29)}$	$17_{(152)}$

*The numbers in parentheses are bases for percentages.

About a third of the self-employed belonged to occupational associations in five of the eight towns. They reported no memberships in the Ghanaian towns and two-thirds of the self-employed in Abeokuta belonged. They were significantly less likely than the wage employed to belong to work associations in Aba, but in the other three Nigerian towns and Banjul the self-employed are slightly more likely than the wage employed to have such an affiliation. Thus, self-employment cannot be seen as a disincentive to such associations. Differences are related to the entrepreneurial environment of a particular town. Whereas Tema and Ashaiman have relatively little self-employment and much of this is among insecure newcomers, most of the self-employed in Abeokuta are lifetime or at least long-term residents and they contribute over two-fifths of the male labor force. Thus, they have had both the time and the opportunity to develop the dense network of relationships on which such an association flourishes.

Given the small numbers involved, none of the wage employment sectors has significantly more associational membership than the others, but in Ajegunle and the Gambian towns government employees are somewhat less likely to belong to an occupational association than those working for private employers. This is rather surprising, given the relatively well-developed unionism among government white collar workers and the difficulty of organizing small firms, but it is probably explained by the larger proportion of laborers in government employment. Time on the job also makes no apparent difference; new employees are as likely as long established ones to belong to a union. More important differences are found between firms, which probably reflects employer attitudes toward such associations.

An aspect of trade unionism that differs in Nigeria from most developed countries is the continued membership of administrators. A bank manager, a treasurer, and a prison superintendent reported belonging to their workers' union. Regardless of whether they play an active role, such broad membership would probably discourage aggressive action by the union. Overall, the data provide convincing evidence that unions as presently constituted do little to raise the class consciousness of the majority of workers.

B. Informal Contacts

Some employees, such as watchmen, laborers, and soldiers, have more opportunity to socialize on the job than others. Aside from some of the self-employed, the most isolated are probably operatives who control separate machines and work at piece rates. Respondents were asked about activities that could take place at work but not necessarily while on the job: eating with workmates and whether they sat and talked with mates fairly frequently. In Nigeria, they were asked to differentiate whether such activities had taken place at work or elsewhere.

Talking and eating with workmates are much more common on the job than outside working hours. Most men reported some informal contacts with mates at work, but less than a quarter said they frequently sat and talked with men from work at other times. (Talking is the most common way of spending spare time.) Ghanaians appear to have less contact with mates than Nigerians, but the data are not precisely comparable. Responses to a more general question about seeing workmates off the job showed that about 30% of factory workers in Accra and Tema, compared to 34% in Kumasi, 51% in Takoradi, and 77% in rural factories had such contacts (Peil, 1972: 172). This suggests that workers in provincial towns see more of their mates than those in large cities or new industrial towns, but this difference was not observed in Nigeria.

In the two Ghanaian provincial towns, nearly a third of the workmates seen outside working hours were also kin. Tema workers seldom had kin employed at the same firm, but 40% of the friends mentioned by workers in four Nigerian factories studied by Amachree (1968: 235) were both workmates and kin. This reminds us that companions who happen to be workmates are often chosen on other grounds. Even though workers associate off the job with mates, the salient content of the link may not be work but kinship, ethnicity, religion, or some other ascriptive factor.

Table 3. Informal Contacts with Workmates, Men in Wage Employment (Percentages)

Activity	Ajegunle	Kakuri	Ashaiman	Tema
Share Meals[a]				
Never	32	36	73	47
Only at work	64	54 ⎫	27	53
Away from work	4	10 ⎭		
Total	100	100	100	100
Talk Frequently				
Never	6	3	26	14
Only at work[b]	69	76	57	74
Away from work[c]	25	21	17	12
Total	100	100	100	100
Talk with 5 + mates	45	60	19	9
N	119	125	162	133

a. Ate together in the last week. Ashaiman and Tema: "workmates or other friends."
b. Ashaiman and Tema: rarely or sometimes.
c. Ashaiman and Tema: often (location not asked).

Insofar as this is so, the relationship may have no effect in raising consciousness of their position as workers.

Kakuri men find it somewhat easier than men in Ajegunle to see mates off the job because they live much closer together, but the differences are less than expected. The environment of Kakuri and Ashaiman seems to promote contacts with somewhat larger numbers of mates than Ajegunle or Tema. This might be useful in developing worker consciousness, but the number of men involved in such groups in Ashaiman appears to be rather small to have much effect and men in Ashaiman were more likely than those in Tema to say they had nothing to do with workmates.

Amachree (1968: 235) found that unskilled Nigerian factory workers (in Lagos and Ibadan) generally prefer to associate with kin outside the factory; even the minority who listed mates among their friends were overwhelmingly likely to mention kin. The few semiskilled workers in his samples mostly listed workmates, but nearly three-quarters of these were also kin. Skilled workers were more even in their selection of kin and non-kin, but older men tended to choose kin who were not mates, perhaps because they were beginning to think of returning home.

Very few men in the studies reported here mentioned kin among their close friends, perhaps because of the way the question was phrased. Differences by age and occupation in the level of association with workmates are generally small and vary considerably from one town to another. Professionals seldom share a lunch break with colleagues the way manual workers do, but they are overrepresented among men who spend their spare time talking with coworkers. No unskilled workers reported sharing meals away from work and they seldom talk with mates off the job, though the majority do have these contacts at work. Semiskilled workers were least likely to report talking with five or more mates in Ajegunle (35%), but most likely in Kakuri (68%); employment in a factory seems to be less important than differences in the urban environment.

In Ghana, unskilled workers were more likely than other men to report no contacts and semiskilled workers to say they talked with five or more mates, but the differences between occupations were very small. At each occupational level, men in Ashaiman were about twice as likely as those in Tema to spend time with five or more mates. Thus, the Ashaiman men who do decide to socialize seem to find it easier to do so than men living in Tema.

This greater sociability of Ashaiman residents appears to be due to structural factors rather than personal characteristics. In both towns, contacts with mates tend to increase with education and workers who have come from southern Ghana, are Christian and have lived in the town for more than a year (but less than eleven years) are more likely to have such relationships. Thus, workers with the least resources in education, occupation, urban experience, and language find it most difficult to develop friendly relations with workmates, or are less interested in doing so. But these are more likely to live in Ashaiman than in Tema. Those who avoid these problems, or manage to overcome them, may find the type of housing available and the common experience of adverse conditions in Ashaiman conducive to the formation of congenial relations.

As many of the large manufacturing firms provide bus transport for Ashaiman workers, waiting for the bus and riding it daily might be another source of regular contacts with mates. However, manufacturing employees in Ashaiman are least likely to have a large number of contacts with coworkers; men in manufacturing in Tema are twice as likely as those in Ashaiman to report numerous types of contacts with workmates. The relationship is exactly reversed for port workers, which suggests that companionship on the long walk to the docks or on private transportation provides more opportunity than company buses to develop acquaintances. There is no consistent difference between men working for different types of employers in Ajegunle.

The data in this section can be summarized by saying that informal contacts between workers tend to be considerably more important than trade union membership. Most workers do form a social relationship with at least some of their workmates. However, social groups, insofar as they exist, involve very small numbers and are therefore difficult to use as the basis of a mass movement; they are probably as important in maintaining traditional values as in building worker consciousness. This conclusion is reinforced by the evidence on contacts with kin, cotenants, neighbors, and other friends, who are a much larger part of the social networks of most workers than are workmates.

III. OTHER RELATIONSHIPS

A. Kin and Hometown Ties

Kinship is a more important factor in West African urban life than it is for most Americans. Although they are usually migrants, most Africans have kin living nearby, visit them frequently, and rely on them for the security which can be obtained from social welfare provision in developed countries. While about a third of the workers in Ajegunle and Kakuri were close enough to workmates to think of them as friends and/or see them regularly outside working hours, about four-fifths in Ajegunle and three-quarters in Kakuri had kin in town and most saw these at least once a week. More than a third of the men in these towns had eaten with kin not living in their household during the previous week; Kakuri workers were as likely to see their kin daily as to visit frequently with mates outside working hours. Only two-fifths of the men in Ashaiman and Tema had kin in the area, but a third of these saw their kin daily and another third more than once a week. Thus, for those who have them kin are at least as much a part of social life as workmates, and this applies to men at all occupational levels.

Many men also interact frequently with people from home. Since most migrants plan to return home eventually, relationships with friends met in town may be less important than maintaining a place in the hometown network. Young migrants (who have little or no status at home to defend) and the well-educated (who can usually look forward to a pension) tend to be less concerned than older men who are thinking of returning in the next decade, but a high proportion of urban residents have such contacts, if only because long-established friendships are usually rewarding.

Older men tend to be most active in hometown improvement associations, to act as nodes of communication networks, and to feel most obliged to attend hometown funerals (see Kaufert, 1976: chap. 7). But most men visit home at least once a year if it can be reached in a day's travel and send money in emergencies if not regularly. They pay school fees for younger siblings and the children of siblings and accommodate visitors to the town, who may stay for a few days or several months (see Peil, forthcoming: chap. 5).

Given frequent comments in the literature on the propensity of the elites to cut themselves off from the mass of the population (i.e., Weinrich, 1976: 131; Jeffries, 1978: 181), the strength of kinship ties at all levels must be affirmed. On the whole, those who have more to give contribute more, though manual workers sometimes give a higher proportion of their income than many professionals. However, the total given (in kind, time, and advice as well as cash) is difficult to calculate, as is the spirit in which it is given. There are no consistent differences between men in various occupations in the four industrial towns in the frequency with which they see kin; distance and the strength of ties appear to be more important than income or position in society.

Support for parents and siblings is a much stronger duty than support for the extended family. Reporting on extensive studies in Ghana and Nigeria, Caldwell (1976: 233) says that nearly 70% of his respondents got some assistance from their children and most of the rest were either so well off that no help was needed or had no adult children. Parents need not be old, ill, or poor to receive help; children feel it is their duty to repay their parents if they can. Even professionals' children are helped by the older ones when these finish their schooling and find jobs (Caldwell, 1976: 243).

Another aspect of hometown links is membership in hometown improvement associations. Tribal unions have been banned in Nigeria and

Mali as politically divisive and have never been very popular in Ghana, but the small association dedicated to maintaining contacts of migrants with their home has continued to be important in many parts of Africa. In all four industrial towns, membership in primary associations (including those based on ethnicity, clan, and family as well as hometown) was higher than membership in occupational associations, sometimes by as much as 2:1. Some members attend meetings of these societies once or twice a month, whereas once a year or only in emergencies is enough for attending trade union meetings. It is the primary association that passes on news of events at home (through the informal network as well as at meetings) and provides support for members against the exigencies of urban life if their kin are unable to help.

Membership tends to be selective of those who have the most to gain. About a quarter of the men in the Ghanaian towns belonged, compared to two-fifths of those in Ajegunle and Kakuri. The most active members are likely to be self-employed traders/businessmen or manual workers over thirty-five who have an interest in hometown politics and are beginning to make plans for their return home. Newcomers, the young and well-educated, prefer to escape from the influence of their elders, get the help they need from kin, and join other types of associations such as those connected with the churches or catering for recreational interests.

B. Cotenants and Neighbors

To a certain extent, contacts with other people met in town are a substitute for kinship and hometown relationships. Some men choose to spend much of their spare time maintaining primary networks; others prefer a broader range and build an active social life with people who are, to a varying degree, strangers.[3] Many people do some of both.

Respondents were asked a series of questions about their contacts with people living in the same house or the same neighborhood and about their close friends to find out to what extent they associated with people like themselves. Lastly, there were a series of questions about how they would handle specific problems like needing money or a job or trouble with the police. These provide data about their main sources of support in emergencies. Scales developed from these data (see Peil, forthcoming: chap. 6) are useful in assessing the different levels of sociability of men in various occupations and employment sectors.

Houses and neighborhoods are usually much more crowded and heterogeneous in West African towns than in America. There are a few housing estates for the elites or special groups of employees such as miners or railway workers, but most workers have one or two rooms in a house shared by five to ten households—people of varying occupation, income, ethnicity, religion, and so on. Two or three people per room is normal for most towns. An important reason why so few workers form occupational communities is that they have an opportunity to interact frequently and casually with people of different status and sector from themselves. The successful entrepreneur next door is more likely to be seen as an example of what ordinary men can achieve than as a despised capitalist, exploiter of the masses. (The man or woman probably does exploit kin or others who work for him or her, but they will also be able to get training, loans, and advice from their patron; see Lloyd, 1975.)

Tema is an exception in that almost all its houses are government owned. They have been built in the Western pattern which separates families by the rent they can afford to pay, and therefore neighborhoods are much more homogeneous than in other towns. The houses are also smaller and, though crowded, offer less opportunity for socializing with cotenants or neighbors. Thus, it is not surprising that Tema residents know fewer of their neighbors than people living in the other towns; only a quarter of the men said they knew at least ten neighbors. Ajegunle was next lowest, with 29%. This is a very dense[4] and competitive town, where many residents spend hours every day getting to and from work and where social relations are sometimes strained. In comparison, 39% of the men in Ashaiman and 51% of those in Kakuri knew at least ten of their neighbors well; many could name a far larger number.

Much spare time is spent in casual conversation with cotenants or neighbors. Only about a tenth of the men in these towns don't talk regularly with cotenants and about a fifth with neighbors. Thus, most have as much contact with these people as with workmates. Most respondents associated regularly with considerably more cotenants, neighbors, and friends living elsewhere in town than with workmates. These contacts are often with people of different socioeconomic status, and are likely to influence their attitudes, values, and behavior. As a result, factory operatives, clerks, and teachers probably have a clearer idea of what other people in the society (market traders, craftsmen) think about proposed collective action than is the case in a developed society. Several successful strikes have been actively supported by market women, and strong disapproval is often a signal for failure (see Jeffries, 1978: 195–196; Sami, 1978: chap. 8). When Gambians were asked whether incomes should be more equal than they are now, a frequent reason for saying yes (by people at all social levels) was that everyone uses the same market; Nigerian secondary pupils used the same example.

The few members of the elite who opt out of these relationships lose considerable prestige and elicit the kind of class reaction that outside observers often assume is felt toward all people in such positions. However, it is precisely because so many successful men have come from humble origins and maintain contacts with ordinary members of the society (especially kin and people from home, but often including a wide circle of other clients and potential supporters) that the general reaction to them remains so favorable. The situation may be changing; the elite seem to be reacting to the wide-ranging pressures on them by narrowing their support to close kin, and new housing developments make it easier for them to live a more isolated life. Severe inflation and shortages of essential commodities in Ghana have created a significant boundary between the haves and the have-nots, though this boundary does not correspond neatly with status distinctions and varies from one commodity to another. Nevertheless, recent years have shown that the fall of politicians, businessmen, and even senior civil servants can be as rapid as their rise; the elite ignore this lesson at their peril. While mixing is supported by strong cultural values and isolation sanctioned by lost status and support, there are likely to be few (though notable) deviants.

C. Friends

Respondents were asked to provide demographic information on "the people you move with/see often." Most gave details on two to five close friends. These data provide many examples of close relationships across what would in England be class boundaries. An electrician in The Gambia listed two government ministers as close friends. They are about his age and live nearby; he talks with them about three times a month. A prison superintendant listed his car mechanic, with whom he spent most Saturday mornings. An elderly prophet listed a university vice chancellor. They didn't see each other often, as the vice chancellor only visited home occasionally, but they had been friends since childhood. An engineer in Ajegunle listed another engineer, two clerks, a receptionist, and a self-employed trader, all of different ethnic groups and met through work, kin, a party, a cotenant, and on a bus. A teacher mentioned three people from home: another teacher, a clerk and an electrician. Thus, friends come from many sources, and new friends made at work are only a small part of most friendship networks.

There may have been some tendency to list one's most prestigeous friends, but the data suggest that men in high status occupations are almost as likely to list people who are probably below them in occupational status as the unskilled are to list up. In both cases, social activities appear to take place with reasonable frequency. Many unskilled workers have friends who are traders, which they often hope to become themselves.

Table 4 shows that about a quarter of the self-employed and nearly half of the men in wage employment in seven towns listed at least one work-

Table 4. Occupational Heterogeneity and Sources of Friendships, by Type of Town, Occupation and Employment Sector (Percentages)[a]

Friends	Unskilled		Semiskilled		Skilled		Commerce		Clerical, Uniformed		Professional, Administrative	
	I[b]	S[c]	I	S	I	S	I	S	I	S	I	S
Any are workmates	48	38	63	36	44	34	34	33	39	26	62	32
Friends' occupations												
All same level as R[d]	34	36	39	27	34	26	38	32	25	26	22	30
Manual and nonmanual	43	39	41	54	76	59	50	38	55	21	44	19
Met												
At home, school	59	52	54	48	56	43	44	51	53	59	62	48
At work	27	38	47	36	56	43	53	41	45	28	47	27
In town	59	46	56	52	79	61	56	51	61	57	62	59
Total[3]	145	136	157	136	191	147	153	143	159	144	171	134
N	144	56	114	44	80	104	32	109	51	98	32	93

	Self Employed		Law, Defense		Port		Other Government		Manufacturing		Other		Total
	I	S	I	S	I	S	I	S	I	S	I	S	
Any are workmates	19	26	90	42	59	44	38	34	65	64	44	37	40
Friends' occupations													
All same level as R[d]	31	33	29	33	33	44	32	25	33	36	30	26	30
Manual and nonmanual	47	42	33	17	52	22	53	34	40	57	42	38	40
Met													
At home, school	43	48	71	42	70	78	59	49	59	71	51	52	52
At work	29	39	62	50	48	33	35	28	45	57	41	40	38
In town	46	57	48	33	48	33	74	58	57	50	63	52	56
Total[e]	118	114	181	125	166	144	168	135	161	178	155	144	146
N	72	196	21	12	27	9	34	199	140	14	59	73	856

a. Apprentices, domestic employees, and men who claimed to have no friends have been omitted.
b. I = industrial towns: Ajegunle, Kakuri and a small sample interviewed in Ashaiman in 1970.
c. S = service centers: Aba and Abeokuta in Nigeria and Banjul and Serekunda in The Gambia.
d. Unskilled, skilled, etc.
e. Totals are over 100% because many men met their friends in more than one place.

93

mate among their friends; quite a few of the self-employed have no one who could be described as a workmate. In most categories, friends were somewhat more likely to have been met at work than to be among current workmates; some men find friends among customers and a few friendships are carried over from previous jobs. Although neither was very common, more people mentioned friends they had worked with in the past than people they had shared a house with. Thus, the ties of workmates, once developed, appear to have more lasting importance than those between cotenants or neighbors. The latter may interact frequently for a time, but once propinquity is lost the tie lapses. Interaction at work is regular and predictable. If it is also fairly intense, long lasting, and based on mutual support, it can sometimes survive separation for a considerable time.

In most occupational categories, men in industrial towns are at least somewhat more likely than those in service-center towns to have workmates among their friends. This is because of the much higher proportion of wage employment in industrial towns and the larger firms found there. The differences are particularly notable for the semiskilled and professionals. In industrial towns, these are mainly operatives in manufacturing and doctors or teachers in government service; in other towns there are more self-employed drivers and men in traditional professions (mallams and healers) who work alone. Among the wage employed, it is the factory workers and (in industrial towns) soldiers and dock workers who are most likely to find friends among their workmates.

This suggests that these sectors are likely to be more fruitful as a base for worker consciousness than government employees or workers for commercial or construction firms. Even in these cases, however, it must be remembered that the one or two friends who are workmates often also represent other categories; they are from the same village and/or ethnic group or have similar interests outside work such as being fellow church members. Their views are also balanced by friends who work elsewhere, often in very different types of jobs.

About a third of the men mentioned as friends only people of the same occupational level as themselves. More heterogeneous friendship groups were more common; two-fifths of the respondents' friendships included both manual and nonmanual workers. Note that only a minority of professionals and administrators are socially isolated. This is less likely to happen in industrial than in service-center towns; in both, a high proportion mentioned friends from home and childhood. Clerical workers are relatively more selective than the average worker in service-center towns, but in industrial towns the majority mix freely with manual workers (who tend to have about the same income). At the other extreme, unskilled workers are not, on the whole, socially isolated either. They are slightly above average both in listing people like themselves and men in nonmanual jobs as friends.

Imoagene (1976: 165–166, 182–183), who studied ex-politicians, businessmen, and higher civil servants in southwestern Nigeria, found that only about half the friends they listed were of the same occupation as themselves. About a sixth were more than one occupational level above or below the respondent, and the majority had a different level of education. One explanation of this is that 34% of the friendships originated in childhood and schooling, compared to 21% that started at work. Politicians had more contacts with kin and listed somewhat more friends than either civil servants or businessmen.

On the whole, the heterogeneity of friendship networks is more related to opportunities and cultural expectations than to an individual's socioeconomic position. (Where towns are largely homogeneous in religion or ethnicity, so will friendships be; where they are heterogeneous, so will friendship networks be.) There is a tendency for the heterogeneity of friendship groups to increase with education, level of occupation, and income and to be greater for wage than for the self-employed. However, the differences are often not significant and are partly based on greater opportunities which people of greater resources have for interacting with a wide variety of people. Although the numbers in the samples are small, it is clear that professionals and administrators who live in segregated housing have a narrower range of friends than those who live with the rest of the population. Thus, new elite housing estates, which are being built in all of these countries, will probably increase class consciousness by segregating people by income.

The data on source of friends show clearly that work is less important than either home or urban experience. Over half of the workers in my studies had friends from each of these sources, compared to less than two-fifths who had found friends at work. Home is least important for the self-employed (both traders and craftsmen) and most important, surprisingly, for soldiers and dock workers. Work is a better source in industrial than in other towns, perhaps because the ethos of the town makes work a more important part of people's lives or because so many are recent migrants who share the experience of socialization into a new way of life. Service-center towns (the majority in Africa, it should be remembered) tend to have a well-established core population that maintains traditional values and patterns of recreation. Kin are more available (both in town and in the nearby hinterland) and work is therefore less important as a source of identification. Some people have more than one occupation, depending on the season or the opportunities; this is less possible in towns centered on industry.

The proportion of men living in service-center towns who said they met their friends in town is somewhat misleading, since many (especially in Abeokuta and Banjul) had been born in the town. For them, home friends were also town friends, though an attempt was made to distinguish friends of childhood from those met as adults. Skilled and nonmanual workers appear to have the easiest time finding friends in town. The latter tend to have a better command of English than manual workers and thus can communicate fairly easily across ethnic boundaries, but many manual workers (especially in Ghana) know more than one local language, so access to resources (the income to pay for commercial recreation and the time to enjoy it) are probably a more important advantage, especially for professionals.

Skilled men in self-employment, either full time or as a part-time supplement to wage employment, sometimes attract hangers-on who spend their spare time talking and occasionally helping. They also make contacts because it is good for business. For example, tailors and photographers face severe competition, and customers are more likely to come from acquaintances, some of whom become friends. Policemen and port workers in service-center towns appear to make the fewest urban friends. The former are frequently transferred and often mistrusted; the latter were few in number and often in jobs such as fishing, which meant long hours away from the ordinary contacts of the town.

Mutual support is an important component of friendship both because of the frequent need for such help and the strong norms that support it. Thus, the extent to which workmates or other friends are asked to help when money is needed or some other emergency is faced is an additional check on the strength of the relationships. Cohen (1972: 272) found that the union members he interviewed were about equally likely to ask a workmate or another friend for a loan (about 25% each); nearly twice as many would ask kin or someone from their own ethnic group. In Ajegunle and Kakuri, very few men specified a workmate *per se* as a preferred source of help for a series of problems, but about a fifth said they would get help from a friend (who was sometimes also a workmate).

Kin were usually seen as potentially more helpful than friends in Ajegunle, but somewhat fewer men in Kakuri had kin in town so they were more dependent on friends. Men in Ashaiman were about as likely to go to a friend as to kin; many had no kin nearby. Thus, it is not enough to just work together; a stronger bond, usually built up over an extended period of time, is necessary before mutual dependence can be relied on (see Pons, 1969: 211). Although voluntary turnover is now quite low, the uncertainties of business in developing countries mean that many workers lack the opportunity to build up such friendships with their mates.

The Sociability Scale measures breadth rather than depth of social interaction. Points are gained for contacts with neighbors, cotenants, workmates, and other friends based on talking frequently, eating together during the past week, visiting rooms, giving a party, membership in associations and the number of close friends—or, in Ghana, drinking with others—(see Peil, forthcoming: appendix C). Table 5 shows that occupation and employment sector make a significant though small difference in sociability, with a notable difference between the Nigerian provincial towns and the others.

The distinction between self- and wage employment is less likely to be significant than the finer differentiation of employment sector, but may be a safer basis for prediction than occupation because of its greater consistency. Occupations with low means in one pair of towns sometimes have high means in another pair, and the same applies to employment sectors. For example, professionals and administrators have a higher than average mean score (13.25) in the Nigerian provincial towns, a lower than average mean score (9.88) in the Nigerian industrial towns, and a mean score slightly below average for the Gambian (10.83) and Ghanaian towns (8.43). The self-employed, on the other hand, are consistently if not always significantly below average in sociability. This is partly because many lack workmates and thus lose the points that socializing with mates would provide. But, in addition, their working time is less predictable and their hours are often longer; they have less "free" time than wage employees to spend with friends.

The law/defense sector is at least somewhat below average sociability in all four pairs of towns. The difference is most notable in the Nigerian provincial towns and The Gambia, where there were few from this sector in the samples, but the consistency suggests that even soldiers and policemen who live with the general public are to some extent segregated from them. Potential friendships are hindered by mistrust and misuse of power as well as a lack of understanding of the law and its application. The question on what the respondent would do if he had "trouble with the police" showed that a surprising number of people have direct or indirect

Table 5. Variance in Sociability Score Explained[a] by Employment Variables, by Type of Town

Towns	Occupation	Employment Sector	Self/Wage Employment
Nigerian industrial	.057[b]	.055[b]	.045[b]
Ghanaian industrial	.046[b]	.018	.022
Gambian	.075[b]	.078[b]	.057[b]
Nigerian provincial	.024	.101[b]	.003

a. Eta^2
b. = $p < .01$

contacts with policemen or lawyers, but such contacts are only used in emergencies. Periodic transfers encourage policemen and soldiers to socialize with each other. This should not be overemphasized, as the differences seldom reach statistical significance, but overall they are worth noting.

D. Drinking

Both Grillo (1973) and Jeffries (1978) found it very useful to their research to socialize with railway workers in bars and give the impression that workers spend much of their spare time drinking with friends. There are many bars in most towns; they can be opened by men who have only a small amount of capital and hope to support themselves in this congenial way (see Hart, 1973: 79–80). Pons (1969: 152) describes their role in neighborhood relations and the way drinking relationships are sometimes formalized. Thus, the opportunity for drinking is widely available. However, drinking appears to be less frequent and more selective than is usually assumed.

There are far more bars in Ashaiman than in Tema, but only a minority of men in either town reported drinking (41 and 34% respectively). Availability made more difference to the frequency of drinking than to whether or not residents did it. While about 10% of drinkers in both towns only participated just after pay day, those in Ashaiman were more likely than those in Tema to drink during the week as well as on weekends; some Tema men go out to Ashaiman on weekends for the local brews available there.

Drinking is usually a social activity. Very few reported drinking alone or only at home. About a tenth of the men drink with one or two other men, about two-thirds join with three to five others, and the remaining fifth usually share with more than five.

The most striking characteristic that distinguishes drinkers from non-drinkers in Ghana is religion. Only three out of fifty Muslims said they drank. Unskilled and semiskilled workers were less likely to drink, and those who did were less likely to join workmates in a drink, than skilled or clerical workers. The only other significant characteristic was rural/urban background. Men who had lived only in towns were less likely to drink and to drink with workmates than men who came from rural areas. As the difference is stronger in Ashaiman than in Tema, the traditional role of palm wine, millet beer, and other local drinks in village life is probably being carried into the town, whereas men who grow up in towns are more likely to see liquor as a bottled, expensive beverage.

There is less information on drinking in Nigeria and none on The Gambia; no specific question was asked because of Muslim sensibilities. Those who mentioned drinking in connection with activities with kin or friends or over the past four days included 41% of the men in Ajegunle, 38% in Abeokuta, 32% in Aba, and 29% in Kakuri. Religion made less difference to drinking in Nigeria than in Ghana. Very few Muslims drank in Kakuri, where Islamic influence is strong, but they were as likely as Christians to mention drinking in Ajegunle and Abeokuta. (There were no Muslims in the Aba sample.)

Wage employees and especially semiskilled workers are most likely to drink with friends; this included 63% of the semiskilled in Abeokuta and 46% in Kakuri. Nonmanual workers came next, and unskilled workers are least likely to drink. They have the least money to spend, but they are also most likely to be Muslim and so can make the necessity of abstention a virtue. Men under twenty-five were less likely to report drinking than older men in all four towns; monogamously married men were at least somewhat more likely to drink than either single men or the polygynous. The young, single man is often just getting on his feet economically and has little money to spare; married men in the 25–34 age category tend to have fewer family responsibilities than older men, and thus have somewhat more time to sit in bars.

While there is probably considerably more drinking than was reported here, especially at home on the occasion of weddings, funerals, and community celebrations, it seems likely that drinking in town is selective and that a large proportion of the population do relatively little of it. Therefore, it seems wise to be cautious in generalizing from the frequenters of bars to the whole population.

IV. CONCLUSION

Dahrendorf (1959: 273) argues that workers in post-capitalist societies put their work and their social life into separate compartments. The job is left behind at the factory gate and occupation has relatively little effect on social personality. The data from these studies suggest that occupation does make a difference to the social relations of workers in industrializing societies, but that the society probably has a much greater effect on the workplace than vice versa and that the factory *per se* is probably less relevant to these workers than to employees in industrialized countries. Insofar as this is true, there appear to be severe limitations on the spread of class consciousness from large, bureaucratically oriented workplaces to the general population. Not only is the job (and attitudes related to the relations of production) left behind at the gate, but social relations based on other norms are brought into the workplace.

The data used here have not been collected with a view to testing this hypothesis, but they provide fairly strong evidence for it. With a few notable exceptions, men in wage employment are only sporadically interested in trade unions. The majority get to know mates at work but only a minority have more than one or two mates who are close enough friends to spend considerable time with away from work. The mates that do become friends are often selected on ascriptive grounds; they are kin, or the relationship develops because they come from the same area or ethnic group. This situation may be temporary, the result of a labor force which is not only first generation but seldom has more than ten years on the job. But a comparison of men in various age and experience categories suggests that change will require more than time. While only a minority of the population are involved in such work and while urban residents maintain close ties with home, an environment favorable to the development of workplace-based values does not exist.

There are now many studies of the importance of kinship in working class communities in America and England, but the ties which African workers maintain with their kin and home appear to be broader, less localized, and operative at all social levels. Kin in the neighborhood are often seen daily. Contacts with the extended family at home are maintained through visits to and from the town and through messages; every traveler carries a burden of communication. Many home communities work actively to ensure that they are not forgotten by their migrants, and their collective influence on the towns is considerable. Most workers intend to return home in their old age, and many find social relations with kin and people from home (and the attitudes they promote) as important as new, work-based friends and ideas.

Contacts with cotenants and neighbors are less important, but they generally support established rather than new norms. The mixed housing common in most towns is important for maintaining contacts across incipient class barriers and demonstrating the possibility and rewards of social mobility. The lesson of most neighborhoods is that attachment to an employer or workplace is likely to be less rewarding than individual entrepreneurship, unless one is educated well above the average. For the elite, the lesson is that status and prestige come from followers, and these require a "we" rather than "they" position. Traditional norms continue to be highly valued, and those who set them aside may suddenly find themselves in need of the security which only ascriptively based support can give.

Friendships are more commonly based on home or urban than on work contacts and frequently cross socioeconomic boundaries. Though related to overall sociability, occupation is relatively unimportant as a basis for friendship. The self-employed appear to be somewhat narrower in their contacts than the wage employed, but the sociability of employees is, on the whole, only inconsistently or insignificantly related to the sector that employs them.

Railway workers and miners, the most work-conscious groups in West

African societies, have not been included in these studies. The evidence from the groups that have been included, often in considerable numbers, is that work-consciousness (insofar as this is reflected in social relations) is as yet poorly developed. If changes in social structure must await the development of mass movements arising from workplace relations, they will be very slow in coming. Increasing inflation and economic differentiation, blocked mobility and the level of responsiveness of national and local government to public demands, will probably affect the rate at which class consciousness develops in these societies to a greater extent than the influence of workers in industry or trade unionists. So far, these data seem to explain quite well the "conservatism" (Waterman, 1976) and "populism" (Sandbrook and Arn, 1977) of West African workers.

ACKNOWLEDGMENT

The research reported here was supported by grants from the U.K. Social Science Research Council, the Nuffield Foundation, the Centre of West African Studies of Birmingham University and the U.S. National Institute of Mental Health. See Peil (1972; forthcoming) for details of methods and samples.

NOTES

1. I use "worker" to include everyone who works (is in the labor force) rather than in the more limited sense of wage employees because otherwise most West Africans who work would not be classified as workers.
2. He drops the phrase from the revised version (Kraus 1979).
3. See Mayer (1962) for a discussion of this dichotomy among South African workers. The choice there appeared to be more clear-cut than it is in West African towns.
4. About 150,000 per square mile and averaging more than three people per room.

REFERENCES

Amachree, I. T. D.
  1968 "Reference group and worker satisfaction: studies among some Nigerian factory workers." Nigerian Journal of Economic and Social Studies 10: 229–238.
Caldwell, J. C.
  1976 "Fertility and the household economy in Nigeria." Journal of Comparative Family Studies 7: 193–253.
Cohen, R.
  1972 "Class in Africa: analytical problems and perspectives." Pp. 231–254 in R. Miliband and J. Savile (eds.), The Socialist Register 1972. London: Merlin Press.
  1974 Labour and Politics in Nigeria. London: Heinemann Educational Books.
Crisp, J.
  1978a "The labouring poor, trade unions, and political change in Ghana: some empirical and conceptual observations." Manpower and Unemployment Research 11: 93–100.
  1978b "Union atrophy and worker revolt: labour protest at Tarkwa Goldfields, Ghana,

1968–69.'' Paper presented at African Studies Association Conference, Baltimore, Md.

Dahrendorf, R.
1959   Class and Class Conflict in Industrial Society. Stanford: Stanford University Press.

Davies, I.
1966   African Trade Unions. Harmondsworth, Middlesex, U.K.: Penguin.

Epstein, A. L.
1961   ''The network and urban social organization.'' Rhodes-Livingstone Institute Journal 29: 29–61. Reprinted in J. C. Mitchell (ed.), Social Networks in Urban Situations. Manchester, U.K.: Manchester University Press, 1969.

Goldthorpe, J. H., D. Lockwood, F. Bechhofer, and J. Platt
1969   The Affluent Worker in the Class Structure. London: Cambridge University Press.

Grillo, R. D.
1973   African Railwaymen. London: Cambridge University Press.

Hart, K.
1973   ''Informal income opportunities and urban employment in Ghana.'' Journal of Modern African Studies 11: 61–89.

Hinchliffe, K.
1973   ''The Kaduna textile workers: characteristics of an African industrial labour force.'' Savanna 2: 27–37.

Imoagene, O.
1976   Social Mobility in Emergent Society: A Study of the New Elite in Western Nigeria. Canberra, Australia: Australian National University Press.

Jeffries, R.
1978   Class, Power and Ideology in Ghana: The Railwaymen of Sekondi. London: Cambridge University Press.

Kapferer, B.
1972   Strategy and Transaction in an African Factory. Manchester, U.K.: Manchester University Press.

Kaufert, P. A. L.
1976   Migration and Communication: A Study of Migrant-Villager Relationships in a Rural Ghanaian Community. Ph.D. dissertation, Birmingham University, U.K.

Kerr, C. and A. Siegel
1954   ''The interindustry propensity to strike—an international comparison.'' Pp. 189–212 in W. Kornhauser, et al. (eds.), Industrial Conflict. New York: McGraw-Hill.

King, K.
1977   The African Artisan. London: Heinemann.

Konings, P.
1978a   ''Political consciousness and political action of industrial workers in Ghana: a case study of Valco workers at Tema.'' Afrika-Studiecentrum, Leiden, Netherlands, Mimeograph.
1978b   ''The political potential of Ghanaian miners: a case study of AGC workers at Obuasi.'' Afrika-Studiecentrum, Leiden, Netherlands, Mimeograph.

Kraus, J.
1977   ''Strikes and labour power in a post-colonial African state: the case of Ghana.'' Paper presented to Seminar on Third World Strikes, The Hague, Netherlands.
1979   ''Strikes and labour power in Ghana.'' Development and Change 10: 259–85.

Lewis, B. C.
1976   ''The limitations of group action among entrepreneurs: the market women of Abidjan, Ivory Coast.'' Pp. 135–156 in N. J. Hafkin and E. G. Bay (eds.), Women

in Africa: Studies in Social and Economic Change. Stanford, Calif.: Stanford University Press.

Lloyd, P. C.
1975 "Perceptions of class and social inequality among the Yoruba of Western Nigeria." Pp. 189–204 in H. I. Safa and B. M. duToit (eds.), Migration and Development: Implications for Ethnic Identity and Political Conflict. The Hague, Netherlands: Mouton.

Mayer, P.
1962 "Migrancy and the study of Africans in town." American Anthropologist 64: 576–592.

Melson, R.
1971 "Ideology and inconsistency: the 'cross-pressured' Nigerian worker." American Political Science Review 65: 161–171.

Mitchell, J. C.
1956 The Kalela Dance. Manchester, U.K.: Manchester University Press for the Rhodes-Livingstone Institute.

Oyeneye, O. Y.
1979 The Apprenticeship System in Southwestern Nigeria: A Case of Human Resource Development. Ph.D. dissertation, Birmingham University, U.K.

Peace, A.
1979 Choice, Class and Conflict: A Study of Southern Nigerian Factory Workers. Brighton, Sussex, U.K.: Harvester Press.

Peil, M.
1972 The Ghanaian Factory Worker. London: Cambridge University Press.
Forth- Cities and Suburbs: Urban Life in West Africa. New York: Africana Publishing coming Company.

Pfeffermann, G.
1968 Industrial Labor in the Republic of Senegal. New York: Praeger.

Pons, V.
1969 Stanleyville. London: Oxford University Press for the International African Institute.

Priestley, M.
1965 "An early strike in Ghana." Ghana Notes and Queries 7: 25.

Sami, E.
1978 The Social Status of Primary Teachers: A Case Study of the Rivers State of Nigeria. Ph.D. dissertation, Birmingham University, U.K.

Sandbrook, R. and J. Arn
1977 The Labouring Poor and Urban Class Formation: The Case of Greater Accra. Montreal: Centre of Developing-Area Studies, McGill University.

Sandbrook, R. and R. Cohen (eds.)
1975 The Development of an African Working Class. London: Longman.

Smock, D. R.
1969 Conflict and Control in an African Trade Union. Stanford, Calif.: Hoover Institution Press.

van der Horst, S.
1964 African Workers in Town: A Study of Labour in Cape Town. Cape Town, S.A.: Oxford University Press.

Waterman, P.
1976 "Conservatism amongst Nigerian workers." Pp. 159–184 in G. Williams (ed.), Nigeria: Economy and Society. London: Rex Collings.

1978   "A comment on 'The labouring poor and urban class formation'." Manpower and
       Unemployment Research 11 (1): 81–86.
Weinrich, A. K. H.
1976   Mucheke: Race, Status and Politics in a Rhodesian Community. Paris: UNESCO.
Wolpe, H.
1974   Urban Politics in Nigeria: A Study of Port Harcourt. Berkeley, Calif.: University of
       California Press.

CASTE, VILLAGE, FACTORY, AND WORKER IN WEST BENGAL, INDIA*

Morton Klass

When an Indian countryman becomes an employee in an Indian factory, he learns to operate complex machinery and he adjusts to factory regulation; he may well join a labor union and a radical political party. At the same time, however, he is likely to remain a fully integrated member of an extended family, of an agriculturally oriented village, and—most particularly—of a traditionally organized caste marriage-circle. This juxtaposition of continuity and change is likely to occur even when the countryman removes to a factory far from his native village, but it may be studied in sharpest perspective when factory and village are in proximity.

During 1963–1964, I conducted a year-long study of community structure and culture change in an area of West Bengal, India, just north of the

Research in the Sociology of Work, Volume 1, pages 105–130
Copyright © 1981 by JAI Press Inc.
All rights of reproduction in any form reserved.
ISBN: 0-89232-124-5

important industrial center of Asansol (Klass, 1978). In that study, particular attention was given to one village (protectively assigned the fictitious label "Gôndôgram") and its adjacent factory (fictitiously labeled "Das-Walters Bicycle Factory"). The factory had been constructed on land much of which had been purchased from Gôndôgram landholders, and—as a partial recompense for the loss of the land—most male adults in the village were employed in and around the factory.

Villagers regretted the loss of riceland, but they were eager for work in the factory for this was not a region of wealthy agricultural communities; Asansol, the westernmost subdivision of Burdwan District, has been noted throughout the past century and a half for coal mining and industry, but not for agriculture. The town of Asansol itself is built around major heavy and light industrial plants (steel mills, locomotive works, etc.) and sits athwart both the Grand Trunk Road and the Great Eastern Railway. Apart from industry and collieries, however, the region to the north and south of the town is characterized by undulating terrain and infertile and inadequately watered farming land. A rice crop is produced for market (and garden produce for home use) in most of the surrounding villages, but there is only one crop a year and it is rarely a bounteous one. A large part of the rural population, therefore, looks to colliery and industry for additional income, but jobs are scarce.

At the time of the study, there were 673 persons residing in Gôndô-gram, reflecting 96 households and 9 *jatis* (castes, or other ethnic groups).[1]

The composition of the village may be represented as follows:

Table 1. Village Composition

Jati name	Number of households	Persons
Brahman	32	225
Napit (Barber)	2	7
Śutrodhór (Carpenter)	6	75
Śūri (Distiller)	8	90
Dhopa (Washerman)	4	25
Dom	1	5
Bauri	31	171
Santal	11	71
Muslim	1	4

Brahmans—calling themselves "Kanauj" Brahmans—constituted the dominant landholding caste of the village; though in principle a "priestly" people, in fact they devoted their collective attention, before the coming of the factory, to the production of rice for market. Each household (usually of brothers, their wives, and children) controlled its own land and the sale of its crop, and the Brahman households varied from prosperous to marginal. In a very few of the wealthiest homes, where substantial education had been possible, there were men who worked in supervisory positions in colliery or factory, but such men were rare and rice agriculture was the mainstay of all but one or two Brahman households.

The Brahmans, however, were not permitted by the rules of their own jati to perform the tasks of agricultural production (plowing, harvesting, etc.), and for these they depended upon the services of men, women, and children of the Bauri jati. The Bauris of Gôndôgram belonged to a jati of agricultural laborers that is found throughout much of West Bengal and Bihar. Brahmans and other high-ranked castes consider Bauris ritually unclean and so they constitute an example of what is variously termed in the literature on India as an "untouchable," "Harijan," or "scheduled" caste. They reside apart from other castes of the village (in Gôndôgram there were three peripheral Bauri neighborhoods, or "hamlets"), and before the coming of the factory almost all Bauri families worked, on a yearly contractual basis, for different Brahman landholders. Bauri men served as field laborers, their wives and daughters as house servants, and their pre-adolescent sons as herdsmen of Brahman-owned cattle. Most Bauri households tended to be nuclear family; sons would move out of the house soon after marriage.

The presence of Carpenters, Distillers, and Washermen in the village in substantial numbers reflected the fact that this had long been an area of other-than-agricultural employment opportunities. The Distillers had migrated to the area originally to sell fermented palm liquor to colliery employees, and Carpenters had sought work in mill and mine, while Washermen had tried to ply their ancestral occupation. Few were successful, however, before the coming of the factory: most village Carpenters supported themselves by a combination of intermittent carpentry work for wealthy landholders and rice cultivation on small plots of land. Those who had no land worked as agricultural day laborers. Distillers had turned to shopkeeping and small-scale ricegrowing. Washermen had no land and little call for their services; most worked as agricultural laborers.

Only the (then) one Barber family followed exclusively its ancestral occupation, serving Brahman and other high-caste families in Gôndôgram and in neighboring villages. The Muslim worked as a laborer, while the Dom could pick up only occasional extra money as a musician, depending for the most part upon his wife's earnings as village midwife and his own as a day laborer. Santals, representative of a so-called tribal group once prevalent in the area, had been successful in the past in finding jobs as coal miners, and for many years had only resided in Gôndôgram, in peripheral neighborhoods near those of the Bauris, taking no part in the social and economic life of the village. In the period just before coming of the factory, however, many collieries closed down while others became automated, and many of the Santal men were reduced to working as day laborers (at planting and harvest times) for Brahman landholders.

This, then, was Gôndôgram before the factory was built: a rice-producing village controlled by Brahman landholders. Bauri laborers performed most of the agricultural work, though some of the rice production, and some of the field labor, derived from the other castes to be found in the village. There was a social as well as an economic hierarchy, again with Brahmans at the top, and with Bauris and Santals at the bottom. The members of each jati represented in the village belonged to a marriage-circle of families residing in specific villages scattered throughout the area, and no two marriage-circles included the exact same set of villages.

The village jatis differed in more than just the composition of their marriage-circles; each had its own rules of permissible behavior, diet, and occupation. They shared a common rule of virilocality, however: at marriage, girls went off to live in their husbands' homes. And, though most of the jatis had no formal rule of village exogamy, almost all marriages were in fact contracted between boys and girls of different villages (see Klass, 1966, 1978).

In 1951, the Das-Walters Bicycle Company was established on land to the southeast of Gôndôgram. The arrival of the factory disrupted the lives of many villagers, most particularly because a substantial amount of riceland belonging to many Brahman and Carpenter families was acquired by the factory. Even more than a decade later, landholders expressed bitterness about what they considered the inadequacy of the payment they had been forced to accept.

But the coming of the factory was disruptive and disturbing in other ways, for many villagers. For them, it was an alien entity, too close to the village for comfort. Neither the European nor the Indian dimension of the factory was within their experience. The Das-Walters Company was an affiliate of a larger British company, which controlled all aspects of production and manufacturing quality. All such matters were supervised personally by one senior official, the "Works Manager," a British engineer appointed by the British home office and responsible only to that office. Otherwise, the staff was Indian, but the senior officers were of the "Das" family, or otherwise representative of the Bôiddô (Vaidya) jati, deriving ultimately from the Bengali-speaking region that was first East Pakistan and then Bangladesh.

Opposition and conflict in the village increased to the point where senior (Indian) members of the factory management felt obliged to try to do something about it. They attended a meeting of village men and announced that they considered themselves, henceforth, to be "sons of Gôndôgram." A job of some kind in the factory, they promised, would always be available for any boy of the village. The factory would assist, too, in efforts of the village to improve itself.

As factory officials recount the meeting, they appear to have viewed themselves as addressing the "village"—all the men, that is—without observable internal social distinctions, but the village response to the meeting varied according to jati membership. Brahmans—who considered Gôndôgram to be "their" village—were somewhat interested by the the offer of assistance in community improvement, but they dismissed the offer of jobs with some irritation. They saw themselves as farmers, not as manual laborers.

Carpenters did not consider the offer of jobs as sufficient compensation for lost land, but they had no intention of spurning the offer. Distillers were also interested in the possibility of employment, but even more intrigued by the opportunities for income in other ways, particularly by providing liquor for factory workers. Washermen, too, hoped for the opportunity to return to their traditional jati occupation. Few if any Bauris were present at the meeting, or were ever aware of any promise of employment. Santals apparently had no interest whatever in the factory, nor any awareness of the meeting.

At the time of the study, the factory employed approximately 2,790 persons in the manufacture of bicycles. Of these, 2,135 were in the category "semiskilled operators"—those who work on the assembly lines or performed the other basic manipulative tasks of production and assembly. All other employees of the factory—from senior management to the most menial of "sweepers"—made up the remaining 655.

Table 2. Factory Employment

Division	Positions	Persons Employed	Wages, per month (in rupees)
Office and	Officers & Comm. Ass'ts	30	450 (and up)
Administration	Clerks	185	190 (average)
	Peons	27	115
Works and	Tech. Ass'ts, Managerial, etc.	62	425 (and up)
Technical	Supervisors, Charge-hands	103	265 (average)
	Semi-skilled Setter,		
	Worker or Operator	2135	210 (average)
	Mazdoors	248	110

Two hundred and forty-two persons were employed, at the time of this study, in "Office and Administration". Twenty-seven of these, those in the lowest category, were "peons," equivalent to Western "office boys" or "messengers." One hundred and eighty-five were "clerks" receiving an average remuneration of Rs. 190 per month. They were expected, at minimum, to have attended secondary school. The rest of the office staff ("commercial assistants" and "officers") were required to have graduate or professional training.

In "Works and Technical" 2,548 persons were employed. Two hundred and forty-eight of these were unskilled laborers, categorized in the records as "mazdoors," who carried supplies and materials to the various production departments and carried away the completed work.

Some 2,135 persons were in the category "semi-skilled worker, setter and operator" and received, each, wages averaging Rs. 210 per month.[2] A reading ability "up to class VIII Standard" (roughly equivalent to the American eighth-grade level) was formally required for such jobs, but in practice the ability to make out instructions and directions on machinery (with assistance) was considered adequate. Over these people were 103 "supervisors or chargemen" who were expected to have increasing levels of engineering training and experience, and were paid accordingly.

In addition to those employees described above, there was a large but shifting number of people employed in various menial minor capacities, and on a limited, or part-time, basis. These included "sweepers" (who not only swept floors but cleaned toilets), servants of various kinds, and canteen employees. They were both male and female, and numbered about one hundred people.

Other people were employed in activities generated by the presence of the factory, though their incomes did not derive directly from the factory. About 500 people, mostly road-gang laborers, were employed by various contractors for work in and around the factory—building and maintaining roads, putting up new workers' quarters, and so on. About fifty people, it was estimated, operated (or were employed in) the various shops and stalls acceptable to the factory and located in its vicinity. And, finally, there was the unacceptable, or frowned on, periphery—in theory not present at all but in fact very much a part of the factory-supported economy: purveyors of illegal liquor, prostitutes, beggars, thieves, and so on.

At the time of study, the Das-Walters factory produced, daily, between 900 and 1,000 completed bicycles, plus spare parts for separate sale.

The officials of the factory, all educated urban Indians, had little personal experience of village life. They believed that the "villager," before the coming of the factory, was a rice farmer, each man tilling his own field, each family self-sufficient, and each village an isolate providing for all the needs of its members.

There was little awareness of the socioeconomic complexities of village life and of the interrelationships between villages. Views on most matters relating to village life were expressed in simplicities. "Caste" for example was a pernicious and backward practice, condemned by Gandhi and every right-thinking Indian, still surviving in the more benighted rural localities (such as Gôndôgram, unfortunately) but rapidly disappearing everywhere. Similarly, traditional village religion was viewed as a naive adoration of Vedic divinities with offerings of flowers and food. Actual village ceremonies, frequently involving animal sacrifice, shocked and dismayed those officials who encountered them.

The "villager," said officials, thus may have led an idyllic life in days gone by: the coming of the factory "spoiled" him, and he has proved a burden to the factory. Many officials regretted the promise of jobs for villagers, made at the time of the establishment of the factory.

Three reasons are advanced in explanation of the dissatisfaction with "villager" as factory employee:

(1) *Laziness and Absenteeism*: The local Bengali villager, say factory officials, is an indifferent worker at best. He exhibits no interest in his equipment or his work; he shows no initiative. Absenteeism, the officials claim, is much more frequent among local people than it is among those from outside the district, recruited through the labor exchange system.

Some officials will acknowledge that when they speak of "laziness" or "indifference" they have village Brahmans in mind; few had any complaint to make, on that score at least, about Carpenters or members of other non-Brahman jatis. Brahmans, it was said, were as a group unwilling to work at any manual job, and were always requesting transfer to office work, even when they were clearly unfit for it.

All officials agreed, however, that "absenteeism" characterised *all* men of Gôndôgram—of every caste—and indeed all men from all the local villages, when compared with nonlocal employees. This was advanced as a major reason for the present reluctance to employ local people in greater numbers.

(2) *Caste Exclusiveness*: Factory officials of Indian origin insist that they subscribe in no way to notions of "caste"; they add, too, that the laws of India proscribe the maintenance of caste distinction and discrimination. They note that British-born officials are totally uninterested in caste distinctions, and they point out that caste restrictions and observances interfere with the flow of modern business. For all these reasons, they say, "caste" is officially ignored in the factory: no official or application form ever inquires into caste identification—even mere curiosity on the part of a clerk might be grounds for dismissal, they say. Requests for

employment couched in terms of caste preference or restriction are likely to be rejected.

Even more: recognizing that men of the same caste may tend to congregate together, as a matter of policy officials try to separate men of like caste and mix together those of different ones. This is possible, of course, only when officials have some intimation of caste identity; given the official policy, such intimation—they claim—is rare.

Despite all this, and to the intense dismay of the officials, there is a noticeable tendency for men of like caste to cluster together in the factory. The tendency, moreover, was said to be particularly characteristic of local people, and most particularly of the workers coming from Gôndôgram. Officials were baffled and discouraged by the fact that, despite all their efforts, time after time a particular department would come to be made up of men of one particular caste—often, in fact, of close relatives.

Officials usually become aware of this only when a death occurs in the household of one of the employees in such a department. This will impose many restrictions upon a man for the period of mourning—and the period of mourning may be anything from ten to thirty days, depending upon the caste. During this period, diet is restricted, certain activities are enjoined, and time for prayer and contemplation may be necessary. An employee in mourning inevitably poses problems for the factory; even when he returns to work, after a period of absence, he must be reassigned for a time to other, lighter work, for many believe that injuries—particularly the shedding of blood—must be avoided at all costs during mourning. Still, officials perceive the inevitability of the situation, and indeed share many of the sentiments, and so they do all that they can for the individual mourner.

What upsets them, however, is when a death occurs in the household of one employee—and most of the members of his department announce that, as close relatives and caste-brothers, they intend to join him in his period of mourning! And it is such an announcement, with its inevitable attendant stress and confusion as management attempts to cope with the problems caused by one entire department dropping out of the chain of production, that is usually the first intimation the factory has that the department has been taken over by men of one jati.

The response of the factory, after the initial dismay, is to attempt to break up the concentration, or at least water it down through the introduction of new people of different origins. From that point on, vacancies are filled only by men from other parts of India—presumably of different jati.

Such efforts, officials report glumly, rarely seem to work. For some unknown reason, they say, such new employees turn out to be more than usually unsatisfactory; their quotas remain unfulfilled and the complaints about the quality of their work are many. Such new men tend to be dismissed for incompetence with much greater frequency than is the average, or they themselves resign—or beg to be transferred elsewhere. The point is, say the officials, "they don't stay," and a department once taken over by cousins and caste-mates tends to remain that way despite all efforts on the part of the factory officials.

While this is a problem at all times, at all levels, and with employees from all over India, officials insist that "local people"—and particularly the inhabitants of Gôndôgram—give the most trouble. Many of the Brahmans of Gôndôgram who are employed in the factory as "semiskilled operators" work in the enameling department; many of the Carpenters work in the chain department. These two departments, particularly, have precipitated severe crises more than once, because of deaths and the resultant protracted mourning.

(3) *Clamor for Employment*: Given the first two complaints that factory officials have about "local people" it is understandable that they are somewhat reluctant to employ them in great numbers. Nevertheless, the officials remember their early promise to find jobs for "sons of the village" and claim they will continue to do so, if without any real enthusiasm. Unhappily, from the factory viewpoint, villagers not only insist upon the jobs promised to them—in addition they cheat, say officials, constantly bringing in outsiders, from villages far from Gôndôgram, and insisting that these are all "sons of the village."

Again and again, officials say, a man of Gôndôgram will show up, an embarrassed adolescent boy in tow, insisting to all that this is indeed his son—where had they received the erroneous impression that he had no more grown sons? Factory officials note that they could make an issue of these frauds (and may have to in the future), but since the villagers are so insistent, in the end, usually, some job is found for the boy.

There was a characteristic *village* response to the factory; apart from individual idiosyncratic responses, members of each caste represented in the village responded in terms of the caste's needs and internal pressures. The categories of employment found by members of each village caste are presented in Table 3. What follows, here, is an examination, caste by caste, of attitudes and reactions to employment in the factory.

The Brahmans of Gôndôgram, we have noted, were not interested at first in the offer of employment in the factory. One or two men, with sufficient education, applied for and received clerical positions, and a few others requested jobs for "sons"—in every case, impecunious distant relatives.

Within a year or two, however, Brahman attitudes underwent a shift. The yearly income of a semiskilled operator, they discovered, compared favorably with the net income of any but the richest of rice farmers in the

Table 3. Factory Employment by Village Castes

Village jatis	Brahman	Barber	Carpenter	Distiller	Washerman	Dom	Bauri	Santal	Muslim
Total no. adult males	48	3	14	17	5	1	36	14	1
Clerk	5								
Stores clerk	3								
Peon				1					
Foreman or Charge-hand	1								
Truckdriver	1								
Operator	24	1	7	7	1		1		
Mazdoor				2	1		5		
Canteen or other menial							9		1
Road gang, Construction						1			
Peripheral employment	2		1	7	3		1		
Collieries, other factory	5		1					1	

neighbourhood. Further, such income did not require the participation of the family; one man could work while the rest of the family saw to the fields, and so his income was totally an addition to previous earnings. Brahman men of Gôndôgram, of all ages and of all degrees of education and family income, began to clamor for the jobs "that had been promised them." The jobs they wanted, in fact, were without exception non-manual. If nothing else were available, or if the Brahman lacked sufficient education, he would be willing to accept the position of stores clerk—but what he wanted was to work in the office in some kind of clerical capacity. What the factory needed, however, was semiskilled operators on the assembly line.

None of the Brahmans working as operators expressed any real interest in the work (men in the enameling department said they actively disliked it; it was hot and smelly, dangerous, and generally unpleasant). All were disappointed that they had not acquired office jobs. Some blamed their failure on the machinations of other, more fortunate, Brahmans, who kept them out of the office, but most admitted they were simply not qualified; the educational attainments of older Brahmans were low, particularly in English.

All Brahman men interviewed insisted that things would be different for their children—if it were at all possible to do something about it. Children of Brahmans were encouraged to stay in school, to try for secondary schools. Frequently, the money earned in the factory was put aside in large part (when there were other sources of income) for children's schooling. It was hoped that children would become accountants, senior clerks, engineers, technicians—anything but operators like their fathers and older brothers.

All Carpenter men over the age of eighteen, and a few under, had worked, prior to the coming of the factory, in their traditional occupation—carpentry. They fixed carts, built doors and window frames, and repaired other items made of wood. For some, the trade represented their sole source of income, for others it was a welcome addition to whatever they made from their rice fields.

When the factory first came, many of the Carpenters were deprived of land and took the factory's promise of employment very seriously. A number of the older men sought and received immediate employment in the work of construction. Their job it was to erect the bamboo scaffolding as the walls went up. They worked at other construction carpentry tasks as well, and when the factory was ready to open applied for work inside. Almost all were assigned to the category "semiskilled operator" and given the necessary three months training before taking up their permanent duties. Many other members of their marriage-circle, from other villages nearby, were employed in the factory, having started out in much the same way in early construction work. The chain department, in fact, was made up almost entirely of Carpenters, and they were substantially represented in the frame department.

Carpenters report that they find the work undemanding, if uninteresting, and the working conditions quite pleasant, particularly when they can work surrounded by caste-brothers. The wages, most attest freely, are far superior to anything they could have hoped to earn following their traditional occupation, and none would voluntarily leave the factory to resume the trade of village carpenter. For their sons, apart from one man whose son showed some promise of eventual achievement in a technological institute or perhaps even an engineering school, Carpenters wish for nothing more than that the boys be given jobs similar to their own on the assembly line, preferably in the same departments.

And yet, having said all this, some Carpenter men go on to express a measure of sadness. Work in the factory is certainly well-paying, they note, but it is also dull and unsatisfying. It cannot compare with the pleasure of repairing a broken cart—or the deep satisfaction a man could feel when building a new one, working in the cool morning hours in the yard in front of his house with the children watching and neighbors walking by, joking and gossiping. There was true pleasure, a Carpenter will say, in working with the tools he inherited from his father, and in teaching his sons the ancient trade. Now the boys are not interested in learning to become carpenters, for they—like their fathers—hope they will go to work in the factory. And, after a hard day's work, who has time to teach the boys? In many Carpenter homes, the tools are rusty and neglected.

There were eight Distiller households in Gôndôgram. From them came ten men who worked directly for the factory; seven as operators scattered in various departments, two as "mazdoor" or helper, and one in "staff"—but in the most menial of all clerical positions, that of peon, or office boy. Seven other men from Distiller households were employed in the periphery of the factory. Three of these admitted that their work consisted of purveying liquor to the factory workers; the others would say only that they worked in "shops," but it was common belief in the village that they too sold liquor, if illegally.

The attitudes of the Distillers are more difficult to encapsulate than those of other jatis in Gôndôgram. The man who is a peon is proud of his status and hopes his sons will follow him into clerical positions. The operators show no particular pride or enthusiasm for their work, and those who express the hope that their children will follow them into the factory wish them to be clerical workers rather than operators. But most Distillers would prefer, if given the opportunity, to be independent entrepreneurs. Selling liquor is what they know best, but any kind of successful storekeeping would be acceptable.

Meanwhile, more money is coming into Distiller homes than ever before, because of the advent of the factory, and a good part of this money is being channeled into education for their children. They have an advantage over Carpenters—as the latter note with irritation—for Distillers in Bengal are a "scheduled caste" officially, and thus entitled under law to apply for the seats in schools and universities and the civil service jobs set aside for members of such castes.

In general, unlike Carpenters and Brahmans, the Distillers of Gôndôgram have no regrets for the past; the present has its difficulties, and there will be more in the future, but there are also new possibilities for success and fortune, and the Distillers are seeking them out.

There were five adult men in the four Washermen households of Gôndôgram. Of these, one worked as an operator in the wheel department and one as a menial laborer for the factory. The three others, assisted by the women of their families, washed clothes, primarily for the officers of the factory.

The Washerman operator is of course proud of his position and income, and is respected by other members of his jati. For most members of the jati, however, the coming of the factory represented a wonderful opportunity to resume their traditional jati occupation, that of washing clothes. Before the coming of the factory, the Washermen—landless, and living in a poor village—frequently supported themselves by working as field laborers for Brahman households. They have always considered themselves first and foremost "Washermen" but there was little scope for plying their trade. Only Brahmans in Gôndôgram ever gave out washing, and then only special, rarely worn holiday garb. With the factory-induced prosperity, however, some Brahman households are sending out more clothes than heretofore, although never enough to maintain a household of Washermen. But the higher staff officers of the factory in their compound not too far from the village have become major customers. Their families, in comparison with village families, wear many clothes and all is sent out—and the Washermen of Gôndôgram have a monopoly on the laundry work.

The Washermen of Gôndôgram, therefore, are completely happy about the coming of the factory. Now, at last, they can engage in their favorite and traditional occupation—they can feel like Washermen again—and as they see it there will always be work for themselves and their children.

Gôndôgram had one Dom household, containing one adult male; in the past he worked for different men in the village as a day laborer. With the coming of the factory he has been employed, off and on, as an ordinary laborer for various construction contractors, most particularly those who work on the roads.

Of the two Barber households in the village, one was the traditional one whose members had served the village over generations. The eldest son of this household was employed as an operator in the factory and was deaf to all entreaties to return to barbering. His younger brother also planned to seek work in the factory, and so their old father had been forced to come out of retirement to serve his old clients in the village. He had also brought in a young caste-brother from a distant village who now served the village as barber. This last gave no indication, at the time of the study, of a desire to give up the profession for factory employment. The old man was pessimistic, however; he was proud of his family occupation and sorry that his sons would not follow it, but he acknowledged that the money was better in the factory.

It appears that closeness of residence to the factory was an important factor for the Bauris. Men of this caste of the neighborhood closest to the factory have experienced little difficulty in obtaining regular employment. In the village neighborhood inhabited by Bauris and farthest from the factory, however, Bauri men seemed to experience great difficulty in penetrating the barriers to factory employment. Those Bauri men unable to find work in, or in the periphery of, the factory continued to labor in the fields.

It must be emphasized, however, that few if any of the Bauri men were in other than factory employment out of choice. The overwhelming majority of men of this caste insist they have no desire for agricultural employment; they will accept any kind of work in the factory but they would prefer best of all to work alongside what they perceive to be their most fortunate caste-brothers, as "bearers" (busboys) in the factory canteen.

There can be no doubt, in fact, that in their minds the Bauri men of Gôndôgram have removed themselves from the village and its agricultural way of life. In Gôndôgram, in the past, they were servants—man, woman, and child—working for the Brahmans, without hope of improvement or financial aggrandizement. They were always on the outskirts of village life, excluded from religious ceremony, barred from using the barber or the priests others could summon.

Once employed in the factory, however, even in the most menial of jobs, they are men like other men; for the first time in their lives they have what they regard as adequate salaries, they may eat with men of other castes, drink with them, they are petitioned by labor unions and political parties.

Bauris tend not to make any plans for their children's future, for as they see it once a boy becomes a man he will of course do whatever he wishes to without consulting his parents, but it is fair to assume that they expect their children to opt for the same kind of factory employment. Only one Bauri—the sole Bauri semiskilled operator—talked about the need for education of children so that they might have advantages not available to their parents.

At the time of the study, there were eleven Santal households in Gôndôgram. Almost all the men worked at least part of the year as laborers for contractors associated with the factory. Many of them, too, also augmented their incomes by working as day laborers for farmers in Gôndôgram and in neighboring villages. When necessary, their wives would also work as laborers, in the fields or for road gangs. Only one man, however, claimed that he was employed full time as a contractual laborer, and he was also the only one who worked for a contractor engaged in a construction project far from Gôndôgram and the Das-Walters factory, and only one man claimed to be engaged full time in agricultural work.

Whatever the pattern of employment, therefore, a majority of the Santal men actually perceived themselves as being primarily sharecroppers—raising crops on fields owned by others (for the most part Brahmans). They estimated that such work required only four months of their time, leaving eight months of the year free for employment by contractors. In such households, women worked alongside their husbands as laborers for the contractors, and the entire household participated in the agricultural work.

A decade or so before my visit, I was informed by Santals and others in the village, I would have found few Santals engaged in any kind of agricultural work, apart from their own kitchen gardens. The men had worked, like their fathers and grandfathers before them, as coal miners. The collieries in the area, however, have been closing down—many are uneconomic and others are simply no longer productive—and even in those still functioning at full capacity employment is off as machinery replaces manual labor.

In desperation, Santal men and women accepted day labor assignments in the fields in and around Gôndôgram. Along with all other jatis in the district, Santals believe that agricultural day labor is the least desirable of all available occupations, for both financial and prestige reasons. A Santal could only view day labor in the fields as a misfortune that must be kept temporary, to be replaced by a more dignified and remunerative employment as soon as possible. On the other hand, day labor in a contractor's work gang, while not the most desirable of occupations for a Santal, is certainly acceptable, for it does provide a cash income far superior to that of agricultural labor.

What Santals prefer above all else (and they claim they always have, even generations before) is to farm land on their own, on an individual family basis. There is great pride in being a Santal—pride in having their own language, in being cleaner than Bengalis, particularly those low-ranked jatis with which they usually associate—and they are convinced they have the knowledge, intelligence, and industry to be successful farmers.

When, with the coming of the factory, the landholders of Gôndôgram began to find themselves hard-pressed for agricultural labor, the Santals stepped eagerly into the breach. The Brahmans would have preferred to have the Santals simply replace the Bauris as laborers, but this the Santals would do only with extreme reluctance. On the other hand, they were eager to undertake sharecropping, and with the entire family participating could do well at it.

The Brahmans' reluctance gave way before the absence of viable alternative. Also, Brahman men were now working in the factory in increasing numbers, and the raising of a crop by the employment of laborers requires for success the continual presence of an adult male as supervisor. The only alternative was an increase in tenant farming in one form or another, and the Santals constituted the obvious choice.

The Brahman's reluctance was more than matched by Santal enthusiasm; most Santal men dream of controlling enough land under one form or another of sharecropping so as never to have to work as laborers for others again. And some Santals even dream of someday even *owning* the land themselves—which may help to explain the depression of the Brahmans about the state of agriculture in Gôndôgram.

The factory management confesses itself at a loss to explain how men of the same caste manage to cluster in a given department, given the employment regulations, but the problem did not prove a difficult one to investigate. An older Carpenter of Gôndôgram, one of the first of his jati to work for the factory and to be employed in the chain department, was perfectly willing to discuss the matter.

He explained that when the factory buildings were being set up he had been employed, like others of his jati, in the construction work, setting up scaffolding. When construction was completed, he applied for permanent employment and was assigned—purely by chance—to the chain department (just as the first Brahmans to be hired as operators were assigned to the enameling department). A new man hired as operator is given three months training in the work of the department to which he is assigned; this means, for the most part, learning to operate the equipment in use in that department. In the chain department, for example, there are punches to produce the chain link units, and other machines to assemble the links and eventually the lengths of bicycle chain. After the training period, the Carpenter began to work in the chain department, as he has ever since.

Each day, in the early afternoon, there is a work break in the factory for "tiffin" (tea and some food). It became the pattern for a younger brother of the Carpenter to bring the working man his daily tiffin. Sitting near the machine, waiting for work to resume, the employed Carpenter would explain the nature of his work to his younger brother. If no official were around, or if none objected, he showed his younger brother how the punch worked—and even allowed him to work it for a few moments, on occasion.

Then, some months later, when a vacancy occurred in the chain department, the older Carpenter could go to the foreman and point out that he knew of a candidate for the job who would not need the full three months' training, for the man already knew how to operate the equipment. His brother was brought in, tested, and was awarded the job.

In similar ways, other relatives were brought in, or transferred to, the chain department. *Bhalo ache* ("it is pleasant"), say the Carpenters, for caste-brothers to work side by side, at whatever task. And in much the same ways, for exactly the same reason, the Brahmans have come together in the enameling department, the Bauris in the canteen, and so on.

And, as the factory officials have noted, once such a caste concentration takes place, it is almost impossible to break it up, much as they would like to. This is quite true, Gôndôgram men of all jatis admit; if a "stranger" (that is, a man of a jati other than their own) is appointed to a department which some jati has come to think of as its own province, the outlook is bleak indeed.

Men of the ensconced jati treat him rudely or ignore him completely. None will help him or advise him. Sometimes, in fact, they will actively harass him. His personal possessions may disappear or be damaged, his work may show inexplicable errors. The charge-hand—the low-level supervisor ranking just above the operators but responsible for the quality and quantity of the department's work—must for his own preservation protect and support the older workers. Not infrequently, he is in fact a member of the same jati and therefore a leader in the campaign to keep the department a jati preserve. The new man's work is rejected as unsatisfactory more frequently than is usual. He finds himself reprimanded for shortcomings, and the slight relaxation of rules, the winking at small violations common in such situations, are not for him.

Eventually, almost inevitably, the unwanted new man is separated from the department. He may be fired, because after all there have been many complaints about his work and his behavior. More likely, he will plead for transfer, and it will be granted—not so much for his sake but rather to bring tranquility and good production back to the troubled department. Some men, in such situations, have even resigned and left the factory.

One way or another, however, the alien is forced from the department, and the caste-brothers are once again happy in the company of their own.

Factory officials are aware of such caste concentrations where the jatis involved are of local derivation. This is because events in the home villages can have particularly devastating effects upon production. The phenomenon, however, is by no means restricted to local jatis, such as the Brahmans, the Carpenters and the Bauris of Gôndôgram. One official—in a discussion of caste in the factory—shamefacedly volunteered the information that almost all the "sweepers" of the factory (those who clean the floors and most particularly the toilets and washrooms) were of the *Mæthôr* (Sweeper) jati.

Attempts to prevent this segregation, a particularly unpleasant one for educated, sensitive Indians who have taken the teachings of Gandhi to heart, have been uniformly unavailing. The problem is, it was explained, that few but Sweepers apply for such work.

And, then, even when a man of some other jati, driven by desperation, does take on the employment, "he does not stay." He lacks the skill and knowledge the Sweepers have had since early childhood, and of course he lacks his own brushes and pails. But, most serious of all, reported the official, he is resented by the Sweepers, who feel he had taken a job that belongs properly to one of their jati. They make life so miserable for him that eventually, just like the men inserted in the "Brahman's" enameling shop and the "Carpenter's" chain department, he leaves in discouragement or is fired.

And if caste concentrations occur on the lowest level of factory employment as well as on the assembly lines, one might expect them to occur in the highest echelons, and they do. As has been noted, the Indian family that constitutes the major shareholder—the Das family—are of the *Bôiddô* (*Vaidya*) jati. Almost all the higher officers of the factory, and many of the junior ones, exhibit names characteristic of this jati.

Once, before the time of this study (according to a story current in the factory), a number of Panjabi engineers were brought to the factory. It is said that, while their skills were badly needed, there was opposition to their hiring expressed by some officers, who appeared to feel that the skills of engineers to be recruited in Bengal were more than adequate. The Panjabis had been attracted by high salaries, but nevertheless within six months the last of them had resigned and departed from the factory with the bitter comment that "Bengalis and Panjabis don't work well together."

And, finally, it must not be assumed that any of the foregoing is peculiar to the Das-Walters bicycle factory; works-managers and personnel managers from many different factories in the Asansol area report exactly the same kinds of "caste" problems at all levels of employment.

Carpenters and Brahmans of Gôndôgram, employed as operators in the factory, are aware of official unhappiness at their attendance records. Some argue that they think the complaints are unfair, since they feel they are not absent from work a greater number of times in toto than other workers; others admit that they understand the officials' complaints, but say they have little choice in the matter.

Interestingly, there is merit to the argument that men of Gôndôgram do not in fact take sick leave more frequently than others. One factory official, after bemoaning the attendance records of local people, offered to demonstrate his point and produced attendance records which he claimed were characteristic. One was the attendance record of a local person, a resident of Gôndôgram—no better and no worse than the others, according to the official—and the other what he felt was a typical attendance record for a nonlocal and non-Bengali operator.

Given the official complaints, it was startling to note that the Gôndô-gram operator had been absent for only twenty days during the year—for which times he claimed to be sick—and for five other days for unexplained reasons; a total of twenty-five absences for the year. The non-Bengali operator, however, had been out thirty-three times during the year claiming to be ill, and four more times for unexplained reasons, for a total of *thirty-seven* absences!

When this was pointed out to the official, he shrugged and commented that these were not the significant items in the record; what troubled him, he said, was the *distribution,* not the *number,* of absences. From this perspective, it was true that the two records were very different indeed. The non-Bengali took all his days of sick leave—with and without pay—during the months of January and February, and his four days of "casual leave" were divided equally between December and March. In other words, from the end of December through the beginning of March, he was absent almost continually; part of this was annual leave, part was sick leave with pay, and the rest was simply absence without pay. From April through November, however, he was not absent from work for a single day.

The Gôndôgram man, on the other hand, was absent from work for a few days—from one to seven—in almost every month of the year; only August, September, and December showed a perfect attendance record for him.

According to the official, when a nonlocal person employed in the factory returns to his home for his annual leave, one may be certain that he will not return on time. A letter is likely to arrive, or even a telegram, reporting that he has taken ill (and so must use up his sick leave), or that there is illness or other disaster at home requiring his attention even if he must be absent without pay. The official said that the pattern holds at all levels of factory employment, and he personally attributed it to the reluctance of mothers everywhere to see their sons depart again after only a brief visit home.

Whatever the reason, however, he said that the factory had come to expect the behavior and was not particularly inconvenienced by it; after all, the absent worker had been temporarily replaced for his scheduled leave, and the replacement could stay on until he returned without causing additional expense to the factory or adverse effect upon production. The local man's pattern, on the other hand, was much more disturbing to the factory—even if it did not add up to as many absences in the year— because a man unexpectedly away from his machine for a day or two is simply not replaced, and therefore production in his department will be affected accordingly.

The problem, of course, is that the men of Gôndôgram, like most other local people, live at home. If there is an emergency in the family's fields—at time of planting or harvesting—his presence will be demanded. If a child is ill, or someone dies—or even if a marriage takes place in a kinsman's household in some distant village—he is likely to have obligations and responsibilities that will prevent his going in to work. Much the same things are probably taking place at the home of the non-Bengali in his village (say, in Bihar), but he is not at home and so his people must somehow manage without him. Whatever can be postponed, such as marriages and engagements, are of course put off until he returns on leave—which is another reason why he has difficulty in breaking away when his leave is over.

Most of the factory officials understand the true basis of the local villagers' absenteeism, despite the mutterings about laziness and sickliness. But while they understand, they are not prepared to condone. True, there is absenteeism among nonlocal people attributable to drunkenness, venereal disease, and other factors associated with life in the workers' quarters, while few if any of the local people are troubled by such things. This of course was what the factory had hoped for originally, but now the management must equate production loss due to such causes with production loss due to local villagers' absenteeism. It was my impression that they preferred the former.

For the villagers of Gôndôgram, the factory has become a major life factor. In many ways, it has replaced the rice crop as that which determines the state of one's fortune or well-being. It is a direct or indirect source of income for almost every household, and for many it is perceived as an avenue for future advancement for themselves or their children.

And yet, it is also an alien element, an intrusion upon the old patterns and relationships of life. For some, this fact constitutes a threat, for some it is a source of exhilaration. For all, the implications of the factory's presence must be constantly explored and adjusted to.

For those who once controlled the village—that is, the Brahmans—the factory is obviously an alternative economic power source. Once, they themselves controlled the only source of income and of food—land for the growing of rice—and all who wished to articulate with that source had to do it through them. They were the source of labor in the fields, and of rice and money in exchange for services. All who owned no land and who had no outside source of income (and that was most of the village) had to turn to the Brahmans, and thereby recognize and accept their authority. The coming of the factory, therefore, provided an alternative to the Brahmans—and this of course had its impact upon the authority of the Brahmans in village life. In addition, however, the factory also provided new opportunities for Brahmans too; some of them have been quicker than others to see this.

In their feelings about the factory, therefore, the Brahmans are somewhat divided. All agree that its presence tends to be disruptive of old ways; there is a division as to whether or not this is a good thing.

Interestingly, one of the favorite factory complaints about the villager introduces us to one of the areas of change. As we have seen, officials complain that the Gôndôgram villagers are dishonest; they take unfair and unnecessary advantage of the factory's promise to employ "the sons of Gôndôgram" by bringing in boys from villages all over the district and insisting that these are actually their own sons.

From the villager's perspective the difficulty arises out of the fact that it is the duty of the head of a household to seek husbands for all marriageable girls in that household. Both Brahman and Carpenter heads of households in Gôndôgram report sorrowfully that the coming of the factory has added a new and most awkward dimension to their marriage inquiries.

A Gôndôgram guardian from one of these jatis makes his inquiries as do other men of his marriage-circle (see Klass, 1966), and after the usual formalities, sits down with the father of the boy to discuss the thorny matter of dowry and other gifts. Gôndôgram men report that, more and more frequently, the boy's guardian announces that they need not waste time on the matter; he is prepared to agree to an astonishingly small dowry, and in a few cases has even hinted that he might be persuaded to forego dowry entirely.

All he asks is that the girl's guardian take steps well within his power to safeguard the future of the young couple. Since it is common knowledge throughout the marriage-circle (both Carpenter and Brahman) that

Gôndôgram men have special access to jobs at the bicycle factory, he asks only that the girl's guardian must arrange for employment for the prospective bridegroom.

If the Gôndôgram guardian can do that, the marriage is assured. If he fails—and it has become increasingly difficult—the boy's family charges bad faith, and negotiations are often broken off acrimoniously.

Gôndôgram Carpenters and Brahmans find themselves caught in a painful squeeze. On the one hand, factory employment has become a condition for obtaining bridegrooms for Gôndôgram girls. Indeed, in an increasing number of cases, it has become a condition for obtaining brides for Gôndôgram boys! Men of other villages, seeking spouses in Gôndôgram for their daughters, have raised the issue of jobs for the girl's brother! Some Gôndôgram men resolutely resist this demand (arguing that it is the place of the boy's father to make demands, not the other way around) but some have given in, and there are those who fear for the future. And on the other hand, the factory has become less and less generous.

Gôndôgram men can put up with accusations and even insults; they do need those jobs, however. But what with increases in automation, deceleration of expansion activities, and a growing hostility toward Gôndôgram, the outlook is not good. During the year of the study, men were satisfied if they could obtain menial jobs for prospective bridegrooms—though once it would have been as operators, only—and a few marriages were delayed while guardians continued desperately to petition the factory.

One Gôndôgram Carpenter said gloomily that he feared, should the factory ever turn its back completely, that no more Gôndôgram girls would be able to get married.

Neither the Santals nor the Bauris had any problem in this regard, since men of neither jati were aware of any factory obligation, and Distillers reported only minor problems.

Bauris, in fact, are universally enthusiastic about the presence of the factory. Apart from employment possibilities, they see the factory as providing them with the opportunity for getting out from under Brahmanical control, something that is stressed as important particularly by the younger men. For them, the factory has introduced a new horizon, unimagined by their fathers. They are no longer circumscribed by village and by agricultural labor; even those who have not yet achieved the success of factory employment—those still locked into the fields as agricultural laborers—dream only of leaving agricultural employment of every kind behind them and joining the industrial proletariat.

The last two words are used advisedly, for the Bauris who have gone to work in the factory have attended meetings, have been approached by union organizers, and have in some cases chosen political sides—and have gone on to recruit among their fellows in the village.

The Bauri who was employed in the factory, or in factory-related contractual labor, claimed that he was now free to vote as he pleased, and often indicated an intention of voting for a Communist candidate.

But if the Gôndôgram Bauri turned to Communism, he appeared to do it in terms of the references and values of Gôndôgram. One young Bauri man, for example, told me that in his view Bauris had a legitimate source of grievance against Brahmans. Once, he said, his ancestors—the original Bauri inhabitants of Bengal—had owned all the agricultural land of Bengal. Somehow, in a way the young man admitted he could not explain, the Brahmans had acquired control of all the land. Now the Bauri people were without land, but he was convinced that one day they would rise up and take back what properly belonged to them.

This tale—recounted by only one village Bauri—may be idiosyncratic and it may reflect a personal reworking of other tales, told by men of other castes, of supposed Brahmanical wrongdoings. I would note, however, that this young man worked in a factory-related job and had spent much time in or near the factory at political meetings. It is likely, therefore, that he had been exposed to—and had assimilated—a Marxist explanation of the expropriation of property by the landed and governing class. And, if that were the source of the tale, it is certainly significant that there is no place, in the account as he gave it, for men of any other disenfranchised caste: according to him, the land belonged originally to *Bauris,* and to the *Bauris* it must and will return.

This aneceote, I would argue, presents in microcosm the broad range of dilemmas faced by the villager of every caste. We see within it the pressure upon him—and his own willingness—to accept new explanations and interpretations. And we see, too, the conflict and confusion engendered by traditional values and loyalties, from which he cannot easily turn away. And finally, if we look closely, we see a hint of future confrontation.

The Bauri who claims—sincerely—to have turned his back on Hinduism and "caste" and other things that he associates with Gôndôgram remains nevertheless very much a part of his caste—and his caste continues to constitute for him an important boundary of self. Bauris associate primarily with Bauris, partly because few others will associate with them, but also out of choice. They help each other to the best of their ability to get jobs, particularly in the factory canteen, where Gôndôgram Bauris constitute an important element among the "bearers."

In much the same way, as we have seen, members of other castes cluster together in particular factory departments and activities, much to the distress of the factory management. Traditional values, loyalties, and aspirations still govern the lives of the people from Gôndôgram, as indeed they do for others in the factory, from management to "sweeper."

The difficulty is that all the villagers, of every caste, are being deluged daily with pressures to accept and conform to new and contrary values, and they are being asked to demonstrate new and conflicting loyalties.

The older men find, in the factory, that they must work with and eat with men not only of different castes but sometimes of alien castes, from distant regions, and even of other religions. Meat is served in the canteen; the fact that meat is present constitutes a problem for vegetarians, and the kind of meat served may not always be acceptable to those who are permitted to partake of flesh. Muslim employees have complained that, though they may eat goat meat, the animal from which it comes must be slaughtered according to the rules of their religion.

Again, while Indian villagers work hard indeed at times, the patterns and pulsations of agricultural work are very different from those of the factory. A farmer and his laborer may, on certain days, begin work before dawn and continue past dusk—on another day they may find it necessary to work only in the morning, at a leisurely pace, and be able to take a long rest after noon. To say, further, that one starts "early in the day" is to offer an approximation of the time one begins work; it is very different from punching a timeclock at 8:30 AM precisely. The regularity and preciseness of factory worktime pose problems for the man from the agricultural village—and so, as we have seen, does the factory's inability to acknowledge that he occasionally needs time off to attend to his own crop, or to his daughter's wedding.

Not only are caste and village values and relationships strained by exposure to the factory; severe stresses are experienced within the tightly knit family characteristic of all but the lowest castes. As young men take up jobs in the factory, they become alien and somewhat frightening to their parents. Carpenter men, for example, are delighted to work in the factory, and equally delighted to have their sons work there, but they are troubled because the young men have no interest in learning to use the ancestral carpenter tools, or in watching to see how a bullcart may be constructed or repaired. The Carpenters fear, with some reason, that within a generation or so, the ancestral occupation will have been forgotten forever.

The village Barber expressed a similar grief. He had always assumed that his two sons would replace him in time, dividing between them his substantial network of clients in Gôndôgram and neighboring villages. Both young men opted to work in the factory, however, and their father was compelled to seek a distant relative, from a village far away, as his successor.

Many older Brahman men are particularly disturbed because their sons, upon taking up employment in the factory, begin to associate with young men of different castes and strange ways. The Brahman youths are quickly introduced to smoking and card-playing, and perhaps (say the older men) to other vices. The village practice, particularly among Brahmans, was for all members of the family to contribute their earnings to the central family purse under the supervision of the family head. Once they begin to work in the factory, however, young men insist upon retaining a portion of their salaries to spend as they please. This may seem eminently fair and reasonable to Western-oriented persons, such as members of the factory management, who support the young men, but it is extremely unsettling for many of the more conservative Brahmans, who perceive it as destructive of family structure and prospects.

Before the coming of the factory, national political issues did not loom large in the minds of the villagers. Brahmans were most interested. Almost exclusively, they supported the Congress Party, and used their influence among those non-Brahmans in the village who bothered to vote to gain votes for that party. There is a feeling in Gôndôgram, among men of all castes, that one owes some loyalty to the political party supported by one's patron.

Men employed in the factory, however, no longer consider the village Brahmans their patrons, and this is particularly true of the Bauris. Representatives of many political parties vie for the support of the factory employees, and in their efforts they utilize particularly the labor unions. The Das-Walters factory, like many others, is heavily unionized, but the employees belong to a number of competing unions, each supported by, and frequently founded by, a particular political party.

This means, of course, that village friendships and loyalties are challenged by party and union loyalties. Strikes and walkouts are frequently called in support of party positions on state or national issues, as against specific worker versus management grievances within the factory. Village men of different union-and-party may therefore find themselves in serious conflict as one group downs tools and marches out while the other group stays on the job.

And, with all this change in village perception and relationship, there are other problems that lie in wait in the future. Children, as we have seen, are turning rapidly from village occupations and values, seeking eagerly to find places for themselves in the industrial universe. The pattern of change varies sharply from caste to caste; the fact of change does not.

We have noted that heads of household are experiencing difficulty in acquiring jobs for sons-in-law. Part of the reason for this is that the management is reluctant to hire more laborers from the countryside. Another reason, however (and perhaps not entirely unrelated), is that automation has cut and continues to cut the number of laborers needed, despite increases in production. Many factory officials, and not only in the Das-Walters factory, say freely that they look forward to the time when advances in automation will make it possible to cut the size of the work force drastically—when only a skeleton staff of technicians will be required to service the machines.

What will happen, then, to the son of the Gôndôgram villager, particularly if he no longer knows his ancestral occupation, has broken with traditional values, and is unwilling—or unable—to return to the ways of the village?

ACKNOWLEDGMENT

*Much of the material in this chapter is excerpted, by permission of the publisher, from Morton Klass, *From Field to Factory: Community Structure and Industrialization in West Bengal*. Copyright © 1978 by ISHI, Institute for the Study of Human Issues, Inc. Philadelphia.

NOTES

1. A dozen years earlier, when the factory was built, the population of the village was smaller, but the composition was essentially the same: few have left the village, and few have moved in.
2. At the time the study was conducted, 4.76 Indian rupees was worth one U.S. dollar.

REFERENCES

Klass, Morton
   1966   "Marriage Rules in Bengal." American Anthropologist 68: 951–970.
   1978   From Field to Factory: Community Structure and Industrialization in West Bengal.
            Philadelphia: Institute for the Study of Human Issues Press.

WORKING-CLASS
CONSCIOUSNESS: CHILE
1970-1973; GERMANY 1918-1920

Henry A. Landsberger

I. INTRODUCTION

The spectre which, according to Marx, haunted Europe in the 1840s was not only that of communism specifically[1] but, more broadly, the threat of revolutionary action by Europe's still small but growing industrial working classes. And whether or not such a revolutionary threat existed then, exists now, or might appear in the future in this or that society has continued to be a hotly debated issue. These questions arouse passion because—as Marx intended—the answers to them have implications for what should actually be done, now and in the near future, and for what should have been done in the past. The issue is not merely a matter for intellectual speculation.

Research in the Sociology of Work, Volume 1, pages 131–169
Copyright © 1981 by JAI Press Inc.
ISBN: 0-89232-124-5

Nothing illustrates better both the complexity of the facts concerning working-class consciousness, and the passion with which its analysis is undertaken, than does the case of Chile. The last few years of democratic civilian government in Chile, i.e., up to the military coup of September 11, 1973, were times when those broad and complex strata often referred to in oversimplified fashion as "the" working class were about as free to express themselves in deed and word as they have ever been anywhere. At the same time, the very turmoil of those years—not to mention the permanent, intrinsic difficulty of establishing what the "consciousness" of a certain group is—makes an assessment of its mood difficult.

It is to an assessment of the mood of the Chilean working class in the period preceding and following the victory of Dr. Allende's *Unidad Popular* that this chapter is devoted. We have added, however, a short section dealing with the state of mind of Germany's working class in the period 1918–1920 (a period comparable to the Chilean in ways which we shall explain) in order to test whether the conclusions we draw from the Chilean data might be more generally true.

To specify more precisely what we might wish to establish about the mood of the Chilean working class in the 1960s and early 1970s, let us return briefly to Marx. For he was the first major social theorist to accord to working-class consciousness a central role in the explanation of social events. We cannot, in the confines of this chapter, and given its purpose, present a detailed exegesis of his thoughts on the topic. This would be a difficult task in any event, for in the case of this as in that of most of his central concepts, he discusses it in several of his writings but is systematic and definitive about it in none. As Caute, a sympathetic commentator observes: "Marx did not achieve any sustained analysis, and, as was often the case, penetrated the problem [of working-class consciousness] with more power than refinement" (Caute, 1967: 86).

It is, nevertheless, worthwhile to summarize briefly his ideas on working-class consciousness, for they have influenced, however indirectly, almost all discussions of, and empirical research into, the state of mind of industrial workers, even if the researcher may not have been aware of it. And that has been the most usual situation. Even in the case of Chile, research reports do not usually begin with a systematic exposition of Marx's views on the changing nature of working-class consciousness in order to relate empirical findings to them, even though this would not be difficult to do. Indeed, the following summary of Marx's views is presented precisely because it is hoped that the reader will find it stimulating to keep in mind the question: "to what extent does this or that piece of evidence indicate that the Chilean working class had reached the degree of intense self-conscious alienation, and the degree of more positive revolutionary consciousness, which Marx thought of as heralding, as being both a precondition for and a cause of, a socialist revolution?"

At the risk of laying ourselves open to the charge of oversimplification, we shall attribute the following views to Marx.[2] In the period immediately preceding revolution:

1. There is a sense of intense alienation from the following aspects of the existing system: (a) the work process, i.e., intense dissatisfaction with the tasks that the job requires; (b) the product; (c) the wage system *qua* system as a symbol of the worker's alienation; (d) the employer-factory-owner-capitalist; (e) fellow workers; (f) himself as a person; (g) humanity as a whole; (h) his family, the state, religion, prevailing moral norms, and all institutions as they currently exist in bourgeois society. This is the definition of, and these are the indices of, alienation most systematically put forward by Marx in *Economic and Philosophical Manuscripts* (McLellan, 1977: 77 ff.).[3] This is the state of "misery conscious of its spiritual and physical misery" described also in *The Holy Family* (McLellan, 1977: 134–135).

   The question for purposes of this chapter is, then: how intensely were workers dissatisfied with their jobs? with their employers? with the Chilean state?

2. In addition to specific dissatisfactions, but because of their range and intensity, Marx postulates, in the *Communist Manifesto,* for example (McLellan, 1977: 230–231), that workers will become aware that these are the outgrowth of capitalism as a system. They will become aware of the exploitative nature of that system as a whole *qua* system, and the fact that the private ownership of the means of production (the "relations of production") is anachronistic in relation to the necessarily socially interrelated structure of the technical system of production ("forces of production"). Marx describes this, for example, in *The German Ideology* (McLellan, 1977: 177ff.).

   To what extent—in our context—did Chilean workers explicitly reject the capitalist system as a whole?

3. Workers will have a growing sense of unity with their fellow workers and with the rest of the proletariat as all become equally de-skilled and equally insecure in their jobs because of the advance of technology, and because of ever more extreme swings of the trade cycle, especially its "bottom" half. Workers become a class "for" themselves, according to the famous phrase in *The Poverty of Philosophy* (McLellan, 1977: 214).

4. The unity of workers and their recognition of the evils of the system *qua* system will result in the establishment of a workers' movement in which trade unions, not concerned merely with temporary economic gains ("economism" and "trade unionism") but highly active politically, will play an essential role. This is described, for example,

in a letter to Bolte in 1871 (McLellan, 1977: 387). But Lenin, in *What Is To Be Done?* (see Tucker, 1975: 12–114) expresses even more clearly the idea of trade unions as a political mobilizing force which should not be permitted to confine itself to purely economic issues.

How loyal to their unions did Chilean workers feel? To what extent did they wish them to play a role in politics, and in raising the political consciousness of workers?

5. Both the logic of the situation in which they find themselves (and their awareness of that logic) and the activities of their own organizations will make workers increasingly aware that a revolution—a total change in the socioeconomic system—and not merely incremental improvements and reforms are necessary to free them from their state of alienation and *de facto* bondage. The *Communist Manifesto* portrays the growth of revolutionary consciousness particularly vividly (McLellan, 1977: 227–230), but it can also be found in *Economic and Philosophic Manuscripts* and in many other writings.

On the issue of incremental reform vs total change, where did Chilean workers stand?

6. As both consequence and cause of the revolutionary consciousness just described, organized worker activity of a confrontational kind—prerevolutionary activity of all kinds, "revolutionary praxis," directed against the bourgeois state and capitalist employers—will become ever more frequent (*German Ideology*, McLellan, 1977: 179).

What were the positions of Chilean workers on the commission of illegal acts, including the use of violence?

We shall not order the information we have strictly in accordance with these questions. We shall present it, rather, ordered in historical sequence, i.e., beginning in the early 1960s and moving toward the 1970s. Within this sequential framework, we shall present the information by source. This may mean, in some instances, research-study-by-research-study. It means in other instances, presentation event-by-event, e.g., data from earlier and later elections, or data from statistical series on strike activities. And in many instances, the interpretations of what the data imply about worker consciousness will not be ours, but those of knowledgeable observers, including those of Dr. Allende himself, and experienced officials from the communist and socialist parties, who were the mainstay of the *Unidad Popular* (U.P.) coalition that won the September 1970 election.

One further point needs to be made in connection with the issue of what kind of evidence is appropriate if one is to address the questions raised by a Marxian definition of working-class consciousness. That point concerns the use of survey instruments to obtain information about workers' attitudes. Again, the scope of this chapter does not permit the kind of sophisticated discussion that this issue deserves, and the more basic one of how, in general, one "gets at" consciousness. Let us simply assert very provocatively, that we firmly reject at least one-half of the accusation (and the accusation is often made) that the use of such attitudinal measures is a sign of superficiality of which only a bourgeois sociologist could be guilty, someone who does not grasp the complexities of the concept of "consciousness." Attitude surveys of workers' revolutionary consciousness are used by Marxist sociologists, and are certainly cited by them, when the results support a Marxist position. Among the best known examples is Zeitlin's (1967) study of Cuban workers. But we shall use in this chapter attitude surveys of Chilean workers which have been cited by Marxist-oriented writers to substantiate the thesis that Chilean workers had arrived at, or were at least close to, a state of revolutionary consciousness in the late 1960s and early 1970s. And that, at bottom, is the question to which this chapter addresses itself: had they, or had they not?

We take a far less dogmatic stand on the issue of whether attitude surveys—by whomever used—are superficial or not. The very fact that we use voting and strike statistics, well-known incidents and events, and the interpretation of all of these by knowledgeable observers, indicates that we regard all kinds of data as both useful and limited. We are thoroughly eclectic and catholic in our use of and confidence in various data collection methods. We find it difficult to imagine that there is a single royal road to the assessment of a phenomenon as intractable—by its very nature and definition—as the consciousness of a group.

II. WORKING-CLASS CONSCIOUSNESS IN CHILE: 1960–1973

A. The Chilean Labor Movement

Chile has been, since the beginning of this century, one of the most highly industrialized countries of Latin America. It has for decades ranked about fourth or fifth out of twenty-three in the share of its Gross Domestic Product added by manufacturing. Percent of the labor force employed in industry is slightly below 20%, however, and has been stagnant for a considerable period of time. But even that puts Chile ahead of most Latin American countries (United Nations, 1964).

Its trade union movement was—together with that of Argentina—the oldest on the continent. It goes back to a series of mutual aid and "resistance" societies established in the middle and late nineteenth century.[4] Their conversion to full-fledged unions was marked, as in Europe, by ferocious repression and considerable bloodshed at the turn of and in the first part of this century. A significant sector of Chile's working class was, therefore, in some way conscious of its interests at a very early stage. Twenty percent of the labor force was unionized by 1973. And since mid-1950, a single trade union confederation—CUT—has spoken for the unions—more or less!

Moreover, the structure of Chile's political party system followed class and ideological cleavages with exceptional clarity. On the left, its Communist party (PC) is one of the oldest (founded in 1921) and the largest and best organized on the continent. But it had already been preceded by a series of Socialist, Workers', Left Democratic, and other parties. The PC's rivals on the left—anarchists at earlier times, a Socialist party (PS) since 1931—follow comprehensible, classical European lines in many respects. (The Socialist party is unusual, however, in having followed, since 1965, a more extreme line than the PC, i.e., it is not equivalent to the French or Italian Socialist parties, let alone the Social Democratic parties of Northwest Europe.)

These parties were followed on the political spectrum by more-or-less reformist, more-or-less centrist parties (the Radical party, later in part displaced by the Christian Democrats, the PDC) and these in turn have always had ideologically clear-cut parties on their right: the Liberal and Conservative parties, which merged into the National party (PN) in 1966. Understandably, close relations have existed between trade unions on the one hand and the left and center parties on the other, with the rivalries between the parties reflected in tension and rivalries among and within the unions.

With a relatively "mature" (by Latin American standards) industrial structure at its base, the history of the Chilean working class and its organizations gave every sign of being among the most coherent and developed not only in the region, but by world standards. It is this that has drawn world interest to its fate, and it is this maturity, too, that it shared with the working class of post-World-War-I Germany and its parties and trade unions. The underlying question (to put it somewhat provocatively) is, therefore: if we were to find that the working class of these two countries lacked revolutionary fervor, what working class can be expected to be revolutionary?

We turn now to various studies of the mood of Chilean labor, ordered, very roughly, in historical sequence, and beginning in the early 1960s. This was the "take-off" period for a process of political mobilization which was to end in disaster in the 1970s.

B. A Base-Line Study: Union Leadership at the Grassroots

We begin with the Landsberger-Barrera-Fuchs-Toro survey (1964) of 231 blue collar union leaders, conducted in 1961–1962. A survey instrument using mostly closed questions was used in face-to-face interviews lasting from ninety minutes to three hours. Respondents constituted either the universe (in Concepción and Valparaiso) or a systematically chosen sample (in Santiago). The reason for citing it first is not (only) egocentrism, although I do think it was and still is the most systematic effort of its kind. I cite it also because it was historically the first study of the type of unionism prevailing in Chile until 1973 that employed survey techniques and focused on the then-current situation. Previous studies had been historical and qualitative. Note that it covered blue collar unions, the putative bulwark of radicalism. It did not include white collar unions, which were often regarded as the (only?) stronghold of Christian democracy in the labor movement. In various ways, therefore, it is a kind of benchmark study. The key results relevant to the study of Chilean working-class consciousness are as follows:

1. A notable demonstration of the strength of reformism (PDC adherence) as against radicalism—if belief in the socialist-communist FRAP (later: UP or *Unidad Popular*) can be taken as a measure of the latter. As we shall see, "FRAP" adherence is in fact a very generous estimate of "radicalism" [see 4. below]. The "Totals," i.e., bottom *line* of Table 1, show that PDC sympathizers—as early as 1962—were presidents of a quarter of all locals, while FRAP (UP) sympathizers were presidents of half. Thus, the PDC, PS, and PC were each about equal in representation. The final 25% declared themselves either as noncommitted or—to the extent of fewer than 10%—adherents of the Radical party and of the two right wing parties, the Liberals and the Conservatives. While there might have been persons reluctant to confide their radical politics among this 25%, our young, modestly dressed, and carefully selected Chilean interviewers did not, at that time, consider this to be a frequent reason for that response.
2. "Economistic" goals (see Table 1, Goals 1 and 9) predominated in the minds of leaders of all political loyalties. Marxian "consciousness raising" goals (5 and 6) began to figure only in second and third place, even for FRAP-oriented officials.
3. "Community improvement" and "education" (typical "right-of-moderate" goals) were important second and third place goals: as important as "consciousness raising."
4. Party loyalty does not differentiate between emphasis on one kind of goal or another. Contrary to expectations, leaders loyal to Marxist parties did not pursue a "consciousness raising" goal more than others. Hence, caution is indicated in interpreting votes. Perhaps some of PDC candidate Radomiro Tomic's supporters (in the presidential elections of 1970) were really quite radical, as is often (and,

Table 1. "Thinking about the Next Three to Five Years: Which of the Following Objectives Should Your Union Try to Reach? List the Three Most Important in Order."

	First Place			Second Place			Third Place		
	NC[a]	CD[b]	FRAP[c]	NC	CD	FRAP	NC	CD	FRAP
1. Economic betterment	63	64	59	2	9	10	7	4	5
2. More respect for union by industry	7	4	4	21	8	11	5	11	9
3. Unification and strengthening of Chilean labor movement	7	13	13	16	19	23	12	8	10
4. Educational and moral betterment	16	6	8	16	25	23	16	21	15
5. Awaken political conscience of workers	—	—	2	2	0	7	0	0	8
6. Greater solidarity among workers	—	9	7	16	25	8	12	23	12
7. Social activities	—	—	1	5	0	1	7	6	8
8. Betterment of surrounding community	7	2	4	9	15	11	26	15	24
9. Better working conditions	—	2	2	12	—	5	14	13	7
TOTALS	100(43)	100(53)	100(99)	100(43)	100(53)	100(99)	100(42)	100(53)	100(98)

Source: Landsberger, 1968:234.
  a. Noncommitted
  b. Christian democrats
  c. FRAPists

138

Table 2. Opinion on Probability That Workers Would Benefit from Current Development Plan, by Group (Percent)

	Noncommitted	Christian Democrats	FRAPists
Workers to benefit:			
Fully	9	0	6
Quite a bit	35	38	16
A little bit	52	50	70
Not at all	4	13	8
TOTAL	100(23)	100(24)	100(63)

Source: Landsberger, 1968:238.

in part rightly, in our opinion) asserted by those disappointed in Dr. Allende's support. But then, too, perhaps some of Dr. Allende's 36% was *not* an indication of any great degree of radicalism.

5. The far from complete coincidence between party loyalty and adherence to the ideology for which the party supposedly stands is further illustrated by Tables 2 and 3. The ordering in the two middle categories of Table 2 do indeed follow party lines as expected. Far more Christian Democrats (38%) than FRAP (16%) believed that workers would benefit "quite a bit" from (then-) current national development plans. But the expected positions are inverted at the extremes, and perceptions of the trend in inequality (Table 3) while clearly showing party-effects, still do not show anything close to a one-to-one coincidence. Moreover, leaving aside party comparisons, thirty-three of the 100 union leaders believed that workers would benefit "fully" or "quite a bit" from the then-current development plans, formulated by a right-center government coalition to which at most 10% of the leaders felt any political allegiance. Depending on one's numerical tastes, one can consider 33% to represent "much" or "little" confidence in this establishment-dominated regime. Percen-

Table 3. Opinion on Whether Differences Between Rich and Poor are Increasing or Decreasing, by Group (Percent)

	Noncommitted	Christian Democrats	FRAPists
Decreasing	34	21	13
Static	23	36	19
Increasing	43	43	68
TOTAL	100(44)	100(53)	100(100)

Source: Landsberger, 1968:238.

Table 4. "What Do You Think would
be the Best Way to Achieve the
Economic and Social Progress
which Chile Needs?"

	%
Through an immediate total restructuring of the presently existing institutions.	34
Through a restructuring of existing institutions which, though not total and immediate, would take place at least in not too long a time.	44
Through a gradual evolution of existing institutions.	22
Maintaining the institutions as they are to-day.	0

Source: Landsberger, 1963:25.

tage figures carry no automatic descriptions with them. This writer
thinks it indicates a substantially *divided* opinion.

6. Finally, and most pointedly, on the issue of the radicalization of blue
collar workers: Table 4 presents answers to the question: "How do
you think the social and economic progress which Chile needs can
best be obtained?" Once again: my reading of that table is that it
shows a degree of radicalism which I would describe as being simultaneously substantial and yet surprisingly little. Thirty-four percent
of all union presidents (42%—only 42%!!—of the socialist-
communist FRAPists, 28% among Christian Democrats) wanted the
"immediate and total restructuring of today's institutions." Another
44% opted for change in the "not too distant future," while 22%
would be happy with "gradual evolution," i.e., a percentage which
was two-thirds of the 34% who wanted immediate change. Once
again this indicates to us a very wide range of views, containing a
substantial but far from majoritarian radical segment. Note that
respondents were not asked to balance the benefits of rapid change
against any kind of cost such as the possibility of violence. We shall
see below that response rates change dramatically when such possible costs are included.

Because of its timing at the beginning of the fateful '60s, precisely
the moment when "mobilization" began, and because of its systematic nature, we might regard this study as a bench-mark and ask
of later studies: did they turn up convincing evidence to indicate a
substantial shift to the left? Did they indicate anything else except
what we found: a very wide range of opinions?

C. Studies of the Mood of Labor in the Mid- and Late-1960s

Studies of the attitudes of workers, and of slum dwellers, conducted at later points in time do not, in fact, indicate any need to modify this picture of a working class with a solid, but not a majority (or, possibly, on occasion just barely a majority) core of radicalism. At no time was it large enough to justify referring to the revolutionary consciousness of "the" i.e., united, Chilean working class.

The most comprehensive survey of politically relevant attitudes among Chilean rank and file blue collar union members was conducted by Patrick V. Peppe in 1967. We are deeply grateful to him for giving us access to the data. He has reported some of its results (Nash and Corradi, 1977: 92–109). But in our view, the relatively limited number of questions and answers reported on by Peppe, as well as the interpretation he gives them, emphasize unduly the degree of working-class radicalism present at that time. We report the results of the survey at some length because the questions asked cover most of the six "dimensions" of revolutionary consciousness that we have proposed as composing the concept as a whole. Peppe's sample included 260 blue collar workers, 85% male, and all unionized. They were typical factory workers in the sense of being mostly semiskilled and unskilled, and were thoroughly urbanized: 80% had never worked in agriculture.

On the critical issue of *relations between workers and owners:* 21% of respondents thought the latter had been "greatly" concerned for workers, 38% that they had been concerned, but not enough; and 40% that they had not been concerned. Roughly equal proportions, i.e., about one-third, thought relations between owners and workers would in the future be better, the same, or worse. This is not a picture of working-class consensus on an antagonistic stand vis-à-vis employers.

On the issue of alienation from the work *process and machinery,* only 34% thought the effect of modern machinery had been harmful: 41% that it would be beneficial. Sixty-one percent liked their work "a lot." However, in the kind of reversal that sometimes happens in surveys, 63%, i.e., a majority, thought it would be "bad" to install *new* machinery and only 32% thought it would be "good."

Concerning *property, i.e., private ownership of the means of production,* and specifically to whom factories should belong: 48% of these unionized blue collar workers thought factories should belong to their present capitalist owners, only 15% that workers should own them, 20% that the government should. Thus, generalized hostility to private ownership of the means of production was not at all widespread in the sphere which was of most immediate interest to them. However, 85% wanted to see U.S.-owned copper mines state controlled, and 90% were in favor of the expropriation of large farms: 60% with compensation given to owners, 30% without. The high degree of radicalism on these two positions should not, in our opinion, be ascribed to any substantial degree to "working-class consciousness." Rather they represented a kind of national consensus at the time, certainly including both the left *and* the massive center of Chile's political spectrum. President Frei's Christian Democratic government was, during these years, in the process of implementing a program of agrarian reform as well as controlling and even taking over the copper industry. The differences between Frei's progressive center position on these two issues and that of Dr. Allende's "Popular Unity" was mostly one of pace, not of principle. Even the right-wing nationalist party ultimately voted to nationalize copper!

With respect to *working-class unity,* 82% said "yes" to a generalized statement whether factory workers and peasants had "common interests" (not a very demanding indicator); but only 43% felt a work stoppage or strike should be called to support workers in another company in the same industry: 53% would limit themselves to giving economic help. For workers in other industries, rather fewer would strike, more would give economic aid. There is a good deal of solidarity. But it is hardly overwhelming.

Trade unions were rather ambivalently viewed. Reactions to union leaders as persons was quite divided: half thought they had more good qualities than bad, the other half thought the contrary. As for their own participation: 75% described themselves as attending all union meetings and 40% said they had helped in elections, made recommendations in union meetings, etc. But almost 80% did not want to become union officers: perhaps because they realized that half their fellow workers would not hold them in high regard?

In view of the fact that Marx saw unions as ultimately being beneficial to workers only if they went beyond economic demands and concerned themselves with the distribution of power in society, the question of how workers perceived the relationship between unions and politics is a crucial one. Asked whether or not unions should participate in politics, the majority (52%) were indifferent: but more thought they should not (29%) than that they should (19%). As individuals, only 12% read the communist and socialist dailies; only 33% found political and economic news the most interesting; 95% said they did not participate in a political party, an almost unbelievably high figure, but quite similar to figures for the U.S., where party activists are also few and far between, especially among the working class.

Even more mind-boggling (but really quite congruent with other analyses based on data rather than observers' impressions) are the actual choices between parties and candidates. In the then most recent presidential election, that of 1964, more of these unionized blue collar workers had voted for reformist Christian democrat Frei (35%) than for socialist Allende (27%). A third had not voted at all. And, even when asked whom they admired most on the left, only 15% named Dr. Allende: when asked to name the three people in Chile they admired most, none chose Allende, 25% chose Frei.

Not surprisingly, in view of this, as many thought the Christian democrats had helped workers more than any other party as thought the left coalition had (15% in each case: 20% thought no party had: 15% thought the right and right-center had!). Indeed, when asked what they admired most about Chile, of those who specified anything, the largest percentage (23%) praised its democratic system and political liberty.

As for *power more generally,* 22% of these blue collar workers believed that workers had "much" influence on the government, another 38% that they had "some." An equal percentage (39%) believed workers had no influence.

On other questions, a steady, but never overwhelming, majority did indicate powerlessness: 52% believed the government favored industrialists and capitalists (only 21% thought that it favored workers); 57% believed that rulers would not give workers what they deserved (only 41% believed they would).

On the matter of *economic subsistence* (material misery), 45% judged that their wages covered their needs, and 60% believed that, compared to three years previously, i.e., before the election of President Frei, they were now either better off or no worse off. Very few had been unemployed for any length of time.

As for economic injustice in its broader, national-political setting: when asked what they felt was most unjust in Chile, 56% did not answer, and while 20% referred to low wages, fewer than 5% referred to *differences* between rich and poor. "Inflation" garnered 10%, but neither various kinds of inequality (of opportunity, before the law) nor "external dependence," garnered any substantial adherents. Economic difficulties in an inflationary situation had not, apparently, resulted at that time in any massive and really intense class antagonism as distinct from concern with one's own situation. It clearly had not led to much questioning of the system.

Goldrich and his collaborators conducted a study of slum dwellers (persons living in so-called *poblaciones*) in Santiago in 1965 (Goldrich et al., in Horowitz, 1970: 175–214). Percentages ranging from *61% to 85%* were strongly against "social changes which provoke disorder," let alone the deliberate use of violence. Between 51% and 76% agreed "strongly" that "our system of government is good for the country." At the same time, however, between 44% and 62% agreed strongly that "only if things change very much will I be able to affect what the government does." We feel justified in taking slum dwellers as "proxies," so to speak, for industrial workers, because the extreme Left claimed, in the early 1970s, that these *poblaciones* were at least as radical as the average industrial worker. During the last few months of the UP government, the *comandos comunales* based in these settlements were, indeed, sometimes regarded as more radical. Yet, such systematic evidence as we have, at least from earlier years, gives no indication of any great desire on their part to mount a revolution and unleash all the turmoil it implies, as distinct from "wanting change."

Three further studies of industrial workers were conducted in the latter half of the 1960s of relevance to the issue of working-class consciousness as we have defined it.

First, we have the 1968 survey of 450 workers conducted by Lalive and Zylberberg, as described by J. Samuel Valenzuela (1976). Only 13% of their industrial workers were in favor of a "genuine revolution, violent if necessary," while 60% were in favor of "change and progressive reforms." Valenzuela, no apologist for the political right, comments on this study—and more broadly—as follows:

> Despite appearances to the contrary stemming from a tendency to shroud trade-unionist conflicts in Marxist terminology, the existence of a revolutionary consciousness was, by the end of the 1960s, a minority phenomenon among Chilean workers. The Central Unica de Trabajadores' (CUT—the Chilean labor confederation: HAL) principle that "the capitalist regime should be replaced by an economic and social system which abolishes private property" was, for example, rejected by 66.7% of Lalive's and Zylberberg's sample of 448 industrial workers . . . A majority of the workers (60.4%) chose the reformist option. The right-wing slogan ("the country needs a strong leader") received nearly twice as many preferences (21.7%) as the revolutionary alternative ("Chile needs a genuine revolution, violent if necessary": 13.3%) (Valenzuela, 1976: 158).

Also, in 1968, Alejandro Portes conducted a study of slum dwellers, on which McDaniel and I have commented at length elsewhere (Landsberger and McDaniel, 1976: 510–512). Sixty-two percent thought a "popular revolution" would be bad or very bad; only 33% thought it good or very good. On another, similar question, also posing the issue of violence, the break was 70% vs 27% and on a third, 75%:23%. Only 23% thought it important that diplomatic relations be broken with the U.S.; only 40% thought it important to establish them with Cuba. And while 62% did think it would be important to expropriate the rich—yet in the Lalive-Zylberberg survey, 67% rejected the CUT program to abolish private property.

Finally, we should mention Goodman's 1968 study of industrial workers (Goodman, 1978). Once again, it can best be summarized as showing a wide range of views. Goodman—thus, in essence confirming one of Peppe's results—found more workers thinking better of their boss than of their union (49%) than vice versa (44%). And as for identification with fellow industrial workers, he found that 56% of his blue collar workers would rather have been white collar workers, and only 43% blue collar. Goodman is quite explicitly critical of those who have given "a collective 'yes' " to the question whether workers had a collective sense of themselves as a class in situations where governments were in power representing worker interests, such as post-1959 Cuba and Chile during the popular unity government. For he found "a lack of cohesion among workers, even in a cultural-historical situation that many analysts had described as moving toward the left" (Goodman, 1978: 3).

D. Working-Class Consciousness, 1970–1973

We come now to the most overtly turbulent period in Chilean history:[5] the three years from September 1970, when Dr. Salvador Allende, a Socialist, was elected president of Chile, to September 11, 1973, when the Chilean armed forces overthrew his government in a brief but, for Chile, bloody, coup which Dr. Allende did not survive.

To document what we believe happened to working-class consciousness during these years, we will have recourse not only to attitude surveys. We will use also voting and strike statistics, accounts and interpretations of critical events such as particular strikes, the general comments and interpretations of observers close to labor and sympathetic to it (ranging from Dr. Allende himself and officials of the two main parties of this 'Unidad Popular' coalition—Communists and Socialists—to representatives of the extreme left) and other information.[6]

Radicalism at the polls. Let us first clarify to the extent possible the degree of working-class political consciousness as manifested by the support that Dr. Allende received from working-class voters in the 1970 presidential and subsequent elections. It should be recalled that Dr. Allende received just over 36% of the votes nationwide, about 1.2% more than his right-wing runner-up, and 3% less than he had received in 1964.[7]

In some mining districts such as the traditional communist strongholds of Coronel and Lota, his vote reached the 70–80% range. By contrast: in the huge Anaconda-owned copper mine in the North, Chuquicamata, he received only 43%, and in another, 41%. A reasonable estimate would be that he received 50–60% of the working-class vote overall. This is a generous estimate when compared with the reported results of a survey conducted a month before the election. In such polls, individuals are, of course, questioned directly, instead of inferring from electoral districts, which is a dubious procedure. The survey indicated that only 51% of industrial workers supported Dr. Allende (Smith and Rodrigues, 1974).

Later voter surveys, in 1972 for example, reported fewer than 50% of "lower-class respondents" favoring Dr. Allende. They also reported relatively small percentages of this group (27%) evaluating his performance as "good," and relatively high percentages as holding the U.P government as "partly" or "wholly" responsible for "the climate of violence prevailing in the country" (40%).

But these figures, all from the weekly *Ercilla*, which was not friendly to the government, and reporting on polls which, in retrospect, could also be questioned, need to be put alongside actual voting statistics. Dr. Allende received 50% overall, countrywide support in the municipal elections of 1971. And even in the March 1973 Congressional elections, the UP parties retained the support of 43% of all voters. These voting results could not have been achieved (especially in the face of declining middle-class support) but for very substantial working-class voting (see also A. Valenzuela, 1978: 86–87). A 2:1 ratio in the UP's favor throughout these years seems a reasonable, if generous, guess, especially since this was also the ratio in the famous 1972 national elections for the Central Trade Union Confederation (CUT). There, Christian Democrats appear to have obtained just under a third of the vote, the PS and PC's candidates about two-thirds; the extreme left about 2%.[8]

In sum, the facts—as distinct from their interpretation—seem clear. A mature working class, such as the Chilean, will vote quite substantially for the candidates of left-wing parties. They do so for Labour in Britain, and for the SPD in Germany today (and the SPD and KPD in pre-Hitler Germany).

But voting is a very limited act: it is costless (hence does not in itself prove a high level of commitment) and its exact meaning is not clear-cut. As we have already noted in connection with the study of local union officers: voting for and even identifying with a party does not necessarily imply either understanding of, much less support for, some of its more sophisticated ideological positions. Critics of all political hues have long expressed their reservations about parliamentary systems because they relegate the citizen to being a mere episodic voter: an act considered by many to be meaningless and trivial.

Quite apart, then, from the fact that a minimum of 40% of the working class did not vote for Dr. Allende in 1970, the issue arises: how can we establish more precisely what support for him really meant? Did it indeed represent growing political awareness of the destructive nature of the whole capitalist system? Or was it, rather, indicative of support for a government which was perceived as likely to satisfy short-run consumption demands, both narrowly economic and those of a more general, "quality of life" kind, such as demands for health care, education, and leisure? Our interpretation is that workers voted chiefly—not exclusively, but chiefly—for higher consumption both in its more narrow economic and its broader form.

1. Labor's "Economism"

At one particularly critical juncture, the government itself certainly acted upon the premise that labor's vote was economistically determined, and in that sense almost literally "purchaseable." Despite possibly adverse economic repercussions, it decreed a 35% raise in wages in December 1970, three months before the March 1971 municipal elections. The reason was, as Pedro Vuskovic (Minister of Economic Affairs) said a year later:

> —economic policy is subordinate, in its content, shape, and form to the political need of increasing the Popular Unity's support. There is an imbalance between the level of electoral support with which the Government came to office and the size of the groups which will benefit from the Government's programmes. Accordingly, a central objective of economic policy is to widen political support for the Government, to the extent this is compatible with other aspects of the programme (Zammit, 1973: 50).

Other participants in the conference at which Professor Vuskovic spoke also agreed that "a short-term policy of material benefits to build up the basis of support for future change was necessary and simpler than the immediate pursuit of irreversible structural changes" (Zammit, 1973: 83).

One indicator of worker consciousness—although its meaning is perhaps even less self-evident than the meaning of a vote—is the *degree of strike activity*. Chilean strike statistics are good, and certain ratios can be calculated from them which permit tentative interpretations to be made, confidence in which can then be strengthened by drawing on comments made at the time by knowledgeable actors and observers.

The facts are quite clear (Table 5). Strike activity as well as union membership (Table 6) increased dramatically during the two years (1971 and 1972) of UP government for which there are complete statistics. As Table 5 shows, the number of strikes in 1971 almost tripled as compared with 1969 and went up by another 20% in 1972, while the total number of workers involved in strikes increased 31% in 1972 over 1971. And strikes in the increasingly important socialized and public sectors constituted a very substantial proportion of strike activity. In 1972, 29% of all man-days lost were lost in the public sector.

Were it not for the intense strike activity in the public sector, it would be possible to interpret this increase in strike activity as indicating height-ened conflict between an increasingly militant working class and its his-

Table 5. Strikes 1959–1972

Year	Col. (1) Number of strikes	Col. (2) % Increase over previous date, on per-annum basis	Col. (3) Total number of workers involved	Col. (4) % Increase over previous date, on per-annum basis	Col. (5) Total number of mandays lost	Col. (6) % Increase over previous date, on per-annum basis
1959	204	—	82,188	—	869,728	—
1960	245	20	88,518	8	N.A.	—
1963	416	23	117,084	11	N.A.	—
1965	723	37	182,359	28	N.A.	—
1966	1,073	48	195,435	7	2,015,253	19
1969	977	− 3	275,406	13	972,382	−16
1971	2,709	88	302,397	5	1,414,313	23
Number, and as % of total, in public sector*	(332; 12%)		(50,431; 17%)		(132,479; 10%)	
1972	3,289	21	397,142	31	1,654,151	17
Number, and as % of total, in public sector*	(815; 25%)		(135,037; 34%)		(476,965; 29%)	

Source: Landsberger and McDaniel, 1976:520, Table 3.
*Separate subtotals for the public and private sectors were given only in Dr. Allende's presidential messages. If the totals for previous years did not include public sector strikes—and we believe they were included—then this table exaggerates the increase in strike activity between 1971 and 1969. Even then, however, the very high strike activity in 1971 and 1972, and the high and increasing percentage of it taking place in the public sector, are revealing. See text.
References: 1959–1969: Mensaje del Presidente, May 1970, pp. 366, 368–69; 1971: Mensaje del Presidente, May 1972, pp. 853–854; 1972: Mensaje del Presidente, May 1973, pp. 788–789.

Table 6. Number of Unions and Members by Type; Percentage of Increase over Previous Years; and Percentage of Labor Force in Unions, 1955–1972

Year	Professional Unions[a]			Industrial Unions[b]			Agricultural Unions[a]			Total[a]			% Union Labor Force
	No.	Members	% Increase[c]	No.	Members	% Increase[c]	No.	Members	% Increase[c]	No.	Members	% Increase[c]	
1955	1,495	140,373	—	660	162,937	—	22	1,877	—	2,177	305,192	—	12.1
1960	1,144	108,687	-22.4	608	122,306	-24.9	18	1,424	-24.1	1,770	232,417	-23.9	10.1
1964	1,207	125,929	15.9	632	142,958	16.9	24	1,658	16.4	1,863	270,542	16.4	10.3
1966	1,679	161,363	28.2	990	179,506	25.6	201	10,647	542.2	2,870	350,516	29.6	12.8
% Annual Increase over 1964			14.4			12.8			271.0			14.8	
1970	2,569	239,323	28.1	1,440	197,651	10.1	510	114,112	971.2	4,519	551,086	57.2	19.4
% Annual Increase over 1964			15.0			6.4			1,130.0			17.3	
1972	3,511	282,181	17.9	1,781[c]	213,777[c]	8.2	709	136,527	19.6	6,001	632,485	14.8	22.2
% Annual Increase over 1970			9.0			4.1			9.8			7.9	

Source: Landsberger and McDaniel, 1976:518, Table 2.
a. From Tables 2–4, Mensaje Presidente Allende Ante Congreso Pleno, May 21, 1973, pp. 793–94.
b. From Table 5, Mensaje del Presidente Allende Ante El Congreso Pleno, May 21, 1972, p. 861.
c. Calculated by authors.

toric antagonist, capital. But when the strikes are, essentially, against a worker-based government, such an interpretation becomes impossible to sustain unless one thinks of the UP government and its relatively gradualist policies as representing some kind of betrayal of the working class, and of workers in explicit protest against such a betrayal. But while some extreme left interpretations have come close to imputing betrayal to the UP, as described, for example, in Roxborough, O'Brien, and Roddick (1977: 220), even the left has not gone on to interpret worker militancy as explicitly and consciously directed at the government for that reason.

The government itself, including Dr. Allende, and above all the Communist party—which played a restraining role throughout—as well as the CUT, certainly interpreted the strikes as motivated by the short-sighted search for immediate economic benefits, and as a very grave threat to the government. The obvious pleasure with which Dr. Allende referred in his May 1972 Presidential Message to the very slight decrease in strike activity in the first three months of 1972 is just one indication of how much concern strikes were arousing.

Just a few weeks after Dr. Allende's election, when the copper miners in Chuquicamata went on strike for a 70% wage increase, Dr. Allende berated them as a "labor aristocracy." A year later he again visited "Chuqui," and complained bitterly that unauthorized strikes there had cost the country $36 million in 1970 *after* settlement of the earlier strike; and that a further $12 million had been lost by the time of his next visit in October 1971. Strikes, and production losses in the copper mines due to other labor problems, such as the careless handling of machinery, were a constant worry to the government throughout the UP regime. The disciplining of a worker, in Chuquicamata, for abandoning his workplace and causing costly damage (for the second time) resulted in an immediate and then a further ninety-six partial strikes and several general strikes there in 1972 alone (Zapata, 1975: 56; Gall, 1972). In 1973, in connection with a seventy-five-day strike in Chile's other major copper mine—El Teniente—Dr. Allende was quoted as saying, after the strikers had invaded the Ministry of Labor: "If the workers do not understand the process of change through which we are living, I'll simply go, and then you'll see the consequences" (*Ercilla*, May 30, 1973, No. 1976: 8). At a later point he said that "Neither revolutionary consciousness nor morality exists among the workers." Earlier, in January 1973, he made his presidential headquarters for two days in the nationalized textile plant *Sumar* in order to resolve labor problems there and attempt to dampen excessive wage demands, including the demand that workers be paid in goods which they could then sell on the black market.

Nor was Dr. Allende alone. Leaders of the Socialist party (not to mention the PC) and the CUT itself repeatedly expressed extreme concern about workers' wage demands. The CUT listed the limitation of salary increases as well as of prices as the first task of the workers (*La Nacion*, October 30, 1972: 16); it declared that it would send teachers from its union school to train workers to understand their responsibility to raise production and have profits go to "all of Chile" (*Puro Chile*, December 5, 1971, Supplement:20). And the socialist president of a blue collar union admitted that his party had taught workers to be "economistic" and that in order to change this, "we're letting the workers in on the problems of the plant. If they know how much is spent and produced, they'll know how much they can ask" (*Ercilla*, July 26, 1972: 27).

It is clear, then, that workers' wage demands indicated almost a boundless degree of economism and were interpreted as such by a wide range of observers who wished it were otherwise.

2. Leisure, Freedom from Authority, and the Abolition of Status Denigration

Higher wages were not, however, the only "good" being increasingly demanded by workers in this three-year period. Widespread absenteeism, indiscipline at work, and aggressive behavior toward supervisory, technical, and managerial personnel, as well as toward high status groups in general, were all commented upon by sympathetic observers. In order not to lengthen this paper unduly, we will not cover these topics with references to various particular situations. The reader may rest assured that this could easily be done.

Rather, we wish to give an interpretation to absenteeism, indiscipline, and hostility toward those regarded as having higher status, which is less negative than the valuation stimulated by these particular words and phrases—an interpretation which links them to Marx's ideas about the nature of man, alienation, and freedom. Absenteeism is, after all, not only a way of fleeing a disliked task (alienation from process), it is also one avenue for expanding the time available for leisure, for engaging in non-work-related activities. At least, this is so unless the time is used to earn additional income; e.g., by selling goods in the black market. (This did in fact occur on a scale sufficient to arouse a great deal of concern on the part of the government including Minister Vuskovic and Dr. Allende himself. Indeed, the government at one point planned to institute special penalties for absenteeism, black market activities, and other forms of economic misconduct by workers.)

Increased indiscipline at work, such as disobeying rules and ignoring instructions from supervisors, were also widely remarked upon as bedevilling the economy, not least in the newly socialized sector (APS—"area of social property"). But this, too, can be conceptualized less negatively as freeing oneself from authority wherever encountered. And the kind of provocativeness shown to professionals who, though in the same organization were not in a direct authority relationship, can be conceptualized as a challenge to society's traditional prestige hierarchy, which places rank and file workers below almost everyone, at least in the work setting. In hospitals, physicians felt various infringements on their status and status-linked perquisites to be so intolerable that they went on a forty-eight-hour work stoppage in one of Santiago's key hospitals in June 1973. They included in a bill of demands presented to the government in August 1973 one which stipulated that the "campaign of contempt" against physicians be stopped.

It would seem, then, that the demand of workers for higher relative status, and for respect from others, for freedom from the constraints of rules and authority figures, and for release from irksome labor may be pursued not only against class antagonists. They may also be pursued against, or at least to the severe detriment of, a government partly elected by workers, which is attempting to implant a new social structure or laying the groundwork for doing so. At this stage of urgently wanting "freedom from"—from new duties and responsibilities, perhaps, as well as from really irksome constraints—workers may not even value highly the opportunity to participate in new decision-making structures especially set up for them.

On December 7, 1970, three months after the presidential elections, the new government signed an agreement with the CUT (Central Confederation of Labor) setting out so-called Fundamental Norms which would govern workers' participation at all levels, from national planning to plant-level administration. It would apply, especially, to the new "Area of Social Property," i.e., the state-owned sector which was to be drastically expanded. By early 1973, it consisted of 250 firms and accounted for 80% of industrial production according to one source (*The Economist*, Feb. 24, 1973: 14–15), although according to another, it consisted of 320 firms with only 35% of industrial production (Zimbalist and Stallings, 1973: 10).

The predominant evaluation of the participation program was, at the time, that it was functioning rather poorly even where it had been installed at all. Formal installation had occurred in only 170 plants, and in only thirty-five of these was there genuine worker involvement (Zimbalist and Stallings, 1973: 12). Even American observers sympathetic to the idea of mass participation such as Petras (1973) did not see Chilean workers as desirous of involving themselves even where the opportunity was there to do so. Zimbalist and Stallings (1973: 12) warned of the "severe implications" consequent on the UP's failure to "develop the latter variety of working-class consciousness."[9]

Experienced Chileans such as Luis Figueroa, President of the CUT, and many others, shared this view (*El Siglo*, April 9, 1972, Supplement: 8–9). Apparently, the combined desire for more material wealth, and for freedom, even from the constraints implied by the acceptance of new, positive responsibilities, was stronger than the psychic returns from such new decision-making responsibilities that workers could envision.

Whether in the form of strikes or of absenteeism and indiscipline, workers seemed to have a need to express restlessness and negativism, to assert themselves even against "their own" government. If such a pent-up need is indeed a necessary consequence of the *ancien regime*, it does not augur well for a smooth transition to socialism even as far as workers are concerned, let alone other classes. And this brings us to the question of a "latent revolutionary consciousness" and the possibility of its "exploding," as discussed by Mann (1973: 40ff.), referring especially to the ideas of Robin Blackburn and Henri Lefebvre.

3. The Explosion of Revolutionary Consciousness?

For there is one series of events in this whole complex, contradictory, and confusing three-year history to which we have so far not referred. It is the establishment of so-called *cordones industriales* (literally: "industrial belts," but perhaps "bulwarks" or "barricades" is closer to the real meaning, since they did often take over and block streets as well as organize factory takeovers). These were locality-based organizations, grouping together workers from various plants in a district. The first of the *cordones* was established in June 1972 in the Los Cerillos industrial district of Santiago in support of workers striking in one of the plants. But they spread to other parts of Santiago, and to other cities, as the year progressed, and especially during "the bosses' " strike in October 1972.

The *cordones* for a long time were not controlled by the CUT, much to the latter's discomfort, nor by the established political parties, especially not by the relatively cautious Communists. Their demands for institutional restructuring clearly went substantially beyond what the government intended to do for the time being. They called for, and implemented, further factory takeovers. They called for a Popular Assembly parallel to Parliament, an original UP plank which the government had quickly abandoned. They called for a takeover of urban real estate, not only agricultural land; they attacked the bourgeois judicial system. They advocated worker and peasant control over the bureaucracy, and over production in general. And their support of the government of Dr. Allende was proclaimed as going only "so far as it interprets the struggles and mobilizations of the workers" (Roxborough, et al., 1977: 170–171).

The establishment of "communal commandos," based on town sectors, soon followed. These had their origin in, but went far beyond, the neighborhood-based, so-called People's Supply Committees (JAPs) which the government itself had set up in late 1971 to help distribute equitably the increasingly scarce supplies of food and other staples. The

cordones and *comandos,* on the other hand, sprang up—and soon feder-
ated—in total independence of the government or of any other previously
existing organization, although the MIR and the Left-Socialists, of
course, welcomed them. In essence, the *comandos* and *cordones* began to
crystallize into a parallel system of power. They soon issued statements
critical of the CUT and of the government, especially Minister Millas'
plan, proposed in January 1973 to return illegally seized factories to their
private owners.

By mid-1973, after the attempted coup (half-hearted) of an armored
brigade on June 29, the CUT decided to attempt to co-opt the *cordones*
rather than cold-shoulder them. But the government, half willingly, half
under implicit pressure from the military, refused to sanction continued
activism on the part of these organizations, even as a counterweight to the
June 29 mutiny. Nor did the government back the *cordones* against the
truck owners, when they began their second strike at the end of July 1973.
Lack of government encouragement was certainly among the reasons
why the *cordones* did not maintain their upward momentum, though it
would be wrong to think of them as decaying. However, on September 11,
hearing no clear call to resist, and/or because of the loss of momentum as
well as lack of organization and arms, neither the *cordones* nor any
substantial sector of the working class offered widespread resistance to
the army coup.

The *cordones* could certainly be interpreted as expressing several of the
dimensions of revolutionary consciousness: (1) a recognition of capitalism
as an interrelated system in which political, economic, and judicial institutions are all intertwined; (2) recognition, at least at the level of declarations, of the identity of the interests of the working class, (3) recognition
of the opposed interests of the bourgeoisie; (4) awareness of and action
upon the need to confront the bourgeoisie actively and, in short, (5)
awareness of the need to move toward a revolution as fast as possible.

The questions are: How widespread and how deep was involvement in
the *cordones*? Who formulated their militant ideology? To what extent
were individuals who were (more or less) active in the *cordones* also
committed to their ideology? In other words, to what extent was this a
focused attack specifically on the bourgeoisie and capitalism rather than
the release of pent-up aggression and other feelings, which would choose
a wide range of even friendly targets? In the sense that nothing like this
had ever happened before in Chile, the *cordones* certainly did represent a
more intense level of (general) militancy. And this might indeed have been
an example of the kind of latent revolutionary consciousness, ready to
"explode," to which Blackburn and Lefebvre had drawn attention.

But it is very difficult to decide between these two interpretations—that we are dealing specifically with revolutionary consciousness and not with a more generalized, relief-seeking militancy and, in any case, how much of an increase in militancy? Did militancy increase from embracing 2% of the workers to embracing 4%? Or 10%? or 40%? And beyond the level of declarations, and of establishing organizations at a time when official repression was not to be feared: what did it mean? What did it imply about the possibility of further action?

We have no very conclusive answers to these questions. Objective evidence does not exist about such critical matters as the number of workers involved in the *cordones,* let alone about the degree of their involvement. Indeed, it is difficult to imagine what kind of clear-cut evidence could ever be adduced to establish that a person, or a group, is committed at one level rather than another.

Observers who were close to the scene were divided in their evaluations, and sometimes even the same person's assessment differed from one time to another. Some observers, such as Winn (1976), saw a dramatic increase in radicalism both in extent and in level. Others, such as Petras (1976), were clearly much more cautious. Zimbalist and Stallings (1973) in an article written days before the coup emphasize both rising worker radicalism and also continued "economism." But on the question of spontaneity and whose ideology the proclamations of the *cordones* really represented, they make the following interesting comment:

> The revolutionary action of the working class, although not organized by the government *per se,* was not spontaneous. Local cadres of the PS, MAPU, MIR, IC and PCR (Revolutionary Communist Party—not the official PC:HAL) were largely responsible for the agitation and leadership of the working class during October (Zimbalist and Stallings, 1973: 6).

Above all, J. Samuel Valenzuela and Arturo Valenzuela, who have weighed carefully as much as possible of the evidence pertinent to the question of "how much working-class radicalism?" conclude, in essence, "not much." Arturo Valenzuela cites evidence to the effect that even in *Nuevo La Habana,* a shanty town controlled by the MIR, clientilistically oriented economism rather than ideological commitment predominated (A. Valenzuela, 1978, f.n. 66:126). J. Samuel Valenzuela, in an essay specifically dealing with the labor movement, concludes the section dealing with the period immediately before the coup as follows:

> It is thus not surprising that organized workers supported the Allende government when political pressures from the Right threatened it. While many workers did so out of a commitment to fundamental change, for most it was a question of defending an administration from which they expected to receive the greatest benefit (Valenzuela and Valenzuela, 1976: 164).

And with reference to the *cordones* specifically and the question of "how many workers were really involved?" Arturo Valenzuela sums up the situation as follows:

> Despite the enormous publicity [given] to the *cordones*, they never constituted a massive force. . . . Though perhaps five thousand workers were mobilized, that number was a small fraction of the Santiago working class. In interviews with the author, a sociologist from the University of Chile who was working closely with the Cordon Los Cerillos put the active members at only a few hundred. The account by Patricia Santa Lucia . . . which paints a picture of a strong movement in the text, reveals the weakness of the cordones in an appendix which attempts to list cordones and their membership (A. Valenzuela, 1978, f.n. 58: 131).

This portrayal is supported by Hugo Blanco, the Peruvian Trotskyist, who, as late as June 1973, reported that the MIR had little support among urban workers in the establishment of the *cordones*.

In our opinion, changes in working-class consciousness during the three turbulent years of UP government can best be described as follows: (1) There was a general, but not overwhelming shift to the (non-extreme) left. Otherwise the UP surely could not have increased its support at the polls from 36% in September 1970 to 43% in March 1973. The latter, however, represented a recession from the 50% high-water mark of March 1971: the customary "off year" let down, if nothing else. (2) There surely was an increase in the support of revolutionary positions, but all carefully thought-through evidence, and all objective evidence—such as votes in union elections—indicate that the increase was not large, and that support for the extreme left remained small. (3) There is at least as much evidence from the results of various union elections that, in the last few months before the coup, the strength of moderate views, i.e., PDC adherents, increased. And it was always vastly superior to the extreme left. (4) Thus, polarization more than anything else characterized the working class in 1973, as it did the rest of Chilean society.

In the case of Chile, this polarization did not replace a previously unified central position. It represented, rather, a more clearly visible crystallized set of "extremes"[10] which had always existed, albeit in a more low-keyed form, on either side of a mildly left working-class majority posture. The two "extremes" had become much more active and vocal, but there is no indication that they had really changed very significantly in size. There is no evidence that the ideology represented by the *cordones* and the MIR attracted even 10% of workers. And there is no evidence that the Christian democratic position ever attracted fewer than 25% (or more than 35%) of workers.

E. Chilean Working-Class Consciousness: A Summary

Word portraits of groups should not be advanced with exaggerated certainty when they are based, as they are in this instance, on very different kinds of information, drawn from different subgroups (union leaders, industrial workers, shanty town dwellers) and over a span of ten years. Nevertheless, this very heterogeneity of method, time, and group may lend confidence to one's conclusions when the evidence always seems to support them.

As one juxtaposes Marx's ideas of working-class consciousness (especially in the period immediately preceding revolution) with what we know about Chile, the balance sheet looks somewhat as follows:

(1) A government like that of the early 1960s, i.e., an essentially conservative, establishment government, does not inspire widespread confidence that its policies will benefit working people, or that working class people can do much to influence it. There is a vision of an unfriendly, unresponsive system.

(2) Political alienation in that sense, however, did not lead working-class respondents to withdraw their support for Chile's political system as a whole—its then regnant presidential and parliamentary system, based on competing political parties. Many were aware and proud of Chile's democratic tradition. Their realistic perception that many politicians were feathering their own nests and/or representing interests opposed to theirs was not enough to arouse massive skepticism of the system as a whole. One also needs to remember that there are probably many groups in society—small businessmen, farmers—who do not feel that the state is adequately looking after their interests. Workers, quite correctly, are likely to see this as being the case more strongly than other groups. There may be a point beyond which a quantitatively more intense disillusionment changes into a qualitatively different total alienation. Somehow, the survey statistics and other indicators do not give us the feeling that the Chilean working class ever reached that degree of alienation.

(3) The above assessment is strengthened by the absolutely consistent results indicating that the Chilean working class, in its great majority, did not believe in a violent overthrow of existing institutions. All surveys bear this out. And even if the proportion who accepted violence increased up to a level of 10% or even 15%, that may indicate that there is enough support so that one *can* make a revolution in the right circumstances. It does not mean that "the" working class wants it to happen.

(4) There is a consistent, unresolved division of opinion among workers (and their leaders) as to whether unionism and politics should be linked.

To many it clearly makes sense, both in terms of long-term ideological plans and also in terms of the immediate practical desirability of influencing the government. However, many workers do not like the mixture of the two, for the even more practical reason that it tends to divide an already weak labor movement. It also increases the chance that union leaders will be perceived as unresponsive to their members' wishes. This would represent a loss of confidence which that relationship can ill bear, in view of the low evaluation that, as Peppe's study shows, union leaders receive from their members even when compared with the members' employers. The politicization of the labor movement that Marx had considered essential was regarded as an evil by many workers. And confidence in the union leadership was not great, nor was the union movement a symbol of working-class unity. It was a divided movement.

(5) Resentment at employer-owner-capitalist (call it what you will) was not particularly intense. However, we need to acknowledge that the observer's frame of reference plays as large a role in arriving at this kind of conclusion as do the facts "out there." I start from the position that there is a rather high baseline of resentment among workers—lowly or high—in any society we yet know, over uninteresting tasks, arbitrary authority, inequitable rewards, and insufficient attention to one's own peculiar position and needs. This may not be true of the alternative societies that we can design in our imagination, and that we would like to see established. In these, everyone is satisfied, by definition of our imaginations. But we know nothing about the practical possibilities of their existing and, for that reason, they do not constitute a very helpful baseline for judging what is to be considered a "high" level of dissatisfaction with one's work, wages, employer, etc. If that is the case, the kinds of results obtained by Peppe and by ourselves concerning such issues as optimism about future relations of labor to management do not strike us as indicating any exceptional degree of alienation. When 60% of industrial workers think that employers have been concerned about workers (even if 38% felt: "not enough"); when 61% like their work "a lot"; 50% do not want to see their owners expropriated—then it is not appropriate, in our opinion, to speak of extreme alienation nor growing revolutionary consciousness, especially when highly divided political loyalties and a good deal of skepticism about unions and parties (including left wing parties) is added to the picture.

Above all, what comes through at the level of working-class behavior during the Allende years is the desire for consumption here and now, regardless of national repercussions. This was very similar to the manner in which the U.S. public, and most other publics, are acting with respect to energy and income demands as this is being written. Consumption was defined by workers not only—though largely—in terms of more goods and services. It was also defined in terms of freedom from work, from rules and direction, and from personal denigration. According to Marx, that is inherent in our natures, though he thought of us as containing an element of caring for others and for the community as a whole, a good deal, but institutionally not sufficient amount of which apparently was also seen in Chile during the early 1970s.

The transition to socialism is known to be made difficult by capitalists. Marxist economists have long predicted that a half-socialist and half-capitalist economy will be difficult to run, as capitalists lose the incentive to invest (which is very different from sabotage, of which there was much accusation in Chile but little hard evidence adduced). Perhaps we need to be aware also of difficulties on the worker side. The desire and actual demands for a better life, material and otherwise, are ready to burst forth as soon as a sympathetic government is seen to be in place. Such resentment against the system as has been built up is also then likely to burst forth, lashing out at all restraints: those emanating from a friendly government, not only those stemming from the class enemy. The components of the kind of working-class consciousness Marx envisioned do not necessarily evolve in the coherent manner he expected, and they may be out of phase with the gradual political evolution that he, in his later life, envisioned, but for which his theory of working-class consciousness, formulated much earlier, did not make allowance. In addition to a law of "Unequal Development," which Trotsky formulated for societies, we evidently need a law of "Unequal Development" for the subjective level of working-class consciousness.

III. GERMAN WORKING-CLASS CONSCIOUSNESS, 1918–1920

The main value of a comparison between two countries, and two eras, as different from each other as Chile in the 1970s and Germany in 1918 are as follows:

A. The Parallels: Chile and Germany

First: Both countries had organizationally well-developed, historically long-standing working-class movements both in the form of trade unions and in the form of political parties with strong support among workers and close links to their trade unions. In both countries, however, this triangular relationship [class-party(ies) -union(s)] was not without complications.

Second: In both countries, governments with a socialist orientation, and certainly rooted in the working class, came to power: in 1918 in Germany, in 1970 in Chile. Yet in both countries, the question immediately arose: how fast, if at all, did the two governments really want to move toward a socialist society? and above all: did they put retention of the good will of the middle class and of the armed forces ahead of, or behind, the more substantive goals of advancing toward socialism? In other words, was the government willing to risk a confrontation?

The obverse of this issue is whether the extreme left (the Spartacists under Luxemburg and Liebknecht) or the Majority Socialists under Ebert and Scheidemann better represented the mood of the working class. This is equivalent to the point made by the extreme left with respect to Chile: that Senator Altamirano (leader of the Left-Socialists), the MIR, and other extreme groups should have broken formally with the remainder of the UP to lead the working class into a revolution, once it became apparent that Allende and the Communist party were unwilling to do so, or to do anything whatever that might foreclose the possibility of an agreement with the PDC and the Army. This is the kind of position taken by Roxborough, et al. (1977). Others, of course, argue the exact opposite: that Allende and the PC should have broken formally with their own left, since not doing so—it turns out—saved nothing, while doing so might have salvaged the system from total destruction. It is the latter policy, of course (breaking with each other) which was pursued by the two extreme wings of the Social Democratic party in Germany, but not by the critical center (the so-called USPD).

Ryder (1967) treats this point extensively, coming up with a conclusion which some would repeat for Chile. He devotes much of his final analysis to the role of the Independent Socialists (USPD), the "center" of the socialist spectrum, and their leader Haase. Ryder summarizes sympathetically the argument that the inevitability of this "great tragedy" (Ryder, 1967: 270) might have been halted had the USPD and Haase "backed by the right and centre of the party, had the courage then to repudiate the putschists and extremists. . . . [But] by making concessions to an ultimately insatiable left wing, the party's leaders may well have simply postponed a split which they could not avert. Had they been bold and decisive enough to divide the party at a time when such a move could still have affected the fortunes of the German revolution, they would at least have . . . based [the split on] German needs." The actual sentence reads: "at least have prevented the split from being organized by Moscow for reasons based on Russian rather than German needs." In Chile, there was no split, nor any Moscow responsible for one. We extract the idea that a split based on German (Chilean, *mutatis mutandis*) needs would have been appropriate, and that the center of the socialists should have made it.

Third: Both countries experienced a rash of what were, at the time, euphemistically called "extra-legal" activities of a politically significant kind, in some of which members of the working class clearly played an important part. There were, of course, substantial differences between Chile and Germany. In Chile, nonviolent takeovers of factories and farms, and the passive blocking of roads was all that happened. In Germany, on the other hand, there were very serious armed uprisings on the part of both the extreme left (e.g., the so-called Spartacist revolt of January 1919 in Berlin) and on the part of the extreme right (e.g., the Kapp Putsch in 1920). Left-inspired uprisings occurred—to name but a few—in the region of Munich, Leipzig, and Halle, and ended in the spring of 1920 in the Ruhr Valley. There was, too, in both countries, the phenomenon of parallel power. In Germany, these consisted of workers' and soldiers' councils, the Revolutionary Shop Stewards' Committee, and others; in Chile, in the industrial *cordones* and the neighborhood *comandos* and their federations. With respect to all of these, the question at issue is: how many workers were really involved? with what kind, and degree, of ideological commitment?

Fourth: In both countries, these socialist regimes came to an end without succeeding in implanting major institutional changes. In Germany the socialist governments petered out in the mid-twenties, though the atmosphere continued to be a disturbed one, with political assassinations, street confrontations, etc. But a right wing coup—i.e., Hitler's ascent to power—did not occur until some time later, in 1933. In Chile, the military and the right intervened directly to oust the UP government, dismantling a substantial proportion of the institutional changes that had been undertaken.

From the point of view of the issue of working-class consciousness, two points are of interest. One is, of course, the obvious substantive one of the degree to which the German working class was or was not imbued with 'revolutionary consciousness' in the period 1910–1920. Much as in Chile, the Ebert-Scheidemann "Majority Socialist" regime was accused by the extreme left of betrayal—of agreeing to demands from the Army, and from civilian bourgeois groups, to which there was no need to agree given the psychological readiness of the working class. This, too, was the accusation against Dr. Allende from mid-1972 onwards whenever he engaged in negotiations with the Christian Democrats, or invited representatives of the Armed Forces into the government. What, exactly, was the state of mind of the German working class?

The second point, as in the case of Chile, is methodological: what kind of evidence exists for Germany to answer the substantive question we have just posed?

B. The Question of Evidence and Data

The evidence available for an analysis of why the revolution didn't happen, and what the working class, both rank and file and leadership, contributed to that fact, is far greater for Germany than for Chile. There are vastly more and better records of every kind except surveys, in which those who are convinced that radicalism exists on a large scale generally place least stock—hence they will not miss this particular form of evidence!

The German data have been analyzed over a period far longer than necessarily can be the case for Chile, by many more scholars. And even those who appear to wish to sustain that the German working class was "revolutionary" seem to be forced to conclude that:

1. The evidence for *any* dogmatic assertion about the state of mind of the German working class simply is not there. It is interesting to note that an historian as traditional as Geary, in the kind of data he uses and his manner of using it, decries the absence of "hard, quantitative data" (Geary, 1978: 270).
2. Such evidence as does exist justifies the conclusion that a wide range of views existed among the German working class, and that it cannot be described as "predominantly" revolutionary.

If this is true for Germany (where Marxist thinking and the idea of revolution was closer at hand and in which the imperialist establishment had suffered a disastrous military defeat, causing terrible suffering among the working class) we should expect the same in the case of Chile. Its working class had not suffered comparably, nor had it seen its masters defeated. The idea of a working-class revolution might be expected to be further away than in a Europe which had known 1789, 1848, and 1870. Obviously, such *a priori* reasoning needs to be supported by whatever evidence there is, as we hope to do.

C. The Mood of the German Working Class

Concerning now our substantive point: by far the most comprehensive recent attempt to reevaluate the degree of radicalism among the German working class in the period after World War I—indeed, from 1848 onward—is Barrington Moore's *Injustice: The Social Bases of Obedience and Revolt* (1978), a book devoted entirely to that problem. Moore obviously was writing with the Marxian thesis in mind—"catastrophe as the necessary prelude to utopia" (Moore, 1978: xvii)—toward which he is "skeptical." And while Moore's skepticism is known to antedate this book, he cannot be considered, even remotely, a hard-bitten anti-Marxist merely looking for new examples to prove his point. And his choice of Germany, like mine in this essay, was similarly based on his regarding the German working class as having been subjected to "some of the most important things that have happened to workers in other countries . . . but in more intense form" (Moore, 1978: xv).

Moore's evaluation of the evidence, including the judgment of others who have investigated the issue, is similar in essence (not in detail) to the theses which we maintain about Chile.

Moore sees workers protesting less about the system as a whole than about their working conditions, especially about extreme authoritarianism, personal abuse, and denigration. It was the recent, and young, migrant to the city (as in Hamilton's 1967 study of French workers in the 1950s), not the experienced members of the working class, except for craftsmen threatened by mechanization, who became radical. But in any case, Moore's position is that "the different forms of radicalism all appear to have been a minority current among German workers most of the time" (Moore: 320). In subsequent pages, Moore states that the leaders of the plant-council movement and the workers involved in it gave no evidence of working toward a revolutionary uprising even if some "political outriders" did, and that even the largest of the armed uprisings—the "Red Army" of the Ruhr, with its possibly 80,000–120,000 men between March 13–20, 1920—was essentially defensive, sparked as a reaction to the extreme-right Kapp Putsch. This is reminiscent, of course, of the reaction of the *cordones* to the June 1973 *tancazo*. In Germany the workers even tried to enroll in the security forces under conditions that made this an indication that they did not regard the situation as a revolutionary one. As in Chile, Moore stresses that "Even in the heat of battle, proletarian unity was evidently a myth; the reality was sectarian struggle" (Moore, 1978: 345). And finally,

Over and over again the evidence reveals that the mass of the workers was not revolutionary. They did not want to overturn the existing social order and replace it with something else, least of all one where ordinary workers would be in charge. They were, however, very angry. They were backed into a corner and fought in self-defense. The defense turned rather unexpectedly into a brief offensive. Even then it is clear that many of those workers who were not under arms had no interest in turning the struggle into a revolution. The revolutionary ingredient, such as it was in the whole struggle, was something that only a minority of the local political leaders tried to impose on the whole movement (Moore, 1978: 351).

This may be too extreme a judgement. Certainly Geary's 1978 essay, to which we have already referred, is intended to pull the literature back from an extreme non-revolutionary interpretation. But Geary neither can, nor wishes to, do more than refute the extreme thesis that only war weariness and the desire for political democracy (Geary, 1978: 267) were at the root of the unrest of those years.

Geary makes a convincing case for including a definite radical current as one of a very wide and complex range of postures in Germany's working class. But it should include, too, according to Geary, a goodly place for ignorance and confusion. The slogan of Kiel's socialists: "Scheidemann for President, Liebknecht for Minister of Defence" (Geary, 1978: 271) would have corresponded in Chile to: "Carlos Briones for President, Miguel Enriquez to the Ministry of the Interior." And, again as a precursor of Chile, Geary notes how many workers were thoroughly fed up with factionalism ["Down with fratricide! Workers' unity without leaders" was one slogan (Geary, 1978: 272)]. And even when protesting the killing of leftist workers, they did not wish this to be interpreted as support for any particular faction (Geary, 1978: 272). But in the end, he concludes: "It would be arrant nonsense to claim that what was involved in these struggles was a real threat of revolution in Wilhelmine Germany" (Geary, 1978: 280).

A brief return to Moore. The final part of his book opens with a comparison of Germany in 1918 with the two 1917 revolutions in Russia. And once again Moore questions the attribution of too much importance to the proletariat, especially a radicalized subsection of it, in the evolution of events. Even leaving aside the collapse of the Tsar and the officer corps, and the weak bureaucracy and middle class, on the side of the "revolutionaries" it was the desertion of the soldiers, the fury of hungry consumers, the peasants, next to all of whom workers (and Lenin and the Bolsheviks) played an important role—but no more than that (Moore, 1978: 357–375).

IV. AN UNCONVENTIONAL CONCLUSION

Chile, Germany, Russia. Their working classes showed an enormous range of opinions, with radicalism substantial but never overwhelmingly strong. About the U.S. and Great Britain the issue can scarcely be seriously raised. About France we have the dashed hope of 1968, and even about those events, interpretations must remain tentative.

Academics nevertheless still continue to ask: why was the working class (read also: the peasantry) not revolutionary? Implicitly, that formulation presumes that it "should normally" have been. But is there really continued justification for that way of putting the question, with all the possibly erroneous avenues of analysis to which it may lead (e.g., the search for who's to blame for the lack)? Is not that formulation more a reflection of the ever-green utopian and romantic hopes of some of us, rather than would be a more open-minded formulation: what explains what we find to be the facts about working-class consciousness? That formulation permits, but does not automatically drive us into, explanations involving false consciousness, repressive tolerance and the like. Like medieval alchemists, we continue to search for revolutionary gold and for some catalytic situation which would reveal it or make it spring into existence. And just as there were some intellectual benefits from alchemy and the pursuit of gold, so are there some from the pursuit of "revolutionary consciousness." But these benefits do exhaust quite quickly. We intellectuals don't make particularly good tacticians, nor prognosticators. We should keep to what we do best. What that is may not be very easy to formulate: interpretation, analysis, comparison, generalization are some of the words that come to mind. But it surely cannot lie in a continued attempt to search for the evidently nonexistent. And if, for heuristic purposes, any base line is to be adopted against which to judge the level of consciousness of the working class of a particular country, that of Selig Perlman's "job and wage conscious" worker and unionism may after all be, if not true in any absolute sense, at least a more realistic one than the image of a Marxian "revolutionary conscious" worker (Perlman, 190–210).

ACKNOWLEDGMENT

*A shorter, less detailed version of this paper was presented at the Workshop on "Urban Working Class Culture and Social Protest in Latin America" organized by the Latin American Program of the Woodrow Wilson International Center for Scholars, Washington, D.C., November 30–December 1, 1978.

NOTES

1. "A spectre is haunting Europe—the spectre of Communism": the opening words of the *Manifesto* of the Communist Party, published in London in February 1848, before the June uprising in Paris which ushered in a series of revolts all across Europe.

2. It is puzzling (and we are not being arch in using that word) that books by Marxist writers dealing with class consciousness often deal more scantily with working-class consciousness than one might have expected. Meszaros' *Aspects of History and Class Consciousness* (Meszaros, 1972) to which an array of brilliant Marxist scholars contributed has none devoted to the working class, but does contain a chapter in which bourgeois class consciousness is analyzed: Ralph Miliband, "Barnave: A Case of Bourgeois Class Consciousness," Ch. 3, pp. 22–48. A part of Hobsbawm's chapter (Ch. 2, pp. 5–22, "Class Consciousness in History") deals with working-class consciousness, but less for its own sake than to illustrate a more general point (common also to bourgeois class consciousness) about the complex relations between organizations and class consciousness. Hobsbawm focuses most on early working-class movements and on the dangers of the post-revolutionary (e.g., Soviet) situation: least on the immediately pre-revolutionary situation. Meszaros' own chapter (Ch. 6, "Contingent and Necessary Class Consciousness," pp. 85–127) is an exegesis of Marx's ideas on working-class consciousness, not a discussion of where the concept stands today, both theoretically and, above all, in terms of its relation to empirical reality. This criticism does not, however, apply to Michael Mann's *Consciousness and Action Among the Western Working Class* (London: Macmillan, 1973) which weaves empirical data into summaries of theoretical discussions to support the author's own sophisticated position.

3. We shall take as many as possible of our citations from David McLellan's *Karl Marx: Selected Writings,* since it is readily available.

4. For a highly readable history, see Alan Angell, *Politics and the Labor Movement in Chile* (London: Oxford University Press, 1972).

5. A substantial potential for turbulence may—or may not—have existed below the surface since 1973. But it has not been overt.

6. Some of the information in this section is taken from Landsberger and McDaniel, 1976, supplemented by material that has become available since 1975.

7. Most observers agree that the voting figures indicate that Dr. Allende's success was due, ironically, to a continuation of a resurgence of the right combined with our increase in polarization, i.e., a weakening of the center. There certainly was no massive shift to the left of any kind. Any shorthand summary to the effect that "the Chilean people had turned to . . ." would be totally unjustified (Ayres, 1976; Prothro and Chaparro, 1976; Powell, 1973). All these writers also go out of their way to stress the very weak degree of radicalism, readiness for revolution, etc. among Chile's working class, and its high degree of political division.

8. The vote is surrounded by a good deal of controversy. It took weeks to count, and announce, the results!

9. An evaluation of the participative experience published much later is considerably more positive in tone. But it does not really address itself to whether or not the experience had been positive on the whole and on the average. Rather, it analyzes the correlates of greater or lesser success regardless of the overall average (Espinosa and Zimbalist, 1978).

10. It is awkward to use the word *extreme* to denote the position of PDC-oriented workers. Nationally, the PDC—which itself spans a range of views—occupies a center, or just left-of-center position. Within the labor movement, it is a large minority to the right of labor's center of gravity, though by nowhere near as much as the MIR was to the left.

REFERENCES

Angell, Alan
1972   Politics and the Labour Movement in Chile. London: Oxford University Press.
Ayres, Robert L.
1976   "Unidad popular and the Chilean electoral process." Pp. 30–66 in Arturo Valen-

zuela and J. Samuel Valenzuela (eds.), Chile: Politics and Society. New Brunswick, N.J.: Transaction Books.

Blanco, Hugo
1974 Cited in Les Evans (ed.), Disaster in Chile. New York: Pathfinder Press.

Caute, David (ed.)
1967 Essential Writings of Karl Marx. New York: Macmillan.

Espinosa, Juan G., and Andrew S. Zimbalist
1978 Economic Democracy: Worker Participation in Chilean Industry, 1970–1973. New
York: Academic Press.

Gall, Norman
1972 "Copper is the wages of Chile." American Universities Field Staff, West Coast,
South America Series XIX 3: 1–12.

Geary, Dick
1978 "Radicalism and the worker: metal workers and revolution, 1914–1923." Pp. 267–
286 in Richard J. Evans (ed.), Society and Politics in Wilhelmine Germany. New
York: Barnes and Noble.

Goldrich, Daniel, Raymond B. Pratt, and C. R. Schuller
1970 "The political integration of lower-class urban settlements in Chile and Peru." Pp.
175–214 in Irving L. Horowitz (ed.), Masses in Latin America. New York: Oxford
University Press.

Goodman, Louis Wolf
1970 "Blue collar work and modernization." Ph.D. Dissertation, Northwestern University, Evanston, Illinois.
1978 "Notes on the study of Latin American blue collar workers." Paper prepared for
the Workshop on "Urban working class culture and social protest in Latin America." Organized by the Latin American Program of the Woodrow Wilson International Center for Scholars, Washington, D.C., November 30–December 1.

Hamilton, Richard
1967 Affluence and the French Worker in the Fourth Republic. Princeton, N.J.: Princeton University Press.

Landsberger, Henry A.
1963 El Pensamiento del Dirigente Sindical Chileno: Un Informe Preliminar. Santiago de
Chile: INSORA, Universidad de Chile (Publicacion No. 17).
1966 "The labor elite: is it revolutionary?" Pp. 256–301 in Seymour Martin Lipset and
Aldo Solari (eds.), Elites in Latin America. New York: Oxford University Press.
1968 "Do ideological differences have personal correlates? A study of Chilean labor
leaders at the local level." Economic Development and Cultural Change 16:
219–243.

Landsberger, Henry A., Manuel Barrera, and Abel Toro
1964 "The Chilean labor union leader: a preliminary report on his background and
attitudes." Industrial and Labor Relations Review 17: 399–420.

Landsberger, Henry A., and Tim McDaniel
1976 "Hypermobilization in Chile, 1970–1973." World Politics 28: 502–541.

Mann, Michael
1973 Consciousness and Action among the Western Working Class. London: Macmillan.

McLellan, David (ed.)
1977 Karl Marx: Selected Writings. New York: Oxford University Press.

Meszaros, Istvan, ed.
1972 Aspects of History and Class Consciousness. New York: Herder and Herder.

Miliband, Ralph
1972 "Barnave: a case of bourgeois class consciousness." Pp. 22–48 in Istvan Meszaros

(ed.), Aspects of History and Class Consciousness. New York: Herder and Herder.

Moore, Barrington
1978   Injustice: The Social Bases of Obedience and Revolt. White Plains, N.Y.: Sharpe.

Peppe, Patrick
1976   "Parliamentary socialism and workers' consciousness in Chile." Pp. 92–109 in June Nash, Juan Corradi, and Hobart Spalding, Jr. (eds.), Ideology and Social Change in Latin America. New York: Gordon and Breach.

Perlman, Mark
1958   Labor Union Theories in America. Evanston, Ill.: Row, Peterson.

Petras, James
1970   Politics and Social Forces in Chilean Development. Berkeley and Los Angeles: University of California Press.
1976   "Nationalization, socioeconomic change and popular participation." Pp. 172–200 in Arturo Valenzuela and J. Samuel Valenzuela (eds.), Chile: Politics and Society. New Brunswick, N.J.: Transaction Books.

Portes, Alejandro
1971   "Political primitivism, differential socialization and lower-class left radicalism." American Sociological Review 36: 820–835.

Powell, Sandra
1973   "Elections and the radical left: the rise of Salvador Allende, 1958–1970." Presented at the Latin American Studies Association, Madison, Wisconsin, March 1973.

Prothro, James W., and Patricia E. Chaparro
1976   "Public opinion and the movement of Chilean government to the left." Pp. 67–114 in Arturo Valenzuela and J. Samuel Valenzuela (eds.), Chile: Politics and Society. New Brunswick, N.J.: Transaction Books.

Ryder, A. J.
1967   The German Revolution of 1918: A Study of German Socialism in War and Revolt. Cambridge, U.K.: Cambridge University Press.

Smith, Brian H., S. J., and Jose Luis Rodrigues
1974   "Comparative working-class political behavior." American Behavioral Scientist 1: 59–96.

Tucker, Robert C. (ed.)
1972   The Marx-Engels Reader. New York: Norton.
1975   The Lenin Anthology. New York: Norton.

United Nations
1964   The Economic Development of Latin America in the Post-War Period. UN Publications #/CN.12/659/Rev. 1. New York: United Nations Publications.

Valenzuela, Arturo
1978   The Breakdown of Democratic Regimes: Chile. Baltimore: Johns Hopkins University Press.

Valenzuela, Arturo, and J. Samuel Valenzuela (eds.)
1976   Chile: Politics and Society. New Brunswick: Transaction Books.

Valenzuela, J. Samuel
1976   "The Chilean labor movement: the institutionalization of conflict." Pp. 135–171 in Arturo Valenzuela and J. Samuel Valenzuela (eds.), Chile: Politics and Society. New Brunswick, N.J.: Transaction Books.

Winn, Peter
1976   "Loosing the chains: labor and the revolutionary process, 1970–1973." Latin American Perspectives 8: 70–84.

Zammit, J. Ann (ed.)
1973 The Chilean Road to Socialism. Austin: University of Texas Press.
Zapata, Francisco
1975 Los Mineros de Chuquicamata: Productores o Proletarios? Cuadernos del CES No. 13, Centro de Estudios Sociologicos, El Colegio de Mexico, Mexico D. F.
Zimbalist, Andy and Barbara Stallings
1973 "Showdown in Chile." Monthly Review 25: 1–24.
Zeitlin, Maurice
1967 Revolutionary Politics and the Cuban Working Class. New York: Harper & Row.

THE INTERPLAY BETWEEN CLASS
AND NATIONAL CONSCIOUSNESS
IN HAWAII, 1850–1950

James A. Geschwender

The primary focus of this paper is an analysis of the interplay between class and national consciousness in Hawaii between 1850 and 1950, but it also includes an extended section dealing with the period from 1778 to 1850 because of its relevance. It is assumed that one may not understand the interplay between class and national consciousness without first understanding something about the interplay between class exploitation and national oppression to which they are linked. Consequently, a larger portion of this paper is focused upon the development and experience of exploitation and oppression than upon consciousness *per se*. The theoretical premises embodied in this analysis were developed during two decades of research of the interplay between nation and class in the American racial stratification order as applied to the historical experi-

Research in the Sociology of Work, Volume 1, pages 171–204
Copyright © 1981 by JAI Press Inc.
All rights of reproduction in any form reserved.
ISBN: 0-89232-124-5

ences of Black Americans (Geschwender, 1977; 1978). It is expected that
the framework so developed will prove useful in the analysis of racial
stratification in other societies.

I. THEORETICAL PREMISES

The analysis of racial stratification, as presented herein, rests upon a
series of theoretical premises. It is assumed that race and ethnicity are
purely social categories created by a given society at a particular historical moment. Race is normally defined in physical or genetic terms, while
ethnicity is defined in cultural terms. The same group may be variously
labeled as a race or an ethnic group at different times. Consequently, it is
possible to use *race* and *ethnicity* as interchangeable terms following
existing societal definitions. It is assumed that the social categories of
race and ethnicity emerge out of a situation of economic contact which is
often embodied in the labor process. The existence of a world-economy
with its associated global capital, commodity, and labor markets is
assumed (Wallerstein, 1974; Petras, 1976; 1979; Hopkins and Wallerstein,
1972; Bonacich, n.d.; Portes, 1978). Over the past several centuries the
capitalist economy has gradually expanded from its region of initial development in Europe to incorporate larger and larger portions of the
globe. Regions more recently incorporated into the capitalist system were
not incorporated as equal partners to the regions where capitalism originated.

The primary relationship within capitalism is between capital and labor.
A portion of the population is stripped of all means of earning a livelihood
except for the sale of its labor power (i.e., becomes proletarianized). This
segment of the population then must enter the labor market and sell its
labor power to capital. The terms of the exchange are unequal. Capital
purchases labor power at a cost (wage) sufficient to insure the reproduction of labor as determined, in part, by current standards of socially
defined needs. The labor so purchased is used by capital in the production
of commodities. The value produced through the application of labor is
greater than the price paid by capital and the remainder, after subtracting
costs of equipment and raw materials, is surplus value appropriated by
capital. Some of the surplus value is reinvested to feed the expansion of
the productive process and some takes the form of profit and is con-
sumed.

A second key relationship within the capitalist world-economy is the
relation of core to periphery. As the capitalist world-economy expands
from its centers of capital accumulation, it incorporates more and more
areas into the system and simultaneously develops an international division of labor. The newly incorporated areas tend to be producers of

primary products and/or suppliers of labor power, while the core areas become the centers for the most advanced technological applications to manufacturing processes. Exchange between core and peripheral areas tends to be unequal to the disadvantage of the periphery. Just as capital accumulates surplus value as a result of the labor process, the core extracts capital from the periphery through unequal exchange. Different standards for wage levels develop in the core and the periphery. Workers in the periphery tend to be paid a great deal less for their labors than do workers in the core. This has implications for both the flow of capital and of labor. Competitive capital is constantly faced with the need to reduce costs of production. Some of the more typical means of accomplishing this objective include rationalization of production, exportation of capital to areas of cheap labor, and importation of cheap labor to areas of capital concentration.

The concept of a global market assumes that all persons within the scope of the capitalist economy are potential sources of labor power. This is not to say that all are, at any given time, either engaged in wage labor or directly involved in capitalist production, but there is a possibility that they may be so incorporated. They may be forced into the labor market by being forcibly driven off the land, through the disruption of their economic order, or through the development of surplus population as a consequence of either excess rates of reproduction or land deterioration. It is also possible that they might simply be captured and forced into servitude. Once having become proletarianized, labor may move anywhere within the economic system. There is a tendency for labor to move from the periphery to the core (from low- to high-wage zones) during periods of capital expansion and from the core back to the periphery during periods of capital contraction.

The relation of core to periphery, as of capital to labor, is an economic relation, but this relation is overlaid with a set of political relations. State boundaries do not coincide with the economic boundaries between core and periphery. Any given state may include both core and peripheral regions; but states tend to be, on the whole, more core-like or more periphery-like. It has become a relatively convenient shorthand to refer to core states and peripheral states although this is an oversimplification. Core and periphery are relational terms which should not be used to categorize regions in any absolute sense. There are multiple linkages between regions such that each may be core in relation to one or more peripheral areas and/or periphery in relation to one or more core areas. Those regions that simultaneously stand as core and periphery in different economic relationships are often referred to as semi-periphery. States that comprise such areas, or that are complex enough to encompass both core and peripheral regions (although in economic relationships with different partners), tend to be called semi-peripheral states. The description of a given state as being either core, periphery, or semi-periphery is a time-bound description. As the world-economy evolves and changes, states may readily move from one category to another as a consequence of changes in their internal economic features or their relations to external states.

The political actions of the state interfere with the economic relations between core and periphery (Poulantzas, 1973; 1975). The state is never simply an instrument of capitalist domination internally, nor a simple representative of capitalist interests externally. The state is an arena within which class struggle takes place both between capital and labor and between fractions of capital. The resultant state policies reflect the relative power positions of the various combatants. In capitalist societies capital as a class possesses more power than labor and has the greater voice in shaping state policies. However, it cannot shape them solely as it wishes. The various alternative sources of power must be taken into account. Nor is it normally the case that capital speaks with a united voice on all issues. There are serious areas of disagreement within capital, and state policies cannot fully satisfy the desires of all fractions of capital. Consequently, state policies may variously facilitate, regulate, or inhibit the free flow of capital and/or labor both within and between states.

We must examine the formation (creation, emergence) of racial and ethnic groups within this larger process. Racial/ethnic groups have been created during the expansion of the world-economy both as a consequence of the flow of capital from core to periphery and as a consequence of the movement of labor from periphery to core, from periphery to semi-periphery, or from semi-periphery to core. Park and his students did an excellent job of analyzing the creation of races as a result of the expansion of European capital (for a discussion of their collective works see Geschwender, 1978: ch. 2). Europeans first came into contact with non-Europeans (nonwhites) in the course of European expansion in search of new markets and later as a consequence of the search for raw materials and/or labor. Contact led to economic competition, which often escalated into conflict. Behavioral differences between Europeans and non-Europeans tended to be defined in racial terms. The greater economic and/or military power of the Europeans was utilized in establishing relations of superordination-subordination which, in turn, were rationalized by an ideology of racism that developed in conjunction with conflict. Biological differences are not an essential feature of this process. There was no basic difference between the creation of races as a result of European movement into the Pacific and the creation of ethnic groups as a consequence of English movement into Ireland. The exact form of race/ethnic relations differs according to the situation of contact. Race/ethnic relations take on rather different characteristics in situations of trade as opposed to settler farming colonies or plantation societies, and they also vary according to the extent to which labor is more homogeneous or heterogeneous in racial/ethnic composition.

There is no basic difference between racial/ethnic groups formed through migration or through core expansion. Migrations of people take place because there is a shortage of labor of a certain type in a given location and a surplus labor supply in another location. The resultant relocation normally brings into contact two peoples who differ in some overt manner, be it behavioral or physical. An essentially economic relation of capital-labor coincides with a social relation which has come to be defined in racial/ethnic terms. An ideology of racism develops as a rationalization for particular forms of economic exploitation.

There is more likely to be a multiplicity of workers of different ethnic origins in the immigrant labor situation than in those areas newly incorporated into the world-economy. Consequently, workers may define themselves either in terms of class or racial/ethnic identity. Either choice carries implications regarding the nature of struggle. It is to the advantage of capital to keep workers divided into groups smaller than the total working class. Consequently, it often attempts to elicit the development of national (racial/ethnic) consciousness rather than class consciousness. This may be facilitated by segregating ethnic groups by occupation, work location, or sector of the economy; the payment of different levels of wages to members of different groups; and the use of members of one racial/ethnic group as scabs to break strikes carried on by the members of a different group.

Labor has sometimes collaborated in this process. Where capital pays different wages to members of different ethnic groups, members of the better-paid group become afraid that wages may be undercut, they may be displaced by cheaper labor, or cheaper labor may act as scabs against their strikes (Bonacich, 1972; 1976). Consequently, they tend to take a protectionist view toward their jobs and an exclusionist policy toward the members of the other racial/ethnic group. In turn, the excluded group increases its level of in-group solidarity and becomes increasingly hostile toward members of the better-paid ethnic group. A struggle takes place within the ranks of labor that inhibits any common struggle against capital.

That is not to say that no class struggle occurs where labor is fractionated by race and/or ethnicity. Just as wars of national liberation may take place in the colonial-imperial context, workers of a particular racial/ethnic group may organize to bring together all who simultaneously share the same class and the same racial/ethnic identity to pursue their common interests (Geschwender, 1977). These common interests will normally be a blend of class and national interests and may at times lead to alliances with other workers in class-oriented struggles or to alliances with coethnics in racially/ethnically-oriented struggles. Let us now apply this perspective to the analysis of the historical interplay between race and class in Hawaii.

II. HAWAII ENTERS THE WORLD-ECONOMY

Hawaii remained outside the orbit of the capitalist world-economy until relatively late. The first European[1] contact came in 1778, when Captain Cook accidentally stumbled upon the islands (Daws, 1968: 1–28). The island chain soon came to serve as a provisioning stop for merchant ships (Stevens, 1968: 1–12; Kuykendall, 1938: 82–99; Daws, 1968: 168–172). A number of Europeans settled in Hawaii to service ships during provisioning stops, but they were soon joined by a variety of others, including sailors who jumped ship while in port. The fur trade was established on the West Coast of North America by 1785. The trade soon came to be dominated by Americans who reached the West Coast by sailing around Cape Horn. They then followed a circular trading route which came to include Hawaii as a major port of call.

The presence of sandalwood in Hawaii was discovered by merchants involved in the fur trade and a booming sandalwood trade was developed with China beginning in the early 1800s. The trade was dominated by Americans until the supply of sandalwood became virtually exhausted by 1830. The first New England whaling ship arrived in Hawaiian waters in 1819, and Hawaii soon became a prime location for whalers to take on provisions and to winter their ships. The number of whaling ships visiting Hawaii increased to several hundred at the peak of the trade. Whaling, primarily operated by American capital, stimulated a further growth in local commerce and dominated the Hawaiian economy until it was destroyed by the American Civil War and the increased use of petroleum products which followed thereafter. The mercantile class that developed in Hawaii to service these various forms of economic activity was also predominantly American. The high degree of involvement of American capital in Hawaii was soon followed by a corresponding degree of political involvement. Political relations will be discussed below.

A. Consequences of Contact for Hawaii

The increased incorporation of Hawaii into the world-economy and the beginnings of capital penetration into Hawaii had an impact upon the Hawaiian society. Land ownership traditionally resided with the ruling monarch (Kelly, 1956: 11–49). The king would give grants of land to the higher alii (Hawaiian royalty) who, in turn, might give smaller grants to the lesser alii, and eventually grants were given to the commoners for their use. Each of these grants was revocable at the will of the grantor. These grants were linked to a system of taxation in kind and labor. The social order was buttressed by both a secular order with its civil sanctions and a religious order which used kapus (taboos) as means of social control.

The indigenous economy was seriously disrupted by the sandalwood trade (Lind, 1938: 41; Kuykendall, 1938: 88–91; Kelly, 1956: 89–100). Kamehameha[2] sought to purchase large amounts of goods from the outside and pay for them in sandalwood. He diverted so much of the people's efforts to the cutting and carrying of sandalwood that famine became widespread. Kamehameha saw the folly of this course of action, ordered a cutback in harvesting sandalwood, placed a kapu upon the younger trees to preserve the resource of the future, and ordered the people to engage in farming. A severe financial crisis hit the United States in 1819, shortly after the death of Kamehameha. Liholiho succeeded Kamehameha and allowed the chiefs to have a share in the sandalwood trade, thus reducing the amount of centralized control. American commercial interests saw Hawaii as a potential answer to their financial problems and launched a campaign to sell commodities to the Hawaiian chiefs, taking payment in sandalwood. So much of the energy of the commoners was deflected into the sandalwood trade that food production again fell off, the natural economy was seriously undermined, and sandalwood was so overcut that the supply became virtually exhausted by 1829.

Contact between Hawaiians and Europeans also proved detrimental to the physical survival of Hawaiians as European diseases were introduced. Syphilis, gonorrhea, measles, the common cold, pneumonia, smallpox, and probably cholera all contributed to an erosion of the Hawaiian people (Renaud, 1973: 13; Kuykendall, 1938: 14–15, 356, 386, 411–413; Fuchs, 1961: 13). The entire population of Hawaii, including foreigners, reached a low of 54,000 in 1876, as compared to an estimated 200,000 to 400,000 Hawaiians at the time of Cook's landing.

The role of kapus in the system of social control was also undermined (Daws, 1968: 55–60; Kelly, 1956: 89–92; Kuykendall, 1938: 65–70, 76, 102). Europeans in Hawaii were not always willing to comply with the kapus, and the Hawaiians were not always able to enforce appropriate sanctions against foreigners. It is probable that the people's confidence in the kapu system was undermined by the example of outsiders violating kapus with impunity. This is speculation but the events of 1819 are well documented. Kamehameha died and Liholiho ascended to the throne. Kaahumanu, a woman, was appointed as kuhina-nui (prime minister). She and Keopuolani, the mother of Liholiho, were able to persuade Liholiho to publicly eat with them and other women at a feast during which foods normally denied to women were served. This was immediately followed by a royal order to destroy the heiaus (temples), burn the idols, and end sex-related eating rules. The kapu system was destroyed for all intents and purposes.

B. The Coming of the Missionaries

The first missionaries arrived from New England in 1820. The Hawaiian people were declining as a race, their economy was disrupted, and the religious system was in turmoil. The Hawaiian culture was undergoing rapid and dramatic changes as a consequence of contact with Westerners. The missionaries made an advantageous move into the existing void (Tate, 1960; Kuykendall, 1938: 100–116; Stevens, 1968: 24–31). The missionary contingent brought with them four Hawaiian youths, including the son of the king of Kauai, who had been studying at the Foreign Mission School at Cornwall, Connecticut. They gained Liholiho's permission to remain in Hawaii and to proseletyze. Much of their early activities was spent in winning acceptance from the alii but they also made strenuous efforts in other directions:

> Missionaries set up the first printing press west of the Rockies, developed the Hawaiian alphabet, established schools throughout the Islands, printed textbooks, translated the Bible into Hawaiian, and promoted constitutional government under the Kingdom. By 1832, only twelve years after their arrival, 53,000 pupils were studying under their supervision; by 1846, 80% of the people could read. Missionaries brought Christianity to the Islands on a mass-production basis, the peak years of 1839–41 resulting in the admission of more than 20,000 Hawaiians to the church (Fuchs, 1961: 12).

From the beginning the missionaries devoted a disproportionate amount of their time and energy to providing the chiefs and their families with general and religious education. They developed a great deal of political influence, which became formalized in 1836 when the Rev. William Richards was appointed as advisor and teacher to the king. This continued the trend away from autocracy. Kamehameha had ruled with the advice of a council of chiefs, but under a new tripartite system, power was divided between the king, the kuhina-nui, and a council of chiefs having legislative power (Kuykendall, 1938: 145–147). The missionaries strongly believed that economic development, establishment of the commercial production of sugar, and the employment of Hawaiians as wage labor would have positive moral impact upon the Hawaiian people. From the very beginning, Richards advised that sugar be developed as the foundation for a capitalist agriculture. This development, however, hinged on the development of a system of private land ownership.

III. THE DEVELOPMENT OF A SUGAR INDUSTRY

Richards, in association with other missionaries and with Hawaiians (many of whom were educated by missionaries), achieved a series of changes in governmental structure. Many of these changes, directly or indirectly, bore on the question of land. The Declaration of Rights and associated laws passed in 1839 guaranteed people security in their lands and possessions and access to due process (Kuykendall, 1938: 160). In 1840 the government took over operation of the elementary schools and passed a constitution which created a national legislature and established representative government. It also subtly modified the philosophy regarding land ownership. The king no longer owned land in his own right but was merely the steward for the chiefs and the people who actually owned it. Organic Acts were passed between 1845 and 1847, which consolidated the existence of a cabinet, a judiciary, and a civil service system. The 1852 constitution gave the right to vote to all adult citizens, native born or naturalized. This period saw a dramatic increase in the number of Europeans directly participating in the Hawaiian government from fourteen in 1844 to forty-eight in 1851—twenty-five of the latter were Americans (Daws, 1968: 108).

A. The First Need: Land

The most important changes in this time period were related to land (Stevens, 1968: 32–45; Kuykendall, 1936: 267–298; Fuchs, 1961: 14–17; Kelly, 1956: 105–142; Lind, 1938: 46). California and Oregon were being settled during the decade of the 1840s. This stimulated trade between Hawaii and the American West Coast. The discovery of gold in California and the ensuing population explosion enlarged the potential market for sugar and other produce and, in the minds of the haoles,[3] made the solution of the land question critical. Missionary pressure led to the granting of increasing numbers of long-term leases during the thirties and forties and in 1846 to the experimental selling of land in fee simple in Manoa Valley and the Makawao District of Maui. But the major change came in a series of legislative acts—collectively called the Grand Mahele or division—which between January 1848 and July 1850 divided all land into crown lands owned by the king (984,000 acres), governmental land controlled by the legislature (1,523,000 acres), and land given to the chiefs (1,619,000 acres) and commoners (28,000 acres). Aliens also were given the right to purchase land in fee simple.

Shortly after the mahele was completed, land started gravitating into haole hands through a variety of types of transactions. In some cases fraud was involved; in others, bad deals were made by Hawaiians who undervalued land ownership because they viewed land as something to be used in common and not something to be possessed by an individual. Both commoner and chief were subject to having their land alienated. In addition, the government sold much of its lands, and roughly 65% of the acreage sold went to haoles. It is difficult to determine exactly how rapidly and how much of the land came under the control of haoles. It is clear that in 1896, 57% of the land that was taxed was in European hands and that by 1936 only 6% of land originally going to commoners remained in the hands of Hawaiians or part-Hawaiians. Both missionaries and their descendants participated in the acquisition of land for speculation and for the development of capitalist agriculture. Land became concentrated in very few hands, most of whom were haole.

These changes did not go unnoticed by the Hawaiian people, who were not overly pleased with these developments. Much dissatisfaction was expressed over the amount of land coming under European control and the number of naturalized Europeans moving into government. Maui was a major center of the unrest. Beginning in 1845 prayer meetings were held, protests organized, and petitions signed against foreigners. It was urged that they be barred from becoming naturalized citizens and, naturalized or not, that they be excluded from any official governmental position. Rumors circulated in 1848 about plans for a Hawaiian attack upon the fort in Honolulu and the killing of all foreigners. Nothing concrete materialized, but it is clear that a strong level of national consciousness was building among the Hawaiian people.

B. After Land—Markets

The successful development of capitalist agriculture requires three basic components: land, labor, and markets. The material above describes the manner in which planters solved the land problem. The sugar market was opened by the settlement of the American West Coast, and it was greatly expanded when the American Civil War disrupted production within the United States as well as truncating normal sources of supply (Kuykendall, 1953: 140–149). However, the American government took a protectionist approach toward domestic sugar, and Hawaiian sugar producers seeking to enter the American market were confronted by a tariff. There seemed to be two alternative routes: annexation or reciprocity (Stevens, 1968: 85–186; Tate, 1963; 1968; Kuykendall, 1953: 220–230, 247–251; 1967: 17–115). Annexation had its advocates but it would have posed some problems with the Hawaiian labor system (see the discussion below of the Masters and Servants Act). Serious discussions between Hawaii and the United States with the intent of concluding a reciprocity treaty were begun as early as 1847 but did not bear fruit for almost three decades. During this period various proposals for reciprocity treaties were drafted and discussed but none culminated in a treaty. Finally, in 1873 the pot was sweetened for the United States by including in the proposal the possible cession of Pearl Harbor to the United States for use as a Pacific naval base.

When word of the possible cession reached the Hawaiian people, there was a mass upsurge of unrest and protest. The proposal to cede Pearl Harbor was withdrawn but the unrest intensified. It became necessary on February 13, 1874, for King Kalakaua to request the landing of 150 American Marines to keep the peace. Stevens states that:

> . . . it cannot be questioned that the landing . . . became a decisive factor in maintaining the peace against the threat of revolution. While the force was used at the request of Kalakaua, the fact remains that it was in the interest of maintaining the "paramount" position of the United States (Stevens, 1968: 118–119).

There was a growing belief within the United States government that Hawaii was important to American interests. While some fractions of U.S. capital stood to lose by the approval of reciprocity (e.g., beet sugar and rice), others stood to gain (e.g., California sugar refineries and interests involved in the conduct of trade itself). It was also coming to be recognized that Hawaii was strategically located in the Pacific from both a military and a commercial perspective. The tide of sentiment in the American legislature began to favor reciprocity. Unrest among Hawaiians made it impossible to include the cession of Pearl Harbor at the moment but there was an underlying expectation that, if reciprocity were granted now, Pearl Harbor could be acquired by the United States at some point in the not too distant future. A reciprocity treaty was approved by the Senate of the United States on August 14, 1876.

Reciprocity proved to be a tremendous boost to the sugar producers of Hawaii. Sugar production increased from 26,072,429 pounds in 1876 to 63,584,871 pounds in 1880, and 171,350,314 pounds in 1885 (Stevens, 1968: 141). This growth in the economy did not prevent a corresponding growth in Hawaiian-haole tensions. Hawaiians did not share in the gains derived from economic growth. By March, 1878, the Hawaiian Ministry was three-fourths American by birth; Hawaiians were increasingly concerned regarding growing American influence; and many were afraid that current developments would lead inevitably to a loss of independence for Hawaii. By 1880, unrest had developed into a nationalist movement in politics. A concurrent economic downturn made government debts and taxes increasingly important issues. It should be noted that some of the government debts were developed as a consequence of recruiting labor to the islands to work on the sugar plantations.

Ironically, the rise of Hawaiian nationalism and its political expression helped to stimulate counter moves that proved to be more powerful.

Haoles were also concerned with the growing cost of government and were concerned with the increased number of Hawaiian nationalists elected to office. Their residual Puritan attitudes were further upset when the government began licensing the sale of opium. A group of foreigners came together and formed the Hawaiian League, which armed themselves and used threats to force Kalakaua to accept a new constitution. The constitution provided for the election of members to the House of Nobles by persons meeting certain property conditions, extended the franchise to non-Hawaiian citizens residing in Hawaii, barred Chinese and Japanese from voting, reduced the size of the popularly elected lower house to the same size as the House of Nobles, made cabinet members *ex officio* members of the legislature, and made it possible for the legislature to override the king's veto. In short, it made haoles dominant in the legislature and made the king subservient to it. Hawaiian anger was great and an aborted revolution followed.

In the meantime, the sense of the importance of Hawaii to the United States continued to grow among American officials. The renewal of the reciprocity treaty was debated in the Senate during 1885 and 1886 with the principal opposition coming from cane and beet sugar interests. An amendment was added to the treaty prior to its final approval by the United States Senate which called for the cession of Pearl Harbor to the United States. This provision did not cause any great concern in the newly structured Hawaiian government despite the fact that Kalakaua was so strongly opposed that he swore never to sign any treaty containing such a clause. The reform cabinet approved the treaty and Kalakaua, recognizing his powerlessness, reluctantly approved it. The sugar growers got renewal of the reciprocity treaty and the Americans got Pearl Harbor.

The renewal of the reciprocity treaty proved to be less valuable than had been anticipated by the sugar growers. In 1890 the McKinley Tariff Bill became law. It removed the tariff on sugar and gave a two-cents-a-pound subsidy to domestic production. Thus the reciprocity treaty became worthless to Hawaiian sugar interests. They could enter the American market only on the same grounds as all other foreign sugar and were placed at a competitive disadvantage *vis-à-vis* domestic producers. The sugar interests attempted to have the McKinley amendment changed but they increasingly came to the view that the only way to assure themselves of access to the American market was for Hawaii to be annexed to the United States so that Hawaiian sugar could be treated as domestic sugar. This desire for annexation was further fueled by an aborted revolution in 1889 which had the goal of deposing Kalakaua and replacing him with a ruler who would reassert Hawaiian sovereignty.

The Harrison administration looked favorably upon the annexation of

Hawaii to the United States. The planters, concerned over the McKinley Tariff and rising Hawaiian nationalism, began to seriously plan for a revolution to overthrow the monarchy and pave the way for the annexation of Hawaii to the United States. It appears clear that they received private assurances from the Harrison administration that annexation would follow a successful revolution. Kalakaua died and was succeeded by Queen Liliuokalani, a nationalist who objected to the "bayonet" constitution of 1887. In January 1893 she announced her intent to promulgate a new constitution similar to that of 1864, restoring the monarchy to control over the House of Nobles and restricting the franchise to Hawaiian citizens. This was the final stimulus needed by the planters. Their revolution was carried out in bloodless fashion on January 16 after American naval forces had been landed to "keep the peace and protect American property." In fact, they served to insure the success of the revolution.

Unfortunately for the planters, their revolution coincided with the election of Cleveland and a change from a Republican to a Democratic administration in Washington. Cleveland urged the restoration of Queen Liliuokalani to her throne. The planters refused and decided to go it alone. They formed the Republic of Hawaii, which existed as an independent republic until new elections returned a Republican administration to Washington. Prosperity for the Hawaiian Republic was assured in 1894, when the United States Congress passed the Wilson-Gorham Tariff, which restored a duty on foreign sugar, eliminated the domestic subsidy, and retained the reciprocity treaty with Hawaii. This enabled sugar interests to operate in a profitable manner until annexation took place in 1898.

C. Land and Markets, But Where's the Labor?

While the sugar interests solved the problems of land and markets, neither would be of much value unless an adequate supply of labor could be obtained. The Hawaiian people had effectively been proletarianized. They had lost their land and were now able to earn their sustenance only through the sale of their labor power. Several authors state that Hawaiians did not like plantation work, did not react well to its discipline, or were otherwise unsuited for it (Fuchs, 1961: 70; Daws, 1968: 178–179; Lind, 1967: 7). They imply that this was one of the factors that forced planters to look elsewhere for labor. The truth of the matter lies elsewhere. The total number of Hawaiians and part-Hawaiians declined from 66,984 in 1860 to 51,531 in 1872 and 47,508 in 1878 (Nordyke, 1977: 134–135). Yet these are the very years that sugar production was being stimulated by the American Civil War and by the passage of the reciprocity treaty. The Hawaiian Immigration Society (1874) collected information that revealed that in 1873 there were 3,786 laborers working on thirty-five sugar plantations, of which 2,627 were Hawaiian men and 364 were Hawaiian women. Thus Hawaiians constituted almost four-fifths of the plantation labor force, and more than one out of every two able-bodied Hawaiian men were so employed at the time.[4] This does not suggest that Hawaiians were unwilling to work on plantations but rather suggests that the expansion of sugar production combined with the decline in the Hawaiian population to require an external search for labor.

IV. LABOR RECRUITMENT

There was much debate over the solution to the growing labor problem. A private contingent of sugar planters arranged for the importation of approximately 180 Chinese laborers in 1852 (Kuykendall, 1953: 178–195; Daws, 1968: 179–182). This did not prove adequate. Many planters urged the government to ascertain planters' needs and desires and then use its official powers to obtain the needed amount of labor. Kamehameha V believed that immigration was more complex than simply satisfying the labor needs of the planters. He argued that the state should be concerned with the declining population of Hawaiians and that it should act to attract settlers of a similar or cognate race (e.g., Polynesians) that could intermarry with the Hawaiians and replenish the race. Thus in 1864 the legislature established a Bureau of Immigration with the power to regulate all immigration to Hawaii. This did not make the planters happy, as they did not wish to have any state interference with their decisions in this area, although they sought state aid in carrying out their endeavors.

The Bureau of Immigration became the instrument of state policy with regard to immigration. This policy had three prongs. One was to seek labor to meet the growing needs of the Hawaiian sugar industry. The second was to seek a cognate race of settlers which would intermarry with and replenish the Hawaiian people. The third (reflecting the concerns of the growing stable and respectable haole community in Hawaii) was to seek individuals who would contribute to the development of a stable, family-oriented population. There existed an obvious strain among these three state interests. The desire for a stable, permanent settler population was usually interpreted as meaning Europeans. Yet it was quite expensive to import people from Europe, and many who were imported would not accept plantation life nor remain in Hawaii (Nordyke, 1977: 32–34; Kuykendall, 1967: 133–135). The desire to replenish the Hawaiian race should have meant other Polynesians, but the haoles who were entrusted with enforcing this objective had a primitive understanding of race. All Pacific islanders, including Japanese, were seen as of the same racial stock. The desire for labor meant a desire for cheap and easily controlled labor whatever the source.

The control factor is probably the most important criterion in selecting labor for plantation work (Thompson, 1970; Lind, 1938: 210–243). It is normally the case that plantation labor is selected from a group that is racially different from the plantation owners and located in a geographical area other than where the plantations are situated. This is thought to ensure maximizing the degree of docility or powerlessness. The Hawaiian sugar planters were quite aware of the need for a controllable labor force and utilized a number of techniques of control. Some involved legislative acts and some involved racial "divide and rule" policies in both patterns of recruitment and in treatment of employees.

Sugar was sufficiently important to the economy that the state could be persuaded to import workers in needed numbers, but sugar interests were not always free to pursue their workers when and wherever they pleased. Most labor importation was conducted under the Masters and Servants Act, which appears to have been modeled after the laws governing the control of sailors while at sea (Coman, 1963). The act provided for penal labor contracts enforced through the courts. Persons who absented themselves from work illegally (either by running away or by "pretending to be sick") could be forced to serve double the time of their absence. In practice the lunas (overseers) usually determined who was or was not capable of work. Simple refusal to work could be punished by prison terms at hard labor. In actual practice much of the labor discipline took place on the plantations without reference to, or resort to, the law. Lunas carried and used black snake whips. Punishment was immediate and often harsh. Management might "fine" workers as much as a month's earnings for relatively mild transgressions. The concern for worker discipline was not misplaced, as working conditions were harsh and unattractive. Many workers had not anticipated these working conditions and would not have remained long without some form of compulsion.

A. China

The planters turned to China as the first major source of labor external to the Hawaiian Islands (Fuchs, 1961: 86–105; Kuykendall, 1967: 119–122, 135–153; Nordyke, 1977: 24–29). The first Chinese contract laborers arrived in 1852, but the first group brought in by the Bureau of Immigration came in 1865. All in all, some 54,000 Chinese, mostly male, were imported into Hawaii. Not all remained in Hawaii. Some 27,000 departed between 1870 and 1898, alone. Nevertheless, they increased in number from a handful in 1850 to 2,000 in 1876 and 26,000 in 1900. The increases became a subject of concern to many. There were several cases of organized protests among Chinese workers on sugar plantations but, for the most part, the Chinese responded to the harsh working conditions in an individualistic manner. China was not a unified nation at the time. There was no developed sense of nationalism and there was no great concern on the part of the Chinese government to protect the interests of the Chinese emigrees.

Thus, the typical response of the Chinese was to serve out their contracts and leave the plantations as rapidly as possible. Many left to return to China, many moved to the mainland, some went into agriculture, often as rice farmers raising the staple to be sold to the plantations, and many others moved into the city. White artisans, mechanics, tradespersons, and other workers did not want to compete with Chinese labor and sought protection. Others had never envisaged the Chinese remaining in Hawaii as permanent residents and were appalled by the prospect. This was not the group which they hoped to see intermarry with the Hawaiians and replenish the race. There was also fear of the various social problems that were always associated with populations of men with few women. Still others were afraid that the Chinese were going to take over politically. Consequently, there was a concerted drive to control the Chinese, reduce their numbers and seek an alternative source of workers to undercut their influence and act as a counterbalance. Hawaiians also expressed their opposition to further Chinese immigration. Chinese businessmen opposed the immigration of coolies as they included "bad men," but they sought the recruitment of more Chinese of a better class.

B. Japan

The signing of the reciprocity treaty opened up the West Coast market and created an increased need for workers at the same time that the exodus of Chinese from the plantations produced a declining labor force. There were almost 6,000 Chinese plantation workers in 1886 but only 4,000 in 1902. The sugar growers sought a more stable labor force from Japan (Fuchs, 1961: 106–132; Nordyke, 1977: 35–39; Kuykendall, 1967: 142–185; Wakukawa, 1938). About 180,000 Japanese migrated to Hawaii and almost half remained permanently. A group of 148 was imported in 1868, but problems developed and Japan closed further labor immigration until 1885. Japanese workers soon became the most numerous group among plantation laborers although the work force remained mixed. Wages varied by ethnic origin, with Japanese workers paid at the lowest rates. Work camps were segregated by race, with the worst housing reserved for the Japanese.

C. Worker Resistance

Signs of Japanese labor militancy were found almost from the beginning of the resumption of immigration in 1885. Between 1890 and 1899 thirty cases were reported in the newspapers in which Japanese workers collectively rose up to punish harsh lunas or struck in protest of their actions. Some incidents involved as many as 250 workers. It seems probable that many additional incidents went unreported out of a fear of stimulating increased "problems." Equally significant are the reported cases of violence within the Japanese work force which had the apparent intent of creating labor solidarity. Workers were physically punished by coworkers for violations of work limitation agreements and for failing to support demonstrations against the employer.

Annexation to the U.S. took place in 1898 and was followed by the Organic Act of 1900 which brought a termination of the penal-contract labor system and a major work stoppage on the part of the Japanese. While this is sometimes described as a celebration of the "freedom" brought by American labor laws, it appears to have been a strike action designed to force planters to acknowledge workers' rights to leave the plantation when they chose to do so. Plantation operators proved adaptable. Some forced labor remained, despite its illegality. Brute force was often used to keep Japanese workers on the plantations. The penal-contract was replaced with a crop-sharing contract, but the standard of living of affected Japanese workers *declined*. However, the Japanese workers were now legally free to leave the plantations and many did so. A series of minor strikes took place between annexation and 1908, but they were largely uncoordinated and likely to be aimed at individual grievances rather than class rights.

D. Divisions Among Workers

The first plantation trade union movement was formed in December 1908, with the Japanese in Honolulu providing aid to Japanese on the plantations. The Higher Wages Association launched an unsuccessful strike in May 1909. One of the factors that contributed to its failure was the opposition of the conservative *Issei* (the immigrant generation) who believed that "the action of the agitators was detrimental to the good reputation of the Japanese who resided under the protection of the United States." It is worth noting that those who held this view were persons who had achieved a measure of success in Honolulu and were in a position to identify with the dominant economic order as it existed in Hawaii. A second factor which contributed to defeat was the use of Portuguese and Hawaiians as strikebreakers. The strikebreakers were paid a wage twice as high as had previously been paid to the Japanese workers. It is also worth noting that, while the strike was beaten, it was immediately followed by improvements in wages and working conditions on the plantations. Plantation owners became quite concerned by the display of labor militancy and sought countermeasures.

The growing Japanese population stimulated many of the same fears that had earlier been created by the Chinese but in a more intensified form. The sugar planters were disappointed to find that Japanese workers proved to be far more militant than had the Chinese. The first group of Japanese immigrants came in the year of the Meiji restoration and many of the later waves came from areas that had experienced peasant unrest and turmoil. Japan was a unified nation and the workers possessed a sense of nationalism. The Japanese government was proud and concerned about the fate of its emigrees, so it monitored conditions and exerted some influence in their behalf—although less than might have been desired. Thus there was an objective basis for the development of unity and labor militancy among the Japanese workers. From the beginning the planters feared this unity and sought to undermine it. They strongly believed that their program of divide and rule was the best single tactic, as illustrated by the following editorial, which appeared in the newspaper after a 1906 strike at Waipahu plantation:

> A more obstreperous and unruly lot of Japanese than Waipahu is cursed with, are not to be found in these islands. . . . The Japanese Counsul, once all-powerful among laborers of his race in Hawaii, meets insults and threats on every hand. . . . To discharge every Jap and put on newly imported laborers of another race would be a most impressive object lesson to the little brown men on all the plantations. . . . It would subdue their dangerous faith in their own indispensability. So long as they think that they have things in their own hands, they will be cocky and unreasonable. . . . Ten or fifteen thousand Portuguese and Molokans in the fields would make a vast difference in the temper of the Japanese (*Pacific Commercial Advertiser*, Jan. 16–22, 1906, cited in Fuchs, 1961:210).

One response to Japanese labor militance was a series of unsuccessful attempts by Hawaiian officials to persuade the United States Congress to modify the Oriental Exclusion Act to allow a limited number of Chinese to be imported into Hawaii for agricultural purposes only. They would then be frozen in Hawaii, forbidden to go to the mainland, and barred from nonagricultural (i.e., nonplantation) work. However, others feared any form of increased Oriental immigration. Laws were passed keeping Orientals out of civil service and charging higher license fees for Orientals in a number of crafts, and informal pressures were used to discourage any employment of Orientals in more desirable occupations. Nevertheless, the planters needed more labor in order to keep pace with growth in the sugar industry and movement off the plantations. American laws forbade the binding of workers to plantations, the Oriental Exclusion Act prohibited further immigration from China (the sugar growers failed to get it modified), and the Gentlemen's Agreement eventually barred further immigration from Japan. The sugar growers sought a labor supply which would be cheap, available, likely to remain on the plantations and, above all, controllable.

One may get a sense of the degree of docility desired in laborers from a letter printed in the newspaper during an earlier (1894) discussion of the possible recruitment of American Blacks to solve the labor shortage. This statement should be read in light of the degree of "militance" exhibited by American Blacks on the mainland in 1894.

> The time has been when a Negro could be ordered and even driven; but the time has passed. . . . A Negro will not submit to a scolding or cursing while in the discharge of his plantation duties, and prides himself upon a freedom to "talk back" when abused by his employer. This would most likely displease a luna, whose charge had been the management of a set of Chinese who never dared venture a reply. (*Pacific Commercial Advertiser*, March 15, 1894, cited in Fuchs, 1961:207).

E. Philippines

The Bureau of Immigration and the planters then turned to the Philippines as a source of legally importable workers with the proper degree of poverty and a rural agricultural background to make a docile labor force (Melendy, 1977: 17–108; Nordyke, 1977: 41–44; Fuchs, 1961: 138–149). Filipinos were free to immigrate as American nationals and were from the same type of poor agricultural society that had provided the bulk of the Chinese and Japanese immigrants. Filipinos were more similar to the earlier Chinese immigrants than to the Japanese in the sense that the Philippines had not developed a high degree of national unity and solidarity. Filipinos were divided by language into Ilicono, Visayan, and Tagalog speakers. These groups came from different parts of the Philippines, differed somewhat in background social characteristics, and shared a degree of mutual distrust and hostility. The planters could, and did, play upon these differences in order to inhibit the development of solidarity and militance. Filipinos were, in part, recruited in order to keep Japanese workers in line, but their importation was also a response to a labor shortage caused by Japanese leaving the plantations in large numbers. Between 1902 and 1922 the numbers of Japanese on the plantations declined from 31,000 to 17,000 despite continued immigration from Japan. By 1937 two out of every three plantation workers were Filipinos.

Serious attempts to recruit Filipino laborers began immediately after the 1909 Japanese strike on Oahu. Approximately 800 were imported in 1909 and more than 4,000 followed in 1910. The Hawaii Sugar Producers

Association (HSPA) continued their recruiting efforts until 1925, by which time there was a large enough supply of voluntary immigrants coming to its Manila office to enable them to rely entirely upon this source. Between 1909 and 1931, 112,828 Filipinos came to Hawaii, of which 38,946 returned home and 18,607 went on to the West Coast. Immigration declined to negligible levels during the Depression and World War II. The HSPA did bring in 7,360 Filipinos in 1945 in a dual attempt to attract a number of plantation workers before Philippine independence cut off the supply and to beat back the unionization drive of the International Longshoremen's and Warehousemen's Union (ILWU). It was felt that the recent Filipino immigrants would be more resistant to unionization than the older residents of Hawaii and that their harsh wartime experiences under Japanese occupation would make them less willing to cooperate with Japanese-Americans in a class-oriented movement such as the ILWU. However, the ILWU infiltrated the crew of the ship bringing the Filipinos to Hawaii and had them virtually all signed up as union men before the ship docked. This discussion of the role of the ILWU is continued below.

V. THE STRUGGLE AGAINST DOMINATION

The strategy of divide and rule based upon race worked quite well (Melendy, 1977: 85–108; Probasco, 1965; The Federation of Japanese Labor in Hawaii, 1920; Reinecke, n.d.; Fuchs, 1961: 206–240; Manlapit, 1930; Kurita, n.d.; Lane, 1971; Lind, 1938: 233–243). In 1916 the Japanese acted as strikebreakers in a strike carried on by Hawaiian and Filipino workers. For the Japanese remaining on the plantations the period between 1916 and 1920 was a time of increased labor unrest and labor organization. At the same time, the Filipinos organized a separate union. In 1920 the Filipinos called a strike and asked for labor solidarity on the part of the Japanese. The Filipino strike began on January 19 and Japanese workers were harassed by striking Filipinos. The Japanese union called for an indefinite layoff on January 22, which they changed to a full strike on February 1. The Japanese vacillation was partly the result of their uncertainty as to whether this was the most advantageous time for a strike. They had requested that the Filipinos delay the strike a short while, but the request was not honored. It appeared that ethnic hostilities were diminishing when the Japanese joined the strike, but this was proven wrong when the Filipino strike leader called off the strike and ordered the Filipinos back to work. They refused to go, so he declared the strike on again. Japanese-Filipino relations were further strained by this sequence.

By mid-February the majority of Oahu's 5,871 Japanese and 2,625 Filipino sugar workers were on strike. The strike was less successful on the outer islands where plantation owners and police felt less restrained in the use of violence and coercion. A campaign was launched against Japanese workers while Filipinos were ignored. The newspapers attacked the strike as an attempt to take over Hawaii for Japan. Japanese workers were evicted from their plantation houses. A flu epidemic hit the displaced workers. Health authorities evicted them from their places of refuge for "reasons of health and sanitation." The children of strikers had been excluded from the public schools during the strike. The strike was beaten after 165 days. The plantation owners made no concessions. They announced that no nonstrikers or strikebreakers would be fired to make room for returning strikers. All strike leaders were blacklisted and some were jailed.

The strike defeat increased the rate of Japanese migration off the plantations. In 1919 there were 24,791 Japanese sugar workers but only 12,781 in 1924. The strike also had two other apparently conflicting results. Wages were increased shortly after it ended, wage differentials by race were reduced, and plantation living conditions were greatly improved. At the same time, laws were passed between 1919 and 1923 making illegal "criminal syndicalism, anarchistic publications, and picketing." Apparently workers were to be kept docile through a combination of the carrot and the stick.

The 1920 strike was the last major attempt at multinational labor unity prior to World War II, but it was not the end of Filipino worker militance. In 1924 there was an all-Filipino strike, which lasted for eight months and involved 3,000 workers. Repression was even more intense than it had been in 1920. In one incident alone 101 strikers were arrested, sixty sentenced to jail, and the strike leader received a two-to-ten-year term on trumped-up charges. The strike was beaten. Labor strife continued sporadically into the thirties and culminated in 1937 with the last major national strike. The Filipino workers, under the leadership of an all-Filipino union—the *Vibora Luviminda*—struck Puunene Plantation on Maui. The strike is noteworthy in that the union, for the first time ever, was able to force the planters to negotiate and sign a contract arrived at through collective bargaining. The contract was vague and conveyed little in the way of direct benefits to workers and several strike leaders were tried and convicted on conspiracy charges, but the union still claimed a victory. Others have described the strike as a defeat for workers and a case could be made for either position. However the achievement of a negotiated contract was an important opening wedge toward the organization of labor.

A. The Growth of a Class Orientation

There was about this same time some growth of class-oriented worker activity in Hawaii (Thompson, 1951; Fuchs, 1961: 354–376; Perlman, 1952, Johannessen, 1956; Henderson, 1941; Aller, 1957; Anthony, 1955;

Allen, 1950). The *Voice of Labor* was published as a militant class-conscious paper between 1935 and 1939 under the leadership of left-oriented maritime workers. Most of the serious labor organizing took place on the docks and among maritime workers, although it gradually spread into the urban centers of Honolulu and Hilo. Most of these activities were under the leadership of the ILWU which was charged, not without some validity, with being a communist-dominated union. Jack Hall and the ILWU were planning an organizing drive among plantation workers when they were interrupted by the outbreak of World War II. The war period proved immensely important in increasing plantation-worker receptivity to the union. Hawaii was placed under military rule and plantation workers spent a major portion of the war either officially frozen into their jobs or unofficially prevented from moving to other jobs. Their wages were frozen. At the same time, large numbers of defense workers were imported to Honolulu from the mainland and paid high wages. Prices rose rapidly, making conditions difficult for plantation workers on fixed incomes. In some cases, the military "rented" workers from the plantations to work on projects alongside the mainland imports. Plantation workers would see their employers make a profit directly from their labor and see mainland workers doing the same job for much more money. It is not surprising that the war's end found plantation workers angry, bitter, and receptive to unionization.

The ILWU was aided in its drive by a favorable ruling of the NLRB, which in October 1944 found between 50 and 60% of plantation employees to be industrial workers subject to the provisions of the Wagner Act. It was further aided by the passage of "the little Wagner Act" in Hawaii on May 21, 1945, extending the same rights to agricultural workers that industrial workers enjoyed under the Wagner Act. The growth of the ILWU was rapid and culminated in 1946 with a major test of strength between the union and the sugar planters. The union demanded a significant wage increase and an end to all perquisites and vestiges of paternalism. The sugar planters were willing to consider the wage package but not the end of perquisites or other infringements on "management prerogatives." The strike lasted seventy-nine days and ended with a total union victory. The ILWU, espousing an ideology of class unity and class militance, became a major economic force in Hawaii.

B. National Struggle Continues

At the same time as this revolution was taking place on the labor front, a similar one was taking place on the political front (Fuchs, 1961: 323–353; Inouye, 1967; Coffman, 1972). The end of World War II found the Japanese population to have come of age in a real sense of the term. They were now predominantly a citizen population and comprised the largest single ethnic block among eligible voters. Prior to the war, politics was firmly in control of the Republican Party, which was dominated by the sugar factors. Thus any effective political challenge could only come through the revival of the Democratic Party. Japanese-Americans, led by veterans of the 100th Infantry Battalion and the 442nd Regiment, came together with John Burns to try to rebuild the party. At the same time the ILWU and Jack Hall sought a political outlet for their growing economic power and also turned to the Democratic Party. The two forces alternately fought one another and worked together against their common enemy until the Democratic Party became the dominant party in Hawaii and established a record of significant and widespread social reforms. Success, however, has not produced a unified Democratic Party. The same factions in existence thirty years ago may be seen today, along with some new ones.

While it is outside the scope of this paper, it should be noted that the revolution in Hawaii was short-lived. The Democratic Party has achieved virtual total dominance over the political scene and Japanese-Americans have become the dominant group within it, yet it has largely lost its crusading spirit. There is little evidence of any continued concern with class issues or the expansion of workers' rights. The ILWU has suffered a similar fate. It paid a very high price during the red-baiting period of the late '40s and early '50s. Perhaps it became so concerned with surviving that it forgot *why* its survival was important. At any rate we may now observe the ILWU operating in concert with the sugar factors to promote sugar subsidies, protective tariffs, etc. But that is the subject of a different paper.

VI. CONSCIOUSNESS: CLASS OR NATIONAL

This chapter has been primarily concerned with the interplay between class and national consciousness in Hawaii between 1850 and 1950. We traced developments within a fairly typical colonial pattern. Plantation societies need land, markets, and labor. The missionary influence led to the development of private property and the distribution of land among individual owners. Within a few decades the majority of all agriculturally valuable land was in the hands of Europeans. Developments in the United States created the potential market. The indigenous population was too small to provide the needed labor supply. Even if it had been sufficient, it probably would not have been relied upon as the sole or even major source of labor. It is characteristic of plantation societies that labor is recruited from racially and culturally different peoples in order to maximize the control factor. Labor was recruited from a number of different sources, each of which was kept segregated from one another and paid different amounts of wages in order to prevent unity from developing. Strikes by members of one national group were fought with strikebreakers recruited from one or more other national groups.

The workers, for the most part, responded by developing national consciousness rather than class consciousness. Strikes occurred along national lines and workers were often aided by their conationals who were in different class situations. The few early attempts to form class-conscious movements were readily split through exploitation of national consciousness. The one ultimately successful attempt to build class consciousness across national lines required the efforts of an ideologically motivated, militant cadre. The ILWU and its radical allies were indispensable in this endeavor. They were also aided by favorable organizing conditions created by the treatment of labor during the war. Nor can it be said to have been entirely successful in building a class conscious labor force in Hawaii. The ILWU became a powerful force and agricultural workers in Hawaii became the highest paid in the world, but racial tensions remain strong and show no signs of dissipation.

The historical experiences of Hawaiians were such that they were far more prone to identify as Hawaiians rather than in terms of their class membership. Outsiders came in, introduced diseases which led to their virtual extermination, alienated their land, destroyed their economy, displaced their religion, and finally overthrew their government and seized their country. It is not surprising that a high degree of national consciousness developed. This consciousness was reinforced by the fact that Hawaiians were largely excluded from the opportunities to succeed in the new Hawaii. In 1950 the infant mortality rate was sixty per thousand live births for pure Hawaiians and twenty-six per thousand for part-Hawaiians (Lind, 1967: 106). Filipinos were the only ethnic group to have a higher infant mortality rate (thirty-one per thousand). The median income of males with income for 1949 was $2,369 for Hawaiians and part-Hawaiians combined, which was lower than the median income of any other ethnic group with the single exception of Filipinos (Lind, 1967: 100). This understates the extent of Hawaiian deprivation because part-Hawaiians are much better off economically than pure Hawaiians. Filipinos were also the only ethnic group to exceed the proportion of Hawaiians employed as laborers or to have fewer professionals drawn from their ranks. It is true that many Hawaiians did develop a degree of class consciousness and were quite active in the organizational drives and strikes of the ILWU, but it is also understandable that as of 1950 Hawaiians were far more prone toward national than class consciousness.

Filipinos, Japanese, and Chinese by no means exhaust the list of ethnic groups brought to Hawaii as laborers, but they are both the largest and the most crucial ones for our purposes in examining the interplay between class and national consciousness. There is one additional group whose experiences shed some light both on the nature of consciousness and also on the nature of racial/ethnic identity. This group is the Portuguese. Portuguese were brought to Hawaii in two waves (Nordyke, 1977: 30–32; Kuykendall, 1967: 122–126; Felix and Senecal, 1978). The first wave, numbering approximately 12,000, was recruited between 1878 and 1887 in response to the anti-Oriental (primarily anti-Chinese) agitation. The second wave came after annexation. United States law barred Orientals from becoming naturalized citizens (although their children born in Hawaii would be native-born Americans). The Bureau of Immigration wished to recruit to Hawaii people who were eligible to become American citizens. Consequently, almost 13,000 additional Portuguese were recruited between 1906 and 1913. The Portuguese were one of the few Caucasian groups to come to Hawaii to work on the plantations and who, in sizable numbers, remained in Hawaii as permanent residents.[5]

The Portuguese were Caucasians but were never defined as haoles. To this day the resident population is socially divided into haoles and locals, with the latter category encompassing all nonwhites. Portuguese are normally included in the "local" category. It is probable that this categorization resulted from their location in the labor force. Portuguese were paid more than Orientals but less than haoles when performing similar work. They were also frequently used as lunas or first-line overseers but only in very rare cases were they elevated to plantation management positions. Thus the Portuguese played the role of the classic middleman minority (Bonacich, 1973). They were located in the economic system between the haole capitalists who owned and operated the plantations and the Orientals who formed the bulk of the laborers. This position as buffer between two different racial/ethnic groups with different positions in the economic order led the Portuguese to be classified socially as something different from either. They were not Orientals and they were not haoles— they were Portuguese.

Little has been said to this point regarding the state of consciousness of haole workers. It is difficult to get reliable data because statistics on Caucasians do not always distinguish between haole civilians, Portuguese, military personnel, and military dependents. Available information indicates that Hawaii had a very small civilian haole working class during the relevant time period (1850 to 1950). Most haoles were in upper- or middle-class locations and could not be expected to display any sense of working-class consciousness, although they did exhibit a high degree of racial or national consciousness. There was a relatively small number of haoles working in craft occupations, on the docks, in the warehouses, and as seamen. Craft workers tended to take a protectionist view toward their occupations, but haoles in the other three occupations were involved in the building of multiracial unions and did display a degree of class consciousness.

The Chinese left the plantations during the period when Honolulu was growing, and many were able to move into small business or other occupational niches which provided an opportunity for upward mobility. By 1950 they occupied a collective position in the economic order second only to haoles. Consequently, they developed an individualistic orientation although they retained enough racial consciousness to share resources for their common good. These opportunities in Honolulu had largely disappeared by the time that the Japanese left the plantations. As of 1950 they were still concentrated in the working class although some were beginning to take advantage of the educational opportunities provided by the G.I. Bill and prepare for professional careers (Yamamoto, 1979). They played an active role in building the ILWU. Filipinos were still concentrated in plantation agriculture in 1950 and formed the largest single component of the ILWU membership. Segments of each of the latter groups retained a sense of national consciousness, but the success of the ILWU helped to forge class consciousness during the course of its struggles.

VII. THEORETICAL CONCLUSIONS

This paper has considered two of the types of relationships that may be created between racial/ethnic groups: the first, which develops as the consequence of the expansion of the capitalist system, and the second, created as a consequence of labor migrations. The contact between Europeans and Hawaiians illustrates the manner in which racial/ethnic relations are forged in the course of capitalist expansion. In fact, it actually illustrates three subtypes of relationships that might be created in this manner. The first, the trading subtype, developed when Hawaii was first brought into contact with the expanding capitalist world-economy. This was the trading relationship of unequal exchange in which, for the most part, Europeans exploited the existing stratification order in order to extract surplus from the Hawaiians although some contact was made directly with the Hawaiian people. This subtype of relationship includes as examples the trading activities of Cook's crew, fur traders, merchantmen, whalers, and those persons involved in the sandalwood trade with China. In each of these cases the Europeans attempted to enrich themselves, but in so doing they set in motion processes that altered the existing stratification order to the disadvantage of the commoners.

The second, the land clearance subtype, developed when Europeans alienated the land from the Hawaiian people. This form of relationship almost inevitably develops when colonizers attempt to develop a settler colony and wish to use the land for their own purposes. It becomes necessary to clear the indigenous population from the land. The actual techniques vary from case to case (e.g., the Kikuyu in Kenya, the Irish in Ireland, the Native Americans in the United States, the Caribs in the Caribbean, the Hawaiians in Hawaii) but the net impact is the same. The land that was used to sustain non-Europeans is taken over and used for the benefit of Europeans. There may be very little interaction between groups, but this situation may still be classified as a type of race relations as both groups remain part of the same social system (although one exists on its fringes) and one group is deprived to the extent that the other monopolizes existing resources. Relations are real, if indirect.

The third, the proletarianization subtype, developed when the Hawaiian people were proletarianized and made to become wage laborers in order to sustain themselves. In a very real sense, then, the latter two subtypes are closely linked. The alienation of the land from the Hawaiian people simultaneously proletarianized them. However, the two processes are not always so closely linked. The Caribs were not proletarianized— they were exterminated. The Koi and the San peoples in Southern Africa experienced a similar fate. Native Americans had their lands alienated and were partially exterminated. The survivors were not incorporated into the economy as wage labor for a full century or more. Thus it is clear that the two subtypes of relationships are theoretically independent although each involves an extraction of surplus from the colonized peoples.[6] The gains to the colonizers in the latter case come about in the form of surplus value extracted during the production process.

While all three forms of racial/ethnic relations involve Europeans gaining at the expense of non-Europeans, it should be emphasized that race/ethnicity is not the crucial factor operating. It could be argued that racial/ethnic differences are almost irrelevant to the process—almost, but not quite. The driving force in each of these three situations is the expansion of the capitalist world-economy and the incorporation of newer areas into it. The extraction of surplus value via unequal exchange takes place through the market place and is a normal part of merchant capitalist practices. The alienation of the land is justified by an ideology that stresses development, progress, the virtues of work, etc., but it is still done in order to facilitate the development of capitalist agriculture. The proletarianization of a people and the extraction of surplus value through wage labor is the classic form of capitalist exploitation. Race and ethnicity are only involved in the development of an ideology of rationalization or justification. Observable differences form the basis for the development of social categories of race and/or ethnicity. Evaluative notions become attached to social differences and these, in turn, become the justification for a pattern of exploitation. It is not necessary to capitalism that racial/ethnic differences exist or that an ideology of racism emerge, but they do make the system function more efficiently and do provide a convenient justification for more intense forms of exploitation. These forms of relationship are not conducive to the development of class consciousness and are much more likely to result in the growth of national consciousness. Struggle is less likely to take the form of class struggle and is more likely to take the form of wars of national liberation. However, the latter, because they are anti-imperialist, are also ultimately anti-capitalist.

Each of the types of race relations discussed above developed as Hawaii was incorporated into the world-economy in a periphery-to-core relationship. The second broad type of racial/ethnic relationship illustrated in this paper results from a semi-periphery-to-periphery (or core-to-periphery if one prefers not to use the concept of semi-periphery) relationship. That is, the establishment of capitalist agriculture in Hawaii made Hawaii into a center of capital accumulation such that it was more core-like *vis-à-vis* some areas of the world (e.g., Japan, Philippines, China) although it remained more periphery-like *vis-à-vis* the United States. Thus the type of racial/ethnic relations that emerged with the importation of Chinese, Japanese, and Filipinos into Hawaii was specifically created by the existence of a global labor market through which labor normally, in times of capital expansion, flows from areas of cheap labor (e.g., the periphery with minimal degree of capital concentration) to areas of higher degree of capital concentration (i.e., the core with higher wage levels). Some such flows are relatively voluntary in that they are motivated by economic necessity but involve a high degree of free choice and individual decision making (e.g., Irish Catholics to the United States and part of the Filipino migration to Hawaii). Others are totally involuntary in that they involve capture and forced transportation (e.g., Africans to the New World). Contract recruitment of labor falls in between the two ends of the continuum (e.g., Chinese, Japanese, and most Filipinos to Hawaii).

Racial/ethnic relations that come about in this manner are often much more complex than those created by the incorporation of new areas into the capitalist world-economy. They frequently involve a multiplicity of racial/ethnic groups, each of which exists in a relation of labor to capital which is overlaid with a second relation of racial/ethnic minority to majority group. The social categories of race and ethnicity emerge in exactly the same manner in either context, just as an ideology of racism is equally likely to emerge and will, once developed, perform the same function. Initially the splits between capital and labor and majority-minority will largely coincide. However, as generations pass the two lines of cleavage may begin to diverge somewhat although they will always retain some relation to one another. The situation is made more complex by the presence of a number of different racial/ethnic groups so that lines of cleavage are also created along racial/ethnic lines within the proletariat. These lines of cleavage may be manipulated by capital as a means of facilitating the exploitation of labor as a whole. Hawaiian sugar planters kept workers of different national groups segregated from one another and encouraged them to see each other as enemies. They did this by varying wage levels by national identity, by using workers of one national group as scabs to break the strikes conducted by workers of other national identities, and by using members of one group (i.e., Portuguese) as straw bosses or first-line supervisors where they were explicitly charged with maximizing the production of laborers of different group identities.

There is little question that these tactics encouraged the development of national consciousness and hindered the growth of class consciousness among the various segments of the working class in Hawaii. Portuguese wished to distinguish themselves from Orientals and to be accepted as haoles. Japanese and Filipinos had little trust of one another and often acted to the other's detriment. Filipino members of one language group acted as strikebreakers against Filipino members of another language group (Fuchs, 1961: 235). However, it is attributing too much power to the capitalists to give them credit for all cases in which national consciousness impeded the development of class consciousness and manifested itself in one segment of the proletariat taking actions to the detriment of others.

It is necessary to understand that the class struggle is very complex and is waged in many different ways. If members of one ethnic group see that others are used to undercut their position *vis-à-vis* capital, to strike out against that group and exclude them from the labor market is really an attempt to strike at capital by removing one of its weapons. One segment of labor improves its bargaining position *vis-à-vis* capital at the expense of a weaker segment of labor. Such acts may be described as shortsighted in that they are divisive, impede the development of class unity and are contrary to class interests. However, such developments normally occur when prospects for a unified class movement are quite remote, they are harmful to capital and, thus, are an integral part of the class struggle at a given historical moment. It is in this light that one should interpret the actions of the haole mechanics and clerks in urging the exclusion of Chinese from Hawaii. These actions are fratricidal but they are, nevertheless, part of the class struggle. It is more difficult to interpret scabbing and strikebreaking in the same light as such actions are both fratricidal *and* play into the hands of capital. Nevertheless, they develop in the same social context and represent attempts to improve some workers' positions *vis-a-vis* capital.

This paper has also illustrated the fact that it is very difficult, but not impossible, to overcome national consciousness and form a class-conscious movement. It can be accomplished providing the right set of socio-historical circumstances combine with the activities of a cadre of militant, ideologically motivated activists. The ILWU had within it a body of highly committed radical activists who were willing to risk much in order to achieve significant social change in Hawaii. They worked hard and long and many suffered in their endeavor. It is not possible to analyze historical situations on a "what if?" basis with any degree of confidence. Yet, it seems reasonable to state that the efforts of the ILWU would have been much less successful if they had not come so close on the heels of World War II. The combination of the naked oppression of Hawaii's labor and the oppressive wartime experiences of the Japanese-American community in Hawaii contributed to this success. It is true that Hawaii's working class was always highly exploited and that such exploitation was always quite visible. However, it seems likely that the experiences of World War II highlighted that exploitation in such a fashion that workers could not help but recognize its class basis. It would have been especially difficult to fail to recognize this with the presence of the ILWU and associated radical activists who were constantly presenting a class analysis in vivid terms. Class unity did not come about overnight or as a result of purely verbal blandishments. It began in a tentative fashion and was largely forged in struggle, and especially in victorious struggle. The strikes that were fought and won on a multinational class basis after generations of failed national strikes proved, more than anything else could, the value of class solidarity.

The same time period also demonstrated that national struggles may be progressive forces which have their place in a struggle against oppression. The returning Japanese-American war vets came together on a basis of national unity, not class solidarity. Yet their efforts to organize themselves politically and overthrow the political domination of the planter class helped to bring about significant changes in Hawaii. The rise of the Japanese-dominated, reform-minded Democratic Party to political power paralleled the rise of the revolutionary ILWU on the economic scene. The two reinforced one another for a time and helped to create a new Hawaii. It is true that in time the dynamism for change waned and the new Hawaii stagnated short of a truly equalitarian society, but it is much closer to that objective than the old Hawaii (i.e., the Planter's Hawaii) could ever have become. The story of the decline in the dynamism for social change and the continued role of race/ethnicity in the new stratification order in Hawaii is the subject of another paper.

VIII. AN AFTERWORD

The research reported in this paper was conducted for two purposes: to further our understanding of the nature of race and class in Hawaii through the use of theoretical ideas formulated in the course of studying the historical experiences of Black Americans and to assess the extent of wider applicability of those ideas. The earlier work focused on the interaction between class exploitation and national oppression and the associated interplay between class and national consciousness as bases for emerging lines of struggle. It was always intended that the theoretical concepts and interpretations, which involved an analysis of race/ethnicity in labor force terms within a broader context of a capitalist world-economy, would have applicability to racial/ethnic relations wherever capitalism impinges. However, any such claim was always subject to the criticism that the historical experiences of Black Americans are unique and that any theoretical explanation of their experiences must be similarly unique. It is true that the historical experiences of Black Americans are unique. It is equally true that the historical experiences of all ethnic groups are unique in all their details. This paper suggests that the same processes that account for the historical experiences of Black Americans also account for the historical experiences of Hawaiians as well as Japanese-Americans, Chinese-Americans, Filipino-Americans, and Portuguese-Americans in Hawaii. Additional research should demonstrate that these processes are equally valuable in explaining the historical experiences of all racial/ethnic groups in all areas of the world incorporated into the capitalist world-economy, even if only incorporated in a peripheral manner.

ACKNOWLEDGMENTS

This paper is the product of research supported by Grant Number 5R01MH2847902S1 from the Center for the Study of Metropolitan Problems, National Institute of Mental Health, and by a fellowship from the National Endowment for the Humanities. The paper has benefited from comments received from my co-participants in a global labor market seminar at the Fernand Braudel Center (Trevor Abrahams, Robert Bach, Mark Beittel, John Casparis, Ray Davis, William Martin, Elizabeth McLean Petras, Alusio de Rosa, Jim Toth, Isidor Walliman, Immanuel

Wallerstein). It has also benefited from comments and criticism received from Barry Rigby and William Canak.

NOTES

1. The term *European* is used herein in the racial/ethnic sense and not in reference to continent of origin. It includes both Europeans and Americans and may presently be used interchangeably with "haole." The original meaning of "haole" was "without breath," meaning someone who did not speak Hawaiian. It later came to be loosely interpreted as stranger or foreigner and gradually took on the meaning of "Caucasian" (Nordyke, 1977: 29).

2. It may prove useful to have a sense of the Hawaiian Succession. Kamehameha (sometimes called Kamehameha I or Kamehameha the Great) unified the Hawaiian Islands, completing the process around 1812. He was the first king and was succeeded by Liholiho (Kamehameha II) at his death in 1819. Liholiho died in 1824 and was succeeded by Kauikeaouli (Kamehameha III), who was nine years old at the time. He, in turn, passed away in 1855 and was succeeded by his nephew and adopted son, Alexander Liholiho (Kamehameha IV), who passed away in 1863 and was succeeded by Lot Kamehameha (Kamehameha V). The death of Lot Kamehameha in 1872 brought an end to the Kamehameha dynasty and brought Lunalilo to the throne until his death in 1874. Kalukaua followed as king and ruled until his death in 1891. He was succeeded by Queen Lilioukalani, who ruled very briefly until overthrown by the Planters' Revolution in 1893.

3. See note 1 for the definition of *haole*.

4. This statement may appear inconsistent with the population of Hawaiians living at the time. However, it is based upon the definition of an "able-bodied male" used by the planters. The Report of the Secretary of the Hawaiian Immigration Society stated very clearly that they were restricting the applicability of the term to males under forty years of age and were inclined to exclude all those close to that age. In short, an able-bodied male is one whom the planters believe is able to withstand the rigors of plantation labor and whom they are thus willing to hire.

5. Other Caucasians brought to Hawaii as laborers included 100 white Americans, 327 Austrians, 84 Italians, a few Scots, 1,400 Germans, approximately 600 Scandinavians, 110 Molokans, and over 2,000 other Russians from Harbin, Manchuria (Nordyke, 1977: 29–35).

6. This is a debatable point in that many scholars would argue that the two processes are essentially the same and that it does not make a basic difference whether surplus is extracted during the productive process or the exchange process so long as it takes place within a capitalist economy (Hopkins and Wallerstein, 1977: 121–122). I am not convinced of the value of expanding the meaning of proletariat in this manner, but I remain open on the question.

REFERENCES

Aller, Curtis
   1957   Labor Relations in the Hawaiian Sugar Industry. Berkeley, Calif.: University of
          California.
Anthony, J. Garner
   1955   Hawaii Under Army Rule. Stanford, Calif.: Stanford University.
Bonacich, Edna
   1972   "A theory of ethnic antagonisms: the split labor market." American Sociological
          Review 37: 547–559.

1973 "A theory of middleman minorities." American Sociological Review 38: 583–594.

1976 "Advanced capitalism and black/white relations in the United States: a split labor market interpretation." American Sociological Review 41: 34–51.

n.d. "International labor migration: a theoretical orientation." unpublished.

Coffman, Tom

1972 To Catch a Wave: Hawaii's New Politics. Honolulu, Hawaii: Honolulu Star Bulletin.

Daws, Gavan

1968 Shoal of Time: A History of the Hawaiian Islands. New York: Macmillan.

Felix, John Henry, and Peter F. Senecal (eds.)

1978 The Portuguese in Hawaii. Honolulu, Hawaii: privately published.

Fuchs, Lawrence H.

1961 Hawaii Pono: A Social History. New York: Harcourt, Brace and World.

Geschwender, James A.

1977 Class, Race, and Worker Insurgency. New York: Cambridge University Press, American Sociological Association: Arnold and Caroline Rose Monograph Series.

1978 Racial Stratification in America. Dubuque: William C. Brown.

Hawaiian Immigration Society

1874 Report of the Secretary, July, 1874. Honolulu, Hawaii: Hawaiian Immigration Society.

Henderson, C.J.

1951 "Labor—an undercurrent of Hawaiian social history." Social Process in Hawaii 15: 44–55.

Hopkins, Terence, K., and Immanuel Wallerstein

1977 "Patterns of development of the modern world-system." Review (Fall): 111–145.

Petras, Elizabeth McLean

1976 "Towards a theory of international migration: the new division of labor." Washington, D.C.: Paper delivered at Smithsonian Conference on the New Immigration.

Petras, Elizabeth McLean with the collaboration of James A. Geschwender and John Casparis

1979 "Migration flows within a global market." unpublished.

Probasco, Herbert A.

1965 "Filipino labor unions and the 1920 plantation strike in Hawaii." unpublished.

Portes, Alejandro

1978 "Migration and underdevelopment." Politics and Society 8: 1–48.

Poulantzas, Nicos

1973 Political Power and Social Classes. Tr. and ed. Timothy Hagan. London: New Left Books.

1975 Classes in Contemporary Capitalism. Tr. David Fernbach. London: New Left Books.

Renaud, Bertrand R. with the assistance of Tu Duc Pham

1973 Population Dynamics in Hawaii. Honolulu, Hawaii: University of Hawaii, Economic Research Center.

Reinecke, John E.

n.d. "The 1920 Japanese strike." unpublished.

Stevens, Sylvester

[1945] American Expansion in Hawaii, 1842–1898. New York: Russell and Russell.
1968

Tate, Merze

1960 "The early political influence of the Sandwich Islands missionaries." The Journal of Religious Thought 17: 117–132.

1963   "Sandwich Island missionaries and annexation." The Journal of Religious Thought
       20: 137–145.
1968   Hawaii: Reciprocity or Annexation. East Lansing, Mich.: Michigan State Univer-
       sity.
Thompson, David E.
1951   "The ILWU as a force for interracial unity in Hawaii." Social Process in Hawaii
       15: 32–43.
Thompson, Edgar T.
1970   Plantation Societies, Race Relations, and the South: Selected Papers of Edgar T.
       Thompson. Durham, N.C.: Duke University.
Wakukawa, Ernest K.
1938   A History of the Japanese People in Hawaii. Honolulu, Hawaii: The Toyo Shoin.
Wallerstein, Immanuel
1974   The Modern World System: Capitalist Agriculture and the Origins of the European
       World-Economy in the Sixteenth Century. New York: Academic Press.
Yamamoto, George
1979   "The ethnic lawyer and social structure: the Japanese attorney in Honolulu."
       Social Process in Hawaii 27: 38–50.

COMMUNITIES OF MINERS IN UPPER SILESIA:
TRADE UNIONS, THE CATHOLIC CHURCH, AND NATIONALITY CONFLICT, 1865–1914

Lawrence Schofer

Why were miners' unions in pre-World War I Upper Silesia so late and so slow to develop? The first large long-lived union began to gain ground for the first time after 1908, though union-led strikes had occurred in 1889 and 1905–1907 and would occur in 1913. There had been all kinds of workers' organizations in earlier years, usually Polish-speaking ones with a devotional slant. The various workmen's circles of the 1870s, 1880s, and even after often had ties to the church. The largest of them all, the Society for Mutual Aid (Związek wzajemnej pomocy), slowly cut its ties to the German Catholic church and its political expression, the Center party. German-speaking groups like the Social Democratic Union of German

Research in the Sociology of Work, Volume 1, pages 205–226
Copyright © 1981 by JAI Press Inc.
All rights of reproduction in any form reserved.
ISBN: 0-89232-124-5

Miners and the liberal Hirsch-Duncker unions made little headway. In 1908 the floundering Society for Mutual Aid merged with two other Polish groups to form the Polish Professional Union (Zjednoczenie Zawodowe Polskie—ZZP), and only in the next few years did trade unionism play an outstanding role in Upper Silesian mining.

Many of the people who today ask about the peculiar pattern of trade unionism in Upper Silesia are in fact Social Democrats themselves. They wish to know why a movement with such great successes in other industrial areas met with such abysmal failure in Upper Silesia. This essay constitutes a preliminary effort to use existing historical literature in a way designed to understand this situation.

One problem in answering this question lies in the way the question is posed, for it assumes that workers naturally gravitate toward trade unions. Clearly that is not so. One can argue that a trade union forms a kind of broad community structure which provides a place in society for its members. Other kinds of communities are possible, and Upper Silesia proved a testing ground for many of these—the settled rural community, miners as a world unto themselves, the firm as a community in the spirit of paternalism, the Catholic church, Polish nationality, the trade union, the society of Social Democracy. Some of these lay linked with the past, some with the developing industrial society. Because of the slow rate of migration into Upper Silesia and because of the cultural pecularities of a Polish mining area in the Prussian state, the old style was slower to break down than in some other areas. As change came, it did not uproot the old culture as happened elsewhere. In particular, attachment to the Catholic church and a growing sense of Polish self-consciousness created new social and cultural patterns.

I speak here not of a community in a narrow sense, but of a broad background that sets the patterns in which one lives; it is a subculture in the way that term has been used for German Social Democrats in the German Empire (Roth, 1963). The unwritten rules of the community set the bounds on how people lived, how they related to one another, how they behaved at work. Many of their customs and traditions originated in an earlier period before industrial capitalism set the tone of industrial relations, and many profound adjustments had to be made in the new era. So widespread were the changes that the old subculture broke up, and newer social movements vied with each other to fill the gap. In other areas of Germany, the Social Democratic party and the Social Democratic trade unions often proved successful in creating a new framework for industrial workers. Among miners in the Ruhr, the Catholic church through its allied trade unions found it possible to retain the allegiance of a good proportion of local men. Poles in the Ruhr before the First World War formed a relatively compact group, concentrated occupationally in mining and geographically in specific towns. Though they created their own social groups and economic organizations, in the long run the pressure to assimilate overcame their separateness (Klessmann, 1978: 145–171). In Upper Silesia the social struggle turned out to be more complex, for here the German environment was not so overpowering. Whatever the outcome, the Social Democrats failed to gain more than a tiny foothold; the new subculture came to have values quite divergent from those regnant in other industrial areas (Schofer, 1975 and reviews in Crew, 1977; Długoborski, 1976; Tenfelde, 1977a; see also Stearns, 1976; 251, 260, 266).

When speaking of Upper Silesia, one has several possibilities for reference points for communities. The Polish-speaking population springs immediately to mind; but Roman Catholicism, so crucial an ingredient of Polish self-consciousness, crossed nationality boundaries. Local Germans were Catholics, too, and the lines of allegiance lay intertwined here. Socialists and trade unionists appealed to an international class feeling, an allegiance that also transcended the presumed parochialism of nationalities. Practically speaking, no Poles belonged to the industrial bourgeoisie, but many Germans did indeed stand in the ranks of the local proletariat. And then there were the miners, an occupational group with many traditions and a long memory. All of these competed on many levels for the loyalty of the Upper Silesians, but some were more successful than others.

I

Like miners everywhere, the coal, lead, and zinc (primarily coal) miners in Upper Silesia formed a distinct group within a larger society. In the decades around the turn of the twentieth century, they possessed a specific style of life, set of customs, working habits, language, and jargon that set them off even from other working people. Their Polish was not only different from that spoken elsewhere, mainly in its conservatism and resistance to foreign influences (Pater, 1969), but they infused their talk with Upper Silesian dialect pronunciation and with the kind of specialized vocabulary characteristic of miners in many climes (Tenfelde, 1977b: appendix). They maintained a set of traditions similar to those of miners elsewhere in Germany, but these too had an Upper Silesian slant—miner brotherhoods, uniform, celebrations of St. Barbara's Day, and so on. And of course there were the lifestyle items—frowning on work by wives (Piotrowski, 1962), the large number of children (Haines, 1975), the attachment to landholding (Schofer, 1974: 39–59), the desire to keep a pig

or goat (the "miner's cow") (Ligęza, 1964). They also had a sense of
dignity, of pride in their jobs, and of the difficulties inherent in them. This
sense of importance dated far back in time to when miners formed a
specially privileged estate within society. In the nineteenth century those
privileges rapidly dropped away, but miners maintained a pride of being
sustained by their social customs as well as by their jobs. Newcomers to
the occupation even in the late nineteenth century picked up the old
notions and incorporated them into their outlook on the world.

Legally, mining in Prussia entered the free-enterprise era with the new
legislation culminating in the general mining law of 1865, when the state
renounced its control over hiring and firing. Owners were free to run their
enterprises as they saw fit, while miners lost their status as a separate
estate in society. Miners' special privileges were being eroded all through
the early nineteenth century; now the miners officially entered the free
labor market, free in the sense of freedom to move, freedom to apply for
work anywhere. Freedom, however, did not mean total emancipation
from the past. More and more historians have been emphasizing the
relevance of past traditions and popular culture to the lives of workers in
industrial society (Tenfelde, 1977b; Gutman, 1977). In a way, the story of
Upper Silesian miners from 1865 to 1914 involved the setting of a free
labor market with workers who were not entirely comfortable with the
new arrangements and with employers who were constantly attempting to
mold those workers into pliable forms.

The lack of large-scale migration into the developing industrial region of
Upper Silesia constituted a major element in the peculiar social development of the area. Newcomers simply did not come. They did not come
from German areas like East Prussia and Pomerania, which were export-
ing people wholesale to other labor markets; nor did they come from
Polish-speaking Posen, which might have been assumed to be a likely
source of supply. New workers for the mines and mills hardly even came
from Lower Silesia; individuals from Oppeln, barely 100 kilometers away,
had to be considered "long-distance" migrants.

Why didn't they come? Upper Silesia had long had the reputation of
being a wild, unsettled, foreign place. Previously peopled by Polish
peasants and marked by few cities to relieve the glumness, at the end of
the nineteenth century the area was still considered a Polish island with a
number of drab industrial towns. To be sure, these towns now were
generally populated by a German-speaking majority, but they all suggested Charles Dickens' repugnant "Coketown." However, a reputation
about living conditions could not by itself have sufficed to turn away
prospective workers. The Ruhr basin certainly had its share of grimy
hovels, and language conflicts have not held off migration to other developing areas.

Table 1: Number of Employees in Upper Silesian Mining, 1852–1913

1852	14,025
1865	28,526
1885	54,726
1900	83,064
1913	135,858

Source: 1852 and 1865, Zeitschrift für das Berg-, Hütten-, und Salinenwesen, annual
volumes; 1885, 1900, 1913, Zeitschrift des oberschlesischen berg- und
hüttenmännischen Vereins, annual volumes.

One must perforce turn to the managers of the Upper Silesian enterprises to see how they went about recruiting miners. Too often accounts
of workers neglect the role of employers in the process of the formation of
an industrial labor force. These entrepreneurs and top managers play a
key role in determining the course of industrial relations. In Upper Silesia, these men at the top were without exception German; the people at
the bottom, the workers, were primarily Polish. In the low-level supervisory ranks, Germans and German-speaking Poles received preference,
while Germans occupied all important positions further up in the evolving
bureaucratic hierarchy. Upper Silesian mineowners in the mid-nineteenth
century were peculiar in that most of them were landed magnates, including some of the richest families in Germany (Prince of Pless, Hohenlohe,
Ballestrem, Donnersmarck, Schaffgotsch), and some of these industrial-
manorial princes remained active in their firms long after the need for
capital forced incorporation on most of them. Subsequent Polish nationalist propaganda included an anti-Semitic note, but practically every mining
employer of note was a German, usually Roman Catholic, including the
later Zentrum president of the Reichstag, Franz von Ballestrem. As the
firms grew, new managers came in, instituting more highly structured
chains of command. They did not recast recruiting patterns, however.

That immigrants did not come suggests an environment quite dissimilar
from that in the Ruhr and in the other major industrial complexes of
Europe. Upper Silesia provided a continuing Catholic and Polish environment for miners, even if they were fresh off the farm. While new industrial
migrants to the Ruhr faced severe cultural problems, new workers in
Upper Silesia could more readily tap into a pre-existing network founded
on a familiar language and a familiar religion. This is not to minimize the
difficulties encountered in Silesia, but merely to emphasize the enormous
and sometimes insuperable hurdles faced in the Ruhr (Klessmann, 1978:
83–144).

In spite of the strangeness of the West, a number of Silesians chose to
forsake the low pay of the East and to move. Improved transportation
and communications were serving to make migration to western Germany

Figure 1.   Eastern Prussia and Neighboring States, 1914.

Note: The areas named were Prussian regencies (Regierungsbezirke). The province of Silesia consisted of the regencies of Liegnitz, Breslau, and Oppeln. Oppeln comprised administrative Upper Silesia. *Source:* Reprinted with permission of the University of California Press.

easier after the 1870s, and the short but bitter mining strike of 1889 inaugurated a trend of sizable post-strike emigration (Schofer, 1975: 72–77). Availability of jobs and wages are perhaps the best initial predictor of movement between labor markets, and Upper Silesia fared very poorly in that regard. Though wage rates in Upper Silesian coal mining rose over time, those in the Ruhr consistently stayed a good deal higher. Average

Figure 2.   Oppeln Regency, 1914.

G   GLEIWITZ
Z   ZABRZE
B   BEUTHEN
K   KATTOWITZ
1   BEUTHEN CITY
2   KÖNIGSHÜTTE
3   KATTOWITZ CITY

OPPELN   REGENCY

----- County boundary

Upper Silesian
industrial region

Note: The areas named were counties. The Upper Silesian industrial region consisted of the southeastern counties outlined on the map.
Source: Reprinted with permission of the University of California Press.

wages per shift in Upper Silesia in the 1889–1914 period were lower than the average in every other bituminous mining area of Germany except for Lower Silesia. Almost until 1900 even the Ruhr surface workers, occupying the very lowest rung in the hierarchy of adult mine workers, earned a shift wage higher than that of skilled miners (hewers and haulers) in Upper Silesia; after 1900 these Ruhr surface workers continued to be paid at a rate not much lower than the Upper Silesian hewer-hauler average (Schofer, 1975: 105).

Put in a very simplified way, the decision makers did not offer enough to outsiders to warrant overcoming their reluctance to enter the area. Before the end of the 1880s there seems to have been little problem in satisfying local demand with local workers. The approximately 55,000 miners in 1885 had grown up locally, some descended from mining families, most from peasant families (Schofer, 1975: 14–15). A situation probably existed of "unlimited supplies of labor," in which there were so many applicants for work that wages hardly moved; all that was needed was a slight pay incentive to leave agricultural employment (Lewis, 1963). The situation was shifting, however, and the strike of 1889, similar to that in the Ruhr, marked the end of unchallenged employer dominance of the labor market.

What then were the recruitment policies adopted to meet local needs, especially after 1889 when the cries of a shortage of labor resounded incessantly? Mining companies resorted to a whole range of measures, all calculated to divert attention from their pay scales by creating a new kind of work community. Some local firms leased out plots of land to their workers in the hope of creating a settled labor force and with the intention of holding down wages. Agricultural employment is sometimes regarded as the antithesis of industrial work (including mining), but the perception prevailed in Upper Silesia that a miner with his own plot would prove to be a steadier and more reliable worker. Local miners needed less, contended the managers, because of ". . . agricultural side-occupations, cheaper cost of living . . . cheap rent in mine housing, leasing of arable land, rent-free potato patches, etc." (Denkschrift, 1890: 70). In particular in the counties of Pless, Rybnik, and Tarnowitz (the southern and eastern ends of the area) close to half the mining and smelting workers possessed fields and a quarter or more owned animals (Sattig, 1892: 21). The marriage registers of the towns of Rosdzin and Schoppinitz in more industrialized Kattowitz county showed predominantly agricultural background for newlyweds in the 1870s and industrial backgrounds in the 1890s (Reichling, 1941: 3). In the main management after 1889 abandoned policies encouraging farming by miners, but in some outlying areas—such as Mittel-Lazisk in Pless county—the connection of low wages with supplemental farm income lay imbedded in the local landscape (Gąsiorowska-Grabowska, 1962: 354–355).

Other forms of tying workers to a particular firm were tried, in particular the propagation of the concept of the industrial family (*Arbeiterstamm*). This oft-used term embodied the notion of a "family" of employees and employers at a particular plant or firm; the idea was to create a new community to substitute for the older agricultural society.

Except for the workers at the small mines of the Prince of Pless, however, miners and smelter workers of Upper Silesia received little reinforcement for this appeal to their loyalties. Prince Hohenlohe, the Donnersmarcks, and the other old families did little to warrant respect for a paternalistic policy. New managers like Gustav Higer (Vereinigte Königs-und-Laurahütte) and Adolf Williger (Kattowitzer AG für Bergbau und Hütten-betrieb) thought in terms of supply and demand, not in terms of their industrial families (Schofer, 1975: 79–84).

New sources of workers were sought locally. Specifically, women and children, who did not have the mobility of young males, were drawn into mining work. Although women were banned from underground work in Germany in 1868 and from other types of mining in subsequent years, Upper Silesian employers received temporary permission to continue employing them ("temporary" lasted until 1922). Zinc mining in particular, but coal mining too, used large numbers of women, and in 1912 women (primarily unmarried) comprised 5% of all Silesian miners (including the Lower Silesian coal basin) (ZBHS, 1912). Children too remained a definite part of the local scene, numbering almost 5% of all miners in all of Silesia in 1912 (JRGB, 1912). In contrast, no women and almost no minors worked in Ruhr mines in 1912 (*Statistisches Jahrbuch*, 1914).

One last alternative to newcomers materialized in the increasing numbers of foreign seasonal laborers brought in after 1890. Nonresident aliens had been expelled in 1886, but both agricultural and industrial employers in the Prussian east lamented a shortage of hands for work. The numbers of Poles allowed into Upper Silesia (after 1905 Poles and Ukrainians) fluctuated, but from 1896 on they constituted a sizable portion of the work force: 3–5% up to 1904, 10% or more from 1905 on (Schofer, 1975: 26; Brożek, 1966).

In all these areas recruitment policies nurtured the locally born labor force. The foreign seasonal workers could never form a community of their own. They had to leave the area for a specified period each year; they had no families with them; they barely could converse in German (the Ukrainians did not even have Polish). In contrast to these "guest workers," women and children belonged to a viable community, but by definition they had little mobility; in almost all cases they lived with spouse or parents.

Other arrangements supported the inbred nature of the work force. A shortage of housing was crucial in limiting possibilities even for short-range migration. Companies did make some attempts to construct quarters for workers, both family houses and dormitories. Georg von Giesche's Erben opened its much publicized Gieschewald colony in 1906, a village designed according to old Upper Silesian peasant patterns and designed to support the company's Arbeiterstamm. Dormitories, however, were much more common, even though they thoroughly disrupted family life (Schofer, 1975: 84–91).

All of these social circumstances promoted the localism of the miners: little immigration, minimal recruitment outside Upper Silesia, employer encouragement of peasants in the mines, the notion of the industrial family, a shortage of housing for newcomers. In addition, specific cultural traditions reinforced the separateness of the Upper Silesian mining community, in particular the self-consciousness of miners, the Roman Catholic church, and Polish national or ethnic identification. In these areas changes were unavoidable; here the political parties and workers' organizations competed for the loyalty of the Upper Silesians.

II

There is little need to go on at length about the individuality of mining communities (Brepohl, 1957; Lantz, 1958; Tenfelde, 1977b; Trempé, 1977; Trist, 1951; Erikson, 1976). Tales of their work traditions, their anecdotes, their slang, their family customs, their holidays—in short, their popular culture—are legion (Ligęza, 1958; 1964). Miners in Upper Silesia regarded themselves as a group apart from the rest of society. Only they, or at least the underground workers among them, experienced the darkness, the hardships, the camaraderie, the dangers involved in mining. They also harkened back to earlier conditions of miners as a separate social estate. The remnants of past glory were only vestigial, like uniforms and specific holidays; nonetheless, miners stood apart from other groups in society. Even newcomers tended to adopt the trappings of the old, a process simplified by the local provenance of the Upper Silesian labor force. New recruits had grown up in the vicinity of this world, and they probably adapted easily to the older traditions. Moreover, many people were probably hired on the basis of recommendations of those already employed; patterns of previous acquaintanceship no doubt facilitated the move into the miners' culture (Rees, 1966).

The peculiarities of Upper Silesia lay in customs familiar from other isolated regions and from mining areas but here expressed with Upper Silesian Polish accents. On St. Barbara's Day they paraded in the traditional black uniforms with gold buttons; when comrades died they paid tribute in traditional ways. One of the most characteristic Upper Silesian habits unfolded in the desire for land, either as kitchen gardens or as something more extensive tilled by other members of the family. As noted above, mineowners attempted to exploit that yearning for land as a means of building a committed labor force, but that proved to be a tough row to hoe. Above all else, the real uniqueness of Upper Silesia in Germany emerged in the practically universal membership in the Roman Catholic church and in the Polish nature of the population. In the early years of industrialization these two elements lay so intertwined that one could speak of a Catholic Polish mining subculture in Upper Silesia. However, tensions developed with the growth of the mining labor force, the politicization of the church through the Center party, and the nascent Polish self-consciousness. New communities began to develop as the old alliance of church and Pole showed signs of strain; supplementary movements, including Christian and Social Democratic trade unions, vied for the allegiance of the Upper Silesians. These newcomers never supplanted the church, but the impact of the "atheist" socialists forced the church to take stands on social issues, stands that over time no longer automatically reflected employers' interests.

That the Poles of Upper Silesia should identify themselves with the Poles of Posen or with Poles in Russia or Austria-Hungary seemed incredible to German observers in the twentieth century. German politicians continued to speak derogatorily of "water Polaks," and Polish nationalist feeling was deemed an alien element imported by outside agitators from Posen. Even Posen Poles in the 1880s and 1890s proved reluctant to recognize the significance of the Silesian Poles, and local activists borrowed a cue from Italian nationalists by adopting the slogan "Silesia fara da se" (Silesia will act by itself). After about 1900, however, only Germans deceived themselves into negating any significance for Polish nationalism in Upper Silesia; the election of the outspoken radical nationalist Wojciech Korfanty to the Reichstag in 1903 signaled to all groups in Germany that Polish nationalism had come of age in Upper Silesia (Orzechowski, 1975).

To speak of "Poles" in Upper Silesia leaves some questions unanswered. After all, some Germans worked there, not only as supervisors but also as ordinary workers. In retrospect nobody knows exactly who was German and who was Polish; some people did not know themselves. Names provide no clue, for German given names were required by law. Employee lists are filled with Johanns and Friedrichs coupled with Slavic surnames like Nowitzki and Gatzki. Hugo Bonikowsky turned out to be the executive director of the mine owners' trade association! In addition, many of the local people probably would have had trouble identifying themselves as either German or Pole. Many considered themselves simply "Silesian," while others saw the road to social mobility paved in German. They adopted the German language and joined German organizations, though the atheist socialists made little headway among them. This transitional group is a fascinating one, although hard to trace. It is likely that a number of lower-level supervisors moved up via this route, but presently it is hard to say more than that. It is however conceivable that the spreading of Polish national feeling from the 1890s on may have limited this assimilation. In contrast Poles in the Ruhr, especially after World War I, either emigrated or were swallowed up by the majority culture (Klessmann, 1978, 172–177).

The first stirrings of Polish cultural activity appeared in the 1860s. As mining employment rose, Poles began to come into more extensive contact with their fellows, and many responded to offers of expanded social and cultural communication. That banding together received an impetus from the Kulturkampf of the 1870s, when the mother church seemed threatened by an overbearing German Protestant establishment.

The most well-known of the early opinion leaders was Karol Miarka, editor of the influential newspaper *Katolik*. By organizing Polish social clubs and by invective in his writings, Miarka hoped to counter the pernicious, atheistic appeal of the socialist-oriented trade union organizers then entering the area. Miarka's group maintained close ties with the Catholic church, whose priests saw the need to minister to the Polish-speaking population. One cannot speak of "nationalism" in any sense, but *Katolik* and the Polish circles managed for the first time to arouse a certain self-respect among the hitherto neglected Poles of Upper Silesia.

Allegiance to the Roman Catholic church remained a hallmark of local Polish groups, even when Germanizing tendencies grew in intensity in the German-dominated hierarchy (diocese of Breslau). Priests emerged on both sides of the issue, like Father Franciszek Przniczyński, who ran a relatively anti-Center oriented newspaper (*Gazeta górnośląska*) until it collapsed in 1886 (Pater, 1969: 142–157). Similarly, Father Stanisław Radziejewski edited *Katolik,* the most important Polish local newspaper in Upper Silesia in the 1880s. The Germans wanted Radziejewski out, and eventually the newly confirmed archbishop of Gnesen reassigned him back to Posen in 1886. German nationalists did not even want him in a parish bordering on Silesia, and in 1888 he became house priest of Prince Ferdinand Radziwiłł. This new post left him much free time to continue his campaign to make the Polish language more respectable, and in 1888 Bishop Georg Kopp of Breslau banished him from Silesia altogether. Kopp over the years became increasingly strident in his opposition to Polish nationalist activity; his work made it ever more difficult for clerical groups like the *Katolik* element to maintain unquestioning allegiance to the Center (Pater 1969: 117–119).

To be sure, there was more to Catholic life than association with a political party. While Kopp and the upper hierarchy may have urged Germanization, the lower clergy of priests and their vicar assistants recognized their primary responsibility to be the souls of the faithful. For that task they needed the Polish language and Polish customs. They ministered to a Silesian Polish population and in the main did not feel it useful to use their energies in political and cultural battles. The priests preferred to incorporate the message of Polish nationalism into the context of God's word rather than fight the nationalism directly; atheistic socialism was the enemy, not the slightly misguided Polish nationalist spokesmen.

Polish nationalist activity in Posen and in Russian Poland had a conservative cast, for its leaders stemmed from the landed nobility. In contrast Upper Silesian nobles were Germans; Poles here had not even developed the middle class of professionals and tradesmen who usually provide the major support for incipient nationalist movements. The Polish renascence in Upper Silesia developed not in areas with the greatest numbers of Poles, but in the areas of their greatest concentrations. That meant the population of mining settlements, and it gave the local movement a distinctive coloration. As the German government toned down the anti-Catholic campaign from the late 1870s on, it accelerated its anti-Polish activities. This new policy led the workers in these densely populated areas not to abandon the Polish language but to seek moral support in Polish organizations. The new policy also propelled the Polish petite bourgeoisie in these townlets—the artisans, the traders, the few shopkeepers—to feel their Polishness more acutely. The social circles of the 1870s gave way in the 1880s to workmen's circles and to chapters of the Society of St. Aloysius. Increasingly the local branches of these groups became forums for debate between Polish elements and the pro-Center Party clergy. In 1893 for the time Polish candidates opposed Center men in elections for the national parliament and Prussian diet. The new sort of Polish subculture was coming of age, and it included a specific niche for workers; they were not yet attracted in any numbers by Social Democratic blandishments.

Of course there were many attempts to organize workers. The lean years of the 1880s witnessed a number of groups, such as the Christian Union of Workers in Kattowitz (Chrześcijański Związek Robotników w Katowicach), but they were all short-lived (Gąsiorowski-Grabowska, 1962: 207–211). They faded quickly, primarily because the supply of labor so exceeded demand that little pressure on employers was possible. Labor conflict remained far more important on the plant level than on the plane of industrywide organized protest. The major exception in these years came in 1889, a year of significant strike activity in all the major German mining areas. Action in Upper Silesia lasted only five days, but almost one-third of the local mining force participated (Jonca, 1952). Wages improved markedly thereafter, and a new Polish workers' organization emerged—the Society for Mutual Aid. *Katolik* stood intimately tied to the new group, which was more a mutual benefit society than a full trade union.

The Polish movement in Upper Silesia was now increasing its ability to provide for a whole range of needs of the local population in the developing economy: an influential newspaper, a large-scale workers' organization, social circles, consumer cooperatives. It is essential to emphasize that the Roman Catholic church continued to form a central element in almost all the local movements and organizations. This was true of the older mining culture as well as of the *Katolik* group and even to a certain extent of the radical Polish nationalist movement that emerged in the 1890s. The fledgling Polish Social Democratic party had to adopt church forms (newspaper articles like "The Ten Commandments for Workers" and "The Worker's Catechism") to get a start in the area (*Gazeta robotnicza,* August 12, 1893: 4; February 11, 1893: 1); even then the socialists never became a strong group except in a few localities. Intolerance of Polish differences surfaced even among the Social Democrats of Germany, who found it difficult to take seriously the separatist claims of Upper Silesian comrades. The local Polish party moved in and out of affiliation with the national party. Despite years of devoted organizing work by August Winter and others, Upper Silesia never became a pillar of socialist strength.

The Catholic church in Germany was no stationary monolith. Once the anti-Catholic campaign of the 1870s was over, church and party leaders moved to capture for the Center party positions of strength in the German political system. On the local level, priests undertook not only moral but also political roles in guiding the faithful. In Upper Silesia that meant sympathizing with the Polish population. However, church personnel were not immune from the increasingly rabid nationalism of Imperial Germany, a nationalism that manifested itself in land expropriation laws and language and education policies directed against Poles, in the racist Eastern Marches Association, in the Slavic-Jewish expulsions of 1885 and 1905, in mounting anti-Semitism. The new intolerance could be seen in the activities of Bishop Kopp of Breslau, although in German eyes he probably passed for a moderate. On the parish level, priests were in a quandary as to how to serve the local population and simultaneously to further the interests of the church as expressed by the Center.

Against some Polish leaders the task was simple. The Polish socialists were easy to depict as godless; the same was to some extent true of National Democracy, the Polish nationalist organization. The outstanding figure here was Wojciech Korfanty, self-styled tribune of the Polish workers. His election to the Reichstag in 1903 from an industrial district shocked German observers, who for the first time had to reckon with an indigenous Polish nationalism in Upper Silesia.

> Today it is not enough for a [parliamentary] delegate to be only a Catholic; it is not enough to be only a worker; it is not enough to be a Pole begging for the favor of the Germans. Today we need a Polish delegate, in body and soul a Pole and a Catholic,

who denounces the Germanizing priests; a Pole and a worker who knows not only the financial but also the spiritual needs of the working people . . . (Orzechowski, 1965: 70. Citation of letter to editor in Polish newspaper, 1903)

So went the call for Korfanty. He was deemed a radical, a man who pictured himself as a champion of the workers. Although probably elected with socialist votes, he was never an acknowledged socialist, and his policies became gradually more moderate until he went into temporary political decline after 1910.

Korfanty's success stemmed from his ability to portray himself as a man of the people, someone who knew their sorrows and their needs. With some mining experience himself, Korfanty claimed an affinity with the Polish industrial workers. He came on as a down to earth "socialist" as opposed to the Social Democrats, who campaigned with a more abstract and complex socialist program. Moreover, he delivered his speeches in Polish as opposed to the German of many of his opponents. Finally Korfanty could emphasize that the big entrepreneurs were exclusively German, while the workers were mainly Polish. Thus he could combine nationalist protest with a kind of class protest, something that the German Social Democrats could not or would not do for fear of offending the German workers. And the Polish socialists? They too suffered from their association with the German party as well as from their consistent rejection of clerical authority.

National Democracy was bigger than Korfanty. Although many of his speeches referred to his special role as defender of miners and smelter workers—such as those he made as a delegate to the Prussian diet—the movement as a whole seemed more petit bourgeois than proletarian. Anti-German and anti-Semitic pronouncements, attacks on Center policy but not on the church itself, declarations of Polish independence, support of Polish cooperatives and "Buy Polish" policies—all these did not suggest a socialist revolutionary movement. Big capital may have been the enemy, but only because it was German or Jewish big capital. An enormous gap separated these nationalists from the Polish socialists (Orzechowski, 1965: 88–133, 208).

For all the flashiness of the Korfanty group, the bedrock of Polish consciousness in Upper Silesia seems to have lain in the *Katolik* circle. With traditions going back to the 1860s, this newspaper and its editors stood as one of the three pillars of political activity in the area. (The others were the Center party and National Democracy.) Earlier a mainstay of the Center-oriented Polish movement, under the editorship of Adam Napieralski, the newspaper became an independent force with strong but often strained ties to the Center. In fact, a history of Napieralski's policies expressed in *Katolik* and in the other organs of his newspaper empire record the ebb and flow of relations between the Polish movement and the Catholic church hierarchy (Czapliński, 1974). The strength as well as the weakness of the Napieralski coterie lay in their determination to stick close to the church and the Center. Poles were a Catholic community, they believed, and it was important to maintain ties with the house of God. This strategy formed a mainstay of *Katolik* policy even when Napieralski could perceive that the majority of the 400 priests in Upper Silesia, though stemming from Polish families, had succumbed to the "German spirit" (Czapliński, 1974: 74).

One of the major organizational affiliates of *Katolik* was the Society for Mutual Aid. Formed in the aftermath of the 1889 strike, it started as a mutual aid society for Poles and evolved with spasmodic growth into a kind of trade union. At first there was little talk of a proletarian-bourgeois dichotomy. The group had no strike fund, and most of its activity consisted of formulating complaints to local government and to local entrepreneurs as well as providing death benefits for member families. As late as 1902 a large proportion of the officers were merchants, innkeepers, artisans, and newspaper dealers (Orzechowski, 1964: 44).

Yet workers did not break away; they did not flock to the Social Democratic miners' union (Alter Verband), nor were they especially receptive to other organizers (liberal and German Christian unions). The Alter Verband never succeeded in organizing more than a few thousand workers, while the Organization of Catholic Unions enrolled primarily artisans, often including owners of small shops. These workers, both Germans and Poles living in urbanized areas north of the industrial heartland, stood a great distance from the more recently formed industrial proletariat.

During the stormy strike years of 1905–1907, rival unions engaged in some common action, but no long-term cooperative effort developed. Membership in labor organizations, summarized in Table 2, reflected the latent and manifest conflict between the Poles and Germans. The Social Democratic union grew slowly, from fewer than 1,000 to about 2,600 members in 1913, and membership in 1913 included only about 500 people in Polish-speaking locals. Occasionally it was credited with adding to worker unrest, but that was all (Gąsiorowska-Grabowska, 1962: 381–382). On the other hand, the church-oriented, Polish-speaking Society for Mutual Aid did enroll quite a few members, growing from 4,000 members in 1896 to about 14,000 in 1900, only to subside soon after (Gąsiorowska-Grabowska, 1962: 436–437). After the strike years of 1905–1907, the society went into temporary decline, dropping to under 4,000 members in 1908; but that date marked a turning point in organization. The Society for Mutual Aid merged with Polish trade unions in the Ruhr and Posen to form the Polish Professional Organization (ZZP), and from then on membership climbed rapidly, albeit sporadically. Before the defeat of the great

Table 2.   Membership in Unions of Miners in the Upper Silesian
Industrial Region, 1902–1913

Year	Union of German Miners (Verband Deutscher Bergarbeiter-Social Democratic) Number of members
1902	925
1903	800
1904	1939
1906	1937
1907	2288
1908	2371
1913	2625
1913 (Polish only)	480

Year	Organization of Catholic Unions (Berlin wing) Total number of members	Members of Polish groups
1905	10,117	?
1906	17,546	1065
1907	19,471	2128
1908	25,742	2728
1913	?	4129
1913 (all of administrative Upper Silesia)	?	7078

Year	Polish Professional Organization (ZZP) Number of members	
1910	10,574	(miners)
1911	4,523	(smelter workers)
1913	20,451	
1913 (all of administrative Upper Silesia)	20,712	

Source: Compiled from yearbooks of the Verband Deutscher Bergarbeiter and scattered archival sources in Opole, Katowice, and Wroclaw by Felicja Figowa, Związki Robotników Polskich w bylej Rejencji Opolskiej w przededniu Pierwszej Wojny Swiatowej [Polish labor unions in the former regency of Oppeln on the eve of the First World War] (Opole, 1966): Union of German miners—pp. 14, 17, 19, 51; Organization of Catholic Unions—pp. 29, 48–50; ZZP—pp. 12, 43–48. Reprinted with permission of the University of California Press.

strike of 1913 caused a depletion in the ranks, about 10% of the entire local labor force in heavy industry enrolled in the union (Szerer, 1968: 28–32, 38–47).

Christian trade unions in the Ruhr basin remained strong, and that same church-oriented outlook emerged clearly in Upper Silesia. Miners were reluctant to abandon their Catholic ties, a phenomenon not unlike that of other German areas. The interlocking of Catholicism and Polish consciousness, so vivid since the seventeenth century, led miners and other workers in Upper Silesia to cling to one of the most important elements in their culture. Even the so-called secularism of National Democracy could not dispense with the church, and nationalism in Poland to this very day has retained religious ties apparent almost nowhere else in Europe. *Katolik,* the Society for Mutual Aid, the church (including the Center party), and subsidiary organizations provided a firm community in which Upper Silesian workers could survive. The Social Democratic subculture threatened them with its anti-clericalism and its obvious Germanizing tendencies (Ritter, 1975). The local population did not see the need to turn to such an outside group.

Industrial relations did not continue peacefully, of course. Upper Silesian managers proved to be perhaps even more intransigent than their Ruhr counterparts, if that is imaginable. The Society for Mutual Aid did eventually become a union, and it did lead the major coal strike of 1913 (Schofer, 1972; Feldman, 1966: 91, 360, 374). Workers were changing their outlook and their expectations, but they were not shucking off their Polish Catholic community. That community stood fast in an industrializing world. The Center party may have harbored many Germanizers, but the Catholic clergy still looked after their flocks. *Katolik* may have railed against Center support of Prussian anti-Polish policies, but Napieralski and his supporters were never willing to relinquish their ties to the church. The Polish community was a Catholic community, which developed institutions sufficient to withstand the onslaught of the industrial world. The Free Trade unions and the Social Democrats seemed German and atheist; the Polish-Catholic-worker community never successfully collaborated with the trade union-socialist-worker community.

ACKNOWLEDGMENTS

This essay is dedicated to Hans Rosenberg, teacher of a generation of social historians. Many thanks to Al Rieber for comments on an earlier version of this essay and even more for a stimulating interchange of ideas over a number of years. Wacław Długoborski wrote a valuable critique of the earlier essay, and Hans Mommsen helped me clarify a number of points. Some of the work for this essay was supported by a grant from the American Philosophical Society.

The German-language version originally appeared in a volume published by the Europäische Verlagsanstalt.

REFERENCES

Brepohl, Wilhelm
1957 Industrievolk im Wandel von der agraren zur industriellen Daseinform dargestellt am Ruhrgebiet. Tübingen: J. C. B. Mohr (Paul Siebeck).

Brożek, Andrzej
1966 Robotnicy spoza zaboru pruskiego w przemyśle na Górnym Śląsku (Workers from beyond the Prussian partition area in Upper Silesian industry.) Wrocław: Ossolineum.
Crew, David
1977 Review of Schofer 1975. In International Labor and Working Class History xi: 44–46.
Czapliński, Marek
1974 Adam Napieralski, 1861–1928. Wrocław: Ossolineum.
Denkschrift
1890 "Denkschrift über die untersuchung der Arbeiter - und Betriebsverhältnisse in den Steinkohlen-Bezirken." Zeitschrift des oberschlesischen Berg- und Hüttenmännischen Vereins xix: 57–132.
Długoborski, Wacław
1976 Review of Schofer 1975. In IWK: Internationale Wissenschaftliche Korrespondenz 117–122.
Erikson, Kai T.
1976 Everything in Its Path. Destruction of Community in the Buffalo Creek Flood. New York: Simon and Schuster.
Feldman, Gerald
1966 Army, Industry, and Labor in Germany, 1914–1918. Princeton, N.J.: Princeton University Press.
Figowa, Felicja
1966 Związki Robotników Polskich w byłej Rejencji Opolskiej w Przededniu Pierwszej Wojny Światowej (Polish labor unions in the former regency of Oppeln on the eve of the First World War). Opole: Instytut śląski.
Gąsiorowska-Grabowska, Natalia (ed.)
1962 Źródła do dziejów klasy robotniczej na ziemiach polskich (Sources on the history of the working class in the Polish lands), Vol. II. Warsaw: PWN.
Gazeta Robotnicza
(Polish socialist newspaper).
Gutman, Herbert G.
1977 "Work, Culture, and Society in Industrializing America." Pp. 3–78 in Gutman, Work, Culture and Society in Industrializing America. New York: Knopf.
Haines, Michael
1975 "Fertility and Occupation: Coal Mining Populations in the Nineteenth and Twentieth Centuries in Europe and America." Ithaca, N.Y.: Cornell University Western Societies Program Occasional Paper no. 3.
JRGB
Jahresberichte der königlichen Regierungs- und Gewerberäte und Bergbehörden.
Jonca, Karol
1952 "Strajk na Górnym Śląsku w roku 1889" (The strike in Upper Silesia in 1889). Przegląd Zachodni viii: Studia Śląskie 369–402.
Klessman, Christoph
1978 Polnische Bergarbeiter im Ruhrgebiet 1870–1945. Göttingen: Vandenhoelk & Ruprecht.
Lantz, H. R., with the assistance of J. S. McCrary
1958 People of Coal Town. New York: Columbia University Press.
Lewis, W. Arthur
1963 "Economic Development with Unlimited Supplies of Labour." Reprinted in A. N. Agarwala and S. P. Singh (eds.), The Economics of Underdevelopment. New York: Oxford University Press.

Ligęza, Józef
1958   Ludowa Literatura Górnicza (Popular literature of miners). Opole: Śląsk.
Ligęza, Józef, and Maria Żywirska
1964 · Zarys kultury górniczej: Górny Śląsk, Zagłębie Dąbrowskie (Outline of a mining
        culture: Upper Silesia and the Dabrowa basin). Katowice: Śląsk.
Orzechowski, Marian
1965   Narodowa demokracja na Górnym Śląsku (do 1918 roku) (National Democracy in
        Upper Silesia to 1918). Wrocław: Ossolineum.
1975   Wojciech Korfanty. Biografia polityczna (Wojciech Korfanty. A political biogra-
        phy). Wroclaw: Ossolineum.
Pater
1969   Ruch Polski na Górnym Śląsku w latach 1879–1893 (The Polish movement in
        Upper Silesia, 1879–1893). Wroclaw: Ossolineum.
Piotrowski, J.
1962   "Attitudes Toward Work by Women." International Social Science Journal xiv:
        80–91.
Rees, Albert
1966   "Information Networks in Labor Markets." American Economic Review lvi:
        559–566.
Reichling, Gerhard
1941   "Der Uebergang vom Bauern zum Arbeiter beim Aufbau des oberschlesischen
        Industriegebietes. Gezeigt am Beispiele von Rosdzin-Schoppinitz, Kr. Kattowitz."
        Schlesische Blätter für Volkskunde iii: 1–29.
Ritter, Gerhard A. and Klaus Tenfelde
1975   "Der Uebergang vom Bauern zum Arbeiter beim Aufbau des oberschlesischen
        im letzen Viertel des 19. Jahrhunderts." In Heinz Oskar Vetter (ed.), Vom
        Sozialistengesetz zur Mitbestimmung. Zum 100. Geburtstag von Hans Böckler.
        Cologne: Bund-Verlag.
Roth, Guenther
1963   The Social Democrats in Imperial Germany. Totowa, N.J.:
Sattig
1892   "Ueber die Arbeiterwohnungsverhältnisse im oberschlesischen Industriebezirk."
        Zeitschrift des oberschlesischen Berg- und Hüttenmännischen Vereins xxxi: 1–50.
Schofer, Lawrence
1972   "Patterns of Worker Protest: Upper Silesia, 1865–1914." Journal of Social History
        v: 447–463.
1975   The Formation of a Modern Labor Force: Upper Silesia 1865–1914. Berkeley,
        Calif.: University of California Press.
Statistisches Jahrbuch
        Statistisches Jahrbuch für den preussischen Staat.
Stearns, Peter
1976   "The Unskilled and Industrialization: A Transformation of Consciousness."
        Archiv für Sozialgeschichte xvi: 249–282.
Szerer, Barbara
1968   "Klasowe związki zawodowe na Śląsku w przededniu Pierwszej Wojny
        Światowej" (Class trade unions in Silesia on the eve of the First World War).
        Studia i Materialy z Dziejów Śląska ix: 7–56.
Tenfelde, Klaus
1977a Review of Schofer 1975. In Archiv für Sozialgeschichte xvii: 642–646.
1977b Sozialgeschichte der Bergarbeiterschaft an der Ruhr im 19. Jahrhundert. Bonn-Bad
        Godesberg: Verlag neue Gesellschaft.

Trist, E. L. and K. W. Bamforth
  1951 "Some Social and Psychological Consequences of the Long-Wall Method of Coal Getting." Human Relations iv: 3–38.
Trempé, Rölande
  1970 Les Mineurs de Carmaux, 1848–1914. Paris: Editions ouvriers.
ZBHS
    Zeitschrift für das Berg, Hütten, und Salinenwesen.

CLASS STRUCTURE, THE SEXUAL DIVISION OF LABOR, AND WORKING-CLASS CONSCIOUSNESS IN SPAIN

John R. Logan

One of the most consistent pressures for political reform in Spain today, eclipsing the brief attempt by the first post-Franco government to maintain authoritarian rule with a democratic facade, has been the re-emergence since the 1960s of an independent working-class movement with strong popular roots. Especially in industrial centers such as Barcelona, Madrid, and Bilbao, the labor movement is based on a growing class consciousness in the sense of readiness to participate in collective conflict as well as alienation from the regime and its institutions. My problem here

Research in the Sociology of Work, Volume 1, pages 227–247

will be to trace the roots of this phenomenon in the social situation of workers, and particularly in the major social transformations that were in progress during the 1960s and early 1970s. I will examine two categories of change. The first, which has a substantial tradition in sociological research, is change in class structure, principally rural-urban migration and upgrading of skill and wage levels within the class. In addition, and in a more exploratory mode, I examine the changes in the sexual division of labor, comparing class consciousness among men and women workers in the same industry and questioning the effects of recent rapid increases in women's labor-force participation.

My main source for this study is a set of interviews with textile workers in Barcelona that I directed in 1971. Despite the difficulties of interpreting a survey conducted during a period of repression, these data provide a unique insight into the perceptions of individual workers. Their main limitation is that they should be analyzed within the context of the life situation which workers experience.[1] I am convinced that social structure and class consciousness interact closely, as workers' perceptions must be continuously tested against their experiences in encounters with family and friends, fellow workers, employers, the state, and labor militants.

I. THE CLASS POSITION OF URBAN WORKERS

The contemporary process of industrialization of the Spanish economy is well known. Stimulated by foreign investment, international loans, tourism, and remittances from emigrants in Common Market countries, the economy grew at an average rate of 9% annually during the first decade following the "economic liberalization" undertaken by the Opus Dei cabinet in 1957.[2] My interest here is in the two major shifts in class structure that were generated by industrialization. First, there was a massive movement from rural to urban working-class occupations, as some one and a half million migrants were brought into the major urban centers of Catalunya, Madrid, the Basque region, and the Levante. The proportion of the active work force employed in industry rose from 25% in 1950 to nearly 40% in 1970, while the proportion in the rural sector dropped from 40% to 26% in the same period.[3] Second, within the urban sector there was a general upgrading of skill levels and standard of living. The proportion of industrial workers officially classified as "unskilled" fell from 28.1% to 19.8% (1964–1970) (INE, 1965; 1972), real wages of industrial workers rose about 7% annually, and large numbers of workers for the first time entered the market for such products as automobiles, televisions, and refrigerators. Although I would also stress that urban workers have achieved their present standard of living on the basis of long working hours (a sixty-hour week is common) and reliance on wages from all family members (many working-class children begin regular employment by age fourteen), there is no doubt that there has been considerable upward movement within the working class. These patterns were especially clear in the early 1970s, before the onset of the current recession.

To anticipate the impact of these fundamental structural changes on workers' consciousness of their class situation requires a more detailed examination of the stratification system. This is because both rural-urban migration and upgrading of skill and wage levels (to which I will for convenience apply the term *affluence*) can under different conditions both deflect and accentuate class consciousness.

Within the framework of a class analysis, there is general agreement that recent migrants are likely to be relatively conservative and individualistic in their orientations, except in the rare cases in which they bring a radical political culture into a highly politicized urban setting. The relevant characteristics of recent migrants in this respect are their lack of experience and knowledge of the urban class structure, and the concealment of their class position by their perception of past gains and expectation of future mobility (Lopes, 1960; Huntington, 1968: 278–283). However, migrants are at the same time much influenced by their subsequent experiences in the city: becoming more conservative in a context of high mobility (the Mexican case according to Cornelius), or more class conscious where class boundaries are more rigid (Cornelius, 1969: 833–857; Nelson, 1969).

There is similar ambiguity in the effects of affluence. In studies of advanced industrial capitalism many researchers have posited a process of "embourgeoisement" as workers approach middle-class income levels, become increasingly skilled and educated, move away from traditional working-class communities, find high chances for mobility through public education, and aspire to middle-class social status. Affluence, however, is not the same social phenomenon in all societies. In many countries the creation of a small, highly skilled and well paid industrial work force is accompanied by the expansion of a heterogeneous marginal lower class; this is the pattern associated with dependent development in countries such as Brazil. Here class consciousness within the "worker aristocracy" is oriented toward the defense of its position of relative privilege and wage demands which can be achieved within the existing structure rather than toward structural change (see Touraine, 1961: 389–707). Or, even where economic growth is sufficient to satisfy the aspirations of most workers, it may—if not matched by relaxation of barriers to movement into the middle class—result in the radicalization of the most affluent workers, by generalizing the experience of "partial upward mobility."[4]

In Spain, rural-urban migration and affluence have been accompanied by the growth of a new middle class of sales, service, and office workers, which allows a new channel of upward mobility for manual workers, and

especially for women. Therefore by 1966, the proportion of nonmanual
workers with urban working-class fathers had grown to 16% compared to
10% in 1960 and rose to 22% by 1969. However, since the urban working
class itself expanded at a high rate due to rural-urban migration, the actual
probability of such upward mobility for a given manual worker's son
decreased during the period. Thus the recent growth of the lower middle
class has not kept pace with expansion of the working class (FOESSA,
1970:586–588).[5] For sons of urban working-class fathers, the proportion
who entered non-manual occupations dropped from 33% in 1960 to 27% in
1969. This was even more severe for migrants: for sons of rural working-
class fathers, that proportion dropped from 38% to 17% in the same
period.

The results of another set of surveys (INE, 1965; 1972) indicate that
what chances for upward mobility of skilled workers do exist are increasingly dependent upon attainment of post-primary education. In 1964,
only 2–3% of skilled workers had reached beyond primary education,
compared with 32% of middle-level workers (technicians, middle management, and white collar employees). By 1970, with no change among
skilled workers, the figure for middle-level workers had increased to 38%.
Such a trend would not increase barriers to interclass mobility if educational opportunities were expanding adequately for working-class children. In fact, the Spanish government has made rapid improvements in
elementary education. But between the ages of twelve and fourteen the
proportion of children in school drops from 83% to 40%, largely due to a
change in the class distribution of students.[6] The lack of opportunities for
secondary education for working-class children is directly reflected in the
geographic distribution of schools. For example, in the region of Barcelona, the school enrollment capacity per 10,000 population in 1970 was
361 in the central city compared to around sixty in the working-class
suburbs ringing the city.

Whether movement into the growing lower-middle class occupations
could be considered upward mobility for a skilled industrial worker is in
itself uncertain. Some recent survey data suggest that it cannot (DATA,
S. A., 1973). In the province of Barcelona, 56% of skilled workers already
considered themselves to be lower-middle class or higher (compared with
only 24% of unskilled workers). This class identification is supported by
the fact that in Spain as a whole, while skilled workers on the average
have lower incomes than artisans, small shopkeepers, and other occupations that might be considered middle or lower class (around 9,000 vs
12,000 ptas. monthly in 1970), the difference is slight compared to the gap
between these and the upper-middle class or upper class occupations
(with average incomes around 30,000–40,000 ptas. monthly).

Perhaps more revealing than actual incomes is the amount that persons
believed necessary for their lifestyle. The *perceived* income needs of

skilled workers are identical to those of lower-middle-class occupations, somewhat higher than those of unskilled workers, but considerably lower than the perceived needs of all other groups. Unskilled, skilled, and lower-middle-class workers shared the sense of earning less than they needed, while higher groups reported higher incomes than needs.

In sum, the trend in class structure through the 1960s has been negative from the perspective of both affluent workers and migrants: (1) the chances for interclass mobility are contracting, especially for migrants, (2) the chances of what could be *perceived* as upward mobility for affluent workers are even smaller, and (3) the educational system seems to reinforce rather than to undermine the class boundaries.

It would be a mistake, however, even more so in an authoritarian state, to define the class position of workers in entirely economic or occupational terms. Workers as a class were among the vanquished in the civil war which brought the Franco government into power, and the organization of the corporatist state was partly designed for the purpose of institutionalizing the victory of the propertied classes. The implication here is that the working class became to a considerable degree defined by its exclusion from, and opposition to, the state.

In the simplest terms, where the state is perceived to be allied with management in the control of industrial conflict, such conflict is likely to spread beyond what might be termed "conflict consciousness" or "militancy" to involve opposition to the regime. That is, the state itself politicizes industrial conflict and lends perception of class position a political dimension. The same economic class structure could in other political contexts be associated with quite different class relations. In semidemocratic systems (for example, Chile in the 1960s) the labor movement may become the ally of political parties competing for influence *within* the system, and the political dimension of class consciousness is expressed in attitudes supportive of these parties. This may have been occurring in Spain in the late 1970s. Or in populist authoritarian states (Brazil and Argentina in the 1940s) the mobilization of workers becomes a source of support for a paternalistic regime, manifested in nationalism or personal loyalty to the head of state. In short, political exclusion was a critical dimension of the class position of workers in the period studied here, creating a link between two classical dimensions of class consciousness in the Marxian sense: factory militancy and opposition to the state.

II. CLASS STRUCTURE AND CLASS CONSCIOUSNESS

The characterization of Spanish society in the previous section provides some expectations about the effects of large-scale migration and increasing affluence on working-class consciousness in this country. These expectations are tested below by examining the association of indicators of class consciousness with migrant status, income, and other personal attributes of workers, drawn from the 1971 survey of textile workers. Some introductory remarks are necessary to describe the survey sample, the indicators of key variables, and methods of statistical inference.

The sample is comprised of 357 men who were employed in one of four textile firms in Barcelona province in 1971. These include two of the most important firms in the region (employing over 2,000 workers each), located in both the Bajo Llobregat (Prat and Cornellá) and the traditional textile centers around Sabadell and Tarrassa, and representing the spinning and weaving, washing and dyeing, and petrochemical sectors of the industry. Interviews were conducted in the workers' homes, where interviewers were generally well received, although close to 4.0% of the original sampling list could not be included in the study, either because they could not be located or were reluctant to participate in the study (a problem that developed as it became known within the community that some kind of investigation was being conducted). While this is not a random sample by any means, I believe it is representative of an important sector of the working class in the province.

Two dimensions of class consciousness have been measured. The first is *class militancy*, indicated by response to the question: "Do you believe that in principle the strike is a legitimate way for workers to make their demands heard?" (yes or sometimes/no) The second is *politicization*, the attribution of problems to or opposition to the political system, indicated by response to the question "What do you believe should be done in Spain to make things go better?" (Change the system of government or leadership./ Make little or no change in government.) In this study these indicators of militancy and politicization have a positive correlation of .24 (p < .001).

The tables presented here are selected from two previously published articles, where the associations have been described in greater detail (see Logan, 1977: 386–402; 1978: 1159–1178). At several points in the text I provide estimates of the statistical significance of multivariate associations. These are based on Goodman's (1973: 1135–1191) model for the analysis of contingency tables. The significance levels (one-tail) are the probability that corresponding beta parameters in the saturated model equal zero in the population from which the sample was taken. These statistics are not reliable for a nonrandom sample, however, and are provided only as a guide for distinguishing between strong and weak relationships. The advantage of the Goodman model is that it evaluates multivariate relationships without requiring normally distributed variables, interval measurement, or homoscedasticity.

A. Class Consciousness of Migrants

Workers have been classified into four categories of urban experience: recent and established migrants, sons of migrants born in the province, and native workers. The cutting point between recent and established migrants is at ten years' residence in Barcelona; this is the point at which differences in militancy and politicization appear. As shown in Table 1, there is among migrants a tendency for those who have been in the city longer to be more militant and more politicized. Established migrants are more class conscious than either recent migrants or natives.

There are at least two broad class-based interpretations of this finding: that migrants are socialized by contact with the urban working class or that there is some aspect of their own urban experience that makes them more aware of their class position.[7]

The socialization hypothesis supposes that migrants learn class consciousness from other urban workers. Therefore among recent migrants the more class conscious should be those with some prior urban experience, and the greater increase in class consciousness should occur within those factories in which workers are better organized and more aggressive.

The first inference is examined in Table 2, section *a*, where migrants are classified according to the size of the town *from which* they emigrated. Although the effect is only significant for militancy, it appears that the most militant and politicized workers are those from larger towns. The effect seems to be somewhat weaker among established migrants (i.e., the influence of prior socialization declines with time), but this difference as measured by the interaction of time and size is not significant.

It is also possible to compare recent and established migrants in different factories. There are enough migrants for this comparison only in the two largest factories, which provide a sharp contrast. One is located in the industrial suburbs, where workers are exposed to all of the currents of organized protest in the region; it has experienced strikes and factory demonstrations in recent years, and the management-supported slate was

Table 1. Militancy and Politicization
by Migrant Status

	% Militant		% Politicized	
Migrant status:				
Recent migrants	34%	(67)	19%	(67)
Established migrants	39	(118)	36	(118)
Sons of migrants	34	(80)	40	(80)
Natives	34	(85)	29	(85)

Table 2. Militancy and Politicization by Tenure and Other
Characteristics of Migrants

	% Militant		% Politicized	
	Recent	Established	Recent	Established
a. Size of prior town				
Under 5,000	23% (40)	34% (73)	15% (40)	33% (73)
5,000–50,000	44 (16)	50 (30)	13 (16)	40 (30)
Over 50,000	44 (9)	42 (12)	44 (9)	50 (12)
b. Factory context[a]				
"Radical"	39% (33)	49% (55)	27% (33)	47% (55)
"Conservative"	25 (20)	23 (30)	5 (20)	33 (30)
c. Family income				
Under $150	31% (29)	36% (39)	7% (29)	23% (39)
$150–$230	28 (25)	45 (45)	24 (25)	39 (45)
Over $230	50 (8)	33 (24)	25 (8)	42 (24)
d. Skill level				
Unskilled	29% (48)	35% (63)	15 (48)	40% (63)
Skilled	47 (19)	44 (55)	26 (19)	24 (55)
e. Conditions of emigration[b]				
Forced migrants	46% (28)	34% (41)	29% (28)	32% (41)
Voluntary migrants	21 (24)	39 (52)	4 (24)	39 (52)

a. Large factories only, see text.
b. For definition, see text.

soundly defeated there in the 1975 union elections. The other is isolated in a village at the fringe of the metropolitan area and has no militant tradition.

These differences are reflected in Table 2, section *b*: the effect of workplace on both militancy and politicization is highly significant (p < .01). However, it seems that the effect of the factory context is *immediate,* as it is found even among recent migrants. The hypothesis of continued socialization is weakly supported on the dimension of militancy, as militancy increases only in the more militant factory while politicization increases about the same in both factories. However, the interaction effect of time and factory is not significant even for militancy.

Thus there is some evidence of *pre*socialization and of *immediate* effects of the factory context. But the greater class consciousness of established migrants compared to recent migrants cannot be explained in terms of socialization, and we are led to examine instead the class experiences of migrants themselves. It is hazardous to generalize too widely about these experiences, as they surely vary considerably both among countries and among individual migrants. It is usually presumed that migrants are relatively poor and unskilled, and that they have less opportunities for social mobility than do natives. These characteristics are found among the textile workers studied here. And yet—perhaps because of the rapid expansion of the industrial working class—many migrants do advance quickly within the class. For example, 49% of established migrants in the present sample are skilled workers, compared to 30% of recent migrants; only 36% have a family income under $150/month compared to 47% among recent migrants.

A simple argument would propose that migrants become class conscious due to their material deprivation; therefore the poorest should become the most class conscious. But as Table 2, section *c*, demonstrates, militancy (p = n.s.) and politicization (p < .01) are if anything associated with *higher* income, and the differences between recent and established migrants are not consistently related to income level. (This association with income level is analyzed in detail below.) It might alternatively be argued that migrants (who are Spanish-speaking in a region in which Catalán is predominant) are subject to the experience of ethnic discrimination. In the present sample, however, the majority of migrants denied the existence of discrimination, and this variable is not directly related to class consciousness.

Others have argued that migrants perceive deprivation only as a temporary condition, a stage in an urban career, so that poverty is not understood as a class problem. Evidence of a willingness to accept present sacrifices in return for future gains is evidenced by the many cases of migrants who live poorly while saving to send for their families or to buy an apartment. This is especially likely among those who have voluntarily chosen to migrate as a conscious project of mobility. According to Touraine and Ragazzi the political behavior of these "voluntary" migrants will be marked by:

> . . . the desire for further mobility, which is to say, the wish to consider industrial work as only an indirect and unavoidable way of satisfying a desire for social mobility which is generally unassuaged by this first success (Touraine and Ragazzi, 1961).

From this viewpoint, which is consistent with the general notion of relative deprivation, the increase in class consciousness should occur mainly among those migrants whose aspirations for mobility are blocked. This is presumably the case of migrants who remain unskilled manual workers. Table 2, section *d,* seems to confirm this reasoning. Increasing class consciousness is found only among the unskilled (the interaction of politicization, skill, and tenure is statistically significant, p < .05).[8]

Another test of this interpretation can be made by operationalizing Touraine's distinction between what I will call "voluntary" and "forced" migrants. In Touraine's view, the voluntary migrant is likely to be one who was never unemployed in his home village, who left on his own rather than as part of a mass exodus, and who left without the pull of a firm job offer in the city "tempting his fate." In Table 2, section *e*, migrants have been classified as voluntary if they meet at least two of these three conditions. The result is straightforward. Class consciousness is relatively high among recent forced migrants, and remains at the same level or drops somewhat over time. Among voluntary migrants, however, it is initially quite low but rises sharply. This interaction effect of conditions of emigration and time in Barcelona is statistically significant with both dimensions of class consciousness.

B. Affluence and Class Consciousness

Table 3 shows the relationship between class consciousness and two dimensions of class position of workers, family income and skill.[9] It should be noted that skill and income are not intercorrelated in the present sample; this is because the pay differentials among workers within an industry are small, and even an unskilled worker may have a "high" family income if other household members are working or if he works overtime or holds two jobs (which is common). The distinction between these two dimensions of affluence is important, because while income has a significant positive association with militancy and politicization, skill does not.

The finding that skill is not associated with class consciousness is contradictory to the hypothesis of affluent militancy, which I began to develop in the discussion of class structure above. One would expect that workers at the top of the occupational hierarchy would be the most aware of the obstacles to further upward mobility and therefore the most class conscious. The present result may be explained in several ways. The textile industry itself is not the most advanced or best-paying industry,

Table 3.   Militancy and Politicization by Skill and Income.

	Monthly Income (ptas.)		
	Less than 10,000	10,000–15,000	Over 15,000
1. Militancy			
Unskilled	29% (38)	27% (26)	41% (22)
Semiskilled	24 (33)	36 (45)	47 (19)
Skilled	33 (27)	53 (19)	50 (22)
Highly skilled	38 (24)	30 (36)	40 (15)
2. Politicization			
Unskilled	29% (38)	38% (26)	50% (22)
Semiskilled	15 (33)	36 (45)	47 (19)
Skilled	15 (27)	32 (19)	32 (22)
Highly skilled	25 (24)	39 (36)	47 (15)

and some workers may intend to use their present employment as a bridge toward a better position in metallurgy or automobile plants. It is also possible that some of most skilled workers have hopes of achieving a supervisory position within the factory. The most convincing explanation in my view is the relative unity of workers' experiences regardless of skill level: workers at all levels report considerable pessimism regarding the chances of mobility within the factory, and all workers are part of a single bargaining unit and are equally affected by the outcome of negotiations.

In any case, class consciousness *is* related to the income dimension of class position: workers with higher incomes are more militant (p < .06) and more politicized (p < .001). But what is the politically relevant meaning of income? It is not the present standard of living; this is clear, for example, from the fact that controlling for ownership of home appliances, a car, an apartment, or savings account does not affect the relationship between income and militancy or politicization. Nor is it a matter of leisure time or functional literacy, since neither the number of hours worked nor frequency of newspaper reading is related to class consciousness. Rather the effect of income is intertwined with perceptions of mobility and changing expectations concerning what should be a worker's position in the society.

The leftist political parties prior to the Civil War consciously appealed to the "working class" for support, but as described in the discussion of class structure a majority of skilled industrial workers consider themselves to be "middle class." In the present sample, 40% reported their family to be "lower-middle class" or "middle class" rather than "working class" or "lower class"; the proportion is 51% among high-income workers. Given that middle-class identification among workers is usually found to be associated with conservative politics, it is important to explore the meaning of upward class identification among Spanish workers and to see how that meaning has changed for new generations of workers.

Table 4 shows the relationship between class identification, income, and generation (dichotomized according to whether one entered the work

Table 4. Proportion Identifying as
"Middle Class"
by Income and Age

	Age	
Income	20–39	40 and over
Less than 10,000	38% (47)	21% (68)
10,000–15,000	43 (65)	42 (53)
Over 15,000	69 (32)	33 (33)

force before or subsequent to the recent period of industrialization). Those who identify as middle class are the workers with higher incomes (p < .01), and younger workers (p < .001). In addition, there is a significant interaction effect: high income is more closely tied to middle-class identification for younger than for older workers (p < .04). Affluence then, particularly for those who entered the work force during the period of affluence, is linked to a new perception of class apparently based upon standard of living rather than occupation.

Yet paradoxically, as shown in Table 5, these young, high-income, "middle-class" workers are also the most "class conscious." That is, class identification in itself has no direct effect on class consciousness as defined here; its effect depends upon workers' age and income (this interaction effect, however, is statistically significant only for militancy). Middle-class identification is associated with greater militancy and politicization for young and high-income workers, but has the opposite effect on older and lower-income workers.

Evidently "class" has a new meaning for new generations of workers. For older workers, whose perceptions were first formed in a period of poverty and a tradition of clearly identifiable, militant "working-class" unions, it is rare to identify as middle class even with a middle-class income; those who do so are the more conservative workers of that generation. For younger affluent workers, who have entered the work force in a period of increasing prosperity, when the working-class political movement is only beginning to take shape again after the Civil War, middle-class identification is a symbol of expectations of a social position (upward mobility, quality public services and public education, social status and security) which is increasingly closed to them. For such workers, it is radicalizing.

Table 5.   Militancy and Politicization by Income, Age, and
Class Identification

	20–39		40 and over	
	Working class	Middle class	Working class	Middle class
1. Militancy				
Less than 10,000	38% (29)	33% (18)	31% (54)	15% (14)
10,000–15,000	35 (37)	36 (28)	48 (31)	23 (22)
Over 15,000	30 (10)	55 (22)	50 (22)	45 (11)
2. Politicization				
Less than 10,000	24% (29)	33% (18)	15% (54)	15% (14)
10,000–15,000	30 (37)	46 (28)	35 (31)	27 (22)
Over 15,000	40 (10)	59 (22)	27 (22)	36 (11)

III. THE SEXUAL DIVISION OF LABOR AND CLASS CONSCIOUSNESS

The analysis reported above was replicated for a sample of 119 women workers in the same firms. Generally the relationships of class consciousness with migrant status, skill, and income are the same among women, and the main difference is that on both indicators of class consciousness, the mean for women is significantly lower than the mean for men. While in the male sample 36% were categorized "militant" and 32% "politicized," the proportions among women were only 27% and 11% respectively.

Political sociologists have consistently found that women, even working women, are more conservative than men (see Duverger, 1955; Hamilton, 1967: 311–314), and their conservatism is often—although with little evidence—attributed in some way to their social position or the "sexual division of labor":

> Marriage places the woman, even today, in the situation of a minor. When she lives exclusively in the home—and at this time the great majority of married women have no profession—her interest is generally subordinate to that of men. The occupations to which she is limited, due to the time which they require and their very nature, close her into a mesh of routines and keep her separated from the problems of public life (Dogan and Narbonne, 1955: 187).

From one point of view, the political differences between men and women are due primarily to their different occupations and would not be found so strongly, for example, among workers in the same industry or factory. Even women who work in factories, however, may be under pressure to minimize their investment in the workplace. Within a society in which the family-centered conception of the woman's role prevails, outside employment may create what has been called an "emergency of status articulation" (Coser and Rokoff, 1955: 535–554) the woman has to decide whether to give priority to her status as worker or to the competing demands of her status as wife-mother-daughter. The pressure to conform to the latter status has clear implications for the working woman's relation to political conflicts arising out of the factory, and a change in social norms would therefore imply a change in political attitudes:

> Women workers generally worked during the time of their lives before and after the years of childbearing and child-raising, so that they were not considered and did not seem to consider themselves permanent workers. The whole society united to say that the man's income was primary and that the woman's was only secondary . . . It is to be expected that women, as they become more integrated into the workforce, will begin to act more and more like workers with their own special interests that they will actively defend (Peterson, 1971: 1–22).

The reasoning behind these comments is that the sexual division of labor extends to politics and class conflict, affecting even women who have entered the work force. This reasoning seems particularly applicable to a country such as Spain, where since 1938 it was state policy (explicit in the Fuero del Trabajo of the Franco regime) to "liberate married women from the shop and factory," and where suffrage for parliamentary elections was limited to male heads of households. It is suggestive that in responses to another interview question regarding neighborhood politics (whether it would be proper to organize a protest group if the municipality ignored problems of the neighborhood), women in this sample were significantly *more* likely than men to answer in the affirmative. There is apparently a political division of labor between men and women. That it is possible to maintain such a division is illustrated by the case of an older working housewife who, pressed for an explanation of her approval of local protests, explained that "union makes force." The same woman was opposed to industrial conflict or governmental reform.

A. Sex Roles and Working Women

The overall changes in levels of employment of women in recent years seemingly contradict these observations. Between 1950 and 1970 the proportion of women active in the labor force (ages 15–64) jumped from 14% to 30%.[10] But detailed examination of the age distribution of changes in women's employment and the kinds of occupations to which women have had access shows remarkable stability in the division of labor.

A national survey of Spanish women in 1969 revealed that although 91% approved of work outside the home for a single woman, about half opposed such employment for a married woman and five out of six opposed employment of women with small children. A majority of those who were themselves employed asserted that they worked only to help out the family and their husbands: "It seems as though the housewife who works needs to justify herself somewhat for doing so, for stepping outside the role which traditional norms assign her" (FOESSA, 1970: 1062).

The age distribution of increases in employment is consistent with these values (see Table 6). In 1950 the highest rates of labor force participation were found among younger women, ages 15–24, progressively lower in higher age groups. By 1966 the proportion working had increased among all age groups, but most rapidly among women under twenty-five (more than doubling) and least in the 25–34 category, which includes the largest share of women with small children (increasing just under 50%). These differential increases reflect also the greater time demands on married women and especially those with children, as well as the motivation of young single women to become more independent of their parents. But

Table 6.   Evolution of Women's Labor-Force Participation by Age
1950–1966*

	15–19	20–24	25–34	35–44	45–64	Total 15–64
1950	19.6	21.3	16.3	12.0	13.7	14.0
1960	27.1	28.2	16.7	22.8	16.5	20.3
1966	40.6	45.3	23.9	21.2	21.3	26.5

* Proportion active of total female population.
Source: FOESSA (1970: 176).

the result is that the great increase in women's employment has conflicted
less with values concerning the place of women—and therefore presumably required less transformation of those values—than might be im-
agined.

The old norms concerning the proper *kind* of employment seem also to
have been maintained, although detailed information on occupational
status by sex is not available except for recent years. At present women
constitute the majority of workers in personal services, primary education, and the traditionally female textile and garment industries. Those
who find nonmanual jobs are over-represented as salespersons, office
workers, and semiprofessionals (27% of the labor force in these occupations), but under-represented as professionals and business executives
(about 10% in these categories (Duran, 1972: 131, 171). Thus again the
pattern of employment reflects less a change in women's social position
than an adjustment to new economic opportunities in a pattern consistent
with old values.

In the present sample I have looked for evidence of generational
changes in these values, controlling for differences in family situation.
This control is necessary because younger women are much more likely
to be single or to have no children, and they could by virtue of this fact
alone have a different perception of work or face different kinds of social
pressures regarding work.

As indicators of their orientations toward work, women were asked two
kinds of questions. The first reflects attitudes toward the proper role of
women: "Do you think it is right for a married woman to work outside the
home to bring in extra income?" The other questions probe their subjective commitment to their status as worker. First, "If your family did not
need your income to cover each month's basic expenses, would you still
keep working?" Taken alone this question has the defect that some
women, especially younger women, see work as highly instrumental but
temporary; they should not be considered job-committed even though for
the moment they would continue working. Therefore the question has
been used in conjunction with another asking whether they expect still to

Table 7. Approval of Married Women's Employment and Job
Commitment by Age and Family Situation

	Age	
	17–29	*30 and over*
a. Proportion approving employment		
Unmarried	52% (27)	30% (10)
Married, no children	60 (10)	71 (7)
Married with children	55 (9)	57 (49)
Widowed	—	78 (9)
b. Proportion job committed		
Unmarried	41% (27)	60% (10)
Married, no children	20 (10)	71 (7)
Married with children	11 (9)	20 (49)
Widowed	—	44 (9)

be working outside the home for the next five years. They are classified as
job-committed only if they answered affirmatively to both questions.

Table 7 presents the association between these items and age and
family situation. The variable of work approval is not significantly related
to either age or family status. As might be expected, job commitment is
substantially (and significantly) lower for married women with children
than for other women, but controlling for family status there is actually a
significant tendency for older women to be more job committed than
younger women. Thus job commitment, rather than increasing from generation to generation, appears to increase with age. Disaggregating the
index of job commitment, it was found that younger single women were
slightly more likely than older single women to say that they would
continue working if they did not need the income, but they were the least
likely category of women to think that they would still be working in five
years. Work for this newest generation is perceived to be a temporary
arrangement, useful as a way of gaining some independence or to have
pocket money or to save for marriage; most young women even today
look forward to marriage as a social advancement and a liberation from
work.

B. Sex Roles and Class Consciousness

Among many of the women in this sample there is a contradiction
between the fact of their employment and their professed beliefs regarding the role of women. One young woman asserted that "women have an
equal chance to find a good job because they have emancipated themselves in society. But work is for men; women's place is in the home."

Her case is not unique. Of the *married* women 38% said that it is not right for a married woman to work even if she has no young children.

These traditional notions of womanhood manifest themselves in the factory in a variety of ways. One question in the survey asked women whether they would prefer a man or woman to represent them in the *Jurado de Empresa,* which is a directly elected union body at the factory level. The worker representatives on the Jurado handle routine grievances, in some factories conduct wage bargaining or negotiations concerning the application of the national contract, and increasingly organize job actions by workers. Although women usually constitute a separate section in the factory and therefore are represented by a woman in the Jurado, about half in the present sample indicated preference for a man. Their reasons reveal their own evaluation of the differences between the sexes:

1. "Employers will listen to him more." "They pay more attention to a man." (five respondents)
2. "It is man's work." "It seems right." (six respondents)
3. "Men are more capable." "They know more." "They are more professional." (nine respondents)
4. "They have a stronger character." "They demand more, having to support a family." "They have more solidarity." (eleven respondents)

Finally, there is evidence that the sexual division of labor affects the class consciousness of women workers. In Table 8 militancy and politicization are both shown to be associated to some degree with measures of marginality from the work role (job commitment and approval of women's employment). Although only job commitment has a statistically significant effect, the pattern supports the conclusion that the low class consciousness of women is at least partly due to the pressures that keep them marginal to their role as industrial workers.

IV. CONCLUSION

Regarding the impact on class consciousness of increasing employment of women, this research emphasizes the stability of a traditional division of labor in which women are contained in a domestic sphere of activity. Undeniably the employment of women has affected some aspects of Spanish society, allowing working-class families to raise their standard of living, providing greater freedom for young women within their family of origin, etc. There is nonetheless no indication that the changing economic function of women has as yet substantially altered basic conceptions of

Table 8.   Militancy and Politicization by Approval of Married
Women's Employment and Job Commitment

	Job commitment		
	High	*Medium*	*Low*
1. Militancy			
Approve	31% (26)	7% (28)	7% (15)
Disapprove	20 (10)	3 (29)	0 (11)
2. Politicization			
Approve	27% (26)	36% (28)	20%(15)
Disapprove	30 (10)	24 (29)	18 (11)

their proper social role. These conclusions are strikingly consistent with the results of recent research on the integration of women into the work force of other European countries nearly a century ago (see Scott and Tilly, 1975: 36–64). Given the difficulties in changing the social position of women even as a major goal of a revolutionary government (the experience of Cuba, for example),[11] it seems likely that working women in Spain will continue to have only a marginal participation in the labor movement even with the passing of the conservative regime.

These results also suggest that both migration and affluence have contributed to increasing class consciousness among individual workers in Barcelona, and provide some insight into the character of this class consciousness.

After an initial period in which migrants are especially conservative or apathetic, they become among the most class-conscious workers. Upon finding employment, they are much influenced by the political context of the factory in which they work, but the subsequent process of increasing class consciousness cannot be attributed to continuing contextual influences. Nor does the class consciousness of established migrants appear to correspond to material deprivation in an absolute sense. The evidence presented here supports instead the view that recent migrants are conservative because they seek to interpret their situation in a manner consistent with their perceptions of and hopes for personal advancement within the existing class structure. Their later class consciousness represents the disillusionment of their expectations and an attempt to redefine their social positions.

A similar interpretation can be made of the perceptions of affluent workers. Here, particularly among the postwar generation, militancy and politicization are a protest against the obstacles to further mobility and recognition of the adversary role of the state. In analyzing both migration and affluence, it appears that the need for collective action is most recognized by workers whose past mobility has revealed the limits to individual advancement in the existing system. The political economic strategy of the Franco regime—to promote economic expansion while repressing industrial conflict—was therefore ultimately self-defeating. Industrialization and repression were the structural bases for the development of class consciousness which the state could not finally contain within an authoritarian framework.

Since 1971 Spain has undergone both structural and conjunctural changes. The legalization of strikes, dissolution of the state-controlled Organización Sindical and its replacement by unions linked to the socialist and communist parties, and partial displacement of factory conflicts by political negotiations at the national level are radical changes in the mode of articulation of class interests. The limitation of emigration to Common Market countries and prolonged recession of the Spanish economy have combined to raise unemployment, presumably affecting especially the lower sectors of the working class. The conclusions reached here, therefore, are already a part of the history of the labor movement, and the field is open for new research.

ACKNOWLEDGMENT

This research was supported by National Science Foundation Dissertation Grant GS32-343.

NOTES

1. Some recently published studies of class conflict and labor organization in Spain describe this context. See Morcillo, et al., 1978; de Elejabeito, et al., 1976; and Maravall, 1978.

2. For an excellent summary of economic policy and conditions in that period, see Anderson, 1970.

3. Except where otherwise noted, statistical data referred to below are taken from the compendium of information published by the Fundación Foessa, 1970.

4. A similar reasoning is applied to intellectuals and the middle class in traditional societies by Germani, 1966.

5. Note that Giner, 1968, also concludes that "the steady growth of the working class still outbalances whatever upward mobility there is in that stratum." He believes, however, that affluence will eventually integrate the working class into society. "The seeds of a consumer economy of western style are already planted in the Iberian Peninsula and Spain's very high rate of industrial output after 1959 could in the long run severely modify the revolutionary impetus . . . of its lower classes."

6. In the year 1962–1963, when approximately 50% of the urban population was working class, the proportion of students who were from working-class families dropped from 32% at age of twelve, to 21% at age fifteen, 14% at age seventeen, and 6% at the university level (FOESSA, 1970: 953).

7. There are other differences between recent and established migrants which might have accounted for differences in class consciousness, without involving an influence of time in the city. Recent migrants are younger, more likely to be from the south of Spain, and more

likely to be "voluntary" migrants in the sense defined below. None of these differences accounts for their lower class consciousness. On many other characteristics the two groups are similar: size of place of birth, prior work experience, initial skill level in Barcelona, and father's occupation.

8. Soares, 1964, reports a similar result for Brazil. In his interpretation, "Feelings of relative reward are replaced by feelings of relative deprivation as urban living makes socioeconomic inequality more visible. The rewarding comparison with a rural life fades into the past, and gives way to a damaging comparison with higher standards of living."

9. The low income level of less than 10,000 ptas. monthly provided a bare subsistence, most of which was spent on food, while a high income level (over 15,000 ptas.) approximated that of a middle-class family. "Unskilled" workers include those who performed routine manual labor. The "semiskilled" generally operated simple textile machinery requiring no more than a week's learning. "Skilled" workers are primarily those whose positions required an apprenticeship of up to 3 years, such as machinists, mechanics, and electricians, as well as most positions in the ramo de agua (the washing, bleaching, and dyeing sector). The "highly skilled" are those with seniority in skilled occupations, and also include "contramaestros" who perform supervisory work.

10. The source here is FOESSA, 1970: 176. Official census figures for 1970 based upon a 1% sample show a labor force participation of only 27% in the 15–64 age category, virtually the same as reported by FOESSA for 1966. The government's figures, however, have been said to underestimate women's employment for various reasons. A useful review of state policy regarding women is provided by Duran, 1972.

11. Apparently the Cuban government under Castro was unable to undermine traditional male attitudes toward women. See Oleson, 1971.

REFERENCES

Anderson, Charles
    1970   The Political Economy of Modern Spain. Madison, Wis.: University of Wisconsin Press.
Cornelius, Wayne, Jr.
    1969   "Urbanization as an agent in Latin American instability." American Political Science Review 63: 833–857.
Coser, Rose, and Gerald Rokoff
    1955   "Women in the occupational world: Social disruption and conflict." Social Problems 18: 535–554.
DATA, S.A.
    1973   Estructura social básica de la población de España y sus provincias. Madrid: Confederación Española de Cajas de Ahorro.
de Elejabeito, Concepción, Carmen de Elejabeito, Ignacio Fernández de Castro, and Germán de Trasalva
    1976   La clase obrera, protagonista del cambio. Madrid: Elias Querejeta.
Dogan, Mattel, and Jacques Narbonne
    1955   "Les Françaises face à la politique." Cahiers de la Fondation Nationale des Sciences Politiques.
Duran, Maria Angeles
    1972   El trabajo de la mujer en Espana. Madrid: Tecnos.
Duverger, Maurice
    1955   La participation des femmes à la vie politique. Paris: UNESCO.
Fundación Foessa
    1970   Informe sociológico sobre la situación social de España 1970. Madrid: Edicusa.

Germani, Gino
1966 "Social and political consequences of mobility." In Neil Smelser and Seymour Martin Lipset (eds.), Social Structure and Mobility in Economic Development. Chicago: Aldine.

Giner, Salvador
1968 Continuity and Change: The Social Stratification of Spain. Reading, U.K.: University of Reading.

Goldthorpe, John, David Lockwood, Frank Bechofer, and Jennifer Platt
1969 The Affluent Worker in the Class Structure. Cambridge, U.K.: Cambridge University Press.

Goodman, Leo
1973 "Causal analysis of data from panel studies and other kinds of surveys." American Journal of Sociology 78: 1135–1191.

Hamilton, Richard
1967 Affluence and the French Worker in the Fourth Republic. Princeton, N.J.: Princeton University Press.

Huntington, Samuel
1968 Political Order in Changing Societies. New Haven, Conn.: Yale University Press.

INE
1965 Encuesta de la población áctiva.
1972

Logan, John R.
1977 "Affluence, class structure and working-class consciousness in modern Spain." American Journal of Sociology 83: 386–402.
1978 "Rural-urban migration and working-class consciousness: The Spanish case." Social Forces 56: 1159–1178.

Lopes, Juarez Rubens Brandão
1960 "O ajustamento do trabalhador a industria." In Bertram Hutchinson (ed.), Mobilidade e Trabalho. Rio de Janeiro: Centro Brasileiro de Pesquisas Educacionais.

Maravall, Jose María
1978 Dictadura y disentimiento politico. Madrid: Alfaguara.

Morcillo, F. Almendros, E. Jiménez-Asenjo, F. Pérez Amoros, and E. Rojo Torrecilla
1978 El sindicalismo de clase en España 1939–1977. Barcelona: Ediciones Peninsula.

Nelson, Joan
1969 Migrants, Urban Poverty, and Instability in Developing Nations. Cambridge, Mass.: Harvard University Center for International Affairs.

Oleson, Virginia
1971 "Leads on old questions from a new revolution: Notes on Cuban women, 1969." In William Goode and Cynthia Epstein (eds.), The Other Half. Englewood Cliffs, N.J.: Prentice-Hall.

Peterson, Brian
1971 "Working-class communism: A review of the literature." Radical America 5: 1–22.

Scott, Joan, and Louise Tilly
1975 "Women's work and the family in nineteenth century Europe." Comparative Studies in Society and History 17: 36–64.

Soares, Glaucio
1964 "The political sociology of uneven development in Brazil." In Irving Horowitz, Revolution in Brazil. New York: Dutton.

Touraine, Alain
1961 "Industrialisation et conscience ouvrière à São Paulo." Sociologie du Travail 3: 389–707.

Touraine, Alain, and Orietta Ragazzi
1961 Ouvriers d'origine agricole. Paris: Editions du Seuil.

WORK, WORKERS AND
MODERNIZATION IN THE USSR

T. Anthony Jones

With the maturation of the industrial economy, and the social modernization that has accompanied it, work has taken on a new significance in
Soviet society. As the rate of economic growth has declined, labor productivity has become the focus of much concern and debate in the Soviet
Union, an issue made even more important by the failure of technological
innovation to keep pace with the increasing level of demand for products.
As a result, work and workers are more significant for the future of the
USSR than they have been since the Revolution. The importance of
workers, moreover, extends well beyond their contribution to production. They have been affected by changes in the general society, and they
now have increasing expectations for tangible improvements in their
standard of living, as well as far greater expectations for their children's
future. As in other industrial societies, the stability of the regime will
increasingly depend upon its ability to meet these demands. In Eastern

Research in the Sociology of Work, Volume 1, pages 249–283
Copyright © 1981 by JAI Press Inc.
All rights of reproduction in any form reserved.
ISBN: 0-89232-124-5

Europe, it is already clear that workers are a political as well as an economic force, and the regimes in these societies are well aware that their future depends upon developing a *modus vivendi* with workers. While Soviet workers are a long way from being as effective a pressure group as workers are in Poland, they nevertheless have come to achieve considerable (even though mainly indirect) influence on public policy.

At the center of the labor problem is the question of productivity, since without an increase in productivity a wide range of societal goals (i.e., improving consumption levels, social and educational programs, meeting national security needs, and so forth) will be difficult, if not impossible, to achieve. Soviet policymakers and those who advise them have come to realize, however, that productivity cannot be considered in isolation from more general issues in the life of the worker, both on and off the job. As a result, during the last fifteen years there has been a rapid rise in research on the sociology of work. Consequently, we now know more about workers and their activities than at any time since the Revolution. In spite of this, however, the Western literature on this topic has remained surprisingly small. While a number of studies (ranging from the popular to the academic) appeared between the time of the Revolution and the death of Stalin (for example, Fairburn, 1931; Freeman, 1932; Gordon, 1941; Dallin and Nicolaevsky, 1947; Schwartz, 1951), the post-Stalin period has produced surprisingly few studies (among them Kaplan, 1968; Dewar, 1956; Galenson, 1955; Brodersen, 1966; Conquest, 1967; Berliner, 1957; Sacks, 1976; Lane and O'Dell, 1978). While the economics literature on wages, the labor force, and general economic aspects of labor is extensive, very little attention has been given by Western sociologists to the characteristics of work as they affect the worker, or to the position of the worker in Soviet society at large. Workers have also been neglected by those who have tried to develop theories of social processes in the USSR. For example, discussions of interest-group influence typically ignore workers (Skilling and Griffith, 1971), although this is not the case in discussions of Eastern Europe (Lane and Kolankiewicz, 1973). This lack of attention may be understandable given the relative quietude of Soviet workers as compared to those in Eastern Europe, although Soviet workers are less quiet than many suppose. Such neglect, however, ignores the possibility that influence may occur in less direct ways than through public confrontation.

This brings us to the question of consciousness, and whether the relative absence of worker militancy in the USSR means that Soviet workers are more "atomized", or whether their form of consciousness differs from that found elsewhere. Unfortunately this question cannot be answered directly, since Soviet sociologists have not investigated class consciousness among workers (or if they have, it has not been published openly). Therefore, it is necessary to approach the issue indirectly by making inferences from the available information on the worker's life both on and off the job. In this paper, I shall attempt to establish some generalizations regarding the situation of the Soviet industrial worker (agricultural workers, therefore, will not be considered). On the basis of a survey of some of the more recent Soviet literature in the sociology of work, I shall argue that contrary to the considerable emphasis given by Soviet theoreticians to the importance of job content and the characteristics of the work group as determinants of worker consciousness, the available evidence would seem to suggest that the factors that have the greatest effect on workers' values and activities are those that are extrinsic to the job and the workplace. It will be suggested, however, that as a consequence of changes already underway (increasing technological innovation, rising educational levels, continual differentiation within the working class, some decentralization of the economy, and the changes in management-worker relationships that these factors will produce), workplace factors will have a greater effect on worker consciousness and activity in the future. In conclusion, some of the implications of these changes for authority in the enterprise, and for the effect workers may have on the wider society, will be suggested.

I. WORKERS AND THE STRUCTURE OF EMPLOYMENT

During the last few decades, the Soviet occupational structure has been experiencing the same general changes that have occurred in other industrial societies, albeit in a modified form. As the economy has grown, those employed in manufacturing industries have decreased relative to other occupations. Thus, the share of workers in industry has fallen from 36.5% of the labor force in 1960 to 33.3% in 1977 (*Statisticheskii ezhegodnik stran-chlenov soveta ekonomicheskoi vsaimopomoshchi,* 1978: 400— hereafter cited as *Statisticheskii ezhegodnik,* 1978). During the same period, the service sector has increased its share of the labor force from 15.2% to 22.2% (*Statisticheskii ezhegodnik,* 1978: 395). Consequently, even though the absolute number of industrial workers increased from 27.4 million in 1965 to 35.4 million in 1977 (*Statisticheskii ezhegodnik,* 1978: 400), they represent a relatively declining stratum in Soviet society. Structurally, however, this sector is of increasing importance since it will be expected to increase its productivity to meet growing demand.

As the industrial work force becomes relatively smaller, a change in its composition also occurs as mechanization reduces the need for many of the purely manual tasks that are performed without the aid of machinery. Between 1959 and 1975, the percent of industrial workers engaged in such manual work declined an average of 1.65% per year, so that by 1975 about 58% were classified as machine workers, the plan being to increase this to 65% by 1980 (*Ekonomicheskaia gazeta,* No. 48, November, 1978). Mechanization has been slow in coming to the ancillary work force, however, and this ties up a great deal of labor. For example, 80% of the workers who move materials and warehouse them have no machines at their disposal. This requires so much labor that it has been suggested by some that the mechanization of these jobs would save four or five times more labor than increasing the mechanization of the productive process itself (Manevitch, 1978). In spite of increasing mechanization, therefore, the absolute number of workers doing unskilled and hard manual labor continues to grow both in production and in ancillary spheres. Moreover, insofar as there is an increase in the service and light-industry sectors, the demand for manual labor increases, since these sectors are labor intensive rather than capital intensive. Because these sectors of the economy continue to retain labor, the supply of workers for new industrial plants has to come from turnover and unorganized migration, thus increasing the problems of already established enterprises (Maslova, 1978). Even where mechanization occurs, however, demand for labor may not decline, particularly when new multioperation technology requiring more labor is introduced (Danilov, 1977).

As a result of these factors, the Soviet worker is in a unique position as compared to workers in most of the nonsocialist industrial societies. Soviet workers find themselves in a seller's market, at least as far as employment of some kind is concerned. This is because the USSR suffers from a general shortage of labor resulting from a combination of demographic factors, employment policies, the rate of technological innovation, and the form of Soviet industrial organization.

The demographic contribution comes from a long-term decline in the rate of natural increase, which has fallen from 13.2 per thousand in 1940, to 9.2 per thousand in 1970, to 8.9 per thousand in 1976 (*Narodnoe khoziaistvo SSSR za 60 let,* 1977: 73). The decline has been greatest in the most industrialized areas. For example, whereas the rates in 1976 were 29.7 in Tadzhikistan and 28.2 in Uzbekistan (relatively underdeveloped republics), the more urban, industrial Russian, Estonian, and Latvian republics had rates of 5.9, 3.1 and 1.7 respectively (*Narodnoe khoziaistvo SSSR za 60 let,* 1977: 73). Thus, industrial needs for labor can only be met by relocating industry to the areas of highest increase, or by encouraging migration, both of which involve economic and political problems. The question of future labor supply is also made more complex by the fact that its decline is not entirely due to a fall in the birth rate (which has actually increased a little in the 1970s), but rather to an increase in the death rate, which rose from 7.3 per thousand in 1965 to 9.7 per thousand in 1977

(*Statisticheskii ezhegodnik*, 1978: 10). (This increase has occurred not only among the elderly, but also among those in their thirties, forties, and fifties as well.)[1] As a result of these demographic changes, the rate of growth of the labor force is declining: thus, whereas the number of workers increased by 22% in 1960–1965, it did so by only 14% in 1970–1976 (Geliuta and Staroverov, 1977: 19). Finally, industry's traditional source of new labor, the agricultural sector, has ceased to be a significant contributor; indeed, agriculture is itself experiencing a labor shortage, especially of young workers.

In addition to demographic factors, the labor shortage is also due to the official Soviet policy of full employment. This works in two ways: firstly, by putting pressure on managers to reassign displaced workers rather than to fire them, and secondly, by encouraging women to seek full-time employment. As a result, there is now no reserve pool from which more labor may be drawn. Whereas in 1959 82% of all ablebodied adults were employed or were in full-time education, by 1970 this had increased to 92.4% (Danilov, 1977). This is probably an upper limit, and it may actually decline somewhat in the future, especially if there is an increase in those in higher education, or if an increasing number of women take maternity leave to catch up with delayed childbearing. As a result, additions to the work force will have to come from school-leavers, and they already account for more than 90% of the growth in employment in the 1970s, as compared to only 29.1% in 1961–1965 (Danilov, 1977). Even this source cannot be relied upon, however, since the number of young people will decline as the smaller birth cohorts of the 1960s come of age. Thus, while young people provided 2.7 million new workers in 1977, they will provide only 1.8 million in 1979, 1.5 million in 1980, and even fewer in later years (Bachurin, 1978). The situation will also be worsened by an increase in the retirement rate as the earlier large birth cohorts reach retirement, although moves are already afoot to bring back pensioners into the labor force and to retain those who are eligible to retire.

The organization of the Soviet enterprise also contributes to the labor shortage. Not only do the production plans for the economy and the enterprise encourage the misuse of labor, but the rewards that managers receive are related to the number of workers in the enterprise. There are also frequent changes in the production plan as the economic ministries continually attempt to adjust the economic plan for the system as a whole, and this often means an increase in the need for labor at short notice. In addition, the lack of smoothness in the production process, and the increase in pace at the end of each month, poor calculations of the amount of labor needed by the work process, the need to supply workers for seasonal work outside of the factory (to help with planting or harvesting or to work on municipal construction projects), and making the size of the bonus funds dependent upon the size of the wage fund, all encourage managers to hoard labor and so contribute to the overall shortage. One recent report cites managers in a number of major cities as saying that they could reduce the number of workers in their plants by 15%–30% if the vagaries of the plan were abolished, and if they were not required to provide labor for seasonal projects (quoted in *Current Digest of the Soviet Press*, Vol. XXX, No. 16, 1978). Clearly, hoarding and the labor shortage are mutually reinforcing, since managers will hoard more and more workers as the chances of replacing them diminish with increasing shortages.

Rather than increasing the efficient use of labor, moreover, the shortage encourages waste. Because of the shortage, especially of unskilled workers, many people with high levels of training are used to perform menial, unskilled, and semiskilled tasks. The Soviet press frequently publishes complaints by engineering and technical personnel that their time is needlessly wasted. They may be sent to work on construction sites, but then remain idle for days while work at their enterprise gets behind. Since taking workers away from machines directly disrupts production, more skilled specialists are often sent instead. Complaints such as that of a graduate of the Bauman Higher Technical Institute in Moscow (the Soviet equivalent in prestige to M.I.T.) are typical:

> There isn't a thing I haven't done: I've dug ditches, picked up garbage, and painted window frames. . . . The plant is now being retooled, and a new system is being introduced to enhance production efficiency and quality; one would think that an engineer's talents are no less essential here than, say, in cleaning the streets (*Pravda*, May 4, 1978. Quoted in *Current Digest of the Soviet Press*, Vol. XXX, No. 22, 1978).

In a comment on this and similar complaints, the chief designer at the plant pointed out that not only was this a waste of talent, but also a cause of low morale and discipline problems. Since there is a shortage of labor at the disposal of local city and borough administrators, they are obliged to use the personnel of local industries to perform cleaning tasks and to build housing and various other facilities, but in the absence of careful coordination and distribution much of this requisitioned labor is underutilized or left idle.

There have been many suggestions for overcoming the shortage of ancillary workers, including the suggestion of one economist that college and high school students be drafted as part-time or summer workers. Some classes, he suggested, could be moved to the evening to enable students to work during the day! (*Literaturnaia gazeta*, August 30, 1978). While suggestions such as this cannot be taken too seriously, they do illustrate the urgency of the problem, the economic costs of which are considerable. For example, the Central Statistical Administration has estimated that one-third of all whole-day shutdowns, and one-half of all shift shutdowns are due to labor shortage (Maslova, 1978). Part of the problem, however, lies not just in a shortage of people, but in their distribution, since, although large cities experience a shortage of industrial workers, many small and medium-sized cities have a surplus. This situation is perpetuated by the official policy on urban growth, which still attempts to prevent migration to metropolitan areas in an effort to spread the population more evenly over a large geographic area.

While it is at least conceivable that changes in urban policy, and in the policy of maintaining full employment, may ease the situation a little, long-term solutions are not yet in evidence. Clearly, the greater use of technology would reduce the need for labor, but the economy does not have sufficient strength to provide the necessary capital investment. Moreover, buying foreign technology not only is expensive, but also creates economic ties with other nations, which have important political implications. Increasing the birth rate will provide more workers, but this takes from fifteen to twenty years to have any effect, and in the meantime it will decrease the labor supply as women take time off for childbearing and childrearing. Thus, current calls for an increase in maternity leave and in family allowance payments (Manevitch, 1978) are likely to worsen the situation rather than to improve it.

Apart from the implications of the labor shortage for the general economy, it has significant effects on workers. Firstly, a full-employment economy puts workers in a good bargaining position and provides a general context of security within which they can operate. Secondly, it influences their on-the-job activities, for (as we shall see later) it contributes to discipline problems and to high turnover rates.

As the labor shortage has been becoming more acute, the workers themselves have been undergoing some important changes. Since the death of Stalin, and especially during the 1960s and 1970s, a new type of industrial worker has been emerging. As has been the case in other industrial societies, economic development has created a stratum of industrial workers that is significantly different from that found during the industrialization drive of the 1930s and 1940s. Because of the small size of the working class at the time of the Revolution, the program of rapid industrialization initiated by Stalin in 1929 necessitated the recruitment of workers from the only available source, the peasantry. For an entire generation the mines, mills, and factories were manned by people who had gained their skills on the job, by people who came from families where there was no tradition or experience of working in industrial occupations. From the 1950s on, however, the ranks of industrial workers have been filled by the children of these workers of peasant origins, and they have brought with them an inheritance of skills, education, and expectations that is radically different from that of their parents. This has provided benefits for the economy, but it has also given rise to a new set of problems.

The changing makeup of the industrial labor force which has been occurring in recent years may be illustrated by the findings of a study of seven mechanical engineering factories in Leningrad, undertaken between 1965 and 1976–1977. Firstly, with rising levels of education in the society in general, the new workers have achieved more years of education than their predecessors. Thus, whereas the average number of years of schooling completed was 8.2 in 1965, this had risen to 8.8 in 1976–1977. Moreover, although only 28% of the workers in these factories in 1965 had received complete secondary or specialized secondary education, in 1976–1977 50% had achieved this level (Konstantinova, et al., 1978: 7). Figures for the USSR as a whole show that 78% of those classified as manual workers in 1977 had received at least some secondary education, as compared with only 32.2% in 1959 (*Narodnoe khoziaistvo SSSR za 60 let,* 1977: 56). Moreover, many workers are enrolled in evening and correspondence courses at institutes and universities, with the result that in some factories up to a third or more of engineering-technical workers have received some higher education (Geliuta and Staroverov, 1977).

As a result of an increase in educational levels, young workers are now more likely to have received their occupational preparation in a formal educational setting rather than while on the job, as was the case for older workers. Thus, whereas in 1965 67.7% of the workers under nineteen years of age were trained entirely on the job, this had fallen to 15.3% by 1976–1977 (Konstantinova, et al., 1978: 7). These changes have also meant a narrowing of the educational gap between highly skilled and unskilled workers, for whereas the former had 2.2 years of education more than the latter in 1965, they were only 1.4 years ahead in 1976–1977 (see Table 1).

Figures on the social origins of the Leningrad workers as of 1976–1977 also illustrate the extent to which recruitment increasingly has come to be from the urban, industrial working class, for 83% came from an urban background, and 38.8% were children of industrial workers. That social origins influence occupational placement, however, is obvious; whereas 69% of the unskilled workers surveyed came from farm or unskilled backgrounds, this was true of only 28.3% of the skilled machine workers (Konstantinova, et al., 1978: 11).

Not only do the new industrial workers have more education than the previous generation, but they are also part of a more "stable" and "mature" work force. As we can see from Table 1, in 1976–1977 all workers except the most highly qualified had more years of experience in their occupations than was the case in 1965; also, all groups had been employed at their current factory longer than was the case in 1970. This is

Table 1. Changing Characteristics of Workers in Seven Factories in Leningrad, 1965 to 1976–1977

Occupational Level	Educational Level: Average Number of Years Completed			Average Number of Years in Current Occupation			Average Number of Years in Current Factory		
	1965	1970	1976/77	1965	1970	1976/77	1965	1970	1976/77
Unskilled	6.5	5.6	7.7	7.0	9.6	8.5	—	10.2	10.8
Skilled machine workers	8.2	8.4	8.7	8.3	9.4	11.5	—	9.0	11.3
Skilled manual (other than machine workers)	8.3	8.7	8.9	11.1	10.3	12.7	—	9.4	11.9
Highly qualified workers who combine mental and manual work	8.7	9.8	9.1	13.9	10.2	13.5	—	9.9	15.5

Source: Konstantinova, et al., 1978: 10

257

further evidence for the belief that the experience and situation of industrial workers are sufficiently different from those of earlier generations to have created a new set of expectations. Whether or not this constitutes a new worldview is debatable, since this would involve a change in perspective on a wide range of topics, and it is too early to know whether this has in fact occurred. It may reasonably be argued, however, that these new characteristics have already led to new forms of behavior at work, and that they also appear to be influencing some wider aspects of workers' activities.

II. THE SCIENTIFIC-TECHNOLOGICAL REVOLUTION AND ITS IMPACT ON WORK AND WORKERS

While the growth of education and urbanization in Soviet society has been affecting the social characteristics of workers, the so-called scientific and technological revolution has been changing their lives at the workplace as well. The growth of mechanization and automation has required workers not only to develop new skills, but also to become more flexible in the range of tasks they are able to perform. At the same time, they must be willing to undergo retraining as the work tasks become different and more complex.

During the period 1965 to 1975, the number of mechanized lines in industry as a whole increased from 42,947 to 114,108, while the number of automated lines increased from 5,981 to 17,072 (*Narodnoe khoziaistvo SSSR za 60 let,* 1977: 150). These changes have meant an increase in the "mental" component of job tasks and have given rise to the emergence of a new type of worker, the so-called worker-intellectual. This new worker has been defined as being highly skilled and as being "employed in the most complicated fields of physical work the greatest components of which are of [an] intellectual nature. At their working places these workers operate complicated machinery, which calls for the knowledge of a technical college or a higher educational institution (institute or university)" (Gheliuta and Gogoliukhin, 1974: 170). These workers are said by ideologists and theoreticians to be the vanguard of the new working class, a class which is gradually being transformed by the "intellectualization" of labor as a result of the scientific and technological revolution. This is said also to be part of a long-term process whereby the working class and the intelligentsia will fuse into a single class. Indeed, the major trend in the further development of Soviet society is precisely this, *"the drawing together of all classes, groups and layers of working people by the character of work"* (Rutkevitch, 1974: 25, emphasis in the original). As the distinctions between manual and mental work diminish this is allegedly accompanied by a diminution of differences in the sphere of distribution (i.e., consumption). This involves both increasing equalization of incomes and increasingly similar patterns of consumption and leisure use. This theory is surprisingly similar to a thesis current in the West in the 1950s and 1960s, which claimed that the working class and the middle class were beginning to fuse, that the worker was experiencing "embourgeoisement." In the Soviet case this might be referred to as "intelligentsification," but the underlying assumption is the same, namely that technological change is leading to the homogenization of society. However, data on the lifestyles of workers do not support the theory any better in the Soviet case than Western data did in the case of "capitalist" societies.

Currently, worker-intellectuals only account for approximately 4% of all workers, although in some plants (mainly in the chemical and metallurgy industries) they may be as much as 44% of the work force (Gheliuta and Gogoliukhin, 1974: 174). Given the speed with which technological innovation is proceeding, it is unlikely that workers of this type will significantly increase their share of the general labor force during the next decade or so. Moreover, partial automation (which accounts for a significant part of technological innovation) does not markedly increase the mental component of jobs, and may actually make the job more monotonous. In addition, partial automation also tends to retain a high percentage of unskilled workers, and so it does not lessen the labor shortage (Kolbanovsky, 1974).

Although the widespread, socially transforming effects of technological change predicted by official theory will almost certainly not occur during the remainder of this century, technology is already the major determinant of job creation, about two-thirds of all new jobs during the last twenty years having resulted from the increasing complexity of equipment (Lane and O'Dell, 1978: 14). This has meant an upgrading of the general skill level of workers, as shown by the fact that whereas in 1962 37.7% of all industrial workers were classified as being at skill levels I and II (on a six-point scale, six being the highest skill level), this had fallen to 28.1% by 1972. Likewise, those at levels V and VI increased from 13.5% to 21% during the same period (*Rabochi klass razvitogo sotsialisticheskogo obshchestva*, 1974: 81). In spite of this upgrading in classification, however, many workers still perform tasks below their official skill levels.

While increasing mechanization and the upgrading of skill levels have been occurring, they have not done so at a rate necessary to maintain earlier rates of increase in productivity, which rose by only 4% in 1976 compared to 6% in the early 1970s (Lane and O'Dell, 1978: 14). Technological innovation has also failed to keep pace with the rising educational level of workers, with the result that many of them (especially young

Table 2. Educational and Skill Levels of Industrial Workers
According to Age

Age	Years of Education	Official Skill Level (average)	Skill Level of Job Actually Performed (average)
Up to 19	9.60	2.47	2.47
20–24	9.88	3.00	3.10
25–29	9.98	3.64	3.49
30–34	9.59	3.87	3.54
40–44	8.03	4.42	3.74
50–54	7.49	4.20	3.64
60 +	7.28	4.54	4.03

Source: Konstantinova, et al., 1978: 14.

workers) have jobs whose requirements are below that which their educational level would warrant. This is illustrated by the results of a study
done in 1976–1977 of workers in Leningrad (Table 2). Although the
youngest workers have an average of more than two years more education than older workers, they are from 1.73 to 2.07 skill grades below
them. While a stress on job seniority would lead one to expect this, the
lower official levels of those in their twenties and thirties shows that
technological developments and mechanization have not led to the replacing of older workers by better educated, younger workers, a subject of
contention by younger workers in the Soviet press. It is not surprising,
therefore, that 65% of the young workers surveyed in this study did not
feel that their skills were being adequately used, nor that they reportedly
had lower levels of productivity (Konstantinova, et al., 1978: 15). The
data in Table 2 also demonstrate a frequent finding of such research,
namely the underutilization of skills among those aged thirty and above,
all of these age groups reporting that their actual job tasks merited a lower
rank of skill than that which they officially possessed. However, care
should be taken in interpreting these data, since management apparently
uses job-reclassification as a way of giving wage increases and of rewarding seniority, and so higher skill grades may not necessarily be the result
of workers having more skills. There are signs that the seniority system is
being undermined, however, as reflected in the frequent protests by
workers that they are not being promoted because they lack formal
credentials, and that they are being pushed to one side in favor of those
who do. This has even led to the development of a black market for fake
diplomas, which workers may buy in an attempt to gain promotion (or
even, reportedly, to keep from being replaced) (Izvestiia, March 14,
1972).

III. MATERIAL CONDITIONS, LABOR TURNOVER, AND WORKERS' VALUES

The utilization and distribution of labor in the USSR is in principle accomplished through the general economic plan which is drawn up by the ministries and central planners. The plan, in its specification of factor usage and enterprise location, determines (in general) what kinds of jobs will be available, how many there will be, and how they will be allocated by sector and region. Labor is not envisaged as being part of a market system and attempts are made to distribute workers through a combination of assignment and choice, various material and ideological incentives being used to move labor to those areas where it is most needed. Ironically, however, the principle of full employment (and the current overemployment of labor) has begun to undermine this planned system of allocation, and there are signs that the development of a labor market is well under way. The emergence of such a market has been noticed and commented upon by a number of Soviet social scientists (e.g., Levin, 1973), although it would be perhaps more accurate to describe it as a proto-market, since entry is still rather restricted, and bargaining is strictly circumscribed by central controls. However, it is significant that it is emerging at all, and if it continues, it is likely to have profound effects on society and on the economy. For our purposes, the element of the proto-labor market of greatest concern is that of labor turnover, since this is most closely related to the question of worker consciousness. Labor turnover is relevant here insofar as its patterns, and the factors that determine the choices and decisions underlying these patterns, can tell us something about the values and goals of workers.

Labor turnover in the USSR is considerably more frequent than it is in other industrial countries, for whereas in the late 1960s and early 1970s the rate was about 5% in the USA and in West Germany, official Soviet figures for that period put it at about 21% (Teckenberg, 1978: 194). Most of this turnover is unplanned and unregulated, and it has the effect not of creating a more efficient distribution of labor, but rather the reverse. While the national rate is about 21% per year, there are wide variations between industries and regions, ranging from 14.8% in the metal industry to 35.7% in the food industry, and from 15.7% in the central RSFSR to 39.8% in Tadzhikistan (Rusanov, 1971, quoted in Teckenberg, 1978: 195).

Labor turnover has been a topic of increasing concern during the last two decades, for as work processes have become more complex, the economic costs of turnover have become greater. Estimates of these costs vary, but that of Sonin (that turnover is responsible for up to 20% of the losses in industry, and for rather more than 20% in construction) is typical (quoted in *Current Digest of the Soviet Press*, Vol. XXIX, No. 38, 1977).

In Belorussia alone in 1977, direct losses resulting from turnover came to 2.5 to 3 million workdays (Skarupo, 1977). The costs of this turnover result not only from a loss of productivity as newcomers adapt to their new occupation (productivity declining by up to 20% during a worker's first few months in a new job), but also to lost time between jobs. Partly this is due to the problem of finding a suitable job in a desirable area, but it is also due to the complicated process through which workers have to go when changing jobs. Medical examinations, obtaining approvals and signatures for paperwork, and other official requirements, can be a time-consuming process (for example, at one mine in the Ukraine new employees need to obtain no less than thirteen signatures before they can begin work), and this further delays re-employment (*Trud,* March 4, 1978). A study of turnover in Borisov done in 1974 found that although 57.5% of workers had a break between jobs of less than two weeks, 24.4% took from two to four weeks, 11.2% took from a month to a year, and 2.5% took over a year to obtain another job (Skarupo, 1977). Another study of machine engineering and construction workers done in 1970–1971 found that, compared to the mid-1960s, they were taking longer to find new jobs (Antosenkov and Kupriianova, 1977).

The reasons for the high level of turnover are complex.[2] One factor that has been shown to affect it is the size and character of the enterprise. Thus, turnover is less in large enterprises than it is in small ones, ranging from 7.9% in those employing 10,000 or more workers to 40% in those employing 250 or less (Teckenberg, 1978: 197). Although there has been (as far as we know) no systematic research on this relationship, the explanation probably lies in a combination of material and organizational factors, rather than in differences in job content. Workers in a large enterprise engage in a trade-off between sociopsychological rewards and material rewards. The larger size involves a loss of contact with management, greater anonymity, and greater subjection to a bureaucratic form of organization, but it also means the possibility of higher income (because of the greater size of the wage fund and the bonus fund), more facilities and services (especially housing), and more opportunity for mobility within the enterprise. This last factor not only means that more opportunities for promotion may be present, but also that should new processes reduce the demand for labor, there is a greater chance that displaced workers can be given another job within the enterprise, rather than their having to leave. These extrinsic factors would account for lower turnover in that they promote a general feeling of security and of opportunity and encourage a high level of job satisfaction. While this argument is plausible, however, we shall have to wait until Soviet researchers address this issue in more detail before we can know how accurate it is.

A further contributing factor to turnover is the sex-ratio of an enterprise or an area. In some towns the predominance of industries that employ mainly women means that women greatly outnumber men, and this causes women to leave for other areas where this imbalance does not exist (*Pravda*, April 20, 1977). This has led some economists to advocate that plans for industrial siting and urban development should create a mix of employment opportunities that will maintain an overall balance between males and females (Kostakov, 1976).

The second major factor associated with turnover is that of job satisfaction, with some research reports claiming that this explains as much as 36% of the variance (Popova, 1973: 270). Whether or not it has such a strong influence as that, it is clear that job satisfaction has been becoming a more significant factor in workers' behavior since the 1950s. With increases in the level of education, and with the introduction of more complex technology, workers apparently have become more concerned about the content of work. Surveys have repeatedly shown that scope for creativity is highly valued by workers, especially by those who are younger or who have more education; those with less education, however, tend to value wages to a greater extent (Slesarev, 1974). Research has also shown that job satisfaction is positively correlated with skill and the degree to which tasks require complex decision making, and negatively correlated with the performance of physically laborious tasks. For example, a recent study of industrial enterprises in Borisov found that 54.3% of those workers who were in jobs which required heavy physical labor without the aid of machinery expressed dissatisfaction with their jobs, compared to 11% of those engaged in mechanized work and 1.5% of those performing automated work (Skarupo, 1977). In a study of young workers in Leningrad, job dissatisfaction was found to be as high as 80% among unskilled workers, who, of course, are precisely those who perform the heaviest manual work (Iadov and Kissel, 1974: 85).

Findings such as these would lead one to expect that turnover would be greatest among the unskilled and the young, and this is indeed the case. As we shall see, however, job satisfaction is not simply a reflection of the technological content of the work tasks, but is rather due to the degree to which the material rewards that the worker receives are seen as "just". This raises the issue of the criteria according to which workers judge the value of the jobs they perform, and of the direction in which these criteria are developing. We can, I think, discern an answer to both of these questions in data on the expectations and behavior of young workers. According to research by Kotliar and Talalai (1977), workers under thirty change jobs four times more frequently than those in their thirties, and ten times more frequently than those over fifty years of age. Also, 34% of all new workers who are secondary school graduates quit during their first year, and another 16% quit in their second year. This high turnover rate among young high school graduates is due to the fact that although 80% of them have no vocational training, they do have high expectations regarding level of pay, interesting jobs, and good working conditions. Because of their lack of formal skills, many of them are given unskilled and heavy, manual jobs, since these are in demand by the enterprise. Even those who received on-the-job training in more skilled work have a higher turnover rate than those who received formal training in a specialized (technical) secondary school, and they were an average of one skill level lower than the latter group. Even among those with formal skills, however, 20% were in jobs other than those for which they were trained, and this leads to some turnover even among these workers. All of these factors help to explain why two-thirds of all turnover is accounted for by young workers (Kotliar and Talalai, 1977). The problem, of course, is that changes within industry have not kept pace with the increasing expectations which result from greater length of formal education. Because industry is especially short of less-skilled (especially ancillary) workers, even if young workers improve their skill levels this does not mean that promotion is assured; even now, many workers are actually performing jobs that are below their official skill levels. However, if industry does not change sufficiently to meet some of the job expectations of the new generation of workers, then worker unrest may begin to express itself in ways other than turnover, perhaps even political activities.

The third and fourth factors most associated with labor turnover are material factors, namely wages and access to goods and services. While these factors are probably the most important factors underlying turnover, the strength of their effect varies depending upon their interaction with the previous two factors we have mentioned. Thus, when services and access to adequate housing are satisfactory, then job satisfaction becomes a relatively more significant factor. In older enterprises in larger cities where services are relatively plentiful, job satisfaction and wages are more important motivations, and workers move in search of better conditions, better pay, or a promotion. For example, research in Leningrad (an old, well-established industrial city) has found that workers most frequently cite working conditions as the reason for changing jobs (35.7% say this), compared to 27.5% who cite housing and living conditions, and 21.4% who mention wages. Only 3.7% mention the work process itself as a reason (Blyakhman, et al., 1965: 142). In newer enterprises in more remote areas, or in small towns or settlements, material factors assume the greatest importance. The lack of housing and services gives material, external factors a dominant role in motivating turnover, since in the face of the general problems of living this creates, job content becomes less important; even wages assume a secondary position, given the fact that money alone cannot provide access to goods and services. Illustrations of this general rule may be found in research on workers in Novosibirsk (Antosenkov, 1969), and in Ufa (Aitov, 1972), among others. The issue of housing is an especially troubling problem for many workers, especially young workers, both married and single. A recent study of young workers in over a hundred enterprises in Belorussia and the RSFSR found that although 42% of those aged 20–24, and 80% of those aged 25–29, were married, only 8.9% of all workers in these age groups had their own home. Even among those aged thirty and over only 66.5% had their own home. Moreover, of those workers under thirty years of age who needed dormitory accommodation only two-thirds actually received it, with a total of 29% of this age group living in dormitories (Kotliar and Talalai, 1977). Even those fortunate enough to live in a dormitory experience problems, for although it is inexpensive (about four rubles a month, or approximately 3%–4% of income) conditions are often poor. There are constant complaints about overcrowding, overly strict regulations, poor facilities, insensitive and irresponsible management, and lack of anything to do. Boredom is a frequent problem, and in areas where outside recreational facilities are poor or lacking, drunkenness becomes a major problem (*Trud*, November 18, 1977; *Molodoi kommunist*, May, 1977). (Indeed, drunkenness among workers is such a general problem that it has been estimated that if it were eliminated in the workplace alone it would increase productivity by 10% [*Komsomol'skaia Pravda*, May 17, 1978]). These problems associated with housing cause workers to move from job to job, and this may produce turnover levels as high as that recently found at one enterprise in the Gorky region, where 4,000 out of a total of 9,000 workers leave every year. Investigation of the reasons for this high level showed that the lack of local housing forced workers to commute long distances from remote towns and villages, and that there were insufficient stores, services, and day nurseries to meet their needs. This not only resulted in a high turnover rate, but also produced low morale, poor work performance, and a general dissatisfaction with life (*Pravda*, April 15, 1977).

Another material factor is that of wages, although there is a complex interaction between satisfaction with wages and education, a survey of research in this area showing that both absolute and relative wage levels have an effect on job satisfaction and turnover. As the absolute wage level increases, wage and job satisfaction also increase, although this rise in satisfaction is less among workers with more education (Aitov, 1972). In sum, therefore, education and income determine job satisfaction, which in turn affects labor turnover.

Although research done in the 1960s showed that income was positively associated with job satisfaction (e.g., Zdravomyslov, et al., 1970), it has only been in the last few years that the idea of a relativistic "norm of income" has been developed and investigated. Recent research by Rabitskii (1978) has attempted to demonstrate that such a norm exists, and that there is a "potential turnover pool" that is created by this norm. The median income for given skill levels is used to distinguish two groups—those above and those below median income, the latter being defined as the group of potential job-changers. This is an advance over earlier research in that skill level is controlled for. The results of this research have shown that those in the potential group do have lower productivity, lower quality of output, and greater discipline problems. They also participate less in work-improvement ("rationalization") schemes, and less in the social life of the enterprise (Rabitskii, 1978). More studies will be needed in order firmly to establish the existence of a "norm" of income, but the findings to date are certainly in agreement with other research on the importance of income as a determinant of workplace behavior. Moreover, the Rabitskii approach helps to explain a frequent finding of research on labor discipline, namely that workers with poor discipline records are twice as likely to mention their dissatisfaction with wages (while also being less involved in social activities of various kinds) than is the case with workers with good records (Podorov, 1976).

Finally, there have been attempts to discover which elements of the organization of the workplace may affect turnover rates. In one such study of workers in metallurgical enterprises in Western Siberia, it was found that the degree of solidarity of the work group (measured by the extent of cooperation and mutual aid) was positively related to the degree of satisfaction with wages, although the researchers were unable to show which factor was cause and which effect. However, it was shown that departments and shops with low solidarity also had the greatest discipline problems and the highest turnover rates (Patrushev and Shabashev, 1975). Given what we know from other research, it is likely that dissatisfaction with wages is the cause of low solidarity rather than the reverse being the case. Indeed, Soviet sociologists have begun to realize that job content and work-group relations are not the most important causes of job satisfaction and turnover, and they have been placing increasing emphasis on the importance of extrinsic factors (Iadov and Kissel, 1974). The same conclusions are now being drawn from research on the determinants of labor productivity, and it is clear that the earlier stress on the importance of job content (construed in a narrow, technological sense) was misplaced (Iadov and Kissel, 1974). Recent research in the Perm area has shown that workers' satisfaction with their general situation and wage level together explain 32% of the variance in productivity, compared to 29% in the case of level of mechanization, skill level and education (combined into a single index), and 11% in the case of job content, level of creativity, labor discipline, and turnover (again, combined into one index) (calculated from

Gerchikov, 1979: 185). Thus, the importance of extrinsic factors is increasingly being recognized. In addition, some recent research has begun to suggest that autonomy in the work sphere may also be a better predictor of productivity than job technology, although it is too early to know if this factor will prove to be as strong as are the material factors (Tikhonov, 1976).

What has begun to emerge from recent Soviet research and surveys of the literature is a fairly uniform hierarchy of priorities among workers, with pay, conditions, and interesting work being the most important factors; the size of the enterprise, scale and type of output being next; job related conditions (good workmates, an easy pace of work, etc.) being next; and factors related to security (pensions, job security, medical services) being least important (Kolodizh, 1978). The low priority given to security is clearly due to the situation of full employment in which workers find themselves, and this makes Soviet workers rather different from workers in the West. At the same time, Soviet conditions have also created a rather instrumental orientation to work, although this is lessened to the extent that workers have achieved more formal education and more skills. As a result, for most workers internal (work) considerations play a relatively minor role in their evaluation of their general existence, and the external factors of income, housing, and services are apparently of greatest concern. For those workers who have achieved a satisfactory level of living, however, internal factors assume a greater importance.

A final illustration of the hierarchy of priorities among workers may be found in the results of a study conducted in 1977 in Khar'kov. Although the focus of the research was on the role of discipline in the work group, it also shows the relative importance given to material versus workplace concerns. The researchers asked sixty-seven shop leaders and 824 workers in two factories to indicate which punishments for infractions of discipline they thought would be most effective. Scoring was on a five-point scale, with five being most effective, and one least effective. As we can see from Table 3, there was considerable agreement between workers and shop leaders that monetary penalties and the loss of one's place on the housing list would be the most effective penalties. Social pressures at the workplace were considered relatively unimportant measures by all groups, while workers gave more weight to dismissal or loss of summertime vacation than did the shop leaders. Although job security is not generally considered a worrisome issue by Soviet workers, a dismissal for discipline reasons would make it difficult for them to obtain an equally good or better job elsewhere, and this would involve a wage penalty in addition to a disruption of one's life. Also, appearing before a Comrades Court is probably given more weight than censure in the workplace since

Table 3.   Assessments of Effectiveness of Various Sanctions for
Infractions of Discipline

	Shop or Department Leaders		*WORKERS* *Machine-Engineering Factory*		*Tractor Construction Factory*	
SANCTION	*Rank*	*Score*	*Rank*	*Score*	*Rank*	*Score*
Deprivation of monthly bonus	1	4.47	3	4.26	2	4.43
Demoted on waiting list for apartment	2	4.44	1	4.68	1	4.56
Deprivation of share in yearly bonus of enterprise	3	4.33	2	4.44	3	4.24
Have case discussed in Comrades Court	4	4.16	5	4.24	5	4.20
Dismissal	5	4.00	4	4.25	4	4.20
Have case discussed at workers' meeting	6	3.80	10	3.55	7	4.00
Transfer to lower paying job	7	3.75	6	4.05	6	4.02
Individual discussion with shop leader	8	3.74	8	3.76	9	3.85
Move vacation time from summer to other month	9	3.54	7	3.86	8	3.86
Criticism in factory newspaper or radio	10	3.32	11	3.43	11	3.49
Announce an official reprimand	11	3.15	9	3.65	10	3.60

Source: Reznikov, 1978: 63.

it is a more public situation, and it may involve some further penalty. The
general implication of these figures, however, is that they show the
importance of material factors for workers, and the relative weakness of
constraints at the workplace. Results such as this cast doubt not only on
Soviet sociologists' emphasis on the importance of social relations at the
workplace as a factor in the behavior of workers, but also upon the
general, official pursuit of subjective controls. In spite of attempts to use
propaganda and socialization to firmly anchor the worker in a collective
(i.e., the work group), wages and living conditions are still the primary
motivating forces in a worker's life.

IV. WORK AND THE STRUCTURE OF AUTHORITY

Changes in the backgrounds of workers and in the nature of the work they
perform have resulted in the emergence of developments that have occurred in other industrial nations in recent years. These developments

may be summarized under the rubric of "the democratization of work," and although Soviet conditions have prevented very extensive development the fact that it has emerged at all is in itself of great interest.

First, let us look briefly at the organizational context in which the process of "democratization" has begun. Soviet industrial enterprises, like those elsewhere, are characterized by a hierarchical form of organization in which people in the lower levels are subordinate to the dictates of those at higher levels. The basic division is between managers and workers, and decision making is both formally and actually in the hands of the managers. The principle which controls this organization is that of "one man rule" (*edinonachalie*). This means that in principle the responsibility and accountability for a work unit is assigned to a specific individual, and in return these individuals are given the right to demand compliance by those under them. Thus, the enterprise may be seen as a pyramid of units, each of which is controlled by a single person, with the enterprise director having the ultimate authority. All unit leaders are appointed or removed at the discretion of the director, and everyone is directly subordinate to only one person. The director holds this position on the authority of the appropriate Ministry, which alone has the ability to appoint, transfer, or fire an enterprise director. Although this system of organization is said to be based on the Leninist theory of management, it is clearly not too different from industrial organization in the West.

The production goals of the enterprise are set by the Ministry to which it is subordinate, with targets being determined by the national economic plan. The budget, production output goals, pricing, and the delivery schedules are decided by the Ministry, and the task of the director and of his managers is to coordinate the activities of the plant in order to meet or exceed the targets set for the enterprise by the plan. In doing this, the director is supposed to place the interests of the society (in the form of the plan) above those of the enterprise or of those who work in it.

It has frequently been noted (e.g., Yanowitch, 1977; Berliner, 1957) that this form of organization was developed for, and adopted in, a situation that was very different from that which exists today. During the period of rapid industrialization in the 1930s and 1940s, the absence of both an experienced working class, and a large enough supply of trained managers and specialists, made it necessary to build work discipline into the organization of the enterprise, since discipline could not be counted upon at the level of the individual worker or supervisor. With changes in both the make-up and background of the work force, however, the old system has become more and more dysfunctional for performance, and as a result there are continuing attempts by economists and planners to introduce innovations that solve the problem without weakening the principle of one-man rule.

One way in which people have tried to introduce changes has been to urge greater attention to those aspects of the existing system that allow for participation by workers in decision making. In principle, one-man rule has always included the principle of "collegiality" (Yanowitch, 1977: 139ff), meaning that discussions of problems at the plant or unit level should involve workers as well as managers, and that the latter should take the opinions of the former into account. Using this principle of democratic centralism as a source of legitimation, there have been pressures since the 1960s to make participation a reality, although to date these pressures have been successfully resisted by managers and the central authorities.

Although worker participation in any real sense has yet to develop, a more indirect input by workers is being achieved through the adoption of aspects of the human-relations approach to enterprise organization. Soviet management theory has now been amended to include the principle that the new work situation calls for a form of organization that takes into consideration the social relationships, attitudes, and interests of workers. While this does not represent the replacement of a one-way flow of communications by a two-way flow, it does mean that the messages must be devised in such a way as to anticipate those factors that will increase their chances of being implemented. In a sense, this is an indirect form of democratization, since it is a mechanism for representing (at least partially) in the decision-making process the interests of workers. In addition, it also represents a movement away from external controls over work towards internal (self-regulated) controls, since it includes the expectation that the performance of work tasks will rely more on the initiative of the worker and less upon the orders of a unit boss.

The relative change in direction of communication flow which the new human relations approach involves can be seen in the greater emphasis given to "improvement in the psychological climate of the collective" (Yanowitch, 1977: 142). This calls for a new style of management, one which relies less upon authoritarian controls and more on sensitivity, friendliness, consideration, and on keeping people informed of events that affect the enterprise. Thus, in addition to questions of technological feasibility, managers now have to consider questions of social and psychological feasibility, and it is this need that has led to the rapid growth of factory sociology during the last decade.

The indirect democratization that the new Soviet management theory involves shows no signs of supplanting the principle of one-man rule—indeed, its purpose is to make it more effective by manipulating the situation more rationally. Even though the old system is being merely amended, however, there is little evidence about the extent to which managers have actively adopted the new approach; one may infer from the frequent complaints about management, however, that the old system is still very much the mode. Indeed, it would be surprising if managers did other than resist this change, since the rewards for making it are uncertain, and in the past managers have found that officially sanctioned innovations can prove very costly for the individual enterprise and those who run it (e.g., the Shchekino experiments of the last decade). Moreover, as long as the external environment of the enterprise remains unchanged, internal changes frequently prove difficult or create worse problems.

Although in principle the Soviet enterprise has always been participatory, it has been only in recent years that research on workers' participation has occurred. Unfortunately, Soviet research on participation is very different from that undertaken in Yugoslavia, since Soviet sociologists have restricted their research to looking at participation in schemes such as workers' competitions to increase output, improve product quality, or invent better tools or ways of doing things; and to such activities as taking part in voluntary work, or engaging in sociopolitical activities such as attending meetings, taking courses and giving talks to schoolchildren. There have been (as far as we know) no studies of the actual influence workers may have on decision making, although research has been done on whether workers "feel" that they have an influence on decisions. The results of research on these topics have been much as we would have predicted, with workers with higher levels of education and skill reporting more involvement in competitions, voluntary work, and sociopolitical activities, and also reporting that they feel they have more influence on major decisions (Arutiunian, 1971; Ermuratskii, 1973; Oligin-Nesterov, 1973; Iovchuk and Kogan, 1972; Mukhachev and Borovik, 1975; Kuznetsov, 1974). In the absence of research on actual participation, however, it is impossible to know how much influence workers really have, or whether the debate on participation has modified the system of "one-man management" to any extent.

What research there has been on attitudes towards workers achieving greater participation, however, shows that management and workers have very different ideas on the matter. Thus, surveys that have asked if respondents were in favor of management (including the director) being elected by the workers, have found that two-thirds of the workers thought it a good idea, whereas 70% of the top management thought it was a bad idea (Yanowitch, 1977: 154). Managers, therefore, may be expected to resist strongly any attempts to democratize the factory that would threaten their security and challenge their authority. As a result, it is likely that increased participation will occur through piecemeal evolution, rather than through rapid and radical change. Already there have been innovations in deciding how enterprise "profit funds" are distributed, with the union having gained an equal right in making this decision; the next step would be to distribute portions of the fund to separate departments and shops for them to disburse according to their own agreed-upon decisions. The next step would be the involvement of the union, and later of worker committees at the shop level, in decisions affecting technological changes and, perhaps, the production plan itself. Although these developments lie some time in the future, a debate on these issues is already in progress.

One thing is sure, and that is that the solutions tried will not involve any thoroughgoing decentralization of decision making—thus, nothing like the Yugoslav form of industrial organization will be tried in the foreseeable future. Instead, one may expect a continuation of the current development of "scientific management" (including human relations techniques), which protects the leading role of management; indeed, the centralized system of economic planning and allocation remains an effective barrier to decentralization within the enterprise. Once the parameters have been set by the plan, the scope of decisions is narrowed to such an extent that only the minutiae of enterprise activities may be debated. Ironically, although any further decentralization of the economy (especially an increase in the role of the market) would facilitate democratization at the workplace, the workers would pay for this with greater insecurity, since meeting market demands in a competitive situation would reduce overemployment. Since worker security is an acknowledged benefit of the Soviet situation, it is unlikely that workers will be eager to press for innovations that would weaken their position in this respect.

We may summarize the foregoing as follows. With increasingly complex technology, the functional position of the worker changes. There is a shift from routine and predetermined performance activities to a stress upon evaluation and decision-making activities. This means that workers need to know more about basic scientific and engineering principles than was formerly the case, and that they have greater responsibility for the production process itself. This necessitates a change in social relations at the workplace, especially in the relations of authority. The old system of "one-man management," devised for a situation in which most tasks were routinized and specific, is not suited to a situation in which tasks overlap and responsibilities widen. This has widespread implications for the whole system of authority in the enterprise, and there are already signs that new relations are in the process of being defined.

V. COLLECTIVE ACTIVITY AMONG SOVIET WORKERS

Unlike the activities of workers in Poland, very little is known in the West about collective activity among Soviet workers. There have been a number of descriptions of strikes, protests and slowdowns (Boiter, 1964;

Holubenko, 1975; Haynes and Semyonova, 1978), but we do not know the precise frequency with which such events occur, nor how workers themselves view them. "Regular" Soviet sociologists have not investigated this area (or, at least, they have not published accounts of such research), but it is quite likely that sociologists employed by the Party or by the KGB have done so, since the purpose of having sociologists in these agencies is precisely to investigate (but not to publicize) politically sensitive issues. In spite of the lack of systematic information, however, we know enough to make some preliminary generalizations. (See Holubenko, 1975, for a brief summary of our knowledge to date.)

First, it would appear that strikes and demonstrations are more likely to occur in the provinces than in major centers such as Moscow and Leningrad. While we cannot be sure of the reasons for this, it probably is due to greater shortages of goods and services, to less control by the KGB, and to less concern among the leaders because the periphery is less visible (both internally and externally) (Holubenko, 1975). It is also likely that potential trouble is' spotted and headed off in the central areas precisely because it is more visible, and so management would be more sensitive to issues that could escalate into general action by workers. This would help to explain the second generalization, namely that workers' activities in the provinces are more likely to involve violence, and tend to last longer, than those at the center. If trouble develops in a major city, it is dealt with quickly and flexibly, as illustrated by the handling of the following incident in Kiev:

> In May 1973, thousands of workers at the machine-building factory on the busy Brest-Litovsk Chausee went on strike at 11:00 a.m. demanding higher pay. The factory director immediately telephoned the Central Committee of the Communist Party of the Ukraine (C.P.U.). By noon, a member of the C.P.U. Politburo arrived at the factory to evaluate the situation. He met a delegation of workers and immediately promised to fulfill their demands. By 3:00 p.m. the workers were informed that their salaries were to be increased, and most of the top administrators of the factory were dismissed (Holubenko, 1975: 9).

Following such an incident, investigators will move in, and those workers considered to be agitators or leaders are then dealt with in secret (being sentenced to a prison term and/or exile).

By contrast, incidents on the periphery may last for several days, may involve the use of troops and specially trained and armed security police, and may result in many deaths and casualties (some reports alleging that hundreds have been killed in a number of incidents). The problem, however, is that our knowledge is based upon second- and third-hand accounts, and descriptions of the same incidents often vary in essentials. The existence of collective action among industrial workers, though, is beyond dispute, the following (see Holubenko, 1975: 11–17) being a list of some of the incidents for which there is documented evidence of some kind:

1956: During the period which has come to be known as "the thaw," workers at factory meetings reportedly criticized the privileges of "the ruling elite."

1959: Riots occurred in the Temir-Tau metallurgical complex in Kazakhstan, sparked by pay cuts and food shortages.

1960: Similar events to those in Temir-Tau occurred in the Kuzbas region of Siberia.

1961: A strike by workers in Rostov-on-Don to protest the currency reforms.

1962: In reaction to an increase in dairy and meat prices, strikes, demonstrations, and riots occurred in Grosny, Krasnodar, Odessa, Donetsk, Iaroslav, Zhdanov, Gorky, Kiev, and among workers at the Moskvich Auto Factory in Moscow. There were also riots at the Budenny Electric Locomotive Works in Novocherkassk, whose workers were joined by women from the local textile factory and by students. After soldiers and the KGB had fired upon the crowd (allegedly killing several hundred) the riot ended, and martial law and a curfew were imposed.

1967: Workers at the Khar'kov Tractor Factory walked off the job.

1970: Workers in Kaliningrad, Lvov, and some cities in Belorussia struck in sympathy with the Polish workers' strikes (these cities are all close to the Polish border).

1972: Thousands of workers in Dnepropetrovsk went on strike in September for higher wages and a higher standard of living; several were allegedly killed. One month later more strikes broke out.

1973: A two-day strike among factory workers in Vytebsk over new work norms and a 20% cut in wages. Also, work stoppages occurred among construction workers in Moscow and Leningrad.

While our knowledge of these incidents is fragmentary, it is clear from what we do know that they were occasioned by concern over wages and living standards, and not by on-the-job or job-related issues. That workers are mainly concerned about external conditions is illustrated in a petition taken to Moscow in 1969 by a deputation of workers, in which their major complaint was about local housing conditions ("Kiev workers protest to the Central Committee").

The pattern of protest which these events portray further illustrates the argument that the form of organization of the Soviet enterprise and its place in a centrally planned economy have removed many of the sources of contention that lead to worker unrest in the West. Since economic reform of a decentralizing kind would re-introduce these elements, we would expect to find an increase in purely locally sparked strikes. It is conceivable, however, that the regime would actually benefit from this, since the greater income differentiation among workers which a more demand-oriented enterprise would create, together with a lessening of job security for the most marginal workers, would considerably lessen worker solidarity. Also, and more importantly, it would shift protest away from the central authorities towards local management. Any increase in market factors, therefore, may be expected to increase lateral conflicts (between workers and management) and to decrease vertical conflicts (between workers and the Party).[3] The current absence of the diffusing (and defusing) mechanism that the market would create makes the regime extremely wary of allowing conflict to develop, or to last for long once it has emerged.

VI. CONCLUSION

The emphasis in this paper has been on the general situation within which Soviet workers operate, and on the material conditions that influence their values and activities. Indeed the central argument has been that it is these factors (general context and material conditions) that are most important for an understanding of workers' motivations. It now remains to summarize the position taken above and to make some suggestions regarding future developments.

First, it is unlikely that there will be a major change in the overall employment situation in the foreseeable future. The labor shortage will almost certainly persist, and so workers will continue to benefit from the security that this produces. Some planners and economists have called for the development of "a system of manpower reserves" and a redistribution of the workforce in order to solve the problem, but what this amounts to is the creation of unemployment and the control of migration and labor turnover. Since the regime cannot control these processes now, and since deliberate unemployment can only be created if there is a massive reorganization of industry, these solutions are unlikely to occur. Moreover, while greater material incentives may produce some relocation of labor from areas of oversupply to areas of scarcity, this too has its limitations. Thus, wages themselves are less of an issue than access to housing and services, and these are precisely the things most lacking where labor is needed. The current state of the economy is unable to provide the enormous capital expenditure such a re-allocation would need in order for it to work.

With regard to the situation within the enterprise, as the expectations of workers increase, and as the emotional demands of modern technology grow, then greater attention will have to be given to workplace conditions. Already factories are having to provide reductions in the level of noise, the introduction of air-conditioning, rest and relaxation facilities, and so forth, in an effort to lessen strains on workers. At the same time, higher levels of skill and education mean that greater attention will have to be given to job enhancement. While some moves in this direction are being made (including the tentative introduction of flexible work hours similar to the systems that have developed in other industrial societies [*Literaturnaia gazeta*, January 4, 1978; February 15, 1978]), they are not likely to increase rapidly as long as the shortage of labor (especially less-skilled labor) persists. Without job enhancement and the introduction of more skilled tasks, however, the unused capacity of young workers will continue to create problems.

This raises the issue of work-group solidarity and its effect on productivity. Increasingly during recent years economists and sociologists have called for economic planning to incorporate measures to increase solidarity, including such measures as increasing skill levels, increasing workers' participation in decision making, and job enhancement (Patrushev and Shabashev, 1975). While these changes may improve productivity via an increase in work-group solidarity, they are likely to be much less effective than an improvement in wages, housing, and services. The path to greater productivity and worker contentment lies less in on the job issues than in the general position of the worker in a wider social context, in spite of the fact that on the job factors are becoming *relatively* more important as workers become better educated. Job enhancement and the further reduction of unskilled jobs would certainly help (especially in the case of young workers), but probably less than giving more attention to services, facilities, and consumption. This, of course, would require either a major shift in resource allocation, or economic growth, which in turn requires an increase in productivity. Ironically, attempts to improve economic performance through decentralizing reforms such as the Shchekino system will in all likelihood *increase* conflict, since they will give management more discretion, and hence will expand the range of issues for possible negotiation.

In recent years writers such as Teckenberg (1978), and Lane and O'Dell (1978) have stressed the importance for workers' general views and activities of their relationships to the enterprise, although whereas Teckenberg stresses conflict, Lane and O'Dell stress integration. Moreover, Lane and O'Dell suggest that Soviet workers are not alienated or "privatized," but rather that they typify a type of worker they call "incorporated." This type of worker has a degree of solidarity with the factory, accepts authority if it is efficient, participates in improving production, and "is closer to the administration both socially and politically than the worker in capitalist society" (Lane and O'Dell, 1978: 50). This, I think, is to give too much emphasis to the extent to which the worker is either ideologically or socially involved in enterprise life, although the provision of housing, services, and various other benefits by the enterprise probably does make the Soviet worker rather more of a corporate being than the Western counterpart. However, I do not think that workers are as incorporated as Lane and O'Dell would suggest, or at least it is less a factor in their consciousness than are issues of income, housing, and consumption. When it comes to important, life-deciding activities (such as changing one's job, forming a family, going on strike, joining in collective action) the worker's main orientation is towards these material factors, and not to the work collective or to the occupation itself.

I am in agreement with Teckenberg's emphasis on the importance of extrinsic factors, but I would not agree with his contention that the available research data show "a considerable degree of conflict in the firm" (Teckenberg, 1978: 210). This is not to deny that conflicts within the firm exist, nor to suggest that workers and management do not have conflicting interests. Indeed, Soviet research has shown that workers do express dissatisfaction with supervisors and management (Rusalinova, 1972). The very hierarchical form of organization and the degree of discretion allowed to supervisors in allocating jobs, creating job descriptions, and setting wage rates would be expected to produce a conflict of interest. It is necessary to take a larger view, however, in order to understand the general position and consciousness of the Soviet worker. One of the consequences of the Soviet system of central planning has been to significantly *diminish* conflict between workers and management, since both sides know that the rules of the game are not negotiable, and that the levels and range of wages and salaries have been determined by outside agencies. Add to this the benefits that accrue to workers from the current system (job security, an easy work pace, low levels of stress, protection from market forces), and one can see that most sources of conflict within the enterprise have been avoided (McAuley, 1969). In such a context extrinsic factors may be expected to be of greater importance than intrinsic factors, and this is apparently the case. In a sense, therefore, the current movement in the Soviet firm towards a human-relations approach to work is misguided, since it is more suitable for the future (when workplace relations and job content are expected to become more important as younger, better-educated workers become a majority in the industrial labor force), rather than for the current situation in which workers are highly instrumental in their approach to work.

There are already a few signs that Soviet sociologists are themselves beginning to face this issue. For example, in a recent survey of research on the sociology of work, Podmarkov (1978) has called for more attention to the general situation of the worker, and to the development of macro-social theories to relate the currently fragmented variables in a systematic way. This is a necessary admonition, but his call for the development of concrete suggestions by sociologists to solve problems of turnover, discipline, and productivity is less likely to be heeded, since to be effective they must go beyond tinkering with relations in the workplace. As we have attempted to show here, the "consciousness" of Soviet workers, insofar as this is indicated by our limited knowledge of their values and activities, is determined more by their general position in society than by their experiences at the workplace; indeed, I would go further and argue that the latter are greatly determined by the former. In this respect, a more detailed study of the extrinsic influences on the effects of workplace technology would be a contribution to the current debate in the West on the relative importance of (or interaction between) intrinsic and extrinsic factors (Shepard, 1977).

Trying to predict the future, even in the short term, is a hazardous undertaking, and in the case of the Soviet Union it is a notoriously unreliable venture. With this in mind, I would argue that the future of the Soviet worker is likely increasingly to resemble that of workers in Eastern Europe, who have become in recent years both direct and indirect interest groups. They are direct in the sense that they are willing to engage in collective action to defend their interests, and they have proven themselves effective in challenging official policies. The indirect interest-group mechanisms operate through the institutionalization of a proactive policy-making process, whereby policies come to be designed in such a way as to avoid unduly antagonizing the workers. In practice this means that the workers' interests are taken into consideration, at least minimally, by policy makers. I would argue that this has already occurred in the Soviet Union, and that it can be expected to become strengthened in the future. As we have seen, Soviet workers have also shown themselves willing to engage in collective action, although to date they have yet to form the mass movement that Polish workers have developed. To our knowledge, there has never been a concerted, nationwide protest in the USSR as there has in Poland. However, there are signs that the conditions for such a movement among Soviet workers are already developing. Just as the development of a hereditary intelligentsia has produced a dissent movement among this stratum, so also may the development of a hereditary stratum of industrial workers lead to a similar development. This would mean a shift from sporadic strikes and demonstrations aimed at specific issues, to more persistent and ongoing demands (backed by organized collective action) for institutional changes. This does not mean that workers would challenge Party rule, but rather that they would call for organizational changes at the level of the enterprise and for better linking mechanisms between workers and the Party, which would enable workers' interests, desires, and demands to more systematically shape policies. Such a process is already underway in Poland (de Weydenthal, 1979), and although the Gierek regime is resisting the demand for institutional change it is unlikely that he or his successor will be able to prevent it from occurring. While the Soviet Union is still some way from this level of worker demand, it is already presaged by the debate on worker participation that has been underway for the last decade. Although many leaders in both Poland and the USSR fear the political consequences of such a move, it will (ironically) probably enhance the legitimacy of the regime in the long term. Firstly, this would result from the increase in productivity that greater worker involvement would be expected to produce, which in turn would enable workers' demands for a higher standard of living to be met. Secondly, it would help to defuse some of the discontent that would result from the lessening of job security a more efficient economic system would produce, since conflict with the Party would be reduced if such changes were "negotiated" rather than imposed. It is unlikely that Soviet workers would resist change as strongly as Western workers have done (by featherbedding, strict job delineation, resistance to job-reducing technology, and similar actions), since the general labor shortage would prevent unemployment from becoming a serious problem. Moreover, since the state is the sole employer, displaced workers can be absorbed to a degree not possible in capitalist or mixed economies.

This brings us to the possibility that insofar as Soviet workers become a more active group, and insofar as they gain greater access to decision making within the enterprise, the Soviet system will become strengthened. Far from being the graveworms of the Revolution, which the dissenting intelligentsia could possibly become, a dissenting industrial working class would help the regime by strengthening the economy. Although workers may be in favor of a change in authority relations in the enterprise, in the national arena they are likely to remain economistic in their demands. Thus, despite the hopes of many of those on the left in the West, the Soviet worker may yet turn out to be the savior of the Party; and this would be the final irony.

NOTES

1. This refers not to just an increase in the number of deaths among younger people, but to an increase in their death *rate*. Moreover, this is affecting mainly young (under forty-five) males, whose death rate is about three times higher than that of young females. The reasons for this steady increase during the last fifteen years are uncertain, although it has been suggested by Murray Feshbach of the U.S. Bureau of the Census that it is due in part to the high rate of alcohol use in the USSR. It is also likely, however, that it is due to the

environmental and physiological disruptions that have accompanied industrialization. Whatever the causes, the reality of the increase and its economic consequences are beyond dispute.

2. There is a methodological problem with much of the research on turnover, since Soviet sociologists rely upon official categorization of the reason for job termination. Thus, the factory management may give as the official reason displacement due to less need for labor, the disappearance of the need for a particular skill, discipline problems, poor work, or the personal wish of the worker. If management can claim that termination is voluntary, then it is absolved of responsibility for finding the worker another job, or of having to negotiate with the trade union (or even the courts) for a legal dismissal. This makes it difficult to know how much turnover is by choice and how much by involuntary termination.

3. The terms *lateral* and *vertical* are used here to distinguish between conflicts between two or more groups regardless of their power or position in an organization, and conflicts between social groups and the central political authority. Thus, conflict between managers and workers would be in this sense lateral, whereas conflict between workers and the Party or the State would be vertical. This is not meant to deny that the enterprise is hierarchical, but rather to emphasize conflict relations at the societal level.

REFERENCES

Aitov, N. A.
    1972   *Teknicheskii progress i dvizhenie rabochikh kadrov.* Moscow.
Antosenkov, E. G.
    1969   *Opyt issledovaniia peremeny truda v promyshlennosti.* Novosibirsk.
Antosenkov, E. G., and Z. V. Kupriianova
    1977   *Tendentsii v tekuchesti rabochikh kadrov.* Novosibirsk.
Arutiunian, Iu. V.
    1971   *Sotsial'naia struktura sel'skogo naseleniia SSSR.* Moscow.
Bachurin, A.
    1978   "Zadachi uskoreniia rosta proizvoditel'nosti truda." *Voprosy ekonomiki* 8: 3–14.
Berliner, Joseph S.
    1957   *Factory and Manager in the USSR.* Cambridge, Mass.: Harvard University Press.
Blyakhman, L., and O. Shkaratan
    1977   *Man at Work.* Moscow.
Blyakhman, L. S., A. G. Zdravomyslov, and O. I. Shkaratan
    1965   "Problemy upravleniia dvizheniem rabochei sily." In A. G. Zdravomyslov and
           V. A. Iadov (eds.), *Trud i razvitie lichnosti.* Leningrad.
Boiter, A.
    1964   "When the kettle boils over." *Problems of Communism* XIII, January/February:
           33–42.
Brodersen, Arvid
    1966   *Labor and Government in Soviet Society.* New York: Random House.
Conquest, Robert
    1967   *Industrial Workers in the USSR.* New York: Praeger.
Dallin, David J., and Boris I. Nicolaevsky
    1947   *Forced Labor in Soviet Russia.* New Haven: Yale University Press.
Danilov, L.
    1977   "Sokrashchenie ruchnogo truda: vazhnyi faktor ratsional'nogo ispol'zovaniia tru-
           dovykh resursov." *Kommunist* 9: 39–50.
Dewar, Margaret
    1956   *Labour Policy in the USSR: 1917–1928.* London: Royal Institute of International
           Affairs.

Ermuratskii, V. N.
1973 *Sotsial'naia aktivnost' rabotnikov promyshlennogo predpriiatiia*. Kishinev.
Fairburn, William Armstrong
1931 *Forced Labor in Soviet Russia*. New York: Norton.
Freeman, Joseph
1932 *The Soviet Worker*. New York: Liveright.
Galenson, Walter
1955 *Labor Productivity in Soviet and American Industry*. New York: Columbia University Press.
Geliuta, A. M., and V. I. Staroverov
1977 *Sotsial'nyi oblik rabochego-intelligenta*. Moscow.
Gheliuta, A. M., and S. P. Gogoliukhin
1974 "The formation of a new type of worker." In M. N. Rutkevitch and W. Wesolowski, et al. (eds.), *Transformations of Social Structure in the USSR and Poland*. Moscow and Warsaw.
Gerchikov, V. I.
1979 "Otsenka urovnia sotsial'nogo razvitiia proizvodstvennogo kollektiva." *Sotsiologicheskie issledovaniia* 1: 175–185.
Gordon, Manya
1941 *Workers Before and After Lenin*. New York: Dutton.
Haynes, Victor, and Olga Semyonova (eds.)
1978 *Workers Against the Gulag*. London: Pinto Press.
Holubenko, M.
1975 "The Soviet working class." In *Critique: A Journal of Soviet Studies and Socialist Theory* Spring: 5–25.
Iadov, V. A., and A. A. Kissel'
1974 "Udovletvorennost' rabotoi: analiz empiricheskikh obobshchenii i popytka ikh teoreticheskogo istolkovaniia." *Sotsiologicheskie issledovaniia* 1: 78–87.
Iovechuk, M. T., and L. N. Kogan (eds.)
1972 *Dukhovny mir sovetskogo rabochego*. Moscow.
Kaplan, Frederick I.
1968 *Bolshevik Ideology and the Ethics of Soviet Labor, 1917–1920: The Formative Years*. New York: Philosophical Library.
n.d. "Kiev workers protest to the Central Committee." Pp. 71–77 in *Critique: A Journal of Soviet Studies and Socialist Theory*.
Kolbanovsky, V. V.
1974 "The impact of scientific and technological progress on the working class structure in the USSR." In M. N. Rutkevitch and W. Wesolowski, et al. (eds.), *Transformations of Social Structure in the USSR and Poland*. Moscow and Warsaw.
Kolodizh, B. N.
1978 "Prestizh predpriiatiia v obshchestvennom mnenii zhitelei goroda." *Sotsiologicheskie issledovaniia* 3: 110–117.
Konstantinova, N. P., O. V. Stakanova, and O. I. Shkaratan
1978 "Peremeny v sotsial'nom oblike rabochikh v epokhy razvitogo sotsialisma." *Voprosy istorii* 5: 3–18.
Kostakov, V. G. (ed.)
1976 *Trudoviye resursy: sotsial'no ekonomichesky analiz*. Moscow.
Kotliar and Talalai
1977 "Kak zakrepit' molodye kadry." *Ekonomika i organizatsia promyshlennogo proizvodstva* 4: 26–43.
Kuznetsov, E. M.
1974 *Politicheskaia agitatsiia*. Moscow.

Lane, David, and George Kolankiewicz (eds.)
1973   *Social Groups in Polish Society*. London: Macmillan.
Lane, David, and Felicity O'Dell
1978   *The Soviet Industrial Worker: Social Class, Education, and Control*. New York: St. Martin's Press.
Levin, A. I.
1973   *Sotsialisticheskii vnutrennii rynok*. Moscow.
Manevitch, E.
1978   "Vosproizvodstvo naseleniia i ispol'zovanie trudovykh resursov." *Voprosy ekonomiki* 8: 38–48.
Maslova, I.
1978   "Effektivnost' ispol'zovaniia trudovykh resursov." *Voprosy ekonomiki* 8: 49–59.
McAuley, Mary
1969   *Labour Disputes in Soviet Russia, 1957–1965*. Oxford, U.K.: Clarendon Press.
Mukhachev, W. I., and V. S. Borovik
1975   *Rabochi klass i upravlenie proizvodstvom*. Moscow *za 60 let*.
1977   *Narodnoe khoziaistvo SSSR za 60 let*. Moscow.
Oligin-Nesterov, W. I.
1973   *Ispol'zovanie ekonomicheskikh zakonov sotsializma i upravlenie proizvodstvom*. Moscow.
Patrushev, V. D., and V. A. Shabashev
1975   "Vliianie sotsial'no-ekonomicheskikh uslovii truda na sotrudnichestvo i vsaimopomoshch' v proizvodstvennom kollektive." *Sotsiologicheskie issledovaniia* 4: 83–91.
Podmarkov, V. G.
1978   "Sotsiologicheskie issledovaniia v promyshlennosti." *Sotsiologicheskie issledovaniia* 2: 33–39.
Podorov, G. M.
1976   "Opyt sotsiologicheskikh issledovanii trudovoi distsipliny na predriiatiiakh Gorkovskoi oblasti." *Sotsiologicheskie issledovaniia* 4: 72–78.
Popova, I. M.
1973   *Sotsiologicheskie problemy upravleniia sotsial'noi deiatel'nost'iu*. Moscow.
Rabitskii, A. I.
1978   "Sotsial'no-psikhologicheskie aspeckty zarabotnoi platy i potentsial'naia tekuchest'." *Sotsiologicheskie issledovaniia* 2: 71–77.
Rabochi klass razvitogo sotsialisticheskogo obshchestva
1974. Moscow.
Reznikov, P. P.
1978   "Distsiplina truda kak factor sotsial'nogo razvitiia proizvodstvennogo kollektiva." *Sotsiologicheskie issledovaniia* 2: 58–63.
Rusalinova, A. A.
1972   "Nekotorye voprosy formirovaniia vsaimootnoshenii v proisvodstvennykh gruppakh." *Chelovek i obshchestvo* 10: 94–101.
Rusanov, E. S.
1971   *Raspredelenie i ispol'zovanie trudovykh resursov v SSSR*. Moscow.
Rutkevitch, M. N.
1974   "Social structure of socialist society in the USSR and its development towards social homogeneity." In M. N. Rutkevitch and W. Wesolowski et al. (eds.), *Transformations of Social Structure in the USSR and Poland*. Moscow and Warsaw.

Sacks, Michael Paul
1976 *Women's Work in Soviet Russia: Continuity in the Midst of Change.* New York: Praeger.
Schwartz, Solomon M.
1951 *Labor in the Soviet Union.* New York: Praeger.
Shepard, Jon M.
1977 "Technology, alienation and job satisfaction." In *Annual Review of Sociology.* Palo Alto, Calif.: Annual Reviews.
Skarupo, Z.
1977 "Sokrashchenie tekuchesti i uluchshenie ispol'zovaniia rabochei sily." *Planovoye khozyaistvo* 6: 118–125.
Skilling, H. Gordon, and Franklyn Griffiths (eds.)
1971 *Interest Groups in Soviet Politics.* Princeton, N.J.: Princeton University Press.
Slesarev, G. A.
1974 "Socio-demographic groups within the Soviet working class." In M. N. Rutkevitch and W. Wesolowski, et al. (eds.), *Transformations of Social Structure in the USSR and Poland.* Moscow and Warsaw.
Statisticheskii ezhegodnik stran-chlenov soveta ekonomicheskoi vsaimopomoshchi.
1978 Moscow.
Teckenberg, Wolfgang
1978 "Labor turnover and job satisfaction: Indicators of industrial conflict in the USSR." *Soviet Studies* April: 193–211.
Tikhonov, A. V.
1976 "Vliianie proizvodstvennoi samostoiatel'nosti rabochego na otnoshenie k trudu." *Sotsiologicheskie issledovaniia* 1: 31–44.
Weydenthal, Jan B. de
1979 "The workers' dilemma of Polish politics: a case study." *East European Quarterly* Spring: 94–119.
Yanowitch, Murray
1977 *Social and Economic Inequality in the Soviet Union: Six Studies.* White Plains, N.Y.: M. E. Sharpe.
Zdravomyslov, A. G., V. P. Rozhin, and V. A. Iadov (eds.)
1970 *Man and His Work.* White Plains, N.Y.: International Arts and Sciences Press.

THE COLLEGE-EDUCATED
BLUE-COLLAR WORKERS

Richard Hamilton and James Wright

I. INTRODUCTION

Some recent works have noted the emergence of a rather unusual and unexpected phenomenon: a growing proportion of the blue-collar labor force reporting at least some college education (Hamilton, 1972: 212–214; Hamilton and Wright, 1975). Survey evidence for U.S. adults shows that the proportion of manual workers reporting one or more years of schooling beyond high school has risen from about 4% in 1952 to about 17% in 1974. In the industrialized societies of Western Europe, on the other hand, university-educated, blue-collar workers are virtually non-existent.[1] Despite the unique position of the United States in this regard, and despite the sharp trend just noted, little is known about the background, experiences, outlooks, or politics of the group. Accordingly, the purpose of this paper is to present descriptive evidence from recent U.S. surveys on the college-educated working class.

Research in the Sociology of Work, Volume 1, pages 285–335
Copyright © 1981 by JAI Press Inc.
All rights of reproduction in any form reserved.
ISBN: 0-89232-124-5

II. SOME INITIAL PERSPECTIVES

What expectations might be entertained at the outset about college-educated workers? Perhaps the most intuitively appealing hypothesis has been provided by Westley and Westley (1971):

> As we have indicated elsewhere, surveys have shown that the more educated the blue collar worker, the more likely he is to be dissatisfied with his work, and the more he will want to make some of the decisions connected with his job. . . . This worker has then become, or is becoming, alienated from society. . . . To sum up, we have suggested that the effect of affluence and increased education on the status system of modern industry is to erode the legitimacy of this system. This, in turn, means that the involvement of the modern, affluent, highly educated worker is weakened and is unsatisfactory to him. (1971: 118, 122)

This conclusion does seem a plausible one. Here are persons whose aspirations have been raised and who then, unexpectedly, have either "fallen" into the blue-collar ranks or else have not "risen" into the white-collar ranks as they may have hoped. One might well anticipate, as with the Westleys, that the reaction would be one of dissatisfaction or dismay. Many who have commented on the situation of "the young worker" predict more dramatic reactions—anger, resentment, and a striking out at the system that has frustrated them. Some have predicted rightist reactions, that is, an attraction to George Wallace (e.g., Krickus, 1971; Simon and Gagnon, 1970) while others anticipate a mobilization to the left (e.g., Garson, 1972; Aronowitz, 1973).

III. DATA AND PROCEDURES

The Westleys' conclusions are based on a small number of cases since very few workers with more than a high school education appeared in national samples a decade or more ago.[2] Most of the claims made by other commentators about young workers have been based on odd-lot or catch-as-catch-can sampling methods. Now, however, the number of college-educated workers appearing in national studies is sufficient to allow a detailed exploration of their attitudes and outlooks. That is the primary aim of the present paper. In the process we will examine the attitudes and outlooks of young workers generally, including also those of low and middling educational achievement. We will also undertake some exploration of the attitudes of downwardly mobile workers. Where it is useful, some comparison will be made with equivalent segments of the non-manual rank.

Data for this report are taken from the 1972, 1973, and 1974 General Social Surveys of the National Opinion Research Center. These surveys are based on probability samples of the noninstitutional, voting age population of the forty-eight contiguous states.[3] For this analysis, the three surveys have been merged, thus tripling the normal sample size to yield a total of 4,601 respondents. Our specific focus, however, is on a much smaller subset of cases. First, since most of the discussion of new developments in the working class has dealt primarily with male workers, females have been omitted from the analysis. Secondly, since the determinants of attitudes and outlooks in the black population are quite different from those affecting white workers, blacks have also been excluded. We have also excluded retired respondents and those who reported that they were students, members of the armed forces, or foremen. This leaves 1425 economically active white males to provide the basis for our analysis. A preliminary analysis of women's attitudes is to be found in Wright, 1978. A more detailed analysis of the attitudes of both women and blacks will appear in Hamilton and Wright, forthcoming. A replication of the present study based on the Survey Research Center's Quality of Employment survey (1972–1973) may be found in Hamilton and Wright (1979).

For the initial steps of the analysis, respondents were divided by occupation into manual (or blue-collar) and nonmanual (or white-collar) categories. Each of these categories was then further subdivided on the basis of educational attainment into those with less than a high school education, those who had completed high school, and those who had at least some college education beyond high school. In the latter case, we are dealing only with college or university education in the conventional sense, since the question specifically asked respondents not to include "schooling such as business college, technical or vocational school," etc. In the following discussion, it should be kept in mind that the "college-educated worker" category includes those with only one or two years of education beyond high school (by far the most common case) as well as a small number who had completed college and even a few who had completed some years of graduate education. Thus defined, the college-educated workers constitute one-twelfth of all economically active white males and about one-sixth of the manual workers in that category.

IV. RESULTS

A. Backgrounds

We will consider first some descriptive data on the backgrounds of college-educated workers (Table 1). The findings indicate the ways in which they are similar to and different from other segments of the working

Table 1. Background Characteristics
(Economically Active White Males)
NORC General Social Surveys 1972, 1973, 1974

Respondent's Occupation:	White Collar			Blue Collar		
Respondent's Education:	Less than high school	High school graduate	Some college	Less than high school	High school graduate	Some college
Background Characteristics						
Age:						
18–29	17.8%	26.0%	27.2%	19.3%	39.8%	51.7%
30–39	12.3	23.3	24.6	17.7	21.1	18.6
40–49	27.4	19.9	22.5	24.5	16.3	15.3
50–59	20.5	23.3	17.1	25.5	16.7	11.9
60 or more	21.9	7.5	8.5	13.0	6.1	2.5
N =	(73)	(146)	(426)	(322)	(246)	(118)
Father's Occupation:						
white collar	18.8	36.2	51.7	9.8	13.4	37.1
blue collar	57.8	46.9	37.9	61.7	67.7	51.4
farm	23.4	16.9	10.5	28.6	18.9	11.4
N =	(64)	(130)	(391)	(266)	(217)	(105)
When 16 years old family income was:						
above average	12.7	14.4	21.1	7.6	11.8	27.1
average	54.9	64.4	54.5	52.0	60.2	55.9
below average	32.4	21.2	24.4	40.4	27.9	17.0
N =	(71)	(146)	(426)	(317)	(244)	(118)

Marital status:					
single	9.6	10.2	12.9	8.7	19.5	27.1
married	82.2	83.0	82.4	83.2	72.4	66.1
divorced or separated	5.4	6.8	3.5	6.6	6.9	4.2
widowed	2.7	—	1.2	1.6	1.2	2.5
N =	(73)	(147)	(427)	(322)	(246)	(118)
Labor force status*						
full-time work	82.2	85.7	90.9	73.0	82.9	73.7
part-time work	11.0	2.0	3.7	7.1	5.3	15.3
unemployed	1.4	6.1	2.3	8.4	8.5	6.8
N =	(73)	(147)	(427)	(322)	(246)	(118)
Kind of job:						
nonmanual	100.0	100.0	100.0	35.1	47.6	46.6
craftsman				41.0	29.7	27.1
operatives				13.0	8.5	9.3
laborers						
service				10.9	14.2	16.9
N =	(73)	(147)	(427)	(322)	(246)	(118)

* Does not add to 100% because of some unemployeds, some laid-off, or not at work because of illness, vacation, or strikes.

class. The following discussion says nothing about the causes of their high level of educational achievement; the purpose, rather, is to provide an initial description of their origins and current situation to be used for later elaborations of the findings.

As might be expected given the trends, the college-educated workers are disproportionately young, just over half of them being under the age of thirty. Conversely, the oldest segment of blue-collar workers are those who did not complete a high school education. In one respect, then, the college-educated group *is* the "working class of the future." As the older and less educated workers retire, the proportion of college-educated manuals will necessarily rise. At the same time, however, percentaging the table in the other direction shows that the modal experience of young workers is "completed high school." Because of the close relationship between education and age, these two variables will, in a later discussion, be considered simultaneously.

Roughly three-eighths of the college-educated workers report that they came from white-collar families. An additional eighth originated in farm families, and the remaining half report working-class backgrounds. Those originating in white-collar families would, in the conventional terminology, be the "downwardly mobile" group, and for them, there must be a double frustration. Reared in a middle-class familial context and having taken the first steps towards assuring themselves of a similar situation as adults, they nonetheless find themselves located in what are presumably less desirable manual jobs. The group is thus an important part of the "proletarianized" middle class. Given the discussions of downward mobility one finds in the received literature, their outlooks must be characterized by intense frustration, hostility, and resentment.

For the half originating from working-class backgrounds, the frustrations would presumably have a somewhat different character. These would be the working-class children reared on the belief that college was the route into the middle class. Having taken some steps in that direction, they find their aspirations and mobility blocked; they are "forced" back into the less prestigious, more onerous, and less-well-paid blue-collar jobs. Thus, their frustrations may well be based on what one author calls the "false promises" offered by the society (Aronowitz, 1973). Despite their considerable efforts, the society has defaulted on its premise of a comfortable middle-class life.

Some mention might also be made of an "opposite" group on the white-collar side of the table, the white-collar workers with less than a high school education. As shown, the majority of them came originally from blue-collar families, and despite their lesser educational "achievements," they have nonetheless been "rewarded" with white-collar work. The reactions of both segments will be explored later in this article.[4]

A question was asked about the financial situation of the respondent's family when growing up. There was a predictable tendency for the college-educated (in both white-collar and blue-collar segments) to have come from "above average" backgrounds, a condition which no doubt facilitated their achieving this relatively high level of education. For the current college-educated blue-collar workers, those originating among affluent backgrounds should, again, sense a special frustration. Their downward mobility would be rather pronounced, not a modest "fall" from a lower-middle-class status.

At this point, some mention can be made of the amount of education received by those going beyond high school. Two measures are available: (1) the number of years of schooling beyond high school; and (2) any degrees or diplomas acquired. As indicated, the vast majority of college-educated blue-collar workers are college dropouts: 33.1% completed only one year beyond high school, and an additional 44.1% completed only two. Only about 15% of the group received four or more years of post-secondary education. In terms of certification, somewhat more than 80% report earning only a high school diploma; their "extra years," in short, produce nothing in the way of a credential that might be traded in the job market for more prestigious or rewarding work. Approximately 4% had completed a junior college degree, 11% a bachelor's degree, and 2% (three cases out of 118) a graduate degree.[5] For the most part, then, the college-educated workers appear to be people who had begun college but dropped out in the first or second year. A tiny proportion, on the other hand, are true "achievers" in the sense that they had achieved the entire "basic package."

The college-educated working class is disproportionately single; in fact, they are more than twice as likely never to have married than the college-educated middle class. It is not possible to say with certainty what this pattern represents. On the whole, working-class people tend to marry earlier than middle-class people; this is especially true of working-class girls. The working-class male who "digresses" from the usual life-cycle pattern for one or more years of college may thus find it necessary to postpone marriage past the time that is "normal" in the class. If, after that postponement, one then returned to a working-class community and milieu, one might encounter some difficulties in locating an available and acceptable mate.[6]

Finally, we can briefly mention the labor-force activities and current employment of the college-educated workers. Reflecting their disproportionate youth, note first that they are more likely than any other segment to be employed in part-time work. Beyond this, their distribution among skill categories is, for all practical purposes, identical to that of the high-school educated blue-collar workers. One might anticipate that the individuals who were downwardly mobile or those who had "left" their class to acquire an academic education would not have learned the skills necessary for "success" within the working class. Given the training normally offered in the first couple of college years, one would anticipate that they would be employed as operatives or possibly as laborers when either "arriving" or "returning" to the working class. But, surprisingly, nearly half of them (46.6%) were employed as craftsmen, the percentage in this case being larger than in either of the other working-class categories. They had the smallest representation of the three segments in the operatives category. There was a very slight overrepresentation in service occupations.[7]

B. Income and Satisfaction

The college-educated workers report somewhat higher earnings than other blue-collar workers (Table 2). Approximately three in eight reported earnings of $15,000 or more as compared to only one in eight among the less-than-high school group. The differences vis-a-vis the high school graduates are not very great. There is a bimodal tendency in the income distribution of the college-educated, the low-income mode probably reflecting the larger proportion of part-time workers. The college-educated workers, on the whole, make less than the equivalent middle-class group. But then too, the much-discussed "blurring of class lines" is also indicated inasmuch as a large protion of these blue-collar workers earn more than many persons in middle-class occupations.[8]

There is very little distinctiveness to be reported with respect to the college-educated workers' perceptions of the trends over the last few years. Two-fifths reported that things were getting better. An equal-sized group said things had stayed the same. And one-fifth said things were getting worse. But approximately the same distribution was found in other working-class segments with only the high school group, by a smallish margin, giving somewhat more optimistic reports.

When asked to assess their incomes relative to other families, the responses of the working-class segments generally reflected the average levels of income indicated above, that is to say, there was a modest tendency for the college-educated to report their incomes as above average.

In summary then, one may note that the college-educated working class has been somewhat better rewarded than other workers. There is also some subjective recognition of that difference. At the same time, however, it must be noted that half of these workers see their incomes as only average, and one-fifth see them as below average. Only about three in ten feel they are above average. Put somewhat differently, this means that this category of relatively well-educated persons contains a solid majority who view their financial rewards as average or less than average. For this reason too, one might anticipate considerable dissatisfaction.

Given those expectations, the actual result will come as something of a surprise since there is essentially no variation in the pattern of financial satisfaction between the three working-class segments. A quarter of the college-educated workers report that they are pretty well satisfied, half say they are more-or-less satisfied, and a quarter say they are dissatisfied. They are slightly less likely than the high-school educated to report that they are pretty well satisfied. That difference in support of the resentment thesis, however, depends on the responses of four individuals.

How do the college-educated workers feel about their work? Does one find widespread dissatisfaction? Again, the result is an unexpected one (at least from the perspective of the received theorizing) in that they are again only marginally different from the other workers. All three working-class categories show majorities satisfied with their work, the basic pattern being two-fifths very satisfied and another two-fifths moderately satisfied. The image of raging hatreds and seething hostilities does not appear in this evidence. The equation of education plus blue-collar work equalling intense dissatisfaction is borne out in only 6.1% of the relevant cases. And that percentage is no different from the equivalent figures for the other categories of workers. The best evidence of dissatisfaction in this group involves those who were "a little" dissatisfied, the difference here amounting to roughly five percentage points.

Much the same pattern comes through in the responses to a question on personal happiness. In this case, one-quarter of the respondents said they were very happy, over half said they were pretty happy, while just under a fifth report they were "not too happy." Compared to the high school group, one does find a slightly smaller percentage in the "very happy" category and some increase in unhappiness. This latter difference (three percentage points) is not what one would call compelling evidence in support of the resentment thesis.

The middle-class categories, it will be noted, were generally more satisfied with their financial situation and their work and they were somewhat more likely to report being "very happy." These class differences, on the other hand, are not of enormous magnitude. The college-educated middle class, who as noted make much more money than their working-class "peers," show only a ten percentage point difference in satisfaction with income. In terms of overall happiness, they are even less distinguished. They are not the happiest category, and, moreover, their distinctiveness vis-a-vis the college-educated workers is a small one, amounting to approximately ten percentage points.

One group of special interest for our purposes is the less-than-high-school white-collar category. If the college-educated workers, by the

Table 2. Income and Various Measures of Satisfaction
(Economically Active White Males)
NORC General Social Surveys 1972, 1973, 1974

	White Collar			Blue Collar		
	Less than high school	High school graduate	Some college	Less than high school	High school graduate	Some college
Total family income:						
"In which of these groups did your total family income, from all sources, fall last year—(1971-2-3)—before taxes, that is?"						
$20,000 or more	15.7%	15.0%	34.1%	4.5%	8.7%	19.8%
15–19,999	11.4	20.0	2.3	8.1	20.7	17.1
10–14,999	32.9	44.3	24.5	31.5	36.2	21.6
8–9,999	20.0	7.9	8.8	19.8	14.7	12.6
6–7,999	5.7	5.0	5.1	11.4	7.3	12.6
less than 6,000	14.3	7.9	5.2	24.7	12.5	16.2
N =	(70)	(140)	(408)	(308)	(232)	(111)
Trend in financial situation:						
"During the last few years, has your financial situation been getting better, getting worse or has it stayed the same?"						
getting better	45.2	58.2	60.0	33.4	49.2	38.3
stayed same	37.0	27.4	27.1	43.3	37.7	40.0
getting worse	17.8	14.4	12.9	23.2	13.1	21.7
N =	(73)	(146)	(420)	(314)	(244)	(115)
Relative financial standing:						
"Compared with American families in general, would you say your family income is—far below average, below average, average, above average, or far above average?" (Categories collapsed)						
above average	29.2	22.6	49.9	7.8	15.9	28.8
average	47.2	65.1	41.8	60.9	66.1	50.8
below average	23.6	12.3	8.0	31.3	17.9	20.3
N =	(72)					

present financial situation, more or less satisfied, or not at all satisfied."

pretty well satisfied:	37.0	27.2	34.8	27.1	29.3	25.4
more-or-less satisfied:	42.5	52.4	49.2	44.5	45.5	48.3
not satisfied at all:	20.5	20.4	16.0	28.3	25.2	26.3
N =	(73)	(147)	(425)	(321)	(246)	(118)

Satisfaction with work:

"On the whole, how satisfied are you with the work you do—would you say you are very satisfied, moderately satisfied, a little dissatisfied, or very dissatisfied?"

very satisfied	52.9	48.2	61.0	42.9	42.4	37.7
moderately satisfied	33.8	41.1	28.8	41.2	39.0	40.4
a little dissatisfied	7.4	8.5	6.7	10.3	10.6	15.8
very dissatisfied	5.9	2.1	3.6	5.6	8.1	6.1
N =	(68)	(141)	(420)	(301)	(236)	(114)

Happiness:

"Taken all together, how would you say things are these days—would you say that you are very happy, pretty happy or not too happy?"

very happy	34.2	39.5	33.2	30.1	38.5	25.4
pretty happy	49.3	50.3	57.9	52.8	56.1	55.9
not too happy	16.4	10.2	8.9	17.1	15.4	18.6
N =	(73)	(147)	(425)	(322)	(246)	(118)

Marital happiness:

"Taking things all together, how would you describe your marriage? Would you say that your marriage is very happy, pretty happy, or not too happy?"

very happy	61.1	79.1	68.9	65.8	71.3	66.7
pretty happy	33.3	17.9	30.1	31.6	26.9	25.9
not too happy	5.6	3.0	1.9	2.5	1.9	7.4
N =	(36)	(67)	(219)	(158)	(108)	(54)

Character of life:*

"In general, do you find life exciting, pretty routine, or dull?"

exciting	55.6	40.2	63.2	38.7	48.4	53.8
routine	40.0	58.5	34.6	56.0	48.4	44.9
dull	4.4	1.2	2.2	5.2	3.1	1.3
N =	(45)	(82)	(269)	(191)	(161)	(78)

* Used only the NORC 1973 and 1974 studies.

295

conventional standard, are those who have been unjustly denied social mobility, then this category consists of those who have been unjustly rewarded with that mobility. Although they are the most poorly rewarded segment of the middle class, coming in somewhat below the college-educated workers in terms of family income, their levels of financial satisfaction and of satisfaction with work are well ahead of those of the college-educated workers. And also in their overall estimate of happiness they come in ahead of the college-educated workers although the differences are not very large.

There are two other measures of possible relevance here. The 1973 and 1974 NORC studies asked questions about marital happiness and about the general "tone" of life. The variations in marital happiness between the three working-class categories are again very small. The dominant response, chosen by two-thirds of the college-educated workers, was "very happy."

Many accounts have portrayed blue-collar work as routine, dull, and repetitive. Unfortunately the NORC question focused on the respondent's *life* as opposed to the narrower job focus. For what it may be worth, a minority, 44.9%, of the college-educated workers found life "routine" and only one respondent (of seventy-eight) found his life dull. The rest, by a slim majority, chose the word "exciting" to describe their lives. Within the working class, the choice of this option varied *directly* with the level of education.

The basic conclusion to be drawn from this evidence then is one of essentially no difference between the college-educated workers and their less-educated peers in the satisfaction expressed with (1) their financial situation; (2) their work; (3) their marital happiness; and (4) their overall happiness. The expectation of "alienation," of dissatisfaction, of anger or resentment is supported by only the most miniscule of percentage differences, none of which was statistically significant.

C. Attitudes Towards Work—A Diversion

A frequently discussed subject, one accompanied by both praise and lament, is the subject of work motivation: the "old" work ethic, so one hears, is dead. The NORC General Social Surveys again provide us with some relevant evidence.

When asked what it takes "to get ahead," whether it is a matter of work, or of luck (plus help from others) or both combined, majorities of both classes and at all educational levels put the emphasis on "hard work" (Table 3). One cannot, of course, say anything about a trend on the basis of a single cross-sectional study, but there should be little doubt about the general sense that "hard work" is *the* necessary means for "getting ahead."

Table 3. Attitudes Towards Work
(Economically Active White Males)
NORC General Social Surveys 1973, 1974

	White Collar			Blue Collar		
	Less than high school	High School graduate	Some college	Less than high school	High School graduate	Some college
Most important to get ahead: "Some people say that people get ahead by their own hard work; others say that lucky breaks or help from other people are more important. Which do you think is more important?"						
hard work	62.5%	55.4%	64.8%	63.7%	62.9%	60.5%
work and luck	22.5	27.7	26.7	25.3	30.2	27.6
luck	15.0	16.9	8.5	11.1	6.9	11.8
N =	(40)	(83)	(270)	(190)	(159)	(76)
Would work if rich? "If you were to get enough money to live as comfortably as you would like for the rest of your life, would you continue to work or would you stop working?"						
continue work	68.3	71.2	80.2	65.7	67.5	74.7
N =	(41)	(80)	(273)	(181)	(157)	(75)
Characteristic most preferred in work: "Would you please look at this card and tell me which one thing on this list you would most prefer in a job?"*						
high income	15.6	16.9	11.4	22.6	15.1	12.8
security	8.9	7.2	1.5	14.7	10.7	6.4
free time	6.7	1.2	5.5	10.5	5.0	7.7
chance of advancement	33.3	18.1	15.0	19.5	22.6	15.4
feeling of accomplishment	35.6	55.4	66.7	32.6	46.5	57.7
N =	(45)	(83)	(273)	(190)	(159)	(78)

* Actual wordings: High income; No danger of being fired; Working hours are short; Lots of free time; Chances for advancement; Work important and gives feeling of accomplishment.

But the question is ambiguous. People may recognize work as a means to an end without themselves subscribing to that end. The study does not ask directly about striving for success; it does ask, however, whether the respondents would continue working if they had enough money to live comfortably for the rest of their lives. Majorities in all segments said they would continue working. Some might suspect that "education" undermines work motivation; but as it turns out, education and the work-preference are positively correlated in both classes. The relationship with age will be considered in a later discussion.

Another question allows exploration of a different dimension of the work motivation question; it asks what respondents wish to receive from their work, whether a high income, job security, free time, a chance for advancement or a feeling of accomplishment. This question yields a result that is very clearly consonant with some of the claims made about the post-industrial society; the percentage putting a "feeling of accomplishment" first varies directly with education, this being the case in both the middle and the working classes. A clear majority of the college-educated workers reported that they wanted this "feeling of accomplishment." It was the less-educated workers who placed the emphasis on "traditional" concerns, that is, on income, security, and a chance for advancement.

The college-educated workers, it has been noted, "ought" to feel dissatisfied—but do not. We now find that they seek a feeling of accomplishment in work and yet are located in less-prestigeful and presumably less-attractive blue-collar jobs.[9] This too should be a source of dissatisfaction—at least that is what one would surmise, given the claims that blue-collar work is dull, routine, and onerous. It was possible, of course, to sort out that subset, the college-educated workers who sought "accomplishment" in their work and to enquire of their job satisfactions. Where 37.7% of the entire category reported they were "very satisfied" with their work, among those wishing a feeling of accomplishment the figure was 50.0%. Another 29.5% said they were moderately satisfied.[10] Thus, the analysis that argues that the college-educated will seek different things from their work is accurate. But it is mistaken in the belief that those things will not be found in blue-collar work. The argument, in other words, would seem accurate in its prediction of a "new" or "emergent" development but errs in its prediction of the consequences.

D. Class Identification, Politics, and Related Attitudes

What does the evidence indicate with respect to the class identifications of college-educated workers? Do they identify with the middle class? Have they perhaps "picked up" that identification in the course of their education? Or do they reject that possibility? Do they instead link up with "the workers," serving perhaps as a new vanguard? The evidence shows that a majority of them identify as working (or lower) class (Table 4). At the same time, however, it should be noted that middle- (and upper-) class identifications do increase with education. It would be a mistake to read too much into such "identifications." Previous research in the area suggests that for many it is a rather peripheral concern. This "identity" does not serve as an "anchoring point" or as a basic beginning point for their lives or their political actions. For some the middle-class identification reflects their middle-class origins. For others it appears to reflect little more than a sense of relative affluence.

A brief glance at the other "side" of the table also tells a useful lesson. Almost half of the respondents in the less-well-educated middle-class segments identify themselves as working (or lower) class. Findings similar to this have appeared in all comparable studies from 1949 to the present. This finding is of more than average interest only because of persistent refusal on the part of social critics, commentators, and social scientists to recognize the fact. As a consequence they are in no position to think through the possible implications.[11]

How do the college-educated workers respond politically? Do they turn to the right or to the left? Other than a tendency for them to be political independents (with a strong lean toward the Democrats), they show little distinctiveness. One might take that as a sign of "new things" except that this is a younger group and the young generally are more likely to be independent (Campbell, et al., 1960: 162; and Schreiber, 1971).

College-educated workers were more likely to have voted in the 1972 election, a finding that will occasion little surprise. The 1972 election did provide the setting to test the assumption of a liberal-left tendency on the part of these workers. As in the 1964 election, 1972 voters were offered "a choice, not an echo." If this group were liberal-to-left on the issues and favored a general countercultural direction, they clearly had the McGovern option. All three working-class segments, however, voted against McGovern and instead gave clear majorities to Richard Nixon. Looking at the admittedly small percentage differences, one will note that the support for McGovern actually declined among the better-educated segments. The same pattern is also to be seen among the nonvoters (considering their expressed preferences); there too, majorities in all segments rejected McGovern and the level of rejection increases with education. Although the percentage differences and the case bases are small, it should be kept in mind that, following the lines of the "alienation" argument, this group should have been well ahead of the other workers in their support for McGovern.

Approximately three in ten of the college-educated workers were Republican identifiers to begin with or were independents leaning toward the

Table 4. Class Identification, Politics, and Related Attitudes
(Economically Active White Males)
NORC General Social Surveys 1972, 1973, 1974

	White Collar			Blue Collar		
	Less than high school	High school graduate	Some college	Less than high school	High school graduate	Some college
Class identification:						
middle, upper	50.6%	54.5%	80.0%	24.4%	30.5%	42.7%
working, lower	49.3	45.6	19.9	75.7	69.6	57.2
N =	(73)	(147)	(426)	(320)	(246)	(117)
Party identification:						
strong Democrat	16.9	10.6	8.2	23.6	12.8	12.8
weak Democrat	29.6	24.6	18.3	29.3	30.8	24.8
independent Democrat	11.3	13.4	16.6	8.1	17.9	19.3
independent	8.5	16.2	9.4	12.1	15.4	13.8
independent Republican	16.9	12.7	16.3	6.7	8.1	10.1
weak Republican	5.6	17.6	22.1	14.1	12.4	11.0
strong Republican	11.3	4.9	9.1	6.1	2.6	8.3
N =	(71)	(142)	(416)	(297)	(234)	(109)
Voted in 1972*						
percent yes	64.3	71.1	87.8	55.7	64.6	71.4
N =	(42)	(83)	(271)	(185)	(158)	(77)
Percent of voters for McGovern*	30.8	24.1	34.2	44.1	41.5	40.4
N =	(26)	(54)	(219)	(93)	(94)	(52)
Percent of nonvoters favoring McGovern*	41.7	17.6	32.1	46.8	32.7	30.8
N =	(12)	(17)	(28)	(62)	(49)	(13)
Abortion—						
if wants no more children? "Please tell me whether or not you think it should be possible for a pregnant woman to obtain a *legal* abortion if she is married and does not want any more children?"						
Approve:	54.9	49.0	64.4	36.9	43.7	58.3

300

Free speech for atheist: "If . . . a person wanted to make a speech in your city . . . against churches and religion, should he be allowed to speak, or not?"

	59.7	78.2	90.4	52.5	71.5	76.9
N =	(72)	(147)	(427)	(322)	(246)	(117)

Free speech for communist: "Suppose (an) admitted communist wanted to make a speech in your community. Should he be allowed to speak, or not?"

	57.7	68.7	82.0	43.4	55.9	73.3
N =	(71)	(147)	(422)	(316)	(245)	(116)

Opposes laws against racial intermarriage: "Do you think there should be laws against marriages between Negroes and whites?"

	66.2	74.8	85.1	49.8	62.0	75.0
N =	(68)	(143)	(423)	(311)	(242)	(112)

Would not object: "How strongly would you object if a member of your family wanted to bring a Negro friend home to dinner? Would you object strongly, mildly, or not at all?"

	66.2	72.1	84.0	59.9	64.4	71.3
N =	(71)	(140)	(425)	(317)	(239)	(115)

Courts too harsh: "In general, do you think the courts in this area deal too harshly or not harshly enough with criminals?"

	3.3	6.0	4.9	3.0	3.8	8.8
N =	(60)	(116)	(305)	(265)	(186)	(91)

Oppose capital punishment: "Do you favor or oppose the death penalty for persons convicted of murder?"

	29.9	26.4	29.9	26.9	24.7	28.7
N =	(67)	(144)	(412)	(308)	(239)	(115)

Communism as form of government:* "Thinking about all the different kinds of government in the world today, which of these statements comes closest to how you feel about communism as a form of government?"

worst kind	57.1	44.0	23.4	51.1	46.3	39.5
no worse than some	31.0	35.7	37.4	30.5	35.2	25.0
all right for some	9.5	19.0	33.3	15.3	13.6	31.6
good form of government	2.4	1.2	5.9	3.2	4.9	3.9
N =	(42)	(84)	(273)	(190)	(162)	(76)

(continued)

Table 4. (Continued)

	White Collar			Blue Collar		
	Less than high school	High school graduate	Some college	Less than high school	High school graduate	Some college

Confidence in people running:*

"I am going to name some institutions in this country. As far as the *people running* these institutions are concerned, would you say you have a great deal of confidence, only some confidence, or hardly any confidence at all in them?"

	Less than high school	High school graduate	Some college	Less than high school	High school graduate	Some college
Major companies						
great deal	40.9	43.4	41.9	35.4	32.7	28.2
only some	45.5	51.8	46.3	48.7	55.3	56.4
hardly any	13.6	4.8	11.9	15.9	11.9	15.4
Organized labor						
great deal	27.3	11.9	9.2	23.0	28.4	15.4
only some	50.0	52.4	57.0	56.1	51.2	59.0
hardly any	22.7	35.7	33.8	20.9	20.4	25.6
Organized religion						
great deal	34.9	47.0	30.9	42.7	37.1	39.7
only some	39.5	44.6	54.6	41.1	49.1	46.2
hardly any	25.6	8.4	14.5	16.1	13.8	14.1
Military						
great deal	54.8	40.5	21.4	55.0	42.1	30.8
only some	33.3	46.4	55.4	36.6	40.9	50.0
hardly any	11.9	13.1	23.2	8.4	17.0	19.2
Ns +	(42–44)	(83–84)	(270–276)	(187–192)	(159–162)	(78)

* Only in 1974 and 1975 studies.

302

Republicans. It would appear that they were joined by a large part of the Democratic identifiers and by many independents. This statement merely notes the fact; it does not provide an explanation. It might be that the "breakaway" was due to the position of the unions, or to the widespread opposition to McGovern expressed in the nation's newspapers. Or it might be that the analyses of the working-class situation offered by the commentators and the critics are mistaken. Some of the offerings in the McGovern "package" may have repelled rather than attracted; some themes may have been taken as an insult.

Lest one assume that the college-educated workers are "primitive" hard-hat conservatives (on the model of the cultural critic's stereotype), it is useful to explore some related attitudes. The college-educated workers, more so than the other workers, are likely to take the "educated position" on abortion, they are more likely to favor free speech for an atheist and for an admitted communist (two questions originally used by Stouffer in 1955); they are more likely to oppose laws against racial intermarriage and they are less likely to object to a Negro dinner guest.

The "standard package" liberal (or leftist for that matter) would agree with all the positions offered in the above paragraph. They would also be likely to feel the courts were too harsh in their sentences and they would oppose capital punishment. But in these respects, the college-educated workers, along with substantial majorities in all segments of the white population, take separate paths; the latter feel the courts are too lenient and they favor capital punishment. Only small differences are to be noted by education with respect to the former issue; no clear pattern exists with respect to the latter.

Two of the General Social Surveys contained questions on communism as a form of government. This might provide some indication of the workers who are "fed up with the whole ethos of the industrial system."[12] One does, in fact, find a tendency for the educated workers to say that communism "is all right for some," that coming together with a decline in the percentage considering it the "worst kind" of government. But there is a question to be raised as to whether that is a reaction to their work (linked to the resentment, the frustration, etc.) or whether that stems instead from the education. The presence of an identical pattern in the middle class strongly supports the latter view; it appears to be education that gives rise to this expression of "tolerance."

Another way of approaching the question of disaffection involves the confidence respondents express in the people running various "established" institutions. When asked about the persons running "major companies," workers do indicate less confidence than is expressed in the middle class. Among the workers there is a decline in the level of confidence associated with education, but this amounts to an overall seven percentage point difference and all of that is between those having a "great deal" and those having "only some" confidence. The third option, "hardly any," was chosen by 15.4% of the college-educated respondents.

The college-educated workers indicate less approval for the leaders of unions than for the leaders of major businesses. One-quarter say they have "hardly any" confidence in the labor leaders and only 15.4% have a great deal of confidence. This response, however, is difficult to interpret since it could have either a rightist or a leftist thrust to it.

Somewhat less ambiguous is a question about confidence in religious leaders. Two out of five of the college-educated workers express a great deal of confidence in this leadership group, a level of approval which is ahead of both business and labor leaders. There is an element of ambiguity here, too, in that the leaders referred to could be "swinging priests" on the one hand or very traditional fundamentalist ministers on the other. In passing, it should be noted that some of the *dis*satisfaction with religious leaders does not express a withdrawal from or a rejection of traditional institutions. Some of that dissatisfaction was expressed by regular church-goers.

There was a decline in confidence in military leaders associated with education, most of this involving the expression of limited confidence as opposed to outright rejection. Again, it would be a mistake without further investigation to assign this to leftist dissatisfactions. Some evidence from the previous decade showed education to be positively correlated with support for "tough" military options (Hamilton and Wright, 1975b). And again, it would be a mistake to attribute the result to determinants within the working class, since the same pattern appears within the middle class.

How do these results add up? One point is immediately clear; the claims of alienation, of dissatisfaction, of resentment, and of rejection of the "system" do not gain serious support in any context. In some respects, the college-educated workers respond as do other blue-collar workers. And in other respects, they respond as relatively well-educated persons, in much the same way, that is, as the college-educated persons in the middle class. In no context do they appear as a radical "vanguard."

The presentation thus far has focused on the "marginal" distribution, that is, on the overall distribution of attitudes of the college-educated segment. It is useful at this point to carry the analysis at least two steps further, to explore the pattern by age (since much of the popular analysis has focused on the young workers), and also by class background.

E. The Young Workers

Sociologists William Simon and John H. Gagnon (1970) open their discussion with the statement that: "To a degree possibly never experienced before, ours is a society whose image of youth is one of discontent and alienation." The situation of working-class youth they feel to be even worse, since that image is of middle-class youth. Working-class youth must face their problems without the guidance provided by such a "model." As a consequence:

> His [the working-class youth's] participation is rather episodic and largely nonorganizational, passionate rather than programatic. In content, his stance tends to be defensive and protective rather than offensive and expanding. And in his present mood he feels increasingly cornered and slightly paranoid. . . .
>   Behind it all, however, and with very little language with which to describe it, he is a classic instance of alienated man. He feels powerless and often feels himself to be the object of manipulation, someone who is exploited and poorly served by the central institutions of his society (Simon and Gagnon, 1970).

An account of the much-discussed strike of the General Motors' Lordstown, Ohio, plant in March 1972 opens with the statement that:

> . . . More and more young workers now seem to be fed up with the whole ethos of the industrial system. Freer in spirit than their fathers, they often scorn the old work ethic and refuse to be treated like automatons. . . . Their anguish and boredom are likely to worsen in the next few years. . . (Garson, 1972).

Similar conclusions are drawn by the political scientist Ronald Inglehart (1971) (deriving them from the theories of psychologist Abraham H. Maslow, 1954). The goals of the young, he indicates, "no longer have a direct relationship to the imperatives of economic security, . . ." and as a consequence, he suggests that "intergenerational political conflict is likely." In this case, it should be noted, he is focusing on middle-class youth, for whom "economic security may be taken for granted." Another author, drawing on Simon and Gagnon and on his own conversations with young workers, applies the claim more generally—"Today job dissatisfaction is prevalent among workers who have been reared in an era of prosperity and are but dimly aware of the depression." As a consequence, he sees "A growing number of young workers [who] seem to be becoming politically restive." (Krickus, 1971: 505)

The task here is to see whether the available evidence supports such claims. There are two principal comparisons we wish to make. First, following the main concern of this article, we will examine the situation and responses of the young educated workers, contrasting them initially with the young but less-educated segments. The second comparison will be between the young and the older workers, the focus, once again, being on the educated segments within those age categories, those who, presumably at least, provide us with a glimpse of the future. For the purpose of this discussion, the young workers are those of ages eighteen to twenty-nine and the older workers are those thirty or over. Once again, it should be kept in mind that we are dealing with white economically active males.

In most respects, the young educated workers showed the same background traits discussed above. They are more likely than the other young segments to have had fathers in middle-class occupations and to have come from families with above average incomes. Approximately half of them were single, a figure well above that of the other working-class segments, and one-fifth of them were employed only part time. Their current family incomes were somewhat higher than those of the other younger segments, but the differences were not great, and, one must remember, the needs are different given the differences in marital status. Although the differences in income were not large, the college-educated were more likely, by a fair-sized margin, to report above-average incomes, a fact that might reflect these different needs. More of them identified with the middle class than was the case with the other two segments. At the same time, however, it should be noted that a majority identified themselves as working class. Their higher level of middle-class identification, once again, might reflect their origins and/or to a lesser extent their current financial status.

Another point deserving of at least a passing mention is that the young better-educated segment has a higher proportion of Catholics than the other categories. This might be a function of the place of origin; those in cities, such as is generally the case with the Catholics, have a better chance to gain a higher education than the Protestants, who, disproportionately, are located in small towns and in the countryside.

Turning to the satisfaction-dissatisfaction questions, one finds a tendency for the better-educated young workers to express a middling satisfaction, that is, taking the more-or-less satisfied position (Table 5). They have the smallest percentage of the three categories expressing outright dissatisfaction. This finding, on the whole, is not too surprising. They are, on the whole, somewhat better paid than other workers and they do show some recognition of that fact. And then too, as the saying goes, "It's not the money, it's the job." (This is the subtitle to the Garson article, 1972.) For that reason, therefore, it is necessary to look at job satisfaction. But here one finds "not a nickel's worth" of difference between the three segments. Far from discovering a solid block of dissatisfaction among the young educateds, one finds a solid block of satisfaction with one-third being very satisfied and another two-fifths expressing moderate satisfaction. That leaves approximately one-quarter dissatisfied, most of them being only a little dissatisfied. Moreover, approximately the same level of dissatisfaction is found in each of the three younger segments. Were one to pay attention to small differences, one finds that the extreme case, very dissatisfied, runs inversely with educational achievement rather than

Table 5. Satisfactions by Age and Education: Blue-Collar Only (Economically Active White Males) NORC General Social Surveys 1972, 1973, 1974

Age:	18 to 29 years			30 years or over		
Education:	Less than high school	High school graduate	Some college	Less than high school	High school graduate	Some college
Financial situation:*						
pretty well satisfied	22.6%	28.6%	24.6%	28.2%	29.7%	26.3%
more-or-less satisfied	38.7	38.8	55.7	45.9	50.0	40.0
not satisfied at all	38.7	32.7	19.7	25.9	20.3	33.3
N =	(62)	(98)	(61)	(259)	(148)	(57)
Job satisfaction:						
very satisfied	38.3	33.0	32.2	44.0	48.6	43.6
moderately satisfied	38.3	38.3	42.4	41.9	39.4	38.2
a little dissatisfied	13.3	19.1	18.6	9.5	4.9	12.7
very dissatisfied	10.0	9.6	6.8	4.6	7.0	5.5
N =	(60)	(94)	(59)	(241)	(142)	(55)
Happiness:						
very happy	29.0	21.4	19.7	30.4	33.1	31.6
pretty happy	54.8	60.2	62.3	52.3	53.4	49.1
not too happy	16.1	18.4	18.0	17.3	13.5	19.3
N =	(62)	(98)	(61)	(260)	(148)	(57)

* See Table 2 for question wordings.

positively. One is, to be sure, speaking here of trivial differences. The result is of importance only in that it stands *in opposition to* the assumptions of Maslow, Inglehart, et al.

Another measure, this one asking about general happiness, does indicate some malaise among the young educated workers. But this has more of the character of a dark cloud than of a general storm warning. Specifically, the educated workers are more likely than others to say they are "pretty happy" as opposed to "very happy," the latter choice being more frequent among the poorly educated. There is, again, "not a nickel's worth" of difference in the proportions saying they are "not too happy." The responses to the previous question about job satisfaction suggest that this feeling of malaise is not to be attributed to job-related concerns.

A second direction of comparison is between the young and the older workers. Some greater dissatisfaction with their financial situation is expressed by the older educated workers. One-third expressed outright dissatisfaction as opposed to only one-fifth among the equivalent younger group. It should be noted that the difference here depends on a small number of cases. All of that difference between the older and younger college-educated segments depends on eight respondents. This result is of some significance, nevertheless, since most commentators anticipate a difference in the opposite direction. Hence, the finding is a bit more "weighty" than would at first appear.

It is of some interest in this connection to note how the popular theorizing has everything turned around. Those commentators focus on the young educateds as the dissatisfied group, when, in fact, it is the young poorly educated who are most dissatisfied with their earnings. The commentators argue a gradual "adjustment" to their situation on the part of the older workers. That claim is consonant with the evidence for the older less-educated workers (and there is some good reason for that, as we shall see); it is not adequate, however, as a description of the older educated segment.

The above describes the financial satisfaction of workers but, as is frequently noted, that presumably is not at the center of worker concerns. Turning, therefore, to the "heart of the matter," to job satisfaction, we find higher levels of job satisfaction in all older working-class segments. Again, however, as with the young, the differences by education prove to be very small. The highest level of dissatisfaction in the older category is found among the older educated workers, but here one is dealing with 18.2% of the total, most of them expressing only "a little" dissatisfaction. Education, in short, does not account for much variance at either age level. It is, contrary to all the bold assertions, an extremely weak predictor of working-class satisfaction or dissatisfaction. (See also Sheppard and Herrick; 1972: 116, for a similar result.)

Table 6. Attitudes Toward Job by Age and Education: Blue-Collar Only
(Economically Active White Males)
NORC General Social Surveys 1972, 1973, 1974

Age:	18–29 years			30 or over		
Education:	Less than high school	High school graduate	Some college	Less than high school	High school graduate	Some college
Most important job characteristic:						
meaningful work	22.9%	40.6%	47.4%	34.8%	50.5%	67.5%
advancement	31.4	25.0	18.4	16.8	21.1	12.5
job security	22.9	14.1	13.2	12.9	8.4	—
high income	17.1	18.8	10.5	23.9	12.6	15.0
short hours	5.7	1.6	10.5	11.6	7.4	5.0
N =	(35)	(64)	(38)	(155)	(95)	(40)
If rich, would:						
continue to work	85.7	73.4	83.3	61.0	63.4	66.7
stop working	14.3	26.6	16.7	39.0	36.6	33.3
N =	(35)	(64)	(36)	(146)	(93)	(39)

A similar result appears in the examination of overall, or life, satisfaction as expressed in response to the happiness question. The levels of reported happiness are higher in two of the older segments (among high school graduates and the college-educated). But, again, the differences by education between the three older segments are trivial.

The stress in the above paragraphs should not lead one to overlook the fact that middle-class satisfactions were generally higher (not shown in Table 6). But, while noting the fact of "class differences," it must also be indicated that these differences were not very large. In general, one is talking of ten percentage point differences, as, for example, in the case of financial satisfactions. One area in which sizable differences did appear was in their reports of trends in financial situations over the last few years. Here, the differences in the two better-educated segments amounted to twenty and thirty percentage points, with the middle-class groups being the more likely to report things getting better. The inverse pattern was not one of the working-class situation getting worse. Most of the difference involved merely a larger proportion of workers saying things had stayed the same.[13]

The Maslow hypothesis does gain substantial support in one context. Respondents were asked what they valued most in their work. There is a very pronounced relationship between education and choice of the option "work important and gives a feeling of accomplishment" (referred to as "meaningful work" in Table 6). Within the young working-class segment, the percentages putting this in first place (among five items) increased from 22.9% to 40.6%, and then to 47.4% among the college-educated. Similar patterns are to be found among the older workers (and also in both the young and older middle-class segments).

At this point, however, the support for the Maslow hypothesis ends. Where many have argued that this is a "new" thing, part of a significant new trend, interestingly enough, the older educated workers are more likely than the equivalent young workers to give this item a first-place ranking, the difference in this case amounting to twenty percentage points. The same pattern appears in the other education categories; it is the older segments who are more likely to give this item the first-place rank. Younger workers by comparison place relatively more stress on "chances for advancement" and job security ("no danger of being fired"). There is, of course, good reason for this placing of the priorities.

Another point at which predictions and reality diverge involves the reaction to the interest in meaningful work. Where the "critical" commentators assume that respondents are not able to realize that goal, the respondents themselves report high job satisfaction.[14]

One final observation is worth noting in this connection. One hears much discussion of the decline in work motivation; the young, it is said, no longer share the same work ethic that made America what it is today. If that were the case, it should be indicated in the response to the following question: "If you were to get enough money to live as comfortably as you would like for the rest of your life, would you continue to work or would you stop working?" Sixty-three percent of all respondents said they would continue working. No trend statement, obviously, can be supported with any such single-shot inquiry. But it is possible to contrast the young and the older males, those being discussed here. In both segments, the proportions who would continue working were higher for the sample as a whole, and, of striking relevance for the point under discussion, the younger respondents were more likely to indicate support for the "work ethic" than the older ones, the respective percentages being 78.6 and 70.0.

One may specify that result somewhat. The younger workers in each category of education were more likely to continue work if rich than were the equivalent old. Of special note is the case of the young educated workers (those who presumably have picked up those other values, the "new" or post-industrial goals); 83.3% of them indicated they would continue working as opposed to "only" 66.7% of the equivalent older workers. The greatest willingness to withdraw from the labor force was found among the poorly educated older workers; even there, however, three-fifths said they would continue working.

If one were to take these results at face value, it would suggest a need to worry about the work motivations of the *older* generations. It is their renunciation of "traditional values" that poses the problem. (Or, seen from the vantage point of the counterculture, it is the younger group who pose the problem; they refuse to give up the traditional values that have already been abandoned by millions of forty and fifty year olds.) There is, however, another possible reading of this result, one which is possible, plausible, and consonant with the available evidence.

F. Some Alternative Interpretations

Contemporary studies, with some degree of frequency, have found attitudes or behaviors to be related to age. In most introductory statistics courses, it is pointed out that such findings are subject to two divergent interpretations. It could mean that there is a trend in process (in this reading younger persons are seen as *shifting away* from "traditional" patterns; they are, for example, more tolerant of racial and ethnic minorities, or they come to support the Democrats). Or, the same result could occur because of changes over the life cycle. In this case, it is argued that with increasing age something happens to cause a change of position (for example, with increasing conservatism, one *shifts to* the Republicans).

Both hypotheses have been put forward in discussions of job dissatisfaction. On the one hand, it is argued that a new and different generation is present on the scene. Making the link to the higher levels of education (which presumably liberate people and elevate the levels of their demands) a higher level of dissatisfaction is predicted among contemporary youth than was the case in previous eras. Simultaneously, one offers a life-cycle hypothesis, namely, in time there will be a "wearing down" of these demands; the youth ask much, but, a few years on the job, the increasing burden of family responsibilities, and a growing sense that there is "no way out" lead the one-time rebels to lower their demands and to adjust to life as they find it. This dual interpretation allows the "critical" analyst to argue that young workers dislike their work and that although older workers "accept" it, it is an acceptance under duress.

There are two difficulties with this analysis. The first, already noted at some length, is that only a minority of the young workers report any degree of dissatisfaction with their work. The stress on working class "youth," on the entire category, is mistaken. And the second difficulty is that the "wearing down" hypothesis has not been investigated, only asserted. Another possibility is that workers find better jobs as they get older. With rare exceptions, the first job is likely to be the least attractive job of one's entire career. In the normal run of things, some upgrading of skill levels will occur; one hears of better opportunities from friends, neighbors, or relatives; and eventually, some upgrading comes with acquired seniority and the possibility of bidding for the better jobs. It is to be expected then that most people will report greater job satisfaction at later points in the life cycle.[15] There is, in short, an alternative, an equally plausible hypothesis to account for the age relationship.

This "job upgrading," like the "wearing down" claim, represents only a possibility: it is an unsupported argument. A cross-sectional study ordinarily does not allow an answer to the problem posed here: which of the alternatives is valid? One could, to be sure, make use of retrospective questions, that is, asking individuals whether they had been "worn down" over the years or whether they now had better jobs. The best procedure, clearly, would be to follow a sample of young workers over time, checking job characteristics, job changes, and job satisfactions. Until that study is accomplished, the best one can do is to recognize that another option is available for the interpretation of these results.[16]

This alternative reading of the significance of the working-class life cycle also helps to interpret the findings in Table 6. Young workers are likely to be at the lowest point of the typical working-class career, and they are unlikely, at that point, to have much job security. As a consequence, it should not come as much of a surprise that they put greater stress on "advancement" and "job security" as important desiderata in their employment. The older workers, with better jobs and more security, are less interested in such matters; it is they who, following the Maslow developmental view, show the "post-industrial" interest in "meaningful work."

The work motivation question (if rich, would continue working?) may also be explained in terms of the life cycle; the workers who are closest to retirement are the ones most likely to say they would stop working. As such, it does not appear as the beginning of a new "world historical" trend, a break with the traditional work ethic. Their response usually comes under a much more prosaic heading; it is ordinarily called early retirement.[17]

G. The Downwardly Mobile

Some of the college-educated workers as we have seen, 37.1% of the total, came from middle-class families. An "ancient" theoretical tradition holds that these persons should resent their "fall" in status. They should also be conservative or rightist in their politics. They should resist integration into their new milieu. And they should be striving to regain their "old" or "former" position.

The NORC studies do not allow us to say much about the backgrounds of the downwardly mobile persons. As compared to the college-educated segment who remained in the middle class, they were somewhat more likely to have come from small towns or rural settings, a fact that might have provided some initial "penalty," for example, in an inferior education. As against that penalty, this group has a remarkably high percentage reporting the family circumstances as having been above or far above average—41.1% did so as opposed to a 24.1% figure among the college-educated workers of working-class backgrounds. None of the downwardly mobile reported coming from families with below average incomes.

Judging from the class identifications, there appears to have been a fair amount of "integration" into the working-class milieu, in that a majority of this downwardly mobile group identified themselves as either working or lower class. While the largest percentage of middle- (or upper-) class identifiers in the working class is to be found here (44.7%), the proportion making this choice is not markedly different from that found among the college-educated workers of working-class backgrounds (42.6%). What is striking is the difference between this group and those college-educated of middle-class origins who remained in the middle class. In that segment, the middle- and upper-class identifications run to 86.1%. The suggestion is that many of the "downwardly mobile" persons made an "adjustment" to their present situation; that is to say, they have accepted it. The lingering affection for the middle class felt by some of them does not necessarily indicate dissatisfaction or resentment. It could mean simply that they are defining class in terms of relative income and in turn are saying where they stand vis-a-vis other workers, the respective percentages for those of middle-class and working-class backgrounds reporting above average current incomes being 35.9 and 25.9.

Are the downward mobiles more conservative? As indicated by party identifications, the answer is no. Republican identifiers (including Independents with Republican leanings) constitute 27.8% of the downward mobile segment as opposed to 24.6% among the college-educated workers of working-class background. The study does not ask about their original preferences, say when growing up; if they were similar to those who remained in the middle class, where 49.0% were Republican identifiers, then again there must have been some "adjustment," that is, a shift in a Democratic direction.[18]

The key evidence, the crux of the resentment argument, would be found in the responses to the various satisfaction questions. Are they satisfied, first of all, with their financial situation? Most said they were more or less satisfied. There were fewer at the "pretty well satisfied" or "not at all satisfied" extremes than among the college-educated workers of working-class origins. But overall the differences were not very large.

The most significant indicator of dissatisfaction with downward mobility would be in the attitude toward one's work. But here one finds nearly half (47.4%) reporting they are "very satisfied" with the work they do and another 36.8% being moderately satisfied. Only 15.8% expressed "a little" dissatisfaction and no one in this category expressed great dissatisfaction. This level of high satisfaction stands in marked contrast to the college-educated of working-class background among whom only 28.8% said they were "very satisfied." Dissatisfaction, in short, was found disproportionately among those of working-class background; the total who were a little or very dissatisfied was 26.9%.

Are the "downward mobiles" especially unhappy with their lot? On the whole there is little at all that is distinctive in their pattern of reported happiness. Approximately one-quarter said they were very happy, one-half said they were pretty happy, and one-quarter said they were not too happy. The latter percentage (23.1) is higher than among the equivalent segment, the college-educated workers of working-class backgrounds (14.8%). That 23.1% figure is the largest expression of unhappiness to be found among any of the six categories of middle-class background or any categories of working-class background. The difference between this downwardly mobile segment and the next closest categories (the two poorly educated worker segments, those of middle- and working-class backgrounds) amount to only four percentage points.

The long and the short of the matter, then, is that this downwardly mobile segment does not prove to be as distinctive as one might have initially expected. Their responses, on the whole, do not suggest resentment, they do not show any pronounced rightist propensities, and there are some suggestions of integration and acceptance of their working-class existence instead of a steadfast rejection of it.

V. CONCLUSIONS AND DISCUSSION

This research has yielded three unexpected conclusions: that college-educated workers are not especially distressed with their situation; that young workers generally are not especially distresed with their situation; and that the downwardly mobile college-educated workers are not especially distressed with their situation.

Given the "rich" theoretical tradition that both predicts and "explains" dissatisfaction for all three segments, some consideration must be given to this finding of *absent* dissatisfaction. It proves useful to begin with the notion of mobility.

Much of the literature on the subject has portrayed the social world as neatly divided into manual and nonmanual categories. Indeed, for heuristic purposes, to address the claims formulated within this framework, we too have adopted that procedure in the present chapter. In what is perhaps the most detailed justification of this claim, the following points were made:

> 1. Most male nonmanual occupations have more prestige than most manual occupations, even skilled ones.
> 2. Among males, white-collar positions generally lead to higher incomes than manual employment.
> 3. Nonmanual positions, in general, require more education than manual positions.
> 4. Holders of nonmanual positions, even low-paid white-collar jobs, are more likely than manual workers to think of themselves as members of the middle class and to act out middle-class roles in the consumption patterns.
> 5. Low-level nonmanual workers are more likely to have political attitudes which resemble those of the upper middle class than those of the manual working class.
> (Lipset and Bendix, 1959: 14–16)

The crux of the argument, the point of difference with the findings here, involves the qualifying phrases, for example the "generally lead to, . . ." the "in general," and the "are more likely. . . ." If one alters some of these assumptions, specifically, if one recognizes and "builds in" consideration of these exceptions, the result is a better model. And from the perspective of that new beginning point, the present findings are not at all unexpected.[19]

Basically, the problem is one of "overlap," that *some* manual jobs are viewed as more desirable than some nonmanual jobs; recognition of that fact opens up other options. It means that in some instances, what has been considered "upward mobility" may in fact be considered by those involved to be downward mobility and vice versa. One might consider the cases of skilled workers (manual) and small shopkeepers (nonmanual). The former works fixed hours, receives time-and-a-half for overtime and doubletime for Sundays and holidays. He gradually acquires seniority within the firm, thus giving him a developing feeling of job security. His ordinary income is well above that of many lower-level white-collar workers—and shopkeepers. Away from the job, he is a relatively free agent, that is to say, he is unencumbered by worries about the firm, about unfinished tasks, etc.

The shopkeeper, by comparison, works long hours. He receives no time-and-a-half. Frequently his family will be drawn into the business as unpaid helpers. His income is a function of the number of people who happen into his shop and of the amounts they spend there. If it is a small and marginal firm, he will have no growing sense of security. Ordinarily his income will be well below that of the skilled worker. The problems of the firm are always with him.

Some questions must be raised: if one moves from being a skilled worker to being a shopkeeper, is that to be counted as an "upward" move? And if the shopkeeper gave up his "independent" status and found employment as a skilled worker, would that represent a loss? Would that be a "fall into the proletariat?" Would that generate *ressentiment*?

Unfortunately, the questions posed here have only rarely been researched. The original assumptions have been taken as sufficiently realistic so as to discourage further inquiry. A study from France, dating from the 1950s, is of some relevance here. It discovered enough deviant cases there to suggest the need for research elsewhere on the quantity of the nonconforming cases (Girard and Bastide, 1957).

If working-class life is uniformly punitive, lacking in rewards, in status, etc., there should be a near-universal drive or aspiration to find another job, presumably one in the middle class. But when respondents were asked—"If you had to begin over again, would you choose the same occupation?"—approximately two out of five blue-collar workers responded with "yes." Approximately the same proportion said no with the remainder being "don't knows" or "no answers." The workers and farm laborers were different from the other categories in that a majority of the latter and a plurality of the non-farm workers indicated they would choose another occupation. The authors lay the stress on this point—"The punishing or dirty character of their work and their modest pay justifies this attitude." They fail to comment on the substantial group of non-farm workers who would not change.

A follow-up question was posed to those who would have chosen another job; for the non-farm workers, that meant to 44% of the total.

Nearly a third of them, 31%, wished another working-class job. A majority of the workers, in other words, chose working-class jobs as their preferred options; 42% chose their current one and another 14% wished another blue-collar position. This does not deny a strong preference for mobility out of the class; some would have preferred to be civil servants, some to be white-collar employees, some to be foremen, etc.

Asked what kind of a job they would recommend to a son who was choosing his occupation, one-third of the workers said they would advise him to become a worker. In this case it is clearly a minority recommendation. The important thing to note, however, is that one is not dealing with a minuscule preference; large numbers, millions in fact, would make that recommendation.

The obverse side of the coin involves the recommendations of the shopkeepers and artisans (*commercants et artisans*), most of whom would be classical "petit bourgeois" independent businessmen. Seventeen percent of them would advise their sons to become workers. That percentage, incidentally, is exactly the same as the percentage who would recommend that their sons become *commercants* or *artisans*. Again, the result, broadly speaking, is consonant with the assumptions outlined above, that is, with one exception, namely, that the proportion counselling "downward mobility" is not minuscule. There are a lot of small businessmen who, somehow or other, see the so-called downward mobility as a step upward.

Would the same findings appear in the United States? Lacking the necessary evidence it is impossible to do anything more than speculate; plausible arguments could be made for both the affirmative and the opposing side of the question. One national survey does indicate that there are some satisfactions to be found in at least one section of the American working class; as these authors expressed it, the skilled workers "have few distinguishing characteristics except that they are the least likely to admit to having any worries at all or to feelings of inadequacy as a spouse" (Gurin, et al., 1960: 225–226). They would certainly be earning well vis-a-vis many "lower-middle-class" persons. And that would mean, when all was said and done, that persons in and around that milieu, those familiar with both the range of working-class and lower-middle-class jobs, could easily find skilled work to be the more attractive of the options. (For the comments of some persons of white-collar origins who have *chosen* blue-collar jobs, see Clark: 1976.)

Lipset and Bendix are correct in their judgments that *most* male nonmanual occupations have more prestige than most manual ones, that *in general* the white-collar positions lead to higher incomes, and that the nonmanual positions, *in general,* require more education than manual positions. The point being made here, however, is that enough exceptions to those generalizations exist as to justify an elaboration of the original model so as to recognize the relative attractiveness of some working-class jobs.

Their fourth point, that even the low-paid white-collar employees "think" of themselves as members of the middle class, deserves some greater attention. This is the least adequately supported of the claims on the list, inasmuch as approximately half of the low-paid white-collar employees identify themselves as "working class" with no evident strain or tension (see note 12). As for the "acting out" of middle-class roles in their consumption patterns, this too is open to some question, although here the precise data necessary to assess the claim are not currently available.

A large portion of the "lower-middle-class" white-collar workers live in working-class areas of the cities. (Hamilton, 1972: 159ff.) It is difficult to believe that they live in a continuous state of opposition to their working-class neighbors. It is difficult to believe that because many of them must be kin to the workers; they must have grown up together with those workers, gone to school with them, seen each other in their leisure hours, been in Sunday school and church with them, and so forth. Given a lifetime of "togetherness," it is hard to imagine a desire to "maintain difference" or to "keep one's distance." Indeed, those white-collar employees identifying as working class probably are those living in these working-class districts. Acting out a different class model in such a circumstance seems unlikely, a hazardous possibility.

The claim that low-level nonmanual workers would resemble the upper middle class politically, more so than the working class, is not borne out in the one study that has attempted to assess the matter. This study found reason to stress the *identity* of outlooks of the lower middle class and the blue-collar workers. The two groups were similar in income patterns over their careers. That means that family incomes increased through to middle age and then fell off in older age categories. This was in sharp contrast to the upper middle class pattern, which was one of steady increase through to retirement. Sharing backgrounds and neighborhoods with manual workers, there would be little in their lives that would or could cause a difference in political outlook. As for living out a different consumption style, with earnings lower than the typical skilled worker, it would be next to impossible to live out the style of the upper middle class. Data for the United States does show the distribution of political attitudes in the lower middle class to be approximately the same as in the working class. (Hamilton, 1972: 214ff, 375ff; Hamilton, 1975: chs. 2, 3).

What does this mean for the study of mobility? It means that a move from the manual to the nonmanual rank might not have any important effects on social or political outlooks. If the "move" were into a lower-middle-class job but one remained in the same neighborhood, then the only "force for change" (if any) would be in the new job milieu. But if that milieu contained persons from the same backgrounds, then here too there would be little incentive to change.

In discussions of "white-collar work," the tendency is to think of downtown offices, of the head offices of banks or insurance companies, or of downtown stores. But much white-collar work is found in or near the factories, in or around the railroad yards, in the yards of trucking firms, in the warehouses outside the city center, and so on. Much white-collar work is found on the main business street of the working-class districts within the cities. The "ambience" there is far removed from that of the executive suite.

Upward mobility, then, might involve a shift from driving a truck to dispatching the trucks. As such, it might mean a "coming in out of the cold," the acceptance of a low level clerical job, one that pays less than driving, but one which at the same time has more security and less wearing working conditions.

What about those who start on the road "upward," who at least begin a college education, and then are "forced" to return to their class of origin? At the moment, one can only speculate about the outlooks associated with this "career line." Most of the college-educated workers have achieved only one or two years of college. If that year or two involved only a marginal attachment to that institution (or to the college life), if the student were in continuous danger of failing, there may have been no change in orientations or goals. There may, in other words, have been no acquisition of upper-middle-class values from which perspective one would then feel frustration and resentment. The very process of failing, or dropping out, or of being "counselled out," involves a shift in orientation to some other occupation and implicitly, to other life goals. In such circumstances, it might be relatively easy to shift to, or to reawaken consideration of, working-class jobs. This may not come as much of a trauma because of the evident impossibility of the new option and because of the known attractiveness of some working-class occupations. The relatively high percentage found in skilled working-class occupations attests to the knowledge of and ability to establish the links necessary for "success" in the working-class milieu.

Not all of the college-educated workers, of course, would be failures or drop-outs. One obvious alternative consideration involves the possibility of "interest." While achieving a higher education, one might discover that the subject matters taught there are not high priority personal concerns. This would be the case with those, as in the frequently cited instances, who are mechanically oriented and like to work with their hands but find themselves working over the meanings of nineteenth century romantic poetry, studying "deviance," or exploring the identity problems of distant minority groups.

What of the so-called downward mobiles? How is one to account for their unexpectedly high levels of satisfaction? There are some peculiarities about the study of social mobility that have long since been observed. There has always been a very striking asymmetry about mobility studies, virtually all attention being given to upward moves and next to none to downward moves. Then too, as late as 1965, one author could write that "we know very little about the part that ability plays in the movement of persons through the class structure" (Eckland, 1965: 735). Although upward mobility is typically portrayed as the normal, the right and proper reward for talent, there is an evident reluctance to consider the further implication—that downward mobility, presumably, is the normal consequence of absent talent. Here too "very little is known" about the process. This is the case even though as Lipset and Bendix have shown (1959: 25), approximately one-quarter of the sons of middle-class parents end up in manual occupations.

For the genuinely downward mobile person (as opposed to the shopkeeper turned craftsman, as discussed above), the process probably begins with poor performance or failure in school. If there is a recognition that one is not succeeding by the standards and criteria of Plan A, one will be motivated to search for an alternative. Since most of these moves are likely to be from the lower middle class to the working class, the "fall" is not very great and in some cases even may be accompanied by some tangible advantages. The main point, however, is that the frame of reference is *not* likely to involve a fixed attachment to and identification with the middle class. Some process of disaffection is likely to have intervened to define that attachment as unrealistic. And if the aspirations have been "lowered" in that process, it might, therefore, be easier to accept, adjust to, and even like the working-class job. That acceptance, put in Durkheimian terms, is a function of the equivalance of the job requirements and ability, that there is no significant gap between the two.

VI. A NOTE ON THE SOCIOLOGY OF KNOWLEDGE

How is one to account for the disparity between the "sense of things" offered by various intellectual commentators and the responses offered by the general population they purport to be describing?

The main argument we have to offer is that fundamentally there is no disparity at all; at the root of the matter there is a simple problem of sampling.

Most attitudes involve some kind of a distribution. Some people, for example, are highly tolerant of minority rights, some are indifferent, some are opposed. If one's sample is drawn disproportionately from the latter, one might overlook the presence of a tolerant majority. This point is so simple as to yield a bored or disdainful "of course" by way of response; it is, nevertheless, the basic "error" which has given rise to the present misconception. There is also a second important source of error, namely a free assumption of a trend on the basis of observations made at a single point in time. This is usually "covered" by some reference to an easily assumed past state or by an equally casual reference to "more and more" (dissent, disdain for work, etc.) or to "growing" dissatisfactions.[20] Some instances of this problem may be helpful.

Barbara Garson, author of the play *Macbird,* wrote an essay for *Harper's* magazine entitled "Luddites in Lordstown." A brief biographical note tells us that she was active in the Free Speech Movement at Berkeley and later "worked for a year in an anti-war GI coffeehouse in Tacoma, Washington." Her investigation, it seems, began with "hanging around the parking lot (of the Lordstown plant) between shifts." Later, inside the factory, she spotted Duane, who had been in the army while she was working in the GI coffeehouse. Duane introduced her to some friends and between them, they supplied two columns of material. Later in the week she spent some time in an "autoworkers' commune" and acquired material for another two columns. Ordinarily, one might doubt the representative character of material drawn from such manifestly atypical sources. But this frankly and openly described "unscientific survey" apparently provoked no pangs of doubt for either the writer or the publisher. This account, moreover, has been frequently cited in other literature, usually without so much as a single word of doubt as to the method. A single suggestion of a frequency distribution does appear in the article, incidentally. One individual appears who seems of a different mind from all the angry young men portrayed throughout the article. He is described in a single paragraph on the fourth of five pages in the course of which he is also treated with some condescension—"He was a cheerful, good-natured lad, and, as I say, he liked the Vega." Not all of the dehumanizing, it will be noted, occurs on GM assembly lines.

It also deserves to be noted, at least in passing, that another source of misrepresentation is operative in this and other such accounts of the Lordstown strike. One takes a given event, a strike in March 1972, and fits that into a larger historical framework. The event is *defined* as symptomatic of the new emergent trend; a categoric type, *the* young worker is telling us something. And there is a willing, uncritical acceptance of this *hypothesis* (for it is nothing more than that). The ease of the acceptance is indicated by the failure to consider any alternatives. The labor relations specialist, Frederick Myers, once casually stated that the Lordstown strike sounded like a reaction to a routine speed-up to him. When one

reviews the extensive popular literature on Lordstown, it is quite remarkable just how precisely this alternative hypothesis fits the case. The plant,
which opened in 1966, had been taken over by a new management group
within General Motors only months before the strike and they were in
process of "rationalizing" the unit, that is, speeding up production. An
action to halt a speed-up is not "something new," it is not an "early
warning signal of a whole series of new convulsions." It is, in fact,
something that has been done for some generations now, for example, at
least since the time of the Luddites mentioned in Garson's title.

The preface to Garson's article notes that the "anguish and boredom"
of young workers are "likely to worsen in the next few years." The
studies that are reported here cover those "next few years." One post-
script to the Lordstown discussion appears in a *New York Times* headline
from March 1975, three years after the strike, "Auto Workers at
Lordstown, Older and Fearful of Recession, Are No Longer Militant" (Stevens, 1975).

How are the results shown in the present article to be reconciled with
the evidence reported by the Westleys? The answer, briefly put, is that
the data offered here are entirely consistent with the evidence they
presented. They have given (Westley and Westley, 1971: 33ff.) results
from a 1963 Canadian Gallup Poll (Canadian Institute for Public Opinion)
which showed the percentages of men satisfied with work by educational
level. This data does show, as they reported, that "the more educated the
blue-collar worker, the more likely he is to be dissatisfied with his
work. . . ." The high school educated blue-collar workers were less
satisfied than the public school educated—by a margin of 6.73 percentage
points. And those who went beyond high school were less satisfied than
those with only a high school education; the margin in this case was
thirteen-hundredths of one percent, with the case base for the "beyond
high school" group being seventeen. Data from the same study (with the
same categories and bases) showed a slight tendency for the financial
satisfaction of the blue-collar workers to increase with education level.

A limited presentation of United States' data (from the Survey Research Center's 1964 election study) shows only the financial satisfaction
of the blue-collar workers with "high school or more," they being compared with two middle-class categories. Since comparison with the less-
educated workers was not possible, that evidence, regrettably, is not
adequate for the present purpose. The Westleys also draw on Arthur
Kornhauser's work (1965: 137). This data also proves to be inadequate for
the present purpose. Kornhauser's highest category of education is
"high school graduates." The case bases upon which his conclusions are
founded are also rather small (nineteen cases for young high school
graduates and seventeen for the middle-aged). This means that the only
usable data for the present purpose is the 1963 Canadian data.

One final point deserves to be noted with respect to the seventeen blue-collar workers in that study who had gone beyond high school: 76.47% indicated that they were "satisfied" with their work. The evidence, in short, is perfectly consistent with the present findings; the level of satisfaction was high and the variations in satisfaction by educational level were very small.

Another work, a much-cited one, one also based on systematic interviewing offers many of the same kind of alarmist conclusions. In the course of a foreword, a preface, and an introduction, one hears of the "genuine depth of worker discontent" and of its "profound implications" (vii) and "explosive potential" (x). "In today's highly regimented, increasingly automated, and deeply impersonal industrial society," the authors tell us, "the human being who has found fulfilling work is indeed among the blessed" (Sheppard and Herrick, 1972: xi). Furthermore, we are told, "a crisis exists. . . ." One is prepared, given such statements, to expect evidence showing intense majority dissatisfaction with work.

In their Chapter 1, which first reviews some of the data, they report the findings of a major study by the University of Michigan's Survey Research Center, a national survey from November-December 1969 and January 1970. The overall percentage with "negative attitudes toward work" in that study, they say (p. 37), was thirteen percent. The rest, presumably, had *positive* attitudes toward work. That dissatisfied thirteen-percent figure says nothing about the degree of dissatisfaction. Some of them may well have been only moderately dissatisfied. Not all of it, surely, is of the magnitude suggested by the invocation of crisis conditions.

In Chapter 2, they introduce their own study, this being a survey of white, male, blue-collar, union members selected from four cities in Pennsylvania. They develop a complex index of what they call the "blues" and on this basis establish that a minority, "nearly 30%" (p. 19), suffers from this malaise. The index incidentally involves a high score on an Aspiration-Achievement Discrepancy Index and reports of little or no real chance of getting ahead on the job. They are then referred to throughout as the "discontented" workers. The choice of the indirect measure is a puzzling one since there was a direct question on job satisfaction/dissatisfaction; this (as reported in a footnote, p. 37) found 22% who "voiced discontent with their jobs."

The data in this study are clearly consonant with the data from the national NORC studies from the 1970s; that is, they *all* show majority satisfaction within blue-collar ranks. The emphasis throughout in the Sheppard-Herrick book, then, is on variations in what is the minority position. The dramatic formulations of the preface neglect entirely the question of the basic frequency distributions. In essence, they treat the minority response as the typical response.[21]

Although the Sheppard-Herrick work involves interviews at a single point in time, this does not stop them from speaking in terms of *trends,* of emerging developments, etc. The one fragment of trend data they present is found in a four line footnote (p. 14): "In Gallup Polls since 1963, the percentage of white Americans expressing satisfaction with their work has been declining—from 90 percent in 1963 to 83 percent in 1971." That result does indicate a decline; it also indicates a high overall level of satisfaction, even in 1971. The significance one attaches to this finding depends on the "interpretative scheme" one brings to bear on the subject. If one links it to education, and assumes that "more and more" people will be educated, it seems reasonable to project that downturn into future decades. If, on the other hand, one recognizes the life-cycle possibility, another interpretation is clearly possible. Young people, we have noted, typically have the lowest levels of job satisfaction. A large cohort was born in 1947; it was the largest generation ever born in the United States up to that time. They would have been 16 years old in 1963. The working-class members of that cohort would have begun their entry into the labor force then, with most of the rest following up in the next few years. The middle-class members of the cohort, who typically would have somewhat more attractive jobs, would not enter the labor force until some years later, after they had completed college (Hamilton and Wright, 1975a). The relatively large cohorts that followed the "forty-sevens" would also have made some contribution to the 1971 Gallup result. Many of them would have been in their first job, the job that is likely to be the least attractive of their entire careers. The significant point in this connection is that a larger percentage would have been in first jobs at that time than was the case in the immediately preceding years.

One might expect the same pattern to develop, to be accentuated even, as the large cohorts of the 1950s enter the labor force. But at this point the decline would be countered by the relatively large cohorts of 1947 to 1950 moving on to better second and third jobs. If this were the case, rather than a continuation of the 1963–1971 trend reported by Gallup, one should expect a new stabilization at roughly the 1971 level. A stabilization of this sort is indicated in the NORC General Social Surveys for the period 1972–1975. Sheppard and Herrick noted that one would be able to assess the trend through a comparison of two large surveys done by the Survey Research Center, the first in late 1969 and early 1970 and the second early in 1973. George Strauss (1974: 78) has summarized the results of that comparison as follows: ". . . There were no significant changes in overall job satisfaction between 1970 and 1973. . . ."

The above summarizes what the evidence has had to say about the overall levels of satisfaction and dissatisfaction. Harvey Swados' Foreword to the Sheppard and Herrick work makes a specific linkage between work dissatisfaction and the higher educational levels of workers (p. ix) as does also the Introduction to that work by Michael Maccoby (p. xxviii). But on page eight of the text, one finds the following statement which summarizes the results taken from the Survey Research Center's 1969–1970 study: "Surprisingly enough, almost identical percentage (sic) of workers among the following three groups expressed dissatisfaction with their jobs: those with an elementary-school education or less, those with a seventh- to twelfth-grade education, and those who had progressed beyond high school." The respective percentages expressing that dissatisfaction were 13, 14, and 13. (See also p. 116 for a summary by education and age.)

One possible explanation for the diversity in the conclusions might be the difference in method. It might be the case that those who "are there," those who talk directly with workers, or who come from working-class backgrounds, or who otherwise know and mix with the workers, come up with one kind of conclusion, while the more distant or bureaucratic survey research comes up with another. Barbara Garson, for example, finds job dissatisfaction nearly everywhere, and much the same can be said for the work of Stanley Aronowitz. But that runs up against the objection that other participant observers have found diametrically opposed results. E. E. LeMasters (1975: 20), for example, who came from a working-class background and engaged in five years of participant observation among skilled blue-collar workers, reports that: "I never heard a single man say that he hated his work—or even disliked it. . . . As a group the men seemed to enjoy their work."[22]

Still another possibility is that the surveys have been asking the "wrong" questions. That possibility has been discussed and explored at length for some decades now without anyone discovering the "right" questions, that is to say, the questions that would turn the modal response from one of satisfaction to one of dissatisfaction. (See Kornhauser, 1946; Herzberg, et al., 1959; Vroom, 1964; Robinson, et al., 1967; Kahn, 1972; and Strauss, 1974.) It should be noted too that in these decades a wide range of questions have been used, some asking for satisfaction or dissatisfaction, some asking if people would choose the same job again, some asking if they would continue working if they did not have to, and so on.

There is good reason to believe that the responses to the basic satisfaction-dissatisfaction questions do exaggerate the levels of "real" satisfaction. Most people answer questions with a relative standard in mind. They are saying: "I am satisfied in comparison to other jobs I have had or in comparison to other jobs that might fall my way." George Strauss (1974: 86) reports an interview he once had with a blue-collar worker who had a routine job. This worker told him: "I got a pretty good job." "What makes it such a good job?" Strauss asked. "Don't get me wrong," he answered, "I didn't say it is a *good* job. It's an OK job—about as good a job as a guy like me might expect. The foreman leaves me alone and it pays well. But I would never call it a *good* job. It doesn't amount to much, but it's not bad." This man would probably answer the work satisfaction question in the NORC studies by saying "moderately satisfied." And that would be his "real" answer in terms of the framework that he has briefly explained.

Intellectuals, especially those of "advanced" ideas, adopt a much more demanding standard—satisfaction relative to some loosely defined and rather inspecific, almost edenic state of unity between Man and Nature, where Work and Leisure are one, where work is joy, fulfillment, and self-realization, not something alien to the self. Since all existing conditions fall short of this standard, they "know" that the right answer to the satisfaction/dissatisfaction question is to be dissatisfied. But for most people, that standard of judgment appears unrealistic and impractical for the organization of everyday life.

It is difficult to see what is served by the repetition of unqualified categoric claims about boredom and outrage in the workplace. Ironically, for all the warm approval given by the ever-helpful culture critics for Communication and for all their lamentation over the barriers to significant Communication, there seems to be a distressing lack of it evidenced in their own writing. Charles Reich, in *The Greening of America*, announces that "The majority of adults in this country hate their work" (quoted in LeMasters, 1975: 20). "For most Americans," moreover, "work is mindless, exhausting, boring, servile, and hateful. . . ." (Reich, this time quoted in Wattenberg, 1974: 16). A representative cross section of Americans have "communicated" an opposite view on this matter (see Table 2 above), and other cross sections have given similar responses in earlier surveys.

One can lead off a chapter, as does Aronowitz (1973: 21), with a quotation from a twenty-year old Lordstown assembly-line worker. He says: "Every day I come out of there I feel ripped off. I'm gettin' the shit kicked out of me and I'm helpless to stop it. A good day's work is being tired but not exhausted. Out there all I feel is glad when it's over." That communication is "real" but it is not typical for the labor force as a whole or for the blue-collar segment thereof.[23] Also present in the blue-collar ranks are some who find the job merely OK, as with the man interviewed by Strauss (cited above). There are also some who, like the carpenter interviewed by LeMasters, 1975: 22–23), feel as follows:

> I tell you, Lee, I get a hell of a kick when I drive around town and see a building I helped to put up. You know that Edgewater Hotel down by the lake? I worked on that sonofabitch fifteen years ago and she's still beautiful. I did the paneling in that dining

room that looks out over the water. Sometimes I drive down there just to see the damn thing—do you think I'm nuts or something?

And from a study by McKenzie (1973: 19, 37), one hears the following:

"After building a home I feel an accomplishment, something to last 100 years or so. I feel I've done something for society."

"I like creating and building things, I like to use my hands and brains, it's constructive work; very satisfying when you see the metal tool that I've built myself as per blueprint instructions." A mason reports: "Satisfaction—seeing a building go up from floor to roof. I've been part of it all." An electrician: "Challenging to see a forest then houses, it's fabulous. Storeys, buildings, grow and you know you've been a small part of it." And a toolmaker: "You make different kinds of tools. It isn't monotonous—everything's different. Sometimes you have to plan out your own work—it's a challenge. It's doing something different always."

Aronowitz, to be sure, is quoting an assembly-line worker, someone in a semiskilled job involving repetitive work; LeMasters and McKenzie are quoting skilled craftsmen. Even there, the "for instances" are misleading. The more systematic inquiries have not found categoric differences but rather have discovered rather limited percentage differences. One evident conclusion is that our knowledge and understanding of these matters is not well served by statements that ignore or deny basic frequency distribution, or worse, which misrepresent them.

ACKNOWLEDGMENTS

Authors are listed alphabetically. We express our appreciation to the National Opinion Research Center, The Roper Public Opinion Research Center, and the Survey Archive for the Social Sciences (University of Massachusetts) for making these data available; and to the University Computing Center and the Social and Demographic Research Institute (University of Massachusetts) for their research assistance. We would also like to thank Mr. John Banks, who assisted in the data analysis. Conclusions and analysis, of course, remain the responsibility of the authors.

NOTES

1. A 1972 study of the adult population in the Federal Republic of Germany failed to turn up a single worker with university experience. Not a single worker had even the *Abitur* (the Gymnasium school-leaving certificate). Two (of 294) had completed work in an advanced trade school (*Höhere Fachschule*) and three had achieved the "mittlere Reife" (tenth grade with a diploma). Aside from another nine cases who had attended a business school, all of the other workers had had either primary schooling alone or primary schooling with a subsequent apprenticeship.

The study in question is the 1972 German Election Panel Study, Wolfgang Gibowski, Max Kaase, Dieter Roth, Uwe Schleth, and Rudolf Wildenmann being the principal investigators. We wish to thank them for the use of their data.

2. This is speaking of the normal sample sizes. An exception to the statement made in the text would be the case of Samuel Stouffer's 1954 study, *Communism, Conformity and Civil Liberties* (1955). It was based on two relatively large national samples, which were then combined for most of the analysis. One presentation based on this study (Lipset, 1960: 109) found 64 college-educated workers out of an 884 total.

3. Technical details on the NORC sampling procedures may be obtained from the study codebooks that are available from the Roper Center, Williams College, Williamstown, Massachusetts or from the Inter-University Consortium for Political and Social Research, at the University of Michigan, Ann Arbor, Michigan.

4. We do not personally subscribe to the arguments presented here. We are merely outlining a conventional way of looking at the subject of class and mobility and noting some "functional" problems that are posed given the assumptions of that perspective. An alternative line of analysis will be offered later in the article.

5. This contrasts with the college-educated middle class where 33.7% had a bachelor's degree and another 25.3% had some graduate degree. The 1972 Survey Research Center election study asked respondents which university they had attended. There were sixty-nine college-educated workers in this sample. In general, the institutions they had attended were not among the most eminent in the nation (e.g. Arkansas State, University of Chattanooga, East Carolina, Farris State, Henderson State Teachers College, University of Houston, McMurray, Newark State, San Diego State, South Dakota State, Tennessee Tech., Valparaiso University, Youngstown University). Two-fifths of them named junior colleges and county or city colleges. A few did come from more prestigious institutions (e.g., one each from MIT, NYU, and Northwestern). No one listed an Ivy League institution, or such institutions as Stanford, University of Chicago, University of Wisconsin (or Michigan, Indiana, Iowa, Minnesota, or Illinois), and no one listed the University of California (any branch thereof).

Burton Clark's study of a California junior college (1960) found very high levels of turnover. The college-educated workers picked up in the samples used in this study are, in part, those who dropped out (or who were "counselled out") at the time of Clark's study.

6. The working-class college-educateds who came from families with average or below average incomes were somewhat more likely to report experience in the United States' armed forces; this would ordinarily mean another two or three years of "digression."

7. Only a partial listing of the occupations is possible here. Among others, we have: Baker; Brickmason (2); Carpenter (8); Compositor (2); Electrician (2); Power lineman; Inspector; Locomotive engineer; Machinist; Air conditioning mechanic (2); Office machine repairman; Radio-TV repairman (2); Motion picture projectionist (2); Painter (3); Plumber (9); Roofer, Sheet-metal worker; Telephone lineman; and Tool and die maker (2). There are also an assortment including: Checker (2); Cutting operative; Dry wall installer; Gas station attendant (2); Metal plater; Mine operative (2); Bus driver; Delivery man; Railroad switchman; Construction laborer; Freighthandler (2); Warehouseman (2); Janitor (2); and Cook (2).

8. There are a couple of standard "read-ins" that come up in such discussions, both involving the question of "reference groups." The skilled workers are supposed to gain a sense of gratification by virtue of their edge over some middle-class persons. And the latter are thought to feel some deprivation or injustice about this state of things. Most of this speculation proceeds without any attempt to ascertain what are in fact the reference groups or what are the respective satisfactions or dissatisfactions.

A less exotic reading of the finding is possible. Skilled workers in large metropolitan cities (where wages and costs tend to be high) earn more than white-collar workers in small towns and rural areas. The carpenter in Chicago, for example, will normally earn more than clerical workers in the rural counties of Mississippi or of Illinois. It seems to us unlikely that the carpenter would get "ego gratification" out of that fact or that the clerk in Natchez or Rock Island would feel distress over it. Rather than making such distant references, it seems more likely that the comparison would be with one's own position at some time in the past or with others in the immediate milieu. Most white-collar workers who grew up in a working-class milieu would be fully aware of the implications of their *choice* of a white-collar job. They would have had both white-collar workers and skilled workers among their relatives and acquaintances when growing up. One chooses the white-collar job with full awareness that the pay is less; it is also easier and one avoids an extended apprenticeship or training period. See Hamilton, 1972: 368–375.

9. The study contained an occupational prestige rating based on the work of Hodge, Siegel, and Rossi (1966). Occupations were given scores ranging from 1 to 90. Within the entire group of white males being considered here, 30.7% had occupations with a rating of 50 or better. Almost all of these, however, were nonmanual occupations. Less than 1% of the blue-collar workers had jobs with that level of prestige. Approximately 70% of the college-educated workers had jobs with prestige scores below 40 in contrast to only one-eighth of the equivalent nonmanual group.

10. Garson's article leads off with a passing reference (1972: 68) to white-collar workers who, she says, "resent toiling at trivia." Aronowitz (1973: 303) refers to their work as "incredibly stultifying and intrinsically meaningless." Most of the more routine white-collar jobs would probably be performed by those with less than high school education and those who were high school graduates. They would, for the most part, be in the "lower-middle-class" jobs. Contrary to the completely unsupported Garson and Aronowitz assertions, one finds (in Table 2) that approximately half of these two groups say they are very satisfied with their work and another third say they are moderately satisfied. Most of them would continue working if they were rich (Table 3).

11. See Hamilton, 1972: 100–102; Hamilton, 1975: 68–69, 104–108, 126–128, and 140–141; Schreiber and Nygreen, 1970; Hodge and Treiman, 1968; Jackman and Jackman, 1973; and Dalia and Guest, 1975. The breakthrough work in this area was that of Richard Centers, 1949: 138–139. A comparative study confirming Centers' finding was that of Buchanan and Cantril, 1953.

For some cases of "non-recognition" of long-since available facts, we have: Arono-witz, 1973: 295: " . . . in the white-collar world there are very few people who consider themselves workers. Instead, they are called, and call themselves, by the higher-status term 'employees.' " Parker: 1972, xx: ". . . Studies of self-classification show that the over-whelming majority of Americans publicly call themselves middle class, whether technician or laborer, blue-collar or white-collar." And Ricci, 1971: 29–30: "One of America's sources of strength in the battle of ideologies is that most of its people, regardless of their income or position in American society, think of themselves as middle class. The result of this widespread outlook is that Marxist theory, which emphasizes proletarian misery, is viewed by most Americans as irrelevant at best and pernicious at worst." Ricci offers some support for this claim; he refers to a study by Elmo Roper that appeared in *Fortune* magazine in January 1947. He has ignored, or is oblivious to, all of the subsequent work in the area. These claims should be seen in the light of the evidence contained in Table 4.

The question working in the NORC study is: "If you were asked to use one of four names for your social class, which would you say you belong in: the lower class, the working class, the middle class, or the upper class?"

12. Garson, 1972: 68. It *might* show they are fed up with an industrial system; then again, it might not, since most Communist regimes aim to industrialize. The opposite of an industrial system would be an agrarian-handicraft system. Unfortunately, the present studies do not allow us to explore this question more closely.

13. The leading review of the class differences question concludes as follows: "Our

findings reveal no great 'cultural chasm' between manual and nonmanual workers and suggest that the distinction does not warrant the great importance often attributed to it in the sociological literature.'' Glenn and Alston, 1968: 381. A later study by Glenn (1974), based on data from the late 1960s, reports a *decline* from the already small manual-nonmanual differences discovered in the data from the middle 1940s.

14. Exactly half of the college-educated workers interested in meaningful work (N = 44) reported they were "very satisfied" with their jobs and another 29.3% said they were moderately satisfied. The young, under-thirty college-educateds interested in meaningful work were only somewhat less enthusiastic, the respective figures for that group (N = 17) being 41.2 and 35.3.

15. The percentages of college-educated workers reporting they were very satisfied with their jobs were: under 30, 32.3%; 30–39, 38.1%; 40–49, 47.1%; 50–64, 50%. This result, obviously, is consonant with both the wearing down and the job improvement hypotheses.

16. Still another possibility involves a change in composition of the age groups. Generally, through differences in fertility or through shifting patterns of immigration, the older cohorts could have a different religious or ethnic composition than younger ones. More specifically, changes in opportunity (for example, in the cost or location of universities) could lead to a change in the characteristics of the younger cohorts of college-educated workers. See Hamilton, 1972: 270–272.

17. The percentages in each age category (as in note 15) of the college educateds who would continue working if rich were: 83.3; 71.4; 66.7; and 61.7. Similar patterns appear in all other classes and education segments. In some cases, however, the work motivation remains high until just before retirement and then plummets. Among the poorly educated middle class, for example, 76.7% of the 50–59 year olds would continue working as opposed to only 45.5% of the 60–64 category.

The same patterns by age can be found with respect to other features of one's life. Young persons, generally speaking, have least choice of jobs and also, a closely related matter, on leaving the parental family, have least choice of housing location. Older persons have more earning power and also have had additional decades in which to pick and choose residential location. Accordingly, one finds increasing satisfaction with one's living place among older cohorts, the retrospective percentages expressing quite a bit, a great deal or a very great deal of satisfaction with "the city or place you live in" goes from 36.8% in the youngest category to 43.8, 75.3, and finally 84.6. Again, it should be noted that this result, like the attitudes toward the job, is ambiguous. It could mean they had found better housing, or it could mean that their standards or expectations had been worn down. We have undertaken some investigation of the questions raised in this discussion; see Wright and Hamilton, 1978.

18. This is all premised on the assumption of a conversion occurring in the course of the mobility. Another possibility is that Democrats are more likely to be downward mobile. This possibility is not as far-fetched as it first sounds. For relevant evidence, see Thompson, 1967 and Wilensky and Edwards, 1959.

19. Lipset and Bendix themselves make note of this difficulty when they say that: "It is important to remember, however, that like all single-item indicators of complex phenomena, this one will necessarily result in some errors; that is, some nonmanual positions which have lower status than some manual occupations will be classified in the high group though they should be in the low'' (p. 17). The comments in the text are not intended to detract from the significance of this ground-breaking work; rather, they are intended as providing the basis for an extension of their accomplishment.

20. We have been using a merged data-set, one which combines the NORC studies of 1972, 1973, and 1974. When the college-educated workers were examined on a year by year basis, to assess the trend assertions, the number of cases was reduced to approximately one-third of the figure we have been using throughout. There are some small fluctuations in

the satisfaction items but no clear overall tendency is evident. See below in the text for SRC trend data.

21. See Bowles and Gintis, 1976, and Christopher Jencks' review, 1976: 18. See also Gintis, 1970: 29, where he says "If there were no loss of income, most workers would choose not to work at all," and compare that with the statements of "most workers" indicated in our Table 3. See also Wright and Hamilton, 1978: note 1.

22. That summary is not entirely accurate. On p. 34 of his work, he reports the comments of a skilled carpenter who tells of the deterioration in the quality of work done over the years. He is quoted as saying: "I don't enjoy the work any more."

23. A leading source on the subject of work in America states that the "classically alienating jobs (such as on the assembly line) that allow the worker no control over the conditions of work and that seriously affect his mental and physical functioning off the job probably comprise less than 2% of the jobs in America." Upjohn Institute, 1973: 13. This volume contains many of the same assertions that have been criticized throughout this article. The assertions follow very closely those of the Sheppard and Herrick volume, a result which is not surprising since they were both members of the "task force" which produced this work for the Secretary of Health, Education, and Welfare.

REFERENCES

Aronowitz, Stanley
1973　False Promises: The Shaping of American Working Class Consciousness. New York: McGraw-Hill.
Barber, James A., Jr.
1970　Social Mobility and Voting Behavior. Chicago: Rand McNally.
Bowles, Samuel, and Herbert Gintis
1976　Schooling in Capitalist America. New York: Basic Books.
Buchanan, William, and Hadley Cantril
1953　How Nations See Each Other. Urbana: University of Illinois Press.
Campbell, Angus, Philip E. Converse, Warren E. Miller, and Donald E. Stokes
1960　The American Voter. New York: Wiley.
Centers, Richard
1949　The Psychology of Social Classes. Princeton, N.J.: Princeton University Press.
Clark, Burton R.
1960　The Open Door College: A Case Study. New York: McGraw-Hill.
Clark, Champ
1976　"White-Collar Kids in Blue-Collar Jobs." Money February: 32–36.
Dalia, Joan Talbert, and Avery M. Guest
1975　"Embourgeoisement among Blue-Collar Workers?" Sociological Quarterly 16: 291–304.
Eckland, Bruce K.
1965　"Academic Ability, Higher Education, and Occupational Mobility." American Sociological Review 30: 735–746.
Garson, Barbara
1972　"Luddites in Lordstown: It's Not the Money, It's the Job." Harper's 244: 68–73.
Gintis, Herbert
1970　"The New Working Class and Revolutionary Youth." Socialist Revolution 1: 13–43.
Girard, Alain, and Henri Bastide
1957　"Niveau de vie et repartition professionnelle." Population 12: 60–63.

Glenn, Norval D.
1974 "Recent Trends in Intercategory Differences in Attitudes. Social Forces 52: 395–401.
Glenn, Norval D., and Jon P. Alston
1968 "Cultural Distances among Occupational Categories." American Sociological Review 33: 365–382.
Gurin, Gerald, Joseph Veroff, and Sheila Feld
1960 Americans View Their Mental Health. New York: Basic Books.
Hamilton, Richard F.
1972 Class and Politics in the United States. New York: Wiley.
1975 Restraining Myths: Critical Studies of U.S. Social Structure and Politics. New York: Sage-Halsted-Wiley.
Hamilton, Richard F., and James Wright
1975a "Coming of Age—A Comparison of the United States and the Federal Republic of Germany." Zeitschrift für Soziologie 4: 335–349.
Hamilton, Richard F., and James D. Wright
1975b "The Support for 'Hard Line' Foreign Policy." In Richard Hamilton (ed.), Restraining Myths. New York: Sage-Halsted-Wiley.
Forth- The American Working Class.
coming
Herzberg, Frederick, B. Mausner, and Barbara Snydermann
1959 The Motivation to Work. New York: Wiley.
Hodge, Robert W., Paul M. Siegel, and Peter H. Rossi
1966 "Occupational Prestige in the United States: 1925–1963." Pp. 322–334 in Reinhard Bendix and Seymour Martin Lipset (eds.), Class, Status, and Power. New York: Free Press.
Hodge, R. W., and D. J. Treiman
1968 "Class Identification in the United States." American Journal of Sociology 73: 535–547.
Inglehart, Ronald
1971 "The Silent Revolution in Europe: Intergenerational Change in Post-Industrial Societies." American Political Science Review 65: 991–1017.
Jackman, M. R., and R. W. Jackman
1973 "An Interpretation of the Relation between Objective and Subjective Social Status." American Sociological Review 38: 569–582.
Jencks, Christopher
1976 Review of Bowles and Gintis, 1976. In the New York Times Book Review. February 15: 17–18.
Kahn, Robert L.
1972 "The Meaning of Work: Interpretation and Proposals for Measurement." In Angus Campbell and Philip Converse (eds.), The Human Meaning of Social Change. New York: Russell Sage Foundation.
Kornhauser, Arthur
1946 "Psychological Studies of Employee Attitudes." In S. D. Hoslett (ed.), Human Factors in Management. Parkville, Mo.: Park College Press.
1965 Mental Health of the Industrial Worker. New York: Wiley.
Krickus, R. J.
1971 "White Working-Class Youth." Dissent 18: 503–506, 517.
LeMasters, E. E.
1975 Blue-Collar Aristocrats: Life-Styles at a Working-Class Tavern. Madison, Wis.: University of Wisconsin Press.

Lipset, Seymour Martin
1960 Political Man: The Social Bases of Politics. Garden City: Doubleday.
Lipset, Seymour Martin, and Reinhard Bendix
1959 Social Mobility in Industrial Society. Berkeley, Calif.: University of California Press.
MacKenzie, Gavin
1973 The Aristocracy of Labor: The Position of Skilled Craftsmen in the American Class Structure. Cambridge, U.K.: Cambridge University Press.
Maslow, Abraham H.
1954 Motivation and Personality. New York: Harper & Row.
Parker, Richard
1972 The Myth of the Middle Class. New York: Harper & Row.
Ricci, David
1971 Community Power and Democratic Theory: The Logic of Political Analysis. New York: Random House.
Robinson, John P., Robert Athanasiou, and Kendra B. Head
1967 Measures of Occupational Attitudes and Occupational Characteristics. Survey Research Center. Institute for Social Research. Ann Arbor, Mich.: University of Michigan.
Schreiber, E. M.
1971 " 'Where the Ducks Are': Southern Strategy Versus Fourth Party." Public Opinion Quarterly 35: 157–167.
Schreiber, E. M., and G. T. Nygreen
1970 "Subjective Social Class in America: 1945–68." Social Forces 48: 348–356.
Sheppard, Harold L., and Neal Q. Herrick
1972 Where Have All the Robots Gone? New York: Free Press.
Simon, William, and John H. Gagnon
1970 "Working-Class Youth: Alienation without an Image." In Louise Kapp Howe (ed.), The White Majority: Between Poverty and Affluence. New York: Random House–Vintage.
Stevens, William K.
1975 "Auto Workers at Lordstown. . ." New York Times. March 19: 28.
Stouffer, Samuel A.
1955 Communism, Conformity and Civil Liberties. Garden City, N.Y.: Doubleday.
Strauss, George
1974 "Workers: Attitudes and Adjustments." In Jerome Rosow (ed.), The Worker and the Job: Coping with Change. Englewood Cliffs, N.J.: Prentice-Hall.
Thompson, Kenneth
1967 "Class Change and Party Choice." Ph.D. dissertation, Madison, Wis.: University of Wisconsin.
W. E. Upjohn Institute for Employment Research
1973 Work in America: Report of a Special Task Force to the Secretary of Health, Education, and Welfare. Cambridge, Mass.: MIT Press.
Wattenberg, Benjamin J.
1974 The Real America. Garden City, N.Y.: Doubleday.
Westley, William A., and Margaret W. Westley
1971 The Emerging Worker: Equality and Conflict in the Mass Consumption Society. Montreal: McGill-Queen's University Press.
Wilensky, Harold L., and Hugh Edwards
1959 "The Skidder: Ideological Adjustments of Downward Mobile Workers." American Sociological Review 24: 215–230.

Wright, James D.
 1978 "Are Working Women *Really* More Satisfied? Evidence from Several National Surveys." Journal of Marriage and the Family 40: 301–313.
Wright, James D., and Richard F. Hamilton
 1978 "Work Satisfaction and Age: Some Evidence for the 'Job Change' Hypothesis." Social Forces 56: 1140–1158.
 1979 "Education and Job Attitudes among Blue-Collar Workers." Sociology of Work and Occupations 6: 59–83.

WOMEN'S SOCIAL CONSCIOUSNESS: SEX OR WORKER IDENTITY

Ida Harper Simpson and Elizabeth Mutran

Women "have no awareness of themselves as an important part of the labor force of this country" (Wolfson, 1929: 124). This observation made a half century ago to explain the low unionization of women workers would find little challenge today. Women have almost doubled as a percentage of the labor force, and women workers no longer are predominantly young and single but now resemble male workers in age and marital status. Yet according to the literature (Brown, 1976), they behave in ways that fit Lockwood's (1966) conception of a deferential worker. They accept subordination and mistakenly identify their interests with those of their superiors. Men are less likely to do so.

Why do women behave differently from men? The answer one gets to this question is that they do so because they are women. In other words,

Research in the Sociology of Work, Volume 1, pages 335–350
Copyright © 1981 by JAI Press Inc.
All rights of reproduction in any form reserved.
ISBN: 0-89232-124-5

335

women's gender affects their behavior; it is unclear whether men's affects theirs. Kanter (1976) has identified three explanations of the ways in which gender affects women's work behavior and consciousness: the temperamental, role-related, and social structural. (For a similar discussion, see Stromberg and Harkess, 1978: 125–133.) All three explanations imply that women are a minority in the labor force and seek to explain their deviation from the majority sex, men. These different explanations of women's social consciousness have not been systematically studied. This paper deals with this neglected subject.

The temperamental view of the female worker is congruent with the functional perspective on the family. The family is a reproductive organization based on sex differentiation of roles within and outside the family. Female functions are procreative and sustenance-oriented; male functions are protective and procurement-oriented. Early socialization implants a feminine character. The character is made up of traits or dispositions that are invariant across situations. Socialization subsequent to childhood may occur but is fitted to the feminine character. The character enables females to perform procreative and sustenance roles. Women can play other roles, but they are best performed if consistent with the feminine character. Work roles differ in the extent to which their culturally prescribed behavior coincides with the feminine character. Regardless of the degree of fit, women will behave *as women*. Women's socialization equips them for female-typed work and disadvantages them for male-typed work. The temperamental view implies that sex identity is so central to the person that other identities cannot overcome its influence. It constitutes a latent identity (cf. Gouldner, 1957). Manifest identities, such as occupational ones, adapt to it.

The role-related explanation of the effects of gender on women's work behavior and consciousness focuses on family-centered roles. Family and work are considered separate institutions that make competing demands on women. The organization of the family and women's familial functions commit women to family roles more than to work roles. Family roles take primacy over work roles and constrain women's work behavior. For example, women are said to scale down achievement aspirations in order to avoid competing with potential mates (Komarovsky, 1946) or to forego demanding occupations in the interests of motherhood and marriage (Rosenberg, 1957; Simpson and Simpson, 1961). When work competes with family responsibilities, accommodations are made in favor of the family. According to this view, sex affects women's work behavior and consciousness indirectly through their giving higher priority to family than to work roles. Women who do not marry can escape the constraints of family roles.

The role-related explanation, like the temperamental one, is consistent with the functional view of the family. But the two explanations differ in that the role-related view sees current role constraints, not prior socialization, as the cause of women's behavior. It is a structural explanation and the structure to which it attributes causation is a woman's current family. It differs from what Kanter calls the social-structural explanation in that it looks at women's role-sets; the structural explanation identified by Kanter locates women only in work organizations and disregards roles in other settings.

The social structural approach explains women's work behavior and consciousness on the basis of their work positions. Gender is important only as it affects recruitment to work roles. Proponents observe that women and men are distributed differently in the labor force. Women are concentrated in a limited number of female-typed occupations. These occupations are in the secondary labor market (Montagna, 1977: 126–142; Grimm and Stern, 1974). They are characterized by limited opportunities and power (Kanter, 1975: 129–205). Women's occupations are subordinate to male ones, and women accommodate to their subordination by behaving in ways characteristic of the disadvantaged. Their behavior is that of a powerless and opportunityless people; there is nothing distinctively female about it (Kanter, 1975: 51–56). Men who are in deadend positions that lack power act like women. What appears as female behavior turns out to be a strategy to deal with subordination (cf. Mills, 1940). In the social-structural view, women's work behavior reflects their work situations and not a latent sex identity or a competing commitment to family roles. This structural explanation is consistent with writings as diverse as those of Marx, Mannheim, Gerth and Mills, and symbolic interactionists.

Which explanation best accounts for women's social consciousness? Our data permit us to examine only the social-structural and socialization hypotheses, but these are the most opposing. The socialization explanation treats social structure as an exogenous variable whose effects, if any, are mediated through sex identity; sex identity determines social consciousness. The social structural explanation reverses the causal sequence; it treats gender as an exogenous variable with only indirect influence on social consciousness, mediated through social-structural placement. Figure 1 shows the causal relations implied by the two explanations. The socialization hypothesis, in assuming a latent female identity that intervenes between work situations and reactions to them, implies that women have low worker consciousness. (By worker consciousness we mean consciousness of themselves as workers, or consciousness derived from their being workers.) The social-structural hypothesis, in contrast, implies that

Figure 1.   Two Explanations of Women Workers' Social
Consciousness

1. *Socialization:*

Social Structure → Sex Identity → Worker Consciousness

2. *Social Structure:*

Gender → Occupational Placement → Worker Consciousness

women have high worker consciousness and react to express it when situations are relevant to their work interests. According to the social structural hypothesis, women's identities are situated (Mills, 1940; Stone, 1962), not latent as in the socialization hypothesis.

A test of the social-structural vs the socialization explanation requires two variables, sex and occupational placement of workers. Sex is the explanatory variable in the socialization hypothesis and occupational placement in the social structural hypothesis. But a simple comparison of men and women in different occupational categories is insufficient, for it cannot show whether gender affects both sexes or only one. A sex comparison might show effects of gender on women, on men, or on both, but we would not know which. To know the effects of gender on women workers, we must vary the work status of women in addition to the sex of workers. (We cannot vary men's work status because nearly all men of working age are workers.) The combination of gender and women's work status yields three groupings for comparison: married working women, housewives, and married working men. We restrict our sample to married persons, nonemployed housewives and full-time employed workers, and to whites because blacks' work histories and traditions differ sharply from those of whites.

Our research strategy is to pair the three groupings with each other and compare the pairs: men vs working women, working women vs housewives, and men vs housewives. We want to see which groupings are most similar and most different in opinions and behavior that vary in relevance to women and to work. The socialization hypothesis predicts that working women and housewives will be most similar; the structural hypothesis would see workers, regardless of sex, differing from housewives. Data for our analyses are the NORC yearly surveys of 1972 through 1978 on the noninstitutional, voting-age population of the forty-eight contiguous states of the United States. The questions used for our analyses were not all asked in all the surveys. When questions were asked more than once we combined them after preliminary analysis failed to find noticeable yearly variations in the responses. Combining the seven surveys yielded sample sizes varying from 261 to 1974, 143 to 766, and 195 to 1695 for men, working women, and housewives respectively.

I. WORKER CONSCIOUSNESS

Six categories of opinions and conduct varying in relevance to work were selected to see whether working women similarly placed occupationally to men and to housewives' husbands would respond more similarly to the men or the housewives. The categories are opinions toward respondents' personal economic and financial situations, work orientations, sex-role orientations, frequency of social visits, voluntary association memberships, and TV watching. If women responded on the basis of worker consciousness, their responses should differ the least from men's; but if they reflected latent sex identity, they should differ the least from housewives'. Both hypotheses require that the comparisons be within occupational categories. The Census occupational categories were used to classify working women and men by their occupations and housewives by their husbands' occupations. Our procedure was (1) to determine the percentage of each occupational category of working women, men, and housewives responding in a given way, (2) to get the percentage difference between the responses for each pairing for each occupational category, (3) to sum the within-occupational-category differences, disregarding signs, for each pairing, and (4) to average these within-occupational-category differences for each pairing because there were fewer occupational categories for working women than for men or housewives. No working women were farmers. This procedure summarizes within-occupational differences in order to compare sex-and-work pairings on the basis of the element (sex or work status) that is common to both members of a pairing. The smaller the difference between the members of a pairing, the more that pair reacted on the basis of its common element.

Table 1 presents the average differences between the members of each of the three pairings. It shows that working women were more like men than like housewives. To simplify the exposition, we refer to a pairing as "most (or least) similar" if its members were most (or least) often *more similar* to each other than were the members of the two other pairings. We refer to a pairing as "most (or least) different" if its members were most (or least) often *more different* from each other than were the members of the two other pairings. On only three of twenty-seven responses were working women and housewives the most similar pairing. Not only were

Table 1. Average Within-Occupation Differences between Men and Working Women, Working Women and Housewives, and Men and Housewives (Percentages and Means)

	Men—Working Women	Working Women—Housewives	Men—Housewives	Smallest Difference
Economic Situations				
Income tax too high	13.42	14.93	7.00	M–H
Government should reduce income differences	7.35	9.76	8.93	M–WW
Satisfied with financial situation	4.20	7.50	3.79	M–H
Financial situation improved	5.24	10.84	10.91	M–WW
Family income above average	8.44	5.74	11.75	WW–H
Number of smallest differences	2	1	2	
Work Orientations				
Satisfied with job or housework	6.24	10.6	8.27	M–H
People get ahead by hard work	4.06	7.50	10.96	M–WW
Low importance on money as preferred job feature	8.08	3.58	6.76	WW–H
Low importance on job security	9.22	6.36	4.73	M–H
Low importance on short working hours	3.00	4.84	5.29	M–WW
High importance on chances for promotion	6.48	8.32	6.42	M–H
High importance on feeling of work importance and accomplishment	6.33	7.42	5.52	M–H
Number of smallest differences	3	1	3	

Sex Role Orientations

Mother working doesn't hurt children	26.80	27.95	7.06	M–H
Wife should help husband's career first	5.47	19.68	20.90	M–WW
Preschool children suffer if mother works	20.00	26.90	8.52	M–H
Better for man to work, woman tend house	13.98	27.72	12.50	M–H
Women should care for house not country	3.10	11.58	9.13	M–WW
Approve women working	9.02	13.16	5.01	M–H
Women aren't suited for politics	6.62	7.86	10.60	M–WW
Number of smallest differences	3	0	4	

Sociability: Spend Evening More Than Once a Month With

Parents	12.75	5.33	2.32	M–H
Sibs	17.37	9.50	4.45	M–H
Relatives	26.80	27.95	7.06	M–H
Neighbors	8.28	5.23	5.03	M–H
Friends	10.86	9.08	6.75	M–H
At bar	7.00	4.45	12.86	WW–H
Number of smallest differences	0	1	5	

Leisure Activities:
Mean number of:

Association memberships	.59	.60	.67	M–WW
Hours TV watched daily	.13	1.27	1.10	M–WW
Number of smallest differences	2	0	0	

Table 2. Numbers of Smallest Differences between Groupings

	Differed the Least	Differed the Most
Men—working women	10	6
Working women—housewives	3	13
Men—housewives	14	8
Total comparisons	27	27

they less similar than the other pairings; they were also the most different one. This is shown in Table 2, which summarizes the numbers of smallest and largest differences in Table 1. Degree of relevance of the items to work did not alter the pattern of similarities and differences between working women and housewives, but it did affect those between working women and men. Working women and men were the most different pairing in frequency of social visits; social visits are the least work-related items, and visiting is sometimes considered more feminine than masculine. Working women and housewives were most similar in visits to bars, which were rare for both.

Clearly, these responses of working women do not reflect a latent sex identity, but neither can we conclude that they reflect only a work identity. Men differed more often from working women than from housewives. Work status separated women but did not pull men and women together. Sex interacts with work status to differentiate working women from housewives and to relate housewives to men. Housewives' social locations are strongly influenced by their husbands' work. The data suggest that housewives' views reflected their husbands' views and the status of housewife. Housewives and working women were the most different pairing in orientations toward sex roles. Housewives, more than other groupings, felt that a woman's place is in the home as a helpmate to her husband and mother of her children.

We conclude there is not an overriding sex identity that transcends work status. Sex and work status interact to build complementary marital interests between housewives and men, but the interaction does not appear reinforcing for working women. Their interests appear to be distinctive. We shall pursue this question further by looking at the class identification of working women, men, and housewives.

II. CLASS IDENTIFICATION

If the social consciousness of working women reflects both their sex and work statuses, their identification should be distinctive. Working women are unlike men, including housewives' husbands, in that they are overrepresented in white-collar occupations. In our sample, white-collar workers

Table 3. Percentages Identifying with the Working Class

| | Objective Status | | |
	White Collar	Blue Collar	All
Men	27.3	65.6	45.6
Working women	47.0	74.1	53.7
Housewives	26.1	58.4	44.0

constituted 50.9%, 74.7%, and 43.4% of men, working women, and husbands of housewives respectively. We take this into account in looking at class identification. The NORC question asked respondents, "If you were asked to use one of five names for your social class, which would you say you belong in: the lower class, the working class, the middle class, the upper-middle class, or the upper class?" We combine the lower and working classes, and the two middle classes and the upper class, to obtain two class identification categories which we label working and middle. Table 3 gives the percentages of working women, men, and housewives of white- and blue-collar occupations who identified with the working class. Working women were much more likely to identify themselves as working-class than were men or housewives. (See Table 4, which summarizes differences shown in Table 3.) Nearly half of all white-collar working women identified with the working class; this was nearly twice the percentage of working-class identifiers among white-collar men and housewives. In the blue-collar stratum, working women were also the most likely to identify with the working class, but here men departed somewhat from housewives in identifying more frequently with the working class, though less frequently than working women. Blue-collar men were intermediate between blue-collar working women and housewives in working-class identification. Again we see the same pattern evidenced earlier regarding worker consciousness. Sex separated male from female workers and work status divided women.

One of the most marked effects of sex and work status on class identification was on false consciousness, a discrepancy between objective

Table 4. Differences between Categories in Identification with the Working Class

Objective Status	Men–Working Women	Working Women–Housewives	Men–Housewives
White collar	19.7	20.9	1.2
Blue collar	8.6	15.7	7.1

Table 5.   Percentages Incorrectly Identifying With Their Objective
Statuses

| | Objective Status | | All Incorrect Identifiers |
	White Collar	Blue Collar	
Men	27.3	34.5	30.7
Working women	47.0	25.9	41.8
Housewives	26.1	41.6	34.7

occupational class and subjective class identification. In the sample as a whole it was slightly more characteristic of women than of men, but working women and housewives differed sharply in the strata where it was most prevalent (see Table 5). Nearly half of all white-collar working women expressed false consciousness, but only about a fourth of the housewives with white-collar husbands did so. In the blue-collar objective stratum, housewives were considerably more likely than working women to have false consciousness. Work status influenced the nature of the false consciousness. The white-collar working women who identified with the working class downgraded their class and the blue-collar housewives who identified with the middle class enhanced theirs.

The pattern that we have found is not an artifact of the broad working- and middle-class occupational classification. Each blue-collar Census occupational category of housewives identified with the middle class considerably more than working women or men in the same category, and each white-collar Census category of working women identified more with the working class than housewives or men in the same category. Working women's propensity for false consciousness stood out most from that of housewives or men in the category of administrators or managers. The percentages of female professionals, managers and administrators, and clerical workers who identified themselves as working-class were respectively, 29.9, 44.4, 55.4. Working women in the "new middle class" were not the only false identifiers.

Why did worker status lead to class degradation among working women while nonwork status led to class enhancement among housewives? We offer three possible explanations of false consciousness among white-collar working women. Perhaps they used the term *working* differently from housewives and men. The NORC question mixes hierarchical designations with a functional one. *Working* describes a function; *lower, middle,* and *upper* refer to places in a rank system. Working women may have used the term *working* to distinguish themselves from nonemployed housewives, since paid work is a significant status that differentiates women.

But this semantic explanation does not account for middle-class identification of blue-collar housewives. It seems less satisfactory in explaining housewives' or working women's false consciousness than a second
explanation which is more consistent with our findings on the interaction
of sex and work statuses: False consciousness of white-collar working
women expressed a class degradation they actually faced in the world of
work, and false consciousness of blue-collar housewives expressed the
class enhancement they sought in their devotion to the housewife role.
Working women in both white-collar and blue-collar jobs are disproportionately in the secondary labor market (Montagna, 1977: 125–142).
They are disadvantaged relative to men in power, opportunities, income,
and other rewards. White-collar women workers who identified with the
working class may have been showing recognition of their objectively low
market position and accommodating to encapsulation in a secondary
labor market.

Still another possibility is that working women identified with classes
based on their husbands' occupations, not their own. Our sample of
white-collar working women had 43.3% married to blue-collar husbands. If
these women identified disproportionately with the working class, the
false consciousness may have been more apparent than real. White-collar
women workers with blue-collar husbands were more likely than those
with white-collar husbands to identify themselves as working class
(Table 6). But only 54.7% of the white-collar working women who identified with the working class had blue-collar husbands and 45.3% had
white-collar husbands. (The table does not show these figures.) We have
seen earlier that blue-collar women were more likely than white-collar
women to identify as working class (Table 3). It appears most unlikely
that working women disregarded their own occupations when they put

Table 6. Congruence of Working
Women's and Their Husbands'
Occupations and Class
Identification of Working Women
(White-Collar Women Only)

	Percentage Identifying with the Working Class
Husband and wife white-collar	35.9
Husband blue-collar, wife white-collar	56.3

themselves in social classes. This conclusion is supported by the findings of Ritter and Hargens (1975). Given the ambiguous position of women in the stratification system, it is not surprising that the bases of class identification are less uniform and probably more complex among working women than among housewives or men.

Whereas we see working women's downgraded class identification as involving the interaction of gender and work, the class enhancement expressed in blue-collar housewives' false consciousness may reflect their identification with the role of housewife. Housewives convert resources provided by the husband into status benefits for the family. Merely to be a full-time housewife is a luxury, and for a husband to have a full-time housewife advertises his ability to support the family. The false consciousness of blue-collar housewives may be based partly on their seeing the housewife role as adding a significant status increment to the work of their husbands. They see their class standing elevated by their being full-time housewives, in contrast to working women whose secondary position in the labor force degrades the objective status of their work. This interpretation of false consciousness among working women elaborates our earlier findings on their worker consciousness.

III. BASES OF CLASS IDENTIFICATION

Our discussion of false consciousness hinged largely on differing bases of class identification. We now examine these in more detail. We have suggested that housewives may base their class identification partly on their husbands' occupational strata. When they do this, they are using a structural criterion. Structural class criteria in our data are occupational prestige as measured by the Hodge-Siegel-Rossi Prestige Score, income, education conceived as a work credential, and union membership. Instead or in addition, people may base their class identification on style of life. Our style-of-life variables are perceived comparison of one's family income with that of American families in general and housewives' education.

When housewives base their own class identification on status increments they add to their husbands' social class, they are foregoing an autonomous identification in favor of a familial one. A familial basis of identification is not autonomous. It is not the property of the individual respondent, but of a family whose members contribute to it and partake of it.

Structural and style-of-life bases of class identification may be either autonomous or familial. Figure 2 gives examples.

We use regression analysis to compare the bases of class identification of the three groupings. Table 7 shows that they differed in ways generally

Figure 2.   Illustrative Class Units and Evaluative Bases

	Class Unit	
Evaluative Base	Autonomous	Familial
Structural (Job-connected)	A Respondents' occupations; income; education as work credential	C Husband as head of household; familial income; spouses' occupational prestige
Style of life (Off the job)	B Education as cultural symbol	D Comparison of family standing relative to others; spouses' education

consistent with findings given above. Men's bases of class identification were the most distinctive. Their identification rested heavily on autonomous statuses connected with their occupations. These were structural criteria rather than familial contributions to style of life. Housewives' class identification was almost totally familial because they had only one autonomous status, education. Housewives' familial evaluative bases were both structural and style of life. Working women differed from both men and housewives. They were more similar to housewives than to men; they had autonomous statuses but education was the only one of them that contributed significantly to their class identification. Working women were unlike housewives, however, in that their main familial class criterion was related to style of life. Their perceived family income and spouses' education were more important for their class identification than for housewives' (.236 vs .178; .028 vs .018). Spouses' occupational prestige was more important for housewives' class identification than the family's actual income and nearly as important as the family's perceived financial standing.

We interpret these findings as consistent with our earlier ones. Work-related autonomous structural bases of identification were the most important ones for working men, but for working women the main criteria were familial and style of life. Housewives' identification depended solely on familial bases, both structural and style of life. Housewives drew on their husbands' statuses to locate themselves in the class system. Working women did not draw much on their husbands' statuses nor on their own; neither their education nor their work supported their class identification. The failure of working women's autonomous statuses to contribute to their class identification reflects the limitations of their jobs in the secondary labor market.

Table 7. Regression Coefficients of Status Characteristics on Subjective Class Identification of Married Full-Time Working Men and Women and Housewives

	Men			Working Women			Housewives		
	Beta	B	S.E.	Beta	B	S.E.	Beta	B	S.E.
Autonomous statuses									
Education	.147*	.066	.021	.125*	.063	.033	.055	.037	.024
Occupational prestige	.102*	.004	.002	.075	.003	.003	—	—	—
Union membership	.004	.000	.002	.004	.000	.003	.032	.003	.002
Income	.120*	.031	.010	−.065	−.014	.014	—	—	—
Familial statuses									
Spouse's education	.099*	.023	.011	.160*	.028	.011	.100*	.018	.007
Spouse's occupational prestige	.038	.002	.002	.074	.003	.003	.185*	.009	.002
Familial income (objective)	—	—	—	.022	.006	.018	.107*	.025	.008
Family's financial standing	.234*	.202	.033	.259*	.236	.052	.164*	.178	.036
R^2	.28			.23			.20		

* Significant at .01 level

IV. CONCLUDING COMMENTS

Our analysis illuminates Wolfson's (1929) observation that women have little awareness of themselves as an important part of the labor force. They lack awareness not because they are women but because of their occupational positions. Their disadvantaged position does not tell them they are important. They see themselves as working in the interest of their families' styles of life rather than to further autonomous work interests.

We have found no evidence to support a view that women's socialization as women accounts for their work consciousness. Their gender affects their occupational recruitment, but their consciousness reflects their structurally limited place in the world of work.

ACKNOWLEDGMENT

We have benefited from suggestions by Richard L. Simpson.

REFERENCES

Brown, Richard
    1976   "Women as Employees: Some Comments on Research in Industrial Sociology." Pp. 21–46 in Diana Leonard Baker and Sheila Allen (eds.), Dependence and Exploitation in Work and Marriage. London: Longman.

Gouldner, Alvin W.
    1959   "Organizational Analysis." Pp. 400–428 in Robert K. Merton, Leonard Broom, and Leonard S. Cottrell, Jr. (eds.), Sociology Today. New York: Basic Books.

Grimm, James W., and Robert N. Stern
    1974   "Sex Roles and Internal Market Structures: The 'Female' Semi-Professions." Social Problems 21: 690–705.

Kanter, Rosabeth Moss
    1975   "Women and the Structure of Organizations: Explorations in Theory and Behavior." Pp. 34–74 in Marcia Millman and Rosabeth Moss Kanter (eds.), Another Voice. Garden City, N.Y.: Anchor Books.
    1976   "Policy Issues: Presentation VI." Pp. 282–291 in Martha Blaxall and Barbara Reagan (eds.), Women and the Workplace. Chicago: University of Chicago Press.

Komarovsky, Mirra
    1946   "Cultural Contradictions and Sex Roles." American Journal of Sociology 52: 182–189.

Lockwood, David
    1966   "Sources of Variation in Working-Class Images of Society." Sociological Review 14: 249–267.

Mills, C. Wright
    1940   "Situated Actions and Vocabularies of Motive." American Sociological Review 5: 904–913.

Montagna, Paul D.
    1977   Occupations and Society. New York: Wiley.

Ritter, Kathleen V., and Lowell L. Hargens
    1975   "Occupational Positions and Class Identifications of Married Working Women: A Test of the Asymmetry Hypothesis." American Journal of Sociology 80: 934–948.

Rosenberg, Morris
1957 Occupations and Values. Glencoe, Ill.: Free Press.
Simpson, Richard L., and Ida Harper Simpson
1961 "Occupational Choice among Career-Oriented College Women." Marriage and Family Living 23: 377–383.
Stone, Gregory C.
1962 "Appearance and the Self." Pp. 86–118 in Arnold Rose (ed.), Human Behavior and Social Process. Boston: Houghton Mifflin.
Stromberg, Ann H., and Shirley Harkess, eds.
1978 Women Working. Palo Alto, Calif.: Mayfield.
Wolfson, Theresa
1929 "Trade Union Activities of Women." Annals of the American Academy of Political and Social Science 142: 120–131.

SEASONAL FARM LABOR AND WORKER CONSCIOUSNESS

William H. Friedland

Forms of organization and levels of organizational activity provide concrete phenomena reflective of forms of consciousness. Consequently the
situation of farm workers in the United States lends itself to the analysis
of the development of consciousness, because farm workers are only just
beginning to manifest *continuing* organizational capacity. While innumer-
able attempts at organization have been undertaken in the past (Jamieson
1945; London and Anderson 1970; Galarza 1977), it has only been since
the mid-1960s that a successful and continuing organization of farm workers has developed that permits a closer examination of the forms of
farm-worker consciousness.

Before turning to an examination of current developments with farm
workers, it is worth recalling the particular social conditions of these
workers. The agricultural sector of the U.S. economy has undergone a
major transformation since the beginning of the century to the point

Research in the Sociology of Work, Volume 1, pages 351–380
Copyright © 1981 by JAI Press Inc.
All rights of reproduction in any form reserved.
ISBN: 0-89232-124-5

where less than 5% of the labor force is engaged in agricultural pursuits.[1] Further, much of the agricultural labor force consists of self-employed farmers with few or no employees. On many farms in some sectors of agriculture, one or two employees represent the total number of workers other than the farm owner-operator. These patterns, particularly found in Eastern and Midwestern agriculture, are different from the prevailing trends in the far South (Florida), the Southwest (Texas and Arizona), and the West (especially California) where the new pattern of agribusiness, characterized by factory-like production and large-scale farms, is increasingly the norm. It is on this latter situation that this paper will be concentrated, examining the character of farm-worker consciousness when employed in large-scale production organizations.

To facilitate this analysis of farm workers, it will be useful to develop a typology based on two dimensions, migration-stability and skill-specialization. With respect to physical mobility, there has been, since after the Second World War, a sizable number of *migrant* agricultural workers who have moved with the crops in three major streams. On the East Coast, one stream originally began in Florida and moved through the Atlantic Coast states ending in New Jersey and New York. In recent years, this stream, originally composed largely of black workers, has shifted in composition as workers from Puerto Rico and from Mexico have entered it. The Midwest stream, composed heavily of workers of Mexican origin, begins in Texas. Workers move widely throughout the U.S. from this base to Washington and California, to Mountain states such as Idaho, but with the major contingent migrating to states such as Wisconsin, Michigan, and Ohio. There is also a stream of workers who move through the three Western states, California, Oregon, and Washington.

A different pattern has become increasingly significant in the past decade in California, Arizona, Texas, and Florida. Here the pattern has become one of *nonmigration* with workers based in a permanent locale, picking up work on a daily, weekly, or seasonal basis. These workers often move considerable distances on a daily basis to find work. And while some may be defined as "migratory" because they sleep away from home in the course of doing their work, their migratory work patterns are much reduced. Often such workers are permanently located in a single place, find all of their work in the general area, and do not migrate at all.

The second basic dimension, skill-specialization, poses some conceptual problems in delineation since all agricultural labor has some skill despite common beliefs that it is simply hard, physical, "stoop" labor. Perhaps one way to get at this factor is to note that in places like California, there have long been workers specializing in distinct activities in agriculture. Although there have been no historical studies, there is one

Figure 1. Types of Agricultural Workers

	Nonspecialized	Specialized
	1	3
Migratory	"Migrants"	Lettuce Harvesters
	"Ditchbankers"	Fruit tramps
	"Pickups"	
	2	4
Non-migratory	Tomato Harvesters	Grape workers
		Citrus workers

study in depth of "fruit tramps," workers who specialize in the harvest of tree crops, especially fruits (Mintz 1971).[2]

Based on these two dimensions, a four-celled typology of agricultural workers has been set out in Figure 1. In each of the four cells, suggested *examples* of types are intended to be suggestive, not exhaustive. The typology will prove useful when we turn to the discussion of types of consciousness manifested by agricultural workers. For the moment it is simply worth noting that organizing activities have been carried on amongst all four types but that success in unionization has occurred, up to the present time only with specialized workers.

Despite considerable interest in agricultural workers over the decades, only a little useful information has been developed in the past decade about these workers and their lives. From these few studies, a picture, but clearly an incomplete one, can be developed of agricultural worker consciousness.[3] The findings of Newby with respect to British agricultural workers are startlingly appropriate to the United States:

> Thus while our knowledge of family farming has a fairly sound basis, non-family agricultural workers have been almost entirely overlooked. The more thoroughgoing capitalist system of agriculture in . . . . England remains unexplored (1972: 413).

More detailed coverage, albeit sporadic, is found in journalistic accounts of farm workers. Although often taking the form either of "horror stories" or "ain't-everything-great," considerable information can be built up through journalistic materials. The development of a systematic body of knowledge about agricultural workers, firmly grounded in social science, however, remains to be accomplished. Such studies could contribute to the development of a sociology of agriculture and to the comparative analysis of production systems.

I. SOME THEORETICAL CONSIDERATIONS

In considering the kinds of consciousness that agricultural workers manifest, it will perhaps be useful to consider two distinctive ways in which this subject has been conceptualized by scholars and practitioners involved with labor movements. First, it is useful to consider the approach taken to the study of consciousness by Marx and Engels and later by Lenin. Second, this approach can be contrasted with that taken by Perlman, one of the pioneers of modern industrial relations theory. These two approaches represent, at least as far as the literature is concerned, two contrasting views of the development of consciousness.

For Marx and Engels, the formation of consciousness in the working class was an inevitable product of a constellation of forces that brought workers as a social category, a "class," into continuous struggle with employers. The structural forces producing conflict were several: the process of physical agglomeration represented something new in the labor process since workers were concentrated in unprecedented numbers as a result of the onset of capitalist production. Added to this, however, was an inevitable process which included the continuous immiseration of the working class as the rate of capitalist profits fell. The reduction of the standard of living of the working class, whether absolutely or relatively in comparison to the bourgeoisie, contributed to the development of struggle. A third structural element had to do with the anarchy of capitalism, the ups and downs of the business cycle and of overproduction and underconsumption. A final feature was represented by the alienation that workers experienced by virtue of their separation from the means of production.

All these features produced amongst workers common understandings irrespective of the differences they had by virtue of different social, ethnic, or racial origins. These experiences created the working class as an *objective* phenomenon; this was the condition in which the working class became, for Marx and Engels, a class *an sich,* in itself.

What is particularly significant about capitalist social relations is that it creates a homogeneous working class:

> Generally speaking, large-scale industry created everywhere the same relations between the classes of society, and thus destroyed the peculiar features of the various nationalities. And finally, while the bourgeoisie of each nation still retained separate national interests, large-scale industry created a class which in all nations has the same interest and for which nationality is already dead; a class which is really rid of all the old world and at the same time stands pitted against it (Marx and Engels 1976, Vol. 5: 73–74).

But Marx and Engels recognized that the creation of the working class objectively was only part of a complex dialectical process. The objective status of the class became transformed through continuous struggle. For, as workers responded to their new life condition, they learned about their homogeneity with respect to each other, on the one hand, and the class opposition to their interests as manifested through their employers, the bourgeoisie. Thus, the process of struggle produced a new state of consciousness of a class *subjectively* or a class *für sich*, for itself.

Marx and Engels retained, to a considerable degree, an inevitablist orientation toward the development of working-class consciousness. For them, consciousness became revolutionary because the common experience of workers brought them into common struggle with all employers.

That the process of transformation of consciousness was not simply mechanistic but implied conscious and deliberate intervention is indicated by the activity Marx and Engels, but particularly the former, undertook with the formation of the International Workingmen's Association (IWA—the First International). Marx recognized the necessity not only for the development of an organizational praxis but one which transcended national lines. Marx became active in the IWA at its inception and maintained an active role until the IWA Secretariat was banished to the New World in his conflict with Bakunin.

While Marx did not write about consciousness development in a systematic way, his orientation toward consciousness and its transformation can be subsumed as follows:

1. The class in itself is transformed to a class for itself through struggle.
2. Transformation is not automatic and the intervention of some agency (e.g., the International) facilitates the development of subjective consciousness.
3. Struggle does not develop in a unilinear manner although it is cumulative; there are ups and downs in the development of struggle and therefore of consciousness.

The major development (or revision, depending on how "classical" one wants to be with Marx) introduced by Lenin was to emphasize the limited consciousness of the working class if left to itself. Lenin more deliberately pointed out that the working class was capable of great spontaneity in its battles with employers. This did not, by itself, lead to a higher level of consciousness in which it recognized itself as a class. Thus, for Lenin, the transition from *an sich* to *für sich* was unquestionably not automatic:

> This consciousness could only be brought to them from without. The histories of all countries show that the working class, exclusively by its own effort, is able to develop only trade union consciousness, i.e., it may itself realise that necessity for combining in unions, for fighting against employers and for striving to compel the government to pass necessary labor legislation, etc. (Lenin, 1943: 53).

Lenin thus emphasized the crucial significance of outside agencies in generalizing the experience of the working class and in demonstrating the relationships not only between workers and employers but also between employers as a social category and the state as their instrumentality. This factor, as well as the specific conditions of Tsarist Russia, led Lenin to a new formulation of the concept of the party. Lenin thereby made far more conscious and deliberate what was, at best, only preconscious in Marx and Engels: the importance of an organized force to intervene in struggle to generalize the character of local conflict and turn it into revolutionary struggle.

Selig Perlman (1949), in essence, agrees and disagrees with the Leninist formulation. Perlman developed a series of arguments that placed the United States in an "exceptional" position in comparison to labor movements in Europe. The factors creating American exceptionalism include the geographical and vertical mobility possible to individual members of the working class that serve to drain off leadership potential, the "free gift of the ballot," intergenerational mobility, and the heterogeneity of the American working class (162–169).

While Perlman's terminology is now somewhat obsolete in his references to the need for "a theory of the psychology of the laboring man" (237), the essential features of his theoretical orientation are clear and remain valid in any examination of the development of consciousness.

Perlman argued for a fundamentally limited and limiting consciousness of workers, of "manualists." Based on a consciousness of scarcity, this stood in sharp contrast to the consciousness of the businessman based on a consciousness of opportunity. Scarcity consciousness of the workers translated into a desire to control those aspects of life over which control was feasible:

> If . . . opportunity is believed to be limited, as in the experience of the manual worker, it then becomes the duty of the group to prevent the individual from appropriating more than his rightful share, while at the same time protecting him against oppressive bargains. *The group then asserts its collective ownership over the whole amount of opportunity,* and, having determined who are entitled to claim a share in that opportunity, undertakes to parcel it out fairly, directly or indirectly, among its recognized members, permitting them to avail themselves of such opportunities, job or market, only on the basis of a "common rule" (Perlman 1949: 241–242, emphasis in the original).

Thus, for Perlman, the salient feature of worker consciousness was marked by (a) a collectivist orientation centered on (b) control over jobs since jobs were the "scarce" commodity for workers but also the commodity related to their experience.

As with Lenin, however, a crucial issue emerged for Perlman with respect to intellectuals since they constantly obtruded on workers with their own concerns. Perlman subsumed the intellectuals as consisting of

three types: the Marxist "determinist- revolutionary;" the "ethical intellectual" encouraging workers to escape from "wagery" to "freedom";
and the "efficiency intellectual," exemplified by the Fabians, seeing
"labor as a 'mass' propelled by the force of its burning interest in a
planned economic order yielding a maximum technical and social efficiency" (282–283). While Perlman was somewhat less than enthralled by
the various types of intellectuals, he regarded them as significant forces
impinging on the development of workers' consciousness, if only by their
ubiquity and persistence.[4]

The essence of Perlman's view of consciousness is very much like
Lenin's but derives from a very different set of standards. Perlman agrees
with Lenin that, left to themselves, workers develop only a limited consciousness. Although he names this consciousness differently from
Lenin, its limitations are notable. Thus we have Perlman's job consciousness based on scarcity vs Lenin's trade-union consciousness based on the
limitations of experience. For Perlman, this level of consciousness is
perfectly sufficient for the requirements of workers; for Lenin, this consciousness is limited and must be transcended by the intervention of an
external, generalizing force, an intellectual force represented by the
professional revolutionaries organized within the vanguard party.

With this theoretical introduction, we can turn to an examination of
seasonal agricultural workers in the United States, bearing in mind the
restrictions that have been set out about the different types of workers
found in agricultural employment.

II. STRUCTURAL FEATURES INFLUENCING AGRICULTURAL WORKERS' CONSCIOUSNESS

To talk about agricultural worker consciousness in the abstract is difficult,
especially in historical perspective. To find ways of assessing consciousness historically, we turn to an historical analysis of specific farm worker
struggles. Jamieson's (1945) remarkable, and long out-of-print, compendium of labor struggles to organize unions is perhaps a useful place to
begin a review of the development of consciousness amongst agricultural
workers.

What is also notable about the diversity of attempts of a staggering
variety of agricultural workers all over the United States to organize
themselves is the amnesia experienced about agricultural workers' organization. This is perhaps because of the localized quality of most agricultural workers' actions; in most cases, attempts at organizing, even
when they took the form of strikes and/or other militant action, rarely
developed a broad understanding in the larger society. This was not only
because of the localized character of the organization but probably be-

cause those who study such phenomena, scholars of labor and unionism, tended to concentrate their studies on workers who were more "important," originally craft workers and later industrial workers.

Jamieson's study has value because its descriptive detail demonstrates the variations occurring amongst agricultural workers as they seek to deal with their life circumstances. For example, the development of crew organization by the Japanese as they entered California agriculture is worthy of note. Similarly, the same Japanese later had to organize to remove the labor contractors as middlemen since their control over the labor supply produced better results for the contractors than for the workers (50–54). Jamieson dedicates a substantial segment of his study to the Industrial Workers of the World and various attempts at organizing by communist trade unions. These fit together with Lenin's and Perlman's discussion involving the intellectuals in organizational activities amongst workers (chapter VI and VIII). But he also deals with organizing share-croppers and tenants (chapter XVII), the cowboy strike of 1883 in Texas (257–260), Catholic unionism in Crystal City, Texas, in 1930 (271–272), the Southern Tenant Farmers Union (chapter XVII), strikes of cranberry workers in the Massachusetts bogs in 1931, 1933, and 1934 (356–363), and strikes among Hardin County (Ohio) onion workers and sugar beet workers in Ohio and Michigan in 1934–1937 (chapter XXI).

What becomes clear through a perusal of these historical studies is that organizing attempts have been the product of "spontaneous" actions by workers themselves as well as the result of intervention by organized "intellectuals" of the IWW, the Communist party, or traditional labor organizations such as the AFL and the CIO. Jamieson summarizes his analysis by emphasizing the diversity of attempts:

> The origin of many rural unions lay in spontaneous strikes, which temporarily brought agricultural workers together to attempt collective bargaining. Many such outbreaks (sic!), however, failed to develop any sort of organization that could function after the strikes were settled. . . . The conditions which made it difficult for seasonal farm workers to organize were the same conditions that made them vulnerable to agitation and strikes. The hardships which they suffered made them a problem group of great public concern, the true "forgotten men" of the thirties. Their extreme mobility, the high seasonality of their work, and the low wage rates all combined to make unionization among them costly and, at the same time, created chronic conditions for the communities in which they lived (Jamieson, 1945: 406).

Probably the most significant features that have impeded the development of any broad form of consciousness of agricultural workers have been the localized character of agricultural labor markets, on the one hand, and the maintenance of high levels of surplus labor, on the other.

Fisher (1953) dealt only implicitly with the first in his study *The Harvest Labor Market in California* but more centrally with the second. Characterizing California as having a "structureless" labor market, being devoid of structural elements such as job rights, skills, and (at the time he wrote) mechanization, the basic strategy of California growers has been to maintain an oversupply of labor to guarantee adequate numbers of workers at harvest time (chapter 1). This strategy was somewhat modified at the time of the bracero program when Mexican labor could be contracted for; under these circumstances, workers could be employed for very short periods of time and tight scheduling of the work force was possible. Yet the bracero program was not very efficient in its usage of labor either (Galarza, 1964: chapter 16). Similar wastage of labor was noted in New York State when black migrant workers were transported in crews from Florida in numbers which effectively wasted their labor (Friedland, 1969).

Given these conditions, it is not surprising that, despite many attempts at organization, relatively little continuous and significant unionization occurred amongst farm workers. Morin (1952) dealt with this problem, concluding that agricultural unionism confronted considerable difficulties until workers could become more concentrated, could break out of cultural isolation, could become more homogeneous and skilled, and could find legislative protection. At the same time, Morin projected that organization would probably occur in labor-intensive crops and probably in loci near industrial centers, citing California, Florida, and New Jersey as possibilities but also including the range livestock areas and the Delta plantations as likely centers for unionism (chapter V).

A systematic assessment of the structural factors inhibiting organization is relevant since these structural features contribute to hindering the development of stratum, group, or class consciousness. Such an examination should consider structural elements of the social relationships in agricultural production. We turn initially to an examination of structural aspects of the overall economy, polity, and society manifested in employment relationships before examining some of the structural changes in agricultural production.

III. IMPEDIMENTS TO THE DEVELOPMENT OF CONSCIOUSNESS

In the literature on agricultural workers, seven factors have generally been subsumed as impeding the development of consciousness and organization.[5]

Maintenance of an oversupply of labor has already been cited. On the whole, the continuous presence of an oversupply of labor has been an important factor in U.S. labor policy. From the middle of the last century, the development of agriculture and of industry called for heavy importation of workers, predominantly from Europe. On the West Coast, importation of labor from Asia represented standard policy despite protest from organized labor. Agriculture often served as a "way station" for imported workers on their way to urban, industrial employment. After the turn of the century, continuous and sustained importation of Mexican workers (albeit in waves) became a "normal" feature feeding labor market needs in Western agriculture as well as Western and Midwestern industry. Similarly, while the focus of Puerto Rican immigration in the East was mainly urban, it had an important agricultural component.

Systematic utilization of coercion where organization did occur. The history of American labor is replete with the application of a wide variety of coercive mechanisms to restrain union organization. The yellow-dog contract, the blacklist, the injunction, the vigilante mob, were all devices extensively applied to inhibit unionism. To these were added some of the most brutal applications of force in the worldwide history of labor. In such circumstances, the application of coercive measures against agricultural workers, whenever they sought to organize, came to be expected as a "normal" aspect of American society.

The exceptional character of American agriculture became a norm in the United States because of a celebrated myth of agrarian democracy with roots in a Jeffersonian ideal. This was translated, by the middle of the last century, into a belief that the dispersed and fragmented character of agricultural production precluded the application of science to improve agriculture. As a result, a complex of legislation was put in train that resulted in the land grant complex of colleges and universities, the agricultural experiment stations, and agricultural extension. Agricultural exceptionalism also took more profound form during the 1930s, as far as workers were concerned, when New Deal protective labor legislation was introduced. As bill after bill was passed providing for union representation through the National Labor Relations Act, for minimum wages and social security, agriculture was considered to be "exceptional" and agricultural workers were exempted from coverage. Thus, it was not until the 1970s that agricultural workers entered the mainstream of American labor by obtaining some coverage in protective legislation.

Agricultural mechanization—While mechanization provides a structuring of the labor force and, in the long run contributes to the development of organization (Friedland and Nelkin, 1972), in the short run it undermines unionism. First, it should be recognized that agricultural mechanization was first present in family farm circumstances which facilitated a concentration process in land and production but not in labor. Second, in those areas where agricultural production began or was sustained on a large scale, mechanization was initially not considered to be important because a steady oversupply of labor existed. In more recent times, however, the presence of mechanization capacity has served as a threat or warning to workers. Thus, in California at the end of the bracero program, rather than confront the problem of recruiting a U.S.-based harvest labor force (Friedland and Barton, 1975), mechanized tomato harvesting was introduced at the end of the bracero program. More recently, when the United Farm Workers undertook an organizing campaign among workers on the mechanical tomato harvester machines, growers quickly turned to electronic sorting to reduce their labor requirements (Schuering and Thompson, 1978).

Social mobility has characterized agricultural employment as the agricultural class structure began to differentiate and some farmers began to be employers. In the early phases of differentiation, agricultural workers saw themselves on the equivalent of a "job ladder" in which they began their careers as workers, accumulated small capital, and began farm operations of their own. The conception of farm labor as a way station on the road to some other activity changed as farm workers found that there was really not very much of a job ladder in agriculture. Indeed, the job ladder was directed *outside* of agriculture since agricultural employment became defined as being at the bottom of the occupational structure.[6]

In different periods in U.S. history, mobility out of agriculture, while profound, also was involuntary. This process occurred, for example, in Southern agriculture with the massive out-migration of blacks after the turn of the century. Movement of blacks was accelerated and a similar movement on the part of white agriculturists became notable during the 1930s when the introduction of tractors reshaped Southern agriculture. As farmers (and farm workers) learned there was little future within agriculture, they turned to other channels of mobility off the farm and contributed to the massive rural-to-urban shift that has characterized the U.S. in the past century. Workers became more concerned with escaping agriculture than with dealing with internal conditions. Accordingly, the structure of social mobility contributed to the retardation of consciousness.

Geographical mobility of farm workers has also contributed to blocking the development of collective consciousness. Thus, Taylor and Kerr (1940) noted, in their study of the San Joaquin Valley cotton strike of 1933, that an essential tactic in facilitating the strike and in strengthening consciousness and identification with the union was to physically concentrate strikers in their own "concentration camps." The physical dispersion of farm workers over space is but one part of their geographical mobility; in addition, many farm workers must move with the crops, as noted earlier, either from a single base or as migrants. Physical mobility is significant in delaying the development of consciousness since workers are insufficiently proximate to one another to develop solidaristic relations necessary for consciousness formation.

Historically, the IWW overcame geographical mobility and dispersion by establishing a degree of control over the means of communication available to the migratory workers of the time. Wobbly organizers utilized the railways and the "jungle camps" around railway junctions as a means to reach the worker "hobos" of the period. The capacity of the Wobblies to spread the word through the railways and the jungles about free speech fights in such cities as Fresno and Spokane is well known. What is perhaps less known is that the IWW also maintained a degree of social control over the communications system by ensuring that hoboing Wobblies could travel with some security over the rails.[7] If the IWW could not control the movements of its members, since mobility was a fact of life for many Western Wobblies in agriculture, the organization could resolve its communications problems by exercising an informal dominion over the transportation network.

At a later stage, Cesar Chavez recognized geographical mobility as a major obstacle toward organizing farm workers. Perhaps accidentally, perhaps deliberately, when he began to organize workers into the National Farm Workers Association (NFWA), Chavez worked amongst grape workers in the Delano area. One characteristic of these grape workers is that they are largely nonmigratory. Most lived in one place, made their homes there, and had stabilized family and social relationships. Thus, Chavez' organizing activities not only did not have to overcome the dilemma of geographical mobility but focused on the homogeneity of the Delano workers in ethnic background, skill levels, and experience.

While geographical mobility contributes to delaying the development of group consciousness, it does not do so in all situations. One category of workers regularly involved in migration who manifest high levels of solidarity are lettuce harvest workers (Friedland, Barton, and Thomas, 1978: 33–35). In this case, workers follow the harvest *as crews* and maintain stable social relationships over time. Thus, the form of geographical migration can contribute or impede the development of group consciousness. This fact came to be recognized in 1970 when the United Farm Workers Union began organizing lettuce workers after lettuce growers signed sweetheart agreements with the Teamsters Union (Friedland and Thomas, 1974). The UFW quickly developed a powerful base of support among harvest workers that continued to be strongly manifested in the 1979 strike of lettuce workers.

Racial and ethnic heterogeneity long played a part in impeding group consciousness, although this factor has perhaps decreased in significance in recent years. Particularly in the situation in which workers must migrate, it is understandable that forms of solidarity based on family and kinship, ethnic similarity, and traditional social forms such as *compadrazco* will be important. To attempt to develop solidarity with other workers with whom one is briefly in contact for a short harvest period, and to attempt to translate such solidarity into attempts at organizing would be foolish.

Because the agricultural labor force has been notably heterogeneous, not only by virtue of its movement patterns in migration but in its ethnic and racial makeup, it is unsurprising that these factors have played a role in hindering the development of any forms of consciousness.

IV. STRUCTURAL CHANGE IN AGRICULTURAL PRODUCTION

Despite the many factors that have been adduced as impediments to the development of consciousness, structural changes in agricultural production have created the preconditions for the development of some forms of consciousness which are currently taking organized form through unionism. Here we will briefly deal with these changes before examining the forms of worker consciousness.

The major sectors of agricultural production within which structural change is occurring are in large-scale production of fruit and vegetable crops. This production sector is concentrated in four states: California, Arizona, Texas, and Florida. Several other states, however, show similar trends in fruit and vegetable production including Ohio, Michigan, New Jersey, Oregon, and Washington. Unsurprisingly, it is within all of these states that some manifestation of union organizing can be noted.

The main structural changes leading to unionization, which are considered here to be an indicator of the development of consciousness, have to do with the growth of agribusiness and the increasing corporatization of large-scale agriculture. Following Morin (1952), we will examine some of the changed conditions that are giving rise to a new consciousness amongst farm workers:

1. While farm workers continue to constitute a very small segment of the labor force, the development of larger-scale agricultural enterprises tends to concentrate them geographically. Instead of workers being spread over thousands of small farms, they are physically located on smaller numbers of large enterprises. Thus, one condition of factory employment, with its concomitant, the plant gate, has begun to occur. This situation describes, in particular, the situation of a significant number of year-round permanent workers of the agribusiness enterprises in the West. It also applies, although to a lesser extent, to seasonal workers

who have developed regularized employment patterns with a number of agricultural employers. It applies least to seasonal workers whose employment is very irregular and other persons who find themselves in agricultural employment temporarily. Parenthetically it can be noted that the massive oversupply of agricultural workers that characterized Western agriculture for many decades has now ended; while some oversupply exists from time to time, in general the kind of oversupply found in the past has now ended.

2. The agricultural labor force has become more homogeneous in ethnic origin in the past two decades. Despite the presence of a wide variety of ethnic groups in California, for example, agricultural workers tend more to be Mexican in origin than ever before. The same is true of workers in Texas as well as workers that base themselves in Texas and move into the mid-continent migrant stream. In Florida, workers are more heterogeneous. Although largely of black origin, in the 1950s there began a continual infusion of Puerto Rican and Mexican workers.

Nationally, then, agricultural workers tend more to be Mexican by origin. Although the number of Mexican workers is increasing, internal differentiation exists among these workers. The Mexican-Americans are different from many of the Mexican nationals who are legally present in the United States. And both categories are *very* different from the undocumented workers illegally in the U.S. Thus, even if the agricultural labor force became totally "Mexicanized," it would not be completely homogeneous in orientation.

3. As production of crops becomes increasingly specialized, the skills of workers within a crop or constellation of crops tend to become more homogeneous. This homegeneity produces some structuring in the character of the labor market.

4. As capital investment in agribusiness increases, labor costs as a factor of production decrease. In such circumstances, agricultural employers, despite their detestation of unions, are prepared to deal with workers as an organized force as long as unions serve as a proper disciplinary device, stabilizing the labor force. This has the tendency to stabilize employment of workers and fix their location in space.

5. Increased mechanization produces significant changes in the structure of the labor force. One consequence is to reduce the number of workers required in the "flash-peak" of the harvest. This contributes to a reduction in the importance of labor as a *cost* factor. It also contributes to some structuring of the labor market, undoing the oversupply and "structurelessness" discussed by Fisher (1953) by requiring employers to have a guaranteed supply of experienced labor available at the crucial periods of

the production cycle. In some cases, mechanization contributes to the maintenance of an oversupply of labor; in other cases, it leads to situations in which a regularized, predictable, and reliable labor supply becomes exigent in maintaining production even if the skills of the workers involved are fairly low.

6. Employer opposition to unionism tends to diminish as the need for a guaranteed, rationalized, and stabilized labor force becomes clear. In addition, large-scale employers are more vulnerable to national publicity if they undertake the kind of union-busting that was once considered tolerable in localized circumstances with localized power elites.[8] Although legal harassment of unions remains notable in Western agriculture and a farm worker was killed during the 1979 UFW lettuce strike, the pattern of systematic brutality and coercion that marked earlier periods in agricultural unionism has declined somewhat.

7. One final change in agricultural labor relations should also be noted, despite being limited to a small number of states: the introduction of legislation mediating relations between workers and agricultural employers. There still is no federal legislation protective of the rights of agricultural workers to organize and, until 1975, only one state, Hawaii, provided such legislation on a statewide basis. In 1975, the adoption of the Agricultural Labor Relations Act in California represented a major shift. Because growers felt the California ALRA was biased in favor of the United Farm Workers Union, they hastened to introduce legislation protective of *their* interests in Arizona, Idaho, and Washington. The repercussions of the California events nationally should not be underestimated. Although the UFW has not favored coverage of agricultural workers under the National Labor Relations Act, the California legislation galvanized agricultural employers in California to endorse incorporation of agricultural workers within the scope of the Act. This has been because California employers feel themselves to be competitively disadvantaged with respect to growers in other states that have legislation that favors growers. These legislative changes mark a decline in the significance of the exceptionalism that has been so notable in U.S. agriculture for so long.

V. FORMS OF AGRICULTURAL WORKER CONSCIOUSNESS

With the structural changes that have occurred in agriculture, new forms of consciousness have begun to develop with agricultural workers. Three basic types of consciousness can be said to characterize agricultural workers. In considering the three types, the caveat made for all typologies should be emphasized: a typology is a subsuming of real life. Social reality occurs in less neat forms than occur in the scholarly typologizing. In addition, a typology does not reflect the fact that differential forms of consciousness can be present in the same population simultaneously, manifesting itself in varying behavior on different occasions dependent on situational contexts. Accordingly, the types presented here should be considered only that, *ideal types*, and real behavior as reflections of the forms of consciousness discussed can be variant from any of the suggested types.

The three types of consciousness can be equated to cells 1, 3, and 4 in Figure 1. The first, the consciousness of hopelessness and despair, describes cell 1, workers who are migratory and unspecialized. These are the workers who capture popular imagination when the term "farm worker" is used. They are represented not only by Steinbeck's Joads of *The Grapes of Wrath* but by real people in the Eastern migratory stream.

In cell 2 are the nonmigratory and nonspecialized workers. This cell constitutes a fairly heterogeneous grouping including workers such as some tomato harvesters, weeders, irrigators, and others. Included in this group are housewives and students who enter the agricultural labor force for varying time periods. The elucidation of their forms of consciousness is equally heterogeneous. Some of these workers, for example those who depend entirely upon agricultural wages for their livelihood or those for whom agricultural employment is an important part of their regular cycle of employment, will have different orientations toward employment than those that are only temporarily employed. Many students, for example, work for a summer or two in agricultural labor but have no long-term commitments to this form of employment. Some workers, therefore, will be oriented toward unionism or can be encouraged in this direction while others will be indifferent or hostile to anything viewed as interfering with plans for a summer of employment.

Cell 3 describes specialized migratory workers such as fruit tramps and lettuce harvesters. These workers manifest considerable solidarity that is usually limited to the immediate group(s) involved. Where consciousness takes organized form, it will be argued, this takes the form of *class* and *conflict*, often thrust on them by employers as they seek to deal with small-scale localized conditions.

Cell 4 refers to specialized and nonmigratory workers such as grape and citrus workers. Such workers find employment in crops requiring steady inputs of labor over much of the year. As a result, these workers experience a common life condition that is broader and involves more people than is found amongst the migratory, specialized workers. Consciousness accordingly is based on the generalizability of their life circumstances.

Organizing efforts have been attempted with all four types of workers but, it will be argued, it is only with the growth of the specialized types (cells 3 and 4) that success in union organizing has occurred. An attempt was made, for example, to organize unspecialized migrants in the early 1960s by the CIO's Agricultural Workers Organizing Committee. This attempt failed miserably (London and Anderson, 1970: chapter 3). Similarly, the United Farm Workers (UFW) sought to organize tomato harvesters unsuccessfully in 1975.

Historically, most attempts at unionization have been directed at migratory workers having some degree of specialization. These are the workers with whom Jamieson (1945) has particularly dealt. The lettuce workers in the 1979 UFW strike also fall into this category. But the most unusual form of organizing, it will be argued, was that developed by Cesar Chavez to organize grape workers in the Delano (California) area in the early 1960s. Chavez' approach was based on the consciousness of common life circumstances and was successful in building a base on which the present UFW emerged.

A. The Consciousness of Hopelessness and Frustration

Agricultural workers may be at the bottom of the social structure but, like most human beings, they are neither unintelligent nor unaware of social realities. Being an agricultural worker is not, for most workers, a matter of choice but is often a product of desperation or a conscious determination to utilize this form of labor as a springboard to other activities. It was this form of consciousness which mainly characterized the black migrant agricultural workers studied by Friedland and Nelkin (1971) in New York State and New Jersey.[9]

Most black migrants considered their life situation to be relatively hopeless. With a realistic perception of their vulnerability to employers and the depredations of their crew leaders, their tendency was to accept the inevitable, whether the inevitable constituted bad weather, a delayed season, the crew leader's deductions from paychecks as well as his recordkeeping (and cheating).

The expressions of this form of consciousness took the form of tendencies towards alcoholism, notable for most of the migrants, and the tentativeness and instability of interpersonal relations. Migrants recognized that they had no social meaning in the world beyond the labor camp; for most, the external society was an anomaly characterized by a lack of predictability into which one ventured only when necessary.

Three forms of adaptive behavior sought to grapple with the hopelessness manifested in daily life. First, migrants would individually give way to tension-releasing activities from time to time, often directed at other migrants but occasionally at a more appropriate source. This form of tension release often took verbal form as with "playing the dozens" (Friedland and Nelkin, 1971: 158–159). Another form of verbal release occurred in jokes and story telling. In an analysis of sixty-five jokes and 148 stories that were collected during field study, Lillian Trager noted that the largest single category of jokes involved "putdowns," in which some person was denigrated, and the most frequent category of stories involved "environmental manipulation," in which the story teller got away with something, escaped a dangerous situation, or beat the system in some way (Friedland and Nelkin, 1971: 153).

The second most important form of grappling with hopelessness was dropping out. For many migrants the trip North was a way to remove themselves from the South and from Florida to a Northern environment and have the crew leader bear the transportation costs. Thus, the arrival of a crew in camp was often marked by immediate disappearance of some crew members while others would wait a week or two to earn a few dollars to carry them over when they deserted the camp. For others, dropping out often was a measure of desperation undertaken because earnings were so limited. All to frequently, because of the delayed or short seasons or the debts owed the crew leader, workers had little or no cash at the end of the week. Movement out of the camp, under these circumstances, was a measure of genuine desperation because workers often had only vague notions of where they were located and had no idea about how to find work elsewhere.

The third form of adaptation occurred relatively infrequently but was found: attempts at organization. Organization occurred, from time to time, spontaneously as workers found themselves being cheated or were put to work in a field for a second or third picking that would be so bad that it would not be worth the effort given the incentive method of payment. Action was *spontaneous* in that workers would refuse to undertake the job or would walk away from it. In most of the cases noted, there was no leadership in these actions nor was there any long or conscious deliberation; a *conscience collectif* manifested itself in a common agreement that no further work should be undertaken. Another form of organizing, but limited to the Florida context, consisted of organizing attempts by a union with accompanying strikes. Here, outside organizers established contact with workers and triggered some kind of job action. No such attempts were found in the North during the time the field study was conducted. A third form of organization was found on only a single occasion and probably represents a deviant case: this was the situation in which the bulk of one crew consisted of workers who were affiliated with a religious group. While the "Church of A to Z" had no formal relationship to the crew, the crew leader, the crew influentials, and many workers belonged to it. In this case, the operation of the crew was significantly different from that found in other migrant labor crews (Friedland and Nelkin, 1971: 237–242).

While these attempts at organizational forms were notable, the prevailing conditions of most black migrants was characterized by hopelessness. Note should be taken, however, of the variations found in a study of Eastern agricultural workers from Jamaica (Foner and Napoli, 1978) who contrasted sharply with the black workers studied by Friedland and Nelkin (1971). The Jamaicans were more confident of themselves and undertook migratory labor in a pattern that fitted with their lives at home. While no studies are available, it would appear that Puerto Rican migrant agricultural workers in the East did not fall into the same kind of hopelessness found amongst black workers. For them, agricultural labor fitted into planned patterns with respect to what they regarded to be their permanent lives in Puerto Rico. Consciousness under these circumstances is circumscribed by the delineation of the agricultural activity as deviant, special, different, but not fundamentally related to the basic pattern of life lived elsewhere, e.g., outside of agricultural labor in the United States.

B. The Consciousness of Class and Conflict

The major form of consciousness that has emerged historically amongst farm workers is consciousness generated through the process of conflict. While agricultural workers lead lives of serious deprivation, as with workers in many other occupational and historical contexts, they undertake to organize themselves for job actions and into unions and, just as frequently, they are the object of external organizers determined to make a contribution to working-class history through farm worker organization.

The forms of consciousness generated through conflict are many. Often, the tendency on the part of scholars studying farm workers' conflict is to come to the conclusion that any firm *class* orientations are products of external agitators or organizers. Taking a position similar to that of Perlman (1949), this analysis holds that, where farm workers do undertake organization on their own, it will be limited to strict economism, e.g., trade unionism and its economic objectives. But, as Jamieson has noted: "Many of the largest, most violent, and most ruinous strikes during the thirties occurred among nonunion workers" (1945: 408).

This point should perhaps be emphasized and underlined. In fact, while unions are not inherently pacifist and are willing to utilize violence, that violence is usually more controlled and directed than violence occurring amongst unorganized workers (or most unorganized bodies). Organization not only provides discipline but normally includes decision-making structures that place violent action within limiting constraints. In contrast, where organization does not exist, when groups form to deal with their dissatisfaction, the concept of limits is undeveloped. In this respect, the absence of organization has greater potential for revolutionary action than exists in cases where organization exists.[10]

Most "normal" organizing, therefore, takes the form of the organizing group, if there is one. In the IWW period, the group consciousness of Wobbly agricultural workers reflected the syndicalist spontaneism of the IWW. In the 1930s, organizing under the ideological camopy of the Communist party produced a more controlled form of organization characterized by simplistic class consciousness. The primitiveness of this consciousness level was often a reflection not only of the state of consciousness of workers but of what the Communist party expected of the workers. Later, as the CIO began organizing farm workers, it reflected traditional, "normal" economism of mainstream US unionism, focused on wages but characterized by a heavy orientation toward militancy dictated by the harsh conditions under which agricultural workers were being organized.

We will return to a final assessment of the consciousness of conflict in the concluding section as we turn to an examination of the forms of consciousness against the theoretical discussion earlier in this chapter.

C. The Consciousness of Life Condition[11]

The preceding discussion of the consciousness of conflict has deliberately eschewed a discussion of the forms of consciousness manifested by agricultural workers in the most recent period, e.g., the organizing effort of Cesar Chavez in California that began in the early 1960s. Although Chavez' organizing reflects, in recent years, the consciousness of conflict, it will be contended that his earliest approach to organizing represents a different form of consciousness still residually present in the present-day manifestations of farm worker unionism, the United Farm Workers (UFW).

The essential thesis is that early Chavez organizing represents an invention of a new social form based on a conceptualization of a form of consciousness different from that traditionally present either in union or community organizing, the latter tradition being the one in which Chavez was trained. This form of consciousness will be referred to here as the consciousness of life condition.

Chavez' personal history is often misunderstood by those who have not examined his work or his organizing efforts carefully. Contrary to popular belief, Chavez never was trained by Saul Alinsky nor did he follow an essentially Alinskyist trajectory in his organizational work. Chavez had his organizational experience in the Community Services Organization (CSO), a Mexican-American community organization concentrated in California among urban Chicanos. CSO reflected the influence of Fred

Ross who was trained by Alinsky. Thus, if Chavez was "Alinsky-trained" it was in the second generation.

In fact, what has characterized Fred Ross' approach to organizing has been variant from that employed by his teacher. Where Alinsky's base theory rests on fundamental Marxist assumptions about conflict, Ross emerged as a master scenarist of organizing, but paid little attention to conflict.

The Alinsky theory of organizing functions on two basic assumptions. The first is that there is an elite structure that utilizes material resources to benefit itself and exploit vulnerable social strata. Alinsky's strategy that flows from this assumption is to create the conditions in which the community becomes polarized so that the elite reveal themselves and the structure of control. It was for this reason that Alinsky, as he became a national figure in the 1960s, utilized himself as a key instrumentality in producing community polarization. By interjecting himself only after a long introductory, money-raising period, Alinsky sought, in an abrasive way, to get the community elite to reveal itself as hostile to any organizing by poor people. The second basic assumption made by Alinsky rests on a belief that much indigenous organization exists in any poor community and the problem of the organizer is to mobilize these indigenous forms.

Chavez' form of organizing stands both of Alinsky's assumptions on their heads, but particularly the first. It is not that Chavez denied the existence of conflict; rather it was that Chavez was very aware of what conflict had produced in earlier farm worker organizing and therefore explicitly avoided a conflict orientation. With conflict to be avoided, Chavez began his organizational activities with the assumption that farm workers experienced a common life condition, having many needs that were not normally satisfied in everyday life.

Farm worker needs were highly varied but they originated in the common life circumstance of being a farm worker. Thus, all farm workers experienced financial needs because their income was not only uncertain but concentrated. There were periods of considerable employment with wages coming in regularly and other periods, fairly lengthy, without employment or income. Similarly, farm workers experienced considerable financial difficulties whenever death obtruded. Dying is expensive and throws an exceptionally heavy burden on a family, particularly since death is often unexpected. Another special characteristic of the group Chavez set out to organize was that these workers were relatively self-reliant in finding employment and did not depend very much on labor contractors. Thus, finding and traveling to work was undertaken by workers themselves, and they therefore needed to have and to maintain their own cars.

One element common to all workers Chavez set out to organize was that they were of Mexican extraction, heavily under the influence of Catholicism, strongly family-oriented with a dominant male heading the family.

Chavez' organizational strategy was built on the recognition of these common factors. Thus, far from building upon a conflict assumption, Chavez began with what sociologists familiar with Durkheim might call the *conscience collectif.*

And although certainly without knowledge of Durkheimian theory, Chavez sought to develop organization based on the consciousness of life condition. In so doing, Chavez flouted the second assumption made by Alinsky about the existence of indigenous organization. In contrast, Chavez appears to have assumed that the movement from Mexico to the United States, while leaving some residual cultural elements intact, had left farm workers relatively isolated in the social structure. Indeed, they did not have access to the normal institutional arrangements that fulfilled the needs of other Americans. When someone died, this constituted a catastrophe to the family. Other people had access to financial reserves or to banks to deal with economic uncertainties. Farm workers did not have this access. Nor did they have much access to the kinds of services necessary to sustain their existence as workers, particularly with respect to movement to employment in their own vehicles.

The Chavez approach to organizing set out to create organization to *fill these common needs* while explicitly avoiding conflict. Chavez recognized that a movement organizing *against* employers would bring their traditional hostility and power down on the heads of the workers. Thus, Chavez organized to resolve the needs of workers as a result of life condition. This took the form of dealing with specific needs of farm workers, building one organization after another: a death benefit society, a credit union, a gas station.

To get a better idea of Chavez' implicit social theory, it is worth noting his orientation toward food and the social obligations that the giving of food provides. No anthropologist, to my knowledge, ever had to explain to Chavez the importance of commensality. But Chavez' instinctive approach was to use the need for food as an organizing tool to develop the bonds of solidarity:

> We didn't have any money at all in those days, none for gas and hardly any for food. So I went to people and started asking for food. It turned out to be the best thing I could have done, although at first it's hard on your pride. Some of the best members came in that way. If people give you their food, they'll give you their hearts (Chavez, 1966).

Although not cognizant of exchange theory, Chavez recognized that he was undertaking an obligation to a farm worker family by asking for food. The occasion became one in which a long discussion began in the house about the union and Chavez notes that this family became one of the cadre elements of the NFWA.

What can be seen in Chavez' approach is distinctly different from the organizing that characterizes Alinsky or Chavez' organizing activities at a later stage. What Chavez did, in theoretical terms, was to develop an implicitly Durkheimian theory of organizing not by explicitly delineating the enemy but by developing bonds of solidarity, singly: each bond reinforcing the other.

One final point can be noted that emphasizes the different approach Chavez took to farm worker organizing: the name of the organization he created at this stage was the National Farm Workers *Association* (NFWA). It was not until much later that the word "union" became part of the name of the organization.

The change in the organization was initiated and its move to explicit trade unionism became clear only after the strike of grape workers was brought to the Delano (California) area by a strike of Filipino workers begun earlier in the Coachella Valley in 1965. NFWA members were confronted by the dilemma of crossing the picket lines of the striking Filipinos, then organized by the CIO in the Agricultural Workers Organizing Committee (AWOC). When the picket lines were recognized, Chavez and the NFWA rapidly moved into the leadership of the strike. However, Chavez has stated on many occasions his reluctance to become involved, feeling that strike activity was still premature for the young NFWA.

From this point on, the organization began to shift and Chavez' organizing strategies became more mixed, reflecting the heterogeneity of his organization (now with a heavy admixture of Filipino workers), the stronger union attachments, and more of a class conflict orientation. But even during the crucial days of the grape strikes of the 1960s, Chavez maintained a heavy emphasis on cultural orientations appropriate to earlier *conscience collectif* organizing. This was particularly the case with his insistence on nonviolence, an orientation with few roots in the history of American labor. While nonviolence may also have been tactically wise, it represented a common viewpoint that many farm workers of Mexican origin experienced and felt *at the time*. It is perhaps notable that, a decade later, in the 1979 lettuce strike, which has involved violence, Chavez has not taken the strong stance on nonviolence that formerly characterized his approach. The transition to trade unionism and to trade union consciousness now appears to be completed.[12]

VI. CONCLUSION

Given the types of consciousness that have been claimed to appear amongst farm workers, what can be said about the different theoretical interpretations of consciousness that have been drawn from Lenin and Perlman?

Initially we can note that there is less of a contradiction between Lenin and Perlman than appears on the surface. Of course, there are profound and vital differences between the two in the inferences drawn from their respective theoretical analyses since Lenin develops a theory of organizing vitally different from Perlman's. What Perlman failed to acknowledge and Lenin recognized was the raw, primal power implicit in spontaneous organization. In a sense, Lenin also missed this point although in a different way. For Lenin, the raw masses, undisciplined by working-class organization, manifest their dissatisfactions with exploitation through periodic blowups. For Lenin, however, these eruptions are easily misled, deflected, or culminate in orgies of destruction without taking appropriate *political* form. Thus, for Lenin, working-class rebellion is not the equivalent of revolution since it does not, by itself, overthrow the existing class structure (which constitutes the classical Marxian definition of *revolution*). To produce change in the class organization of society, a more consciously organized and deliberate force, the party, is necessary.

Lenin's views, of course, follow in the Marxian tradition and resuscitate the older debate between Marx and Bakunin over spontaneity and organization. There exists a long and well-developed tradition having to do with consciousness and revolutionary activity. The primal power of the masses, unfettered by close-knit organization, was understood by Luxemburg (1971) and Trotsky (1971). But the enduring character of vanguard organization remains pre-eminent in the minds of many scholars of revolution.

The argument has been amplified recently by Piven and Cloward (1977) who have taken Michels' precept: "Who says organization says oligarchy (1949: 401)" and developed an analysis of the restraints that organization sets on the raw power of the poor as they move into action. Piven and Cloward (1977) also devote attention to the cyclical character of working-class action, noting that such action is neither constant nor regularized.

What can be drawn from these various analyses, as applied to agricultural workers, is that the forms of consciousness can be highly varied, depending on situational contexts, organizational circumstances, and the degree of collective response at a given moment. Most workers (or poor people or students or anyone else for that matter) confronted by hundreds of police armed with guns, rifles, tear gas, helicopters, mace, and other accoutrements of "social control," exercise hesitation about "seizing state power." But when there are lots of "us" as compared to "them" and we can see that "they" are wavering, the possibilities of profound transformations of the social order come flooding into our "collective" minds.

Thus, agricultural workers, like workers everywhere, experience a variety of forms of consciousness. The particular expressions will be a function of context and organization. One contextual factor producing trends toward class and conflict consciousness rests on the factor of *the organizer*. In the 1930s, for example, a key organization attempting to organize farm workers was the Communist-party-led cannery and agricultural workers unions. With the CP acting as organizer, it is not surprising that a class-conflict orientation was manifested by workers. But this is only one contextual factor contributing to the development of a class consciousness and all that accompanies it.

A second, and probably even more important factor, is the approach that employers take to organizing attempts of workers. Where agricultural employers attempt, as in California in the 1930s to meet worker organization with clubs, cops, and injunctions, it is not surprising that workers move toward a conflict position; after all, little leeway has been left them to develop other approaches.

On a similar note, it is worth noting that Chavez' original approach to organizing was not oriented toward conflict but toward reinforcing tendencies toward solidarity based on common needs. However, the forms of organization were driven toward conflict, not by anything Chavez undertook at the time but by the movement of the strike of Filipino grape workers into the Delano area. Subsequently, when Chavez moved to organize lettuce workers he shifted from the group he had originally targeted for organization after the grape workers were organized, the citrus workers. The UFW was drawn into organizing lettuce workers when their needs and feelings were overrun by lettuce growers desperate to avoid dealing with Chavez and willing to sign sweetheart agreements with the Teamsters Union. As the lettuce workers came into the UFW, the nature of the organization began to change.

Thus what characterized the UFW during the period of grape organization (1967–1970) was less the strike and more the boycott; what characterizes the union in 1979, despite threats of the boycott, is the strike. The boycott represented a continuation of the form of consciousness of life condition geared at urban and liberal masses and calling for relatively light sacrifices. It was less directed at a conflict orientation, despite what managers of supermarkets confronting UFW pickets may say, than the kinds of actions that characterize the union picket line. The form of consciousness that characterizes the base of the UFW, therefore, has shifted since its constituency has changed from grape workers to lettuce harvesters.

This paper has sought to relate the forms of consciousness found amongst agricultural workers to the specific processes of production in which they are involved. It has been argued that the development of a detailed understanding of farm worker consciousness requires the differentiation of this population into different types. Such differentiation provides the opportunity for understanding the various forms of consciousness, and organization, that have appeared from time to time and that exist currently.

ACKNOWLEDGMENTS

A short version of this paper was read to the 1979 annual meeting of the Rural Sociological Society. This paper has benefited from the critical comments of Amy Barton, Anne Fredricks, Robert J. Thomas, and the Editors.

NOTES

1. Problems exist with the determination of the size of the agricultural labor force. While enumeration of farmers may be fairly accurate, there are indications that the number of workers is much higher than reported. Many agricultural workers, particularly in the West, are undocumented, e.g., illegally in the United States. These workers, similar to minorities in urban centers, are persistently underenumerated.

2. Watson (1977) has also written a paper on fruit tramps in the lettuce industry. This study deals with Anglo workers who specialized in packing (not harvesting) lettuce in the 1930s.

3. In the past decade or so, Friedland and Nelkin (1971), Nelkin (1971), Ruel (1972), and Foner and Napoli (1978) have written about agricultural workers in the East. Provinzano (1971) has studied Midwestern farm workers. Peterson (1969), Mintz (1971), and Barton (1978) have provided material on the West.

4. The relationship of intellectuals to masses remains a central problematic not only for Marxists but for others. Gramsci (1971, 5–23) addressed the issue of the organic intellectuals and Mao Tse-tung had to resolve their relations to the masses in the formulation of the "mass line." See Mao's writings during the 1942–1944 period (Mao, 1967: vol. III), especially "Economic and Financial Problems in the Anti-Japanese War (December 1942) and "Some Questions Concerning Methods of Leadership" (June 1943). Selden (1971, chapter 5) provides an excellent summary of this question. This subject was an issue to Pareto (1968) in his discussion of "foxes" and preoccupied Weber (1946).

5. The following discussion has been drawn heavily from Morin (1952) and Fisher (1953).

6. Thus, in a study of occupational prestige hierarchies, Hodge, et al., (1964) found that farmhand occupied the same occupational level as a janitor and was only slightly more prestigious than a soda fountain clerk.

7. Joe Murphy, a Wobbly organizer in the 1920s, in a personal communication, states that he participated in what was, in effect, an IWW police force that traveled the railways in small groups, flashing money rolls to provoke jack-rollers into attempting to rob the money-carriers. When the jack-roller made his move the other group members would move in, disarm him, and provide instant punishment.

8. Jenkins and Perrow (1977) argue that it is the changed importance of liberal urban populations and the mass media that has been responsible for the successful organization of farm workers (in the UFW) after so many decades of failure. See also Jenkins 1975.

9. The material reported for the Eastern states is included here, even though conditions in the East are different from those in the West. Western material similar to that found in the East, however, is available even though it is less systematically presented.

10. Thus Uldricks (1974) notes, in the Russian Revolution of 1917, the significant role played by the *buntarstvo*—the primitive peasant elements, new to the factory system and drafted into industrial employment as the older proletarian elements were drafted into the Russian army. The *buntarstvo* were important precisely because they had not yet absorbed the discipline of the factory or of workers' organizations. As they took to the streets, they introduced a raw and primal power which had, in fact, revolutionary consequences. A similar argument about the constraining influence of organization has also been made by Piven and Cloward (1977).

11. In developing the arguments in this section, I have depended heavily on reports provided by participant-observers of Alinsky organizing, in particular, Jay Schulman, and Chavez organizing, particularly by Jerry Brown and Juanita Brown. Brown (1972) presents some of this material. The literature on Alinsky is not particularly good. He has, himself, described his organizing approaches in *Reveille For Radicals* (1969) and *Rules For Radicals* (1972). Silberman (1964) provides some useful material on Alinsky organizing but I found Schulman's oral reports far more insightful and have depended heavily on them. While considerable material has appeared on Chavez (for example, Dunne 1967; Matthiessen 1973; Taylor 1975; Levy 1975), much of it is hagiographic or uncritically polemical. A senior thesis by John Hartmire (1978) provides remarkable descriptive details on the early period of Chavez organizing. Friedland and Thomas (1974) present a somewhat different view of the UFW than is commonly found in the literature. The author is presently working on a more detailed comparison of Alinsky and Chavez organizing approaches and their theoretical bases.

12. This discussion of Chavez' approach to organizing has dealt exclusively with the early phase of development of the National Farm Workers Association. I have not sought to examine Chavez' organizational approaches in later phases which are *very different* from the early period. The organizing of urban liberal populations for boycotts, the capacity to mobilize liberal and radical Anglo intellectuals for work in urban settings, all constitute an important part of UFW history and of Chavez' changed orientations. Limitations of space preclude their development here.

REFERENCES

Alinsky, Saul D.
   1969   Reveille for Radicals. New York: Vintage.
   1972   Rules for Radicals. New York: Vintage.
Barton, Amy E.
   1978   Campesinas: Women Farm Workers in the California Agricultural Labor Force. Sacramento, Calif.: California Commission on The Status of Women.
Brown, Jerald Barry
   1972   The United Farm Workers Grape Strike and Boycott, 1965–1970: An Evaluation of the Culture of Poverty Theory. Ph.D. Dissertation, Latin American Studies Program, Cornell University.
Chavez, Cesar
   1966   "The Organizer's Tale." In Staughton Lynd (ed.), American Labor Radicalism. New York: Wiley.
Dunne, John Gregory
   1967   Delano: The Story of the California Grape Strike. New York: Farrar, Strauss and Giroux.
Fisher, Lloyd H.
   1953   The Harvest Labor Market in California. Cambridge, Mass.: Harvard University Press.

Foner, Nancy, and Richard Napoli
1978   "Jamaican and Black American Migrant Farm Workers: A Comparative Analysis." Social Problems 25: 491–503.
Friedland, William H.
1969   "Labor Waste in New York: Rural Exploitation and Migrant Workers." Transaction 6: 48–53.
Friedland, William H., and Amy E. Barton
1975   Destalking the Wily Tomato: A Case Study in Social Consequences in California Agricultural Research. Davis, Calif.: Dept. of Applied Behavioral Sciences, University of California. Research Monograph No. 15.
Friedland, William H., Amy E. Barton, and Robert J. Thomas
1978   Manufacturing Green Gold: The Conditions and Social Consequences of Lettuce Harvest Mechanization. Davis, Calif.: Dept. of Applied Behavioral Sciences, University of California. California Agricultural Policy Seminar Monograph No. 2.
Friedland, William H., and Dorothy Nelkin
1971   Migrant: Agricultural Workers in America's Northeast. New York: Holt, Rinehart and Winston.
1972   "Technological Trends and the Organization of Migrant Farm Workers." Social Forces 19: 509–521.
Friedland, William H., and Robert J. Thomas
1974   "Paradoxes of Agricultural Unionism in California." Society May-June: 54–56.
Galarza, Ernesto
1964   Merchants of Labor: The Mexican Bracero Story. Santa Barbara, Calif.: McNally and Loftin.
1977   Farm Workers and Agri-business in California, 1947–1960. Notre Dame, Ind.: University of Notre Dame Press.
Gramsci, Antonio
1971   Prison Notebooks. New York: International Publishers.
Hartmire, John W.
1978   Farm Worker Organizing as a Social Movement. Senior sociology thesis, Dept. of Sociology, University of California, Santa Cruz.
Hodge, Robert W., Paul M. Siegel, and Peter H. Rossi
1964   "Occupational Prestige in the United States, 1925–1963." American Journal of Sociology 70: 286–302.
Jamieson, Stuart
1945   Labor Unionism in American Agriculture. Washington, D.C.: Government Printing Office, Bulletin 836.
Jenkins, J. Craig
1975   Farm Workers and the Powers: Farm Workers' Insurgency (1946–1972). Ph.D. Dissertation, Department of Sociology, State University of New York, Stony Brook.
Jenkins, J. Craig, and Charles Perrow
1977   "Insurgency of the Powerless: Farm Worker Movements (1946–1972)." American Sociological Review 42: 249–268.
Lenin, V. I.
1943   What Is To Be Done? In Selected Works, Vol. 2. New York: International Publishers.
Levy, Jacques
1975   Cesar Chavez: Autobiography of La Causa. New York: Norton.
London, Joan, and Henry Anderson
1970   So Shall Ye Reap. New York: Crowell.
Luxemburg, Rosa
1971   The Mass Strike. New York: Harper & Row.

Marx, Karl, and Frederick Engels
   1976 The German Ideology. In Collected Works, Vol. 5. New York: International Publishers.
Matthiessen, Peter
   1973 Sal Si Puedes: Cesar Chavez and the New American Revolution. New York: Dell.
Mao Tse-Tung
   1967 Selected Works. Peking: Foreign Language Press.
Michels, Robert
   1949 Political Parties. Glencoe, Ill.: Free Press.
Mintz, Warren
   1971 A Search for a Successful Agricultural Migrant: A Study of Five Fruit Harvests on the West Coast of the United States. Ph.D. Dissertation, New York University, University Microfilms.
Morin, Alexander
   1952 The Organizability of Farm Labor in the United States. Cambridge, Mass.: Harvard University Press. Harvard Studies in Labor in Agriculture, No. 2-HL.
Nelkin, Dorothy
   1971 On the Stream: Aspects of the Migrant Labor System. Ithaca, N. Y.: New York State School of Industrial and Labor Relations.
Newby, Howard
   1972 "Agricultural Workers in the Class Structure." Sociological Review 20: 413–439.
Pareto, Vilfredo
   1968 The Rise and Fall of the Elites: An Application of Theoretical Sociology. Totowa, N. J.: Bedminster.
Perlman, Selig
   1949 A Theory of the Labor Movement. New York: Augustus M. Kelley.
Peterson, Cheryl
   1969 The California Farm Labor Force: A Profile. Report published for the Assembly Committee on Agriculture by its Advisory Committee on Farm Labor Research with the assistance of the California Department of Employment.
Piven, Frances Fox, and Richard A. Cloward
   1977 Poor People's Movements: Why They Succeed, How They Fail. New York: Pantheon.
Provinzano, James
   1971 Chicano Migrant Farm Workers in a Rural Wisconsin County. Ph.D. Dissertation, University of Minnesota, University Microfilms.
Ruel, Myrtle R.
   1972 The Migration Episode and its Consequences. East Lansing, Mich.: Michigan State University, Center for Rural Manpower and Public Affairs.
Selden, Mark
   1971 The Yenan Way in Revolutionary China. Cambridge, Mass.: Harvard University Press.
Schuering, Ann F., and O. E. Thompson
   1978 From Lug Boxes to Electronics: A Study of California Tomato Growers and Sorting Crews. Davis, Calif.: Dept. of Applied Behavioral Sciences, University of California. California Agriculture Policy Seminar Monograph No. 3.
Silberman, Charles E.
   1964 Crisis in Black and White. New York: Vintage.
Taylor, Paul S., and Clark Kerr
   1940 "Documentary History of the Strike of Cotton Pickers in California, 1933." Hearings before a Subcommittee of the Committee on Education and Labor, U.S. Senate, 76th Congress, 3rd Session (The LaFollette hearings).

Taylor, Ronald B.
    1975   Chavez and the Farm Workers. Boston: Beacon.
Trotsky, Leon
    1971   1905. New York: Vintage.
Uldrichs, Teddy J.
    1974   "The 'Crowd' in the Russian Revolution: Toward Reassessing the Nature of
           Revolutionary Leadership." Politics and Society 4: 611–623.
Watson, Don
    1977   "Rise and Decline of Fruit Tramp Unionism in the Western Lettuce Industry."
           Paper prepared for the Southwest Labor Studies Conference, Tempe, Arizona,
           March 4.
Weber, Max
    1946   Essays in Sociology. H. H. Gerth and C. Wright Mills, Ed. and Trans. New York:
           Oxford.

LABOR FORCE INTEGRATION
AND SOUTHERN U. S. TEXTILE
UNIONISM

Richard L. Simpson

The labor movement has made little headway among Southern U. S.
textile workers. Probably no more than a fifth of them, if that many, have
ever been paid-up union members.* The long record of union failure is so
well known that its causes have been a routine subject of speculation in
Southern newspapers. Scholars and union officials have ruminated about
them but have not reached consensus.

Analysts of textile union weakness have suggested possible reasons
that fall into four general categories: management control and repression,
characteristics of workers, characteristics of the industry, and characteristics of the unions. These kinds of explanation are not mutually exclusive. All might be valid and none alone sufficient. Our aim is to summarize
and evaluate them and to propose a broader perspective than can sub-

Research in the Sociology of Work, Volume 1, pages 381–401
Copyright © 1981 by JAI Press Inc.
All rights of reproduction in any form reserved.
ISBN: 0-89232-124-5

sume many of their insights: *labor force integration*. Labor force integration is the ways in which members of a labor force are integrated into community and work-based social structures, and the ways in which these structures interpenetrate one another. Differing forms of labor force integration help to explain unionism or its absence. Our focus is on Southern textiles but the discussion will refer selectively to other industries for contrast, chiefly to coal mining and steel manufacturing.

I. MANAGEMENT REPRESSION AND CONTROL

Management practices ranging from the subtle social controls of mill-village life to extremely repressive measures are often cited to explain the weakness of Southern textile unionism.

A. Anti-Union Strategies and Tactics

Managements have used an impressive array of weapons against unions. Companies have fired union activists. Firms are said to have cooperated in well-organized blacklists so that a worker fired from one mill could not get a job in another. The National Guard has been sent to the scenes of strikes in the classic manner of its use in American labor disputes. Law officers have arrested union organizers on trumped-up charges. In one instance reported to the author, a North Georgia sheriff invited a startled new organizer to get acquainted at a local tavern. Two sips into his first beer, the organizer was arrested for public drunkenness and told that the charges would be dropped if he was out of the county by the next morning. He was and they were. In a company-owned village, it is easy to use the law as a weapon: strikers can be evicted from company houses (Pope, 1942: 250), and an organizer who visits workers is trespassing on company property (Herring, 1949: 66).

Managements have threatened to shut down mills permanently to punish workers for voting unions in. Occasionally they actually have done so, as in Darlington, South Carolina in 1957. News of this kind of action spreads fast. It can have a chilling effect on the appeal of unions all across the region.

Extreme violence against unionists has been rare but not unknown. In Marion, North Carolina in 1937, police shot six strikers in the back.

A more benign strategy is to keep a close eye out for budding unionism and nip it by voluntarily raising wages. Workers then feel that a union is not worth the bother. Not many companies are that generous. Even without unions, textile manufacturing is among the least profitable American industries (Newspaper Enterprise Association, 1979: 109). Few of its firms have excess money to spend on higher wages unless forced to.

Roy (1965: 239–240) describes another benign tactic which he labels
"pseudo-paternalism" and union officials call "sweet stuff." Programs of
human relations in industry may fit this label. Less institutionalized forms
of sweet stuff include election-eve speeches, leaflets, and letters describing the harmony that exists and the company's plans to shower largesse
on employees.

If a union does win an election, the management may simply refuse to
bargain with it. In Roanoke Rapids, North Carolina, no contract had been
signed with a union five years after the National Labor Relations Board
certified it in 1974.

Coldblooded management tactics undoubtedly have hurt unionism in
Southern textiles, but they cannot wholly account for its weakness.
Managements elsewhere have tried them and failed. Savage repression
did not, in the end, stop unions in the coal mines of "Bloody Harlan"
County, Kentucky, the steel mills of Homestead, Pennsylvania, or many
other industries and places. For the labor movement to stay so feeble for
so long in textiles, other causes must have been at work.

B. Paternalism and the Mill Community

The social system of traditional textile mill communities is often in-
voked to explain why they have had so few unions. As the analysis goes,
the traditional mill owner's paternalism bred a childlike loyalty in his
workers, sapped their initiative, and made them unreceptive to unions.
Even those who were dissatisfied were conditioned to accept their fates
passively.

Much of the essence of Southern mill villages is captured in the old
rhyme that Roy (1965: 238) cites: "The mill by the rill and Uncle Ben on
the hill." The kindly Uncle Ben resembles the early New England shoe
manufacturers described by Warner and Low (1947: 134–139) in a discussion entitled "The Managers of Men Were Gods." But from the picture
one gets of traditional Southern mill towns, it appears that their paternalism was more thoroughgoing than Yankee City's. Some were near-total
institutions. Herring (1929, 1949) gives perhaps the fullest description.
Companies provided or subsidized workers' housing, trash collection,
electricity, police and fire protection, schools, churches, welfare services,
garden plots, recreational facilities, doctors, and nurses. They sponsored
athletic leagues, bands, Boy Scout troops, lodges, and assorted women's
and men's clubs. Workers bought food and other necessaries from company stores. Owners knew every employee personally, and workers went
to them for advice on family problems. Naturally, the managements ran
the town governments.

Several conditions fostered a Gemeinschaft atmosphere in mill villages and made them ripe for the imposition of a control system based on ecology, social structure, and culture. Many of them were geographically isolated. Nearly all were ethnically and culturally homogeneous; owners and workers alike were God-fearing Protestants of the same ancestral stock. Husband, wife, and children in a family commonly worked in the same mill, and the management turned to them to recommend their kin for new openings (Gilman, 1956: 272).

The management capitalized on these conditions to build an impressive set of controls over workers. Some controls were quite tangible, such as prohibiting saloons. Others operated in the minds of workers, who were apt to feel obligated to the owners for services rendered every hour of every day. Some owners deliberately used the mill villages to create a passive anti-union atmosphere. For others, the only apparent conscious motive was Christian duty or noblesse oblige. The owners' motives do not particularly matter. Their paternalism was a complex social structure that worked against unionism. The structure was self-perpetuating. It generated a culture that supported it. It prevented the growth of indigenous worker-controlled social structures that might form a basis of organized opposition to it (Herring, 1949: 114–117).

For workers who lived in such a place, nothing developed the habit of organizing for any collective purpose besides religion—and that only to a limited degree, for the management furnished money and leadership for the churches (Herring, 1929: 28–30; Pope, 1942: 36–48, 143–161). A management need not play rough against unions when its workers look up to it as a benefactor. It has little reason to fear that people who have never built any kind of organization will organize themselves into a labor union.

But mill-village paternalism is not enough to explain the weakness of textile unionism. For one thing, paternalism has rarely been so complete as in the ideal type we have presented. From Herring's discussions, it appears that company housing was starting to decline at about the same time that company-sponsored welfare work was becoming fashionable, in the 1920s, and that only a minority of mills undertook the full range of welfare services. Except in the very early years, many Southern mills have been located in or near sizable towns, where the workers were not geographically isolated though they may have been a distinct social class. Even where mill owners did run villages, there were sometimes unions (Herring, 1949: 66–79). On the other hand, unions usually were absent from mills where paternalism was relatively undeveloped.

Anyway, paternalism is now almost dead in the industry. Company houses have been sold. Welfare work has been abandoned. Most textile workers now are residentially intermingled with other kinds of workers. Many of them commute long distances to work, while the occupants of the old houses next to a mill may drive off to work in other mills or other industries. With the end of child labor and the diversification of industries and jobs in the South, the family is no longer the unit of labor in the mills. The ethnic and cultural homogeneity of textile labor forces and communities is far less than before: many mill workers are black, and Uncle Ben has been replaced by salaried executives hired from the outside (Herring, 1939; Roy, 1965). Despite all this, there are still few unions. The percentage of textile workers belonging to unions has hardly changed for at least sixty years.

Moreover, unionized industries have had company towns resembling classical Southern mill villages. This has been particularly true in coal mining (Caudill, 1963: 98–111) and steel manufacturing (Brody, 1969: 112–124). Many of these towns appear to have had some of the same preconditions of Gemeinschaft as Southern textiles, especially coal towns where the workers and managers were of the same WASP stock and the communities were even more isolated than most cotton-mill towns. Why did unions flourish in coal and steel towns but not in textile towns? Much of the reason is that in coal and steel, the family was not a unit of labor. Mining and steel mill jobs are men's work. A part of our discussion of labor force integration, below, will analyze the significance of this fact of community life.

II. CHARACTERISTICS OF WORKERS

Some writers have explained Southern mills' immunity to unionism on the basis of cultural values and compositional characteristics of their workers.

A. Individualism

Southern textiles recruited much of its first-generation labor force from rural areas that had kept many elements of frontier culture. In particular, Scotch-Irish Appalachian mountaineers have been famed for sturdy independence (Leyburn, 1962). Yeoman farmers from the mountains were numerous among recruits to upper Piedmont mills. Herring (1929: 22) quotes a typical one as saying he had "never worked a day for any boss man."

Whether they were mountaineers or lowlanders, small farm owners or tenants, Southern country people who entered the mills were imbued with the Protestant Ethic. They believed in hard work as an intrinsic good and a way to get ahead, and they saw the mill with its job ladder as a place where individual effort could pay off. Individualism of this kind is no hindrance to the disciplining of a labor force. The Protestant Ethic supports both. It helps to produce workers who are eager to please management and are not attracted to the collective economic strategy of unionism.

B. Docility

A related argument is that mill hands are a peculiarly docile lot, willingly pushed around like sheep. In the early days they were grateful to mills for jobs and cheap housing (B. Mitchell, 1921). Whatever independence the first generation of workers in some mills may have brought from the farm eroded quickly as they were socialized to the factory. They had no choice but to submit to mill discipline. While their independence lasted, it probably worked against unionism; the union looked like another boss. Succeeding generations grew up in paternalist mill villages and absorbed a culture that stressed nonassertiveness (Morland, 1958). Some mill recruits did not require a dose of factory discipline. They were sharecroppers before they came to the mills, and hence accustomed to a structure that instilled a feeling of dependence and a habit of obedience.

Working-class white Southerners are, in fact, among the nation's most disputatious and violent people. To this day, they are noted for using guns to settle differences of opinion (Reed, 1972: 45–55). This does not contradict the assertion that they relate passively to mill managers. They direct their violence against one another, not against the boss. Southerners' violence has been attributed to a frontier heritage and related patterns, including *machismo* and an actual need to defend one's life and property because the frontier has no law. Another factor in the mill village may have been displaced aggression acting in a paternalist social-psychological atmosphere where the boss was off limits as a target.

So far as we know, this explanation of violence is sheer speculation; but some explanation seems called for when there is solid research evidence that Southern workers are both docile and violent. This one would fit, given the shock that hit rugged individualist hillbillies when they came to the mills and were suddenly subjected to bosses and rules. The displaced-aggression hypothesis resembles a lot of analysis, some of it backed by research, of the in-group violence-proneness of traditional Southern blacks. The blacks developed the elaborate Brer Rabbit system of guile and dissembling as a way to get things from whites, but this did not remove their incentive to violent aggression because it did not alter the basic structure of subordination. The literature does not record that working-class Southern whites created such a system.

C. Southern Rural Culture

If there is anything about rural Southerners as such that has made them resistant to unions, it probably is their rural heritage more than their Southernness. Many urban Southerners have had strong unions for years. Steelworkers in Birmingham are an example. Lubeck (1981) reports that urban experience heightens working-class militancy of Nigerian workers independently of other variables such as duration of factory employment. Stearns (1975: 10–11) reaches a similar conclusion regarding traditionalist Belgian workers who were slower to urbanize than to industrialize. Even agricultural laborers can be unionized, but the job is not easy and is rarely accomplished except under special structural conditions (Friedland, 1981).

D. Women Workers

Around two-fifths of textile employees, including half or more of the operatives, are women (U.S. Bureau of the Census, 1963, 1973). Unions generally find women more difficult to organize than men (Breckinridge, 1933: 164–165). Women tend to be in the secondary labor force, easily replaced if they cause trouble. It has been asserted that most women workers are relatively uninvolved in their jobs, or were in the past. If so, one would expect women to be hard to interest in strenuous efforts to better their lot, including union activity. Textile unions in the past were not always attentive to unskilled women workers (Breckinridge, 1933: 165).

E. Ethnic and Racial Composition of the Labor Force

Many writers have observed that a mixture of ethnic groups in an industry's labor force can impede unionism. It can reduce class solidarity and incite antagonisms against fellow workers instead of management. This happened between Yankee and immigrant steelworkers (Brody, 1969: 119–121; cf. Castles and Kosack, 1973: 123–125). Some steel companies deliberately mixed Russians and Poles, or other hostile nationalities, as a divide-and-conquer strategy (Interchurch World Movement, 1920). Eventually the steelworkers overcame these divisions, but where there were ethnic cleavages they delayed steel unionization. Montgomery's (1972) analysis of the Kensington, Pennsylvania, riots of 1844 shows how managements broke a local weavers' union by exploiting Protestant-Catholic tensions. The unions themselves often have been run by whites, for whites, and have kept blacks out of their industries (Marshall, 1965;

Wolkinson, 1973). Their purpose has been to monopolize jobs for whites, but an effect probably has been to strengthen some unions that might otherwise have been weakened by racial antagonisms. Ethnic mixtures of workers have been common in U.S. textile manufacturing. In New England and Pennsylvania, different nationality groups have often worked at the same or neighboring mills (McMahon, 1926: 15). More recently, mills in the South have become racially mixed. Until about 1960, Southern textiles was virtually a lily-white industry except for a few menial job categories such as sweepers and outside laborers. Since then, white males have been leaving the industry for better-paying work and blacks have been replacing them (Rowan, 1970: 69–115). It will be ironic if the tight-knit mill community gives way to a heterogeneous urban labor force whose union potential is hampered in an almost opposite way by racial cleavage.

Probably all these characteristics of workers have hurt Southern textile unionism, but they are not enough to explain how feeble it has been. Other industries with similar labor force characteristics have had strong unions. Birmingham steelworkers had a biracial union long before the civil rights movement. So did Detroit's automobile workers, many of whom were from the South (Killian, 1952). Unionized coal miners in West Virginia and Kentucky have had the same Southern Protestant, frontier, and rural backgrounds as many textile workers. Outside the South, women in the garment industry have been unionized for decades. Unions have been strong in numerous Northern industries where different nationality groups work side by side or in neighboring plants.

III. CHARACTERISTICS OF THE INDUSTRY

Intrinsic features of textile manufacturing and the way it is organized in the South have been thought to hinder unionization. Some, but not all, of the industry's characteristics have been changing in ways that may be more favorable to unions in the future.

A. Plant Size, Management Structure, and Location

Three characteristics of the industry underlay the early paternalist Gemeinschaft: small size of mills, local ownership, and geographic isolation. Ownership and geographic patterns have changed. Owing to these changes, smallness of mills may not mean all that it once did. The overall effects of the changes on unionism probably are mixed.

With or without paternalism, small establishments are hard for unions to organize (Lockwood, 1968: 101–102). In early Southern textiles, small mills were just one part of an overarching pattern that was inhospitable to unions. In a small, locally owned mill in a one-industry town, workers could know each other and the owner personally. A few overlapping kin networks linked most workers. The owner was apt to be a patriarch or scion of a distinguished local family (H. Thompson, 1906: 67; B. Mitchell, 1921: 131). The community status system supported the authority system of the mill. Paternalism fitted both and could grow up naturally.

Local ownership has waned. Consolidation of the industry in the South began in the 1920s, accelerated in the 1930s, and continues to this day, although the industry is less concentrated than most (Herring, 1929: 19; Herring, 1939; Standard & Poor's, 1979). But the mergers have not increased the sizes of mills much, if at all. Most mills still employ fewer than 100 workers (Rowan, 1970: 13).

Industry consolidation can work both for and against unionism. The net effect is hard to assess. Workers are more easily organized against outside managers representing distant headquarters than against local paternalists (Warner and Low, 1947: 140–150; Roy, 1965: 239). But a big company that operates many small establishments can weather a local strike. It can afford to shut down permanently any one mill that breaches an antiunion policy. On the other hand, outside managers may be accustomed to unionism and not resist it. A rationalized bureaucratic management may even welcome unions as a way to standardize labor relations, especially if it runs numerous small establishments that would be hard to monitor.

Southern textile workers are far less isolated than they once were. In the old days, many of them rarely left the one-industry towns where the range of vision was narrow and no other working conditions or ways of life seemed possible. They had no nearby higher-wage reference groups or union exemplars. If they did grow interested in a union, they knew the company could fire them and leave them with no alternative job. All of this has changed. Villages have become towns or cities with some diversification of jobs. For many workers, automobiles have separated the place of residence from the place of work. Increased education, daily newspaper reading, and exposure to the standard American mass media have broadened mill workers' horizons. A wide range of work conditions and opportunities is visible to them. This has not led many to join unions, at least not yet. A more common response has been to use textiles as an intragenerational or intergenerational way station between farming and higher-paying industries (Norsworthy, 1961; Simpson and Norsworthy, 1965: 220). Should upward mobility out of textiles become blocked, unionism might be a response.

B. Technology and Skill Level

Textiles is a low-skill industry. Low-skill workers have long been noted for unorganizability (Weyforth, 1917). Their tendency when dissatisfied is to change jobs rather than try long-range ways to improve those they have. This tendency is accentuated in textiles, where jobs in different mills are so similar that a worker can move from one to another without having to learn anything new (Herring, 1949: 52). Low-skill labor normally is in surplus supply. Managements can easily replace union activists or assemble strikebreakers.

The main technology in textiles is machine tending. Workers can move around and set their own work pace to some degree. Such work is less alienating than assembly-line or other jobs where the worker is glued to one spot and cannot control the pace of work. The less the alienation, the less may be the appeal of unions, at least to low-skill workers. (Craft workers have low alienation and high union-proneness.) Blauner's (1964) evidence suggests that textile workers' low alienation is a factor in their avoidance of unions. Indirect evidence of the role of technology is seen in the effects of the "stretchouts" of the early 1930s, which led to a flurry of strikes in 1934 all over the South's textile region. Much of what the workers were reacting against was the loss of ability to pace their own work.

Against this reasoning it can be argued that farming, from which most first-generation textile workers came to the mills, allows vastly more freedom of movement and work pace, yet the early mill workers showed few signs of alienation or unionism. Perhaps more important, there have been other industries with as high or higher work satisfaction (Goodrich, 1925; Blauner, 1964: 199–209) but more unionism. Coal mining, printing, and steel manufacturing are examples.

Probably the technology of textile manufacturing does affect job satisfaction favorably and works against unions, partly because of the intrinsic nature of specific jobs and partly because it offers opportunities for advancement. Pay and skill are low in most textile jobs, but the matter is not that simple. Textiles has an age-graded skill hierarchy with several levels of easily learned work—i.e., an internal labor market where a worker can move up with experience (Warner and Low, 1947: 66–89; Rowan, 1970: 7–11; Doeringer and Piore, 1971: 1–40). The ladder may look short from the outside, but from the inside it looks tall and it can be climbed. Upward movement mollifies potential leaders of unionization movements, or buys them off. There is more of a textile skill hierarchy for men than for women, and men have usually been the leaders of unionization in mixed-sex industries. The chance to move up a skill ladder may be less now than earlier because formal education requirements of the best jobs have risen, but it probably remains greater than in most industries.

C. Economics of the Industry

The industry is subject to boom-and-bust cycles. In recent years it appears to have been in a secular decline as U.S. firms have fled to lower-wage countries. The number of U.S. textile employees fell from well over a million throughout the 1940s to 932,000 in 1974 (U.S. Bureau of the Census, 1940, 1951, 1977). Surplus labor is abundant during recessions and in a period of decline. Workers know this and tread cautiously.

Textile manufacturing is a labor-intensive, competitive, low-profit industry. Wages are a high proportion of its costs. (For statistics showing these things, see U.S. Bureau of the Census, 1976, 1977; Newspaper Enterprise Association, 1979.) Union-generated wage increases can be very damaging to a textile firm. The manufacturers have good reason to resist unions vigorously. They are competing in a cut-throat, worldwide business. Its markets are international. Its raw materials and products are cheap to transport. People in any country quickly learn most mill jobs. The industry's high labor intensity, low skill level, cheap transportation, and small plant size have motivated and enabled textile firms to move at short notice to low-wage areas: from New England to the South, then to Korea or Taiwan. Short of this, they can move from union to nonunion places within the South.

Workers understand this, and managers are not loath to remind them of it. It is reasonable to assume that their awareness deters unionism. In these respects, textiles is very different from industries such as coal mining and steel manufacturing. Coal mining is confined to a limited number of fixed sites. Its transport costs are high. Its skill level has come to exceed that of textiles (Trist and Bamforth, 1951). Steel manufacturing has high transportation costs, a greater proportion of high-skill jobs than textiles, and huge capital investments in giant mills. For these reasons, coal and steel firms cannot so easily move across the countryside or the ocean to escape unions—and their workers know it.

On balance, the distinctive characteristics of the Southern textile industry have weakened unionism. The effects of recent changes in them are mixed.

IV. CHARACTERISTICS AND BEHAVIOR OF THE UNIONS

Features of the unions themselves have been blamed for their failure. They have not been strong in the North. Their being based in the North has hurt them in the South.

G. S. Mitchell (1931: 3–5) paints a grim picture of textile unions in the North when the U.S. industry was still centered there. The movement was splintered into feuding fiefdoms which were unable to control their members or collect dues with any consistency. Separate crafts disdained to affiliate with one another, let alone with the common run of operatives. Factory-wide industrial unions sprang up briefly around local grievances, but did not spread or take root. Struggles between left-wing and right-wing factions drained off energy and added to the disunity.

Northern-based, weakly financed unions kept few full-time organizers in the South. The small size and geographic scattering of mills probably contributed to this problem. The parent federations were more enticed by industries where organizers need not roam large territories to find enough potential dues payers to warrant the expense, and where a single plant or a few neighboring ones might yield thousands of members. In any event, much early history of Southern textile organizing is a dreary repetition of the same story. An organizer would be rushed in when there was a spontaneous walkout, sign up workers, then leave, and the union would melt away once the immediate issue had been settled (McMahon, 1926: 24–25; G. Mitchell, 1931: 3).

Southern strikers often welcomed Northern organizers, but sometimes a clever management could turn workers against a union by portraying organizers as bolsheviks, atheists, or at any rate as alien intruders. This happened in the famous Gastonia, North Carolina, strike of 1929 (Pope, 1942). (In this case the organizers *were* bolsheviks.) The CIO-affiliated Textile Workers Union of America unified textile unionism and paid considerable attention to the South after World War II. The failure of the massive CIO Southern organizing drive of the late 1940s may have been partly due to its lack of indigenous Southern leadership. There are rumors that Jewish organizers sent south from New York since the merger of textile and garment unions into the Amalgamated Clothing and Textile Workers Union in 1976 have had trouble establishing rapport with small-town Southern workers. In a low-union region, organizers from outside cannot expect much help or legitimation from local or nearby unionists.

V. LABOR FORCE INTEGRATION AND WORKER CONSCIOUSNESS

We have reviewed four kinds of explanations of the weakness of unions in Southern textiles. All four appear to have some merit, but they are only partial and in some ways unsatisfying. Why, for example, did isolated company towns immunize textile workers against unions when they did not have this effect on coal miners? If the recent racial mixture of the textile labor force has hurt unionism, how could a single union enlist the diverse immigrant strains of the steel mills?

In this section we apply a broader and more analytical perspective which can subsume many of the empirical variables discussed earlier. This perspective is *labor force integration* (hereafter, for brevity, *LFI*): the ways in which members of a labor force fit into community and workplace social structures, and the ways in which these structures interpenetrate one another. The term *integration* need not imply social harmony or a high degree of systemic interdependence. Community LFI and workplace LFI each has four dimensions: power or authority, a class system of earnings and skills, a status order of prestige and deference, and a system of interdependent functions. The power and class dimensions are always present in a workplace or a community, though workers do not always perceive them. The status order and the interdependence of functions may be weak or virtually absent.

Differing modes of LFI, and the extent and nature of interpenetration of community and workplace LFI, help to explain differing degrees of *worker consciousness:* workers' identities that are based more on workplace social structures than on kinship, ethnicity, or other nonwork structures and affiliations. Worker consciousness increases the likelihood of work-based collective action such as unionism. When worker consciousness rests on the general condition of being a worker rather than on specific occupation, it is favorable to industrial unionism rather than to craft unionism.

VI. ASPECTS OF TEXTILE LABOR FORCE INTEGRATION UNFAVORABLE TO WORKER CONSCIOUSNESS

A. The Traditional Textile Community

In the archetypal Southern textile town, workplace and community LFI were strong, mutually reinforcing, and antithetical to worker consciousness and collective action. Mill and community were virtually a single system of authority, class, status, and interdependence. It was a hierarchical Gemeinschaft rooted in the ascribed community system and duplicated in the mill.

The family rather than the individual was often the basic unit of labor. This brought community-based authority and interdependence into the mill. Smelser (1959: 180–224) describes this family pattern as it existed in early English mills. The U.S. pattern in the early days was similar. Not just nuclear families but larger kin networks and groups of neighbors might be recruited into the same mills (Herring, 1929: 20). Families served the owners as agents of labor discipline. Parents disciplined their children, and relatives watched each other to keep up the kin group's reputation as a source of reliable labor. The importing of kin and neighborhood networks into the villages helped to preserve rural patterns of community social control. Unlike the Nigerian situation analyzed by Lubeck (1981), early textiles was not a transformation from patrimonial household relations to advanced capitalist labor relations. It was an adaptation of the industry to preexisting patrimonial systems of sharecropping and dependent, debt-ridden small-scale farming. It imported patrimonialism into the mills and villages.

In these ways the mill and its village combined the structures of family, community, and factory into an all-encompassing LFI. This kind of social integration is not work based. It orients people to identities rooted in the community order more than in workplace social relationships. It inhibits worker consciousness and collective work-based action.

The textile industry has been very different in these respects from industries such as coal mining and steel manufacturing. Workers in those industries, especially coal mining, have lived in isolated homogeneous communities, some of them company owned, but traditional family and community authority were not brought into the work setting. Community LFI was not superimposed on workplace LFI. Work could be an autonomous source of identity. Structures of collective action aimed at altering the social relations of work were not held back by the restraints of an ascribed community order of status and deference.

B. Women Workers

Since the end of child labor, textile workers have been fairly evenly divided between the sexes. Sex consciousness has stood in the way of unified worker consciousness. The sexual division of labor within the mills has aggravated this problem. Men generally have had the most skilled jobs and dominated the unions, and the work-based interests of the sexes have not been the same. Women's interests traditionally have focused more on family and community than on work. Worker consciousness can develop more easily in industries where nearly all workers are men.

C. Technology and Work Groups

Cohesive work teams that arise from closely interdependent work foster worker consciousness and collective action (Sayles, 1958; Friedland, et al., 1978: 33–35). Textile technology limits the formation of interdependent work groups. Mill workers tend large numbers of machines as individuals and are separated by great distances in large rooms. In contrast, coal mining and steelmaking create more cohesive groups. Their production processes rely more than textile technology on directly interdependent workers or work crews (Goodrich, 1925; Trist, et al., 1963; Brody, 1969).

D. Community Organizational Bases for Collective Action

Strong community organizations run by workers may serve as an organizational base for collective action related to work. They train working-class leaders and sometimes give direct help to unions. Textile workers have lacked such an organizational base.

The main indigenous workers' organizations have been religious ones. Black churches furnished top leaders and much of the organizational structure of the civil rights movement, which in turn has facilitated black unionization. Islamic organizations have aided working-class militancy in Africa (Lubeck, 1981). Nineteenth-century English cotton-mill unions drew strength from working-class leadership and organizational experience in nonconformist churches (G. Mitchell, 1931: 84; E. Thompson, 1966: 379–380).

Ethnic organizations and informal structures have provided an organizational base for unions. Friedland (1981) analyzes how Cesar Chavez has used Chicano solidarity in organizing California farm laborers. Kornblum (1974) shows that an ethnically based infrastructure sustains Chicago steelworkers' unionism. Ethnic churches and religious clubs combine two foci of indigenous community LFI and have sometimes directly aided strikers (Warner and Low, 1947: 225–226).

Organizations of workers do not support unionism if the management controls them. They are then extensions of management authority. This was true of the Gastonia cotton-mill workers' churches described by Pope (1942). It is also true of workers' clubs sponsored by management as a part of welfare programs. Management control of workers' churches and other community organizations was a central part of the paternalism that stifled mill hands' worker consciousness. Textile workers have also lacked ethnic organizations because their communities were ethnically homogeneous.

E. Occupational Community vs. Traditional Gemeinschaft

Lockwood (1968: 103) summarizes several studies that suggest that the absence of occupational communities leads to working-class deference and hinders unionism. Why might this be so?

The pattern he describes characterized the traditional Gemeinschaft of Southern textile villages. The Gemeinschaft pattern arises in homogeneous communities like the one transplanted from the farm to the isolated mill village. The consciousness of workers is not occupational. It is undifferentiated, global, and familistic. It involves a total way of life. Kinship and other community ties are more salient than work relationships.

Occupational community arises chiefly in differentiated communities. Members of an occupation set themselves off consciously from others on the basis of their work (Lipset, et al., 1956). Work is perceived as a fundamental basis of social differentiation, perhaps the most salient one for men though not for women. Worker consciousness takes precedence over other consciousness.

Worker consciousness can occur in homogeneous, isolated communities if work—or work that is regarded as meaningful—is reserved to the men and is not a family affair. Among coal miners or small-town steelworkers, working in the mines or mills is what differentiates the sexes and is the main social tie that unites the men. It has the same effect as occupational differentiation within a sex in a more differentiated community. Work-related and sex-related organizations and groups are likely to be the same. A community of this kind is unlike a textile village where community LFI is kin-based and is brought into the mill.

Craft technology favors occupationally based worker consciousness. Craft workers see the social differentiation of the workplace as essentially functional rather than hierarchical, or they see themselves as occupying the top of a worker hierarchy. Strong positive identification with one's function facilitates lateral orientation to workmates based on pride in work, and is conducive to craft unionism. Textile workers lack pride in their function. Local people refer to them as "lintheads," a word that conveys negative status like a derogatory ethnic epithet. They see the mill and community as a hierarchy in which they are inferior to the management and the Main-Street middle class, not only in class but in status (Morland, 1958).

Steelworkers and coal miners form occupational communities and develop worker consciousness to a far greater degree than textile workers. They see themselves as performing a valued function, not just as occupying the bottom place in a hierarchy. What they do is "men's work." It corresponds completely to sex differentiation. In this way it is unlike what men do in a cotton mill, where both sexes work and the major sex-role differences are seen as lying in traditional nonwork spheres rather than in sex-typed mill jobs.

F. Social Immobility and Mobility

The literature gives two opposite views of the amount of mobility out of textile work. Both are right. They reflect different times and conditions. Neither condition is conducive to worker consciousness or collective action because neither orients workers to the class system of a fixed workplace.

A number of older studies report that people who have entered textile work are not likely to leave it, and that their children are apt to follow them into the mills and stay there (Rhyne, 1930; Lahne, 1944; Parnes, 1954; Morland, 1958, 1960). It almost seems that mill work has mysterious qualities that stamp themselves on workers and lock them and their descendants into the mills forever. The evidence in these studies is convincing. The immobility they describe occurred in the past, in isolated mill towns with no jobs in sight outside the mills. The immobility pattern fits the management-controlled patrimonial form of LFI.

Somewhat later studies find a substantial amount of mobility out of textile mills (Simpson and Norsworthy, 1965: 217–222; Rowan, 1970: 28–29). This pattern appears to have become the prevailing one following the breakdown of mill-village isolation and the diversification of work opportunities. Workers now perceive a class system in which they can move, and many do. Textile work now is frequently a step up a ladder that begins with marginal farming or unskilled labor and ends with work in higher-paying industries, for the children of the mill hands if not for the mill hands themselves. When people see themselves as brief sojourners in their industries, they are not likely to develop worker consciousness focused on them.

VII. CHANGING LABOR FORCE INTEGRATION AND THE FUTURE OF TEXTILE UNIONISM

Changes in textile LFI since World War II may have improved the prospects for unions.

A. Work Function and Community Status

The old mill community status order of ranked families has broken up. The connection of work function to community status also has declined. The work functions of people in industrially diversified communities and in geographically dispersed commuter labor markets are parts of unconnected work structures. Jobs in these separate workplaces are mutually invisible and incommensurable. This diversification pulls workers toward consumption-based status symbolism (cf. Lockwood, 1968: 106–108). An orientation toward consumption symbols coupled with an absence of identification with work functions is compatible with bread-and-butter unionism and with industrial rather than craft unionism. Thus the orientations of textile workers fit the nature of the union, the ACTWU. The combination may augur well for Southern textile unionism in the future.

B. Black Workers

The textile labor force is increasingly black. Blacks in the South have often joined unions when given the chance, as in Winston-Salem tobacco factories and Birmingham steel mills. Black Southerners have long had an indigenous organizational base in their churches and lodges. They have a recent history of successful collective action in the civil rights movement. Black organizational skills that were developed through civil rights activism have been applied with success to local politics. These experiences and structures may make black textile workers more attracted to unions than whites have been, and better able to do the organizational work of forming and running unions. The shift to a black labor force may more than offset the strains that a racially mixed labor force puts on unionism. The racial mixture may be temporary anyway. This industry, which once excluded blacks, may become predominantly black.

• • •

All things considered, recent and ongoing changes in Southern textiles may make them ripe at last for unionism. But a union victory could be pyrrhic if it hastened the flight of the industry to low-wage countries. Some companies might not mind moving abroad, but others would prefer to stay in the American South. Even without the push of unions, the industry in this country is declining and not very profitable. Unions and managements have a common interest in keeping their industry alive. If unions come, the two parties may recognize this fact and cooperate in planning ways to protect the industry's health. This would be a new kind of cooperation in textiles, more nearly equalitarian than the paternalist village and based on rationally created structures rather than on patrimonial tradition.

ACKNOWLEDGMENTS

I am grateful to Ida Harper Simpson for suggestions and to Julia Heath, Joan Gutmann, and Vicki Van de Houten for research assistance.

NOTE

*Reliable figures on union membership by industry within states or regions cannot be had, so far as we can tell. Reasonably accurate sources for the nation as a whole show 16%, 21%, and 18% of the blue-collar textile workers belonging unions in 1920, 1960, and 1974 respectively. (We calculate these percentages from data in U.S. Bureau of the Census, 1940, 1960, 1962, 1977.) Authorities commonly assume that unions have penetrated in industry far less in the South than in the North.

REFERENCES

Blauner, Robert
    1964   Alienation and Freedom. Chicago: University of Chicago Press.
Breckinridge, Sophonisba P.
    1933   Women in the Twentieth Century. New York: McGraw-Hill.
Brody, David
    1969   [1960] Steelworkers in America: The Nonunion Era. New York: Harper & Row.
Castles, Stephen, and Godula Kosack
    1973   Immigrant Workers and Class Structure in Western Europe. London: Oxford University Press.
Caudill, Harry M.
    1963   Night Comes to the Cumberlands. Boston: Little, Brown.
Doeringer, Peter B. and Michael J. Piore
    1971   Internal Labor Markets and Manpower Analysis. Lexington, Mass.: Heath.
Friedland, William H.
    1981   "Seasonal farm labor and worker consciousness." In Richard L. Simpson and Ida Harper Simpson (eds.), Research in the Sociology of Work, Vol. 1. Greenwich, Conn.: JAI Press.
Friedland, William H., Amy E. Barton, and Robert J. Thomas
    1978   Manufacturing Green Gold: The Conditions and Social Consequences of Lettuce Harvest Mechanization. Davis, Calif.: Dept. of Applied Behavioral Sciences, University of California. California Agricultural Policy Seminar Monograph No. 2.
Gilman, Glenn
    1956   Human Relations in the Industrial Southeast. Chapel Hill, N.C.: University of North Carolina Press.
Goodrich, Carter
    1925   The Miner's Freedom. Boston: Marshall Jones.
Herring, Harriet L.
    1929   Welfare Work in Mill Villages. Chapel Hill, N.C.: University of North Carolina Press.
    1939   "The outside employer in the Southern industrial pattern." Social Forces 18: 115–126.
    1949   Passing of the Mill Village. Chapel Hill, N.C.: University of North Carolina Press.
Interchurch World Movement
    1920   Report on the Steel Strike of 1919. New York: Interchurch World Movement.
Killian, Lewis M.
    1952   "The effects of Southern white workers on race relations in Northern plants." American Sociological Review 17: 327–331.
Kornblum, William
    1974   Blue Collar Community. Chicago: University of Chicago Press.

Lahne, Herbert J.
    1944   The Cotton Mill Worker. New York: Farrar and Rinehart.
Leyburn, James G.
    1962   The Scotch-Irish: A Social History. Chapel Hill, N.C.: University of North
            Carolina Press.
Lipset, Seymour Martin, Martin A. Trow, and James S. Coleman
    1956   Union Democracy. Glencoe, Ill,: Free Press.
Lockwood, David
    1968   [1966] "Sources of variation in working-class images of society." Pp. 98–114 in
            Joseph A. Kahl (ed.), Comparative Perspectives on Stratification. Boston: Little,
            Brown.
Lubeck, Paul M.
    1981   "Class formation at the periphery: Class consciousness and Islamic nationalism
            among Nigerian workers." In Richard L. Simpson and Ida Harper Simpson (eds.),
            Research in the Sociology of Work, Vol. 1. Greenwich, Conn.: JAI Press.
Marshall, Ray
    1965   The Negro and Organized Labor. New York: Wiley.
McMahon, Thomas F.
    1926   United Textile Workers of America. New York: Workers Education Bureau Press.
Mitchell, Broadus
    1921   The Rise of Cotton Mills in the South. Baltimore: Johns Hopkins Press.
Mitchell, George Sinclair
    1931   Textile Unionism and the South. Chapel Hill, N.C.: University of North Carolina
            Press.
Montgomery, David
    1972   "The shuttle and the cross: Weavers and artisans in the Kensington riots of 1844."
            Journal of Social History 5: 411–446.
Morland, J. Kenneth
    1958   Millways of Kent. Chapel Hill, N.C.: University of North Carolina Press.
    1960   "Educational and occupational aspirations of mill and town school children in a
            Southern community." Social Forces 39: 169–175.
Newspaper Enterprise Association, Inc.
    1979   World Almanac Book of Facts, 1980. New York: Newspaper Enterprise Associa-
            tion.
Norsworthy, David R.
    1961   Mobility Effects of Industrial Growth. Ph.D. Dissertation, Department of Sociol-
            ogy, University of North Carolina. Chapel Hill, N.C.
Parnes, Herbert S.
    1954   Research on Labor Mobility: An Appraisal of Research Findings in the United
            States. New York: Social Science Research Council.
Pope, Liston
    1942   Millhands and Preachers. New Haven: Yale University Press.
Reed, John Shelton
    1972   The Enduring South. Lexington, Mass.: Heath.
Rhyne, Jennings J.
    1930   Some Southern Cotton Mill Workers and Their Villages. Chapel Hill, N.C.:
            University of North Carolina Press.
Rowan, Richard L.
    1970   The Negro in the Textile Industry. Philadelphia: University of Pennsylvania Press.
Roy, Donald F.
    1965   "Change and resistance to change in the Southern labor movement." Pp. 225–247

in John C. McKinney and Edgar T. Thompson (eds.), The South in Continuity and Change. Durham, N.C.: Duke University Press.

Sayles, Leonard R.
1958 Behavior of Industrial Work Groups. New York: Wiley.

Simpson, Richard L., and David R. Norsworthy
1965 "The changing occupational structure of the South." Pp. 198–224 in John C. McKinney and Edgar T. Thompson (eds.), The South in Continuity and Change. Durham, N.C.: Duke University Press.

Smelser, Neil J.
1959 Social Change in the Industrial Revolution. Chicago: University of Chicago Press.

Standard & Poor's
1979 Standard & Poor's Industry Surveys. Textiles: Basic Analysis. Sect. 2. July 19.

Stearns, Peter N.
1975 Lives of Labor. New York: Holmes and Meier.

Thompson, E. P.
1966 [1963] The Making of the English Working Class. New York: Random House.

Thompson, Holland
1906 From the Cotton Field to the Cotton Mill. New York: Macmillan.

Trist, E. W., and K. W. Bamforth
1951 "Some social and psychological consequences of the longwall method of coal-getting." Human Relations 4: 3–38.

Trist, E. L., G. W. Higgin, H. Murray, and A. B. Pollock
1963 Organizational Choice: Capabilities of Groups at the Coal Face under Changing Technologies. London: Tavistock.

U.S. Bureau of the Census
1940 Statistical Abstract of the United States, 1940. Washington, D.C.: U.S. Government Printing Office.
1951 Statistical Abstract of the United States, 1951. Washington, D.C.: U.S. Government Printing Office.
1960 Historical Statistics of the United States. Colonial Times to 1957. Washington, D.C.: U.S. Government Printing Office.
1962 Statistical Abstract of the United States, 1962. Washington, D.C.: U.S. Government Printing Office.
1963 Census of Population, 1960. Subject Reports. Occupation by Industry. Final Report PC(2)-7C. Washington, D.C.: U.S. Government Printing Office.
1973 Census of Population, 1970. Subject Reports. Occupation by Industry. Final Report PC(2)-7C. Washington, D.C.: U.S. Government Printing Office.
1976 Census of Manufactures, 1972. Vol. I, Subject and Special Statistics. Washington, D.C.: U.S. Government Printing Office.
1977 Statistical Abstract of the United States, 1977. Washington, D.C.: U.S. Government Printing Office.

Warner, W. Lloyd, and J. O. Low
1947 The Social System of the Modern Factory. New Haven, Conn.: Yale University Press.

Warren, Roland L.
1973 The Community in America. 3rd ed. Chicago: Rand McNally.

Weyforth, William O.
1917 The Organizability of Labor. Baltimore: Johns Hopkins Press.

Wolkinson, Benjamin W.
1973 Blacks, Unions, and the EEOC. Lexington, Mass.: Heath.

CULTURAL DETERMINISM, TECHNOLOGICAL DETERMINISM, AND THE ACTION APPROACH:

COMPETING EXPLANATIONS OF NEW WORKING CLASS MILITANCY

John Low-Beer

This paper seeks first to clarify three theoretical approaches to the explanation of worker behavior: (1) social structural, situational, or, more specifically, technological determinism; (2) cultural determinism, or explanations in terms of the prior orientations and values of workers; and (3) the action approach, according to which workers' behavior must be understood as the joint outcome of prior orientations and situational

Research in the Sociology of Work, Volume 1, pages 403–433
Copyright © 1981 by JAI Press Inc.
All rights of reproduction in any form reserved.
ISBN: 0-89232-124-5

factors, these latter as interpreted by the actors. In much of the debate of recent years, the second and third of these approaches have been confounded and counterposed against the first, thus confusing the efforts to evaluate the usefulness of each. The first task, then, is to arrive at a clear formulation of each of these approaches, and particularly to distinguish the action approach from the other two.[1]

The second aim of this paper is to evaluate how well these approaches can explain the findings of recent research on the new working class, including the author's own. The new working class thesis is essentially a technological determinist position and has been attacked as such by followers of the action approach. Thus, a discussion of the usefulness of the three approaches is also an assessment of the validity of the new working class thesis.

The new working class thesis was first formulated by Serge Mallet, whose book on this subject was published in France in 1963. Both in Italy and in France in the early 1960s technicians and private sector white-collar workers had begun to strike for the first time. Their militancy followed a long period of quiescence in labor relations which had lasted through the 1950s, and had led Ross and Hartman (1960) to argue that the strike was "withering away" in the advanced capitalist societies. The resurgence of labor conflict captured the attention and imagination of Mallet and other observers, who saw in these educated workers of the advanced sectors a revolutionary vanguard. Mallet titled his book *The New Working Class,* and its influence was such that his usage has by now become widely accepted.[2]

Why did these strikes attract so much attention? The reversal of the decline in conflictuality was itself seen as significant. And the advanced technological settings lent the strikes an added glamor. But beyond this, these strikes prefigured many of the themes of the May Movement of 1968: participatory democracy in the conduct of the strikes, egalitarian and solidaristic demands such as reduction of wage inequalities and abolition of merit raises, and demands for control reaching even into the boardroom to challenge management's right to make investment policy unilaterally.

The new working class theorists explained this new militancy as the result of social-structural and technological changes. Their argument centered on the workplace. Like theorists of the post-industrial society, they pointed to the rapid growth of the knowledge-based industries and the increase in the numbers of technicians and professionals in the labor force. They accepted the descriptions of changes in work given by proponents of the embourgeoisement thesis such as Blauner (1964) and Galbraith (1967), but they saw greater education and involvement in work as leading to higher aspirations and increased conflict rather than integration. Technicians' allegiance to a body of professional knowledge was said to make them cosmopolitan and egalitarian, less dependent on the company and more demanding of it. The teamwork that is a common feature of advanced technology jobs was described as creating horizontal solidarities. Conflict between the rationality of science and the rationality of profit maximization was eventually to lead from militancy over immediate issues to a broader class consciousness.

The new working class thesis broke fresh ground in the debate on the political role of the working class because of its emphasis on relative rather than absolute deprivation as a source of militancy, its focus on power and control dimensions, and its disregard for the traditional manual/nonmanual distinction. But it shared the basic explanatory model of the embourgeoisement and post-industrial society theories, and therefore also shared the basic weaknesses of these theories: the assumption that technology and social structure produce consciousness and behavioral outcomes in a relatively deterministic way, a view of technology as a liberating force with an objectively determined direction of development, and the extrapolation of current trends of economic development and industrial organization without sufficient theoretical analysis of the mechanisms underlying these changes.

If the assumption regarding the impact of technology and social structure is indeed mistaken, the new working class thesis must fall regardless of the outcome of the debate on the other issues. In the literature in English, it was precisely this assumption that was called into question, as it collided directly with the assertions of the action approach, which was gaining acceptance in the years following the publication of Mallet's book. Of course, it is not an assumption original to the embourgeoisement or new working class theses. It is an instance of the idea, pervasive among sociologists, that social structures pattern behavior. Beginning with Marx, the debate on the political role of the working class in capitalist society has turned on analyses of changes in the situation of workers. Although Mallet and Blauner differed in their judgments as to the implications of technological change, they both assumed that an accurate assessment of the future role of the working class in politics could be deduced from an analysis of technological and social-structural changes. We will refer to this view as situational, social-structural, or technological determinism.

How social-structural change leads to changes in behavior is a source of disagreement. Some authors argue that value change is an intervening variable between social-structural change and changes in behavior. Others downplay the role of values, preferring a rationalistic model of the human psyche. But in either case, in the sociology of work and, to a lesser extent, in the field of stratification, Marxist and non-Marxist sociologists alike have focused on social-structural change as their major explanatory concept. Perhaps this is the inevitable result of the sociologist's search for generalizations that apply across all work situations or across all countries.

The attempt to construct such general theories of worker behavior was challenged by theorists following the action approach. They emphasized that differences in the values of workers lead to differences in their behavior even in the face of identical structural constraints and incentives. It is therefore not possible, they argued, to construct a general theory about how technological development and rising incomes affect workers. Cultural differences between countries and regions, and even differences in values and goals among people within a single workplace, lead sweeping theories to fail when applied in contexts different from their original ones.

This criticism of social-structural and technological determinism would seem to accord well with what we will call the cultural-determinist position. The idea that value differences lead to differences in behavior is of course also an old one in sociology. Indeed, according to Talcott Parsons's influential interpretation of the sociological classics in *The Structure of Social Action* (1937), the emphasis on values and value differences was a dominant theme of sociology almost from its inception. Certainly, Max Weber's comparative historical studies of religion and the rise of capitalism had early on taken the position that values are important independent variables, and that differences between the value systems of otherwise similar societies could result in very different patterns of change.

But the action approach goes beyond the simple assertion that it is necessary to take values into account. In emphasizing that "the actors' own definitions of the situations in which they are engaged [should be] taken as an initial basis for the explanation of their social behavior and relationships" (Goldthorpe, Lockwood, et al., 1968a: 184), it rejects the notion that man is passive, shaped by society as by a mold. While agreeing with Parsonian functionalists that man receives his values from society, it criticizes the "over-socialized conception of man" (Wrong, 1961) for failing to take into consideration that man also creates society. In contrast to functionalism, it argues that sociological theory should be based on the assumption that people are active and more or less rational in the pursuit of their goals. This theoretical difference between an action approach and a cultural-determinist approach implies different explanatory paradigms. For the action theorist, behavior cannot be explained exclusively in terms of values or prior orientations, just as it cannot be explained exclusively in terms of situational variables. A person's response is rather the result of the interaction that takes place when an actor with certain orientations encounters a given situation, defines it in his or her own terms, and responds accordingly.

Some recent critics of technological determinism have overlooked this point. Although calling themselves action theorists, they have sought to supplant the criticized approach with an equally straightforward cultural determinism, according to which workers' responses can be understood in terms of their prior orientations, whereas technology is largely irrelevant. In view of these misunderstandings, it seems advisable to consider in greater detail what the action approach is and how it can be operationalized. Only then can we evaluate its usefulness. For the first of these purposes, we shall rely heavily on David Silverman's book, *The Theory of Organisations* (1970), one of the most complete and most frequently cited statements of the action approach.

Drawing upon Schutz and the phenomenological tradition as well as upon aspects of Weber's thought ignored by Parsons, Silverman argues that "while society defines man, man in turn defines society. Particular constellations of meaning are only sustained by continual reaffirmation in everyday actions" (1970: 127). In the context of organizational sociology, this implies that the sociologist must direct attention to, among other things, "[t]he actors' present definitions of their situation within the organization and their expectations of the likely behavior of others with particular reference to the strategic resources they perceive to be at their disposal and at the disposal of others" (1970: 154).

Three areas of research, says Silverman, will be of particular interest to the organizational sociologist taking an action approach: the orientations to work that employees bring with them when they first take a particular job; the strategies they use in pursuit of their ends; and the relatively stable patterns of interaction that emerge out of the coming together of the actors and their encounters with one another (Silverman, 1970: 170, 196). Delimiting the action theorist's concerns in this broad fashion, Silverman is led to praise two groups of studies, each embodying one of the distinguishing aspects of the action approach. On the one hand, he cites with approval those studies that emphasize prior orientations, even though they usually do not take into account how these orientations interact with definitions of the organizational situation to produce varying outcomes. On the other hand, he notes studies that view organizational life as an "ongoing product of human interaction" (1970: 197), in which actors pursue strategies to enhance their positions in the light of the resources available to them, even though these studies often do not take into account the different orientations people bring to their work situations.

The first group of studies shares with the action approach a concern for the ways in which value differences affect workers' behavior. However (and this is not something Silverman notes) most of them also share the

functionalist's "over-socialized conception of man." They assume that
people with certain personality traits, values, or cultural background
behave in certain consistent ways across a broad variety of situations, and
that their behavior in these situations is attributable to the aforementioned
individual characteristics. Of course, there are many instances in which
such an explanatory model is indeed applicable. It seems plausible that
people of rural and small-town origins might be more likely to believe in
the work ethic than people of urban origins (Blood and Hulin 1967); or
that ratebusters might share certain background and personality characteristics; or that Methodism might have had dampening effects on the
militancy and class consciousness of miners in County Durham (Moore,
1975). Nonetheless, this type of reasoning has often led to the *ad hoc*
postulation of a presumed value difference for each behavior difference to
be explained. In this way, behavior differences between groups are
accounted for by presumed cultural and value differences when they
could more parsimoniously be explained by a commonsense rationalistic
model. Conflicting interests and definitions of the situation are assumed to
play no part. For example, the poor are said to be unable to break out of
the vicious cycle of unemployment and social disorganization because of
their values (the "culture of poverty"); democracy is said to be stable or
unstable because of the attitudes and values of the citizens (the "civic
culture"); bureaucratic vicious cycles are said to occur because people
are unable to relate to one another in an open and mature fashion; and so
on. Such explanations escape the Scylla of social-structural determinism
only to be drawn into the Charybdis of cultural determinism.

To the extent that action theorists stress the importance of value differences, their interpretations move toward a cultural-determinist position
and away from their stated stress on rational adaptive strategies. Many
of the same phenomena that the cultural determinists explain in terms of
value differences could be seen as resulting from the adoption of
situationally appropriate strategies by individuals who do not differ in
their basic goals, thus avoiding the need to postulate a particular value
behind each behavior. More important from the position of the action
theorist, studies pointing to value differences as major explanatory variables usually do not see the individual as a rational strategist seeking to
attain certain ends.

The second group of studies cited approvingly by Silverman does
emphasize the rational and active aspects of behavior, but in doing so it
pays little attention to the ways in which people's prior orientations to
work may differ. These studies are typified by the work of Michel Crozier
(1964), who has called his approach "neo-rationalism." The organization
is seen as an "ecology of games," a structure providing each actor with
the counters to pursue certain strategies while excluding other strategies.

As Silverman realizes, the neo-rationalist approach has tended to explain organizational strategies almost entirely in terms of the resources made available to each actor by his or her position, assuming that the ends of all actors are similar: the maximization of monetary rewards, of various forms of power and autonomy, of security, and of status. Although the neo-rationalists share with the action theorists a view of people as actively pursuing their own goals in the organizational setting, they imply that it is the setting that suggests, even determines, the strategies used. In this respect, the neo-rationalist position tends toward that of the situational and technological determinists. Both schools argue that people in similar situations tend to behave similarly. The technological determinists are less explicit about the mechanism whereby this occurs. Some would say that people are molded by their situations, that their values and personalities change. Others, making neo-rationalistic assumptions, say that the logic of the situation, with its incentives and disincentives, its resources and its weaknesses, channels behavior without socializing the person. But whatever the mechanism, it is through an analysis of the situation that one can understand, and perhaps predict, the behavior of people in organizational settings. This idea goes counter to the action theorists' contention that it is necessary to take into account the differing prior orientations and definitions of the situation that people bring to situations.

The action approach, then, distinguishes itself from a social-structural and technological determinism in two ways: by its emphasis on differences in values and orientations to work among workers; and by its view of actors as rational and active in pursuit of their chosen goals. In reviewing the literature of industrial and organizational sociology, Silverman reports many studies finding that values and orientations make a difference, and many using a neo-rationalist approach to describe the strategies and tactics of actors in organizational settings, but very few studies embodying both of these aspects of the action approach. Some possible reasons for this gap will be discussed shortly.

The major recent empirical studies carried out from the action perspective have concentrated on the first point while virtually ignoring the second. Thus, "action approach" has come to signify merely any approach that takes into account workers' prior orientations to work, that is, the value differences among them regarding what they want out of work, and has come to be counterposed against any kind of situational determinism, even of the neo-rationalist variety.

This oversimplification has obfuscated the real issues raised by the action-theoretical critique of systems theory and functionalism. Sociologists identifying themselves as action theorists have attacked the neo-rationalists, with whom they presumably have much in common, and have cited with approval the cultural determinists, with whose over-socialized conception of man they presumably disagree. Action theory has mistakenly come to be identified with cultural determinism.

The tendency to equate the action approach with an emphasis on prior orientation as an explanatory variable was already evident in the first major piece of empirical research in industrial sociology to draw on the action approach, namely the "affluent worker" project of Goldthorpe, Lockwood, Bechhofer, and Platt (1968a, 1968b, 1969). This project had not been designed to test the hypotheses of action theory, nor even the hypothesis regarding the importance of prior orientations. The equation of the action approach with the hypothesis of prior orientations appears to have come about largely by accident. In trying to make sense of the data from the affluent worker study, Goldthorpe and his colleagues were struck by the extent to which their entire sample shared a generally instrumental orientation toward their work. Looking for the reasons for such an orientation, the authors were led to the conclusion that these workers had instrumental attitudes before taking their present jobs, and that many of their reactions to the work situation could be understood only if this prior orientation were taken into account.

The theoretical predilections of the authors led them to describe their subjects' adaptations in rational terms, seeing the trade-off between a more satisfying job and higher pay as a conscious choice. But in fact, their argument that the high value these workers placed on income influenced many of their reactions to work is more compatible with a cultural-determinist position than with an action approach.

The affluent worker study has given rise to a number of other studies (particularly Ingham, 1970 and Gallie, 1978) operationalizing the hypotheses of the action approach in the same way, seeking to show that value differences can lead to differences in work-related attitudes and behaviors. These tests of the prior orientations hypothesis, regardless of their outcomes, are insufficient to confirm the validity of the action approach.

An example, loosely based on our own research on the new working class in Italy, will clarify the difference between the explanatory paradigm implicit in the prior orientations approach and that of the action approach. Suppose a sample of employees has been asked a number of questions concerning (a) how important it is to them to be promoted within the company (an orientation to one aspect of the work situation); (b) how satisfied they are with opportunities for promotion (a definition of their present situation); and (c) the extent of their militancy as evidenced by their participation in strikes (a behavior to be explained). A number of relationships are possible among these three variables. Let us consider two of the more plausible.

In both cases, we assume that the data show that the more dissatisfied the person is with opportunities for promotion the more militant s/he will tend to be. Now let us introduce the third variable, the importance of promotion to the individual. We might find that those with little concern for promotion are more militant than those who are highly concerned about promotion. This set of relationships is shown in Figure 1. It implies that the desire for upward mobility reduces the willingness to participate in strikes.

In this case, there is no interaction between the orientation of the actor and his/her definition of the situation, although both variables have an effect on militancy. The prior orientation (concern for promotion) is an important explanatory variable, but so is the actor's judgment of the situation itself (satisfaction or dissatisfaction with opportunities). The fact that one of the explanatory variables originates outside the work situation is interesting, but the effect of this variable can be understood perfectly well in terms of the cultural-determinist framework. Its introduction refines but does not alter the conclusions regarding the effects of the situation itself.

Suppose, however, that when we control for the importance of promotion we find very different patterns in the two groups. Among those to whom promotion is very important, the level of militancy varies notably with their judgment of the availability of opportunities. If they are sat-

Figure 1.

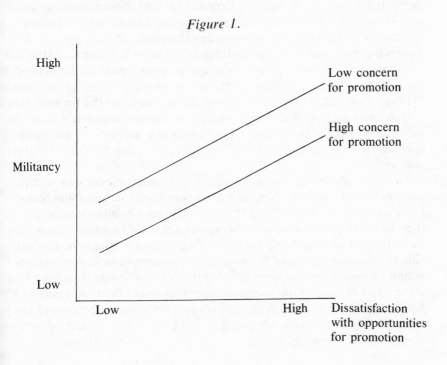

Figure 2.

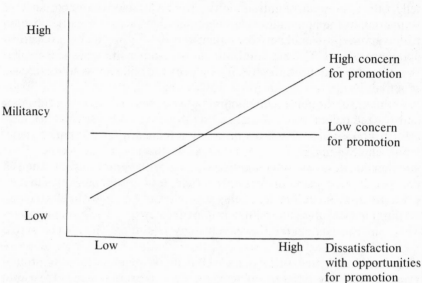

High

High concern
for promotion

Militancy

Low concern
for promotion

Low

Low   High   Dissatisfaction
                                                 with opportunities
                                                 for promotion

isfied with the opportunities for advancement they will be low in militancy, but if they are dissatisfied they will be high. Among those to whom
opportunities for promotion are not so important, satisfaction or dissatisfaction with the available opportunities has little impact on militancy.
This is the set of relationships pictured in Figure 2. In this case, there is a
clear interaction between the orientations of actors and their definitions of
the situation. Neither variable on its own is strongly related to militancy.
Without knowledge of the importance of promotion to the people in the
sample, satisfaction with promotion opportunities would appear to be
only slightly related to militancy. By taking prior orientation into account,
it becomes possible to discern a clear-cut relationship between the other
two variables.

  This type of finding unequivocally supports the contention that it is
essential to know something about workers' prior orientations if their
behavior is to be understood. It also supports the argument of action
theorists that behavior is not determined either by situational factors or
by individual attitudes and values, but can only be understood by considering the interaction of the two. In explaining these interactions, the
action approach has a distinct advantage. Yet Goldthorpe, Lockwood, et
al., as well as most of the subsequent proponents of the action approach,
have concentrated solely on trying to demonstrate the importance of prior
orientations. They have not managed to fill the gap revealed by Silverman's review of the literature.

There is another way in which the prior orientations hypothesis fails to reflect the assumptions of the action approach. It overlooks the point that actors redefine their situations through social interaction and socialization within organizations. The prior orientations hypothesis creates an artificial separation between socialization, presumed to have been completed at some earlier time in the person's career, and action based on values acquired during this earlier time but occurring in the present. Although Silverman, for example, argues for "a view of social reality as socially constructed, socially sustained, and socially changed" (1970: 5), in fact, leading proponents of the action approach such as Goldthorpe, Lockwood, et al., give practically no attention to the processes whereby values and definitions of the situation are changed. Socialization is relegated to the past. In the present there is only rational action. Yet there is abundant evidence that definition and redefinition of situations is a continuous process, and this is as the action approach itself would lead us to expect. This criticism has been developed at some length by Brown (1973) and Daniel (1973) in their discussions of the affluent worker studies. Here we would only note that some of the difficulties encountered in measuring prior orientations have to do with the fact that orientations are never entirely prior because they are constantly changing in response to the job situation. (For an excellent longitudinal study of how the job socializes the worker, see Kohn and Schooler, 1978.) Were action theorists to look more closely at the processes whereby definitions of the situation are created and maintained, they might not find themselves defending the position that all orientations, being freely arrived at, are equally valid. Even Silverman takes this position, which has given rise to the accusation that action theory bolsters the status quo (Daniel, 1969: 375). Presumably a major virtue of the action approach is its dialectical view, a view that should preclude any simple dichotomy between past and present, between prior orientation and present action.

The fact that the prior orientations hypothesis is more compatible with a cultural-determinist approach than with an action approach does not make the hypothesis less important. It is therefore of some interest to ask whether the evidence adduced by the authors of the affluent worker research is sufficient to support their conclusion that the results can best be explained in terms of the prior orientations of the workers. If the evidence from this influential study reveals itself to be less than completely convincing, the importance of prior orientations deserves a fresh look.

Goldthorpe, Lockwood, et al. based their argument on two major contentions: that the affluent workers in their sample tend to be more instrumental in their attitudes toward work than most other workers in similar types of jobs; and that the affluent workers' orientations are relatively homogeneous even across occupational groups and skill levels.

The argument that prior orientations are important is of necessity a relative one, based on comparisons between this sample and others and within this sample itself. Prior orientations are said to be more important than other factors, particularly occupational group and skill level. The evidence provided does not, however, give strong support to the argument.

To take the first contention first: the high level of instrumentalism and interest in the economic (extrinsic) rewards of work among the interviewees is inferred from the analysis of a number of tables showing high percentages of respondents mentioning such factors as important ones in judging a job. Yet such data is of limited value without direct comparisons with the responses of other samples to similar questions. Some comparisons subsequently made suggest that the affluent workers of Luton are not unusually instrumental (Wedderburn and Crompton, 1972: 146; Cousins and Brown, 1975: 70; Platt, 1971). Even among the tables presented in the affluent worker volumes, there are several one might point to in which the intrinsic rewards of work emerge as more important than the extrinsic (for example, Goldthorpe, Lockwood, et al., 1968a: tables 5, 7, 11, 18).

The second contention concerns the homogeneity of the responses across occupational groups and skill levels. If people doing different sorts of jobs respond similarly to questions related to their work, one can only conclude that variation in the work situation does not have a strong effect, or at least that its effect is overridden by that of the shared orientation the workers had before taking the jobs in question. The authors of the affluent worker study do not claim that skill level is unrelated to attitudes. They point out that there are important differences between the skilled and the semiskilled. Nonetheless, they argue, the basic similarity in the responses of the semiskilled, be they process workers, assemblers, or machinists, undermines the claims of the technological determinists. And in summarizing their findings, they emphasize the overriding similarities among all groups in the sample.

The judgment as to whether a particular percentage difference between groups is great or small is inevitably subjective. Yet considering the magnitude of the attitudinal differences between skill levels, and considering also that skill level emerges as more important than nonwork variables as a predictor of instrumentalism, it is hard not to conclude that at least this particular technology-related variable is of great importance. The skilled are consistently less instrumental and economistic than the semiskilled. For example, 49% of the assemblers were "highly instrumental" (according to the scale developed by the authors) as compared to only 16% of the craftsmen; conversely, 54% of the craftsmen were "less instrumental" as compared to only 22% of the assemblers

(Goldthorpe, Lockwood, et al., 1968a: 161, table 72). Even among the three semiskilled groups, there are differences in the expected direction, the assemblers being more instrumental than the process workers and the machinists.

The underemphasis on the work situation is all the more difficult to understand considering that the authors found only weak links between nonwork variables and orientations to work or other work-related attitudes. They report that geographical mobility is not significantly associated with instrumentalism once skill level is controlled for. Downward social mobility is associated with instrumentalism, but less strongly than skill level and only if it is intergenerational rather than intragenerational. The authors suggest that the mid-life family situation of their respondents forced them to give greater weight to economic needs than might people at other stages of life, but the lack of variance within their sample prevented them from testing this plausible hypothesis.

The substantial differences between occupational groups tend, in sum, to belie the argument that the sample is homogeneous in its instrumentalism. Within skill levels, the argument of homogeneity can be made more convincingly. But skill level is, after all, one of the major ways in which technology affects work. The technological determinists, such as Blauner and Woodward, see the effects of technology on worker attitudes as mediated through its effects on skill levels. They may be mistaken regarding the extent to which jobs in continuous process plants are more interesting than those in mass production industries. But this issue is irrelevant to the general question of how or whether variations in the intrinsic interest and skill of a job affect work-related attitudes. The explanation for the finding that skilled workers are much less instrumental than semiskilled is evidently that they find their work more interesting and are more involved in it. As Salaman (1974) has shown in his study of occupational communities, the degree of involvement in work is a very important variable affecting many attitudes and indeed the worker's whole way of life. This observation is confirmed, not refuted, by the data presented in the first volume of the affluent worker study (Goldthorpe, Lockwood, et al., 1968a).

Linking industrial sociology to important issues in stratification, the affluent worker study stimulated interest in the world of work at a time when such interest was very low in the English-speaking world. It also created interest in the action approach. But this interest has centered on the question of the importance of prior orientations, while other implications of the action approach have been ignored.

In essence, the question raised by the affluent worker project is that old sociological chestnut: How important are values? In this case, it is rephrased to ask, how important are values, or prior orientations, or nonwork variables, relative to technology and the work situation? The question is still a live and important one. But the dispute can better be described as being between technological determinists and cultural determinists rather than between technological determinists and action theorists. The action theorist would not be interested in showing that prior orientations are more important than situational characteristics as determinants of workers' reactions. Rather, s/he would seek to show how neither of these factors on its own can explain these reactions, how they result from interaction between the orientations and the work situation.

One part of the debate stimulated by the affluent worker study has revolved around the findings of the study itself (Daniel, 1969; Goldthorpe, 1970; Daniel, 1971; Goldthorpe, 1972; Argyris, 1972; Mackenzie, 1974; Westergaard, 1970). Another part of the debate has gone beyond the affluent worker data to bring new evidence to bear on the question of prior orientations and worker attitudes (Ingham, 1970; Cotgrove and Vamplew, 1972; Wedderburn and Crompton, 1972; Brown, 1973; Daniel, 1973; Gallie, 1978; Low-Beer, 1978). Literatures beyond the confines of industrial sociology are also relevant here: in organizational behavior, the debate between those who give importance to individual differences and those who stress the impact of objective characteristics of the situation (Hackman, 1977; Hackman, Pearce, and Caminis, 1978; Kohn and Schooler, 1978); in political sociology and social and labor history, the debate between those who point out differences in the political traditions of regions or countries with similar social structural characteristics and those who, for example, see similarities among people in the same occupation in different countries (Mitchell and Stearns, 1971; Berger, 1972; Valenzuela, 1979). All these related debates concern the relative importance of values or other psychological properties of individuals on the one hand and social structure on the other.

In this debate, there are only a handful of studies supporting the contention of action theory that interactions of variables are very important. The few studies finding interactions analogous to the one illustrated in Figure 2 are cited repeatedly in the literature. Some of the studies cited in support of the action approach only find differences in the reactions of different groups, not interactions. These findings are compatible with an additive model as well as with an interactive one.

Two studies in the sociology of work literature are frequently cited as evidence of the importance of interactions. One is by Turner and Lawrence (1965), who carried out a survey to determine how various attributes of the job affect worker satisfaction and absenteeism. To their surprise, they found no relationship between the complexity and skill requirements of a job and the satisfaction of the workers. Further analysis revealed two opposite response patterns. Satisfaction among rural or small town workers, predominantly Protestant, tended to be higher in the more demanding jobs. But among urban workers, predominantly Catholic, satisfaction was higher in the less demanding jobs. The authors explained these findings by the greater commitment to American middle-class values among rural Protestant workers.

The second study is one by Blood and Hulin (1967) that confirmed these results. They found opposite reactions to similar jobs among workers in different types of communities (more "alienated" vs less "alienated").

Frequently cited studies by Dalton (1948) and Karpik (1968) have also found differences between rural and urban workers, but their research designs do not enable them to say whether these represent two opposite patterns, as in Figure 2, or whether they are simply additive differences, as in Figure 1.

More recently, a group of studies carried out by J. Richard Hackman and his colleagues has found evidence of both direct and interaction effects (Oldham, Hackman, and Pearce, 1975; Hackman, Pearce, and Caminis, 1978). The studies are about the effects of job enrichment on workers' attitudes and performance. They find that job enrichment has various positive effects, but they also find that workers with strong needs for psychological growth respond more positively than those without such needs. Under one special set of circumstances, using one particular measure of performance, they find opposite trends, the performance of one group improving while that of the other actually worsens. It is only in such cases that prior orientations *must* be taken into account if we are to discern a relationship between the situation and the reaction.

Contrary to the claim of cultural determinists and action theorists, the evidence indicates that one can understand a good deal about workers' reactions by applying a commonsense rationalistic model of human behavior to a knowledge of the situation. Why are the interaction effects hypothesized by action theorists so rarely found to be important? It could be argued that the reason is that most research designs do not allow the researcher even to consider the question of interaction. In order to find interaction, it is necessary to vary both independent variables, i.e., the orientations of the individual and the characteristics of the situation. We have already noted the further methodological problem of measuring prior orientations. The action model assumes that people's values are brought to the work situation rather than determined by it. But in fact, values are also molded by the job situation. The theory would have us isolate a set of relationships that cannot easily be abstracted.

But even were the methodological problems resolved, interactions would probably not be as important as they are claimed to be by adherents of the action approach. The more highly structured a situation is, and the more heavily it impinges on the actors, the less variability there is likely to be in their reactions. This is true for two reasons: first, because such situations tend to socialize people more; and second, because even apart from their socializing impact, such situations contain more powerful incentives and disincentives to which a rationalistic model also would predict less variable responses. The work situation is such a highly structured one, containing powerful incentives. Although there are differences in reactions to such situations, it is not often that these differences consist of opposite reaction patterns such as those pictured in Figure 2.

The rarity of interaction effects brings us back again to the question of the relative importance of work and nonwork variables (i.e., of structure and prior orientations) in accounting for the reactions of workers. Common sense and a number of studies suggest that the more an attitude or behavior has to do with broad social issues and with politics, the more likely it is that it will be affected by nonwork variables. Conversely, the more closely an attitude or behavior concerns the job situation, the more likely it is to be influenced by that situation. Cotgrove and Vamplew, in a study of process workers in five factories in various parts of the British Isles, found that support for unions and attitudes toward management were influenced by political socialization, but that technology played an important role "in determining the meaning and satisfaction derived from work itself" (Cotgrove and Vamplew, 1972: 182). Cousins and Brown caution against assuming "any automatic link between images of the class structure and attitudes toward industrial relations topics . . ." (Cousins and Brown, 1975: 79). Among the Tyneside shipbuilding workers they interviewed, "relative militancy can be associated with individualistic attitudes to personal careers and mobility and a prestige model of the class structure; solidaristic support for the Labour movement with a consensus model of the firm" (Cousins and Brown, 1975: 79). Armstrong points out the cognitive disjunction between the domains of industry and society among the chemical workers he studied (Nichols and Armstrong, 1976: 152). Wedderburn and Crompton (1972) conclude from still another study of a chemical complex that whereas attitudes toward the company were not related to the technology or to the control system, attitudes within the work situation did depend on these variables.

The desire to attack the reigning orthodoxy of technological determinism and the need to stake out a clear position regardless of the complexity of real-world data have led proponents of the prior orientations hypothesis and of the action approach to overstate their case. We have already noted some of the problems of the affluent worker study. But nowhere is this overstatement more evident than in Duncan Gallie's book, *In Search of the New Working Class*. The new working class thesis represents just the type of theory that action theorists and cultural determinists are challenging. It sees technology as the determinant of militancy and radicalism, making no allowance for variations in culture and values among workers. If Mallet's arguments are valid, the propensity toward militancy and radicalism should exist among technicians of all countries. Obviously, this is not the case. But if one considers strictly work-related attitudes, one can discern some similarities among technicians in different countries. Gallie's claim that technology has very little importance for the social integration of the work force within the enterprise, for the structure of managerial power, and for the nature of trade unionism (Gallie, 1978: 295) is as extreme as Mallet's opposite claim.

Let us look more closely at some of the evidence about the new working class. Because Gallie is the major critic of the new working class thesis from the cultural-determinist perspective, and because his is one of the few good empirical studies directed toward the issues raised by Mallet, we will discuss it in some detail.

Gallie starts out by considering the work of Mallet and Blauner, two theorists who claim that technology has determinate effects on working-class consciousness while presenting diametrically opposed views on just what these effects are. Blauner sees automation as leading to the social integration of the worker into the enterprise, whereas Mallet sees it as leading to a renewal of class conflict. As Gallie observes, the very fact of these opposite conclusions casts doubt upon the idea that technology has determinate effects on attitudes. He argues that "[t]he degree of social integration in the highly automated sector will more probably depend on the cultural values prevalent in the wider collectivity to which the workers belong, and on the nature of the institutional structures characteristic of the society in which the automated sector emerges" (Gallie, 1978: 35). His research intends to "evaluate the relative importance of technological determinants on the one hand and cultural variables on the other" (Gallie, 1978: 37). His design compares plants using the same technology in two countries, thus holding technology constant while varying cultural factors. The data come from interviews carried out in four oil refineries, two in Britain and two in France.

Gallie reports major differences between French and British refinery workers. The French workers were more dissatisfied with their salaries and more militant about problems emerging from the organization of work. They tended to see the firm as exploitative, worker-management relations as dichotomous and socially distant, and the authority structure as illegitimate. In comparison, the British had a cooperative image of the firm and of worker-management relations and viewed the authority structure as legitimate (Gallie, 1978: 300).

He also describes major differences in managerial structures and union goals. French management was autocratic, giving worker representatives no power, formal or informal, to influence decision making. While this gave management greater autonomy, it also created problems in motivating and controlling the work force. In contrast, British management allowed more participation to shop floor representatives. This legitimized managerial authority, but gave the work force veto power over many aspects of the organization of work (Gallie, 1978: 302–308). As for the unions, Gallie sees the French unions as primarily interested in heightening class consciousness among the work force so as to encourage them along the road to socialism, whereas the British unions were interested in bargaining with management over specific issues. In this process, they were willing to play a helping role in controlling the work force in exchange for organizational benefits from management (1978: 313).

These observations are undoubtedly very interesting. But Gallie claims too much for them when he maintains that they show the irrelevance of technology. First, it must be pointed out that Gallie's version of technological determinism is largely a straw man of his own creation. The technological determinist does not claim to explain all variation in terms of technology. Cultural differences in the attitudes of workers do not exclude technologically determined differences. As in Figure 1, both a prior orientation and a characteristic of the job situation may affect attitudes independently. Thus, even though workers from France and Britain may differ in their attitudes, a French refinery worker may still have more in common with a British refinery worker than with a French electrician.

Gallie addresses this issue only superficially. At one point, he asks "whether or not technology might enhance or reduce aspirations for control within a given national context" (1978: 146). This question is difficult to answer, he says, because little comparative data is available. However, he did include in his interviews with the French workers three items on attitudes toward worker control from a national survey of French workers. In their responses to these three items, the refinery workers were if anything less favorable toward worker control than the national sample. This appears to support Gallie's argument. But a fuller treatment of the issue is called for in view of its importance and the amount of evidence showing that technology does make a difference. Three items, all on a single content issue and from one country only, do not constitute a large amount of data.

Even given the paucity of data, some further analysis would have been possible. For example, the curious reader can only wonder whether there were differences between the responses of the operators and the maintenance workers, i.e., between the skilled and the semiskilled, on these items. In fact, throughout the book the tables generally present the responses to various items by refinery without further breakdown by type of job. On some issues, Gallie indicates that there were substantial differences between maintenance workers and operators, but on others he does not say whether there were differences or not. Since the variation between these jobs is the only variation in the structure of the job situation within the sample, more systematic analysis along these lines would have been a step in the direction of "evaluat[ing] the relative importance of technological determinants on the one hand and cultural variables on the other" (1978: 37).

In his conclusion, Gallie comes back to the question of variation within a national context to recognize, though only fleetingly and with qualifications, that he has not done justice to it. "Although the critical determinants of worker attitudes clearly lie elsewhere, it may nonetheless be the case that technology has some influence within a specific national context. An examination of whether this is in fact the case would require a different research design" (1978: 300).

Indeed it would! The design, which includes no variance at all in technology, makes it impossible for him to "evaluate the relative importance of technological determinants . . . and cultural variables." Certain research designs lead their authors to certain conclusions while blinding them to others. Gallie's intention from the start was not to "evaluate the relative importance" etc., but to show the importance of cultural factors. This he succeeds in doing, but he fails to substantiate the stronger claim that technology is *not* a significant determinant of attitudes.

A glance at other literature in the prior orientations debate confirms the point that certain research designs are associated with certain positions. Those studies whose design includes several plants with the same technology tend to stress the importance of prior orientations and cultural factors, whereas those studies whose design includes different technologies and a culturally homogeneous work force tend to stress the importance of technology. Obviously, if one variable is held constant in the design, it cannot emerge as a major source of variation.

The classic works emphasizing technology as a determinant of attitudes and behavior are studies of several industries (Sayles, 1958; Blauner, 1964; Woodward, 1965, 1970). Historical studies of the labor movement have delineated different types of unionism, each corresponding to a different technology: craft unionism, mass-production unionism, new working class unionism, etc. (Touraine, 1966; Bauman, 1972; Turner, 1962; Greenstone, 1969). On the other hand, many of the studies giving most weight to prior orientations are studies of one industry, sometimes in different regions (Cotgrove and Vamplew, 1972; Turner, Clack, and Roberts, 1967; Dalton, 1948). Research seriously intended to assess the relative importance of culture and technology would have to include both cultural and technological variation in its design.

Gallie's design creates a further methodological problem which undermines his criticism of social-structural and technological determinism—

the confounding of variation in institutional structure with variation in the cultural values of individual workers. Gallie claims to be showing that "[w]orkers in societies with different cultural patterns . . . interpret similar objective situations in substantially different ways" (1978: 35). In fact, however, the objective situations faced by the workers in the British refineries are quite different from the objective situations faced by the workers in the French ones. Indeed, the descriptions of these differences constitute the most interesting and original parts of the book. Because of this, it is impossible to say whether the attitudinal differences are really due to cultural differences or whether they are simply due to the different situations encountered by French and British workers. Gallie himself attributes many of the attitudinal differences to differences in managerial strategies and institutional structure. A good example of this is the French workers' more conflictual view of relations between workers and management. Because the French management *was* much more autocratic than the British, it is not possible to say to what extent the views of French workers are attributable to cultural factors.

In any case, it is hardly surprising that the commonsense of the French worker is informed by a popularized Marxism whereas the British worker is a pragmatic liberal. No technological determinist could deny that such differences exist, and that the influence of technology is filtered through the prevailing culture. To the extent that technology has an effect, it is within the national context, around the national mean. Furthermore, as suggested above, the effects of the job situation will be more pronounced on attitudes closely related to the job.

Our own findings from a study of the new working class in Italy do not support the sweeping negations of Gallie any more than they do the generalizations of Mallet. The study, carried out in 1970–1971, is based on a sample of eighty-eight technicians in two electronics plants in Milan, one traditionally hierarchical in its authority structure, the other democratic and participatory. The technicians were interviewed in their homes about a wide range of subjects in order to understand the sources of the militancy that arose in the late sixties. The findings indicate once again that attitudes most closely related to work are indeed predictable from a knowledge of the work situation, but that attitudes and behaviors that can be broadly construed as political are not much affected by workplace variation.

In Italy, unlike in countries were the labor movement is less politicized, to participate in a strike inevitably has a political meaning. In fact, the political significance of strike participation overrides its meaning as an action directed toward immediate goals. The individual decision to participate in a strike is a decision to support or not to support the unions, which are viewed as quasi-political organizations. Because srikes in Italy often occur in the middle of the work day and last only a short time, such individual decisions assume a relevance they do not have in countries where strikes shut down an entire plant for a longer period of time.

The political meaning of strike participation is obvious within our sample. Political party identification is the best predictor of strike participation, better even than union membership. It alone explains 29.2% of the variance in strike participation. (For a more detailed discussion of this and following analyses see Low-Beer, 1978.) Political party identification is in turn related to social background. The fact that 58% of the fathers of the men in the sample were blue-collar workers or peasants is far more important in explaining their militancy than the advanced technology of their work environments.

Another important predictor of strike participation is the ambition to move up within the company. Those who say they are interested in becoming bosses are considerably less likely to strike, and this item adds 17.3% to the variance explained by the regression equation. Those interested in moving up also tend to be more individualistic and less solidaristic in their orientations to work and to their peers, and they tend to perceive greater opportunities for mobility. But within our sample, these attitudes are not related to any real variation in opportunities for mobility. In any case, the ambition to advance inhibits strike participation even if the person does not believe that it is possible to get ahead. This is the relationship pictured in Figure 1.

Even though aspirations to move up are not related to opportunities within the range of variation in the sample, it seems likely that as the barriers to mobility faced by technicians have become more and more difficult to surmount, the number of people who maintain such ambitions has decreased. Thus, long-run changes in the work situation have probably affected the availability of technicians for participation in collective actions. Aspirations to move up are also affected by social background. Technicians of working class origins are more solidaristic in their attitudes, and, if not less ambitious—they are not less likely to be attending night school—at least less willing to admit to their ambitions to move up within the company.

Within our sample, social background is much more important than the work situation in influencing the decision to participate in a strike. There are substantial differences among technicians doing different types of work in their attitudes toward the organization and in their satisfaction with their jobs, but these differences have little effect on strike participation.

Attitudes that workers bring to their situations do, then, prove to be the most important determinants of strike participation, but their effects are direct and are not influenced by variations in the work situation. This point is confirmed by analysis of items specifically included to consider the importance of orientations to work. In addition to questions about pay, mobility, intrinsic interest of the job, and so on, we included items from the affluent worker study asking the technicians what are the most important characteristics to look for in a job and how they would rate their present job on these characteristics. Aspects most frequently mentioned were interest, high pay, friends, and career possibilities. For each aspect, a dummy variable was created, grouping together those who said it was important as against those who did not mention it. Analyses were then carried out to see whether orientations to work interacted with judgments about the work situation in the manner predicted by action theorists.

Only one interaction was found between orientations to work and judgments about the job, and it was not statistically significant. A description of how the question was addressed in this case will serve to illustrate the procedure. Technicians who are dissatisfied with their pay are more likely to strike than those who are satisfied ($r = .238$). This tendency is accentuated in those to whom pay is important. A new variable was created to gauge the increase in explanatory power obtained by taking into account orientation toward pay, i.e., to gauge the strength of the interaction. Those who are highly dissatisfied with their pay and consider pay to be important were coded *1*, those who are highly dissatisfied but do not consider pay to be important were coded *2*, and so on, up to those, coded *5*, who consider pay to be important and are completely satisfied. The correlation between the new variable and strike participation rises to .290.

A regression analysis was carried out to test the significance of the interaction effect. The dependent variable was strike participation. The independent variables were (1) the extent of dissatisfaction with pay, measured as the percentage difference between actual pay and what the respondent would consider to be fair, (2) a dummy variable indicating whether the respondent considered pay to be one of the most important aspects of a job or not, and (3) the new variable described above consisting of the interaction between the previous two. The first variable explains 5.7% of the variance in strike participation and has a coefficient significant at the .02 level. But the other two variables add little to the explanatory power of the equation. The interaction variable adds less than 1% to the R^2, and is not even entered into the equation.[3] These findings do not support the contention of action theory that a behavior such as participating in a strike can only be understood by considering how people with different orientations react to particular situations.

The findings do, however, support the prior orientations hypothesis. In the monograph reporting this research, we criticized the new working class theorists for their exclusive emphasis on the work situation.

The weakest point in the new working class theorists' arguments is their conceptualization of the relationship between the work situation and the political situation.
For them, the sources of militancy are exclusively internal to organizations. [Both
Gorz and Mallet] see the generalization from trade-unionistic goals to revolutionary
goals as inevitable. Their arguments are curiously devoid of any references to the
individual or collective histories of workers, their social backgrounds, their political
attitudes, and their prior orientations to work. The causal links between life at work
and life outside of work are all in one direction: from work to other realms. Our
findings, however, show strong causal relationships only in the opposite direction:
from attitudes acquired outside the work situation to militancy in the work situation
(Low-Beer, 1978: 229–230).

At the same time, we noted that some aspects of the new working class
strikes, "namely their emphasis on participation as a means of governing
the strike and on control as a strike objective, cannot be explained by
reference to the preconditions that have always been necessary for any
kind of strike" (Low-Beer, 1978: 210). A leftist background and a disin-
terest in being promoted may make a technician sympathetic to union
action, but these factors are only preconditions, not causes, of strike
action. In order to understand the emergence of new tactics and demands,
we must look at the tensions generated by the work situation. Here we
find some support for situational determinism and for the specific hypotheses of Mallet.

Many of the technicians we interviewed expressed strong discontent
with the organization within which they worked. They complained of
directives being changed without explanation, of a lack of contacts with
technicians and engineers doing related work in other parts of the plant,
and of having to do things without understanding why, and they frequently expressed a desire to work in a more collaborative mode. As predicted by Gorz and Mallet, their involvement in work heightened these
needs instead of meeting them. Discontent of this sort tended to occur in
situations where there was an incongruence between the job and the
organizational structure, for example, where the job was involving and
interesting but the organization was hierarchical and authoritarian, or
where the job was routine but the organization was democratic and
participatory. The involvement that exists in these incongruent situations
leads to an attitude that is demanding, but positive and creative. The
demand is to be allowed to do the job right. This is not something a
profit-oriented company can always allow.

French studies of the new working class (Durand, 1971; Durand and
Durand, 1971; Sainsaulieu, 1972; Maurice, 1965) have come up with
strikingly similar findings. They describe technicians as highly involved in
their work, and see this involvement as leading to "conflictual participation" (a committed but demanding attitude toward work and toward the
organization), particularly when the organizational structure is hierarchical and authoritarian. These studies are organizational in focus, and have

little to say about life outside of work and attitudes toward politics. But they do point out that many of the technicians are of blue-collar origins and share a working-class outlook, while noting, as we have, that the conflict over immediate work-related issues is not related to whatever concern about broader social and political issues they may have.

Among the technicians in our sample, the attitude of discontent with the organization is weakly, if significantly, related to strike participation ($r = .231$). The fact that strike participation is viewed primarily as a political issue accounts in part for the unimportance of work. Our choice of sites and the methodology employed tend to weaken still further the links between strike participation and workplace issues.

In the two firms we studied, the setting of strike objectives and the control of strike actions were in the hands of the unions and their activists within the plant. The white-collar strike had become institutionalized. Its spontaneity was reduced by the diffusion of demands and tactics from other plants and by the strength of the existing union organization. The importance of political attitudes, closely related to attitudes toward the unions, and of other preconditions for a collective strategy were accordingly greater and the importance of immediate causes was reduced.

In contrast, those firms in which new working class militancy was most dramatic were unionized weakly, if at all. The strikes broke out spontaneously, with no prior organizing activity. Most of these firms were highly bureaucratized, and employed large numbers of technicians. The immediate causes of the strikes were more visible in these cases. In one case, the attempt by management to introduce a system of job evaluation provided the spark. In others, the plants were threatened by foreign takeover or by layoffs due to mismanagement. Organizational issues, which under normal circumstances would never be subject to collective bargaining, now became subject to bargaining. In some cases, it was clear to all employees that their jobs were at stake, and middle management participated along with technicians, engineers, and blue-collar workers. The new militancy of technicians on issues of control was evident in these cases. Our decision not to study the sites of the most publicized new working class strikes thus affected our findings in this area.

Taking the individual as the unit of analysis also reduces the weight of immediate causes as opposed to preconditions. The factors influencing the decision of the rank and file to participate in an on-going strike are likely to be different from those motivating the activists who start the strike. A precise assessment of the relative importance of causes and preconditions would require a sample of plants in addition to a sample of individuals. It is not coincidental that the new working class theorists focused on the plant and the strike as their units of analysis. This enabled them to stress organizational tensions and to overlook the importance of preconditions favorable to massive participation and support.

As we have insisted all along, it is to be expected that both prior orientations and the work situation will have independent effects on workers' attitudes and behaviors. We have described the importance of political attitudes and attitudes toward mobility in understanding strike participation. In Italy, and probably in France as well, the decision to strike is more influenced by factors external to the work situation than by the work situation itself. Yet although the aspirations and discontents generated by the job will rarely be sufficient cause for a strike, they will color the behavior of technicians on strike.

Mallet and other proponents of the new working class thesis failed to note the significance of the preconditions encouraging strike participation—the working-class social origins of many technicians and their leftist sympathies, together with the declining opportunities for upward mobility within company bureaucracies—while overestimating the importance of tensions generated by the job itself as causes of the new militancy. Mallet's description of the work situation does prove useful in understanding the themes of power and control prominent in new working class strikes. The feelings of discontent articulated by the technicians in our sample match his accounts well. Increased involvement in work does lead to higher aspirations and to more participation in other aspects of life at work. The professional knowledge of technicians does give them a degree of self-confidence and cosmopolitanism of outlook not possessed by less highly trained workers.

Mallet's errors were to assume first, that greater involvement inevitably leads to greater friction within organizations, and second, that such friction is inevitably translated into militancy. There is a sense in which Gallie is correct when he observes that the effects of technology on social integration are indeterminate. The indeterminacy is, however, only partly attributable to differences in the cultural values or prior orientations of workers. First, organizational structure conditions the impact of technology so that even workers in two companies using the same technology in the same city may face different work situations. Discontent will be generated among technicians if the organizational structure constrains and represses them as they go about their work. In countries such as France and Italy, with traditions of bureaucratic authoritarianism, such discontent will be more widespread than in countries such as Britain or the United States, where management is more likely to realize that there are circumstances under which it can benefit from enlightened policies. If creativity and commitment are more important to the production process than routine labor, democratic management is likely to pay (Low-Beer, 1978: 211–217).

Even given a certain level of discontent with the organization of work, militancy does not automatically result. Other variables enter into play. Among the most important of these are the social backgrounds and political views of the workers, the political traditions and organizations in the area, and the availability of opportunities for mobility.

Where new working-class militancy does develop, its political expression and implications will vary, even though it will everywhere manifest an interest in control over working conditions. In some countries, technicians will be found allied with the working class. In others, their unionism will be narrowly self-interested rather than class conscious in the Marxist sense. In one variant or another, new working-class militancy is already visible in many countries, among teachers, doctors, and other white-collar employees as well as among technicians.

In the course of this discussion of the new working class thesis, we have sought to evaluate three theoretical positions: the situational determinist and its subtype, the technological determinist position; the cultural determinist or prior orientations position; and the action approach proper. Basing ourselves on the evidence presented, we can now draw a few conclusions regarding each.

Situational and technological determinists belong to one or another of two different schools. One school, with which we have not concerned ourselves here, argues that people are socialized by their job situations. Certainly, work does socialize people, but this cannot easily account for the new militancy of technicians. The second school is the neo-rationalist. It argues that people's responses to situations can be understood by applying a commonsense rationalistic model of behavior to a knowledge of the situation. This sort of explanation is appealing in its parsimony. Different behaviors, such as retreatism, satisfied involvement, and militancy are all explained by one model. Occam's razor invites us to see how much can be explained by such a model before resorting to more complex explanations. Insofar as a situation is highly structured and contains powerful incentives, positive or negative, a rationalistic model may go quite far toward predicting behavior. Our review of the evidence indicates that it can account for immediately work-related attitudes and behavior quite well, but that it becomes progressively less adequate as the behavior to be explained is less subject to immediate constraints.

For the cultural determinists, the key to understanding behavior at work is knowing what it is that workers want out of work. Variations in the work situation itself are seen as less important than the values that people bring to the situation. In its recent industrial sociology versions, cultural determinism has gone under the name of action theory. We have argued that this is a misappropriation of the name, because these theorists omit an important aspect of action theory, namely its view of people as actively and rationally pursuing strategies. We have argued further that cultural determinism, with its emphasis on prior orientations, is not incompatible with situational or technological determinism, notwithstanding the attacks of the former school on the sweeping generalizations of the latter. There is no *a priori* logical reason why prior orientations and situational characteristics should not both have effects on workplace behavior. The interesting question that then arises concerns their relative importance in explaining various reactions to work. On this point, as we have just noted, the evidence suggests that the more a response concerns politics and the world outside of work, the more it will be influenced by individual values and prior orientations, and the more difficult it will be to predict the outcome by applying a commonsense rationalistic model.

The action approach combines the neo-rationalism of some situational determinists with an emphasis on prior orientations. According to action theory, people come to situations with different orientations and define them in terms of their own ends. They then use the resources at their disposal to attain these ends. From the action point of view, the idea that cultural values cause people to respond in certain ways is no better a representation of reality than the idea that their responses are determined by the work situation. The response is the result of the interaction that takes place when an actor with certain orientations encounters a given situation, defines it in his/her own terms, and responds accordingly. Interactions between personal values and situations are said to be so important that responses are predictable only if one knows the characteristics of both the person and the situation.

Plausible though the notion of interactions may be, there is little evidence that they are very important in understanding workplace behavior. This conclusion seems warranted even taking into account the problems of measuring prior orientations mentioned earlier. In fact, much variance can be explained simply in terms of the separate (i.e., direct) effects of situational variables and prior orientations. Many work situations are so constraining that they result in fairly similar reactions among most workers, short of radical cultural differences. Other behaviors, such as strike participation among the technicians in our sample, are less influenced by the specific character of the job and are more influenced by the individual values of the workers. Few reactions are influenced by both prior orientations and situational characteristics. The major contribution of the action approach is not its specific explanatory model, but its neo-rationalist emphasis, its view of people as active and rational. This view, which is not, however, unique to action theory, has provided in recent years a needed counterweight to the functionalist emphasis on values and socialization.

The major theoretical contenders remaining in the ring are the cultural determinists and the neo-rationalist technological determinists. Their debate comes down to that old sociological chestnut: How important are values? Our answer is: It depends. Judging from the debate, this answer is unsatisfyingly bland to some. Yet no doubt, if it were not so, the debate would not have lasted as long as it has.

ACKNOWLEDGMENT

I am indebted to J. Samuel Valenzuela for his comments on a first draft of this paper.

NOTES

1. The term *determinism* is not used in a strict philosophical sense here, but only to indicate that the theory in question attributes major direct causal importance to one factor (social structure in the one case, individual properties such as values, prior orientations, or psychological characteristics in the other), often while denying or downplaying the importance of others.

2. This in spite of competing usages referring to very different groups such as the urban poor (Miller and Riessman, 1968).

3. When the regression equation is run without variable (2), the interaction increases the R^2 by 3.4%. The standardized coefficient for this term is .231, significant at the .08 level.

REFERENCES

Argyris, Chris
1972   The Applicability of Organizational Sociology. Cambridge, U.K.: Cambridge University Press.
Bauman, Zygmunt
1972   Between Class and Elite: The Evolution of the British Labour Movement. Trans. Sheila Patterson. Manchester, U.K.: Manchester University Press.
Berger, Suzanne
1972   Peasants Against Politics: Rural Organization in Brittany, 1911–1967. Cambridge, Mass.: Harvard University Press.
Blauner, Robert
1964   Alienation and Freedom. Chicago: University of Chicago Press.
Blood, Milton R. and C. L. Hulin
1967   "Alienation, Environmental Characteristics, and Worker Responses." Journal of Applied Psychology 51: 284–290.
Brown, Richard
1973   "Sources of Objectives in Work and Employment." Pp. 17–38 in John Child (ed.), Man and Organization. London: George Allen & Unwin.
Cotgrove, Stephen and Clive Vamplew
1972   "Technology, Class, and Politics: The Case of the Process Workers." Sociology 6: 169–185.
Cousins, Jim and Richard Brown
1975   "Patterns of Paradox: Shipbuilding Workers' Images of Society." Pp. 55–82 in Martin Bulmer (ed.), Working-Class Images of Society. London: Routledge & Kegan Paul.
Crozier, Michel
1964   The Bureaucratic Phenomenon. Chicago: University of Chicago Press.

Dalton, Melville
1948 "The Industrial 'Rate-Buster': A Characterization." Applied Anthropology 7: 5-18.
Daniel, W. W.
1969 "Industrial Behavior and Orientation to Work: A Critique." Journal of Management Studies 6: 366-375.
1971 "Productivity Bargaining and Orientation to Work: A Rejoinder to Goldthorpe." Journal of Management Studies 8: 329-335.
1973 "Understanding Employee Behavior in its Context: Illustrations from Productivity Bargaining." Pp. 39-62 in John Child (ed.), Man and Organization. London: George Allen & Unwin.
Durand, Claude
1971 "Ouvriers et techniciens en mai 1968." Pp. 7-159 in Pierre Dubois, et al., Grèves revendicatives ou grèves politiques? Paris: Editions Anthropos.
Durand, Claude, and Michelle Durand
1971 De l'o.s. a l'ingénieur. Paris: Les Editions Ouvrières.
Galbraith, John Kenneth
1967 The New Industrial State. Boston: Houghton Mifflin.
Gallie, Duncan
1978 In Search of the New Working Class. Cambridge, U.K.: Cambridge University Press.
Goldthorpe, John
1970 "The Social Action Approach to Industrial Sociology: A Rely to Daniel." Journal of Management Studies 7: 199-208.
1972 "Daniel on Orientations to Work: A Final Comment." Journal of Management Studies 9: 266-273.
Goldthorpe, John H., David Lockwood, Frank Bechhofer, and Jennifer Platt
1968a The Affluent Worker: Industrial Attitudes and Behavior. Cambridge, U.K.: Cambridge University Press.
1968b The Affluent Worker: Political Attitudes and Behavior. Cambridge, U.K.: Cambridge University Press.
1969 The Affluent Worker in the Class Structure. Cambridge, U.K.: Cambridge University Press.
Gorz, André
1964 Strategy for Labor. Trans. Martin Nicholaus and Victoria Ortiz. Boston: Beacon, 1967.
1971 "Techniques, techniciens et lutte des classes." Les temps modernes 301-302: 141-180.
Greenstone, J. David
1969 Labor in American Politics. New York: Knopf.
Hackman, J. Richard
1977 "Work Design." Pp. 96-162 in J. R. Hackman and J. L. Suttle (eds.), Improving Life at Work: Behavioral Science Approaches to Organizational Change. Santa Monica, Calif.: Goodyear.
Hackman, J. Richard, Jone L. Pearce, and Jane Caminis Wolfe
1978 "Effects of Changes in Job Characteristics on Work Attitudes and Behaviors: A Naturally Occurring Quasi-Experiment." Organizational Behavior and Human Performance 21: 289-304.
Ingham, Geoffrey K.
1970 Size of Industrial Organization and Worker Behavior. Cambridge, U.K.: Cambridge University Press.

Karpik, Lucien
1968 "Expections and Satisfaction in Work." Human Relations 21: 327–350.
Kohn, Melvin L., and Carmi Schooler
1978 "The Reciprocal Effects of the Substantive Complexity of Work and Intellectual Flexibility: A Longitudinal Assessment." American Journal of Sociology 84: 24–52.
Low-Beer, John R.
1978 Protest and Participation: The New Working Class in Italy. ASA Rose Monograph Series. New York and Cambridge: Cambridge University Press.
Mackenzie, Gavin
1974 "The 'Affluent Worker' Study: An Evaluation and Critique." Pp. 237–256 in Frank Parkin (ed.), The Social Analysis of Class Structure. London: Tavistock.
Mallet, Serge
1963 La nouvelle classe ouvrière. Paris: Editions du Seuil.
Maurice, Marc
1965 "Determinants du militantisme et project syndical des ouvriers et des techniciens." Sociologie du travail 7: 254–272.
Miller, S. M., and Frank Riessman
1968 "The 'New' Working Class." Pp. 27–34 in S. M. Miller and Frank Riessman. Social Class and Social Policy. New York: Basic Books.
Mitchell, Harvey, and Peter Stearns
1971 Workers and Protest. Itasca, Ill.: Peacock.
Moore, Robert S.
1975 "Religion as a Source of Variation in Working-Class Images of Society." Pp. 35–54 in Martin Bulmer (ed.), Working-Class Images of Society. London: Routledge & Kegan Paul.
Nichols, Theo, and Peter Armstrong
1976 Workers Divided: A Study in Shopfloor Politics. Glasgow, U.K.: Fontana/Collins.
Oldham, Greg, R., J. Richard Hackman, and Jone L. Pearce
1975 "Conditions Under Which Employees Respond Positively to Enriched Work." New Haven, Conn.: Yale University, Department of Administrative Science, mimeograph.
Parsons, Talcott
1937 The Structure of Social Action. New York: McGraw-Hill.
Platt, Jennifer
1971 "Variations in Answers to Different Questions on Perceptions of Class: Research Note." Sociological Review 19: 409–419.
Ross, Arthur M., and Hartman, P. T.
1960 Changing Patterns of Industrial Conflict. New York: Wiley.
Sainsaulieu, Renaud
1972 Les relations de travail à l'usine. Paris: Les Editions d'Organisation.
Salaman, Graeme
1974 Community and Occupation. Cambridge, U.K.: Cambridge University Press.
Sayles, Leonard
1958 The Behavior of Industrial Work Groups. New York: Wiley.
Silverman, David
1970 The Theory of Organisations. London: Heinemann.
Touraine, Alain
1966 La conscience ouvrière. Paris: Editions du Seuil.
Turner, H. A.
1962 Trade Union Growth, Structure, and Policy: A Comparative Study of Cotton Unions in England. Toronto: University of Toronto Press.

Turner, H. A., Clack, G., and Roberts, G.
1967 Labour Relations in the Motor Industry. London: George Allen & Unwin.
Turner, Arthur N., and Paul R. Lawrence
1959 Industrial Jobs and the Worker. Boston: Harvard University School of Business Administration.
Valenzuela, J. Samuel
1979 "Labor Movement Formation and Politics: The Chilean and French Cases in Comparative Perspective, 1850–1950." New York: Dissertation, Department of Sociology, Columbia University.
Wedderburn, Dorothy, and Rosemary Crompton
1972 Workers' Attitudes and Technology. Cambridge, U.K.: Cambridge University Press.
Westergaard, J. H.
1970 "The Rediscovery of the Cash Nexus." In R. Milliband and J. Saville (eds.), The Socialist Register 1970. London: Merlin.
Woodward, Joan
1965 Industrial Organisation: Theory and Practice. London: Oxford University Press.
1970 Industrial Organisation: Behavior and Control. London: Oxford University Press.
Wrong, Dennis
1961 "The Over-Socialized Conception of Man." American Sociological Review 26: 183–193.

THE WEAKEST LINK IN THE CHAIN?
SOME COMMENTS ON THE
MARXIST THEORY OF ACTION

David Lockwood

On the face of it, it seems improbable that there is any such thing as *the* Marxist theory of action. Marxists have, of course, always laid claim to a uniquely privileged understanding of society through their possession of a body of theory which, by its singular unity, transcends the artificial specialisms of "bourgeois" social science. But this claim is surely invalid. It is not simply that Marxism is now in such a state of epistemological disarray that some of its illuminati can deny the very possibility of one of the two subjects in which Marxist scholarship has traditionally excelled, namely, history. It is also that, in practice, Marxism exhibits very much the self-same division of intellectual labour as that of "bourgeois" social

Research in the Sociology of Work, Volume 1, pages 435–481
Copyright © 1981 by JAI Press Inc.
All rights of reproduction in any form reserved.
ISBN: 0-89232-124-5

science. Economic theorists go their several ways without paying much attention to the problems of class formation and class consciousness.[1] Contrariwise, students of the political sociology of class do not as a matter of course relate their work to Marxist economic theory in any systematic way, if at all.[2] Finally, there is a quite distinctive school of "philosophical anthropology" which centres on the concept of alienation (see, for example, Meszaros, 1970; Ollman, 1971; Heller, 1974). Writings on this subject have only the most tenuous connection with the substance of Marxist economic theory, and the majority of leading Marxist political sociologists find the whole notion of alienation of small relevance, if not downright heretical.

Given that contemporary Marxism exhibits such an heterogeneity of persuasion, is it reasonable to suppose that underlying this diversity there is a coherent theory of class action? This is not a question that can be answered within the confines of the present essay without a drastic simplification of the posing of it. But it may be that there is some advantage to be gained from pursuing this matter without too much subtlety, and even with a certain bluntness, since no small part of the discussion that complicates the subject appears in however sophisticated a manner to fudge the basic issues.

From a sociological viewpoint, the most crucial aspect of the problem is the conceptual link between system integration and social integration (Lockwood, 1964); and in Marxism there is only one such link that is at all well forged. What is at stake is quite simply the attempt to relate the economic theory of capitalist accumulation to the political sociology, or the philosophical anthropology, of proletarian revolution. The elucidation of this connection has always been, and still is, the most problematic feature of Marxist theory.[3] The argument that follows has a twofold purpose. The first is to show that the main link between system and social integration has been established by means of a basically "utilitarian" concept of action that leads to unstable and contradictory explanations of conflict and order. The second aim is to show how the most influential exponents of contemporary class theory have "solved" the problems arising from this concept of action either by avoiding them or by rejecting the entire classical Marxist formulation of system and social integration.

• • •

The generally accepted view that, in working out his "law of motion" of the capitalist mode of production, Marx was more indebted to Ricardo than to Hegel is the starting point of the discussion. In particular, the extent to which the Marxian theory of class action represents a modification of what Parsons has called the utilitarian scheme of action will be of prime concern (Parsons, 1937; see also Lindsay, 1925). The two chief distinguishing characteristics of the classical utilitarian position are first the assumption that the ends of actors are "random," and second the assumption that in adapting their means to their given ends, actors are governed by the standard of "rationality." By the time of Malthus and Ricardo, however, the concept of the actor as a rational individual egoist, a view that Parsons attributes to Hobbes, had been replaced by the notion of rational class egoists whose ends are determined by their position within specific relations of production. By this time also the post-Hobbesian solution of the problem of order, which took the form of a political or economic theory of a natural identity of interests, had been replaced by a theory of the natural divergence of interests (Halevy, 1955: 319). The assumption that the ends of actors are random because they are purely idiosyncratic and not subject to social determination had therefore been abandoned. But the idea that ends are random in the sense that they lack moral integration through a common value system is one that persisted, at least implicitly. The problem of moral integration was peripheral to the type of theory that centred increasingly on the antagonisms of interest between capitalists, labourers, and landlords. Moreover, the key assumption that class actors pursued their given interests according to the standard of rationality precluded systematic consideration of the normative determination of action.

Marx may be said to have modified this reconstituted utilitarian framework in two main ways, both of which are related to his claim that his predecessors in political economy treated the modes of action typical of capitalist society as universally valid instead of seeing them as historically relative. First of all, Marx postulates an asymmetry between the ends of capitalists and proletarians in that he ascribes to the latter class the extrasystemic end of its self-abolition. Secondly, this "end-shift" of the proletariat is integrally bound up with Marx's revision of the rationality assumption of the utilitarian action scheme. Corresponding to the asymmetry of the ends of capitalists and proletarians is the assumption of differential class rationality. The distinction between rationality, in the sense of a technologically, or economically, rational adaptation of means to given ends, and "reason," in the sense of a capacity to understand that rational action as just defined can be self-defeating, is a notion already present in the work of Locke (Parsons, 1937: 96), who attributed this higher-order rationality to the propertied classes (MacPherson, 1977: 221–238). By contrast, Marx endows the proletariat with this same kind of reason, and it is, indeed, through its exercise, under conditions created by capitalist accumulation, that the end-shift of the proletariat occurs. These rather compressed introductory remarks on the asymmetry of the ends of class actors and on the distinction between rationality and reason will now be developed in such a way as to bring out the basic source of instability in Marxist explanations of the relationship between system contradiction and proletarian revolution.

• • •

Marx's view of the capitalist class is epitomized by his description of the "rational miser" whose "subjective aim" and "sole motive" is the "restless, never-ending process of profitmaking alone" (1906: 130–131). The rational pursuit of capital accumulation is determined by two conditions. The first draws on the distinction between production aimed at use value and production based on exchange value. In the former case, "surplus-labour will be limited to a given set of wants which may be greater or less" and "no boundless thirst for surplus-labour arises from the nature of production itself" (1906: 219). Production is "kept within bounds by the very object it aims at, namely, consumption or the satisfaction of definite wants, an aim that lies altogether outside the sphere of circulation" (1906: 128). In a capitalist system, however, "the circulation of money as capital is, on the contrary, an end in itself. The circulation of capital has therefore no limits" (1906: 129). The second condition is the competition between capitalists. "That which in the miser is a mere idiosyncrasy, is, in the capitalist, the effect of the social mechanism of which he is but one of the wheels. Moreover, the development of capitalist production makes it constantly necessary to keep increasing the amount of capital laid out in a given undertaking, and competition makes the immanent laws of capitalist production to be felt by each individual capitalist, as external coercive laws" (1906: 603; see also 305).

Marx's rational miser is thus not the product of fixed human nature but of specific social conditions. Nevertheless, the question of whether Marx was correct in accusing his forerunners in political economy of conflating this distinction is unimportant, because his concept of the capitalist as a rational accumulator is, in effect, just as utilitarian in character as his theory that individual capitalists, in rationally pursuing their given ends, unintendedly produce conditions that are irrational from the viewpoint of the capitalist class as a whole. He presents the capitalist only as the "personification of an economic category," but his construct of the rational miser does not differ in its essentials from the concept of the actor which is to be found in theories of the natural identity or divergence of interests put forward by previous writers within the utilitarian tradition. Without this postulate of the capitalist as a rational class egoist Marx's system cannot work. Each capitalist finds himself in a situation whose logic dictates that capital accumulation becomes his ultimate end, and, as a result of his rationally pursuing it, rational knowledge in the form of technology becomes progressively incorporated into the means of production as the chief method of obtaining relative surplus value. And this rising organic composition of capital not only provides the key to Marx's theory of system contradiction but serves to explain how capitalism creates all the major conditions conducive to proletarian revolt.

In turning to the concept of proletarian action the picture becomes more complicated. Like capitalists, proletarians are assumed to act rationally in pursuit of an end that is immediately given by the existing system of production. This is the wage that is necessary for maintaining and producing labour at a level of existence that is either purely physical or one that involves some "traditional" standard of life. And like the class situation of capitalists, that of the proletariat is characterized, initially at least, by competition among workers. But, unlike the capitalist class,[4] the proletariat possesses a higher-order rationality, or faculty of reason, which enables it to acquire an understanding that the rational pursuit of its immediate ends is self-defeating, and that it has an ultimate end, which can only be realized through the abolition of the capitalist system. The nature of this postulated end-shift is identified by the distinction between a struggle over the level of wages and a struggle over the "wages system" itself. The first goal is determined simply by a zero-sum conflict between capitalist and proletarian, "a continuous struggle between capital and labour, the capitalist constantly tending to reduce wages to their physical minimum, and to extend the working day to its physical maximum, while the working man constantly presses in the opposite direction" (Marx and Engels, 1950: 402). From the viewpoint of Marx's theory of human nature, this goal represents the alienated need engendered by capitalist relations of production: "The need for money is, therefore, the real need created by the modern economic system, and the only need which it creates" (1964: 168). By contrast, the extra-systemic end of the proletariat is the unalienated condition of "socialised man, the associated producers, rationally regulating their interchange with Nature, bringing it under their common control, instead of being ruled by it as by the blind forces of Nature; and achieving this with the least expenditure of energy and under the conditions most favourable to, and worthy of, their human nature" (Marx, 1972: 820). According to Marx, this end is not simply an ideal standard but a state of affairs that is already prefigured in the existing society. "The working class ought not to forget that they are fighting with effects but not with the causes of these effects . . . they ought to understand that, with all the miseries it imposes on them, the present system simultaneously engenders the *material conditions* and the social forms necessary for an economic reconstruction of society" (Marx and Engels, 1950: 404). The conditions that make this extrasystemic end of the proletariat attainable are produced by capitalists rationally pursuing their intrasystemic end. The increasing concentration and centralization of capital, the progressive socialization of labour and the growing material and moral misery of the working class are all consequences of the general tendency of capitalist accumulation. But the mediating factor between these conditions and revolutionary action is the proletariat's faculty of reason, its ability to grasp the connection between its immediate and fundamental interests (Ollman, 1971: 114–115; 122–124; 238–239).

This is brought out very clearly by Wright when he says that "Class interests, therefore, are in a sense hypotheses about the objectives of struggles which would occur if the actors in the struggle had a scientifically correct understanding of their situations. To make the claim that socialism is in the 'interests' of the working class is not simply to make a historical, moralistic claim that workers ought to be in favour of socialism nor to make a normative claim that they would be 'better off' in a socialist society, but rather to claim that if workers had a scientific understanding of the contradictions of capitalism, they would in fact engage in struggles for socialism" (1978: 89). Marx did expect that workers would be able to come close to such an understanding, and mainly as a result of their own experience and powers of ratiocination. Indeed, this revolutionary consciousness of the proletariat would be a necessary condition of the success of genuine socialist revolution. His assumption that the proletariat could achieve its historically ascribed end-shift through the exercise of its faculty of reason is a view of action in which the utilitarian source of Marxian thinking merges into the Hegelian. Unlike previous revolutionary classes, the proletariat cannot simply pursue its immediate interests and entrust the consequences of its action to the "cunning of reason." As Lukacs puts it, "the dialectical relationship between immediate interests and objective impact on the whole of society is located *in the consciousness of the proletariat* itself" (1971: 71). The fusion of immediate and fundamental interests comes about, so it is argued, through the process of revolutionary practice in which the proletariat's unfolding power of reason plays a crucial role. As it stands, however, the famous formula that the changing of people goes hand in hand with the changing of their circumstances possesses no more cogency than an incantation. To grasp its concrete meaning requires a specification of the nature of the people and circumstances in question. But before turning to consider what these are, it is necessary to deal with one final issue that arises from the assumption that action is governed by the standard of scientific rationality. This is the explanation of "irrational" action.

Marx's belief that history would vindicate his theory is inseparable from his belief that his theory would prove to be a real historical force in just the same way as the reason of the proletariat with which it had an assignation. But this does not alter the fact that his theory *qua* theory only works by attributing rationality and reason to the actors it creates, and must therefore also be able to account for irrational action. Moreover, it can hardly be said that history has been backward in providing cause for treating this problem very seriously. In general, social theory has found only two main ways of explaining deviations from rational action. The first, an integral part of utilitarian thinking, relies heavily on the concepts of "ignorance" and "error." In other words, irrational action is seen to be due either to the actor's inadequate knowledge of the facts of the situation or to his imperfect understanding of the most efficient, that is, scientifically rational, means of attaining his ends. This type of explanation has always been central to Marxist theory, and it has figured more prominently as the problem of accounting for the aberration of the proletariat has become more exigent. What is referred to here is the analytical promotion of the concept of capitalist ideological domination, and, by implication, that of the false consciousness of the proletariat. This concept has taken different forms, but, as will be seen in due course, the general use to which it has been put has had the effect of creating a high degree of instability in the theory of proletarian action.

The second way of explaining deviation from rational action does not play a systematic role in either utilitarian or Marxist thought. It rests on the distinction between *ir*rational and *non*rational action (Parsons, 1937: 712–713). Whereas the former is defined negatively by the actor's "failure" to conform to the standard of scientific rationality in adapting his means to his ends, the latter is defined positively by the actor's conformity to rules or norms that he regards as obligatory because they embody some ultimate end or value. This type of action, which finds its limiting case in Durkheim's notion of religious ritual, is, therefore, nonrational only in the sense that it is finally inexplicable in terms of ignorance or error. Although some norms may be partly justified as the most appropriate means of attaining proximate ends, and thus capable of being judged according to criteria of scientific rationality, progression up the means-end chain sooner or later reaches a point where the rationale of the rule is grounded in an end that is ultimate in that it is scientifically irrefutable. It is true that ultimate values are still open to rational scrutiny; but, at the same time, it is unlikely that a society made up entirely of moral philosophers would be at all durable. Nevertheless, the fact that most people do not acquire, and seldom change, their ultimate ends purely as a result of logical reflection does not imply that they are simply socialised into an unquestioning conformity to the rules that these values underpin. The view of action now being considered merely serves to bring into focus questions that the utilitarian scheme leaves obscure. The most basic of these is the extent to which the ultimate ends of actors are integrated with one another through a system of common values. This then concentrates attention on the factors that determine the extent to which the values and norms defining the ends and means appropriate to different classes of actors come to constitute conditions of their action in the form of internal, rather than external, constraints. From this perspective, the central problem is no longer that of accounting for deviations from scientifically rational action but rather that of explaining variations in the institutionalization of values.

The position of values and norms within the Marxist theory of class action is very uncertain. Recognition of their significance grows as the evident weaknesses of explanations of ideologically induced ignorance and error call for a much more explicit treatment of the "cultural," as opposed to the "cognitive," obstacles to revolutionary consciousness. In general, however, these cultural factors have been incorporated into the category of ideology. The main reason for this is the lack of a clear distinction between irrational and nonrational action, which rules out the possibility of the rigorous analysis and empirical study of the conditions determining the institutionalization of values. In default of this, the tendency is to resort to an "over-socialised" concept of man, which only accentuates the instability of the theory of class action by encouraging "idealistic" forms of explanation closely resembling those of normative functionalism.

Before examining the way in which Marxism has sought to explain the absence of revolutionary class consciousness by reference to ideological and cultural barriers to proletarian reason, it may be worthwhile to at least indicate how the problem of dealing with normative factors arises directly from Marx's account of the conditions making for proletarian revolt. For the purposes of exposition, it is convenient to separate out three main strands of his argument. First, there is an "economic" theory, which centres on the absolute or relative impoverishment of the working class. Secondly, there is a "sociological" theory, which sees revolution as the outcome of a process of proletarian self-education or praxis. And, thirdly, there is the "philosophical anthropology" of alienation, which locates the revolutionary impulse of the proletariat in the degradation of its species-being.

•   •   •

The most basic question about any past, present, or future material impoverishment of the working class concerns the concept of action that links this condition with working-class revolt. As De Man puts it, "Of what use is it to prove that economic crises have assumed other forms than those foreseen by Marx? What matters to us is whether there really is, as Marx believed, a necessary connection between economic crises and the social revolution" (1928: 23). Impoverishment is, of course, only one aspect of this connection. The other is the way in which recurrent crises that plunge the proletariat into poverty also provide the conditions of proletarian self-education. It may be thought, therefore, that it is factitious to separate the discussion of these two aspects of the problem. But this procedure is not entirely unwarranted, because it is still a common, albeit implicit assumption of Marxist writers that impoverishment, or affluence, *per se,* does have a direct and immediate effect on working-class consciousness. Moreover, as will be seen in due course, this assumption is made less rather than more plausible by the introduction of the notion of self-education, since the latter does not usually take into account the importance of the distinction between human and organizational life spans, and thus confuses the learning embodied in the tradition of a corporate group with the learning of its individual members.

The question of whether Marx predicted an absolute or a relative immiseration of the proletariat is a matter of no great importance in the present context, however controversial it might be from other points of view (Bober, 1948: 213–221 is still the best short account). The main point is that the hypothesis that impoverishment leads to radicalism, or conversely that affluence results in conservatism, is neither empirically supportable nor logically sound. It is not the case that the most impoverished and economically insecure workers are invariably, or even usually, the most radical or that periods of falling real wages and high unemployment are invariably those of working-class radicalism. What is of equal significance is that Marx himself provides the reasons for doubting that there should be a simple and direct relation between the economic condition and the class consciousness of the proletariat. First of all, like Ricardo before him, Marx recognized that the needs of labourers, and hence the value of labour, were variable, determined not only by the conditions of sheer physical subsistence but also by "a traditional standard of life", that is, by "a historical and moral element" (for an extended discussion of this point see Browder, 1959). This means that there is introduced into the very notion of impoverishment a concept of the relativity of deprivation, and that the effects of economic circumstances on class consciousness are mediated by the variability of "moral" factors. Most significantly, in the last analysis, the concept of a "traditional standard of life" involves reference to the phenomenon of status group stratification. Thus, quite apart from the possibility noted by Durkehim that poverty can just as easily lead to fatalism as to revolt because "actual possessions are partly the criterion of those aspired to" (1952: 254)—a consideration that should have entered into Marx's thinking about working-class consciousness from his reading of factory inspectors' reports (Ollman, 1972: 9)—the notion of "tradition" introduces into the Marxian concept of action a normative element of fundamental importance, but one that remains analytically residual.

The systematic nature of this "moral element" becomes more evident if it is accepted that Marx predicted not the absolute, but only the relative, impoverishment of the working class. Whatever the merits of this interpretation, it has far-reaching sociological implications. For unless it is held that it means no more than a purely objective divergence of profits and wages, both of which increase in absolute terms, then the explanation of the feeling of unjust deprivation associated with relative impoverishment must involve reference to the normative interrelationship of the ends of capitalists and proletarians. In other words, the sense of deprivation on the part of the proletariat results not from a comparison of their means relative to their traditionally defined standard of living, but rather from a comparison of their standard of living with that of the capitalist class. If the idea of relative impoverishment does not refer to this kind of comparison, then it is a purely statistical notion with no implications for the action of the proletariat. But if it does have this connotation, then it entails the concept of a status order. If the standard of living of a class contains a moral element, then the relationship between the standard of living of one class and that of another must imply a moral relationship; that is, a status hierarchy which defines the ends, or standards of living, to which different classes may legitimately aspire. Although Marx and Engels were not oblivious of the fact that class solidarity could be impaired by status differentiation, the concept of status entered into their explanations of class action in an entirely *ad hoc* fashion. This has remained characteristic of subsequent Marxist theory; and, as will be seen shortly, the failure to differentiate the institutionalization of status from the general category of the ideological is a main reason why Marxism exhibits a marked tendency to oscillate between two equally untenable schemes of action: at the one extreme, the "positivistic" (of which the impoverishment thesis is archetypal); and, at the other, what can only be called— though in a necessarily limited sense—the "idealistic."[5] At this stage, however, it simply needs to be emphasized that the foregoing criticisms of the impoverishment thesis apply with equal force to the opposite kind of argument which seeks to explain working-class acquiescence or conservatism in terms of relative affluence. Lenin's theory of the "labour aristocracy" is the most striking example of this type of explanation. His idea that proletarian revolution was averted by leading sections of the working class being "bribed" or bought off by their sharing in imperialist "super-profits" is based on the familiar positivistic assumption that reduces the determination of ends to changes in material conditions. Subsequent research has demonstrated the inadequacy of this theory (Moorhouse, 1978). It has also shown that, far from being "bourgeoisified" or indoctrinated with ruling-class ideology, the labour aristocracy constituted itself as a status group—and hence as a reference group for other sections of the working class—through the creation of its own distinctive values and beliefs, which stood at some distance from those of the bourgeoisie (Crossick, 1976; Gray, 1973).

In turning to the second line of argument, namely that which seeks to explain working-class revolt as a process of proletarian self-education, the same kinds of problems arise. The basic weakness of the theory of revolutionary praxis is its neglect of the obstacles placed in the path of proletarian reason by "moral elements" and "tradition." Of particular importance here are first the status incorporation of the working-class movement, and, secondly, the tradition or ritual of the movement itself. In seeking to demonstrate their significance, it is convenient to begin by noting that the concrete meaning of the statement that "In revolutionary activity, the changing of oneself coincides with the changing of circumstances" is to be found in the great importance Marx attached to trade union action as a means of both enhancing proletarian solidarity and altering conditions in such a way as to intensify class conflict. The escalation of trade union action from the level of particular economic struggles to the fight to pass legislation that would generalize the conflict between classes was something he set great store by. Trade unions were the "schools of socialism," the primary mode of praxis through which the end-shift of the proletariat would be realized.

The fact that Marx's theory was not borne out is uncontroversial. When Kautsky coined the phrase *Nur Gewerkschaftlerei* he wrote the epitaph to proletarian reason. And Lenin drove home the point that from then on philosophy would have to work much harder to find its material weapon in the proletariat. To account for this short-circuiting of proletarian praxis, for its fixation at the level of "trade union consciousness," Marxism has had to rely increasingly on explanations that emphasize the role of ideological obfuscation, which results either from a purposive ruling-class indoctrination of the proletariat or from the false consciousness that is generated by capitalist relations of production themselves and affects both capitalists and proletarians alike. In other words, the main recourse has been to the notions of ignorance and error, which, in the utilitarian scheme, are the basic categories for explaining deviations from rational action. The way in which this resort to explanations of class action by reference to ideological constraint introduces a chronic instability into Marxist theory is a matter that will be taken up in the next section. For the moment, interest attaches to a particular aspect of this more general problem: namely, the attempt to account for the arrestment of proletarian praxis at the level of trade union consciousness by reference to the ideological effects of the peculiar civil and political relations of capitalist

446

society. For this kind of argument once again brings into prominence the uncertain position within Marxist theory of the nature of status stratification.

The political and civil relations of capitalist society are held to prevent the emergence of a revolutionary proletariat because they serve to atomize society into a mass of juridically separate individuals and thereby disguise the real nature of class relations and class exploitation. As one writer puts it, "The fundamental form of the Western Parliamentary State—the juridicial sum of its citizenry—is itself the hub of the ideological apparatuses of capitalism" (Anderson, 1977: 29; see also Poulantzas, 1973: 123–137; 210–221; Wright, 1978: 241). And, corresponding to this individualization of political relations, the institutions of private property and free contract have always been regarded by Marxism as having the effect of obscuring the class structure of civil society in an essentially similar manner. Now what is abundantly clear is that these arguments refer to the legal aspect of the status order. Citizenship is no less a part of the status system because it has to do with the equality of civil, political, and social status. On the contrary, it is the foundation of the modern status order, on which are superimposed what Weber refers to as "conventional" status inequalities. In stressing the socially integrative, or at least stabilizing effect of citizenship, then, Marxist theories of the abortion of proletarian revolution are brought into a fairly close approximation to those of "bourgeois" sociology; and in particular to studies that have focused on the consequences for class action of the institutionalization of civil, political, and social citizenship (for example, Marshall, 1950; Bendix, 1964). But Marxism lacks a clear conception of the interrelationship between class and status structures. This is because the analysis of the institutionalization of status has no place in its theory of social integration. The entire problem of status is lost sight of in highly general and essentially functionalist conceptions of ideological domination.

One reason for this neglect is the erroneous view that status consists of purely "subjective" judgements of prestige, which are amorphous, vacillating, and simply ideological products; a view that precludes the study of status groups whose boundaries are maintained through acts of social acceptance, deference, and derogation. But the neglect is also partly attributable to the, again mistaken, idea that, since status implies inequality of social standing, the status of legal equality cannot be part of a status order. On the first count, then, status is regarded as "trivial" and its consequences for class action are assumed to be somehow less "real" than those of the economic structure. And, on the second count, the core, that is, the legal, element of any status relationship is not included in the status system of capitalist society at all. The full implications of this double misconception cannot be gone into here;[6] but it is important, if only briefly, to indicate its bearing on the explanation of "trade union consciousness."

The first point that needs to be made about the supposedly atomizing effects of the political and civil relations of capitalist society is that firm evidence in support of this thesis has still to be adduced. The second point is that there is much evidence that casts doubt upon the thesis. For if workers had really conceived of themselves as juridically discrete and isolated individuals how could they have joined together to form trades unions in the first place? And if workers could overcome this initial ideological obstacle to their collective action what is it that prevents proletarian reason from making the further breakthrough that would shift the interests of the working class from intrasystemic to extrasystemic ends? The formula of trade union consciousness does not provide an answer. Either it merely redescribes the problem, or else it seeks to account for it in a manner that would also fail to explain trade union consciousness itself.

With the benefit of hindsight, it is easy to see why Marx's expectation that the pursuit by trades unions of political goals would have revolutionary consequences was mistaken. And the reason why he was mistaken is very significant. For, in fact, the main end that trades unions have sought to attain through legislative action is that of securing and legitimating their own corporate status: namely, what Marshall refers to as "a secondary system of industrial citizenship parallel with and supplementary to the system of political citizenship" (1950: 44). To dismiss this as mere trade union consciousness may be all very well from the point of view of socialist eschatology. But it is usually the case that the ends of newly formed economic groups, whose position in the status order is anomalous, are in the first instance heavily influenced by an interest in negotiating a definite position within the existing hierarchy of authority and status. It is only when there are no institutionalized means of accommodating this interest that the legitimacy of the status order as a whole is brought into question. This general observation does not imply that the "civic incorporation" of the working class represents an historical end-state, or that the "institutionalization of class conflict" is the final word on the dynamics of class formation in capitalist societies. Its significance lies rather in the problems it poses for the concept of action underlying the theory that praxis is the midwife of proletarian reason.

For one way of defining trade union consciousness is to say that it is a rational, but not a reasonable, response to the situation in which the working class finds itself. This is tantamount to saying that securing the legal rights legitimating the corporate status of trade unions is a rational means of attaining the immediate ends of the working class, but an unreasonable means of attaining its fundamental ends. But this formulation rests on a concept of action that reduces all normative elements in the situation to external means and conditions that rational actors have to take account of. It is, of course, possible to postulate a proletarian actor for whom the acquisition of status rights is purely a means of obtaining other ends. For example, Marx actually did envisage the possibility that an enfranchised working class could vote itself into socialism. The basic flaw in this type of argument, however, is its inability to cope with the "historical and moral element." In particular, it cannot admit that, since the struggle to acquire status rights involves an orientation to "moral elements" legitimating the status order as a whole, the acquisition of these rights results in their having an intrinsic, and not merely an instrumental, value for the actors concerned. This implies, for example, that the institutionalization of "free collective bargaining" is not only a rational means of workers pursuing their immediate interests, but also a mode of action that inevitably takes on a traditional or ritual character by virtue of its having developed within, and at the same time having changed, a status order based on the "moral elements" of citizenship. To dismiss such action as an expression of trade union consciousness, the result of ruling-class indoctrination, and thus by implication as irrational is not just to take a condescending view of the working-class struggle itself; it also ignores the extent to which such action is nonrational in the sense that it involves a positive commitment to normative standards (status rights) which legitimate the immediate means-end relationship, and thus in some degree to the ultimate values from which this legitimation is derived.

The ritual accretions of proletarian practice obstruct the exercise of proletarian reason in two other ways as well. First, there is the familiar tendency towards oligarchy in working-class organizations, which results in goal-displacement. This transformation of organizational means into ends in themselves—a process not unconnected with the interests of leaders in their status within and outside the organization—is the paradigm case of ritual action (Merton, 1957: 149–153). Secondly, adherence to working-class, as to any other, organizations involves a ritual element in so far as there is a disparity between the life span of the organization and that of the member of it. In this disparity lies another main weakness of the thesis of praxis, which tends to confuse the self-education, or learning through experience, of an individual with that of an organization whose capacity to learn is in part a function of its tradition, which is in turn the residue of the experiences and learning of past generations of individuals. It is through the tradition of an organization that a ritual element inevitably enters into the determination of what is rational action for the individuals who compose its present membership. Tradition, status, and ritual signify modes of action which Marxism, like the utilitarian tradition in which it is rooted, is constrained to treat as irrational. While their particular relevance may be very well appreciated (see, for example, Hobsbawm, 1959), they are not factors that occupy a central analytical place within the Marxist theory of action.

The third main type of explanation of working-class consciousness, which centres on the idea of alienation, merits only brief consideration as a theory of proletarian revolt. But it is important to begin by noting that, while the concept of alienation is used chiefly to account for working-class acquiescence, it is also capable of yielding an explanation of working-class revolt. Thus, whatever value it may be thought to have as a dialectical safeguard against every contingency of the class struggle, the fact that contradictory conclusions can be derived from it hardly commends it as a rigorous explanation of class action. The root of the difficulty is to be found in the ambiguity of the two basic terms that enter into its formulation; on the one hand, the concept of "human nature," and, on the other, that of the conditions making for alienation.

As regards the former, it is well known that Marx refers to "human nature in general" as well as to "human nature as modified in each historical epoch." The major difficulty, however, is that the relative importance of these two elements for the action of the proletariat remains highly indeterminate. Fromm expresses this well when he writes "Marx argues against two points of view here: the ahistorical, which postulates the nature of man as a substance existing since the beginning of history, as well as the relativistic, which endows the nature of man with none of its own properties but considers it the reflection of social conditions. However, he never formulated conclusively his own theory of the nature of man to transcend both the ahistorical and the relativistic points of view. For this reason the interpretations of his theory are so variant and contradictory" (1962: 31). As far as the theory of proletarian action is concerned, what is essentially at stake is the extent to which socially determined and false needs inhibit the emergence of the essential need to engage in that "free, conscious activity" which is "the species-character of human beings." Depending on which of these two aspects of need-formation is emphasized, the reaction to alienating conditions can be either passive or active. There is no doubt that Marx laid great stress on the latter response. He writes ". . . the class of the proletariat is abased and indignant at that debasement, an indignation to which it is necessarily driven by the contradiction between its human nature and its condition of life, which is the outright, decisive and comprehensive negation of that nature" (McLellan, 1971: 113). And again "From the start, the worker is superior to the capitalist in that the capitalist is rooted in his process of alienation and is completely content therein, whereas the worker who is its victim finds himself from the beginning in a state of rebellion against it and experiences the process as one of enslavement" (McLellan, 1971: 119). Yet, at the same time, there is ample evidence in Marx's writings to support the opposite interpretation, which has become prominent in subsequent Marxist literature, and which lays much greater stress on the more passive response to alienating conditions, and thereby on the power of these conditions to induce false wants.

Corresponding to the ambiguity of the conception of "human nature," and further confounding the whole issue of the dynamics of alienation in capitalist society, is the problem of whether the conditions making for alienation are to be understood as variable or invariable. If, as is usually the case, the source of alienation is located in capitalist relations of production *per se,* then alienation is global, affecting both capitalists and proletarians alike. Yet it is also possible to argue that, although all workers are alienated, some workers are more alienated than others. The warrant for this is to be found in the passage in *Capital* where Marx writes that "in proportion as capital accumulates, the lot of the labourer, be his payment high or low, must grow worse" and goes on to claim that "all methods for raising the social productiveness of labour" result in increasingly alienating conditions of work (Marx, 1906: 661). Since these methods are technological, and since it is a fact that technologies of production differ in the extent to which they diminish the autonomy of the worker, this introduces an important element of variability into the conditions of proletarian alienation.

Of the theoretical permutations permitted by the conceptual ambiguities just referred to, it is necessary to mention only two. These are the hypotheses about proletarian action that are most frequently to be met with, and which, in their contradictory conclusions, best demonstrate the incoherence of the idea of alienation. The first may be simply stated without comment since it is a strand in the safety-net thesis of the ideological repression of proletarian reason, the discussion of which will shortly follow. It is an argument designed to account for the lack of a working-class revolution in advanced capitalist societies and the unlikelihood of such an event in the foreseeable future. This type of explanation emphasizes the plasticity of the ends of the proletariat and the global character of the conditions making for alienation. In some versions of the argument the extinction of the capacity of the working class to exercise its reason and to comprehend its essential needs is apparently complete; in others, this capacity is regarded as inextinguishable, but too enfeebled to assert itself save by the intervention of an external agency. In marked contrast with this pessimistic view of alienated proletarian passivity, there is a second theory which ingeniously inverts the alternative Marxian thesis that the working class will revolt under conditions of increasing alienation. This interpretation assumes that the essential needs of the proletariat, far from being expunged or deeply repressed, grow more imperative as the nature of work becomes objectively less alienating. It is in the latter respect that ingenuity enters. For, contrary to Marx's expectations, the most dehumanizing conditions of production result in, at most, fractious accommodation on the part of workers; and the longer workers are exposed to such conditions the more pathologically inured to them they become (Argyris, 1957). It is therefore a dialectical *tour de force* to discover that the most radical workers are those who work under the objectively least alienating conditions. Moreover, since these conditions are also associated with the most advanced "forces of production," the theory of "the new working class" (Mallet, 1975) has at least one straw of orthodoxy to clutch at. This is Marx's belief—though one that is hard to square with his view of the tendency of technological development within capitalist relations of production—that human powers and needs would unfold with people's increasing command over nature through progressively socialized production. Underlying the thesis of "the new working class," then, is a concept of "human nature," which postulates some inbuilt hierarchy of needs. It is because workers in advanced technological industries are relatively well paid and secure in their jobs that they are capable of developing wants of a qualitatively different kind from those of other workers: demands for worker control and self-management as opposed to merely "economistic" ones. These interests, which pose the most fundamental threat to capitalist production relations, are also promoted by the nature of the workers' integration into the enterprise. Unlike the passively alienated workers in mass-production industries, the new working class are in a situation where individual labour loses all meaning, where workers' knowledge, skills, and collective involvement in production not only give them a high disruptive capacity but also make them aware of the contradiction between the socialized character of the labour process and the private character of its control. In pursuing their goals, the trade unions of the new working class are able to use new strike methods and are self-educated into making demands that encroach increasingly upon the prerogatives of management, even in areas of financial decision making.

The merit of this argument, which distinguishes it from other theories of alienation, is that it can be refuted; and it has been (Gallie, 1978). It is wrong because it assumes a technological determination of class action which is unable to account for marked national differences in the attitudes and behaviour of workers employed in technologically identical plants. These differences have to be explained by reference to the wider system of industrial and political relations, and in large part by the particular modes of the "civic integration" of the working class. In this respect, the deficiency of the thesis of the alienation of the "new working class" brings to the fore once again the significance for class action of the status order in which class relations are embedded.

• • •

This brief survey of the three main kinds of explanations entering into the theory of proletarian revolution shows that, while they comprise a very versatile set of arguments, all have the same flaw. This is to be found in the assumption that through their power of reason workers will be quick to learn from their experience of capitalist relations of production that their ends can only be realized by the abolition of these relations. Moreover, the fact that material and moral impoverishment, and self-education through collective action, have not led to proletarian revolution in the most advanced capitalist societies now suggests, and not least to many Marxists, that the assumption of proletarian reason is faulty. By according the standard of rationality such a central role in explaining the means-end relationship, Marxism shares the same weakness as utilitarian theory in that it excludes from its purview systematic consideration of nonrational action. In contrast with irrational action, which can always be explained in terms of ignorance and error, nonrational action can only be understood by reference to the normative integration of ends. At the outset, it was stated that the utilitarian scheme treats the ends of actors as "random" in the sense that the question of their interrelationship lies outside the scope of the theory. It was also claimed that the same tendency is characteristic of Marxism. This is now in need of qualification.

At first sight, the concept of ideology would seem to explain why ends are not random and thus demolish the argument that Marxism is a version of a basically utilitarian theory of action. But in order to understand exactly the extent to which this is the case, it is necessary to say something about the main variants of the Marxist concept of ideology. And in doing this, special note must be taken of the way in which the notion of ideology undergoes not only an analytical promotion, but also a qualitative change. Both aspects may be considered as responses to the problem of explaining the lack of proletarian revolution, and hence the failure of proletarian reason.

What might be called the vulgar version of ideologically induced false consciousness originates in certain passages of *The German Ideology* and finds its most extreme formulation in *What Is To Be Done?* It has the following, characteristically utilitarian components. Control over the production of ideas, and thus the ability to inculcate in the proletariat a false consciousness of its position, is one of the means by which the capitalist class rationally pursues its intrasystemic end. This is possible because the ruling class possesses overwhelmingly superior resources for the creation and dissemination of its ideas. In fact, in this theory of social integration, the power attributed to bourgeois ideology is equivalent to the coercive power of Hobbes' *Leviathan*. As far as the subjugated class is concerned, dominant ideas constitute a, presumably internalized, condition of its action, so that it remains ignorant of the means-ends chain that would lead it to recognize its extrasystemic end. With Lenin, what constituted an auxiliary Marxian hypothesis about proletarian action becomes central and axiomatic. Proletarian ignorance is equated with trade union consciousness, and the means of "correcting" this ignorance are conceived of in typically utilitarian terms. It is by systematic "arraignment" and "exposure" that the proletariat can be informed of their real situation; and, as a result of their enlightenment by the revolutionary party in which proletarian reason is enshrined, they will be able to achieve a "socialist" consciousness and embark on their historical mission. What distinguishes this first interpretation of ideology is that, far from raising the problem of the institutionalization of values, it concentrates attention on the cognitive obstacles to revolutionary consciousness and, equally, on the cognitive means by which these obstacles can be removed.

This emphasis on the cognitive element of ideological domination is also characteristic of the second theory of ideology, which has its origin in the concept of commodity fetishism, and which, by contrast with the first, may be termed "sophisticated." But this theory too has very definite underpinnings in the utilitarian theory of action. Most obviously, commodity fetishism is a form of false consciousness which is a "system effect," a consequence of market exchanges. Unlike the vulgar theory of ideology, the fetishism of commodities does not refer to the means by which one class imposes its ideas upon another in order rationally to attain its ends. It denotes the unintended ideological effect produced by the interaction of rational egoists, who, in mediating their relationships through the exchange of commodities, purportedly come to think of their relations with one another as the relations between entities (especially the values attaching to commodities) that possess a life of their own. Individuals are ruled by forces that have the same properties of externality, constraint, and ineluctability which Durkheim, in his phase of sociological positivism, attributed to social facts in general. Marx's theory of commodity fetishism deserves to be called sophisticated for two main reasons. First of all, by contrast with the vulgar theory, it refers to an ideological effect that affects capitalists and proletarians alike. This effect is the unanticipated outcome of a myriad of individual, rational actions, and, like Adam Smith's "invisible hand" of the market, it has socially integrative consequences. Secondly, these consequences are considered to be much more deeply ideological in their nature than any resulting from the attempt of one class to impose its beliefs upon another. This is because commodity fetishism is constitutive of actual class relations and not just an abstract and external justification of them. As such, commodity fetishism is a much more intractable obstacle to the end-shift of the proletariat. It binds the working class into the same system of ideological compulsion that the capitalist class is subject to. The real illusion of commodity fetishism is not that "the direct social relations between individuals at work" take on the character of "material relations between persons and social relations between things" but rather that this condition—which is real—is regarded as inexorable (Lichtman, 1975: 67).

This theory of "systemic" ideology is one whose truth appears to have been regarded as so self-evident among those Marxists who have espoused it that it has been thought necessary only to reiterate the theory instead of proving it. The fact that it is not a theory that finds favour with Marxist historians is particularly unfortunate since it is premised on the existence of market relations which, if they ever existed, are now defunct. Nevertheless, its basic assumption that ideology is effective through its embodiment in everyday class relations is one that has found a new expression in some recent Marxist accounts of proletarian passivity; and most extravagantly in the concept of "ideological state apparatuses." The latter is noteworthy mainly for the fact that, by its indiscriminate attribution of ideological repressiveness to every social institution of contemporary capitalist societies (save for, perhaps, their communist parties), it manages to transform the vulgar theory of ideology into something closely resembling the naive sociological functionalism of the 1950s. From the point of view of Marxism, however, the most objectionable aspect of the rag-bag concept of ideological state apparatuses consists in the damage it does to Gramsci's notion of "hegemony," which has good reason to be treated as the third main variant of the Marxist theory of ideology.

Fragmentary though it is, Gramsci's account of hegemony provides Marxism with the basis of a sophisticated theory of ideology which avoids the positivistic tendencies of the vulgar version. In contrast with the latter, the concept of hegemony places much less emphasis on control over the production and dissemination of ideas as a means by which the ruling class manipulates proletarian consciousness in order to attain its own ends. This view of ideology is due in part to Gramsci's much more subtle and elaborate conception of the functions of intellectuals. But it is due principally to his appreciation of the need for a precise study of how the "grounding" or institutionalization of values and beliefs succeeds in generating a spontaneous, but necessarily imperfect, moral and intellectual consensus. A major consequence of this shift in emphasis is that ideological domination is no longer understood as an easily identifiable, basically cognitive, obstacle to proletarian revolution. False consciousness cannot be equated with a state of ignorance and error that is readily corrigible by the Leninist strategy of an "all-embracing political arraignment" of ruling-class oppression. The very definition of what counts as "common sense" is, as Gramsci puts it, "determined not by reason but by faith," that is, by the individual's attachment to social groups; and, as such, it is not easily alterable by exposure to scientific knowledge. Revolutionary ascendency therefore presupposes a long and arduous struggle to establish a proletarian hegemony which can compete on equal cultural terms with that of the ruling class. This much is evident from Williams's definition of hegemony as "an order in which a certain way of life and thought is dominant, in which one concept of reality is diffused throughout society in all its institutional and private manifestations, informing with its spirit all taste, morality, customs, religious and political principles, and all social relations, particularly in their intellectual and moral connotations" (1960: 587). It is easy to see why this view of ideology should have such a powerful appeal to contemporary Marxism. For what it does is to modify out of all recognition the utilitarian action scheme underlying the vulgar theory of ideology, and, at the same time, it provides a general, sociological formulation of the notion, deriving from the concept of commodity fetishism, that the effectiveness of ideology consists in its systemic nature, in the manner in which dominant values and beliefs are embodied in everyday social relations.

The highly general scope of the concept of hegemony is, however, the source of its main weakness. Gramsci provided the outline of a theory of ideology, the detailed working out of which would have to include a systematic consideration of precisely those moral or normative elements that have remained analytically inchoate within the Marxist scheme of action, and whose effects have been relegated to the category of the irrational. To give the idea of hegemony a cutting edge requires a specification of the modes of institutionalization of values and beliefs, and, more importantly, of the conditions under which such processes are more or less successful in producing a consensual social integration. Gramsci's notion of "contradictory consciousness" might well be the starting point of this investigation (Femia, 1975). But the task has hardly begun. Gramsci's ideas have been incorporated into Marxism in a highly generalized way, with the result that explanations of class action based on them veer towards a form of cultural determinism. It would not be too much to say that Gramsci is the Durkheim of modern Marxism. In most major respects, the concept of hegemony is scarcely distinguishable from Durkheim's concept of the "diffuse" collective conscience which he contrasts with the more specific "government consciousness" (Durkheim, 1957: 79). And just as Durkheim's concept of the collective conscience allowed his successors to construct a sociology that was characterized by an over-integrated view of society and an over-socialised view of man, so Gramsci's concept of hegemony has tempted many Marxist theorists concerned with explaining the lack of proletarian revolution to espouse an equally questionable view of global ideological domination. As one leading Marxist frankly admits, "What is involved is an overstatement of the ideological predominance of the 'ruling class,' or of the *effectiveness* of their predominance" (Miliband, 1977: 53). Miliband draws attention to "the dearth of sustained Marxist work analyzing and exposing the meanings and messages purveyed in the cultural output produced for mass consumption in, say, the thirty-odd years since the end of World War II—not to speak of the virtual absence of such work in the years preceding it" (1977: 49). But it is one thing to show that "the cultural output" is heavily biased towards the maintenance of the status quo, which is what Miliband attempts to show in his earlier work (1969, especially chapters 7 and 8), and quite another thing to demonstrate that this output does have the effects that are claimed for it. In the absence of such evidence, the whole argument of ideological domination, whichever form it takes, necessarily totters on the brink of circularity. For the answer to the question of why the working class does not revolt is that it has a false consciousness of its position due to its subjection to ruling-class ideology; and the answer to the question of what evidence can be adduced to show that the working class is in this state of ideological subordination is that the working class lacks a revolutionary consciousness. Of course, theories of ideological domination never descend to quite this crass level. But, on the other hand, they seldom rise far above it, consisting mostly of plausible, but unsubstantiated arguments about the effects of ideology on this or that aspect of working-class attitudes or behaviour. Most importantly, all theories of the ideological obstacles to proletarian reason have their *raison d'être* in the unquestioned postulate of eventual proletarian revolution. If the general course of proletarian action were not thus prescribed, it would be unnecessary to invent such equally general explanations of the proletariat's deflection from the pursuit of its ultimate goal. In this regard, modern Marxism merely renews and updates the comprehensive insurance policy that Marx himself took out. For within the space of thirty pages of the first volume of *Capital*, he claims first that "The advance of capitalist production develops a working class, which by education, tradition, habit, looks upon the conditions of that mode of production as self-evident laws of nature," and secondly that "with this too grows the revolt of the working class, a class always increasing in numbers, and disciplined, united, organised by the very mechanisms of capitalist production itself" (1906: 761; 789).

• • •

The instability of the Marxist theory of action is manifested by the tendency to shuttle back and forth between positivistic and idealistic explanations of working-class radicalism and acquiescence. The positivistic type of explanation makes it possible, for example, to hold to the belief that the next economic crisis will provide the occasion for the leap in consciousness that fuses the immediate and fundamental interests of the proletariat. At the same time, the idealistic reaction to this utilitarian conspectus can lead to the opposite, pessimistic theory that the working class is sunk in a chronic, an almost irremediable, false consciousness. Depending on which of these two views is preferred, the role of the party differs. In the first case, the party serves as little more than a catalyst of the end-shift of the proletariat. In the second case, revolution being a remote eventuality, it is only through a prolonged ideological struggle that the party, in which proletarian reason is for the time being displaced, can hope to convert the working class to socialism. This oscillation between one conception of the condition of the proletariat and the other is perfectly well understandable if the foregoing account of the instability of the Marxist scheme of action is correct. It is, moreover, not just an abstract, theoretical problem; it has practical, political consequences. For example, writers referring to the same society at the same point in time can arrive at widely discrepant estimates of the radical potential of the working class, as may readily be seen from a comparison of the prognoses of Miliband (1969: 275–276) and Glyn and Sutcliffe (1972: 208–216).

The only remedy of this unsatisfactory state of affairs involves abandoning the assumption that the proletariat *in toto* is identifiable by either a capacity for reasoning that will imminently be actualized or a susceptibility to ideological indoctrination that there is little prospect of alleviating. Positively, this would involve the replacement of global explanations of class consciousness and class action by a much more precise conception of the way in which class interests are, as Parsons puts it, "a function of the realistic situations in which people act and of the 'definitions' of those situations which are institutionalized in the society" (1949: 313). By moving towards such a "voluntaristic" concept of action Marxism would perhaps only be making explicit at the level of its general theory what is normally recognized to be the case by serious Marxist students of particular, historical instances of class formation. It is, of course, unlikely that any such change in theoretical direction would be accompanied by the abandonment of the belief in the revolutionary capacity of the working class. But until proletarian reason manifests itself, it is difficult to believe that forthright Marxist theorists of class action will not sooner or later be constrained to adopt a mode of analysis which, notwithstanding some natural "commodity differentiation," does not differ substantially from that of their "bourgeois" counterparts. In other words, due recognition will have to be given to the fact that the situations in which proletarian rationality operates include normative elements that exhibit great variability in respect of both their content and the extent to which they become internalized conditions of action. Once again, this is not merely an abstract, academic point. It is one that is prerequisite to any attempt to understand which sections of the proletariat are more or less likely to be subject to "bourgeois indoctrination" or open to socialist initiatives.

Surprisingly enough, recent Marxist writings on the class structure of capitalist societies show little sign of the theoretical reorientation just referred to; or even of the recognition of the need for it. The writings in question have two chief characteristics. The first is that they reveal a deep controversy over what are the correct Marxist criteria by means of which definitions of the objective "places" or "locations" of classes are to be arrived at. The second is that they virtually reject the problem of the relationship between class structure and class consciousness/class conflict, either by trying to legislate it out of existence or, and in the end this amounts to the same thing, by treating it as highly indeterminate. As things stand, then, there is on the one hand much conflict over the concept of class, and, on the other, not much in the way of a theory of class conflict.

As regards the definition of class, the anarchy of Marxist analysis is well exemplified by a comparison of the work of Poulantzas and Wright. Of fundamental importance is their disagreement over the relevance of the distinction between productive and unproductive labour, since this is really the only possible conceptual means of establishing a direct link between the economic theory of system contradiction and the political sociology of class conflict. For Poulantzas productive labour is the basic "economic" criterion of the working class. Wright is of the completely opposite opinion, and for three reasons. The first is that Poulantzas's restriction of the notion of productive labour to productive labour involved in material production is totally at odds with Marx's definition of it. The second is that, for the purposes of defining class boundaries, the concept is deficient because it is extremely difficult to establish where productive labour ends and unproductive labour begins. Thirdly, and perhaps most importantly, Wright holds to the view that "It is hard to see where a fundamental divergence of economic interests emerges from positions of unproductive and productive labour in capitalist relations of production. Certainly Poulantzas has not demonstrated that such a divergence exists" (1978: 50). In this, Wright has the support of Braverman who writes that "Although technically distinct . . . the two masses of labour are not otherwise in striking contrast . . . they form a continuous mass of employment which . . . has everything in common" (1974: 423). And in what is perhaps the most notable study of economic divisions within the working class, the productive/unproductive labour concept plays no major role (O'Conner, 1973). In this respect, then, the most elementary notion of what constitutes the economic definition of class is in grave dispute. But this is not the only aspect of Poulantzas's analysis to which Wright takes exception. In what Poulantzas calls the "ideological" criterion of class determination, that is, the distinction between manual and nonmanual labour, the sociologist may perceive some faltering recognition of the significance of status differentiation (1978: 258–259). For Wright, however, such a distinction is completely unacceptable because it means abandoning the tenet of "the primacy of economic relations in the definition of class" (1978: 51). For Poulantzas's third principle of class placement, the "political," which is basically the distinction between supervisory and nonsupervisory labour, Wright has some sympathy, because it approximates his own criterion of class location, which refers to control over what is produced and over how what is produced is produced. He is, however, loath to accept the label of "political" to signify this distinction, which he prefers to regard "as one aspect of the structural dissociation between economic ownership and possession at the economic level itself" (1978: 52).

To anyone not absorbed in it, this debate might appear as no more than a futile logomachy. But this would not explain why the definition of classes is such an important issue for contemporary Marxism and why it should give rise to so much conceptual discord. The answer to the first question is that the definition of class is not simply a sociological exercise but a matter of vital political concern. From the latter point of view, the problem of utmost significance is that of the size of the proletariat, a magnitude that can vary dramatically depending on whether, for example, the productive/unproductive labour distinction (and which particular interpretation of it) is deemed relevant to the determination of class boundaries. Wright calculates that the size of the American proletariat more than doubles if it is estimated according to his criteria (all nonsupervisory employees) rather than by those of Poulantzas, who defines this class more stringently as productive, nonsupervisory, manual labour (1978: 57; 86). In fact, Poulantzas's criteria could reduce the American working class to hardly 20% of the economically active population. And for Wright this is a bitter pill to swallow, because, as he puts it, "It is hard to imagine a viable socialist movement developing in an advanced capitalist society in which less than one in five people are workers" (1976: 23). This is not to imply, however, that Marxist theorists simply tailor their definitions of classes to suit their political needs. Their conceptual disagreement has a real foundation in the fact that the development of capitalism is associated with the declining importance of manual, or blue-collar, workers relative to nonmanual, or white-collar, workers. When the latter threaten to outnumber the former, this raises the crucial question of how to conceptualize the class position of a vast number of heterogeneous functions that cannot easily be identified as either capitalist or proletarian. Politically, it is a question of how many of these white-collar workers can be enlisted in the ranks of the proletariat or counted as its immediate allies. But traditional Marxist categories provide no easy answers. The axiom that within any mode of production there are only two basic class positions and interests requires substantial qualification. This is achieved, for example, by Poulantzas's invention of "political" and "ideological" criteria of class determination and, more generally, by the emphasis that is now placed on "relations of possession" and not just on "economic ownership" (both real and juridical). Through such notions as "political" criteria, "relations of possession," and the "global functions of capital," Marx's observations on "the transformation of the actually functioning capitalist into a mere manager" and on "the double nature" of the "labour of supervision and management" (1971: 436; 383) have come to acquire a central and systematic importance in the definition of class structure. As a result, recent Marxist writings on the class location of white-collar workers employ concepts that are fairly familiar to "bourgeois" social scientists whose work on the formation of the middle classes and on the structure of industrial bureaucracy has been in part a reaction to, and a critique of, an earlier phase of relatively crude Marxist theorizing. And it is not just that these writings use different terms to describe the same phenomena that have for some time past been of interest to "bourgeois" social scientists; it is also mainly on the basis of the research carried out by the latter (into such problems as "white-collar proletarianization" and "the separation of ownership and control") that recent contributions to Marxist class analysis enjoy whatever empirical credibility they possess. This is, after all, not very surprising, since, while both groups of scholars are grappling with the same, highly complicated set of problems, those committed to a Marxist approach are not only fewer in number but usually less concerned with collecting new evidence than with establishing which brand of concepts is most genuinely Marxian in its derivation.

The final point about these discussions of class structure which needs to be brought out is that the whole exercise of defining class "places" and "locations" is of small relevance to the most important problem of the Marxist theory of action: namely, the explanation of the end-shift of the proletariat. Indeed, the most striking feature of the writings under consideration is not that their treatment of the placement of white-collar workers exhibits such a profound conceptual disarray, but rather that they have practically nothing to say about the structure of the core of the working class or proletariat, both of which terms are used interchangeably. While its boundary alters according to the particular definition preferred, the proletariat remains a mysterious entity. Poulantzas is strict in awarding the privilege of proletarian status, but he ends up with a class that is broadly equivalent to the whole of the industrial, manual labour force. Nevertheless, having defined the proletariat to his satisfaction, he finds it unnecessary to investigate its composition. It is as if in his theatre of structural determination the chief actor never takes to the stage but remains hidden in the left wing. Wright is hardly more informative. He states baldly that "the working class (i.e., nonsupervisory, nonautonomous employees) in the United States consists of between 41 and 54% of the economically active population" (1978: 87). This massive aggregate is not subjected to further analysis. It is true that in considering briefly the relation between class structure and class struggle he acknowledges that proletarians differ in their "structural and organizational capacities." Class structure "sets limits of variation on the forms of class capacities," that is on "the ways in which social relations are formed among positions within the class structure" (1978: 105–106). But this determination is very broad: it means that "bourgeois positions, for example, cannot be organized into working-class trade unions or revolutionary socialist parties." Nevertheless, the factors accounting for variations in structural capacity within the limits set by the class structure overall might be thought to be of central importance to the explanation of working-class action. And Wright certainly accepts this in principle. "Class capacities," he writes, "constitute one of the most decisive selection determinations of class struggle. The underlying structural capacities of classes and the specific organizational forms shaped by these structural capacities have a tremendous impact on forms of class struggle" (1978: 103). In view of this, his discussion of the factors explaining variations in the structural capacity of the proletariat is surprisingly short and unsystematic. He mentions four by way of illustration: the concentration of workers in large factories and thus the emergence of "the collective worker"; attempts by capitalists to undermine working-class solidarity through "the creation of job hierarchies, structures of privileges and promotions"; the degree to which workers are involved in occupational communities; and the extent to which "ethnic solidarity" reinforces "the class-based social relations within the community" (1978: 99–100). This list of factors is *ad hoc* and plainly inadequate for a thoroughgoing study of variations in the structural capacity of the proletariat. Moreover, these social conditions play no part in the definition of the location of the proletariat in the class structure, which rests simply on the two criteria mentioned above (nonsupervisory, nonautonomous employees). Why is this? It cannot be that the kind of factors Wright refers to are so heterogeneous that they defy systematic analysis; after all, there is an extensive literature on the subject which shows that this is not the case. Yet for Wright, no less than Poulantzas, the proletariat remains conceptually inviolate. The only conclusion that can be drawn from this is that the structure of the working class is not a matter of ultimate importance because the question of whether the proletariat has a fundamental interest in socialism is considered to be just as unproblematic as that of whether it will eventually realize this interest. In the last analysis, then, it is the objective interest ascribed to the working class as a whole which guarantees its potential unity and makes the detailed analysis of its structure otiose. This does not mean that the diversity of the working class and of its immediate interests is not real, but rather that it is somehow less real than the underlying unity of its basic class location and fundamental interest, which the class struggle will eventually reveal. It is, in other words, still the proletariat of *The Holy Family*.

Remarkably enough, Braverman's study is almost equally uninformative when it comes to elucidating the structure of the working class, which is the task he sets himself (1978: 25). His main concern, however, as is indicated by the subtitle of the book, is to document the moral and material impoverishment of the working class, or as he says its "degradation." His study must be seen then as the latest version of the alienation thesis, and in pursuing it he takes a fairly broad-ranging view of the structure of the working class. For Braverman, the latter consists in the relationship between three sections of the working class: the traditional blue-collar working class of industrial manual workers; the "growing working class occupations" of clerical, sales, and service workers; and the "reserve army" of the unemployed (or subemployed). His argument is that the process of capital accumulation results in an increasing moral impoverishment (i.e., loss of control over the labour process) and/or material impoverishment (i.e., relatively low incomes) among the first two sections of the working class, each one of which is roughly equivalent in size. The mechanization of blue-collar work results in its dehumanization and in displacement of industrial labour, most of which is absorbed into the clerical, sales, and service sector of employment, though some of it is jettisoned into the reserve army of labour. Moreover, even though the extraction, and especially the realization, of surplus value leads to an expansion of employment in the clerical, sales, and service sector, these workers are also subject to increasing degradation as a result of the rationalization and mechanization of their work (particularly clerical employees) and the lowering of their incomes through the pressure on the labour market of the reserve army of the unemployed. If this last section of the working class is defined as including the subemployed, then it overlaps very considerably with the employed working class, and especially with the retail and service sector of employment.

Braverman's view of the working class is very much the same as Wright's. Both reject the productive/unproductive labour distinction as a significant line of intraclass demarcation. Both define the working class as a whole by reference to loss of control over the labour process. And although Braverman's working class appears to have some structure to it in the sense that he distinguishes between factory workers, clerical workers, retail, and service workers, this is more apparent than real because he claims that all these sections of the working class are becoming less and less distinct. As he says "The giant mass of workers who are relatively homogeneous as to lack of developed skill, low pay, and interchangeability of person and function (although heterogenous in such particulars as the site and nature of work they perform) is not limited to offices and factories. Another huge concentration is to be found in the so-called service occupations and in retail trade" (1978: 359). Thus, having set out to investigate the structure of the working class, Braverman ends up with the now familiar picture of a vast proletarian mass. He and Wright reach the same conclusion, but by different methods. For Wright, it is the fundamental, socialist interest he ascribes to the proletariat which secures its unity, despite intraclass differences in structural and organizational capacity and the short-sightedness of its immediate interests. For Braverman, however, the basic common interest of the working class is demonstrated by the fact of its increasing homogeneity and shared degradation.

But has Braverman really demonstrated that the working class has become practically homogeneous in its work and market situation? And are these the only criteria that are relevant to the study of the structure of the working class? As regards the first question, the evidence Braverman adduces in support of his thesis is not very substantial. In his foreword to the book, Sweezy observes that "there is hardly an occupation or any other aspect of the labour process which would not repay a great deal more detailed historical and analytical investigation than are accorded to it in this broad survey" (1974: xii). Broad survey indeed it is. In fact, the greater part of the book is not even a broad survey of the American working class. It is rather a potted history of "scientific management" and technological innovation based on familiar secondary sources which in the majority of instances are concerned less with describing how factory and clerical work is actually organized than with prescribing how it could and should be organized. While Braverman makes good illustrative use of these materials in his account of the "degradation of work," this does not alter the fact that much of his argument proceeds by conflation and by assuming what has to be shown to be the case; it is, in consequence, highly schematic and tendentious. For example, to the basic question posed by his own thesis, of exactly to what degree which sections of the manual and nonmanual labour force are subject to the dehumanizing conditions of work that he describes so graphically in general terms, Braverman has scarcely the beginnings of a definite answer.

Quite apart from this, in so far as the analysis of the situation of the working class is intended to provide a basis for explaining class action, there is no inherent reason why the organization of the work process should be the exclusive focus of investigation. If "what is needed first of all is a picture of the working class as it exists" (Braverman, 1974: 27), then this must emerge from a much more detailed study of the way in which what Wright refers to as "structural capacities" of the working class differ as a result of not only the organization of work but also the interdependence of work and community relationships. This is brought out very well, for example, in a book that was published in the same year as Braverman's: Kornblum's account of the steel workers in South Chicago (1974). There, in the late sixties and early seventies at least, the working class did not take on the shape of a vast homogenous mass. On the contrary, it was composed of a dense network of primary groups which both segregated and aggregated workers whose status differed according to their jobs, ethnicity, and place of residence. And, as Kornblum shows, this infrastructure of primary groups is of vital importance in understanding the dynamics of local union and political organization. More directly relevant to Braverman's particular thesis is the fact that, in the production process, groups of workers differed markedly in respect of the status that attached to different tasks as well as in their autonomy in carrying out these tasks. Now it might be said that Kornblum presents a picture of the working class that is atypical, and that in focusing too closely on the sources of differentiation within the working class, he loses sight of its basic unity. As regards the first point, Kornblum recognises that his study cannot be presented as a " 'typical' working-class community". But at the same time he holds that "South Chicago's diverse population of blue-collar ethnic groups and its range of community institutions are representative of a rather widespread pattern of working-class community organizations in the United States" (1974: 2). In any case, what is regarded as typical or representative of the working class is a question that presupposes a systematic analysis of its structure as a whole; and Marxists such as Braverman, Wright and Poulantzas have not provided this. For them, the proletariat is characterized by its homogeneity; and from this point of view one section of the working class must be just as typical as another. The second point raises questions of a similar kind, since, in the absence of a frame of reference by which it is possible to establish what is of particular rather than of general significance in the study of the structure of the working class, on what basis is it possible to decide which perspective is the more valid: Kornblum's worm's-eye view, which is veridical within its limited range; or Braverman's bird's-eye view, which is the favourite vantage point of the Marxist wishful thinker?

There is, however, one sense in which Braverman's perspective on the working class is insufficiently broad in its scope. This appertains to a point made by Mackenzie who, after referring to "Braverman's failure to consider the *uniqueness* of the United States," goes on to argue that "any analysis of changes in the structure and composition of the American working class should make explicit recognition of the unique as well as the general structural features of that society" (1977: 250–251). Mackenzie's strictures on Braverman apply with equal force to the conceptionalization of class structure advanced by Wright and Poulantzas, even though Poulantzas's distinctive concern with the "petty bourgeoisie" might be thought to reflect something especially characteristic of his own society. For they likewise deny the proletariat any national identity; and thus, in possessing neither a structure nor a history, the proletariat truly acquires the nature of a "universal" class. What is basically at stake here is not so much the uniqueness of this or that society, but rather those aspects of its historical development that can be grasped, through comparative study, in more general terms. Perhaps the most important single point of reference in this respect is the one referred to earlier on in the chapter: namely, the status structure of civil, political, industrial, and social citizenship. The mode of the civic incorporation of the working class is a factor of major significance in explaining national differences in class formation. But once again this involves reference to a "moral and historical" element which has no definite place in Marxist theory; and, in the writings being discussed, this means that the analysis of the status system can play no part in the definition of the position of the working class. The result is that the conceptual sanitation of the proletariat is complete.

This suggests that these modern theories of class structure are still based, at least implicitly, on the classical Marxist action scheme. For in so far as the definition of class structure is intended to elucidate the variability of the class struggle, it must involve some idea of the constituents of social action. That is, it must take account not only of the means and conditions of action (such as control over the labour process) but also of the determination of the ends of actors and of the standards by which they relate means to ends. It is in the latter respect that the status order plays a central role in both the differentiation and integration of ends and the legitimation of means. It must be repeated that this does not entail the assumption that an actor's status situation is an internalized condition of his action. The extent to which he regards its legitimation of his ends and means as binding is variable and is affected by, among other things, changes in his class situation. On the other hand, the status situa-

tion cannot be reduced to the category of those external means and conditions that actors relate to in a purely instrumental manner. In Marxism,
however, this problem of the institutionalization of status does not arise.
Yet just because the concept of status plays no systematic role in its
theory of action, the effects of status can only be taken into account
by treating them in an *ad hoc* fashion or by subsuming them under
the catch-all concept of ideology. The former alternative is evident in
the work of contemporary class theorists.

For example, when Braverman characterizes loss of control over the
labour process as "degradation," he resorts to some idea of socially
invariable and hence completely unproblematic ends akin to Marx's notion of authentic human needs, and it is only by making this assumption
that he can infer the potential of working-class revolt from changes in the
conditions of class action (1974: 139; 151). But, quite apart from the fact
that this conclusion sits uneasily, though familiarly, with his discussion of
the "habituation" of the worker to his alienated conditions of work,
Braverman's explanations of both degradation and habituation take no
account of the way in which the status system inculcates different levels
of expectation of autonomy in work. Once again, this is not to suggest that
variations in these expectations provide a sufficient explanation of action;
the problem is rather to understand how action is jointly determined by
both realistic and normative elements, and particularly by the way in
which changes in these elements are mutually interdependent. In Wright's
work also there are traces of the resort to an arbitrary notion of status.
For example, when he writes that "job hierarchies, structures of privileges and promotions" can operate to "weaken the social relations
among workers within production" (1978: 100), his argument relies on the
general assumption that status differentiation can shape ends in a way that
is inimical to class solidarity. But there is no reason why effects of this
kind should be seen as restricted to "workers within production." So
what is glimpsed here is but the tip of a conceptual iceberg which could
appear anywhere on the chart of class locations. Finally, as was noted
above, Poulantzas's treatment of the ideological division between manual
and nonmanual labour involves a fairly explicit reference to what anyone
but a Marxist would term a line of status demarcation. But again, why
should status manifest itself only at this level of the class structure,
and not, for instance, as Wright suggests, within the working class itself?
The answer is that it is the consequence of Poulantzas's decision that the
ideological criterion of class relates exclusively to the distinction between
manual and nonmanual labour. And to make things worse, it is a decision
that has no clear Marxian warrant.

From this rather lengthy discussion of recent Marxist definitions of
class structure, three main conclusions can be drawn. The first is that,
while the criteria for placing or locating classes are in deep dispute, the

one that there is least disagreement about in principle—namely, the significance of "relations of possession"—raises conceptual and empirical issues of a basically similar kind to those that have occupied the attention of "bourgeois" social scientists in their studies of the bureaucratization of industrial organization. The second notable feature of Marxist class definition is that the classical conception of the proletariat as a unitary class actor survives intact. The working class retains its essential identity either by the ascription to it of a unifying fundamental interest or by the attempt to demonstrate its homogeneity. Thirdly, by concentrating on the means and conditions of action, these definitions of class structure perpetuate a conception of action whose chief defect has always been its failure to take account of the nature and variability of normative elements in the determination of ends and of the means-ends relationship. At the structural level, the most striking consequence of this omission is the abstraction of class relations from the context of the status system of a society. By ignoring these factors, modern Marxism implicitly falls back on a notion of action in which the only significant ends are the given or fundamental interests of class actors, the only norm for relating means to ends is that of rationality, and the only way of explaining deviation from rational action is by reference to ideologically induced ignorance or error.

In raising this last issue, the discussion of the definition of class structure has already engaged with the second main problem it set out to deal with: namely, the question of the relation between class structure on the one hand, and class consciousness and class conflict on the other. It is now time to face this problem directly.

● ● ●

Within classical Marxism, the crucial problem of the end-shift of the proletariat centred on the distinction between a class-in-itself and a class-for-itself. This is a distinction between a class that has objectively defined interests by virtue of its position within the class structure and a class that is an ideologically united and politically organized entity, acting in pursuit of its interests against those of another class. In general, modern Marxism continues to accept this distinction. That is to say, the purpose of the analysis of class structure is to provide an explanation of class consciousness and class conflict. As Wright puts it, "It is all very well and good to clarify the structure of positions defined by social relations of production and to link these to other positions in the social structure. Marxism, however, is not primarily a theory of class structure; it is above all a theory of class struggle" (1978: 97–98). How, then, is the relationship between class structure and class conflict understood?

The first approach to this problem, which is fairly characteristic of writers whose work is almost exclusively concerned with the definition of classes, is in one way or another to avoid it. Braverman, for example, excludes the analysis of class conflict and class consciousness from his discussion altogether. "No attempt will be made to deal with the modern working class on the level of its consciousness, organization, or activities. This is a book about the working class *in itself,* not as a class *for itself.* I realize that to many readers it will appear that I have omitted the most urgent part of the subject matter" (1974: 27). He goes on to say it is not his purpose "to deprecate the importance of the study of the state of consciousness of the working class, since it is only through consciousness that a class becomes an actor on the historic stage" (1974: 29). But the only indication he gives of how this study might proceed is by distinguishing between the "absolute expression" of class consciousness ("a pervasive and durable attitude on the part of a class toward its position in society"), its "long-term relative expression" ("found in the slowly changing traditions, experiences, education, and organization of the class"), and its "short-term relative expression" ("a dynamic complex of moods and sentiments affected by circumstances and changing with them, sometimes, in periods of stress and conflict, almost from day to day") (1974: 29–30). Virtually the same position is taken up by Crompton and Gubbay, whose study is almost entirely given over to the analysis of class position. In asking how "the location in the class structure is reflected in the consciousness of particular groups," their general answer is that there are "no easy answers: the particular structure of the labour market, the dominant ideology, and short-term historical circumstances will all tend to act as intervening variables in the description and explanation of objective location in the class structure and the consciousness, attitudes and behaviour of the groups so located" (1977: 97–98). This list of intervening variables is presented simply to indicate the complexity of the problem and not as a basis for the systematic analysis of it. And in the section of the book where they attempt to discuss class consciousness in rather more detail, their treatment of it relies on an equally *ad hoc* reference to adventitious "secondary structural factors" (differentiation of function, bureaucracy, market and status factors), which, "far from determining the class structure of contemporary capitalist societies," must nevertheless "be systematically taken into account in the detailed empirical analysis of the class structure of any particular society" (1977: 196). Finally, Wright, who gives primacy to the study of class struggle, provides no more than a highly schematic account of how such a study might proceed. This involves a distinction between class structure (which defines the potential objectives of the potential actors in the class struggle), class formation (which refers to the structural and organizational capacities of classes), and class struggle itself, conceived as "the complex social processes which dialectically link class interests to class capacities" (1978: 102). Wright provides brief illustrations of the "dialectical" relationships between these three elements. But the exposition is entirely illustrative of how the schema might be applied. Its "central message" is that "An adequate political understanding of the possibilities and constraints present in a given social formation depends upon showing the ways in which class structure establishes limits on class struggle and class formation, the ways in which class struggle transforms both class structure and class formation, and the ways in which class struggle mediates the relationship between class structure and class formation" (1978: 108). One definition of "message" given by *The Concise Oxford Dictionary* is a "prophet's, writer's, preacher's, inspired communication." Until Wright demonstrates how his schema can provide a systematic analysis of the relation between class structure and class struggle in a given social formation, his advocacy of its usefulness for this purpose must be considered as no more than a message in the sense just defined.

The work of Poulantzas belongs in a different category because it begins by attempting to abolish the distinction between a class-in-itself and a class-for-itself. For him, "classes have existence only in the class struggle," and the latter is not something that is to be treated separately from the analysis of class structure. "Classes do not firstly exist as such and then only enter into the class struggle" (1978: 14). By this he means that classes are not purely economically determined entities which then become transformed into classes-for-themselves at the political and ideological level of class consciousness and organization. According to Poulantzas, this misleading distinction derives from an Hegelian interpretation of Marx, which he foists on Lukacs. The purpose of saddling Lukacs with this error and absolving Marx from it is all too transparent and requires no further comment. What is important about Poulantzas's argument is first that his rejection of the Hegelian "problematic" leads to ambiguity in his concepts of the "political," the "ideological," and the "class struggle," and, second, that the resolution of this ambiguity results in the resurgence of the "problematic" he attempts to dispose of.

To say that classes cannot be defined outside of the class struggle is all very well in so far as it means that class relations are inherently an arena of class struggle and that this class struggle does not necessarily involve class consciousness and class struggle in the traditional sense of a class-for-itself. Moreover, there is nothing objectionable about Poulantzas's argument that class structure is to be defined by reference to "political" and "ideological" (as well as economic) criteria as long as it is remembered that these refer to the supervisory and nonmanual functions which are focal points of class struggle in the social division of labour. So far, so good. The difficulty arises not from this special meaning of political and ideological class struggle being constitutive of class structure but from the fact that class struggle and class consciousness are empirically variable.

Granted that in Poulantzas's terms production relations contain a political and ideological dimension, it is nevertheless the case that this refers to a different order of fact than the political organization and ideology through which the objectively determined interests of a class are expressed or represented at the societal level of the class struggle. Poulantzas is forced to recognize this distinction: "This structural determination of classes, which thus exists only as the class struggle, must however be distinguished from class position in each specific conjuncture—the focal point of the always unique historic individuality of a social formation, in other words the concrete situation of the class struggle" (1978: 14). To exemplify this distinction, take, for example, the working class. Its structural place is determined by reference to aspects of class struggle that constitute class structure: that is by the economic aspect (productive labour), the political aspect (subjection to supervision), and the ideological aspect (manual labour excluded from the "secret knowledge" of the production process). Its "class position," however, refers to " 'Class consciousness' and autonomous political organization, i.e., as far as the working class is concerned, a revolutionary proletarian ideology and an autonomous party of class struggle, refer to the terrain of class positions and the conjuncture" (1978: 17).

What this means is that there is a latent class struggle and a manifest class struggle. There is the political and ideological class struggle that determines the structure of classes, and there is the political and ideological class struggle that is manifested in the forms of class consciousness and political organization specific to class "positions" in the "conjuncture." In other words, by distinguishing between a structural and a conjunctural class struggle, Poulantzas conjures up in a different form the Hegelian spectre of the class-in-itself/class-for-itself that he set out to exorcise. Moreover, his conception of the relationship between the structural determination of classes and class positions in the conjuncture is no less vague. On the one hand, "A social class, or fraction or stratum of a class, may take up a class position that does not correspond to its interests, which are defined by the class determination that fixes the horizon of the class's struggle" (1978: 15). Yet, on the other hand, "structural class determination involves economic, political, and ideological class struggle, and these struggles are all expressed in the form of class positions in the conjuncture" (1978: 16). The problem here is basically that, while Poulantzas admits that classes may not take up positions in the conjunctural class struggle that correspond to their interests, which are determined by their place in the class structure, this discrepancy can only be explained by a systematic study of the specific political and ideological factors affecting "the concrete situation of the class struggle." Since he does not undertake this kind of analysis it is difficult to disagree with the conclusion of one Marxist critic who argues that "Poulantzas's class determination/class position distinction is incoherent and unstable" because the concept of class position in the conjuncture is "not theorized. It is merely a means of hedging any bets made on the basis of class determination" (Hirst, 1977: 133).

In the present context, however, what is most important about Poulantzas's theory of class structure and class consciousness is that the place, interest, and position of the proletariat appears to be entirely unproblematic. It has already been noted that his definition of the class place of the proletariat is such that it constitutes a clear-cut entity: it is at once economically exploited, politically subjected, and ideologically excluded, i.e., productive, nonsupervisory manual labour. Beyond this, Poulantzas has very little to say about the working class. It is excluded from his purview at the outset. But its role in his theory of classes is as crucial as its socialist class "position" is indisputable. As he says, although "these essays do not deal directly with the working class, this class is constantly present"; and it is always present as "the class that is situated beneath the exploitation which the bourgeoisie imposes on the popular masses, and the class to which the leadership of the revolutionary process falls" (1978: 9). It has already been observed that he equates the "position" of the working class with "a revolutionary proletarian ideology," and elsewhere he refers to "The long-term interests of the working class itself, which is the only class that is revolutionary to the end" (1978: 204). Only occasionally is there a glimpse of doubt: for example, "certain ideological elements specific to the petty bourgeoisie may themselves have their effects on the working class's ideology" and "this is even the main danger that permanently threatens the working class" (1978: 289). But his basic assumption is that the interests and position of the proletariat are beyond question. "The class struggle in a social formation takes place within the basic context of a polarization of various classes in relation to the two basic classes, those of the dominant mode of production, whose relationship constitutes the principal contradiction of that formation" (1978: 200). These basic classes are naturally "the bourgeoisie and the proletariat; the only real class ideologies, in the strong sense of this term, are those of these two basic classes, which are in fundamental political opposition" (1978: 287).

The problem of the relationship between the class place and class position of the proletariat—the problem of its end-shift—is therefore solved by fiat. This "solution" has most unfortunate consequences for his analysis of the new petty bourgeoisie, a subject to which Poulantzas devotes a great deal of attention. Given his general theory of class struggle, the new petty bourgeoisie can have no real class position of its own that is independent of "the bourgeois way and the proletarian (the socialist) way" (1978: 297). Its class place is distinguished from those of the two basic classes by reference to the economic, political, and ideological criteria of class determination, and particularly by its intermediate location in bureaucratic structures of authority. Much of what Poulantzas has to say on this score is sociologically commonplace and some of it ungraciously derived; compare, for example, his remarks on "the stupidity of the bourgeois problematic of social mobility" with his subsequent observations on the effects of mobility chances on the consciousness of the new petty bourgeoisie (1978: 33; 280; 284). It is, however, on the basis of this analysis of the structural place of the new petty bourgeoisie that he seeks to identify its class position. As he says, the "structural determination of the new petty bourgeoisie in the social division of labour has certain effects on the ideology of its agents, which directly influences its class positions" (1978: 287). The chief features of this ideology, which unites the new and the traditional petty bourgeoisie at the ideological level, are as follows: it is anticapitalist, reformist, individualistic, and conceives of the state as a neutral arbiter of class interests. But the new petty bourgeoisie is not a homogeneous body. By reference to several broad changes affecting the petty bourgeoisie in general (its feminization, the narrowing of wage differentials between nonmanual and manual labour, the rationalization and mechanization of office work, etc.), Poulantzas seeks to identify three "fractions" of the class that "display the most favourable objective conditions for a quite specific alliance with the working class and under its leadership" (1978: 314). His discussion of the internal differentiation of the new petty bourgeoisie is much more acute than Braverman's treatment of the subject, and not least because Poulantzas's is empirically and sociologically more discriminating. The result is a novel and challenging Marxist interpretation of class structure, which identifies precisely the potential allies of the working class.

But it is at this point that Poulantzas's argument begins to break down. For the class position of those "fractions" of the new petty bourgeoisie whose place in the class structure most closely approximates that of the proletariat depends ultimately on the strategy of the latter class. It is not to be assumed that "an objective proletarian polarization of class determination must necessarily lead in time to a polarization of class positions" (1978: 334). And in fact "the objective polarization which, together with current transformations, marks the class determination of these petty-bourgeois fractions, has not till now been accompanied by a polarization of their class positions. In other words, no alliance has yet materialized between the major sections of these fractions and the working class, based on the specific objectives of a socialist revolution" (1978: 333). Whether this alliance takes place depends entirely on "the strategy of the working class and its organizations of class struggle" (1978: 334). In the last analysis, then, everything depends on the proletariat, the class actor to whom he assigns a "socialist position" *ex cathedra*. That is, until one reaches the penultimate page of his book. For there Poulantzas admits that the problem of how the working class can attempt to establish its "hegemony" over the proletarianized "fractions" of the new petty bourgeoisie presupposes a study of the working class that he has not even begun to make. "For this," he writes, "it would have been necessary, among other things, to undertake a study of the history and experience of the workers' and international revolutionary movement in this respect— of its organizations, of its theories, and the changes in them, on the question of the revolutionary process, of organization (party and trade unions), and of alliances, and finally to understand in more detail the significance of social-democratic ideology and social-democratic tendencies, and their real basis" (1978: 335). In other words, it would be necessary to consider how working-class consciousness is formed not only by the place of the proletariat in the class structure but also by the specific political organizations and ideologies that represent its objective interest. Most importantly, the latter would involve a comparative study of the formation of the working class that took account of "the unique historical individuality of a social formation" and of the cumulative effect on the political organization of the working class of the outcomes of successive "concrete situations of the class struggle."

In conclusion, then, whatever the merits of Poulantzas's analysis of the class place of the bourgeoisie and the petty bourgeoisie, his theory of social classes provides no systematic explanation of class action and does not even begin to deal with the chronic and intractable problem of the end-shift of the proletariat. His belated recognition that the study of specific working-class organizations and their ideologies is essential to an understanding of the way in which the interest of the proletariat is represented in the concrete, conjunctural class struggle introduces a quite abrupt and damaging qualification of his general thesis that the relation between the structural place and the position of the proletariat is unproblematic: that the "long-term interests" of the working class ensure that it is "the only class that is revolutionary to the end." Like most of his fellow theorists of class structure, Poulantzas holds to a fundamentalist conception of the proletariat. Absolutely basic to this idea is the assumption that the proletariat has an objective, long-run, and, however long that run may be, an imperative interest in socialism. The action of the class may deviate from the pursuit of this interest because of a variety of particular social and economic circumstances that influence the course of the concrete class struggle. But, given that its socialist interest is known to be the only "reasonable" end that it can pursue, deviations from this goal must be misrepresentations of its interest and are explicable finally in terms of ignorance or error. This is brought out nicely in Poulantzas's interpretation of the rise of fascism, a conjuncture in which neither social democracy nor communism served the interest of the working class: the former was an "ideological state apparatus" whose role was "to mislead the masses and hold back the revolution," while the latter was itself misled by its "incorrect strategy" based on the theory of social fascism (1974: 147–165).

The demolition of this whole orthodox framework is the aim of the last version of Marxist class theory to be considered here. Its most forceful exponent is Hirst (1977). The crux of his argument is that Marxism is forced to choose between some form of economism, which conceives of the political and ideological struggle as ultimately the expression or representation of class interests that are objectively given by the economic structure, and what he calls "necessary noncorrespondence," which means that there are no such objective interests, but only the interests that are constituted by specific political and ideological forces. Classes as such do not have interests and are not actors, and the basic misconception of economism is its assumption that the real actors in the class struggle, namely political organizations in a broad sense, must necessarily, in the long run, represent objective class interests. Economism is shown to be deficient because the divergence between political representation and objective class interest is all too apparent. One solution of this problem is to accord the political a "relative autonomy," a device that is, in effect, identical with Poulantzas's notion of class position in the conjuncture. But this is merely a sophisticated, but nonetheless theoretically unstable, version of economism. "Once any degree of autonomous action is accorded to political forces as a means of representation vis-à-vis classes of economic agents, then there is no necessary correspondence between the forces that appear in the political (and what they 'represent') and economic classes" (Hirst, 1977: 130). Given the idea of relative autonomy, there can be no guarantee that the political means of representation can be constrained in such a way that they do represent class interests, unless the relativeness of the autonomy is restricted by some kind of "last instance" clause. But the latter means a reversion to economism: "it asserts the primacy of the economy while affirming that politics and ideology cannot simply be reduced to its effects" (Cutler, et al., 1977: 235–236). Moreover, like economism in general, it can provide no satisfactory theory of the "specificity of the political." This has already been shown to be a major weakness of Poulantzas's theory of classes in which the conjunctural class struggle finally emerges as a zone of particularity and contingency. At best, the systematization of the relative autonomy of the political results in a functionalist form of economism, typified by the concept of "ideological state apparatuses" (Hirst, 1977: 131–132; Cutler, et al., 1977: 200–202).

Hirst and his colleagues realize that in rejecting the concept of objective class interest and in espousing the idea of necessary noncorrespondence they adopt a position that "shatters the classical conception of classes" (Cutler, et al., 236). If their argument is accepted—and it is a very cogent one—then many of the most intractable problems of the Marxist theory of class action just disappear. But what of Marxism remains? The broadest statement of intent is that the "connections between social relations, institutions, and practices must be conceived of not in terms of any relations of determination, "in the last instance" or otherwise, but rather in terms of conditions of existence. This means that while specific social relations and practices always presuppose definite social conditions of existence, they neither secure these conditions through their own action nor do they determine the form in which they will be secured. Thus, while a set of relations of production can be shown to have definite legal, political, and cultural conditions of existence these conditions are in no way determined or secured by the action of the economy" (Cutler, et al., 1977: 314). What might seem to be involved, then, is replacing the quasi-Parsonian functionalism of Althusser[7] with a form of Marxism that begins where Weber left off.

● ● ●

Contemporary Marxist theories of social class are in a poor state. There are no doubt reasons why this is the case other than those advanced above. Nevertheless, it might be useful to recapitulate the latter, however much a simplification and exaggeration of certain tendencies of the Marxist corpus they represent. The burden of this essay is that the main weakness of the link between Marxist theories of system and social integration is to be found in the persistence of a basically utilitarian action scheme. One reason why the latter should have been so predominant is that it is fundamental to the economic theory of capitalist development, which is by far the most powerfully developed branch of the subject. Furthermore, in seeking to demonstrate that the proletariat has an objective, scientifically guaranteed interest in socialism, Marxist economic theory has provided the terms of reference for the analysis of social integration. It has set the "norm" against which the rationality of proletarian action must be measured. This, together with the assumption that the proletariat possesses a power of reason commensurate with the task of realizing its fundamental interest, has meant that, from the outset, explanations of conflict and order have taken on a characteristically utilitarian form. The standard of rationality is the major reference point for understanding how capitalists and proletarians adapt their means to their respectively given, intrasystemic, ends, just as the higher-order rationality of reason is indispensable to explaining the transmogrification, or end-shift, of the proletariat. Finally, in the absence of a clear distinction between action that is simply irrational, and nonrational action oriented to the alternative standard of ultimate values, there is no other way of accounting for ostensible lapses from rationality and reason save by recourse to some version of the classical utilitarian notions of ignorance and error.

This theory of action has two basic defects. First, it precludes systematic analysis of the factors determining the extent to which the values and norms defining the legitimate ends and means of actors become internalized conditions of action. The whole problem of the institutionalization of values is inadmissible. Most crucially, this denies Marxism an adequate conception of the status order, the primary focus of the integration of the ends of class actors. The tendency to dismiss both hierarchical and egalitarian aspects of status as ideological reflections of the class structure is not only far too crude to grasp the complicated ways in which the legitimation of status relationships is both contingent upon, and constitutive of, class interests; it is also symptomatic of the second major defect. In so far as normative elements enter into Marxist explanations of action, they do so either in an implicit, ad hoc way, or, as is more usually the case, through their incorporation into the general category of ideology. This is to be expected. By according the standard of rationality such a central place in its explanatory system, and by collapsing the distinction between irrational and nonrational action, Marxism is constantly tempted to lump together as ideologically determined all kinds of apparently irrational behaviour. The concept of "ideological state apparatuses" is only the most egregious example of this. Ideology thus serves an analytical function analogous to that performed by the concepts of ignorance and error in utilitarian theorizing. Even though it locates the sources of irrationality in society rather than in the individual, the theory of ideology has been formulated at a highly abstract level, which befits its chief purpose of providing global explanations of social order. Indeed, in the course of its promotion to account for the absence of proletarian revolution in the most advanced capitalist societies, its conceptual scope has widened to cover ever more disparate phenomena, including not only systems of beliefs and values, but most major social institutions and corporate groups, all of which are seen in some way to be performing ideological functions. At the same time, the precise manner in which, and therefore the effectiveness with which, ideological factors enter into the determination of social action has remained extremely problematic. For these reasons, ideology comes close to being a residual category, resort to which has the theoretically destabilizing effect of introducing into the basic, strongly positivistic, framework of Marxism a type of explanation that approaches the opposite pole of the idealistic scheme of action.

These inherent defects of the theory may help to explain why contemporary studies of class concentrate so heavily on the analysis of class structure and avoid the problem of class action. But this is putting the cart before the horse, because the identification of significant structural factors presupposes an explicit and well-founded theory of action. This is most strikingly evident in the way these studies deal, or rather fail to deal, with the structure of the working class. By reducing to the very minimum the elements that define the basic conditions of the proletarian class situation, it is then discovered that the working class still possesses the homogeneity and potential solidarity requisite to the attainment of its ultimate interest in socialism. But the question of how, under these conditions, the working class will act to realize its final goal, receives no serious attention. To provide an adequate answer would require nothing less than the reconstitution of the classical Marxist theory of action. But far from attending to this task, contemporary class theorists appear to have no clear concept of action whatsoever. So now it is no longer just the case that explanations of the relationship between class structure and class struggle are bound to be unstable and contradictory: the relationship is completely indeterminate.

ACKNOWLEDGMENTS

I am grateful to Duncan Gallie, George Kolankiewicz, and Howard Newby for their comments on the first draft of this paper.

NOTES

1. Consider, for example, the exiguous treatment of the problem of class formation in the most important general expositions of Marxist theory: Sweezy (1949); Baran and Sweezy (1966); Mandel (1975).

2. This applies to both Miliband (1969) and Poulantzas (1973), the two works that have dominated the discussion of the subject in the last decade.

3. It has become increasingly fashionable to argue that Marx did not expect, and that his work provides no grounds for thinking, that socialist revolutions would occur in the most advanced capitalist societies (there is even in circulation an analytical blank cheque called "over-determination," which guarantees that revolutions will occur whenever and wherever the sufficient conditions of their occurrence exist). This view is not in the least convincing. To be sure, during his own lifetime, Marx believed that revolution was imminent on several occasions and in different places. But unless the relation between his theory of system and social integration is held to be a purely contingent one, then the whole logic of his major work points to one and only one conclusion: that the conditions of proletarian revolution will be found in the most advanced, and the most capitalist of capitalist societies. What he has to say on this score in the famous "Preface" to the *Critique of Political Economy* finds identical expression in the *Grundrisse:* "If we did not find concealed in society as it is the material conditions of production and the corresponding relations of exchange prerequisite for a classless society, then all attempts to explode it would be quixotic" (1973: 159). And *Capital* is replete with similar statements. For example: ". . . in theory, it is assumed that the laws of capitalist production operate in their pure form. In reality there exists only approximation; but this approximation is the greater, the more developed the capitalist mode of production and the less it is adulterated and amalgamated

with survivals of former economic conditions" (1972: 175). From this standpoint, the United States has always been the chief embarrassment. To the naming of the factors making for American "exceptionalism" there is hardly any end. But in that case, at what point does one admit that the sociological law of motion of capitalist society has ground to a halt in the sands of historical particularity?

4. It is not altogether clear why capitalists should lack "reason" and be unable to understand that the rational pursuit of their immediate individual ends is detrimental to their fundamental interest as a class. As Elster points out, Marx's account of the introduction of factory legislation sees the process as "partly the result of the political activity of the workers and partly as the defence of the capitalist class against its own members, the idea being that the over-exploitation of the workers might threaten their physical reproduction and thus capitalism itself. The latter explanation either requires the collective interests of capitalists to overcome their individual interests or their long-term interest to overcome their short-term interest. Both ideas, however, are hard to square with what Marx says elsewhere about the possibility of solidarity between capitalists" (1978: 139). While Lukacs seems to suggest that capitalists cannot comprehend the unintended irrationality of their individual rational actions, and, somewhat unnecessarily, that, even if they could, they could do nothing in the way of correcting this outcome that would not further undermine the capitalist system (1971: 61–64), the main solution of the problem is to be found in the role of the state. As Sweezy puts it, "it is not inconsistent to say that State action may run counter to the immediate interests of some or even all of the capitalists provided only that the overriding aim of preserving the system intact is promoted" (1949: 248). And the greater the emphasis on the "relative autonomy" of the state's socially stabilizing function, the more the state acquires the role of "the cunning of reason" as far as the capitalist class is concerned.

5. For the sense in which the concepts "positivistic" and "idealistic" are used in this essay, see Parsons (1937: Chapter II). In brief, "Just as positivism eliminates the creative, voluntaristic character of action by dispensing with the analytical significance of values, and the other normative elements by making them epiphenomena, so idealism has the same effect for the opposite reason—idealism eliminates the reality of the obstacles to the realization of values" (Parsons, 1937: 446). It is only proper to point out that the instability of Marxist explanations of class action has its source in a very general problem which also gives rise to intractable difficulties in "bourgeois" social theory. Despite Parsons's ecumenical notion of "the voluntaristic theory of action," explanations based on the competing concepts of "rational" and "socialised" man appear to be irreconcilable (Barry, 1970: Heath, 1976). In Marxism, this problem is merely magnified because the attempt to provide a unified theory of system and social integration brings out any inadequacy of the underlying action scheme in a much more dramatic fashion than is the case in theories of less ambitious scope.

6. When Lukacs writes that "status consciousness—a real historical factor—masks class consciousness; in fact it prevents it from emerging at all," he limits his observation to precapitalist societies on the ground that in these, in contrast with capitalism, "the structuring of society into castes and estates means that economic elements are inextricably joined to political and religious factors" and "legal institutions intervene substantively in the interplay of economic forces" (1971: 58, 55, 57). But this contrast is exaggerated and represents an over-simplification of Weber's view of the interdependence of class and status formation. While he recognized that societies can be differentiated according to whether class or status relationships are predominant, he did not thereby suppose that in either type of society life chances and life experiences are determined exclusively by either class or status situations. Class relationships are always determined in part by a specific framework of status, and Avineri draws attention to this when he writes that "for Marx the heyday of unfettered capitalism, when economic activity, at least in England, was not encumbered by any limitation at all, pre- or post-capitalist, was short: from the Repeal of the Corn Laws to

the introduction of the Ten Hours Bill'' (1970: 161). But what this fails to bring out is that, even then, capitalism was not "unfettered" and economic activity was not without "limitation." Vital to the understanding of both the basis of, and the limits to, the "free play" of economic forces is "the fact that the core of citizenship at this state was composed of civil rights" (Marshall, 1950: 33). Conversely, even the most rigidly status-ordered societies were never able to establish more than a very imperfect "fit" between the economic prerogatives of different status groups and the actual disposition of economic power. The status order can no more completely immobilize economic forces through legal sanctions than, at the other extreme, class relations, class interests, and class conflicts can wholly break loose from the moral confines of the status system in which they are embedded. This interdependence of class and status relations at the structural level is no less evident at the situational one—even in revolutionary situations, as is strikingly exemplified by the Lemmgen incident in Berlin in January 1919 (Ryder, 1967: 201).

7. The similarity between Parsons's later system of normative functionalism and the covert functionalism of Althusserian Marxism (Cutler, et al., 1977: 201–202) is, on the surface, fairly obvious. Even though the latter cannot stand comparison with the former in terms of analytical development, there is, nevertheless, a striking correspondence between Parsons's concept of the "cybernetic hierarchy" of action, in which values have the "ultimately determining" role, and Althusser's notion of a social totality, which is composed of "relatively autonomous" levels or instances, and which obtains its structural unity through "determination in the last instance" by the "economy" of which of the levels plays the "dominant" role. Marxism has been transformed into a more clearly functionalist form by Habermas (1976), who makes free use of terms such as "functional necessities" and "functional equivalents" and concentrates on certain substantive problems which have long been of central interest to sociological functionalism and "political systems" theory. Although his work is highly tentative and schematic, its most novel feature is the discussion of "legitimation" and "motivation" crises. What Habermas does not seem to appreciate, however, is how closely his general approach to this problem resembles Parsons's theory of "power deflation."

REFERENCES

Anderson, Perry
 1976– The Antinomies of Antonio Gramsci." New Left Review 100: 5–78.
 1977
Argyris, Chris
 1957 Personality and Organization: The Conflict between System and the Individual. New York: Harper & Row.
Baran, Paul A., and Paul M. Sweezy
 1966 Monopoly Capital. New York: Monthly Review Press.
Barry, Brian
 1970 Sociologists, Economists, and Democracy. London: Routledge and Kegan Paul.
Bendix, Reinhard
 1964 Nation-Building and Citizenship. New York: Wiley.
Bober, M. M.
 1948 Karl Marx's Interpretation of History. New York: Norton.
Braverman, Harry
 1974 Labor and Monopoly Capital. New York: Monthly Review Press.
Browder, Earl
 1959 Marx and America: A Study of the Doctrine of Impoverishment. London: Victor Gollancz.
Crompton, Rosemary, and Jon Gubbay
 1977 Economy and Class Structure. London: Macmillan.

480   DAVID LOCKWOOD

Crossick, Geoffrey
    1976   "The Labour Aristocracy and Its Values." Victorian Studies 19: 301–328.
Cutler, Anthony, Barry Hindess, Paul Hirst, and Athar Hussain
    1977   Marx's Capital and Capitalism Today. London: Routledge and Kegan Paul.
De Man, Henry
    1928   The Psychology of Socialism. London: George Allen & Unwin.
Durkheim, Emile
    1952   Suicide. London: Routledge.
    1957   Professional Ethics and Civic Morals. London: Routledge and Kegan Paul.
Elster, Jon
    1978   Logic and Society: Contradictions and Possible Worlds. Chichester, U.K.: Wiley.
Femia, Joseph
    1975   "Hegemony and Consciousness in the Thought of Antonio Gramsci." Political
           Studies 23: 29–48.
Fromm, Erich
    1962   Beyond the Chains of Illusion. New York: Trident Press.
Gallie, Duncan
    1978   In Search of the New Working Class: Automation and Social Integration within the
           Capitalist Enterprise. Cambridge, U.K.: The University Press.
Glyn, Andrew, and Bob Sutcliffe
    1972   British Capitalism, Workers and the Profits Squeeze. Harmondsworth, U.K.:
           Penguin Books.
Gray, Robert Q.
    1973   "Styles of Life, the 'Labour Aristocracy' and Class Relations in Later Nineteenth-
           Century Edinburgh." International Review of Social History 18: 445–452.
Habermas, Juergen
    1976   Legitimation Crisis. London: Heinemann.
Halevy, Elie
    1955   The Growth of Philosophic Radicalism. Boston: Beacon Press.
Heath, Anthony
    1976   Rational Choice and Social Exchange. Cambridge, U.K.: The University Press.
Heller, Agnes
    1974   The Theory of Need in Marx. London: Allison and Busby.
Hirst, Paul
    1977   "Economic Classes and Politics." Pp. 125–154 in Alan Hunt (ed.), Class and Class
           Structure. London: Lawrence and Wishart.
Hobsbawm, E. J.
    1959   Social Bandits and Primitive Rebels. Glencoe, Ill.: The Free Press.
Kornblum, William
    1974   Blue Collar Community. Chicago: University of Chicago Press.
Lichtman, Richard
    1975   "Marx's Theory of Ideology." Socialist Revolution 5: 45–76.
Lindsay, A. D.
    1925   Karl Marx's Capital: An Introductory Essay. London: Oxford University Press.
Lockwood, David
    1964   "Social Integration and System Integration." Pp. 244–257 in George K. Zollschan
           and Walter Hirsh (eds.), Explorations in Social Change. Boston: Houghton Mifflin.
Lukacs, George
    1971   History and Class Consciousness. London: Merlin.
Mackenzie, Gavin
    1977   "The Political Economy of the American Working Class." British Journal of
           Sociology 28: 244–251.

McLellan, David
  1971 The Thought of Karl Marx: An Introduction. London: Macmillan.
Macpherson, C. B.
  1977 The Political Theory of Possessive Individualism. Oxford, U.K.: The University Press.
Mallet, Serge
  1975 The New Working Class. Nottingham, U.K.: Spokesman Books.
Mandel, Ernest
  1975 Late Capitalism. London: NLB.
Marshall, T. H.
  1950 Citizenship and Social Class. Cambridge, U.K.: The University Press.
Marx, Karl
  1906 Capital: A Critical Analysis of Capitalist Production. London: Swan Sonnenschein.
  1964 Early Writings. T. B. Bottomore (Trans. and ed.), New York: McGraw-Hill.
  1972 Capital. Vol. III. London: Lawrence and Wishart.
  1973 Grundrisse. London: Penguin Books.
Marx, Karl, and Frederick Engels
  1950 Selected Works, Vol. I. Moscow: Foreign Languages.
Merton, Robert K.
  1957 Social Theory and Social Structure. Glencoe, Ill.: Free Press.
Miliband, Ralph
  1969 The State in Capitalist Society. London: Weidenfeld and Nicolson.
  1978 Marxism and Politics. Oxford, U.K.: Oxford University Press.
Moorhouse, H. F.
  1978 "The Marxist Theory of the Labour Aristocracy." Social History 3: 61–82.
O'Conner, James
  1973 The Fiscal Crisis of the State. London: St. James.
Ollman, Bertell
  1971 Alienation: Marx's Critique of Man in Capitalist Society. Cambridge, U.K.: The University Press.
  1972 "Towards Class Consciousness Next Time: Marx and the Working Class." Politics and Society 3: 1–24.
Parsons, Talcott
  1937 The Structure of Social Action. New York and London: McGraw-Hill.
  1949 Essays in Sociological Theory: Pure and Applied. Glencoe, Ill.: Free Press.
Poulantzas, Nicos
  1973 Political Power and Social Classes. London: NLB.
  1974 Fascism and Dictatorship. London: NLB.
  1978 Classes in Contemporary Capitalism. London: Verso.
Ryder, A. J.
  1967 The German Revolution of 1918: A Study of German Socialism in War and Revolt. Cambridge, U.K.: The University Press.
Sweezy, Paul M.
  1949 The Theory of Capitalist Development. London: Dennis Dobson.
Williams, Gwyn A.
  1960 "The Concept of 'Egemonia' in the Thought of Antonio Gramsci: Some Notes and Interpretations." Journal of the History of Ideas 21: 586–599.
Wright, Erik Olin
  1976 "Class Boundaries in Advanced Capitalist Societies." New Left Review 98: 3–41.
  1978 Class, Crisis and the State. London: NLB.